D1105516

MANGAS COLORADAS

MANGAS COLORADAS

Chief of the
Chiricahua Apaches

EDWIN R. SWEENEY

UNIVERSITY OF OKLAHOMA PRESS : NORMAN

Also by Edwin R. Sweeney

Cochise: Chiricahua Apache Chief (Norman, 1991)
Merejildo Grijalva: Apache Captive, Army Scout (El Paso, 1992)
(Editor) *Making Peace with Cochise: The 1872 Journal of Captain Joseph Alton Sladen* (Norman, 1997)

This book is published with the generous
assistance of Edith Gaylord Harper.

Library of Congress Cataloging-in-Publication Data

Sweeney, Edwin R. (Edwin Russell), 1950–
    Mangas Coloradas, chief of the Chiricahua Apaches / by Edwin R.
Sweeney
        p.   cm. — (The civilization of the American Indian series ;
v. 231)
    Includes bibliographical references (p.   ) and index.
    ISBN 0–8061–3063–6 (alk. paper)
    1. Mangas Coloradas, Apache chief, d. 1863?   2. Chiricahua
Indians—Biography.   3. Chiricahua Indians—History.   I. Title.
II. Series.
E99.C68M357 · 1998
973'.04972—dc21   98–9616
                                                                                          CIP

Mangas Coloradas: Chief of the Chiricahua Apaches is Volume 231 in
The Civilization of the American Indian Series.

The paper in this book meets the guidelines for permanence and
durability of the Committee on Production Guidelines for Book
Longevity of the Council on Library Resources, Inc. ∞

1 2 3 4 5 6 7 8 9 10

To my wife
Joanne McGarry Sweeney

CONTENTS

ILLUSTRATIONS

MAPS

ACKNOWLEDGMENTS

I would like to take this opportunity to thank the many people who have helped me during my research.

At the top of my list are two people who profoundly affected my decision to write about Apache history. The first is Dan Thrapp, who was the true giant in the field of Apache-military relations. Dan was not only a real friend but also an inspirational mentor. In the same category was Eve Ball, whose works have preserved Chiricahua Apache history from their point of view. Any serious student of Apache history owes a tremendous debt of gratitude to these two remarkable individuals.

Most of my early research was done at the Arizona Historical Society, and I would like to thank its staff, particularly Lori Davisson, the former research historian. Thanks to Joe Parks, former microforms librarian at the University of Arizona Library, and Simeon "Bud" Newman, former librarian at the Special Collections Library at the University of Texas at El Paso. Both guided me to important material about Chiricahua Apache activities in Mexico that was located in their collections.

I have shared many visits to important sites in Mangas Coloradas's country with two special friends from Las Cruces: Dan Aranda and Santiago "Jimmy" Brito. In Arizona, several field trips were made more enjoyable with the company of Rick Collins of Tucson; Larry Ludwig, ranger-in-charge at Fort Bowie; Bill Gillespie of Sierra Vista, and Bill Hoy of Bowie. I would be remiss if I failed to mention the help given to me by Alicia Delgadillo, who accompanied me to Sonora and shared her vast knowledge of Cochise County and of the Chiricahua Apaches. In addition, her door was always open offering a place to stay. I also appreciate the hospitality of Larry and Sandy Ludwig at Apache Pass; Bill and Mary De Stefano of Tucson; Al Gonzalez of Tucson; Bill Hoy of Bowie, Arizona; and Dan Aranda of Las Cruces.

Alan Radbourne of Taunton, England, generously shared his vast knowledge of Apache affairs in Arizona. Thanks also to Berndt Kuhn of Stockholm, Sweden, who compiled a comprehensive list of Apache-white contacts about the time of the Civil War. I would also like to recognize the superb work of Sergio Macedo, of French Polynesia, the artist who created the painting of Mangas Coloradas that is used on the front of this book. And many thanks to Alexander Sudak of Koscierzyna, Poland, one of the real authorities on American Indians in his part of the world.

Several other historians have made contributions for which I am grateful. Author and historian Jerry Thompson of Texas A&M International University in Laredo, Texas, sent me copies of two important letters about Mangas Coloradas. Bill Griffen, a magnanimous person who is the authority on eighteenth- and nineteenth-century Apache relations in the Janos area, permitted me to use his manuscript that contained many items not found in his two important books, *Apaches at War and Peace*, now published by the University of Oklahoma Press, and *Of Utmost Good Faith*, published by the University of New Mexico Press. I appreciate Bill's generosity. I would also like to recognize Boyd Finch of Tucson, whose research on southern Arizona and southern New Mexico about the time of the Civil War is unsurpassed.

I am also grateful to Kathi Plauster, of Milwaukee, Wisconsin, who provided photos; Manuel Valenzuela of Beaumont, California, who shared his reminiscences of growing up in the Sierra Madre of Sonora in the 1930s; Emilio Tapia of Las Cruces, New Mexico, who was reared in the Black Range and conducted me to several obscure locations within these mountains; and new friends Nick and Dolores Ortega of Chis, New Mexico. Thanks also to Lynda Sanchez of Lincoln, New Mexico; my brother Kevin Sweeney, of Stoughton, Massachusetts; and the Sweeneys' best friends in Missouri, Jim and Gwen Ramatowski, of O'Fallon.

Before finishing, I would like to take this opportunity to acknowledge the important work of two individuals. The first is Jo Ann Reece, Associate Editor at the University of Oklahoma Press, who made many suggestions that enhanced the final manuscript. The second is Dr. William "Bill" Betts of Indiana, Pennsylvania. Bill is a retired professor of English composition and literature from Indiana University of Pennsylvania. After reading my book on Cochise, Bill wrote me a nice letter in which he made several important editorial suggestions that have been incorporated into subsequent printings. I immediately asked him if he would be willing to review my manuscript on Mangas Coloradas. Fortunately, he agreed to my proposition, and his expertise has immeasurably improved the final product. Thanks, Jo Ann and Bill, for your vital contributions.

My final acknowledgment goes to my family—my wife Joanne and my three daughters, Tiffani, Caitlin, and Courtney. I bestowed upon my second daughter, Caitlin, the middle name of Chiricahua in order to honor the spirit of these resilient and resourceful people. As she has approached adulthood, I think she has come to understand my reasons for doing so. I would also like to take this opportunity to honor two other important members of my family—my mother, Mary L. Sweeney, of Stoughton, Massachusetts, and my dad, Edwin R. Sweeney, Sr. My mom deserves much credit for raising four children after my dad suddenly passed away some thirty years ago when I was in my mid-teens. Though he knew that I had been fascinated with the American West since I was a young boy, I think he would be surprised to see the direction that this passion has taken me. There was no reason to believe that the son of a Boston railroad worker would some day write books about two of the Chiricahua Apaches' legendary nineteenth century leaders. After meeting General Oliver Otis Howard in 1872, the Chihenne leader Victorio commented: "We think you have had a good father and mother and have been well brought up." I like to think that Victorio would have made the same comments about my parents. Thanks, Mom and Dad.

ED SWEENEY

St. Charles, Missouri

INTRODUCTION

IT is ironic that Mangas Coloradas, who, more than any other Chiricahua Apache chief, wanted to live in peace with Americans, would become one of the most feared of the western Indians. An outgoing and gregarious man who preferred to resolve matters diplomatically, he was the one Chiricahua leader above all others who actually trusted and truly respected Americans. Having a clear conscience, he was normally prepared to talk with them because he had usually advocated peaceful relations with Anglos. In the end, this openness and trust would lead to his death. Like Victorio and Cochise, the two most important Chiricahua Apache leaders in the two decades following his death, Mangas Coloradas did not seek war with Americans. But during his twilight years an intolerable American encroachment came in the form of miners, farmers, and ranchers. They swallowed up much of his country, occupied prime farming areas, devoured the earth by mining, and drove out much of his game. Still he refrained from fighting, for he well understood the consequences to his people. Finally, in late 1860 and early 1861 these intruding forces, with some assistance from the American military, drove the seventy-year-old chief to war. In desperation, in early 1861 he did what any man would do, especially in a society where the prerequisite for leadership was fighting ability—he fought back.

It will likely come as a surprise to most readers that the duration of Mangas Coloradas's warfare against Americans was less than two years, though he had fought a few earlier skirmishes with Anglos in his country and in northern Mexico. Most of his initial acquaintances with Americans had been with frontiersmen—the trappers and hunters—or with the military, both groups, generally speaking, having shown a high degree of integrity and honesty probably because they had a vested interest in maintaining amicable relations. In 1846, Mangas Coloradas had welcomed the American military into his country, because these new arrivals had treated his people with respect and had done nothing really to alienate him. In fact, the Chiricahuas did not earn their reputation for fiercely resisting American encroachment into their country until some fifteen years after American troops, under Stephen Watts Kearny, had first set foot into Apachería.

Just as important to these early friendly relations is the fact that these first American troops had come to fight Mexicans. In 1861, Arizona entrepreneur Sylvester Mowry would declare that he would accept help from any source—including the devil himself—if it meant an ally against the Apaches, whom he compared to rattlesnakes.[1] In 1846, when American troops first arrived in New Mexico, Mangas and his Chiricahuas felt the same way toward Mexicans, but they were not hostile to Americans. They would have aided and supported any force in any fight against Mexicans, whom they detested. After all, the Chiricahuas had battled Spaniards and later Mexicans for almost three centuries. Yet Mangas's tragic end came—and this is the irony—not at the hands of Mexican soldiers nor as a result of Mexican treachery, but instead because of deceit and chicanery by the American military, a black mark that would tarnish relations for years. One contemporary white compared the Americans' execution of Mangas Coloradas to the disgraceful massacre of the Cheyenne Indians at Sand Creek.[2] Certainly the ramifications were the same: Indians' distrust of Americans, especially the military, and American Indian retaliation, which would lead to short-term victories but eventually to total defeat.

Unlike other, better-known Apache leaders, such as Victorio and Geronimo, Mangas Coloradas was truly a Chiricahua Apache chief who conceived and molded alliances to achieve leadership on a tribal basis. In contrast, his son-in-law, Cochise, evolved into a tribal leader not by foresight or a reasoned scheme, but by the strength of his dynamic personality. The tragic Bascom affair at Apache Pass aroused in him such passions to fight Americans that other Apaches were drawn magnetically to his cause. A raging desire for revenge and an inability to forgive those who betrayed him regularly motivated Cochise, the greatest war chief of his nation in his time, to fight Americans for over a decade. For

Mangas Coloradas, however, during his prime years it was the Mexicans, particularly those in Sonora, who generated in him those passionate feelings of hatred and bitterness. He earned his reputation as a war chief and tribal leader in the assaults against them. And yet he did not hate all Mexicans, for he tried to coexist with those living in New Mexico and occasionally made treaties with those south of him in Chihuahua.

His principal enemies resided in Sonora. As early as 1831, when the Chiricahuas went to war with Mexico, Mangas Coloradas, like his son-in-law Cochise and the Bedonkohe fighter Geronimo, came to despise Sonora. Its military had sanctioned activities that encouraged scalp hunting, with genocide of Apaches as the official state policy. This inevitably led to a series of hard fights and a long-standing conflict as each faction mercilessly waged war against the other. Even when some bands sincerely expressed a desire for an armistice, Sonoran military leaders haughtily refused these solicitations, unwavering in their bellicose philosophy. Their treatment of Apache prisoners paralleled the severity and barbarity of the so-called savages. Mexico usually executed its male prisoners and sold the women and children into slavery. If they could entice the Indians in to make peace, they habitually plied them with mescal and other intoxicants and then slaughtered them indiscriminately—men, women, and children. Consequently, the Chiricahuas entered into a fierce war against Sonora. Who could blame them? Many times Sonoran troops clandestinely crossed the border into Chihuahua and massacred Indians whom Chihuahua had offered to protect under a treaty of peace. It was no wonder that Chiricahua leaders, especially those of the Bedonkohe and Chokonen bands, much hated Mexicans, especially Sonorans. Even today, in the remote villages tucked away in the Sierra Madre, the names that twentieth-century Sonorans remember the most are Geronimo and Mangas Coloradas, according to one person who grew up in the district of Sahuaripa in the 1930s.[3]

Mangas Coloradas always distinguished between the Mexicans who lived in Sonora and those who lived in Chihuahua. During the last twenty-five years of his life he directed virtually every major incursion against the former state. Not that he trusted the officials of Chihuahua or always enjoyed good relations there, for that state continued to offer a large reward for his scalp up to the time of his death. It was just that the constant warfare that Mangas carried out against Sonora, as well as that waged by the Sonorans against the Chiricahuas, kept feelings at a fever pitch, for one side or the other always seemed poised to retaliate against the other. For the last thirty years of his life he considered himself at war with Sonora.

Robert M. Utley, distinguished historian and author of *The Lance and the Shield: The Life and Times of Sitting Bull*, insists that every Lakota man of stature consistently exhibited four cardinal virtues: bravery, fortitude, generosity, and wisdom. And his exemplar is Sitting Bull himself. It is Utley's opinion that these traits are more conspicuous in Sitting Bull than in any other Lakota leader. He will get little argument here. Certainly, when it came to wisdom, we are all agreed, the famous chief of the Hunkpapas had no peer.[4]

Now Mangas Coloradas, perhaps better than any other nineteenth-century Chiricahua chief, can be compared to the celebrated Sitting Bull. Both could inspire followers outside their immediate bands to fight their despised enemies—in Mangas's case, the Sonorans, and in Sitting Bull's case, the Americans. Both were served by devoted younger warrior chiefs who occasionally overshadowed their elders' exploits: in Sitting Bull's case, Crazy Horse; in Mangas Coloradas's case, Cochise. Both were propelled by a vision for their people. Both much desired to live in peace, yet both were rudely forced into conflict, and both were treacherously murdered by Americans or by agents of the Americans.

Clearly the four features of character which Utley spells out are the qualities necessary for effective leadership among the Indians. An inspiring chieftain needed to be known as a generous man, as a sagacious man, as incredibly brave and capable of enduring pain and deprivation. And it did not hurt him if his reputation included also the gift of supernatural power.[5] To the extent that these qualities were visible to the tribe was a chief revered. In Mangas Coloradas, as in Sitting Bull, all were conspicuous. These were the qualities of character that determined his every decision. In the history of the Apaches, Cochise and Victorio are the paradigm of the later Chiricahua leaders; Mangas Coloradas and Pisago Cabezón are the models of virtue for the earlier years. Strangely, the more celebrated Geronimo, though he enjoyed a reputation for supernatural power and was a fighter nonpareil, did not demonstrate the other leadership abilities to attract more than an intimately devoted band of followers, most of whom were related by either blood or marriage.

The rise to the status of chief, then, in Chiricahua Apache society was a grueling process out of which natural leaders would emerge during long periods of warfare against their enemies, particularly the Spanish and then the Mexicans, but also other Indians and eventually the Americans. It helped to have the right bloodline, for the son of a chief almost always would receive the proper training, the kind that would ensure that he would follow in the path of his father. Training was not only important; it was vital. Even if the young man was naturally equipped with the essential instincts and wisdom, he had consciously to develop superior fighting skills·and an assertive personality, and he had to put together an impressive record of achievement. In this way only could he earn the respect necessary to attract and retain loyal followers.

Perhaps it is courage that counts for most among the Apaches. And when it comes to courage, every student of Indian life thinks first of Cochise, undoubtedly the bravest Chiricahua fighting man of his time. Historians have little trouble in bringing this out, for we have many eyewitness accounts of the prowess of Cochise in battle and authentic reports of his extraordinary courage. We know that he rode always at the forefront of his warriors, that he led every assault, that he was careless of his own life.[6]

With Mangas Coloradas, however, it is a different matter. Since most of his battles during his prime were with Mexicans, who left behind very few accounts of his individual exploits, it is much more difficult to measure his courage. But certainly it was impressively present. Without great courage he could never have attracted so many followers to his cause. And we do have some testimony. We know, for example, that Mangas Coloradas rode at the head of his warriors during a skirmish with Americans in Sonora in 1849. We know that he led attacks at Janos and Fronteras in 1856 and 1858, respectively. And we know that in 1862, when Mangas was in his early seventies, Private John Teal shot him from his horse as he led an assault against the defense of Apache Pass. There can be no question that Mangas Coloradas did not lack for courage. We can assume without hesitation that he was for his warriors an inspiring figure. We can place him, for this virtue, anyway, in the company of Cochise and Victorio.

But Mangas, clearly, was possessed of these other qualities of character so essential to effective leadership among the Apaches. Was he equipped of a supernatural power? It was thought that every Chiricahua man enjoyed some form of supernatural power, a kind of "guardian spirit," which came in the form of healing ability, clairvoyant powers, superior skills in hunting and raiding for horses, or the expertise necessary to make war. Although it is customary to think that each band included only a few shamans, or medicine men, in reality it was quite the opposite. Anthropologist Morris Opler points out that in historic times nearly every Chiricahua Apache underwent a supernatural experience and thus obtained a ceremony or a ritual from some source.[7] We do not know what form of power came to reside in Mangas Coloradas, for, with an Apache, this was an extremely personal matter, the kind of experience that a man was disinclined to discuss. It is enough to note that beyond his personal power Mangas likely had available to him a powerful shaman whom he could depend upon to protect his war parties and to ward off sickness in camp.

A leader also exhibited generosity, wisdom, and superior oratorical skills that enabled him to speak eloquently and forcefully at public gatherings. He shared food and possessions, practicing self-sacrifice as an example for others to follow. He encouraged his followers to look out for the less fortunate. He was generous with his knowledge and free with advice and had time for anyone who asked. In camp, where most of his time was spent, he advised people how to live, where to hunt, how to care for one another. He counseled his followers to be vigilant for enemies and to overlook petty disputes that were bound to occur from time to time. He acted as a peacemaker on occasion. He displayed his wisdom in many ways. Every few days he would speak to his followers about camp life and the policies that they had chosen to pursue. When other local groups came together, as for social dances and ceremonies, or when the bands joined, as they always did in response to a crisis, it was the band leader to whom they turned. They depended upon the chief to address challenges and to serve as the agent for change. Mangas Coloradas, a man of vision and foresight, in his time as Chiricahua chieftain pointed the way and showed how to get there.

He was not an ordinary man by any standards. Certainly he was a devoted family man who loved his children; for them, according to one observer, he was "willing to make sacrifices."[8] He provided well for his family, as many accounts have suggested. Like Cochise, as noted, he was brave in battle, but also he admired courage when it appeared in his enemies. His demeanor was serious and grave when he appeared in council to represent his people. Yet, like most Chiricahuas, he also occasionally revealed a delightful sense of humor, though clearly the weight and responsibility of leadership, as in Cochise's case, normally prevented him from opening up. Unlike Cochise, he was a gregarious man who liked to bask in the prominence of public life. Among his people and with Americans he was self-confident and ostentatious, trusting and open. Yet to Mexicans he was a pragmatic and cautious man who studied situations closely. He took few unnecessary chances with them.

But perhaps his most significant attribute was his size, estimated at anything from six feet up to six feet seven inches. Actually, according to the surgeon who took precise measurements of his corpse several hours after his death, Mangas Coloradas stood six feet four inches tall (and this was when he was in his early seventies, when he could have lost a few inches). Definitely he towered head and shoulders over the average Apache man, who was five feet six inches tall. How readily impressive Mangas must have been to his people is clear in the doctor's description:

He was a man of the finest physical proportions and qualities . . . as straight as the reed from which his arrows were made. His head and face were formed after the finest and most marked models of his race. The forehead projected sharply and prominently over the eyes. It was unusually high and wide for an Indian. The head was remarkable for width from ear to ear. The cheek bones were large and prominent, and lower jaw massive. . . . His black eyes were very large, and, under the influence of anger, sparkled and flashed like black diamonds. . . . His neck was strong and firm, not gross, giving graceful attachment to a magnificent pair of shoulders and a body measuring forty-three inches in circumference, and clothed with muscles that would have crazed a young and enthusiastic student of anatomy. His limbs were faultless, perfect in proportions and symmetry.[9]

In his prime, Mangas Coloradas attracted followers from each of the four Chiricahua bands. His people looked to him because of his reputation and because of his bitter and uncompromising hatred of Mexico, especially Sonora. The band chiefs were also prominent local group leaders in the traditional organization of Chiricahua society. The local group led by Mangas Coloradas favored the natural springs at Santa Lucía, today known as Mangas or Mangus, about fifteen miles northwest of today's Silver City along the northeastern face of the Burro Mountains. This location placed him between the territory of two Chiricahua bands—the Bedonkohes to the north and the Chihennes east of him. In a way, his local group was a hybrid group, consisting of members with kinship to both bands. In later years, as his daughters matured, Mangas molded other alliances by marrying them off to leaders of other Chiricahua bands and other Apache groups. The most important bond was the one formed in this way with Cochise, the legendary leader of the Chokonen band of the Chiricahua Apaches.

Those readers who have read my biography of Cochise will notice that the structure of this work on Mangas Coloradas closely resembles that of *Cochise: Chiricahua Apache Chief*. Some material in Cochise naturally has found its way into this story about Mangas Coloradas, because the two men were not only allies but also relatives by marriage. When Mangas played a peripheral role, as in his presence during the Bascom affair, I have summarized the events and referred the reader to *Cochise* for the actual details. I have also chosen to employ the same structure in presenting ethnological information, with here perhaps a little more attention to the Chiricahua way of life. Yet the reader will discover a great deal of new and previously unpublished information about Mangas Coloradas and, I hope, will conclude this book with a good sense of what made this remarkable man tick.

The wonder of it all is that the U.S. government throughout these turbulent times continued to handle every Indian nation with an incredibly callous insensitivity. Admittedly, in Mangas Coloradas's case, while the Civil War ripped apart the nation the administration in Washington could afford Indian affairs only the lowest of priorities. Still, the story of Mangas Coloradas is characteristic of the plight shared by all American Indians. In the end he wanted only to be left alone to live in his beloved and beautiful valley at Santa Lucía Springs, which contained good water; afforded good grazing; and included fertile fields for planting corn, nearby mountains in which to gather food staples such as nuts, berries, and mescal, and good hunting grounds. The Washington bureaucracy fortunately did not directly victimize him. It did not behave as abominably as it did in the 1870s when it was responsible for a truly disgraceful treatment of his people, then under Victorio, Loco, and Nana, or as it did in the case of the Nez Percé Indians in 1877 and the Northern Cheyennes a year later, just to mention a few of the many abuses. Instead, Mangas Coloradas forfeited his life to an autocratic military regime in New Mexico that had abandoned its own moral and religious values.

Unfortunately, Mangas's case in its tragedy is but one among dozens, perhaps hundreds, of instances of our senseless mistreatment of the Indian. The Indians lived in the path of what must have seemed at first like an innocuous force simply moving west. Little did they realize that this force was relentless and was bent on an insidious destiny. Its forerunners seemed harmless: hunters and trappers who blazed the trail and usually developed friendly relations with the Indians and their world, for they shared similar ideals. But inevitably, on the heels of these pioneers arrived an influx of miners, ranchers, and, eventually, the military. This steamroller, which systematically moved west, was not governed by conscience. The Indians' ultimate destiny, determined by the wheels of the first wagon train, was to be recorded in blood—the blood of Mexicans, Americans, and Apaches. How dramatically and abruptly their world would change could not have been foreseen by the most sagacious.

Here follows the story of Mangas Coloradas: diplomat, visionary, and war chief. It is a profile of a magnificent Indian, the prototype of the Apache tribal chieftain. In him were come together, harmoniously and beautifully, all of those qualities most valued by the Apache culture. His is the story of a naturally modest people made fierce by misunderstanding and oppression. It is a sad story. It needs to be told.

MANGAS COLORADAS

Chapter 1

AN EIGHTEENTH-CENTURY CHIRICAHUA

MANGAS Coloradas! His name evokes vividly exciting images to students and buffs familiar with the Apache Indians of the Southwest. He was a complex man who combined wisdom and strength with pragmatism and intellect to lead his group of Chiricahua Apaches for almost fifty years. Yet, ironically, we remember him today not for the way in which he lived but for the barbaric and tragic way in which he died, murdered shamefully and premeditatedly by American soldiers after he had come in to parley with these same people. Who was this powerful leader of the Chiricahua Apaches, whose band inhabited southwestern New Mexico and ranged east into Arizona and south into the Mexican states of Sonora and Chihuahua? Who was this man who led his band for over half a century—willingly fighting Spaniards then Mexicans and finally, though reluctantly, Americans during his lifetime? Why did one veteran Chiricahua warrior, who had known Mangas Coloradas, Cochise, Victorio, and Geronimo, consider Mangas "by far the best" of all their leaders?[1]

During the nineteenth century three Chiricahua Apache chiefs occasionally demonstrated tribal leadership over a prolonged period of time. The first was Pisago Cabezón, and he did so from 1831 to 1840; the last was Cochise, the legendary leader and son-in-law of Mangas Coloradas, who provided direction to every Chiricahua band from the early 1860s until the early 1870s. Between these two men was Mangas Coloradas, the subject of this book, who exercised leadership within the tribe for over twenty years, from about 1840 until the early 1860s. This was not leadership in the political and social way that we expect today. The

Chiricahua tribe consisted of four autonomous bands, further divided into local groups and extended family groups. Each band and group had its own leaders. In times of crisis, however, the most dominant of the local group leaders led the band. When the bands united for a common cause, which occurred regularly during the turbulent years between 1831 and the early 1860s, the most respected chief, if he possessed sufficient credibility and strength of personality, led the tribe. During these years Mangas Coloradas filled that role.

The Apaches are members of the Athapaskan linguistic family, which is organized into three geographic divisions: Northern, Pacific Coast, and Southern. The tribes of this language group called themselves Tinneh, Dine, Tinde, and Inde, which translates to "Man" or "People." Anthropologists and historians disagree about the date of the Apaches' appearance in the Southwest. Some (including a recent, thought-provoking study by Richard J. Perry) place their arrival by the late sixteenth century; others argue that they were living in their historic territories by the 1400s.[2]

Linguistically, the Apache nation consisted of seven major groupings. The Jicarillas, Lipans, and Kiowa-Apaches formed the eastern division, and the Navajos, Mescaleros, Western Apaches, and Chiricahuas comprised the western division.[3] The Chiricahuas had virtually no contact with the eastern division. In contrast, the two easternmost of the four Chiricahua bands, the Chihennes and the Bedonkohes, which would have encompassed Mangas Coloradas's followers, had relations, though infrequent, with the Navajos. Mangas's people also had frequent contact with the Mescaleros east of the Rio Grande, whose language and culture more closely resembled those of the Chiricahuas than those of any other Apache tribe. Two Chiricahua bands, the Bedonkohes and the Chokonens, because of their band territory also enjoyed much contact with a few of the Western Apache groups of Arizona, even though those tribes differed in many ways. The Western Apaches practiced agriculture, were organized into clans, and traced their genesis from an emergence from the underworld. The Chiricahuas had none of these beliefs or habits, though after Anglo arrival in the 1850s a few bands did take up planting on a small scale.[4]

The history of the Chiricahua tribe from 1790 to 1863, in particular as it relates to Mangas Coloradas, is the focus of this study.

According to Chiricahua legends and myths, at one time the tribe lived near Ojo Caliente, or Warm Springs, New Mexico, where the members received supernatural powers and learned the customs of the tribe. Afterwards, they divided into bands. The Chihenne band remained, while the other three bands moved south and west to their historic territories. This theory finds support from Richard Perry's recent book, *Western Apache Heritage*, in which he suggests that the Chiricahuas followed the Rio Grande to southern New Mexico, where they separated into bands.[5]

The Chiricahuas consisted of four bands,[6] each inhabiting a well-defined area. Mexicans and Americans knew the local groups of the southernmost band as the Janeros, Carrizaleños, and Pinery Apaches, references to specific locations near which they lived. To other Chiricahuas these were known as the Nednhis, or "Enemy People." The primary homes of the southern band, one of the most numerous of the bands during the early years of Mangas Coloradas, were in the Mexican state of Chihuahua, although the mountains along the present-day United States–Mexico border provided sanctuary. The band occasionally roamed north into southern New Mexico and Arizona.

Mexicans referred to one of the local groups of the southern band as the Janeros because of its friendly relations with the people of Janos, a small town and presidio (or fort) located in northwestern Chihuahua about seventy-five miles south of present-day Columbus, New Mexico. The Janeros' primary leaders from the 1820s through the 1860s were Juan Diego Compá, Juan José Compá, Coleto Amarillo, Láceres, Galindo, and Juh, the last important chief of this band and associate of the notorious Geronimo in the 1870s and early 1880s. The Carrizaleños, probably another large local group of the Nednhis, frequently lived at peace near the presidio of Carrizal, which was some seventy-five miles southeast of Janos. If not a Nednhi local group, then the Carrizaleños represented another Chiricahua band unknown to the Apaches of the twentieth century because Mexican campaigns had virtually wiped them out as a distinct group by the early 1860s. Despite enjoying close ties to the Chihennes, the Janeros local group of Nednhis, and the Mescaleros, they were the most independent of the Chiricahua groups. During Mangas Coloradas's lifetime, Jasquedegá, Cristóbal, Francisquillo, Cigarrito, Cojinillín, and Felipe led this local group.

The second band, commonly known as the Central Chiricahuas, inhabited southeastern Arizona and the northern portions of the Mexican states of Sonora and Chihuahua. They also ranged north to the Gila River, east into southwestern New Mexico, and south into the Sierra Madre in Mexico. From 1800 until 1860 their

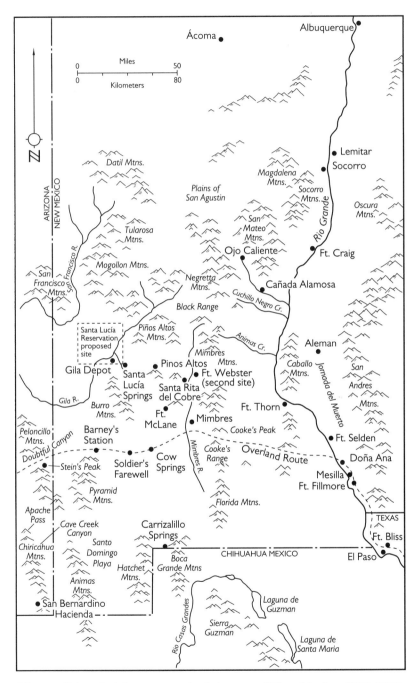

Mangas Coloradas's home range in Arizona and New Mexico, 1790–1863

leaders were Pisago Cabezón, Matías, Tapilá, Yrigóllen, Esquinaline, Miguel Narbona, and Cochise, who married a daughter of Mangas Coloradas in the late 1830s. To the Anglos of the nineteenth century and to Apaches of today, this was the first band called Chiricahuas. To the Apaches they were the Chokonens, which term is unclear in meaning but might translate to the "Cedar People," "Juniper People," or "Ridge of the Mountainside People," all names referring to Cochise's famous strongholds in the Dragoon and Chiricahua Mountains. Because of his close relationship to Cochise, Mangas Coloradas held close ties to this band, particularly during the last twenty-five years of his life.[7]

The Chiricahuas called the third band, which lived north of the others, the Bedonkohes. Probably the smallest of the bands, these people lived northeast of the Chokonens and northwest of the Chihennes along the Gila River and Mogollon Mountains. Their best known leaders during Mangas Coloradas's lifetime were Mahko, Mano Mocha, Teboca, and Phalios Palacio. Although Mangas's affiliation is unclear, he was likely a Bedonkohe by birth. Despite this ambiguity, in his prime this band looked to him for leadership, especially in times of war. In addition, at least two of his brothers became prominent Bedonkohe men; whether they married into the band or were born into it is difficult to determine at this late date. Taking all of the above into account, I would conclude that Mangas was a Bedonkohe by birth who married into the next Chiricahua band that will be discussed—the Chihennes, or "Red Paint People."[8]

The Chihenne band remained the easternmost and most numerous. Nineteenth-century Mexicans and Americans knew them under a variety of names: the Mimbres, Copper Mines, Warm Springs, and all-encompassing Gilas, names describing geographic local group areas where they lived. Their territory lay west of the Rio Grande in New Mexico, and they inhabited the Cuchillo, Black, Mimbres, Pinos Altos, Victoria, and Florida mountain ranges. Their leaders from the early 1800s through the 1860s were Ojos Coloradas, Mangas Coloradas (likely known as Fuerte until the late 1830s), Pluma, Cuchillo Negro (Black Knife), Itán, Ponce, Delgadito, and Victorio.[9]

The Chiricahua tribe's population never exceeded three thousand during Mangas Coloradas's lifetime. Although there was no "formal recognition of the tribe as such," the bands did determine all to be related, having "linguistic and cultural bonds which identify them as one people." Geronimo recalled that the four bands "were fast friends in the days of freedom" and that "only the destruction of all our people would dissolve our bonds of friendship." Although the band was considered more important than the tribe, relationships between members existed in many ways: they usually lived in peace with one another, visited frequently, and often assembled for social dances, puberty rites, and marriages. Occasionally they united for military action or to avenge great wrongs inflicted on them by their enemies. The territory of each band offered reciprocal rights of passage to tribal members. Moreover, the band also served as the political unit of the tribe, and an individual remained a member of the one into which he or she was born unless a man married outside his band, which before 1830 or so was uncommon. In this event, Chiricahua custom dictated that the man live with his wife's people and that his offspring be known by the affiliation of her band.[10]

Each band consisted of three to five local groups, with each of these units containing between ten and thirty extended families. The local group settlement was called a *gota*. The groups took their names either from a natural landmark or from the name of the unit's leader or chief (called a *nanta*), who had achieved prominence because of certain leadership qualities such as superior intellect, exceptional fighting skills, and generosity to the less fortunate of his group. The local groups established their camps at places that provided sanctuary from approaching enemies and easy access to water and grazing. For example, Mangas Coloradas favored the beautiful valley near Santa Lucía Springs, also known as Mangas Springs, located along the northeastern face of the Burro Mountains a few miles below the Gila River. Other Chihenne local groups preferred Ojo Caliente, the Mimbres River, the Mimbres and Black Mountains, Cañada Alamosa, or the Pinos Altos. Unlike the band, the local group was a mobile unit, though its members carried on most economic pursuits (except raiding) within its boundaries. Residence formed the mutual bond between members, but food scarcity, epidemics, internal conflicts, or the death of a leader could sever this relationship.[11]

Chiricahua local groups often consisted of one or more *rancherías*, usually separated by some distance and scattered up and down high mountain valleys at places advantageous for defense and for exploiting the local wildlife and plant resources. As mentioned, these clusters, called extended family groups, normally contained between ten and thirty family units. Each unit, or extended family, which was related through the maternal chain, usually established its home some distance from its neighbor, perhaps as much as one hundred yards away. A Chiricahua informant of Morris Opler described the extended family as a "group of homes occupied by relatives. At the very least an extended family is a father and mother, their unmarried children, and the families of their married daughters." The members of the extended family lived near each other, with each family having its own dwelling. A man's ties and concerns were with the welfare of his new extended family, which was the basic unit of Chiricahua society. Each of these subgroups became known by the name of the family leader.[12]

The various names for the Chihenne band (Gilas, Mimbres, Copper Mines, Warm Springs) were simply local group identifications. According to Gillett Griswold's excellent genealogical study of the Chiricahuas, Mangas Coloradas headed a Mimbres group rather than a Warm Springs group, thus implying that he led one local group of Chihennes who resided near the Mimbres River. Jason Betzinez agreed with Griswold, noting that the Warm Springs local group never recognized Mangas Coloradas as chief. In fact, Mangas had closer ties to the Chihenne groups living near the Mimbres River, but his local group area was some thirty to forty miles west of there, along the Burro Mountains near Santa Lucía Springs. Mangas Coloradas had risen to a local group leader as early as 1814, a Chihenne band leader by 1820, and a leader of the Bedonkohes shortly after. By 1840 he had matured into a Chiricahua tribal leader, particularly for the bellicose groups of Bedonkohes, Chokonens, and Chihennes. At times his influence seemed more pervasive among the Bedonkohes and Chokonens (with whom he had molded an alliance after the marriage of a daughter to Cochise, the up and coming leader of the Chokonens) than among some local groups of his own Chihenne band, who had their own capable leaders such as Delgadito, Ponce, and Cuchillo Negro, men who sometimes adopted policies for their followers contrary to the direction that Mangas espoused for his people.[13]

Besides Santa Lucía Springs, a beautiful area nestled among the foothills and buttes of the Burro Mountains, Mangas Coloradas ranged through what today is known as the Gila Wilderness Area. This includes the rugged Mogollon Mountains, the Burro Mountains, and part of the Pinos Altos range north of present-day Silver City. This country contains six ecological zones and eight primary vegetative types, ranging from the lowland Chihuahuan desert to coniferous groves of spruce, aspen, and pine forest. It

Santa Lucía Springs, New Mexico. A favorite camping area for Mangas Coloradas's local group. (Photo by Kathi Plauster)

varies from an altitude of 4,800 feet near the junction of the Gila and Turkey Creek to 10,895 feet at Whitewater Baldy in the Mogollons. The lower levels are dominated by grasslands and river canyons; the midrange elevations (7,000–9,000 feet) are dominated by mesas, streams, and canyons, with vegetation such as piñon and juniper woodland and ponderosa pines appearing as the elevation nears 9,000 feet; and the upper elevations are dominated by Douglas fir, aspen groves, meadows, and grassy parks. This country provided refuge to Mangas's people during the scorching hot summers, while the valleys and canyons furnished protection during the winters, which were usually mild. Besides sanctuary, this bountiful land furnished much of the food required for the Apaches to subsist. One writer labeled this area as an "Apache version of the modern supermarket with everything from nuts and berries to fruits and fresh meat in the form of rabbit, turkey, and mule deer." In addition, the Chiricahua Apaches' main food staple, the agave or mescal plant, grew abundantly along the lower hills just above the desert plains.[14]

It was into a distinguished family of one Bedonkohe local group that Mangas Coloradas first saw the light of day. At least one existing account has it that Mangas's father was Apache and his mother was Mexican. Given his extraordinary size, and the fact that the Chiricahuas reared captured children as their own, it is conceivable that Mangas had some Spanish blood, though Apache sources discount this ethnocentric view, which, as noted historian Dan Thrapp points out, "probably originated with those who refuse to believe in the intellectual capacity of an Indian." In addition, in Sonora even in the twentieth century it is commonly thought that Mangas Coloradas was "the son of a Mexican woman and an Apache man," according to Manuel Valenzuela, who grew up in the small town of Tacupeto some thirty miles south of Sahuaripa in the 1930s and 1940s. In any event, while we do not know exactly when or where he was born, we can make a good guess that it was in 1790 in the vicinity of Santa Lucía Springs (which the Chiricahuas called Tceguna, "Canyon Spreads Out") in southwestern New Mexico. An Apache retained strong bonds to his place of birth. The parents ensured that the child knew of his or her birthplace and, when near it, would roll the child on the ground to the four directions, the Apaches' sacred number.[15]

Mangas Coloradas's birth came at a time of dramatic changes to the Chiricahua world; the Spanish and Apaches had resolved their long-standing conflict, and peace reigned in Apachería. The Apaches had greeted the Spaniards as friends, but the warlike Europeans had abused the relationship in the seventeenth century, forcing the Indians to fight to preserve their traditional life. The invading Spaniards found that they could neither conquer unconditionally nor convert to Christianity the Apaches as they had other Indian nations. War raged for most of the eighteenth century, with the Spanish adopting one policy after another, ranging from extermination to colonization, in an attempt to pacify the incorrigible Apaches. In 1724, the Marqués de Casafuerte, viceroy of New Spain, dispatched an inspector to report firsthand the conditions of the northern frontier. That report spawned the Regulation of 1729, which became Spanish policy for the next forty years. This new order mandated a different, more humane approach to solving the Apache conflict. Spanish officials decided on a new philosophy to placate the Apaches by treating them honestly and kindly. The Regulation authorized military officials to accept immediately any Apache peace proposals; they would now wage war only as a last resort. Yet it failed miserably, primarily because the Apaches neither respected nor feared Spanish military power, and depredations actually increased.[16]

Realizing that their pacific policies had failed, the Spanish began sending out campaigns to hold back the onslaught during the 1750s. In mid-1751 a Sonoran offensive succeeded in striking a Chokonen ranchería in the Chiricahua Mountains and took several prisoners, including two chiefs. Five years later the Spanish organized another formidable campaign that surprised Chiricahua camps (likely Mangas Coloradas's ancestors) near the Gila River and the Mogollon Mountains; they slew thirty men and captured another thirty-nine. In the late 1750s the Apaches retaliated with relentless raids on Sonora and Chihuahua (then known as Nueva Vizcaya).[17]

The next twenty years were more of the same for the Chihenne and Bedonkohe bands. A chief named Chafolotes, who ranged from the Mimbres River to the Gila River, led one warlike Chihenne group. In June 1769 a Spanish army of seven hundred men destroyed two Chiricahua camps, including that of Chafolotes, in Chihenne band territory, killing sixty and capturing fifteen. One strike begot another in return. The Indians avenged this attack and routed a Spanish force in the Mimbres Mountains. A few years later the Chiricahuas became more audacious. A war party of more than two hundred men attacked the presidio of Janos in 1772. About a year later another war party of three hundred warriors surrounded Janos and severed all outside communications of the isolated presidio. These events were symptomatic of the relationship between Mangas Coloradas's ancestors and the encroaching Spaniards.[18]

The fierce Apache resistance forced Spain to reevaluate its policies. In 1768 royal authorities dispatched Marqués de Rubí to Mexico to assess the critical situation. After a three-year inspection tour, Rubí proposed dramatic changes. Having concluded that the Apaches were implacable enemies, he rationalized that the end would justify the means. He proposed an alliance with all non-Apache tribes and recommended an all-out war of extermination, anticipating the policy of genocide advocated by American General James Carleton one hundred years later. Rubí's suggestions became the model for the Regulation of 1772, which superseded that of 1729 and set down "realistic and uniform procedures." Although this new order failed to accept all of Rubí's extreme ideas, it did adopt his militaristic view as the main point of its policy. The Spanish would wage an aggressive and unrelenting war against the Apaches while retaining its humane policies. In effect, this policy advocated an arrogant benevolence in which the compassionate conquerors would treat all prisoners well because they were potential converts to Christianity. They would incarcerate all prisoners near presidios or send them as slaves to the interior, where Spanish officials planned to enlighten these heathens through education and then conversion. Eminent historian Max L. Moorhead termed this the "most brutal Indian policy ever sanctioned by the king of Spain."[19]

This new Spanish aggression served only to intensify hostilities, and the war raged on through the 1770s and into the next decade. Mangas Coloradas's forefathers undoubtedly participated in the bloody conflict, a gruesome struggle in which neither side seemed willing to give ground. In 1778, Irish-born Hugo O'Conor,[20] commandant-inspector of the Interior Provinces, called "Captain Red" by the Apaches because of his flaming red hair, led a large expedition into Chihenne country and succeeded in killing four and capturing fourteen others. The following spring the Chiricahuas avenged this attack, ambushing a detachment south of Janos and killing fourteen. In Nueva Vizcaya alone, during the five years ending in 1776, Apaches killed an incredible 1,674 Spaniards, captured 154, forced the abandonment of over one hundred ranches, and stole over 68,000 head of stock. This pattern continued into the mid-1780s, when Spain adopted yet another order, the Instruction of 1786.[21]

The Spanish experience of the previous quarter of a century formed the basis for this new policy enacted under the reforms of Bernardo de Gálvez, viceroy of New Spain. The colonists had come to realize that extermination alone was impracticable; instead, they might achieve victory by persuading the Apaches to live in peace near the Spanish presidios. The Instruction took a realistic look into Apache life-ways. It recognized that the Indians' economy consisted of gathering, hunting, and raiding, with the last an important element of not only his society but also his food chain. Perhaps they could subsidize the Apaches with the goods that the Indians normally consumed from raiding, while simultaneously trying to pacify them by turning them away from their native culture. The new policy also recognized another very important factor: that an Apache respected military force and power and that nothing could be accomplished until he was subdued through unremitting war. After all, "a bad peace was better than a good war." The Instruction addressed the fundamental issue of attempting to understand Apache behavior and proved to be the beginning of forty years of generally peaceful but often tenuous relations. It would succeed because it took a realistic and pragmatic approach in first confronting and later dealing with the Apaches.[22]

But relations between the Chiricahuas and Mexico failed to improve immediately. At least one large local group of Chihennes, probably the Warm Springs, whom Moorhead called the "Lower Mimbreños" (which also may have included the Janeros local group of Nednhis), held close ties to the Mescaleros east of the Rio Grande. Together they raided the settlements in New Mexico along the Rio Grande. Moorhead's "Upper Mimbreños," which would have included Mangas Coloradas's local group of Chihennes and the Bedonkohes, remained closely allied with the Chokonens in southeastern Arizona. Their war parties wreaked havoc on Sonora and Nueva Vizcaya.[23]

The Spaniards so fiercely continued their intensive campaigns through the mid-1780s that by 1786 several Chiricahua groups consented to an armistice. That October, El Chiquito, a warlike Chokonen leader, left his mountain strongholds from the Sierra de Peñascosa (the Dragoon Mountains, later made famous by Cochise) and brought his followers to Bacoachi, Sonora. It was an ephemeral truce, however. El Chiquito, a medicine man or shaman whose own followers lived in fear of his power, left the presidio and resumed hostilities the following March. About the same time, east of Sonora, at the presidio of San Buenaventura in Nueva Vizcaya, most of the Chihenne band and many Nednhis had made peace. Their leaders declared that New Mexican troops, allied with the Navajos, had compelled them to leave their homelands for northern Mexico. After a parley with Captain Antonio de Cordero, the Apaches settled near the presidio. Soon after, Mexican officials reported that they had distributed rations to eight chiefs and their local groups, representing some eight hundred to nine hundred individuals.[24]

This truce also proved to be brittle. Two events soon occurred to disrupt it. The first happened when Opata Indians on patrol from Bavispe, Sonora, ambushed a band of Chiricahuas heading to San Buenaventura to make peace. They killed two Apaches and confiscated a large quantity of material. Captain Cordero placated the skittish Indians and restored the stolen property. Shortly after, another Sonoran force jumped El Chiquito's Chokonens and killed a few Chihennes who happened to be visiting his camp. Immediately, the influential Chokonen leader sent emissaries to the Chiricahuas at San Buenaventura, inciting them to avenge this attack. To compound matters, Mantas Negras (Black Blankets), a recalcitrant and warlike Chihenne leader, came in from the mountains and stirred up the hornet's nest, urging war.[25]

On May 21, 1787, the Chihennes and Nednhis bolted from San Buenaventura, killing three Chokonens whom Sonoran officials had dispatched from Bacoachi to act as mediators. The Chokonens succeeded in slaying five men themselves before their relatives disappeared into the mountains. An incensed Captain Jacobo de Ugarte immediately retaliated, twice humbling the Chiricahuas in battle during the summer of 1787, killing twenty-five and capturing ninety-two. Later that fall Spanish troops attacked the village of the bellicose followers of Ojos Coloradas near San Buenaventura, killing five men and two women and capturing one boy. These campaigns, however, failed to restrain the Indians; during 1788 the Chiricahuas, primarily Chihennes and Nednhis, continued to terrorize Nueva Vizcaya. In response the Spanish launched additional campaigns, and the ongoing cycle seemed destined to continue.

By late 1789, however, the relentless Spanish campaigns had forced the Indians to conclude that capitulation and accommodation were better options than imprisonment and death. Some Chiricahua groups made peace at Janos later that year, and the influential Ojos Coloradas followed their cue in March 1789. Two months later, May 29 and 30, his entire group consummated a treaty at Janos. By 1791 most of the Chihennes and Nednhis had agreed to terms; a few indomitable bands remained at large, but authorities considered their numbers insignificant.[26]

A meeting at Janos between Captain Antonio de Cordero and Ojos Coloradas resulted in more than just a truce. Cordero obtained from the important Chihenne leader a wealth of ethnological information about the Chiricahua tribe and other Apaches as well.[27] This data, when analyzed, compares favorably to much of the information gathered by John Bourke in the 1880s and by anthropologists of the twentieth century.

Cordero concluded that the Chiricahuas consisted of three bands: the Segatajen-ne, the Chiricahuas proper (Chokonens); the Tjuiccujen-ne, or the Gileños (Bedonkohes); and the Iccujen-ne, the Mimbreños (Chihennes). He believed that the Mimbreño band, which was the largest in numbers, consisted of two groups: the Upper and Lower Mimbreños. It seems plausible that these two Mimbreño groups were in actuality the bands that would become known as the Chihennes and Nednhis. Those who remained in northern Mexico, the upper unit, lived in peace at Janos and Carrizal, thus representing the two large local groups of the Nednhi band. Meanwhile, the lower unit remained in southern New Mexico, the historic homeland of the Chihenne band, and became further divided into local groups, which would become known as the Mimbres, Warm Springs, and Copper Mines Apaches.

By the early 1790s Spanish military power compelled most of the Chiricahuas to sue for an armistice, which it finally granted under the condition that the Indians live quietly and peacefully in designated areas near Spanish presidios. The Chiricahua groups settled near Janos and Carrizal in Nueva Vizcaya and Fronteras, Bacoachi, and Bavispe in Sonora. The Spanish typically constructed each presidio around a center plaza or parade ground and garrisoned it with fifty to seventy-five troops. They also frequently constructed huts outside the presidio's walls for Indian habitation. Almost at once the conquerors introduced a systematic policy intended to disrupt and destroy the Apache social system. On the one hand they issued rations of corn or wheat, meat, brown sugar, salt, and tobacco at an annual expense of twenty-three thousand pesos. On the other hand, the Spanish furnished gifts of guns, liquor, clothing, and other items with the duplicitous intention of making the Indians totally subservient to and dependent on the Spaniards. They issued inferior weapons that easily broke down, requiring the services of a Spanish gunsmith to repair them. Furthermore, the Spanish hoped the Apaches would neglect their bows and arrows, which they used more effectively than firearms. The whites also dispensed intoxicating liquors so that the Indians would develop a taste for them. "It was at once a highly sophisticated, brutal and deceptive policy of divide and conquer, of peace by purchase, of studied debilitation of those who accepted peace and of extermination of those who rejected it," wrote Max L. Moorhead. However cruel and immoral, he concluded it was "a practical policy and one which offered both races the opportunity for survival."[28]

This system proved to be so successful that more Apaches came in than the Spaniards had bargained for. By the mid-1790s the number of Apaches supported at the presidios had grown to the point that it caused a financial burden. With the outbreak of war between Spain and France, the royal crown had fewer resources to allocate to colonial Mexico. Therefore, the commanding general ordered its administrators to launch a program to curtail and then control expenses. This change in policy posed new challenges for military officials, for they had to accomplish this without alarming the restive Apaches. They somehow had to persuade the Indians that they should return to their indigenous mountains, where they again had to sustain themselves by hunting and gathering. Meanwhile, the Spanish expected the Indians to live in peace under the threat of swift punitive action. At Janos alone, by mid-1796, the number of Apaches living there had dropped to 30 percent of those who had previously received rations, a trend that continued into the 1800s.[29]

Most historians agree that these peaceful relations continued for the remainder of the Spanish period—that is, until 1821—and there is evidence to conclude that they prevailed until 1830. William B. Griffen estimates that perhaps two-thirds of the Chiricahua Apaches participated in the presidio system, also known as *establecimientos de paz,* "peace establishments." He concludes that the cost in controlling the Apaches was far less than the damage that hostilities would have caused and the tremendous expense that punitive military campaigns would have incurred, not to mention the loss in lives on both sides.[30]

It is impossible to state at this late date how all of this affected the young boy who would become known as Mangas Coloradas. We know little about his early years. He was born about 1790, probably in southwestern New Mexico, and his father was undoubtedly an important man at the local group level. Perhaps his parents could have predicted from the beginning that the baby who would become known as Mangas Coloradas would grow into a man of enormous size and strength. The Chiricahuas believed that if the baby "does not cry or cry loudly" at birth, then that child "will grow up to be strong." One or two months after birth, when his parents were sure he would live, he received a name suggested either by the midwife or by an unusual event that distinguished the birth. His Apache name was not known; once he matured and developed into a young man of extraordinary physique, his parents bestowed upon him his Indian name, which likely referred in some manner to his size or strength. According to Grenville Goodwin, "an Apache usually had more than one name: a childhood name, a given name considered the real name, and possibly one or two nicknames acquired in later life." The distinguished anthropologist Morris Opler points out that most Chiricahua names "tend to follow some physical or behavioral peculiarity of the individual bearing it, or it refers to a well-known event in which he was involved." It would be later in life that this young man would receive the name Kan-da-zis-tlishishen, meaning "Red (or Pink) Sleeves." The Mexicans converted this to Mangas Coloradas, or "Red Sleeves," a subject that will be discussed in depth in the coming pages.[31]

Mangas spent much of his youth in his historic territory, living in peace with the Spanish in the Burro Mountains and the region of present-day Silver City. Occasionally his local group or family unit assembled for a journey to one of the frontier presidios and towns to trade or to receive rations. One brother, Phalios [Félix] Palacio, reportedly attended a mission school at Paso del Norte,[32] but whether the youthful Mangas followed his lead is not known. We have some understanding what it must have been like for Mangas Coloradas as a youth growing up at the turn of the eighteenth century. For this we can thank the account of Jason Betzinez, the recollections of Geronimo, the data gathered by anthropologists, in particular Morris Opler, and the extraordinary contemporary reports of Lieutenant José Cortés and Captain Antonio de Cordero, both written in the 1790s. These provide us with an insight into the Chiricahua Apache life-style and culture about the time of Mangas Coloradas's birth.[33]

Mangas Coloradas matured dramatically during this period of peace. His immediate family consisted of his maternal grandparents, parents, and brothers and sisters, but most of their names are not recalled today. Brothers were inseparable if they lived in the same local group. Several of his brothers became prominent men among the Bedonkohe and Chihenne bands. They were Pitfhan, Phalios Palacio, José Mangas (who enjoyed a close relationship with his better-known brother), and Chaha.

Apache society was both religious and ritualistic; ceremonies and supernatural help explained virtually every aspect of everyday life.[34] When a child was a few weeks old, his mother or maternal grandmother pierced the earlobes so that he would "hear things sooner" and obey quicker. Apache parents loved and cherished their children. They rarely administered corporal punishment, although discipline remained ever-present. A parent constantly stressed to his or her child the need to obey one's parents—a principle that the child learned early in life.

As the infant grew, a shaman or medicine man performed several rituals to ensure that the individual followed the same steps in life as had the mythical Apache culture heroes such as Life Giver, Child of the Water, Killer of Enemies, Mountain People and Mountain Spirits, and White Painted Woman. Adults had their own ceremonies, power, and supernatural help to protect themselves; a child, however, could tap into none of these beneficial sources. As a result, the shaman performed ceremonies that not only protected the youth from evil forces but also indoctrinated him about the power of shamans and the importance of prayers, songs, and sacred objects. A baby spent the first six or seven months in a specially built cradle. The mother constructed the cradle of oak, ash, or walnut, using sotol or yucca stalk for the supporting back pieces and employing buckskin to cover the frame. In each phase of construction the shaman prayed that the child would have a long and good life. In addition, he attached amulets, such as bags of pollen or turquoise, to the cradle to protect it. The mother added her own good luck charms, perhaps the right paw of a badger or the claws of a hummingbird, to protect the baby from malevolent forces. In the cradle ceremony, held early in the morning with members of the local group attending, the shaman held it to the four directions, beginning first to the east and then proceeding clockwise back to the beginning, at which point he placed the baby inside. Afterwards the group engaged in a celebratory feast or joined in a social dance.

The next important event in a child's life was the moccasin ceremony. Although held when the child was as young as seven months, it could take place as late as the age of two. As in all Chiricahua ceremonies, a shaman or an individual who knew the rules directed the celebration. Like the cradle ceremony, it also served as a social gathering. After the infant, called Child of the Water, took four ceremonial steps, with the shaman invoking a prayer after each, a great feast was held.

Another important ritual was the spring hair cutting, usually held after the moccasin ceremony. The shaman applied pollen to the child's cheek and head and cut most of its hair, leaving one or more locks. Most Chiricahuas paid close attention to the grooming of their hair, and that included Mangas Coloradas, who, in traditional Apache custom, wore his hair long and below his shoulders.

It was as a youth that Mangas learned about Chiricahua tradition and religion, which focused on the supernatural and emphasized "the virtues of humility and gratitude." His father trained him to be self-sufficient, taught him to hunt, instructed him in the art of warfare, and educated him in the history of his people. His mother taught him about Usen, the Apache supreme being (also called Life Giver), and instilled in him the importance of religion. She also ensured that the lad learned about such culture heroes as the Mountain People, who protected the tribe and were "potential sources of supernatural power." His elders recalled familiar animal stories, such as the adventures of the coyote, an inveterate trickster, from which the boy was expected to learn morals or lessons. The Chiricahuas educated their youths for one reason: to prepare them for the responsibilities of adulthood.

The Apaches were a happy, proud, and fiercely independent people. Their homes, at least for most groups, were wickiups or jacales, circular in form. The women constructed the shelters of either oak or willow tree branches, which they covered with brush, such as bear grass, and animal hides. The home, about seven feet high and eight feet in diameter, was not only practical and economical, but also "warm and comfortable." To afford family privacy, the Chiricahuas would locate each dwelling away from their neighbors, perhaps one hundred yards or so, but close enough to help each other in case of an emergency. The Chihenne band was the only Chiricahua unit to use the tepee, which we normally associate with the Plains Indians, but for the most part that custom disappeared by the early 1800s.

The wickiup had a hole in the center of its roof to act as a fireplace. The women placed pieces of hides on top of the bear grass for waterproofing. Inside, they made beds of grass and brush on which they placed robes and other skins. Their utensils were few but practical: baskets for collecting nuts and berries, pitch-covered water containers, a few dishes and cups, and several bags or parfleches, normally made of deer skin, used to store excess food and clothing.

Although primarily hunters and gatherers, the Chiricahuas did attempt some agriculture on a small scale, cultivating the land on a limited basis. This practice seemed confined to the Chihenne and Bedonkohe bands, particularly the followers of Mangas Coloradas in the later years of his life. Their economy consisted mainly of the game they hunted, the wild plants they harvested (various nuts, berries, and their most important food staple, the sweet and nutritious agave or century plant, whose crowns were baked, dried, and stored), and the stock and loot they confiscated from raiding. The Spanish, as has been discussed, understood the Apaches and decided to supplement their diets with rations in the hope that their raiding would come to a halt.

Apaches were accomplished hunters, and some men exhibited extraordinary skills in bringing down large animals. Herds of mule deer, whitetail deer, antelopes, and even some elk roamed parts of

Apachería. An Apache possessed infinite patience and discipline when stalking game. In fact, one Apache declared that his people could not employ their ingenious methods today, for they were too dangerous. The hunter would often disguise himself by slipping the tanned head of a doe over his shoulders. He would then crawl near the deer, "imitating the motions of a doe." Eventually he would approach close enough to fit an arrow into his bow and drive it into the buck. Yet he would not recommend this practice for today's hunters. Declared one Apache, "Today with so many amateur hunters in the woods this would probably mean sure death, but in those days it was safe enough." Once the hunter returned to camp, he willingly shared his venison with "all who come around," especially the women without husbands, who were very eager for meat."[35]

The Chiricahuas' treks into the buffalo country were infrequent, yet both Geronimo and Jason Betzinez talked about hunting buffalo, and Opler heard an account of a hunt east of Albuquerque. Before white hunters slaughtered the animal almost to extinction, the buffalo did range into eastern New Mexico and southwestern Texas until the early 1870s.[36] Mangas Coloradas likely participated in several hunts during his lifetime, but a trip to buffalo country meant traveling about 150 miles through Mescalero territory, and the Chiricahuas were not always on good terms with that tribe. Likely the majority of their hunts were carried out on those occasions when the Chiricahuas roamed east of the Rio Grande to join their Mescalero brethren in hunting buffalo in southwest Texas. More often, however, they obtained buffalo skins simply by trading with the Mescaleros, at least before 1840, when the two groups seemed to have enjoyed more frequent intercourse.[37]

Though fish abounded in some mountain streams, most Apaches shunned fishing because fish reminded them of snakes. They also refrained from eating bear meat because the bear walked erect and might be the reincarnation of an evil man. An Apache would defend himself, however, and kill a bear if attacked. Of course the hunters also sought out such small mammals as rabbits, opossums, porcupines, and squirrels.

The women gathered fruit, nuts, berries, and wild potatoes and onions. In the Chiricahua diet these items ranked just as important as meat. The Apaches knew many natural food sources that could be found and harvested in the desert and mountains. These staples included the stalk and fruit of the yucca, prickly pear fruit, berries, sunflower seeds, acorns, mesquite beans, piñon nuts, and walnuts. Chiricahua local groups were mobile during those periods when plants and nuts came into season. The plant and berry harvest began in the early spring and continued into the summer, while the harvest for wild nuts began in the fall. Yet the most important food staple was the agave or century plant, also known as the mescal plant, which the Indians gathered and harvested in late spring. This venture was truly a community or local group event. Even the men would participate in the proceedings, dragging the crowns of the plant to a central pit for baking. They also helped dig the pit, gathered the rocks that lined the oven, and provided protection for the temporary settlement. After roasting, which could take as long as four days, the women dried the agave and stored it for year-round use. The Indians used this nutritious and sweet product in a variety of resourceful ways.

A family would collect forty to sixty crowns of the agave plant, which they would store for the coming year. The women, after prying the crown apart from the stalk, trimmed the leaves and then brought the crowns to the pit. One Apache described to anthropologist Morris Opler how they harvested the mescal plant:

> The pit is round, seven feet or more across and three or four feet deep. This hole is lined evenly with rocks. Then a big pile of wood is brought. This is put into the hole in criss-cross layers, first a layer one way and then a second layer the other. It is built up like this until the pit is just about full. Then more rocks are put on top of this wood. Fire is touched to it—from the east side first, then from the south, then from the west, and from the north. Then the woman who did this prays. They let the wood burn to ashes. Then they put the mescal in. Each woman will have a leaf on her mescal heads in a certain place so that she can tell her own. Wet grass goes on top of the mescal, then dirt until no more steam comes out.

According to Opler, "The bottom part of the mescal, the part that is put in the oven, has to be eaten at once unless it is to be dried and preserved. It will spoil if it is not dried." The women peel the leaves off, put them "in the sun to dry," and pound the "softer centers . . . into thin sheets. Juice, drained from the pounded mescal suspended over a receptacle, is poured on the dried mescal sheets and forms a preservative glaze." The Indians store most of the nutritious mescal in this manner, in a "sun-dried, caked state." To be made ready to eat, it can be soaked in water until it softens and then mixed with berries or nuts for consumption.[38]

One prominent historian reports that the Chiricahuas lived in perfect harmony with their environment: "They knew the use of every plant, the habits of every animal, the storing of every item of food—perfect adaptation to environment."[39]

We can easily understand, given such an uncivilized, demanding, and unforgiving environment, why the Chiricahuas were forced to spend most of their time in wresting out a living in simple survival. In other words, even when a warrior remained in camp, he devoted most of his time to the vital economic pursuits of hunting and gathering. One Chiricahua declared that he would "hunt every day" until he got something. "If I have good luck, I can lay off for two to three days."[40] In reality, a man spent very little of his time raiding, a fact that would surprise those whose perceptions of Apaches, or of most other American Indians, for that matter, derive mainly from Hollywood films.

But certainly Mangas Coloradas did learn, and learned well, the economic value of raiding and warfare. Although among the Chiricahuas both were economic pursuits, the terms denote distinct and profound differences. The raid's primary purpose was clearly economic; its objective was to capture livestock for slaughter and food. The war party had two motives: it focused not only on plunder but also on striking the enemy to avenge Apache losses. The Chiricahuas organized most war parties for this reason: revenge. The armistice between them and the Spanish did not alter the manner in which the Apaches trained their youths for adulthood. All Apache children, and especially the boys, went through a formal, vigorous training period designed to prepare them for adult responsibilities.

Because Mangas Coloradas's father had likely been a leading man at the local group level, the local group probably expected Mangas to assume a leadership role, although a youth did not automatically inherit leadership. Family origin provided Mangas Coloradas with status, yet it did not guarantee him rank. A person earned that through his actions and accomplishments. "Ability in war makes a leader," insisted one Chiricahua to anthropologist Morris Opler. "It is easier to get to the front if you are a good fighter." There were no pacifists among Chiricahua Apache leaders. A man could emerge as leader only if he demonstrated superior fighting skills when at war while assuming an active role in the everyday affairs of his local group. He must be willing, even eager, to speak in public and able to supply wisdom in council, to practice fairness in arbitrating disputes between group members, to make personal sacrifices, and to demonstrate a deep sensitivity to the less fortunate members of his group. Many courageous and able fighters lacked the personality, the wisdom, and the capacity for self-sacrifice to become leaders. The son of a chief, however, had an advantage in that his elders had usually provided him with excellent training as a young man, thus preparing him better than most to follow in the footsteps of his father and assume a leadership role.

The training regimen traditionally began when the child was about the age of six or seven. It developed slowly and intensified as the youth became a teenager. A male relative, normally the father, would present the youth with a bow and arrows to begin the process. This enabled the boy to begin hunting small animals and birds. Apache youngsters played competitive games, too, such as hide-and-seek, foot races, tug-of-war, and wrestling, all emphasizing speed, agility, and strength. And of course a boy learned early how to ride, for "there were always some gentle horses" for him to begin with. Ubiquitous in all stages of Chiricahua life were ceremonies, shamans, prayers, songs, and sacred objects, for the child needed all the help he could get until he could develop his own source of power.

Physical fitness, self-discipline, and independence dominated the training process during the next stage of preadolescence. Members of the extended family group advised the youth to take care of himself. Chato, a renowned Chokonen warrior of the 1880s, revealed to one anthropologist how his father had instructed him as he began the training process, probably in the 1850s: "My son, you know no one will help you in this world. You must do something. . . . Your legs are your friends; your brain is your friend; your eyesight is your friend. . . . "[41] The boy began to hunt more, primarily birds and small mammals, and by these experiences developed indispensable skills, such as patience and perseverance and the ability to stalk. To ensure continued success in hunting, the elders advised the boy "to swallow whole the raw heart of the first kill." The teenage boy also became steadily more experienced with horses, learning to care for them and how to ride expertly. In addition, as the youth progressed in his training, the elders assigned to him more responsible scout and guard duties around camp.

By the time the boy reached puberty, from thirteen to sixteen years of age, he was ready to begin formal training as a warrior. He became a *dikohe*, a novice or apprentice warrior. A boy volunteered when he felt old enough and mature enough. His family cautioned him that portentous days lay ahead, filled with challenges, dangers, and hardships. Now the training process assumed a formal and serious tone. Whereas to this juncture the extended family group had assumed full responsibility for the boy's training, now the local group assumed the obligation. The leaders assigned the young man to a shaman who knew about the challenges and perils of war. The training also became more vigorous than before: physical activities, such as wrestling, slingshot fights, small bow and arrow contests, and footraces dominated. The shamans emphasized discipline and obedience. Just as in today's American culture, in which many of our finest athletes and leaders could have been found in their youth on a playground or a ball field, their actions, talents, and skills easily discernible, so it was with the Apaches. Chiricahua culture was no different: future leaders were easily recognizable, and status and recognition originated with these contests. The maturing youth who would become known as Mangas Coloradas must have been most conspicuous among his peers.

Now the young man was ready for the final phase of the dikohe period. When he heard that the leaders were organizing a raiding or war party, he volunteered for duty. A shaman prepared him for the final steps in the training process and cautioned him about the important challenges ahead. The dikohe was an apprentice warrior trying to learn from the experienced men of his group the craft of making war. Of primary concern was the individual's behavior during the raid and his obedience to his leaders. If the dikohe acted suspiciously or exhibited some signs of dishonesty, cowardice, or gluttony, or was unrestrained and had sexual intercourse during one of the first four journeys, the men would label him unreliable for the rest of his life. The leaders assigned him menial camp chores, such as cooking and preparing the warriors' beds, guard duty, and horse-holding responsibilities. The experienced men also protected the novice from danger, for any injury to him would reflect on the party's leaders.

During the first four raids the warriors called the young man Child of the Water. He wore a ceremonial hat for protection and learned special words that the shaman taught him for the occasion.[42] In addition, he had other restrictions: he must drink all liquids through a straw and eat all foods cold. After the fourth raid, which typically could have been one year after his first, unless the warriors disapproved of his performance, the young man joined the ranks of the warriors. Though we know nothing of Mangas's first experiences at war, we can assume that they occurred in the early 1800s, possibly against other Indian enemies, such as the Navajos in New Mexico or the Pimas or Papagos of Arizona. Or perhaps his group raided Sonora, as Chihuahua remained virtually exempt from Apache raids during the first decade of the nineteenth century.[43]

Mangas's dikohe period was undoubtedly a successful one. He had grown into a large and able-bodied young man, much taller and stronger than the average Apache youth. Because he was most probably the son of a leader, he undoubtedly had received excellent training. The dynamic combination of thorough training, a naturally aggressive nature, and extraordinary physical skills catapulted him into the ranks of warriors and very early into a leadership position among the younger men in his local group.

Chapter 2

MANGAS COLORADAS AS FUERTE

COULD Mangas Coloradas have been known by another name during the first fifty years of his life? The evidence suggests such, for no mention of an Apache by that name appears in contemporary Mexican documents until 1842, by which time he had become the acknowledged leader of the war faction of the Chiricahuas. This group would have included some Chokonens, his Santa Lucía local group of Chihennes, and the Bedonkohes. Mangas had attained this prominent position over a gradual period; therefore, it seems reasonable to conclude that before 1840 he was known by another name. If so, he undoubtedly was a man well known to Mexicans and to a lesser extent those Americans who had infiltrated southern New Mexico and northern Mexico during the 1820s and 1830s. An American named Benjamin Wilson claimed that Mangas Coloradas had saved his life in the spring of 1837. There can be no dispute about the date, if we can trust Wilson's recollections, for he noted that the incident took place shortly after the nefarious Johnson massacre of Chiricahua Apaches on April 22, 1837, an event that we will examine in more detail in a following chapter.[1]

So what occupied Mangas Coloradas for the first fifty years of his life? Mexican contemporary documents contain no references to a man by that name before 1842, although there are countless references to Juan José Compá, Pisago Cabezón, and even Chihenne local group leaders Cuchillo Negro, Itán, and Ponce, who were subordinates to Mangas Coloradas in the 1840s and 1850s. Yet we know from Chiricahua Apache oral history that by the early 1830s they regarded Mangas as their most prominent war leader (a position to which a warrior ascended over a gradual period) and that he had been prominent in tribal affairs since 1820 or so. I suggest that he was an important leader within his historic local group and band territory, but known to whites under another name. The most logical candidate, for reasons that we will discuss, and the only one who truly fits, was an important and powerful Chiricahua chief in southern New Mexico named Fuerte, Spanish for "manly, strong, or stout," certainly appropriate words to describe the powerful physique of Mangas Coloradas.

A great deal of evidence exists to support this conclusion. If taken separately, each as just one piece of a puzzle, the facts might not be convincing. Yet, when we consider them as an aggregate, we can form the frame of the puzzle and many of its interlocking pieces, thereby providing enough clues to make a nearly positive identification, or at least to supply the best explanation that can be arrived at at this late date.

To begin with, Fuerte was a chief of the Chihenne band who first came into prominence about 1813, approximately the same time that Mangas Coloradas became a leader, according to the scant Apache oral history. Both seem to have been about the same age. Fuerte's range or local group territory centered on Santa Lucía Springs and included the Mogollon Mountains and Santa Rita del Cobre, identical to that of Mangas Coloradas in the 1840s–1860s. Fuerte enjoyed a close association with Pisago Cabezón, the great Chiricahua leader of the 1830s and 1840s, as did Mangas Coloradas in the early 1840s. Other important Chihenne leaders of the 1830s, such as Cuchillo Negro, Ponce, and Itán, clearly acted in a subordinate role to both Fuerte and Mangas Coloradas. Mexican officials named both men "General" during treaties made in 1832 and in 1843. Fuerte's personality and physique also match that of Mangas Coloradas. Both preferred to keep aloof from Mexicans, choosing to live as traditional Apaches in freedom and away from the scrutiny of presidio life. Yet perhaps the most convincing argument that the two were the same man has to be what the name Fuerte means or implies in Spanish: strong, manly, or stout. Mangas Coloradas was unusually large for an Apache, or even a white man for the early nineteenth century, standing about six feet five inches tall and weighing more than two hundred pounds. Finally, references to Fuerte disappear after 1837 without any mention of his death, while references to Mangas Coloradas begin soon after that time. Other Apache scholars, notably William B. Griffen and the late Eve Ball, concur with my conclusion that Fuerte and Mangas Coloradas could possibly have been one and the same man.[2]

Mangas, a son of Mangas Coloradas. He took an active role during the Geronimo Wars of the 1880s. (Courtesy National Archives)

According to Chiricahua Apache sources, Mangas Coloradas became a chief at an unusually young age. His brother Phalios Palacio told one American that his mother and father had died when he was a young man, probably after 1810.[3] If true, it may have been about that time that Mangas Coloradas left his Bedonkohe band and married into a prominent family of a mixed Chihenne-Bedonkohe group which resided near Santa Lucía Springs, today known as Mangas, northwest of present-day Silver City. Usually parents arranged marriages between bands, especially if they involved sons and daughters of prominent leaders. Perhaps this understanding occurred in the days following a triumphant war party's return to camp, for the Chiricahuas often "turned their victories into a celebration, a dancing and marrying time." This common practice continued during the nineteenth century.[4] The union, which formed strong bonds between the families, was a practice employed by Mangas Coloradas himself with his children in later years. Following Apache tradition, he joined his wife's people, and his responsibilities and obligations bound him to his new extended family. He quickly made a name for himself.

A great leader often possessed some charismatic features that prompted men to follow his direction. Perhaps it was his giant stature and strength which inspired confidence in his followers, or perhaps by acts of generosity he repeatedly showed that he placed the group's welfare above his own. Maybe it was his pragmatic and common sense approach to problems or perhaps his ability as a war leader, for all Chiricahua leaders possessed this attribute. For a man to become a leader in his early twenties, his relatives must have trained him well. He also must have possessed the intellectual qualifications and dynamic personality necessary to lead a warrior race. For example, Juan Diego Compá, brother of the better known Juan José Compá, was in his early twenties when he succeeded his father (El Compá) as chief upon the latter's death in 1795. The great Pisago Cabezón was in his early twenties when he followed the footsteps of his father as leader about 1793. William Griffen's excellent analysis of Apache leaders at Janos in the 1790s reveals that the average age of a Chiricahua chief was thirty-nine. The youngest leader was twenty-two. By the time the Spanish first mentioned an Apache leader named Fuerte in 1814, he was probably about twenty-four or twenty-five years old. Although this was an atypical age for a leader, it was not improbable if he had the bloodline, personality, and qualifications.[5]

The recollections of Jason Betzinez and Geronimo, and the important genealogical work of Gillett Griswold, also reveal one other important detail: Mangas Coloradas became chief of the Bedonkohe band at an early age, probably by 1820 or so, after the death of their beloved leader Mahko.[6]

According to the Chiricahuas, Mahko was the greatest Bedonkohe chieftain of his time. They remembered him as a man of peace, likely because he lived much of his life during the more tranquil times after 1790. His local group territory was the Mogollon Mountains west to today's Clifton, Arizona; there he raised corn and horses, some of which he traded to Mexicans. Although the Apaches disagreed about when he passed from the scene (Betzinez and Griswold thought the 1830s), it would appear that sometime between 1815 and 1820 would be more likely. Geronimo, born in the early 1820s, declared that he never met Mahko, noting that the chief had died when Geronimo's father was a young man. Apache sources all agree that Mahko's death left a tremendous void in leadership among the Bedonkohes. Because they now "lacked a strong leader," they looked to someone outside their band. Mangas, born a Bedonkohe, had many relatives and friends among that band. As head of the hybrid Chihenne-Bedonkohe local group living near Santa Lucía Springs, on the south and eastern limits of Bedonkohe country, he became the logical choice for the Bedonkohes, and they came "under the influence of Mangas Coloradas . . . particularly for war forays into Mexico." Thus, by 1820, Mangas Coloradas, still known as Fuerte, not only dominated his own local group living at Santa Lucía, but also emerged as the prominent chief among the Bedonkohes during times of war. He would retain this status for the next forty years.[7]

As a youth coming to maturity in the 1800s, Mangas Coloradas witnessed a gradual change in relations between his people and the Spanish. His local group, indeed most of his band, had remained encamped in their historic territory, living as they always had except that raiding of Spanish settlements had ceased for the time being. In referring to this time years later, he told an American that the Mexicans had compelled those Indians not living at presidios to "quit the valley and fertile parts to live in mountains and rugged and unfruitful places."[8] To be sure, opportunities still abounded for a young man to enhance his reputation through raiding; this remained an important ingredient in Chiricahua culture. Warriors carried out these forays against other Indian enemies in New Mexico and occasionally against ranches in the interior of Sonora. They ignored travelers and settlements in New Mexico and Chihuahua (then called Nueva Vizcaya), for the Apaches well understood that the Spanish military would vigorously exact revenge for any raids there.

As is the case for most historic American Indians, we know little about Mangas Coloradas's early life. The Apaches had no written records and a cultural taboo about mentioning the names of the deceased. Naturally, this combination presents tremendous problems for the historian. Unfortunately, unlike other Indian tribes, Chiricahua Apaches have little oral history on any individual before 1870. Still, as with any historic figures, there have come down colorful legends and myths surrounding Mangas Coloradas's rise to prominence. In all likelihood some are apocryphal in nature. Nonetheless, the historian must address, analyze, and consider each story, because together they provide the only information available about Mangas's early life.

John C. Cremony, whose writings are often prone to exaggeration and so frequently unreliable, wrote two accounts that discussed Mangas Coloradas's evolution into an important Chiricahua chief. We must view each with caution, yet they are valuable, for we can verify most of the events discussed by Cremony. Cremony's problem was less his creative imagination, though occasionally he could invent a whopping story, but instead his propensity to overstate. In addition to Cremony's writings, in 1873 an important article published in the *Boston Evening Transcript* related incidents of Mangas Coloradas's early life.[9]

The Spanish peace policy had continued into the early 1800s, with large numbers of Chiricahuas remaining near the presidios in northern Mexico. Yet some Chiricahuas had elected to live in the hinterlands, too remote for the Spanish to enjoy any direct control but close enough so that the Indians were reluctant to launch any large-scale expeditions, fearing as they did the strong Spanish military power. Nonetheless, some raiding was done, primarily into Sonora and New Mexico.

It was against the former that Mangas Coloradas, in one of his earliest raids, gained notoriety and emerged as a successful war leader. Exactly when and where the foray occurred is not known for sure, although the period between 1812 and 1815 would be a good estimate. In many details Cremony's account differs from the report published in the *Transcript*, although both accounts ascribe almost superhuman feats to the young warrior. According to Cremony, Mangas Coloradas directed one of his first important incursions into Sonora. During this raid he captured "a handsome and intelligent Mexican girl, whom he made his wife, to the exclusion of his Apache squaws. This singular favoritism bred some trouble in the tribe for a short time, but was suddenly ended by Mangas challenging any of the offended brothers or relatives of the discarded wives." Cremony claims that "two accepted the wager and both were killed in a fair duel."[10]

That all of this took place exactly in the manner described by Cremony is highly unlikely. Mangas Coloradas had several wives during his lifetime, each of whom he treated well and respected, according to Chiricahua Apache morality. Apache men did not mistreat female captives sexually.[11] Occasionally a young woman would fall in love with her captor, and this seems to have been the case with Mangas Coloradas's Mexican wife, known as Carmen. The Apaches normally accepted female captives into their new households, although the captives could cause domestic strife. Even today the Chiricahuas remember the story of Mangas Coloradas's Mexican wife, but the general feeling was that she fit in well with his other wives. Some did not care for her, as demonstrated by the comments of one woman, who recalled that "there was lots of trouble over her. She puts on airs—she doesn't know her place."[12] About the only part of Cremony's story that we can verify is that Mangas did take a Mexican wife during a raid into Sonora; yet the storyteller's anecdote made entertaining reading for his eastern audience.

The account in the *Boston Evening Transcript*, though it differed from Cremony's, was just as sensational. Mangas had just turned twenty years old, thus placing the event about 1810, when he "achieved name, distinction, position, and fame in a single-handed contest with seven Navajo Indian warriors, five of whom he slew and scalped and two saved their lives by a hasty retreat from the scene of bloody contact." Again, this report might be apocryphal, and then again it might contain some elements of truth. After all, the Chiricahuas and Navajos were enemies at this time, and the young Mangas Coloradas, a giant among his people, may have had such a sensational encounter that would have catapulted him into a position of leadership. Yet even if something of this kind occurred, he probably did not slay five men, and definitely did not scalp his victims, for that was not a custom of his people. This story must have appealed to the readers of the Boston newspaper, few, if any, having seen a real Indian, and was typical of the trite impressions produced about Native Americans even today.[13]

Another element of his character undoubtedly aided Mangas Coloradas in his development as a chief: power. In historic times every Chiricahua man possessed special knowledge of some kind of ceremony or supernatural power. The young adult typically received this power in a vision. He employed this new-found asset to safeguard his children and other close relatives who depended upon him for protection. Unfortunately, we know little about Mangas's ceremonies or demonstrations of power, for this subject was a personal and delicate matter among the Apache. Yet we could reasonably assume that his power had something to do with war. Most Apache chiefs were war shamans, with the ability to predict enemy movements, foresee the outcome of expeditions, and protect their men from injury.[14]

Two other important events occurred during Mangas's rise to prominence: first, the Spanish discovered copper in the heart of his country at a place that would become known as Santa Rita del Cobre, located about six miles northeast of present-day Bayard, New Mexico; second, Spain's domination of Mexico was ending. The first breach in the relationship occurred about 1810; Mexico finally gained political independence from Spain in 1821. This event dramatically altered the course of history between the Chiricahua Apaches and Mexico.[15]

Mangas was a young teenager when the Spanish established a settlement at Santa Rita del Cobre, also known as the Copper Mines, in late 1803. The mines lay in the heart of Chihenne band territory, an area that Mangas Coloradas "favored above all others. . . . He loved the greasewood flatlands, the patches of yucca and cacti, the low-lying creosote brush that provided sanctuary for mammals, birds, and . . . the antelope."[16] The Spanish had been unable to exploit the mineral resources of the region during the eighteenth century. According to legend, in the early 1800s an Apache revealed the location of the deposits to Lieutenant Colonel José Manuel Carrasco, formerly stationed at Janos. In 1803 the Spanish founded a settlement there, and the following year troops arrived permanently. The military continued their attempts to control the Apaches in the region, offering them assistance and hoping to win them over with good treatment. To prevent unnecessary conflicts, they required the Apaches to receive permission to hunt in the vicinity. Generally speaking, the Chiricahuas (Bedonkohes and Chihennes) tolerated these trespassers, although open hostilities erupted occasionally. Why these intermittent skirmishes took place is not entirely clear. In all likelihood, competition for local resources and the mere presence of miners carving up the earth troubled the Indians. This increasing interaction between the two races led to difficulties, though the settlement would remain until 1838. During this time Mangas Coloradas, or Fuerte, as the Mexicans knew him, frequently visited, sometimes received rations, and at times led raids against the isolated outpost.[17]

Although peace reigned in Apachería in the early 1800s, local conflicts seemed to sprout now and then between the two races. In 1799 and 1800 a smallpox epidemic exacted a heavy toll on the inhabitants of northern Mexico, who included some Apaches living in peace near several presidios. The arrival of this lethal, contagious disease usually prompted the Indians to abandon the presidios for their former mountain homes. Some left for good, while others eventually returned. In 1803, Spanish intelligence reported that a hostile Chihenne chief named Naranjo was living in the coniferous San Mateo Mountains in New Mexico, north of Ojo Caliente, but he seems to have caused no significant problems to Spanish settlements. That same year Chihuahua sent troops against hostiles reportedly living in the Cobre and Mogollon Mountains, but the agile Apaches easily eluded the slow-moving force.[18]

Mangas's people began to exhibit signs of dissatisfaction in 1807. Having joined the ranks of the warriors, he may have participated in some of these violent events. A large war party of 150 warriors assaulted Santa Rita del Cobre on June 25, 1807, and succeeded in killing one man, wounding another, and driving off a great deal of stock. The following April, raiders ran off some livestock within five hundred yards of the mines, killing a man before Opata Indian soldiers and Spanish citizens repulsed the aggressors. In 1812 the Bedonkohes and Chihennes extended their raids into Sonora before returning to their favorite target in southern New Mexico. In April they twice raided Santa Rita del Cobre, stripping the mines of every head of stock. According to Apache scholar William Griffen, beginning in 1810 "there was a sharp increase in hostilities in some areas," and although "things calmed down after this, the long term was increasing raids in general."[19]

As previously noted, Mangas Coloradas, or Fuerte, first became prominent to the whites about 1814. Early the year before, his Bedonkohe allies had raided Janos, therefore prompting a Spanish campaign into New Mexico in the summer of 1813. Shortly after, the influential leader Mano Mocha, said to be living in the

Mogollons, arrived at San Elizario, about fifteen miles southeast of
El Paso, hoping to make peace. That October he arrived at Santa
Rita del Cobre with a passport that permitted his people to hunt in
safety in the nearby mountains. The military commander had
granted his request despite the belief that his band had committed
depredations in Sonora.[20]

Fuerte was publicly first mentioned in the summer of 1814.
Evidently feeling pressure from Spanish troops, he sent his brother
Pitfhan into Janos to solicit peace, requesting Santa Rita del Cobre
as his peace establishment. If granted an armistice, the Apaches
would settle along the Gila, likely meaning Santa Lucía Springs,
and the Mimbres River. Spanish authorities decided that the
Apaches should be encouraged to remain at peace but that they
should settle in their native territory instead of living near Spanish
settlements. The commanding general expressly forbade them
from settling near Santa Rita del Cobre, though he agreed to recognize peaceful rancherías in the Gila country. There was an advantage to this arrangement, with economics being the primary
motive, for if the Indians were subsisting on their own, the Spanish
would not have to issue rations. In addition, the Apaches would
not reap the benefit of receiving instructions in the use of firearms
and would be left unaware of campaigns sent against them.[21]

Despite this Spanish reluctance to provide rations, Fuerte
brought in his followers to Janos. Numbering 154 individuals, with
58 warriors, they established themselves within the jurisdiction of
Janos. The Indians located many of their rancherías immediately
outside the walls of Janos; they situated others as much as thirty to
forty miles away. Fuerte may have camped at Alamo Hueco or as
far north as the Animas Mountains in southwestern New Mexico.
From there he could send his people in to receive weekly rations.
The appearance of the Chiricahua chief must have impressed the
whites. Mangas had grown into a giant among his people. He stood
close to six and a half feet tall and weighed well in excess of two
hundred pounds. He had an extraordinarily large head, with a
broad forehead; deep-set eyes; large, prominent nose; huge mouth;
and broad chin. His body was long and muscular and perfectly
proportioned. In the monthly report ending June 30, 1815, Mexican
officials listed him as the leader of one group, along with other
Apache notables such as Coyote, Juan Diego Compá, Feroz
(Ferocious), Jasquenelte, and the influential Pisago Cabezón. In all,
these leaders represented a total of 407 Chiricahuas from the
Chihenne, Chokonen, and Nednhi bands. Mangas remained near

Janos until March 1816, for on March 4, 1816, Spanish authorities presented to him and Mano Mocha a gift of thirty-three blankets. Soon afterward, they left, likely because smallpox had again infested the area. They returned to their local group territories just in time to harvest the vital agave before they launched a campaign against Sonora, even then Mangas Coloradas's favorite target.[22]

Mangas Coloradas's followers returned to the Janos jurisdiction in the fall of 1816 and remained there at least until the next spring and possibly into the fall of 1817. Yet about that time another factor emerged to muddy the waters. Mexico's war for independence from Spain had caused serious problems along the frontier. The rebellion had begun in 1810 and had forced Spain to divert troops, resources, and funds from the northern presidios to the interior to quell it. As a result, the Spanish reduced frontier garrisons to skeleton strength, and soldiers went unclothed, unfed, and unpaid. This affected the peace establishments, for they now had fewer resources and presents to issue to the Apaches. Spanish officials had no choice but to curtail the Indians' rations, although they were acutely aware of the potentially catastrophic consequences.[23]

In November 1817 the commander at Janos warned his superiors that he had almost depleted the supply of rations to feed some four hundred Apaches. He urged officials to address that situation immediately; otherwise the local citizens would absorb the brunt of renewed Apache raiding, for no Apache willingly went hungry if the alternative was either to raid or to starve. Although hostilities failed to erupt at that time, this volatile atmosphere proved to be an eerie harbinger of things to come. Rumors abounded throughout the remainder of the decade about the Apaches' intent to commence hostilities. Instead, most of the Chiricahuas returned to their former homes and began to make their living in the traditional style of hunting and gathering, supplemented with occasional raids against other Indians and Mexicans.[24]

In September 1819 a rumor reached Janos that the Coyoteros, which was a generic name for the Western Apaches during the nineteenth century, planned to attack and burn Santa Rita del Cobre. Yet this attack never materialized, and, reportedly, Fuerte led a campaign against the Coyoteros into Arizona, perhaps to punish them for encroaching upon his band territory. Although details are sparse, we know that Fuerte's expedition was a decided success.[25]

For Mangas Coloradas, or Fuerte, relations between the Chiricahuas and Mexico continued to deteriorate during the 1820s. In

1821, Mexico finally won its independence from Spain, but the new government in Mexico City was woefully unprepared to deal with its newly won freedom. Confusion and chaos were the order of the day. The decade of rebellion had drained public treasuries and depleted the funds required to maintain the presidios and the Apaches. The federal government in Mexico City virtually ignored the northern frontier states of Sonora and Chihuahua, and this neglect resulted in the complete breakdown of the defense system, the presidio. For example, at Janos, Chihuahua's government reduced the garrison and compelled the remaining soldiers to live on austere rations and infrequent salaries. Likewise, the system of issuing rations to the Apaches became just as irregular. These precarious times led to conflicts between the two races, for everyone was competing for a share of an ever-decreasing pie.[26]

Mangas Coloradas's response to this seems to have been characteristic: he spent almost all of his time away from Mexican settlements, living securely in his native lands of southwestern New Mexico. In April 1819 he did appear at Janos with a small group of forty-three individuals and received rations. According to the census, he had three women and three children with him; at least one of the women was his wife, and perhaps all three. Dos-teh-seh, future wife of the great Chokonen leader Cochise, may have been among the children. Janos authorities continued to enumerate Fuerte's and Pluma's bands at Janos throughout 1820 and 1821. They consisted of about two hundred in all, with some seventy-five being men. In December 1821, Mexican officials continued to issue rations to 1,423 Apaches in Chihuahua, and although they allocated some one thousand cattle to feed these bands, this amount proved inadequate and some Indians went hungry.[27]

Mexico's independence also caused a drastic reduction in the population of the northern frontier. At Janos the civilian population fell from 2,000 in 1817 to 275 in 1825. The federal government also revised its military administration, dividing Nueva Vizcaya into the states of Chihuahua and Durango in 1823. It continued to garrison the presidios with fewer regular soldiers, which forced local commanders to call up less effective civilian militia. Mexico's frontier, already sparsely settled, suffered further from this erosion of both state and federal control. In addition, Mexican officials repealed the Spanish laws that had forbidden foreigners open access to the frontier. Almost overnight, the Apache frontier saw an influx of adventurers, mostly Anglos, but

Apache Pass, Arizona, was one of Cochise's favorite homes before Anglo arrival. Mangas also camped here on occasion. (Photo by Kathi Plauster)

also others, including Indians such as Delawares and Shawnees, all looking for a stake in trapping, mining, or commerce. This inevitably led to a lucrative trade and the first serious round of Apache incursions into Mexico since the 1780s.[28]

This smoldering animosity exploded in 1824 when Mexicans saw their worst fears realized: an Apache uprising. Fuerte played a minor role in the fighting, which began that summer and was an omen of future developments. The Chokonens living near Fronteras had retired north to the Dos Cabezas Mountains a few miles north of the celebrated Apache Pass in today's southeastern Arizona. That fall, Chiricahua leaders planned several forays into Sonora, eventually striking Fronteras and Bavispe, while Western Apache groups raided south of Tucson and Tubac. Their accomplishments were slight; they stole some stock and killed a few Mexicans. The raiding, however, evoked memories of what Apache terror once had been.[29]

The situation could easily have erupted into a full-scale war, which seemed to Mexicans the Indians' intention. A peaceful Apache at Janos revealed that Teboca, who had left Fronteras, had joined Fuerte and Mano Mocha at Santo Domingo in southwestern

New Mexico. Teboca, a Bedonkohe leader who enjoyed close ties with the Chokonens, in joining with Fuerte at that time corroborates the Apache oral history that the Bedonkohes, in times of crisis, looked to Mangas Coloradas for leadership. A quarter of a century later, Teboca would tell a Mexican official that Mangas Coloradas was his "general" or chief. In any event, another report suggested that the Chiricahuas had joined the Western Apaches, probably the White Mountain band (with whom Mangas was frequently on friendly terms), and had made plans to send a war party into Mexico. Reports also hinted that the Chiricahuas were lurking in the Enmedio Mountains to ambush travelers between Fronteras and Janos.[30]

Despite these rumors, the Indians' hearts were not ready for a full-scale war, at least not yet. Sonora responded by sending troops against the Chokonens in southeastern Arizona; this action, combined with the onset of winter, may have caused the Apaches' enthusiasm for combat to wane. In any case, in December 1824, Juan José Compá and three other leaders requested an armistice at Santa Rita del Cobre. For now, most of the fighting was over. During 1825 a few Chiricahuas drifted back to their peace establishments at Janos, Fronteras, and Santa Rita del Cobre, where Fuerte and his ranchería of 168 persons received rations sporadically for the remainder of the decade, whenever Mexico had the resources available.[31]

Mangas Coloradas was likely at Santa Rita del Cobre in 1826 when American adventurer Sylvester Pattie led a small group of Anglo hunters and trappers into New Mexico.[32] Sylvester's son, James Ohio Pattie, left behind an important and interesting account of their travels that is noteworthy particularly for what it reports about the time they spent at Santa Rita del Cobre in 1826. Relying upon Pattie's description of the head chief of the Apaches, historian Paul Wellman concluded that Mangas Coloradas had met with Pattie. Pattie had some revealing observations about the early Chiricahuas, who after one parley "had painted themselves red." This comment identifies them as the Chihenne band, known among the Chiricahuas as the "Red Paint People."[33]

In August 1826 the Patties arrived at Santa Rita del Cobre only to find that the Apaches had it under siege. On August 1, 1826, two Americans had discovered tracks of six Apaches near the mines. Shortly after, Pattie's men captured two Indians. They released one, sending him to the Apaches with an explicit warning: if the Indians did not come in to parley, the whites would execute their hostage. On August 5 the Chiricahuas arrived, some eighty men in all, under four chiefs. Their presence greatly disturbed the Mexicans at Santa Rita del Cobre, but not the Americans; that did not escape the vigilant eyes of Mangas Coloradas. Although Pattie failed to identify the Apache leaders, an informed guess for three of them would be Mano Mocha, Pluma, and Mangas Coloradas, still known as Fuerte. This was likely his first face-to-face contact with Americans, whom he would come to respect, at once finding out that they were different from Spaniards and Mexicans.

The Apaches did not make any attempt to conceal their contempt for Mexicans, or Spaniards, reciting past acts of betrayal and treachery inflicted upon them by whites. They explained the origin of their most recent dispute. The chiefs described a scenario that would be played out countless times during the next sixty years. It seems the Spanish, or the Mexicans, had invited the Chiricahuas in to Santa Rita del Cobre to make a treaty. Then the whites sprang the trap, "butchering them [Apaches] like a flock of sheep." Only a few escaped to tell the tale; naturally, war followed, for the Chiricahuas had to avenge their dead. They admitted to Pattie that they had raided the mines but declared they would cease hostilities now that the Americans worked them. After making peace, both parties marched to Santa Rita del Cobre, where Pattie "killed three beeves to feed the Indians." After all had their fill, the Apache head chief (likely Mangas Coloradas) presented Pattie with a gift "ten miles square of a tract of land lying on a river about three miles from the mines." Pattie informed the chief that "though the land might be his, he should be obliged to employ Spaniards to cultivate it for him." The head chief, "with a look of great firmness," assured Pattie that the Apaches would not molest the workers. He further declared (and this was consistent with statements Mangas Coloradas would make throughout his life) that he desired peace with Americans because they "never showed any disposition to kill, except in battle." Who was this head chief? Although Pattie does not identify him, his speech, as summarized by Pattie, closely parallels those given by Mangas Coloradas to Americans in later years.

Pattie mentioned the name of only one Apache chief—Mano Mocha, the Bedonkohe leader—yet he clearly did not consider him the principal leader. This seems to point to Mangas Coloradas, or Fuerte, as the chief who made the speech. Several parts of the talk were characteristic of Mangas Coloradas, among them an indelible hatred of Mexicans and Spaniards, a respect for Americans, and a vow to honor any agreements. Mangas Coloradas often expressed these feelings throughout his lifetime.[34]

The final years of the 1820s must have been exasperating ones for Mangas Coloradas. Many of their younger leaders could not recall what life had been like before the peace establishments, when large Apache war parties had devastated northern Mexico. With so many of their leaders having matured during this peaceful period under Spanish rule, they undoubtedly failed to comprehend that Mexico's new regime was but a paper tiger with a weak central government and a depleted public treasury.

These years were equally frustrating for those Mexicans living along the northern frontier. Local civilian and military officials, who feared a general Apache uprising, lacked the capacity to prevent it from occurring. State officials, living in safety in Chihuahua City or Ures, cavalierly discounted the Apaches as a formidable force. After all, it had been almost forty years since large Apache war parties had terrorized the countryside, and few, if any, of these isolated officials expected that the Indians could again dominate the frontier as they had in the eighteenth century. This was neither the first nor the last time that whites would underestimate the determination of Apache people who fought primarily for vengeance. Ignacio Zúniga, a prominent citizen of Sonora, wrote in 1835 that Mexico's war for independence had led to the dissolution of the presidio system, which, in turn, had brought on the Apache uprising of 1831.[35]

All signs suggested that the Apaches were primed for a renewal of hostilities by 1830. Lack of money forced Mexican officials to slash rations further in early 1828, therefore compelling some Apaches to relocate into the Chiricahua, Enmedio, and Animas Mountains, where they planted, harvested mescal, and hunted for subsistence. Pisago Cabezón raised some crops at Alamo Hueco, some four miles north of the present boundary in southwestern New Mexico's panhandle, just south of the Big Hatchet Mountains. In 1829, Mexico expelled Spaniards from the country—a move that further exacerbated economic conditions, because these individuals took with them their cash and technical expertise.[36] Although the Mexicans' lack of assistance left many Apaches disillusioned, some groups of Chiricahuas, under Pisago Cabezón and Juan Diego Compá, remained near Janos. Fuerte and his group remained around Santa Rita del Cobre, and many Chokonens continued to live near Fronteras.

In January 1830 several Chiricahua leaders met with the military commander of Janos and made several requests. First, they wanted their rations to include meat; second, they desired the services of an interpreter; and third, they insisted that Mexicans issue farming tools to them. The commander forwarded their requests to his superiors at Chihuahua City. He authorized the issuance of farming tools and the hiring of an interpreter, but he could do nothing about increasing rations. Finally, in 1831 the Mexican government decided that the expense to sustain the Apaches was prohibitive; it was time for the Indians to learn to support themselves. Therefore, the commanding generals of Sonora and Chihuahua directed a halt to the peace establishments and a cessation of the rationing system. This new policy, combined with an outbreak of smallpox in the Janos area, left the Apaches with no recourse but to return to their former mountain homes.[37]

Almost immediately the Apaches began raiding Sonora and Chihuahua. This was soon to develop into a wide-scale conflict, embroiling most of Apachería from the Mescaleros in eastern New Mexico to the Western Apaches in Arizona. The Chiricahuas were between, and inevitably the most involved. The Western Apaches had begun hostilities against northern Sonora in 1830 with reports from Arispe, San Ignacio, Tucson, and Altar begging for assistance. The government could offer little aid, citing a lack of money and resources.[38] By the spring of 1831 almost every Apache band formerly under Mexican influence had gone to war. Mangas Coloradas, approaching the age of forty and still known as Fuerte, would experience his share of fighting over the next decade. He would become increasingly aloof from Mexico and would develop an unequivocal and passionate hatred of Sonora, a feeling that would persist for the rest of his life.

Chapter 3

THE CONFLICT BEGINS

THE decade of the 1830s was a time of dramatic change in relations between Mexico and the Chiricahua Apaches. The gradual deterioration in this relationship, which had begun with Mexico's war for independence in 1810, continued throughout the 1820s. Fuming bitterness and mutual disrespect finally burst forth in the spring of 1831, and relations between the two peoples were never the same after that. There was no large-scale uprising, nor was there a bloody massacre of a presidio or settlement. Instead, hostilities slowly gained momentum during the decade like a snowball increasing in size as it rolls downhill. By the late 1830s the Apaches held the upper hand, one never relinquished by some Chiricahua bands until their final surrender and subsequent deportation from Arizona in 1886.

Mangas Coloradas reacted characteristically to these changing events. He had never cared for Mexicans but had accepted peace because most of his people, particularly the older Chiricahua leaders, had matured during the peace establishments and knew no other way of life. Now he had reached his prime, and as the war gained momentum so did his reputation. Not every Chiricahua leader embraced this militant policy, for many leaders wanted a return to the status quo. Therefore, as the decade of the 1830s progressed, the Chiricahuas split into factions—one generally consisting of older leaders who favored a return to presidio life and the other dominated by younger, more bellicose leaders who had tasted the fruits of victory and felt nothing but contempt toward Mexico. Mangas Coloradas, still known as Fuerte for most of the 1830s, led the latter group.

During the years following the outbreak the Chiricahuas did agree to several truces. None of them would endure, however, because a penurious Mexican government continued mistakenly to believe that it could restrain the Apaches without providing rations or other assistance. Moreover, and perhaps just as significantly, the conflict had by this time spawned a mutual distrust and antipathy between the two races. Mexico had responded to the Chiricahuas' aggression by sending out large campaigns reminiscent of those of the 1780s. Inevitably, both sides spilled blood, which of course demanded retaliation, and thus followed a cycle of action and reaction that proved virtually impossible to halt. This staccato warfare resulted naturally in philosophical differences concerning the courses to be pursued by each race.

The official Apache policies of Sonora and Chihuahua are a case in point and deserve analysis and discussion. Sonora opted for a vigorous and hawkish approach against the Apaches, one based on vengeance. Rationalizing that extermination was the panacea to the problem, it went so far in 1835 as to pay bounties for Apache scalps. Chihuahua, meanwhile, favored a more peaceful approach, calling out the soldiers to snap the whip against the hostiles to force them to capitulate only as a last resort.

The Chiricahuas were likewise fragmented. Pisago Cabezón, still hardy and vigorous despite his more than sixty years, had previously been a moderate leader. Now, in the early 1830s, frustrated by the events of the previous decade, he reversed directions and became firmly entrenched in the hostile camp. Other Chiricahua leaders, such as Mangas Coloradas, Teboca, Mano Mocha, and an up-and-coming war chief named Tutije, joined the venerable Pisago. Juan José Compá and Juan Diego Compá of the Nednhis, Matías and Relles of the Chokonens, and several Chihenne leaders led the pacific element of the tribe. These divisions virtually ensured the failure of every treaty made between the two cultures during the 1830s and 1840s.

The war began in the spring of 1831. Mexico had quickly learned that the hungry and bitter Apaches remained a formidable force, although the extent of the raiding in the spring and summer of 1831 was not entirely clear. Yet it must have been significant, because both Sonora and Chihuahua drew up plans to quell the rebellion. As early as June 1831, Sonora planned to mount a large force of four hundred men to wage war against the Chiricahuas. However, a paucity of equipment and other problems pushed the expected departure date from the summer to the fall, and the expedition, if indeed it ever got under way, had little success in punishing the Apaches. By October 16, 1831, the Apache devastation had become so widespread that José Joaquín Calvo,[1] the hardline commanding general of Chihuahua, declared war on the hostiles and began preparations for an offensive into Apachería similar to those of the 1780s.[2]

The Chiricahuas made their presence felt in early 1832, launching a war party that spared none in its path. Juan José Compá, hoping for tranquility and a return to peace, sent a messenger to Janos who revealed that the Indians unanimously wanted war but would consider a cease-fire, presumably if the Mexicans agreed to issue rations. He also warned that the Indians had control of the roads between San Buenaventura, Janos, and Carrizal. In late February a Chiricahua war party ravaged the countryside of northwestern Chihuahua, causing widespread terror. The warriors first assaulted the San Miguel and San Diego haciendas and then burned Carretas, killing over fifty people in all. Their success appalled Mexican officials; they had not seen such bloodshed since the destructive Apache forays of the 1770s and 1780s.[3]

In response, a desperate Chihuahua looked for assistance from its sister state to the west. Hoping to protect the northern frontier, it requested reinforcements of one hundred Opata Indians, inveterate enemies of the Apaches, who called them "Strings Coming Up Between His Toes People" in reference to their customary sandals.[4] But Ramón Morales, the hawkish military commander of Sonora, recommended that Sonora deny the request because of the "critical circumstance in which the frontier of this state [Sonora] finds itself." Yet Sonora's governor rejected Morales's arguments and ordered him to dispatch the reinforcements, reasoning that "this objective is beneficial not only to that state but to this."[5]

Meanwhile, the Chiricahuas were active in the triangular region of Fronteras, Bavispe, and Janos. On March 26, 1832, they attacked the horse herd at Fronteras, forcing Morales to send reinforcements. A week later they captured the mail between Bavispe and Janos and collected important information, for many Indians were literate, including Mangas Coloradas's brother Phalios Palacio, who reportedly had been educated at Paso del Norte. About a month later they raided Turicachi, some fifteen miles south of Fronteras, and killed a man. These events prompted Ramón Morales to press the governor for a force of four hundred men for a drive into the Mogollons, where, he believed, the true hostiles were based.[6]

The Western Apaches had also renewed hostilities against Mexico, primarily Sonora. In response, in the spring of 1832, citizens of northern Sonora organized a militia unit to supplement the presidio soldiers. Meeting at Cocospera, about thirty-five miles southwest of the Huachuca Mountains in Arizona, they organized a force called La Sección Patriótica, the Patriotic Section, and elected Joaquín Vicente Elías, a member of the prominent Elías family of northern Sonora, to serve as its leader. In late May 1832 a Sonoran force of one hundred volunteers forged north to Tubac and joined a force under Captain Antonio Comadurán, a veteran and capable officer of the Hispanic Southwest. On June 4, 1832, the mixed force of regular and volunteer troops encountered Western Apaches at Arivaipa Canyon, about fifty miles north of Tucson. According to Mexican reports, the soldiers surprised and then routed the Indians; the whites claimed that they killed seventy-one warriors, captured thirteen children, and recovered 216 horses and mules. The Indians killed one Mexican and wounded twelve others. Sonora had truly scored a one-sided triumph.[7]

Though Sonora's campaign had not affected the Chiricahuas, they soon had to face a determined force from Chihuahua that intended to compel the Indians to sue for peace. Mangas's people had been raiding in the winter of 1832, and although references to him as either Mangas Coloradas or Fuerte for that time have not been found, we can assume that he had led by example, out in the forefront of hostilities. We know that in May 1832 he and Pisago Cabezón led the Chiricahuas against Chihuahuan troops in one of the most significant battles ever fought between the two races. This fight had all the drama and heroics that a truly pitched conflict would entail: hand-to-hand fighting, desperate charges, awesome displays of bravery on both sides, and heavy casualties. By that summer both Apaches and Mexicans had come to recognize Mangas's importance, and soon he would be chosen to act as one of three "generals" to keep peace and to restore order among his people. This selection underscored his growing prowess and significance within the warlike Chiricahuas, in particular his local group of Chihennes, the isolationist Bedonkohes, and the recalcitrant Chokonens, all of whom now looked to Mangas Coloradas for leadership.

The Chiricahua bands gathered along the headwaters of the Gila River, just south of the Mogollons, in the spring of 1832. They considered the Mogollons a sacred place; their cultural myths placed the beginning of life in these mountains. The region consisted of sacred caves and lakes, and the bands collected important medicinal herbs there. The Chiricahuas called the Mogollons Nadazai, which means "Mescal Extends Upward," thus suggesting its economic importance as a source of that important food staple. The Mogollons, whose tallest peaks reached almost eleven thousand feet, also contained rich hunting grounds (elk and deer), lush areas for gathering nuts and berries, and secure places in which to camp. Though chiefly the band territory of the Bedonkohes and Mangas's hybrid local group of Chihennes-Bedonkohes, every Chiricahua band occasionally exploited the region's resources.[8]

It was no coincidence that the bands united in the spring of 1832. Mangas Coloradas and Pisago Cabezón undoubtedly had summoned them to consider a course of action for the upcoming summer. The unexpected appearance of troops from Chihuahua, however, foiled their plans.

Captain José Ignacio Ronquillo, an officer of considerable experience with the Chiricahuas, commanded the expedition. His force of 138 men consisted primarily of regular or presidio troops drawn from Chihuahua's northern outposts of San Buenaventura, Janos, Principe, and San Elizario. He intended to strike a hard blow against the hostiles and to show them that Mexico's military power still existed. Having penetrated the heart of Apachería, Ronquillo's force reached the foothills of the Mogollons on May 21, 1832. There he sent his scouts to ferret out the trail; they encountered a few Chiricahuas and had a brief skirmish with no casualties on either side. Two days later, Ronquillo's troops fought a truly significant and important battle with Mangas Coloradas's and Pisago Cabezón's followers.

According to his windy report, Ronquillo's men performed admirably under perilous circumstances. From the beginning tough challenges had beset his operation. His force had marched from Santo Domingo Playa, situated north of the Animas Mountains between the Peloncillo and Little Hatchet Mountains in extreme southwestern New Mexico, to the Gila River. This was the dry season, and every spring was empty. The lack of water and fatiguing march had worn out both men and horses, who suffered severely from thirst, compelling two-thirds of the force to walk their mounts. Two soldiers "arrived at the river lying across their saddles having died of thirst."

Of his 138 men, Ronquillo could actually bring no more than half his force into the battle, for he had assigned the other half to guard the horses and supplies. The evening before the decisive fight, a brief skirmish took place between the Mexican advance guard and the Chiricahuas, who lost several warriors killed in the sally. Soon after, the Apaches "raised the white flag to parley and I responded in the same manner," wrote Ronquillo. The celebrated Chokonen chief, Pisago Cabezón, and his son Tichac, both armed, approached within ten paces of Ronquillo, who was unarmed. The two leaders talked about making peace, and Ronquillo agreed to wait until noon the next day for the Chiricahuas' response. Likely Pisago had no intentions of making peace, for the confident Chiricahuas outnumbered the Mexicans and had bivouacked within a mile of the Mexican camp. He had succeeded in buying some time until their Bedonkohe and Chihenne allies arrived on the scene.

Early the next morning the Indians again raised a white flag, and a few warriors approached the Mexicans' camp to talk. Soon after, the Bedonkohe and Chihenne leaders under Fuerte and Mano Mocha arrived on the scene. Other prominent chiefs, including Oyá, Pluma, Caballo Ligero, and Boca Matada, accompanied them. They requested a "paper to conclude a peace at El Cobre." Ronquillo obliged their request and produced the document. Then the Apaches returned to their camp, seemingly in doubt as to their next step. Ronquillo kept a close eye on them "with the spyglass," wondering whether he would be fighting the Chiricahuas or escorting them to Santa Rita del Cobre for a formal treaty. It was about noon when a few stalwart warriors gave him an answer.

As the Chiricahua leaders met in council, a small group of four Apaches touched off the proceedings, deciding for their vacillating leaders. They boldly charged the Mexicans' herd, lancing one horse. Ronquillo promptly responded and launched his attack according to plan, because he "could not bear this insult." Alternating charges back and forth and hand-to-hand combat characterized the early stages of the battle, which began shortly after noon and lasted until sunset. Although the Apaches could use their accurate bows and arrows, and did wound Manuel Zambrano in the leg and Diego Saenz in the rump, they inflicted most of the serious wounds with musket fire. Some Indians had mastered the use of this weapon, a result of their years of living in peace at the presidios. Yet despite the Indians' superior numbers and their determination, the discipline and firepower of the Mexican force began to take a toll. The soldiers advanced steadily, taking one Apache position at a time before they eventually overwhelmed the Chiricahuas. It was a rout, not a retreat. Ronquillo placed Indian casualties at twenty-two dead and fifty wounded during the entire conflict. The Apaches had managed to kill three men and wound another twelve soldiers.

The Mexican expedition, according to historian William Griffen, was reminiscent of those of Spanish colonial times. From Ronquillo's perspective, his impressive victory had a salutary effect on the Indians, who now seemed humbled. Within a few months the entire tribe, including Mangas Coloradas, or Fuerte, as he was still known, would sue for peace.[9]

Even some of the Nednhis under Juan José Compá and his brother Juan Diego Compá had participated in the fight along the Gila, somewhere south of the Mogollons, probably north of today's Redrock. Pisago Cabezón had told Ronquillo that part of the Janeros local group of Nednhis had gone to Arizona to enlist the aid of the Western Apaches. Other reports indicated that the Carrizaleño local group had been near Santa Rita del Cobre but had recently left that neighborhood for its old haunts at Agua Nueva, Chihuahua, where they had solicited peace. Jasquedegá and Cristóbal led this group, which represented some sixty-six warriors, probably 250 individuals in all. This local group resided almost exclusively in Chihuahua, between Janos and Carrizal. Few Chiricahuas of the twentieth century had any knowledge of this group (although a study by Harry W. Basehart in 1959 included a reference to them). The explanation is simple. Chihuahuan troops had virtually annihilated them by the early 1860s, and the Carrizaleño local group lost its identity. Its remaining members were absorbed into the Janeros local group under Juh in the early 1860s.[10]

In early July, about six weeks after their resounding defeat, the humbled Chiricahuas dispatched several emissaries to Janos. These messengers soon returned to their people in the Gila country with Chihuahua's proposal. A jubilant José Joaquín Calvo, believing the Chiricahuas conquered, dictated preliminary surrender terms to Colonel Cayetano Justiniani at Santa Rita del Cobre on July 28, 1832.[11] Calvo instructed Justiniani, an experienced officer of the frontier whom the Apaches trusted, to inform the Chiricahuas about the one-sided terms of the treaty. Essentially, the Treaty of 1832 paralleled that of 1810, in which Chihuahua had granted peace to defeated Mescalero Apaches without any government assistance or rations. The Spanish had assigned the Indians to live in specific areas, where they were to subsist on their own by hunting, gathering, and planting. But what might have worked in 1810 had little chance to flourish in 1832. From the start, this unrealistic proposal had no chance of succeeding. The Chiricahuas' only benefit from signing this treaty would be the return of the Mexican troops to their home bases. Yet, without rations the Indians had no incentive to live under Mexican control. One wonders whether either side expected the precarious arrangement to last.

Chihuahua's commander, José Joaquín Calvo, arrived at Santa Rita del Cobre in mid-August. There he conferred with the Mescaleros and Chiricahua leaders from each of the four bands. They consummated the treaty on August 29, 1832. Twenty-nine local group leaders gave their approval. Under the terms of the truce, the Apaches agreed to relinquish all stolen stock in their possession, but this was impracticable, and they returned few, if any, animals. As with the treaty of 1810, Calvo assigned the Apaches to three zones: the Mescaleros from San Elizario to the Sacramento Mountains; the Chihennes and Bedonkohes from Santa Rita del Cobre to the Negrita Mountains, with the Mogollons included; and the Chokonens and Nednhis from Janos north to the Peloncillo and Burro Mountains. Fuerte was named general for the Mogollon region, Juan José Compá was to act as general for the Janos area, and Aquién, which may have been another name for Matías, the Chokonen leader, was to act as general for the Sonoran frontier.[12]

In hindsight, the armistice had a most predictable result. Although it restored temporary order to the frontier, it contained many flaws and from the beginning had little chance to succeed. To begin with, Calvo maintained the parsimonious and hard-line policy of no assistance based on the idealistic belief that the Apaches would somehow sustain themselves without raiding. He refused to make rations a part of the bargain. Just as significantly, and perhaps even more ominously, Calvo erred by overlooking Sonora's interests and, purposely or not, failed to invite representatives from there to participate in the negotiations. The Chokonens and Bedonkohes had become bitter enemies of Sonora, while Mangas Coloradas's Santa Lucía local group of Chihennes had developed the same antipathy. Thus, Calvo's provincial plan had small chance for ultimate success, although the immediate situation improved in some ways.

Chihuahua's Treaty of 1832 also shifted Chiricahua headquarters from Janos to Santa Rita del Cobre, which would play an ever-increasing role in Apache affairs until its abandonment in 1838. Its remoteness from other settlements encouraged clandestine commerce, with the Chiricahuas finding a ready market for the loot they obtained in Sonora and Chihuahua. Often heard during the early to middle 1830s was a charge that "the Americans trade guns and ammunition to the Apaches at Santa Rita del Cobre."[13] Mexican officials named Robert McKnight and James Kirker as two of the prominent middlemen in this practice,[14] and their pernicious influence paved the way for a flourishing but illicit trade. Mangas Coloradas knew both men and would eventually develop a particular disdain for Kirker.

Both races had initially seemed sincere for peace, though the Chiricahuas still hoped that they could persuade the Mexicans to issue rations. In mid-September the commander at Janos released six Apache prisoners, and later that month several Chiricahua leaders expressed a desire to go to Chihuahua City to confer with the governor. Juan José Compá channeled his energies into making a viable peace, working closely with Mexican authorities at Janos and Santa Rita del Cobre. Mangas Coloradas had retired to the Mogollons in late 1832, remaining aloof from Mexican contact despite his title of "general." Unfortunately for both sides, by early 1833 the armistice had begun to disintegrate, and the Chiricahuas renewed their raiding into Mexico.[15]

Mexican officials had recognized the ominous situation and had become uneasy, awaiting the explosion. In February 1833 reports suggested that the Chokonens had returned to their old homes in the Chiricahuas, where they plotted a series of forays into Sonora. Later that month Apaches raided the stock of Rafael Carbajal near San Buenaventura. By May the Apaches had set the frontier ablaze, and for Mangas Coloradas the beginning of a decade of war against Mexico, and Sonora in particular, had arrived.[16]

The pacific Nednhi spokesman, Juan José Compá, mustered all his influence to prevent hostilities. In late April, Sonoran troops under the Opata leader Blas Medrano encountered Juan José's group near the deserted Carretas hacienda tucked just inside Sonora on the road between Bavispe and Janos.[17] Medrano demanded that Juan José return some stock that a few of his young men had stolen. Juan José complied, and Medrano, a lifelong enemy of the Apaches, returned to Bacerac and joined the presidio troops at Bavispe for a patrol against Juan José's ranchería.[18]

In May, Juan José Compá wrote a few letters to the commander at Fronteras, hoping to calm the waters and open negotiations with Sonora, which had not participated in the Treaty of 1832 made between him and Chihuahua. The peace-minded leader offered to meet Sonoran representatives at Fronteras, whose commander believed that they should consider the offer to "avoid the evils that would accompany a new revolt of the peaceful Apaches."[19] Yet it was too late for any humane gestures from either side. Indeed, disturbances at several presidios soon compounded difficult relations, which, in turn, led to the inevitable conflicts. Juan José Compá provided the Chiricahua perception of these events. First, at Agua Nueva, where the Carrizaleño local group of Nednhis had settled, Mexican citizens killed an Apache. The Indians felt that "no justice was done." Consequently, they retaliated, killing several Mexicans and raiding some livestock. Immediately, the Nednhis sent emissaries to other Chiricahua groups, inciting them to hostilities. To make matters worse, Costilla (Rib), a leader living near Bavispe, had a run-in with the commander there, and Juan José Compá felt apprehensive when he visited Janos. Still, he steadfastly promised to send a message to Pisago Cabezón to advise him to give the Mexicans the benefit of the doubt, suggesting that Apaches must have provoked the Mexicans for this to have occurred.[20]

Meanwhile, at Santa Rita del Cobre, the district over which Mangas Coloradas acted as "general," hostilities seemed imminent. Troubles began when Manuel Chirimni, who had been living in peace near there, left the mines to harvest mescal at Carrizalillo Springs. For no apparent reason he had become disillusioned with the armistice. Upon leaving the mines, he sent a messenger to the Chihennes living along the Mimbres River, inviting them to join him on a raid. Shortly after, a small group raided a ranch near Santa Rita del Cobre, running off some stock and killing one Mexican and a sister of Juan José Compá, who for no apparent reason happened to be in the neighborhood. The Mexicans tracked the assailants to Santa Lucía Springs, where the Bedonkohes and Chihennes under Fuerte, Teboca, Geta Matada, and Oyá had established a large ranchería. By the next month Mexican authorities considered each of these leaders hostile. Mangas Coloradas and Pisago Cabezón clearly led the war faction, as they would for the remainder of the decade.[21]

By early June reports indicated that the Chiricahuas had joined in great numbers in the mountains of northern Sonora. On June 2, 1833, they attacked Bavispe, killed a soldier and a citizen, and wounded several more.[22] In July, Pisago Cabezón dispatched two war parties, one against the Navajos in New Mexico and the other against Sonora. Mexican troops achieved a few minor victories over the Chiricahuas that summer. In July one patrol from Chihuahua killed a warrior fifteen miles northeast of Janos near Laguna de la Ascención, and in August another campaign against the Nednhis recaptured some stock. Yet the Chiricahuas, better armed because of the illicit trade at Santa Rita del Cobre, continued to raid Mexico with impunity. In Sonora alone, from the beginning of hostilities in April until October 1833, Apache war parties killed over two hundred citizens. As to Mangas Coloradas's involvement, we can not be certain except to say that he had joined Pisago Cabezón, the most prominent Chiricahua leader of the 1830s. He had become the war leader for his Santa Lucía local group of Chihennes and the Bedonkohes, and he had begun to develop a following among the Chokonens.[23]

Sonora's military could do little to prevent these incursions. Its presidio troops, short on rations, clothing, and cash, had reached a mutinous state. Finally, in September 1833 commanding officers of several presidios convened at the home of Ignacio Elías González in Arispe. Elías González led the disillusioned officers in a barracks revolt against Colonel Francisco Arregui. That October, in a private arrangement, the capable Lieutenant Colonel José María Elías González took control of Sonora's military command. He could do little to improve affairs, however, until he could marshal troops for an expedition into Apachería.[24]

The new year of 1834 dawned with a similar prognosis for Sonora as the Chiricahuas concentrated their forays against ranches and towns of the northern frontier. Pisago Cabezón and Mangas Coloradas directed most of their war parties against Sonora, although one account described a large campaign against Socorro, New Mexico.[25] They had reasons for this strategy. First, Sonoran officials perceived the Apaches as treacherous savages who deserved extermination and accordingly formulated their policies toward that end. In contrast, Chihuahua attempted to control the Apaches by making treaties, feeling peace was better than war. The second reason, and perhaps more compelling, was that Sonora contained well-stocked haciendas and towns situated close to Apachería. Finally, the ongoing war had left both sides extremely distrustful of and vengeful against each other. As a result, this cycle led to a series of never-ending reprisals that continued on until the Geronimo Wars of the 1880s.

Mangas Coloradas probably had a hand in the organization of the large war party that invaded northern Sonora in January 1834. The Chiricahuas, estimated at three hundred, attacked the herd at Fronteras at daybreak on January 8. Captain Bernardo Martínez, with a force of presidio troops and civilians, confidently pursued, thinking he could rout the Indians if he could overtake them. One-half mile east of Fronteras the Chiricahuas swarmed from the hills and almost cut off his command, killing Martínez and three others within sight of the presidio. Afterwards, the Chokonen chief Relles, Tutije (a bold and militant leader of the Chokonen or Bedonkohe band), and Félix (probably Phalios Palacio, the brother of Mangas Coloradas) requested a parley, but no one at Fronteras dared venture out to talk.[26]

In fact, the future of Fronteras deeply concerned civilian officials. Vicente Bustamante, the justice of the peace, pleaded with the governor to send help, declaring that "it is impossible for me to describe the situation that we encounter." If the state neglected his call for assistance, he warned, "this place will have to be abandoned." Furthermore, wrote Bustamante, the Apaches' bravado had appalled the people of Fronteras, who for the previous forty years had enjoyed good relations with the Chiricahuas. "There is presently not one citizen who can work his fields. . . . All are struck by the enemy's determination and his audacity."[27]

After its assault on Fronteras the Chiricahua war party continued south, killing everyone in its path. They cleaned out the ranch of Narivo Montoya and then murdered two citizens on the road to Bacoachi, where they wiped out a party of six men. Next, the war party, now estimated at two hundred, veered southeast to Chinapa, along the banks of the Sonora River, which they boldly occupied, running off every head of stock before retiring toward Arizona. Meanwhile, Sonora assembled a force of two hundred men at Moctezuma but did not pursue the Indians because their men lacked arms and provisions. Finally, in an act of desperation, the famished soldiers turned into an unruly mob and, desperate for food, looted the homes of Moctezuma's citizens, a situation that "embarrassed" Sonora's military hierarchy.[28]

Fuerte was mentioned sparingly in the Mexican documents during 1834. In contrast, Sonoran reports discussed Pisago Cabezón more than any other Apache, probably because he enjoyed more influence within the Chiricahua tribe than any other leader.

The Chiricahuas organized another incursion into Sonora in the spring of 1834. One band of Chokonens ambushed and killed Captain Leonardo León of Tubac near the Babocómari ranch. They returned to rendezvous with other Chokonens and Bedonkohes under Tutije, and likely Mangas Coloradas, at Batepito, some eighteen miles northeast of Fronteras. There the two bands disagreed about their next target. Tutije and his Bedonkohes wanted to attack Fronteras; Matías, the Chokonen chief who had lived at Fronteras during the years of peace, objected and proposed a raid into the interior of Sonora. Finally, the bands separated, with Tutije, Pisago Cabezón, and Mangas Coloradas retiring to the Mogollons in New Mexico. The Chokonens under Matías and Relles returned to their beloved Chiricahua Mountains to harvest mescal.[29]

Rumors were rampant during the spring and summer of 1834 about where the Chiricahuas would strike next. One had it that the Indians intended to attack Tucson; another speculated that they would surround either Tubac or Santa Cruz. Certainly the inhabitants of Santa Cruz had reason for concern. Many had begun to desert their homes, sensing the military's inability to protect them. In mid-July several Chiricahua leaders appeared at the unoccupied Opata mission of Cuchuta, about twelve miles south of Fronteras, and talked with a few vaqueros working a ranch near that site. The cowboys recognized the two leaders: Félix, who as mentioned before was probably Phalios Palacio, Mangas's brother, and Relles. The Apaches cavalierly asserted that they would come into Fronteras in late July to arrange an armistice. Yet for some reason they did not appear as promised; likely their statement was just a ruse to forestall the offensive that Sonora's legislature had authorized Governor Escalante y Arvizu to carry out that fall. Also, this seems to have been a Bedonkohe-Chokonen war party, and the militants of these two bands, who outnumbered the moderates, had no wish to negotiate with Sonora, whom they distrusted. If they were to propose any terms, it would be with Chihuahua, a pattern that would hold true for the next fifty years.[30]

The Bedonkohes, Chihennes, and Nednhis had opened discussions with Chihuahua in early 1834. In late February, Geta Matada had come to Paso del Norte to speak with Lieutenant Santos Horcasitas about the Indians' desire for peace. Evidently the Apaches liked what they heard, for in March seven leaders, led by Fuerte, spoke to Horcasitas at Paso del Norte. This behavior was typical of Mangas, who never felt the same antipathy toward Chihuahua that he did for Sonora. Mano Mocha led the Bedonkohes, and the venerable Jasquedegá led the Carrizaleño local group of the Nednhis. Unfortunately, the details of the conference are vague. Yet they must have sought an armistice, for two months later Captain Ronquillo tried to work out a treaty with the Apaches camped near Santa Rita del Cobre and the Mimbres

River.[31] For some unexplained reason they could not resolve their differences at that time.

In May the Chiricahuas infuriated Ronquillo by stealing 160 horses at Santa Rita del Cobre, leaving the troops without mounts. When not harassing the settlement, they carried on a lively trade, dealing their Sonoran plunder to Santa Rita del Cobre's inhabitants in exchange for powder, lead, and provisions.[32]

With hopes for peace all but gone, that fall both Sonora and Chihuahua organized campaigns to punish the recalcitrants. Chihuahua organized its offensive in response to a Chiricahua war party that on September 28, 1834, had killed two men at Janos and had run off 130 horses. Troops pursued the Apaches and overtook them at the Casas Grandes River. After a brief stalemate, the Mexicans approached close enough to fire several rounds of cannonballs into the unsuspecting Indians. The first missiles caused utter devastation, killing at least six men and wounding some twenty more. Soundly whipped, the Indians fled the battleground. The Mexicans incurred a loss of three dead and two wounded. This defeat, coupled with a rumor that a large Sonoran army was heading for Apachería, compelled some Chiricahua leaders, including Fuerte, to resume negotiations with Chihuahua.[33]

Mexican intelligence had anticipated the Chiricahua plans, thanks to the testimony of a boy who had recently escaped from his captors. According to José Gregorio Madrid, the Chiricahua bands, after a tribal council, had recently dispatched three war parties against Mexico. The one that had raided Janos numbered 136 men, about the same number of men had gone on a foray against the settlements along the Rio Grande in New Mexico to steal sheep, and the third group of 100 men had raided Sonora but had returned after suffering heavy losses. Madrid also confirmed that the Indians' commerce with Anglo-American adventurers had left them well supplied with muskets and powder. He also reported that several Indians had perished from drinking what the survivors believed to be poisoned coffee. They held the Anglo-American traders responsible and vowed to avenge those deaths. Except for the older members of the tribe, who wanted to live in peace, and one local group of the Carrizaleños, the bands wanted war, according to Madrid.[34]

In early October the Carrizaleños under Cigarrito and Jasquedegá sent two emissaries to Paso del Norte and requested peace, which corroborated Madrid's story. Besides the Carrizaleño local group, the Chihennes and Bedonkohes under Fuerte, Caballo Ligero, and Cuchillo Negro had authorized the two Nednhi leaders to speak for them.[35] Why the abrupt change in philosophy is not clear, but one can speculate that they were smarting from their recent defeat by the troops from Janos and thus decided to make an armistice for the winter. Even the involvement of the warlike Chihennes under Fuerte seems uncharacteristic, although a report surfaced that every Chiricahua band favored peace with Chihuahua. This list was a Who's Who of the leaders of the 1830s and 1840s; it included Mangas Coloradas (still called Fuerte), Caballo Ligero, and Itán for the Chihennes;[36] Mano Mocha, Teboca, and Pluma for the Bedonkohes; Tapilá for the Chokonens; and Juan José Compá, Juan Diego Compá, Jasquedegá, and Cigarrito for the Nednhis. Several Mescalero leaders rounded out the impressive list. The principal spokesperson was the venerable sixty-year-old Jasquedegá, who arrived at the head of fifteen Apaches in early November to open formalities. He held several conversations with Captain Ronquillo, the no-nonsense officer who had defeated the Chiricahuas on the Gila nearly two years before. Ronquillo decided to employ unconventional means to coerce the hostiles to make peace. Once the two sides finished the talks, he ordered his subordinate at Paso del Norte to seize Jasquedegá's party and place them in the guardhouse.[37]

Mexican officials had tried this tactic before and would use it again in the future. Sometimes it paid dividends, and sometimes, because there were many unforeseen variables that affected relations between the two races, it failed miserably. This time the latter was the case, and Ronquillo's justice produced the opposite of the intended effect. At that moment still another event occurred which Ronquillo could not have anticipated or controlled. Mangas Coloradas and Pisago Cabezón had turned their thoughts toward Sonora, at which they had become incensed because of a campaign that had captured the Chokonen or Bedonkohe war chief Tutije near the Mogollon Mountains.

Sonora's campaign in the fall of 1834 had been in the planning stages since the early summer. Unlike Chihuahuan officials, Sonoran leaders scoffed at the thought of holding councils with the Apaches, whom Mexican troops had been unable to subjugate. Sonora demanded vengeance, and the subject was so important that Governor Manuel Escalante y Arvizu, described as a "bold man who enjoyed adventure," chose to relinquish his administrative duties to now Vice-Governor Ignacio Bustamante and personally take command for what he hoped would be a climactic strike against the Chiricahuas.

The mixed force of 402 men consisted of cavalry and infantry and even "tame" Apaches from Tucson and Tubac and Opata Indians from Sonora's frontier.[38] Among its officers were Antonio Narbona and José Terán y Tato, two important men destined to become well acquainted with the Chiricahuas.[39] The command established its first base camp at the Elías hacienda on Babocómari Creek, later the site of Camp Wallen, an Arizona fort in the late 1860s. From there the army marched northeast into Chokonen country, arriving at Apache Pass, then called Puerto del Dado, on October 15. There the Opata scouts refused to continue and promptly deserted despite Escalante y Arvizu's threat of execution. To this point the command had found thirteen abandoned rancherías; the Apaches had occupied most of them the previous summer. They discovered three in the Chiricahuas, including two at Apache Pass. The scouts believed that the main body of Chiricahuas had moved north to the Mogollons and Gila River country.

Escalante y Arvizu dispatched most of his force, over three hundred men, on the Indian trail. On October 24, 1834, in the foothills of the Mogollons, probably north of the site of Ronquillo's fight with the Chiricahuas two and one-half years before, the Mexican force succeeded in surprising a small band of Chiricahuas who had just returned from a foray into Chihuahua. Tutije and Vivora led the Indians,[40] and after a brief but hard fight the Sonorans succeeded in capturing the "wicked chief" Tutije and killing two other warriors. The Mexicans withdrew the next day with their considerable prize, as the Chiricahuas considered Tutije one of their important war leaders, rivaled only by Mangas Coloradas at the time. Escalante y Arvizu ordered the Apache leader sent to Arispe and placed on public display. The victorious troops paraded him through the streets as a sign of their great victory. But in terms of results, Escalante y Arvizu's army was ineffective; his efforts had proven fruitless, except for Tutije's capture.

He made his next move to obscure this lack of success. He knew that he held a huge bargaining chip, one that could be an important factor in negotiating with the Chiricahuas. Instead, symptomatic of Sonora's bellicosity, he clearly demonstrated that Sonora viewed extermination as the panacea to the conflict, and he ordered the public hanging of Tutije in the streets of Arispe, which perhaps temporarily disguised the fact that the highly vaunted campaign of 1834 had been a dismal military failure. Tutije's execution served to make relations with the Chiricahuas much worse. It incensed the two greatest Chiricahua leaders of the 1830s—Mangas Coloradas and Pisago Cabezón. They responded in like manner: revenge. One Chiricahua told anthropologist Morris Opler what their men did when one of their principal warriors was killed: "They go after anything, a troop of cavalry, a town. They are angry. They fight anyone to get even."[41]

Tutije's death further hardened the Chiricahua bands into two distinct factions. Pisago Cabezón and Mangas Coloradas headed the group that wanted to avenge Sonora's execution of Tutije and Chihuahua's unjust imprisonment of Jasquedegá's peace contingent. The peace bloc had Juan José Compá as its spokesman but not necessarily its leader. They preferred negotiating with Captain Ronquillo to obtain Jasquedegá's release, after which they would willingly return to the old presidio life.

Historians have credited Juan José Compá with having more influence and prominence than any other Chiricahua Apache leader during the first third of the nineteenth century. That assessment could not have been further off the mark. We must discard the myths that have surrounded him for so many years and attempt to view him according to his contemporary importance. Although countless accounts state that Mangas Coloradas succeeded Juan José Compá after his death in 1837, this was not so. As previously shown, Mangas Coloradas had become an important leader as early as 1814, and at the time of Juan José Compá's death he was already one of the two most influential Chiricahua leaders. Furthermore, the two men were of different bands, and Juan José Compá never achieved leadership except on the local group level of his Nednhi band. The son of El Compá, an important Chiricahua chief who lived at Janos in the early 1790s, Juan José was born about 1786. He was baptized into the Catholic faith in 1794 and attended the presidio school then, perhaps the only Chiricahua to have done so. His father, El Compá, died of natural causes on July 29, 1794, after which Juan José's brother, Juan Diego Compá, emerged as the head of the extended family group. In the early 1830s, with his older brother aging, Juan José sprang into the picture primarily because of three attributes: he was bilingual, literate, and a pacific leader.

Because they had a Chiricahua leader they could talk with, a man who sincerely preferred peace to war, Mexican authorities tried to make him into something he was not—a band leader. He never had a large following; his brother Juan Diego Compá remained the acknowledged leader of the Janeros local group of Nednhis. Yet Juan José Compá appears to have been a sincere and highly principled man trying to serve two masters: his own Apache people, who sometimes distrusted him because of his close relations with whites, and Mexican officials and friends at Janos, who always remembered that he was an Apache—thus, a savage— by birth. One historian labeled him an "information broker." Nineteenth-century Apaches and knowledgeable Mexican officials concurred with that assessment. Colonel Justiniani declared that the Chiricahuas "did not respect him, nor did they pay any attention to him unless it was in the conferences [with Mexicans] where he had to talk to the chiefs." The legend of Juan José Compá had its genesis in the treacherous massacre of him, his brother Juan Diego Compá, and a score of others at the hands of John Johnson, an event that will be discussed in later pages. The Chiricahuas never forgot the nature of the attack, and Juan José Compá came to symbolize early Mexican mistreatment of Apaches, though as far as the Indians were concerned, his death in itself was no more important than that of any of the other unfortunate victims.[42]

Juan José met with Mexican officials at Santa Rita del Cobre in January 1835. He returned the next month and on February 12 discussed conditions with Colonel Cayetano Justiniani, a sagacious officer who had a tremendous amount of experience with the Apaches. Justiniani's report reflected his pragmatic understanding of the Apaches, who had not only agreed to terms, but even pledged to help him fight the Comanches, an inveterate enemy of the Mexicans. The article requiring the Chiricahuas to return all stolen stock proved to be the primary obstacle to an agreement. Unable to enforce this condition, Justiniani recommended its elimination, reasoning that the Indians claimed they had little stolen stock left. Justiniani realized that "a force of eight hundred men well mounted and provisioned for four months" would be required to compel the return of the stolen stock.

Justiniani also recognized the political diversity among the Chiricahuas, for at least three of its bands, all of the Bedonkohes, Pisago Cabezón's Chokonens, and Mangas's mixed group of Chihennes and Bedonkohes, had refused to make peace because of Tutije's execution. Recognizing that this instability would never allow for permanent peace, he addressed this issue with Juan José Compá. The Nednhi leader, who had little influence outside his local group, admitted that he could not speak for those who had boycotted the talks. Justiniani emphasized that Chihuahua would not conclude the armistice unless those who signed the treaty agreed to join the Mexicans against the hostiles. Finally, after a lengthy conference, the Indians agreed "to make war on any of their fathers, sons, or brothers" who refused to make peace. Juan José did obtain, however, a reprieve for the hostiles, persuading Justiniani to give him one last opportunity to bring in the followers of Mangas Coloradas and Pisago Cabezón. He insisted, however, that he would aid Mexican troops against the hostiles if they still refused to make peace. This, of course, was lip service. If push came to shove, Juan José and the treaty-bound Chiricahuas would never have fought Pisago Cabezón's and Mangas Coloradas's followers.

Sixteen Chiricahua leaders representing the moderate faction of the four Chiricahua bands signed the agreement on March 31, 1835. Though a list of those leaders who made peace has not yet been located, we can make a well-informed guess of its contents. Two months later Mexicans took a census of Apaches at Santa Rita del Cobre, and this count, combined with a letter to Sonora's officials that identifies those who refused to make peace, makes it possible to speculate about who were those leaders who signed: for the Nednhis, Juan José Compá, his brother Juan Diego Compá, Francisquillo, and Cigarrito; for the Chihennes, Itán, Cuchillo Negro, Caballo Ligero, Boca Matada, and Geta Matada; for the Chokonens, Relles, Sidé, Matías, and Tapilá;[43] and for the Bedonkohes, Mano Mocha. The only surprises would be the last two leaders, for Tapilá and Mano Mocha normally aligned themselves with the hostile camp. Perhaps they were there acting as the eyes and ears for Mangas Coloradas and Pisago Cabezón, two of the twelve Chiricahua *capitancillos* or chiefs who refused to make peace until they had avenged Tutije's death.[44]

Ronquillo and Justiniani had one other important issue to address: Sonora's participation in the armistice. Consequently, Justiniani sent Matías, the old-time Chokonen leader who had lived for years in peace at Fronteras, to Ures, Sonora. Yet Sonora was in no humor to discuss a truce and refused to recognize Chihuahua's treaty. José María Elías González and Ignacio Bustamante scoffed at the idea of making peace. With such tremendous obstacles, and the ongoing dissension within the Chiricahuas, it was no wonder that the peace of 1835 was destined to be ephemeral in nature despite the sincere efforts of Juan José Compá and Colonel Cayetano Justiniani.[45]

José María Elías González, pictured here later in life, was Sonora's tough but pragmatic military leader, and he understood Apaches. (Courtesy Armando Elias)

Meanwhile, during the spring and summer of 1835, Juan José Compá tried to induce Pisago Cabezón and Mangas Coloradas to come in, but without success. Apache depredations continued at the same levels as in the years before, at least in Sonora. Raiders even struck settlements in Chihuahua, perhaps because the hostile faction wished to undermine the treaty. Furthermore, according to a released captive, the Chiricahuas had vowed to make Chihuahua pay for its imprisonment of Jasquedegá's party at Paso del Norte. The ink was barely dry when they assaulted a ranch near Casas Grandes, Chihuahua, killing Captain Francisco Valles and five other militiamen. Next they went on to El Carmen, where they murdered three more persons. Then, on May 10, 1835, over one hundred warriors raided a ranch near San Buenaventura and stole its entire herd of horses, mules, and burros. Although one report alleged that Juan José Compá had a hand in this raid, he denied it. Justiniani supported the Nednhi's claim, blaming it on Fuerte's and Pisago Cabezón's followers. Another report from Sonora said that Pisago Cabezón had sent war parties against that state and the Navajos in New Mexico.[46]

In response, in June 1835, Sonora and Chihuahua adopted measures consistent with their stated policies. First, on June 12, 1835, a 402-man force under the capable command of Captain Antonio Comadurán, a veteran of Sonora's northern frontier who had a great deal of experience with the Western Apaches, left Fronteras on a scout into Arizona. But the Chiricahuas easily eluded the slow-moving troops, who were usually no match for the nimble Indians. The soldiers returned empty-handed. Elías González, normally a well-composed man, had held high hopes about the campaign's potential. Upon its return, he threw a minor tantrum. In Chihuahua the governor ordered Captain Ronquillo to release Jasquedegá's group, which had been unjustly held at Paso del Norte for seven months. Ronquillo at once authorized Justiniani to set free his captives from Santa Rita del Cobre. While this action undoubtedly appeased the Carrizaleño local group of Nednhis, it was a case of too little too late for most of the Chiricahuas.[47]

The summer of 1835 saw Pisago Cabezón and Mangas Coloradas get their revenge. Pisago, allied with the Coyoteros, or the White Mountain band of Western Apaches, launched large offensives against northern Mexico. Anglo-American traders, led by James Kirker, helped the Chiricahua cause by carrying on a lucrative trade with the Apaches on the Mimbres River. In exchange for powder and other provisions of war, the Indians gave up mules that they had recently stolen in Sonora. In July one band stole most of the horses from San Buenaventura, and the following month it raided Fronteras, Casas Grandes, Ramos, and Janos, killing several people and stealing large numbers of stock. Juan José Compá attempted to distance himself from these depredations but found himself embroiled in the middle between the hostiles and Mexican authorities, who unrealistically expected him to control the militants. Yet the hostiles paid no attention to his words, and he reluctantly conceded that he could not control the activities of those living in the Mogollons and Gila River country. Nonetheless, he sent two messengers to Pisago Cabezón, who openly admitted that his men had been raiding Sonora with Nantanilla, the principal leader of the White Mountain band. Finally, conceding that bringing in Pisago or Mangas Coloradas was a hopeless cause, Juan José suggested that the Mexicans station troops at the Florida Mountains, south of present-day Deming, and in the Chiricahua Mountains. If that were done, the soldiers would be along the main raiding routes of the hostiles and might have a chance at intercepting their incursions. By the fall of 1835, Juan José realized that all hopes for peace had vanished. Accordingly, even he left Santa Rita del Cobre and joined the hostiles.[48]

By the fall of 1835 the Sonoran legislature decided to adopt harsh measures in an attempt to check the onslaught. First, the legislature authorized a bounty of one hundred pesos for the scalp of each Apache male over the age of fourteen. Its troops would subdue the Apaches until they destroyed them. Next, the energetic José María Elías González led a detachment from Sonora that found the Chiricahuas in force near the present-day border of Arizona and New Mexico, probably north of Stein's Peak. This engagement proved to be a virtual repeat of the May 1832 fight except that the Indians were fewer. Even with Pisago's steadying presence, the Mexicans soundly whipped the Apaches, killing ten to fifteen and wounding many others, according to Elías González's report. The Apaches killed three Mexicans and wounded nine others. Despite the one-sided victory, the Apaches' "boldness and discipline . . . with which they made their first two charges," astonished Elías González. By the end of the day, his troops had repelled the Indians' charges. The Sonoran commander attributed the Apaches' change in tactics to the influence of Anglo-American traders, who, he believed, had directed the hostiles. He may have been referring to James Kirker, who, according to rumors, had joined the Chiricahuas at this time.[49]

This defeat served only to incense further Pisago Cabezón, for Elías González believed one of that chief's sons was among the dead. Mangas Coloradas continued to operate with Pisago Cabezón. In early 1836, Elías González received information that an enormous force of Navajos, Utes, and Apaches had joined for an expedition into Sonora, in particular against Bavispe and Santa Cruz. As with most war parties, revenge was the motive of Pisago, "who was bent on vengeance" because of his son's death and the execution of Tutije. Although this force did not appear—the three tribes were not allies—Elías González apparently took the threat seriously.[50]

In the spring of 1836, Chihuahuan officials again approached Juan José Compá and Pisago Cabezón about an armistice. That spring both leaders met the Mexicans at Santa Rita del Cobre, and Pisago, evidently weary of war, pledged to send word of his peaceful intentions to the Bedonkohes and Chihennes. The Chiricahuas, however, distrusted Captain Mariano Rodríguez Rey, for he had imprisoned two warriors named San Juan and Chato.[51] Rey told the Apaches that he would not release them until the Chiricahuas turned over the two Indians who had recently raided the mines. The two young men were Santana, a son of Carro, a Chokonen group leader, and El Adivino (The Soothsayer), whose name suggests that he was a clairvoyant shaman or medicine man. The Apaches partially broke the deadlock when they brought in El Adivino, and Commander Rey released San Juan. Soon after, Chato escaped, and the minor crisis ended.[52]

In an abrupt reversal of its public policy, Sonora had also agreed to talk to the Chiricahuas, who had solicited peace in the summer of 1836. Mangas Coloradas and the Bedonkohes had stayed characteristically aloof, refusing to take part in the discussions and remaining in the Mogollons. On August 30, 1836, five Chokonen leaders—Relles, Matías, Marcelo, Eugenio, and Miguel (probably Miguel Narbona, the war chief of the Chokonens in the 1840s and 1850s),[53] met at the home of Elías González and temporarily accepted fifteen articles of peace. Both parties agreed to reconvene at Fronteras in October to consummate the arrangement.[54]

A perspicacious Elías González understood that Sonora had to provide subsistence to prevent Chiricahua raiding. That September he devoted much of his time and efforts to that end, but his superiors neglected the issue, much to his consternation. Nonetheless, in late October he went to Fronteras, where, to his surprise, he met Pisago Cabezón, freshly arrived from Santa Rita del Cobre.

Pisago had held talks with Captain Ponce de León, assuring the officer that he wanted peace. He admitted that he had no influence over the Carrizaleño local group of Nednhis but that he would do all in his power to convince Fuerte to make peace. Soon after, Pisago left because of an unfortunate encounter between some citizens and a few Chiricahuas. The Indians had entered Santa Rita del Cobre to trade when Mexicans turned on them, killing one woman and two men. Several citizens had murdered one man in cold blood while the other two Apaches were "beaten, stabbed, speared, and shot to death." These murders, which were particularly brutal, marked the beginning of deterioration of Chiricahua relations at Santa Rita del Cobre.

The two murdered men had married into Pisago's extended family group. Incensed at Chihuahua, Pisago Cabezón decided to open talks with Sonora. The Chihenne leaders Caballo Ligero and Boca Matada also participated in the talks. According to Mexican reports, Mangas Coloradas had split with Pisago Cabezón, still opposed to peace with either Sonora or Chihuahua.[55]

Sonora's truce with the Chiricahuas brought a temporary lull in hostilities. In an attempt to bring stability to the frontier, Elías González sent Pisago back to Santa Rita del Cobre to reopen negotiations with Chihuahua. Yet Pisago's visit served no purpose, for both races distrusted and despised each other. In early 1837 reports from Sonora indicated that Fuerte had established his winter camp near the San Francisco River, from which he had sent war parties against Sonora and Chihuahua.[56]

The coming year of 1837 was destined to be historic in Chiricahua Apache–Mexican relations. The conflict would escalate, and the Indians would become even more confident in their ability to make war. Pisago Cabezón's influence would begin to wane, and Mangas Coloradas would emerge as a true tribal leader. Until this time he had been known as Fuerte, but about this time (1837) his enemies discarded the old name, and he adopted the new name. The Chiricahuas would have more than their share of tragedies over the next few years, and it would be Mangas who would serve as the rallying point for those Apaches who demanded vengeance and Mexican blood.

Chapter 4

FUERTE BECOMES MANGAS COLORADAS

PISAGO Cabezón's armistice with Sonora was destined to endure for a short time only, primarily because the important subject of war or peace divided the Chiricahua bands throughout most of the 1830s. The Chokonens, usually the most bellicose of the Chiricahuas, now favored peace. But the Bedonkohes, Nednhis, and most of the Chihennes advocated war. After his truce with Sonora, Pisago had hastened to Santa Rita del Cobre and had requested peace with Chihuahua. There he met Robert McKnight, his old trading partner, and Captain José María Arce, military commander of the post. Arce, who a few years later would be slain by Apaches (probably Mescaleros),[1] was initially sanguine about the prospects for a cease-fire. José Joaquín Calvo, Chihuahua's implacable commanding general, instructed Arce to continue negotiations until the state could hold formal talks. By the time Arce made arrangements, however, the impatient and suspicious Apaches had bolted, perhaps induced by a statement overheard by them at Janos that peace will not be "given them until they are exterminated."[2]

This ill-advised comment, which did not represent Chihuahua's official policy then, set in motion the machinery for the dissolution of any thoughts the Chiricahuas had for peace with Chihuahua. This rancor led to a renewal of hostilities with Mexico and a new cycle of raids, Mexican campaigns, and further retaliation on both sides. The conflict also solidified the positions of Sonora and Chihuahua into a common one, as the latter adopted a new extreme policy—the employment of mercenaries to exterminate Apaches.

For the first time in recent years Mangas Coloradas and Pisago Cabezón had disagreed about the Chiricahuas' course of action.

Mangas despised Sonora and wanted only to be left alone in his country. Furthermore, although Sonora's execution of Tutije had occurred more than two years before, the warlike faction still longed for vengeance. In early 1837, Mangas remained in Mogollon country and may have had a hand in the January 26, 1837, raid on Santa Rita del Cobre, which finally convinced Captain Arce that the Apaches "do not wish peace." Meanwhile, Pisago Cabezón and his Chokonens continued to observe their treaty with Sonora, as some Chokonen local groups spent the winter in the Chiricahua Mountains. Another group camped at Sarampion, known to the Indians as Dziltilcil (Black Mountain), a favorite ranchería site located in the lower Peloncillos due east of the southern Chiricahuas. Marcelo, another Chokonen or Nednhi group leader, spent the winter at picturesque Embudos Canyon, later to be made famous because of American General George Crook's historic meeting there with Geronimo in 1886.[3]

The armistice also led to more frequent interaction between the two former enemies, each of which included individuals who hated the other race. At Fronteras the Chokonen chief Relles had a run-in with Andrés Luna, an avowed Indian hater who was a member of the prominent Luna family. Luna had confiscated several of Relles's sheep after they had wandered into his flock. One might legitimately question how Relles had come to own the sheep, but following the treaty he had made "his mark consisting of cropped ears." Luna refused to return the animals. Relles protested to civil authorities at Fronteras, who passed his complaint along to the governor, noting that Luna "is a man who wants to come out on top and get whatever he wants by fighting with the Indians." The governor ordered Luna to return Relles's sheep. Local conflicts of this nature served to heighten the distrust between the two peoples.[4]

By early 1837 it had become clear that Chihuahua's inability to consummate an agreement would lead to potentially dire consequences. The Chokonens, incensed at Chihuahua's new militaristic attitude, sent raiding parties from their winter homes near Fronteras into Chihuahua. One band returned with over five hundred head of stock. Immediately after, buoyed by the easy pickings, thirty warriors from Marcelo's group left for an incursion. Marcelo, conceding that he was unable to control his young men, soon had another problem. Teboca arrived with a raiding party of Bedonkohes and a few Chokonens, including San Juan, whom Mexicans had just released from Santa Rita del Cobre's prison. Teboca's party had come from the Gila River country, and their appearance stirred up the hornet's nest.

Teboca, a former resident of Fronteras during its peace establishment days, had become an important war leader and close ally of Mangas Coloradas. His party surrounded several Mexicans about seven miles from Fronteras, stripped them, and stole five horses and two hundred head of cattle. One victim, Luiso Romero, clearly identified the Indians involved in the shakedown. He testified that "I know the chief Teboca very well. . . . I have seen him at this presidio several times when he has come here for peace." Both civilian and military officials at Fronteras declared that the Apaches "had laughed at our friendship." Other reports of Apache raiding in the northern frontier reached Elías González, the military commander of Sonora. In addition, from Tucson came information obtained from the Pinal Apaches, a Western Apache band, that the Chiricahuas planned to assassinate Elías González and Captain Antonio Comadurán, the commander at Santa Cruz. After weighing all the evidence, Elías González concluded that the Apaches had broken the peace treaties. He issued an ultimatum: all Apaches not at Fronteras by March 19, 1837, "will immediately thereafter be considered declared enemies." He then suggested that Sonora and Chihuahua take joint punitive actions against the hostiles.[5]

The Chiricahua raids intensified during March 1837. First, the Indians killed a man escorting a wagon train from Janos to Santa Rita del Cobre; next, they struck several ranches in the Janos–Casas Grandes area, where their depredations had prevented farmers from tending to their fields. In Sonora "the frontier towns were helpless" to take any action. Governor Escalante y Arvizu admitted that his government was powerless to stem the tide. Sonora was "destitute of resources, and required assistance in food and money." He did issue another timeworn proclamation, however, hoping to lift the spirits of the citizens living along the frontier. "War to the death of the enemy," proclaimed Escalante y Arvizu.[6]

We can not be exactly certain what role Mangas Coloradas played in the resurgence of hostilities. By the spring of 1837 he had left his winter camps in the lowland canyons and valleys of the Mogollons and had headed south toward the Peloncillo and Animas Mountains. There, according to Chiricahua oral history, he was present during the perfidious John Johnson massacre of Juan José Compá and some twenty-five others on April 22, 1837.

Historians and writers have so much discussed and analyzed the events surrounding the death of Juan José Compá that the story needs no in-depth analysis here. Suffice it to say that John Johnson,[7] an Anglo living in Moctezuma, Sonora, left that place with seventeen Anglos and five Mexicans on April 3, 1837. Escalante y Arvizu had authorized Johnson to hunt down hostile Apaches. No evidence has surfaced to suggest that Johnson's mercenaries, whose reward was half the confiscated plunder, set out specifically to get Juan José Compá. It was apparently purely by chance that Johnson encountered Juan José's Janeros local group of Nednhis, along with some Chokonens and Chihennes, in the Animas Mountains in extreme southwestern New Mexico about ten miles north of the present boundary with Mexico. The Chiricahuas called this range Dzisl-dijole, or "Round Mountain." At least two and probably three Chiricahua bands sometimes camped in these mountains, exploiting the region for hunting, gathering, and as a base to raid into Mexico. The range also contained a number of springs and the highest peak in the area, standing 8,519 feet in altitude.[8]

The Chiricahuas met Johnson's party on April 20, 1837, and the two parties traded goods with each other. The first two days passed with much friendship, according to the testimony of Lautora García, a captive whom Johnson ransomed from the Apaches. Unfortunately, the morning of April 22, 1837, would be different, although the Chiricahuas had no reason to be suspicious. Johnson's party had plotted their treachery the night before; the five Mexicans had refused to participate and left before daybreak. As the Chiricahuas came into Johnson's camp to trade, the whites unleashed their surprise, a small swivel cannon "charged with metallic scraps," which killed or wounded several Indians. Rifle fire from seventeen Anglo marksmen immediately followed as bedlam enveloped the bewildered Indians. When the slaughter was over, the bodies of at least twenty Apaches lay strewn on the field. Among them were the leaders Juan José Compá, his brother Juan Diego Compá, Marcelo, and Guero.[9]

Although contemporary accounts do not mention the presence of either Fuerte or Mangas Coloradas, Apache oral history places him at the scene of the massacre. The informants of Eve Ball told her that Mangas Coloradas was present and declared that after the first volley he had grabbed a baby and fled the scene. Only later, they said, did he realize that "the baby he carried with him was his son." Unfortunately, two of his four wives were not as lucky, for they fell victims of Johnson's insidious chicanery. If all of this is true, the episode definitely left an indelible impression on Mangas Coloradas and much intensified his hatred of Sonora. His personality also seemed to change. Before this he had been aloof and reserved, and as long as the Mexicans left him alone he would do the same to them. After the Johnson affair, he became a more aggressive and vigorous leader who hungered for revenge against Sonora. He took this grudge to his grave more than a quarter of a century later. This change must have been similar to Cochise's metamorphosis with respect to Americans after the Bascom affair in 1861.[10]

Other evidence exists to support this traditional belief that Mangas Coloradas was present at the massacre. First, the Animas Mountains bordered the local group territory of three Chiricahua bands—the Chokonens, Chihennes, and Nednhis. Moreover, in later years Mangas Coloradas bitterly recalled the specifics of Johnson's deed. He said that "at another time a trader was sent among us from [Sonora]. While innocently engaged in trading, often leading to words of anger, a cannon concealed behind the goods was fired upon my people and quite a number killed."[11]

To the Chiricahuas, this was the first in "a series of treacherous attacks made upon us by whites or Mexicans."[12] Clearly, they regarded the deed as one of the worst ever perpetrated upon them, at least until James Kirker got into the act a few years later. The death of Juan José Compá was, in itself, unimportant. He had no influence among any Chiricahua band or group other than his own small extended family group. There was no unusual groundswell of emotion to avenge his death as there had been for Tutije and others. Yet the manner in which his death occurred was significant for two reasons: the way in which the Mexicans had deceived them, and the large number of victims who were women and children. Johnson's nefarious act also signaled to the Chiricahuas that Mexico had adopted a new philosophy in fighting them. It was one thing for their enemies to have defeated them on the battlefield; it was another to have a treacherous attack and wanton slaughter without regard to age or sex simply because the Mexicans could not defeat the Chiricahuas in warfare. Johnson's attack provided an unfortunate precedent for several others that would occur over the next twenty-five years. He had laid the first stone for a new policy: extermination. The ramifications, however, were far from what Mexican leaders had anticipated, for the Chiricahuas, instead of requesting peace or laying down their arms, launched a sanguinary period of retaliatory war parties. During the next five years, with Pisago Cabezón aging, Mangas Coloradas emerged as the undisputed war leader of the three northern Chiricahua bands. And Soquilla, who succeeded Compás as leader of the Janeros local groups of Nednhis, came to defer to Mangas Coloradas.

Mangas Coloradas retired north to the Gila after the Johnson massacre. After a short period of mourning, the Chiricahuas' next response was predictable—revenge, preferably on the parties responsible. Soon after, the Indians wiped out the Kemp party of twenty-two trappers. Then they ambushed a wagon train and killed all twelve men who were en route to El Paso from Santa Fe.[13] It was after the fight with Kemp's party, according to legend, that Mangas donned a shirt with bright red sleeves and thus took on his new name, probably more of a nickname, and became Kan-da-zis-tlishishen, or "Red Sleeves."[14] He may have retained his old Apache name, yet "if a striking new name is acquired, people begin to use it and drop the old name," one Apache told ethnologist Grenville Goodwin. This was likely the case with Mangas Coloradas, as nicknames were those frequently used, for "true given names are likely to be more personal."[15]

A few weeks after the Johnson massacre, Chiricahuas captured an American trapper, Benjamin D. Wilson, and two unsuspecting friends; they were unaware that war had erupted after Johnson's perfidious attack. Years later, Wilson recalled the event:

Everything we had was taken from us. We were marched up to the Apache camp—there we were given to ascertain that something terrible had happened between the Apaches and Americans and that the young warriors were determined to sacrifice us. We expressed our astonishment at the changed conduct of the Apaches, from whom we had ever before received many evidences of friendly feelings. . . . In camp that night the Indians kept up a war dance to the east of the wigwam where Chief Mangas kept us confined. That old chief was opposed to our being sacrificed as he said that he had received many favors from Americans and believed it was to the interest of his people to keep up the amicable relations existing till this time. Our party at this time was reduced to three men. . . . Mangas told us that he had been doing his best to dissuade his men from destroying us but unsuccessfully. Finally at a late hour of the night, Mangas came in greatly excited and said that he had to return to his warriors and one of us must leave, as it was the only one he could save. I asked my men what we should do. One named Maxwell had a sprained ankle and could not walk. The other named Tucker was kind of invalid. . . .

So it was concluded that I should go. . . . I caught up a small buffalo robe and threw it upon my shoulder (the Indians had stripped me of all clothing) and left.[16]

Shortly after, Mangas helped Maxwell and Tucker escape. Why he decided to protect the Americans remains a mystery. One can speculate that he had distinguished between those whites who had harmed his people and those who had not. Yet that does not explain why the Apaches had killed Kemp's party, unless it had committed some frightful act against the Apaches. Wilson's recollections seem convincing in many ways. His mention of the Apaches' war dance, held only when they were out for revenge, seems right, as does his description of Mangas's authority as chief over his furious warriors, who were preparing themselves for war. An Apache leader's control of his men was far from absolute, yet Mangas, as did Cochise in later years, had followers devoted to him who felt confident in his leadership abilities. Notwithstanding this status, Mangas released Wilson discreetly. Mangas's deportment toward Americans seems consistent with his later behavior. He respected and liked most Americans. He recognized that he needed these intrepid adventurers, who brought much-needed guns and ammunition to his people in exchange for the Apaches' booty. At any rate, clearly the Johnson massacre had not embittered the Chiricahuas against all Americans, for over the course of the following year they continued to traffic with non-Mexican groups and even went so far as to allow James Kirker to accompany them on an expedition into Sonora.

The large-scale Chiricahua response did not unfold until the summer of 1837, when warriors struck both Sonora and Chihuahua. On July 8 they assaulted Cumpas, situated on the east bank of the Moctezuma River some twenty miles north of Moctezuma, and killed three persons. Reports implied that the Chokonens were involved, for eyewitnesses had recognized two of Relles's sons. On July 26, 1837, Apaches raided Huepac, on the Sonora River about thirty miles south of Arispe, and cleaned it out of every head of stock in the town's possession. In early August, Apache raiding parties hit Fronteras, striking it on August 7. Troops from Fronteras pursued them and, in a brief skirmish near San Bernardino, killed two Apaches and recaptured their horses.[17]

That fall the Chiricahuas, probably under Mangas Coloradas, beset northwestern Chihuahua. On September 25, 1837, the Bedonkohes captured a young boy, Felipe de Jesús Fuente, from

Galeana. Three days later they overwhelmed a small party near Casas Grandes, killing two and wounding four others. The Mexicans pursued and succeeded in overtaking the Indians. In a running fight, they wounded three Indians before their horses gave out. About this time the Chiricahuas stole eighty cattle and eleven horses from Ramos, a large hacienda some fifteen miles south of Janos. Soon after, they assailed Janos, perhaps because Johnson had retired there after the carnage. Finally, on October 4, 1837, a tremendous war party assaulted El Carmen, a hacienda fifty miles southwest of Carrizal, but did little damage before retiring north. Yet they did strike fear in the hearts of El Carmen's residents.[18]

By late 1837 every Chiricahua band was hostile and committing depredations, and the residents of northern Mexico had become fearful and conscious of a certain helplessness. The Chiricahuas returned to the Janos area in late October, ambushing two men, whom they killed, and stripping two women while they harvested their crops. Six weeks later another Chiricahua war party achieved a major victory at Ramos and killed the justice of the peace and eight others, forcing the hacienda's abandonment. Local populations could do little. For example, in Chihuahua the district of Galeana owned only 129 working firearms, and no one knew when ammunition might run out. The situation was not any better in Sonora. At the small hamlet of Cuquiarachi, a few miles southwest of Fronteras, the citizens had firearms but lacked ammunition. They felt powerless against the "frequency of Apache hostilities."[19]

By the end of 1837 the Chiricahua onslaught had convinced the governors of Sonora and Chihuahua that they must take action to stop the Indians. Simón Elías González, governor of Chihuahua, wrote José Escalante y Arvizu, governor of Sonora (and Tutije's executioner), to propose a joint campaign. They vowed to punish the Chiricahuas, who were "ungrateful after forty-six years of maintaining them in our society and friendship." Elías González's plan called for an army of four hundred men, which, he hoped, would include two hundred Opatas from Sonora, to wage a six-month war into Apachería, using Santa Rita del Cobre as a base of operations. He believed that constant pressure would compel the unified Chiricahuas to sue for peace. But as often happens with grandiose plans, lack of money and political instabilities prevented this one from ever getting off the ground.[20]

The Chiricahuas also had plans for Santa Rita del Cobre. Mangas Coloradas and Pisago Cabezón had decided to evict their tenants, whom they viewed as trespassers on their land. The two great

chiefs could possibly have heard rumors that Chihuahua intended
to close the once profitable mines, whose luster was fading as
rapidly as Mexico's influence in Apachería. As early as December
1836, Mexican officials had ordered that the mines be shut down
because of economics; the cost to extract the ore exceeded its
revenue. Water had also flooded the shafts, thus forcing miners to
spend more time on costly maintenance than on digging for
revenue-producing ore. In today's terms, the mine faced imminent
bankruptcy. If the state government had not subsidized its operations, Mexico would have closed the mines earlier.

With revenues falling, Robert McKnight apparently began to
turn his efforts to the lucrative contraband trade with the Apaches.
In the spring of 1837, Chihuahua's governor brought criminal
charges against him for trading muskets to the Apaches in
exchange for the mules they had obtained during their raids in
Mexico. In early 1838, McKnight resigned, and state authorities
ordered the military commander of Janos to take charge temporarily of Santa Rita's supply center. The Chiricahua hostilities
exacerbated these economic and administrative problems. Raiders
found the settlement easy pickings and preyed on its stock and
citizens without opposition. More than once they severed the communications of the isolated settlement. Mangas Coloradas soon
discovered that Santa Rita del Cobre, totally dependent on supplies
from Chihuahua, was a susceptible target. He decided to exploit
that situation. According to Apache tradition, he vowed that the
Mexicans "shall no longer trespass."[21]

About mid-March 1838, Pisago Cabezón and Mangas Coloradas
summoned Chiricahua leaders to a council, likely held near Santa
Lucía. The Indians, with their confidence soaring, took aim at both
Sonora and Chihuahua. Pisago Cabezón and Mangas Coloradas
resolved to lead one war party of two hundred to three hundred
warriors, consisting of Chokonens, Chihennes, and the Janeros
local group of Nednhis, to concentrate on cutting off the supplies to
Santa Rita del Cobre; they sent a second war party against Sonora
under the *segundos*, or protégés, of Pisago Cabezón and Mangas
Coloradas. Pisago designated Tapilá, a fierce Chokonen war leader,
and Mangas called upon Teboca to lead two hundred Chokonen and
Bedonkohe warriors into Sonora to avenge Johnson's treacherous
act. James Kirker's traders, including Shawnee and Delaware
Indians from Missouri,[22] aided the Chiricahua war parties, ensuring
that the Apaches had new weapons for their expeditions. Kirker, it

has always been supposed, accompanied Tapilá's party into Sonora, lending his expertise to the Apaches.

As Tapilá's party entered Sonora, Mangas Coloradas and Pisago Cabezón executed their plan to take Santa Rita del Cobre. It would not be by force, which was too risky and would cost unnecessary casualties. An Apache fought only on his terms unless protecting his family or fighting for revenge, when he would throw caution to the winds. Instead, Pisago and Mangas decided to cut off the inhabitants of Santa Rita del Cobre from their source of supplies. About every month a caravan of ten or more wagons left Galeana destined for Santa Rita del Cobre; Mangas and Pisago knew this and made plans to ambush it before it reached the mines. They undoubtedly recalled the several acts of treachery carried out against them at Santa Rita del Cobre—including the recent murders of Pisago's two sons-in-law eighteen months before.[23]

For the ambush they selected the rolling hills just south of Carrizalillo Springs, a few miles south of Hermanas, New Mexico, on the Mexican side of the present border. This site lay along the route used by travelers between Casas Grandes, Galeana, Janos, and Santa Rita del Cobre. According to Major William H. Emory, who replaced John Russell Bartlett as boundary commissioner in the early 1850s, the area derived its name from "a series of lagoons formed by many springs, of which fifteen were counted, all affording clear water. They are connected, and all together present a sheet of water from one and a half to two miles long, by from one-third to one-half mile broad, and four to five feet deep; their direction is north to south."[24]

On March 26 the Chiricahuas moved south by way of the Florida Mountains southeast of Deming, New Mexico, where their force was augmented by warriors from a Chihenne local group that had spent the winter there. The Chiricahuas called this range Dzilnokone, meaning "Long, Hanging Mountain." This region was an important base and camping area for one Chihenne local group. With several summits approaching seven thousand feet, the Florida Mountains were also home to large numbers of mountain goats. Leaving there, the war party's route lay south to the Carrizalillo Hills, where Mangas and Pisago prepared their ambush.[25]

On March 30, 1838, Ambrosio Tachan's wagons moved at a leisurely pace toward the springs when, about 3:00 P.M., the Indians suddenly appeared from the hills and swept down on the cattle and mule herds of Narciso Soto and Marcos Escudero that were ahead of the main party. At once the escort and several Americans pursued the Apaches, but the Indians abruptly stopped and defiantly took possession of a hilly area in front of the springs. Seeing that the Indians outnumbered them, the whites halted. According to Mexican reports, the Apaches totaled four hundred—three hundred mounted and one hundred on foot—although that estimate now seems high. Both sides assumed defensive positions, and for the rest of the day and throughout the moonlit night only sporadic gunfire interrupted the stalemate.

About 11:00 A.M. the next day Chato Pisago, a son of Pisago, approached the whites, asking for a parley. Pascual Mora agreed to venture out, but only after hiding a pistol beneath his clothing. Chato told Mora that Pisago wanted to speak with a citizen of Janos. Ambrosio Tachan, the leader of the Mexicans, replied brazenly that if Pisago wanted to talk he should come toward the Mexican positions. After a few tense moments, Gabriel Zapata, trusting Chato Pisago, bravely left the wagons and met the Apaches near their camp.[26]

A few years later American adventurer and writer George W. Kendall met a Chiricahua leader who might have been Pisago Cabezón. If so, his brief portrayal of the great chief is the only one available today. He described Pisago as being about "middle height, strong and well built, some sixty-five to seventy years of age, and with hair as white as snow."[27] Zapata recalled that

> at my request Pisago came down and the two Indians together greeted and embraced me. After speaking about several things in a friendly manner Pisago said, "I want peace. I don't want to fight." I answered saying that although I was only a servant of the hacienda I would risk my hide, and that should they let the wagons and the people pass I would remain with their band until he should receive a guarantee of protection either from Don Roberto (Robert McKnight) or from the Governor. Pisago agreed to this.

This understanding was short-lived and somewhat questionable, for this was a major war party intent on revenge and loot. At this stage another character entered the equation. Bernavé, a renegade Mexican who once had lived at Santa Rita del Cobre, advised Pisago not to agree to anything. Reminding Pisago of the recent atrocities committed by whites on the Apaches, Bernavé shouted, "Don't you remember the Indian women from Sidé who were killed and your own sons-in-law at El Cobre who were beaten to death with sticks there?" At this point Pisago offered "perhaps life and liberty for those you will choose." Yet before Zapata could make a decision, Pisago said that he had to "go see the other captain." Pisago did not mention the identity of this other chief, but it must have been Mangas Coloradas, for according to Chiricahua Apache oral history he had the leading role in this incident. A short time later Pisago returned with other leaders, but not Mangas, and gave Zapata the decision: the Apaches would not make any bargains. Abandon everything and return to Janos and the Indians would not attack the whites. One Apache, Manuel Chirimni, wanted to kill Zapata, but several other Indians protected him. Coche, a Nednhi leader, threw the Mexican "on the rump of a horse and so brought me safely out of the crowd." Either that day or the next (April 2) the whites abandoned the entire train of ten wagons and its provisions and returned to Janos, arriving there on April 3, 1838, with only twenty-two horses.[28]

The commander of Janos reacted immediately, fearing that the Indians would threaten Janos itself. He dispatched two couriers to Bavispe, Sonora, requesting forty men, but the day before, José Manuel Samaniego had sent out a patrol in response to Indian signs north of there, undoubtedly of Tapilá's party. He did forward thirty reinforcements with an artillery piece, however, which must have buoyed the spirits of the residents of Janos. Meanwhile, after the attack at Carrizalillo Springs, Mangas's and Pisago's warriors assaulted the mines in early April, killing several citizens, wounding another, and stealing some mules, donkeys, and three hundred head of sheep.[29] A few weeks later five Apaches threatened a shipment of copper en route to Galeana from Santa Rita del Cobre. They boasted that they would allow the wagons to pass, for they could not eat copper, but upon the wagons' return they would be waiting to confiscate the provisions. On May 6 another train with a seventy-man escort left Galeana destined for the mines. They saw a few Apaches, but no trouble occurred; Mangas and Pisago saw no advantage to risk needless casualties, because they probably had heard that the Mexicans had decided to close the mines. In late June the Mexicans deserted the diggings and transferred the public property to Janos.[30]

Legend has it that Mangas Coloradas and his men compelled the whites to abandon the mines. According to popular belief, the Chiricahuas lay siege to the settlement, thus forcing the inhabitants to leave to escape starvation. As the story goes, while they were en route to their destination the Indians unmercifully fell upon them, slaughtering almost every citizen despite gender or age. This preposterous tale, which evidently originated from the lively imagination of John Cremony (who claimed that he heard the story in Sonora), has also crept its way into Apache oral traditions. Cremony wrote that the Indians cut off and killed "every man, woman, and child" who left the mines "except for four or five." The informants of Eve Ball told her "that many set out for the border, but not one reached it."[31]

No evidence has been found to support Cremony's version or that given to Eve Ball. Another recently published account from the Chiricahua perspective has provided us with the recollections of Dilth-cleyhen, a daughter of the Chihenne leader Victorio, who was in his late teens at the time of the Johnson massacre. She fails to mention any wholesale slaughter of Santa Rita del Cobre's residents. Instead, she notes that Mangas Coloradas vowed to force the "miners and their families to abandon their small adobe homes, even their livestock," therefore leaving "Santa Rita a ghost town." Three contemporary accounts, one by Frederick A. Wislizenus, who journeyed through northern Mexico in 1846–47; another by John Russell Bartlett, an associate of Cremony; and the third by Michael Steck, Southern Apache agent for almost a decade in the 1850s and early 1860s, furnished reliable versions obtained from citizens and, in Steck's case, likely from the Indians. None mentioned anything about a wholesale slaughter. Wislizenus wrote that the mines "had to be abandoned on account of hostile Indians, who killed some of the workmen and attacked the trains." Bartlett was more specific, obviously referring to the incident at Carrizalillo Springs. He carefully described the ambush in which the Indians took the wagons, mules, and horses, "first giving each man who accompanied the train a mule to carry him away. At the same time they sent word to the inhabitants at the Copper Mines, that they would allow no further supplies to reach them and, furthermore, would destroy them whenever an opportunity offered. [Therefore] the people determined to abandon the place." Steck stated that the Apaches killed "many of the inhabitants and the remainder were compelled to fly to safety."[32]

Hostilities continued between 1838 and 1842 except for a brief hiatus in November 1838, when the Carrizaleño local group of Nednhis, along with most of the Mescaleros, made peace at Paso del Norte. Their primary motive was to secure the release of their people held in captivity by Chihuahua, probably the overriding factor in most Chiricahua peace treaties with Mexico during the nineteenth century. Mexican reports indicated that many Chiricahuas were living in the Mogollons, away from the northern frontier.[33]

Meanwhile, in Sonora, its presidios, poorly equipped and sparsely garrisoned, were incapable of either preventing raids or mounting offensives. Beginning in late 1837 political instability prevailed as two rival groups, the Gándaras and the Urreas, began their fight for control of the state. In 1838 a period of eight years of civil war began, a condition that would drive the state into virtual bankruptcy. While Sonora bled, the federalist and centralists groups fought for the privilege of exploiting its resources. The group headed by Manuel María Gándara,[34] a supreme opportunist whom one historian characterized as a "perfidious politician," went so far as to enlist the aid of Sonora's indigenous populations (Yaquis, Mayos, and Papagos) in his quest to rule the state. In contrast, José Urrea,[35] an officer of exceptional intelligence, undaunted courage, unquestioned integrity, and a record of compassion, had returned to Sonora as a national hero after his service with Santa Anna in Texas. He felt jilted when Mexico's President Bustamante passed over him and named Manuel Gándara governor of Sonora. By the fall of 1837 prominent leaders of Sonora met at Arispe and decided to petition Mexico City to allow the state to govern its own internal affairs. One of its significant reforms was to take control of its revenues to use them in their war against the Apaches. Urrea supported this philosophy and was elected governor by a junta in early 1838. Gándara did not take this sitting down, however. After his removal he organized a counterrevolt, and during the summer and fall of 1838 the rivals focused their energies against each other instead of on the Apaches. By the end of 1838, Gándara's coalition had defeated Urrea's forces. Urrea left the state and Gándara proclaimed himself governor.[36]

Despite this chaos, Sonora's military did achieve some small successes. In the summer of 1838 troops killed four warriors near Santa Cruz, a chief and two warriors near Fronteras, and a chief and three warriors near Hermosillo. Yet the Apaches controlled the northeastern frontier, with little resistance from Sonora.[37]

The summer of 1839 was no better. The Indians' audacity increased to the point that they murdered a man inside a house at Santa Cruz, and in August they ambushed and killed two soldiers outside the corral at Bavispe.[38] Finally, in November 1839, Manuel María Gándara led a campaign into Chihenne country. At the Mimbres River the Sonorans surprised an Apache camp and killed

José Cosme de Urrea, Military
Commander and Governor of
Sonora. (Courtesy Armando Elias)

seventeen warriors, including, Gándara believed, Pisago Cabezón
(which proved to be untrue); they recovered 280 horses and mules,
110 head of cattle, and nineteen American rifles. Gándara lost two
men killed and three wounded.[39] Although contemporary documents failed to mention Mangas Coloradas (or any other leader
besides Pisago Cabezón), he likely was in the vicinity, if not
actually present, because of his association with Pisago and the
fact that the battle occurred in his band territory. In any event the
expedition set off another bloody cycle of revenge and retaliation,
although Pisago Cabezón removed his followers to Boca Grande,
north of Janos. In 1840 the Chiricahuas, driven by rage, continued
their depredations in Sonora, where Gándara continued to blame
his impotence on the turmoil caused by internal conflict. "Since
the beginning of the Revolution in 1838, the troops of this department have been occupied in defeating it, thus leaving few troops to
fight the Apaches."[40]

In the late 1830s Chihuahua also suffered heavily from the
renewed Chiricahua raiding. Affairs were at a low ebb; mines were
abandoned, haciendas deserted, and public roads increasingly
unsafe. The state's governor, Simón Elías González, brother of
Sonora's José María Elías González, cautioned that these raids
might force the abandonment of Chihuahua's northern frontier,
particularly the area of Janos, Casas Grandes, and Galeana. The
governor soon became convinced that the Apaches would march

unopposed into the state capital, Chihuahua City, and he felt that his troops could not stop them. Thus, he decided to take action. Its final course differed from that of Sonora, but the objectives were the same.[41]

Recognizing that its presidio troops were no match for the mobile Apaches, Chihuahua opted for a novel approach to its Apache problem: it hired mercenaries, or scalp hunters, as they would become known. This private army, which consisted of some truly unsavory characters—Anglo-American traders and trappers, Shawnee and Delaware Indians, Mexican convicts, and other hard-bitten frontiersmen, would be compensated according to results. Chihuahua would pay a bounty on scalps. The leader of the pack was the ubiquitous frontiersman James Kirker, a "blue eyed, gray haired and gray whiskered man . . . short and stout."[42]

Kirker was a logical choice: he knew Apaches and was thoroughly familiar with their territory and their favorite camping areas. Just as important, he was an opportunistic and pragmatic man usually prepared to take the side most advantageous to him; this time the advantage was in Chihuahuan pesos. During the 1830s he had played both sides: Anglo against Apache and most recently Apache against Mexican (although he claimed that the Apaches had forced him to accompany them after capturing him). Now he would reverse the latter role and join the Mexicans against the Apaches. On June 14, 1839, Angel Trias, president of the municipal council of Chihuahua City, issued an ordinance levying a tax on merchants to support Kirker's outfit. Although this response seemed extreme, public support was overwhelmingly enthusiastic except from Chihuahua's military leaders, who felt that these measures represented a personal assault on their character and efforts.[43]

Kirker's force left Chihuahua City on December 26, 1839. Five days later the governor of Chihuahua made the following announcement:

> The governor has approved the plan to make war on the Indians through the cooperation of Don Santiago Kirker, who is currently in this city. . . . The people of Chihuahua City will assist Kirker with mounts and supplies, for which purpose donations will be collected in this city to cover the expenses. In addition, his excellency, the governor grants to him and his companions the total value of the ownerless horses and half the value of those which are branded, together with the other booty that they may take from Indians, provided that it be done in combat with them, as demonstrated by

the capture or death of one of them. Likewise, the same right is granted to all the residents of the Department who wish to wage a campaign at their expense.[44]

The Chiricahuas soon felt the wrath of Kirker's scalp hunters. Mangas Coloradas's band had remained in New Mexico, seemingly out of the mercenaries' reach. But Pisago Cabezón, who had left the Mimbres country after the attack by Sonoran troops, had no such luck. On December 27, 1839, a small party from Pisago's band arrived at Janos and solicited peace.[45] Pisago, recently defeated by Gándara's troops, wanted a truce. He may have heard that Chihuahua had hired Kirker to campaign against his people. Therefore, his gesture may have been a ploy to thwart the offensive. Or perhaps he just wanted to come in and conduct some business "for the disposal of their booty and the purchase of munitions" as happened under many Apache-Mexican truces, in the words of one contemporary observer.[46] By the time the commander at Janos sent word to Captain Arce in Chihuahua City, Kirker's army had already left toward the Janos frontier. Captain Arce wrote the commander at Janos that he would instruct Kirker to change his base of operations from Casas Grandes to the Carrizal and Paso del Norte region. Kirker did not receive the message, received it too late, or ignored it, for on January 9, 1840, his force, augmented by citizens from Casas Grandes and Galeana, surprised Pisago Cabezón's ranchería in the Boca Grande Mountains, fifty miles north of Janos, and killed fifteen, including ten warriors, and captured twenty others. Among the prisoners was Marcelo, a son of Pisago Cabezón.[47]

The Apaches felt betrayed, for authorities at Janos had assured them they would be safe from Kirker's force if they remained at peace. Pisago would have retaliated except for the twenty prisoners in the hands of Kirker, whom the mercenaries had quickly ushered to Chihuahua City to claim their reward. Instead, Pisago went to the Mogollons to confer with Mangas Coloradas and other leaders, but not before he sent emissaries to Janos to find out the whereabouts of his son and the other members of his group.[48]

Simón Elías González, Chihuahua's governor, was unsympathetic to Pisago's case, believing that Pisago's peace initiative was but a ploy to forestall Kirker's campaign, thus preventing the citizens of Chihuahua from taking the vengeance that was rightly theirs. The governor, however, invited Pisago to come to Chihuahua City to arrange a truce. The venerable Chiricahua leader refused this offer;

instead, he continued to negotiate at Janos in the hope that Chihuahua would return his people.[49]

Meanwhile, Kirker returned to Chihuahua City after his clandestine attack on Pisago's ranchería. After a period of rest and relaxation, on April 5, 1840, he led a force of one hundred men, consisting of "Mexicans, foreigners of several nations, and Shawnee Indians," on another campaign. His crew had evidently worn out their welcome in the state capital. Remarking about their departure, one citizen wrote to the editors of *El Antenor* that most of Kirker's party "are vicious, corrupted, haughty, and undisciplined." This impression was surely accurate, for Kirker had enlisted several of his volunteers from prison.

The next month the roving mercenaries followed the trail of a band of Apaches who had killed three men on the road between El Paso and Chihuahua City. Just before midnight, May 8, near Laguna de Santa María, they surprised the sleepy camp, which proved to be the Carrizaleño local group of Nednhis, and killed six men, captured thirteen women and children, and confiscated 121 horses and mules and four barrels of whiskey.[50]

Kirker's roving death squad did compel those Chiricahuas living within Chihuahua's boundaries to consider a truce in the spring of 1841. Pisago continued to negotiate, hoping to arrange for the return of his people imprisoned in Chihuahua City. In February he sent his trusted subordinate, Tapilá, to Janos. In May the talks heated up. On May 18, José Nancha solicited peace on the behalf of Pisago, but authorities refused to offer any terms unless Pisago himself came in. Meanwhile, Pisago decided to hedge his bets, dispatching another son, Chato Pisago, to Janos, while at Paso del Norte another warrior requested peace for him and Ronquillo, a Carrizaleño leader. Evidently the two sides made some progress, for in mid-June the Chokonen chief Matías and six warriors, with a Mexican escort, arrived in Chihuahua City for talks. Pisago had declined the invitation, claiming that he was too ill for the rigors of travel. In all likelihood he distrusted the Mexicans, fearing treachery.[51]

Meanwhile, shortly after Matías's delegation left Chihuahua City, a report came in that stunned the governor. A large Apache war party, undoubtedly Chiricahuas, had virtually sacked the town of Cocomorachic (located in the Sierra Madre about forty to fifty miles northwest of Guerrero), killing twenty-seven, wounding many others, and capturing at least two children.[52] This raid had the earmarks and signs of a Mangas Coloradas foray (a large war party and a large number of victims), although there is no reliable evidence that it was headed by Mangas. The assault also opened the eyes of Francisco García Conde, Chihuahua's new governor, whose portly physique belied an energetic temperament. Conde promptly resolved on humanitarian grounds to cancel Kirker's contract in favor of reorganizing his presidio and local militia forces.[53]

Conde's decision also paved the way for a new peace agreement with the pacific elements of the Chiricahuas, led by the ageing Pisago Cabezón. Mangas Coloradas would have no part in the preliminary negotiations; he distrusted Chihuahua for employing Kirker's mercenaries and never forgave Sonora for sending out Johnson's scalp hunters, to whom two of his wives had fallen victim. Rage continued to drive him, a deep fuming anger, the result of Mexican treachery and mistreatment of his people. By mid-1842 reports from Mexico unequivocally noted that he was the leader of the warlike spirits, a reputation he would retain for nearly twenty years.

The Chiricahuas were active against Sonora in the early 1840s despite Pisago Cabezón's continued efforts to make an agreement with Chihuahua. From the fall of 1840 until Chihuahua returned his son Marcelo in the spring of 1842, Pisago Cabezón talked peace with the military leaders of Janos. Even after his son's return, Pisago, a pragmatic leader who worked toward goals that were beneficial for his people, continued to talk with Chihuahua about an armistice. Like Sonora and Chihuahua, many older Chiricahua leaders had grown weary after five years of war. Meanwhile, several moderate Chokonen leaders under Matías and Yrigóllen,[54] along with two leaders who enjoyed close ties to Mangas Coloradas (Esquinaline and Teboca),[55] appeared at Fronteras, also requesting an end to hostilities. Like Chihuahua, a war-torn Sonora was eager for peace, but the state was near bankruptcy. Its treasury had exhausted the funds necessary either to feed or to pay its presidio troops. To make matters worse, the forces of Urrea and Gándara were again fighting. In January 1841, Urrea had slipped back into Sonora from Durango. After several months of skirmishes, Urrea fled back to Durango and eventually allied himself with Santa Anna, who had returned to power in the fall of 1841. With his new-found support, Urrea informed Gándara that he was removing him from office, and the tide turned in Urrea's favor for the next few years. This internal anarchy and the Apaches' hostilities had led to poor harvests in 1840 and 1841 along Sonora's northeastern frontier. Meanwhile, food had become scarce at Santa Cruz, Fronteras, and Bavispe, and military successes were infrequent. There was even a rumor that the entire garrison at Santa Cruz had thought about deserting to safer havens.[56]

The prospects for a meaningful armistice improved when Chihuahua agreed to issue rations as part of any agreement. With this prospect, many Chiricahua and Mescalero groups began to filter back to their former peace establishments, agreeing to truces at Janos, Galeana, Carrizal, Agua Nueva, Encinillas, San Elizario, and El Paso.[57] Although most of the Chokonens were talking at Fronteras and Janos, the Bedonkohes, Mangas's local group of Chihennes, and the Janeros local group of Nednhis under Soquilla, successor to Juan José and Juan Diego Compá, initially remained aloof and at war. This faction, led by the powerful Mangas Coloradas, in the prime of life physically and intellectually, harbored a profound distrust and antipathy toward Mexico. Yet the lure of regular rations and the prospect of a safe haven from Sonora's campaigns (Urrea became governor and military commander in May 1842 and promised action against the Apaches) altered the equation, eventually compelling even Mangas Coloradas to reconsider his decision.

Chapter 5

A TREATY AT JANOS

IN 1842, Mangas Coloradas passed the age of fifty. He had not had a single incident or moment that dramatically altered his life, thus dictating his course of future action, but instead had experienced a long history of several unsavory and unforgettable incidents that would profoundly influence his direction for the remainder of his life. His long-standing enmity toward Sonora, now unequivocal and indelibly entrenched, had its roots in events dating back to his early years. Sonora's execution of Tutije in 1834, its participation in the Johnson massacre in 1837, and that state's hawkish philosophy of extermination as the solution to its Apache problems only served to reinforce his antipathy. He did not harbor the same feelings of contempt toward Chihuahua, however, although he still smarted from that state's decision to hire Kirker's mercenaries. He knew many of Chihuahua's civil and military leaders stationed along the Apache frontier. Some he trusted or would come to trust—men such as Colonel Cayetano Justiniani, Lieutenant Antonio Sánchez Vergara, and Chihuahua's Commanding General José Mariano Monterde. Therefore, Mangas would occasionally deal with Chihuahua when he felt it served the interests of his people; Sonora, however, was a different story. Like Cochise and later, Geronimo, he distrusted its military and civil officials. He believed that war with Sonora remained his only option.

In 1842, Mangas Coloradas had clearly become the undisputed leader of the bellicose Chiricahuas. At that time his influence extended even to the Janeros local group of the Nednhi band, now led by Soquilla and Coleto Amarillo, who had been at war since Johnson's massacre. He also continued to lead the Bedonkohes (as

indicated by Chihuahua's references to him as a Mogollon leader)
and his Santa Lucía hybrid local group of Bedonkohes and
Chihennes while maintaining close ties to local groups of his
erstwhile Chokonen allies under Esquinaline, Yrigóllen, Miguel
Narbona, and a rising war chief by the name of Cochise.

What role Mangas Coloradas played during any single battle is
not as clear as that of other fighting Chiricahua leaders such as
Cochise, Victorio, or Juh. Their contemporaries recognized each as
an outstanding war chief whose presence was readily discernible in
any fight in which he participated. What Mangas possessed more
than any other Chiricahua leader, at least from 1842 to 1857, was a
self-confidence, bordering on arrogance, that, like a magnet,
attracted fighting men from every Chiricahua band for incursions
into Sonora. He was a cerebral leader, an organizer, planner, and
diplomat, who led by actions, reputation, demonstrated intellect,
and impressive stature. At this time the war faction of every
Chiricahua band unequivocally supported him. Once the fight
began, he was at the forefront of the engagement. After all, no
Apache leader stood in the background while his men fought. If so,
he would not have had any followers. John Cremony was typically
unreliable and inconsistent when he wrote (1) that Mangas "had
the reputation among all his people of being the wisest and
bravest," and (2) in the same breath, declared that "in action he
was the last to come on the field, and the first to leave if
defeated."[1] This contradiction is not surprising if we remember
Cremony's inherent disrespect for Apaches, which typified the
attitude of American military men of the 1850s and 1860s.

The problem with understanding Mangas's fighting abilities is
with the sources. Those from Mexico were primarily military
reports that occasionally mentioned Mangas Coloradas but contained little information from surviving eyewitnesses, who were
few. Since he lived in peace with Americans for most of his life,
those Anglo accounts that refer to Mangas in battle originated
from a few pitched fights that he participated in during the last few
years of his life, when he was at least seventy years old. At that
advanced age, most Chiricahua leaders left the fighting to the
younger men; the chief would remain in camp, now an honored
patriarch, or, as the Indians liked to put it, one "who commands
for the home."[2] Of course, Mangas did not get the chance to enjoy
the last few years of his life, for he and Cochise would wage a
furious and unrelenting war against Americans, for reasons that
will be discussed later. The Chiricahuas recalled him as a great

leader and warrior, and the mere mention of his name below the border left residents of Mexico aghast.[3] Although not as active in a fight as Cochise (perhaps no other Apache leader was), he acquired a reputation with both friend and enemy as a fearless and stalwart warrior.

Apache parents adored their children. Mangas Coloradas, like his confederate Pisago Cabezón, who had several wives and perhaps as many as fifteen children, had a large family. Though it would be impossible to compose a genealogy at this late date, it seems likely that he had at least four wives, three Apaches (two were reported killed in the Johnson massacre) and Carmen, the Mexican girl he captured in Sonora. He likely sired at least a dozen children and perhaps as many as fifteen. According to John R. Bartlett, an American civilian official, Mangas had nine children when the two met in 1851. Bartlett observed that Mangas "has a large family of bright and intelligent looking children, both of boys and girls, of whom he is very fond, and to whom he is ardently attached. For them and the welfare of his tribe I doubt not that he would be willing to make [sacrifices]."[4]

As his children matured, Mangas arranged for many of their marriages, a custom of the Chiricahuas during his lifetime. Bartlett noticed that other Chiricahuas treated Mangas's family like the aristocracy of the tribe.[5] Family status was important, and a parent tried to match his children to those individuals who showed promise or had comparable rank within the tribe. A young man must possess hunting abilities to provide for his family; for a young woman, a man looked for qualities such as a congenial personality and industriousness. The political status of the extended family was also important. Mangas differed from most Apache men by seeking to arrange political ties outside his own band and, on occasion, tribe. He had at least three daughters by his Mexican wife, Carmen. One married a chief of the Navajos, who lived north of him; another wed a leading man of the Mescaleros, who lived east of him; and he betrothed a third to a war chief of the Eastern White Mountain band of Western Apaches, who lived west of him. This band occasionally journeyed east to the San Francisco River to visit with the Bedonkohes and Chihennes.[6] This man may have been Pedro, an important chief, or possibly Esh-kel-dah-silah, a contemporary of Cochise and one of the "most influential Eastern White Mountain chiefs," according to historian Allan Radbourne.[7] These marriages forged alliances with non-Chiricahua groups and Mangas's followers. Though there are few reliable accounts of these groups cooperating for offensive endeavors, Mangas knew that he had protection from all sides, which allowed him to concentrate on his Mexican enemies to the south.

He employed a similar strategy for his offspring by his Apache wives. By far his most important move was the marriage of his daughter Dos-teh-seh to Cochise, the Chokonens' leading young man of the 1830s. This move forged a tremendous bond between Mangas Coloradas and Cochise's local group of Chokonens—one that would endure for the remainder of Mangas's life. The marriage was likely the cause of great rejoicing, with members from three of the four Chiricahua bands likely attending.[8] Cochise, who may have been a son of Pisago Cabezón, would become a staunch friend and ally of Mangas Coloradas.

Many of Mangas's other children wed prominent Chiricahua men and women, too. His daughter Nah-ke-de-sah married Gonah-hleenah, a Bedonkohe warrior who was a great-grandson of the revered Mahko.[9] Each of his known sons married into eminent families. Cascos, perhaps Mangas's oldest known son, was born about 1820. He married into a prominent Bedonkohe family and by 1850 had risen to a leadership position of that band, one that he retained until Sonoran troops killed him in battle in 1858.[10] Seth-mooda, an important man of the early 1860s, had two wives. The Chiricahuas do not recall the name of his first, but his second wife was Bey-it-tsum, the daughter of the important Chihenne chief Loco. Americans killed Sethmooda in a fight in early 1863 near Pinos Altos, shortly after the death of his father.[11] Another son was probably Luis, or Louis, the Bedonkohe band leader of the early 1860s. In late February 1864 troops of the California Volunteers, with some citizens from Pinos Altos (details are unclear), killed Luis near Pinos Altos, where he had come perhaps under the pretext of discussing an armistice.[12]

At least four of Mangas Coloradas's sons attained important roles among the Bedonkohes and Chihennes after his death. Perhaps the most prominent was Salvador, a Chihenne local group leader in the 1860s whom Americans called a chief but who was not on the same par as Victorio and Loco. A close associate of both Victorio and Cochise, he left the reservation in late 1870 with his famous brother-in-law and was slain in a fight with Americans in the Mogollon Mountains in early 1871.[13] Chastine (Thastine) and Cassori were two other sons mentioned in the mid-1860s, but we know little about their accomplishments. Finally, the youngest son of Mangas Coloradas would take the name of Mangas. Born about 1846, in the late 1860s he would marry Dilth-cleyhen, a daughter of the celebrated Victorio, the Chihenne band leader after the death of Mangas Coloradas. He would be active during the Geronimo Wars of the 1880s.[14] Mangas Coloradas's youngest child, a daughter named Ilth-too-da, was born about 1855. In the 1880s she married a Chokonen man named Astoyeh.[15]

Mangas Coloradas steadfastly refused to join in Pisago Cabezón's peace solicitations in the spring of 1842. In fact, one has to question whether Pisago would have been involved if the Mexicans had not continued to hold his son prisoner. Surprisingly, perhaps because of Kirker's mercenaries, rumors suggested that Mangas might make peace with Sonora but not Chihuahua. Yet this statement, if indeed from his lips, was disingenuous. In February 1842, Bedonkohes and Chokonens under Teboca, Esquinaline, and Yrigóllen appeared at Fronteras and requested a truce. Unfortunately, Sonora's internal problems about who governed the state prevented it from seriously addressing these solicitations.[16] Two months later Vicente, acting as Pisago's emissary, went to Chihuahua City to discuss a treaty. He claimed that he represented twenty-eight leaders from Apache camps along the Gila. Although no itemized list of the twenty-eight has been found, it seems safe to conclude that it did not include Mangas Coloradas, for a few months later he was defiant in his opposition.[17]

While Vicente negotiated at Chihuahua City, Pisago Cabezón dispatched other emissaries to Janos. Vicente soon returned to the Apache camps in New Mexico and, after a brief stay, returned to Janos with two warriors and seven women, arriving there on May 23, 1842. Pisago Cabezón and Manuel (also known as Manuelito) had sent him as proof of "their good faith." Vicente's skittish group remained for two days, then they suddenly departed. They had become concerned about their safety because of the lack of a formal treaty. Without an agreement, they were "afraid that they will be betrayed, just as happened at El Paso."[18] Captain Pedro Madrigal asked Monica, a Chiricahua woman frequently involved with negotiations because of her fluency in Spanish, "the cause of their leaving in such a hurry." She tersely replied that the Indians feared the Mexicans would hold them hostage and use them as had been done with Jasquedegá's party at Paso del Norte a few years before. Furthermore, she revealed that the Indians "were sus-picious that the peace treaties were not legal." Madrigal at once took "precautions for the defense of this place because, as I say, I suspect the Apaches of acting in bad faith . . . and they have seen

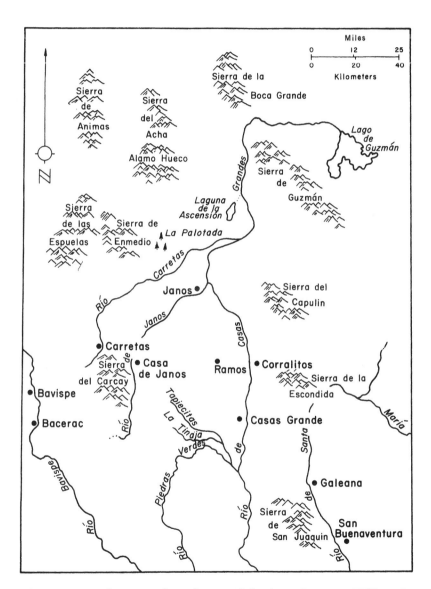

The Janos Jurisdiction and northwest Chihuahua. Courtesy William B. Griffen, *Apaches at War and Peace: The Janos Presidio, 1750–1858* (University of Oklahoma Press, 1998)

that there is no force here to hold them back from acting in their usual crude way."[19]

Despite Madrigal's pessimism, the Chiricahuas resumed talks mainly because they yearned to secure the release of their people held by Chihuahua. Pisago wanted peace, but not at the expense of permanently settling near Janos. He wanted his son back; as for a formal treaty, he would go through the motions, although at his advanced age, and with his health failing, he undoubtedly would have preferred to be left alone in his native haunts instead of settling near a presidio. Chihuahua imposed eight conditions on the Indians before it would sign a formal treaty. The most important articles required the Apaches to return their captives and to assist Mexican troops against hostile Mescaleros and other Chiricahuas who refused to make peace. For its part, Chihuahua, as represented by Governor Francisco García Conde, agreed to release its Apache captives and, in an attempt to ensure that this truce would be more than just ephemeral, decided to offer rations as part of the agreement. Prospects for an armistice looked so favorable that La Luna, the official state newspaper, editorialized: "It is probable, it is necessary, it is useful, and it is urgent." Accordingly, in late June, Conde left the capital for Janos, which he reached on June 27, 1842.[20]

The leaders agreed to the treaty on July 4, 1842, with Pisago Cabezón, Manuelito, and Vicente signing for the Chokonens and Ponce representing the Chihennes.[21] In addition, they claimed to represent Jasquedegá's Carrizaleño local group of Nednhis. With Pisago Cabezón aging and in poor health, the peaceful Chiricahuas named Manuelito "general." The Indians consented to cease hostilities, to deliver all captives, to establish their rancherías near Janos, to help the Mexicans in their war against the Mescaleros and other hostiles, and to register and brand their stock. In exchange, Conde released Marcelo to Pisago's custody. More significantly, Conde, recognizing that the peace treaties of 1832 and 1835 had failed because of Chihuahua's adamant refusal to issue rations, agreed to feed the Indians. He authorized the issuance of rations, which consisted of corn, sugar, meat, and tobacco, to each head of family every fifteen days. Soon after, Conde changed the schedule to weekly. Afterwards, he went south to San Buenaventura and made a treaty with other Chiricahua groups. Although no one could have realized it then, Conde's pragmatic decision to issue rations ensured a successful treaty and a dramatic decrease in the number of Apache depredations in Chihuahua from 1842 to 1844.[22]

Janos, Chihuahua. Mangas agreed to a peace treaty here in the spring of 1843. (Bartlett, *Personal Narratives*)

Mangas Coloradas wanted no part of this cease-fire, although reports suggesting that he might consider an armistice with Sonora were surprising, because he had just returned from a foray against that state. In early May the Chokonens' principal chief, Yrigóllen, sent Matías to Fronteras to warn the commander that hostiles from Chihuahua planned to raid its herd. Meanwhile, as negotiations went on at Janos, a raiding party stole the mule herd of José Varelo near Casas Grandes.[23] In mid-June the Sonoran press reported that a tremendous war party of five hundred warriors (under Mangas Coloradas), "well armed and well mounted," had ravaged the district of Sahuaripa. Though the size was undoubtedly exaggerated, their depredations had compelled the prefect of Sahuaripa to write Governor Urrea that its residents felt they had two choices: to remain and let the Apaches destroy them or to abandon their homes for safer places. Once the people had decided to stay, the prefect pleaded with the governor to send arms, provisions, and mules (the Apaches had taken every one) so that they could protect their families and fight off the Indians. By July, Mangas Coloradas's war party had returned to his ranchería near the Gila River in New Mexico. According to Sonoran reports,

Mangas had sent emissaries to his allies by marriage, the Coyoteros and Navajos, who were also at war with both Mexico and New Mexico.[24]

As both sides probably expected, the treaty was a shaky arrangement at best. Once Pisago had his son back, no one really knew for sure what he might do. He wanted to be left alone, free from controversy, perhaps to live out the rest of his life in his country at peace, away from Mexican settlements. Although some of his band settled near Janos, he remained in the mountains. In addition, the armistice had a problem that both sides needed to iron out, mainly, the refusal of the warlike faction under Mangas Coloradas to recognize it. Since Mangas Coloradas's followers continued to raid, particularly in Sonora, the Janos frontier would remain unstable. Sonoran troops would inevitably pursue the hostiles toward southern New Mexico or Chihuahua, thus setting off the jittery Apaches living in the Janos region. Despite Chihuahua's good intentions, a series of minor crises characterized the summer of 1842. One incident after another almost doomed the agreement before it had a very good chance to succeed.

The Chiricahuas began to filter into Janos a few days after the official cease-fire of July 4, 1842. On July 13, 1842, Collante appeared at Janos with a small group, followed two days later by Chinaca and Vicente, who turned over Justo Delgado, a native of Concepción, Chihuahua. Delgado told authorities that the Indians had moved their rancherías to Boca Grande, about twenty miles south of Carrizalillo Springs just east of the road to Santa Rita del Cobre from Janos. These exchanges helped to persuade the Indians that they could trust Captain Pedro Madrigal, who was really a conscientious and capable officer. Madrigal could not prevent the Chiricahuas from raiding into Sonora, but he had to take action when Mangas Coloradas's followers raided Corralitos on July 14, 1842. By coincidence, Pisago Cabezón and Manuelito,[25] an influential Chokonen chief who had spent much time at Janos from 1810 until 1831, and a group of thirteen warriors happened to be at Janos when Madrigal received news about the raid. Complying with the terms of the treaty to aid Mexican troops against hostile Apaches, Manuelito dutifully took a few warriors and joined Captain Mariano Rey's small detachment. They followed the trail that led straight as an arrow toward Mangas's ranchería in the Burro Mountains. Rey overtook the raiders at the Santo Domingo Playa, a sandy area east of the Animas Mountains, and talked with them. They agreed to turn over the stolen animals, likely because of Pisago Cabezón's universal prestige among the Chiricahuas. It was also possible that the raiders had been unaware of the peace treaty recently signed with Chihuahua, as Mangas Coloradas had been raiding Sonora at the time of the agreement. Whether Manuelito talked with Mangas Coloradas is unclear, yet the former returned to Janos on July 29, 1842, with important intelligence concerning Mangas's intentions.[26]

According to Manuelito, the bands led by Mangas Coloradas, Soquilla, and Ronquillo still opposed peace with Chihuahua. The last two leaders belonged to the Janeros local group of Nednhis, which had waged war since the Johnson massacre. Typically the most pacific of all Chiricahua bands, they were also the one band over which Mangas Coloradas had least influence, because their local group territory was normally in northern Mexico. Yet they were hostile at this time, and Mangas was in an equally aggressive state, so they allied their fortunes with those of Mangas Coloradas's Santa Lucía local group of Chihennes and Bedonkohes. The Mimbres and Warm Springs local groups of Chihennes, under Ponce and others, had made peace at Janos and Paso del Norte. Also peculiar was the rumor that Mangas would consider making peace with Sonora; likely this yarn had come about because of the Chokonens' negotiations at Fronteras and because of Mangas's close relationship with Cochise and Esquinaline. In any event, José Urrea failed to address the Chokonens' offer. Gándara's forces were again challenging his regime, and besides that portending conflict, Sonora lacked cash to pay or feed the presidio troops. Some garrisons had threatened their officers with mass desertions. With no hope on the horizon for either rations or a formal peace with Sonora, later that summer the Chokonens moved east into Chihuahua and north into Arizona and New Mexico.[27]

The hostiles in southern New Mexico, reportedly camped from Alamo Hueco north up the Animas Valley to Santo Domingo Playa, had anticipated a campaign from Sonora, and Elías González, whom Urrea would soon appoint as second chief of the general command, happily accommodated them. He brought a force into northeast Sonora, near the Arizona and New Mexico line, and the presence of his troops endangered the fragile armistice at Janos. In mid-August, Pisago Cabezón arrived at Janos with startling information: Elías González's scouts had cut the trail of Mangas's war party and had followed it into northeastern Sonora. Recalling Kirker's unprovoked attack of a few years before, Pisago feared that Sonora's troops would attack his peaceful ranchería. Captain Madrigal at once dispatched four soldiers to Elías González to inform him about the peace treaty and to remind him that he should punish only those Indians who had committed depredations. Respectfully, the Sonoran commander suspended the campaign and returned to Bavispe. Governor Conde became upset because Elías González "did not ask for the appropriate permission to cross over into the borders of my command." The governor conceded, however, that the Sonoran general "should punish them severely if the charges of which they are accused should be proved true." Two years later Elías González would remember Conde's censure and would take steps to eliminate this problem.[28]

At Janos, Captain Madrigal soon faced another challenge. A raiding party had stolen some mules near Galeana, and according to the Apaches at peace, the culprits were Mogollons (or Bedonkohes) led by a son of Fuerte. Apparently Madrigal understood that Fuerte was Mangas Coloradas, for he rounded up a force to pursue "those of Mangas Coloradas whom I suspect of the robbery." Madrigal also realized that he would have to bring Mangas Coloradas into the fold to have an enduring peace. In September, the peaceful Chiricahuas revealed that Mangas had moved his camp to the Gila and San Francisco Rivers country. In a distinct reference to Cochise's Chokonens, the report added that Mangas has "relations with those known at Fronteras and those who reside in the Chiricahua Mountains."[29]

Mangas Coloradas's next move seems to defy explanation, although it was logical on the surface. The Chokonens' patience had worn thin at Fronteras. Ironically, Sonora could not provide them rations, because "the fields in the immediate vicinity are not cultivated because of the Apache raids."[30] They had heard that Pisago and Manuelito, satisfied with Madrigal's actions, had finally brought their group of 172 individuals (including thirty-two men) into Janos on August 29, 1842.[31] This laid the groundwork for other small groups to come in and eventually attracted the disenchanted Chokonens, who had left Fronteras after a series of difficulties that may have resulted in the spilling of Apache blood. One who had come in was Cochise, likely sent by Mangas Coloradas to ascertain Mexican treatment of the Apaches. In addition, the prospect of rations, good treatment, and a safe haven from Sonora's campaigns appealed to the newcomers.[32]

Captain Madrigal had faced a thankless task and had performed it well, providing the right mixture of fair and honorable treatment while emphasizing that he would punish any party who committed any hostile acts. He also addressed an age-old problem inherent in any Apache-Mexican peace treaty: illicit trade, which, if unchecked, only served to encourage the Indians to raid elsewhere (in Chihuahua's case, Sonora) for booty to exchange on the open market. Unfortunately, the terms of the treaty permitted the Apaches to trade with citizens. Presumably the intent of this article was to encourage the Indians to bring in skins and other native items to exchange. This led to more frequent contact between the races, which inevitably led to local conflicts, as both groups included hard-nosed individuals bent on mischief and, sometimes, vengeance. The other explosive element was alcohol. Governor Conde had strangely ruled that the Apaches could purchase it, perhaps because the Spanish had allowed this practice during colonial times. This was an experiment of dubious value, for the custom often led to violent encounters.

One problem developed when Chato, an inveterate raider notorious for his unruly behavior at Santa Rita del Cobre, had an altercation with two citizens of Janos. In all likelihood either whiskey or a disagreement while engaged in bartering had hastened the conflict. Chato responded by laying waste to the citizens' garden, eating several watermelons and trampling what he did not confiscate. When confronted by Janos officials, he became even more abusive, cursing them out.[33] In September 1842 a man named Selgas had in his possession a horse that Apaches had stolen from the San Elizario presidio. Captain Madrigal investigated immediately and exonerated Selgas of the theft, concluding that "Selgas was here at the time it was stolen." Selgas claimed that he had purchased the horse at Carrizal from a son of José Largo, a brother of the influential Nednhi leader Cigarrito.[34]

After receiving several such reports, all dealing with potential crises narrowly averted, Conde issued an edict to Madrigal that prohibited citizens from trading guns and whiskey to the Apaches. In addition, he delegated to Madrigal the authority to take the appropriate measures to enforce this new order. Conde wrote:

> I have been informed that the residents of the area surrounding your garrison [Janos] consistently do wrong to the peaceful Apaches through selling both firearms and liquor. These wrongs have a great deal of importance because they may so anger the Apaches as to bring about disastrous consequences impossible to prevent. Since this behavior is so pernicious it is necessary that it be avoided at all costs and by making all necessary sacrifices. Therefore, I instruct you to

take military action in those cases against any resident who fails to use the proper moderation in dealing with the Apaches or who continues to engage in the lawless behavior which I have described. The authority of the general commander, who wishes to see this very difficult matter handled, confers upon you full powers to act in the most appropriate manner, not only on the basis of the general principle which I have stated for you, but also in very serious cases, specifically acting to indict individuals with the relevant charges, subsequently establishing the truth and sending the offenders to this capital city to receive the punishment the law provides.[35]

In November, news reached Janos from Mangas's camp in the Mogollons that the chief now wished to discuss peace with Chihuahua. Pisago Cabezón and several warriors, including Mangas's son-in-law Cochise, had been at Janos and had told Mangas about Madrigal's fair treatment. Just as important an issue were the weekly rations given to the Indians. With winter approaching, and having been at war for nearly a decade, Mangas had decided to hear out Captain Madrigal. Although now willing to forgive Chihuahua for employing Kirker's mercenaries, he still distrusted Sonora, which had recently sent out a large campaign to strike Apaches in Arizona and continued to talk about extermination instead of negotiation. The ubiquitous Manuelito, the Chokonen chief named "general" of the Apaches, told Mexican officials at Janos about Mangas's intentions.[36]

In late October a small raiding party of six warriors under Náque pilfered some horses at Casas Grandes. The act incensed Madrigal, because he had given rations to Náque, a member of Pisago's ranchería, for the last several weeks. In accordance with the treaty, Manuelito followed the trail into southern New Mexico. From there it led toward the hostile camps in the Mogollon Mountains before it divided. Manuelito pursued the trail to the Mimbres River, where he unexpectedly found Mangas Coloradas visiting a Chihenne camp on the Mimbres River. Taking advantage of the opportunity, Manuelito conversed with Mangas Coloradas and Pisago Cabezón, who had recently left Janos to confer with the previously hostile leader. Mangas said that he now wished peace for his Santa Lucía local group of Chihennes and for the Bedonkohe band living in the Mogollons. His intentions were sincere, according to Manuelito, who claimed that Mangas exhibited "good disposition and good intentions" toward Chihuahua.[37]

This was truly a significant report, because it afforded Mexicans the opportunity to bring the undisputed leader of the warlike faction to peace. Lieutenant Antonio Sánchez Vergara, who had been instrumental during the negotiations of the previous summer, agreed to undertake the journey. Vergara was one of those peripheral frontier characters whose life touched briefly on that of Mangas Coloradas. The Chiricahuas trusted him, one of the few Mexican officers accorded this respect. Although he sincerely wanted to bring peace to the frontier, Vergara was neither naïve nor peace-hungry. He knew that he faced the nearly impossible task of convincing every Chiricahua band to agree to terms. Yet he also understood that many important leaders, including Mangas Coloradas, had been fighting for almost a decade and had grown weary of war. Furthermore, those Chiricahuas straddling the fence between peace and war may have heard that Urrea, whose forces had repeatedly whipped Gándara's followers, now planned to undertake a major offensive into Apachería. Urrea vowed to remain in the field until his men defeated the Indians. Actually, Vergara shared these sentiments in the event that the hostile Chiricahuas refused to grasp the olive branch. Before Manuelito had delivered Mangas Coloradas's message of peace, Vergara had advocated that Chihuahua dispatch an army to the Mogollons to subdue the hostiles. Yet when he received word of Mangas's change of heart, Vergara agreed to undertake the risky mission of bringing peace to southwestern New Mexico and northwestern Chihuahua.[38]

In company with Manuelito and his brother Torres, sons of Coyote (an important leader of the Janos district in the early 1800s), Vergara, likely with a few Mexican packers, left Janos in late December 1842 or early January 1843. Vergara, whom one historian called a "go-between,"[39] first stopped in the Burro Mountains, where he held parleys with several Nednhi leaders of the Janeros local group, including the previously hostile Soquilla,[40] Bartolo, and Babosa. Normally a pacific group, they had been at war since Johnson's massacre in April 1837. Now eager to make peace, they promised to bring their people to Janos. Vergara's party continued their trek north to the Mogollons, where in late January they met four important Chiricahua leaders: Mangas Coloradas, Teboca, Itán, and Cuchillo Negro. Vergara assured the Indians that the peace treaties at Janos remained in place, though José Mariano Monterde had replaced García Conde as governor. Mangas endorsed the treaty, agreeing to come to Janos by the end of March to meet Monterde and consummate a formal armistice.[41]

Vergara's mission soon paid dividends. In January, Bartolo brought his Janeros local group of thirty-five men, forty women, and sixty-one children to Janos. Bartolo, born in the 1790s, had been a member of Juan Diego's ranchería; therefore, he was likely a survivor of Johnson's massacre. In the coming years he would become overshadowed by other Nednhi leaders such as Láceres and Coleto Amarillo. Meanwhile, friendly Chiricahuas reported that Mangas Coloradas had reached the mountains north of Janos, perhaps the Enmedio Mountains, and was awaiting the arrival of Chihuahua's governor, José Mariano Monterde.[42] Monterde, a native of Mexico City, was a career military man who had recently been the assistant director of Mexico's military college. A man with an impeccable reputation, he was born in 1789 and thus was about the same age as Mangas Coloradas. In early March, Madrigal had informed Monterde that Mangas Coloradas and Itán would soon be coming in. Upon receiving this news, Monterde notified Madrigal that he would leave Chihuahua City about March 11 and planned to reach the frontier presidio by the end of March.[43]

En route, the governor made several stops, likely at Encinillas and Carrizal, to inspect the frontier garrisons and meet Apaches who had agreed to terms. He arrived on March 20, 1843, at Galeana, where he held a conference with local authorities. Like the Apaches, these people were weary after a decade of war and wanted to do all in their power to promote a stable and long-lasting peace. Therefore, they offered to donate land, supplies, and technical expertise to help the Apaches learn to farm. Although their intentions were admirable, and a few Chiricahuas did take them up on the offer, it was an experiment of dubious viability, a naïve idea born of ignorance. The thought of Apaches farming on a sufficient scale to feed themselves was a gross misconception by well-meaning whites, showing their lack of understanding of Chiricahua culture. After spending a week at Galeana, Monterde's entourage left for Janos, arriving there about March 28, expecting to meet Mangas Coloradas, "the *capitancillo* of the Mogollon tribe."

Mangas arrived as promised on March 31, a point that impressed Monterde greatly. The meeting between the Chiricahua tribal leader and the governor of Chihuahua must have been a dramatic affair. Though it flirted with danger, it had exciting implications. On one side stood a superb specimen of Apache manhood—a leader usually aloof from Mexicans, a race whom he distrusted. Opposite him was the governor and commanding general of Chihuahua—an intelligent and perhaps idealistic officer who, unlike most military men (Mexican and American), displayed compassion, empathy, and respect for his onetime enemy. Monterde's character—his honesty and sense of fair play—not only was unique in a military noted for its hatred of Indians, but also showed those attributes greatly revered by Apaches. As a result, as the conference went on, Monterde's actions gradually converted Mangas Coloradas from a skeptic to a believer.

After the initial introductions, Monterde addressed the Chiricahua leaders. Besides Mangas Coloradas, they included Itán, and Fucilito (Little Musket) along with several leaders who had previously agreed to peace: Manuelito, Torres, and Anaya. Recognizing the Apaches' profound apprehensions, the governor conceded that the ferocious war had intensified because of Mexico's committing several "atrocious acts" (alluding to Johnson's massacre and Kirker's scalp hunters). In particular, he noted that Mangas Coloradas openly expressed his acrimony about the perfidious deeds carried out against his people. Monterde's patience, honesty, and open-mindedness eventually imbued the suspicious leaders with confidence. He painstakingly read the articles of the armistice, carefully explaining the ten conditions, as the "leaders wanted no surprises." The agreement was typical of past treaties. In essence, both sides would cease hostilities and agree to "a most sincere peace." Each consented to release their captives, and the Apaches agreed to assist Mexican troops against enemy forces. In return, Monterde would issue rations. The Apaches unanimously elected Mangas Coloradas to serve as "general." He would be the leader responsible for maintaining control of his people. It would be a position that he took seriously.[44]

The Indians also requested that Monterde appoint a commission to go to Sonora to confer with Governor José Cosme de Urrea, thus indicating how seriously they wanted this armistice to endure. Accordingly, the Chiricahuas selected Negrito; the venerable Chokonen peace chief Matías; and Marcelo, a son of Pisago Cabezón, to accompany Peace Commissioner Antonio Sánchez Vergara, who by now had achieved unrivaled credibility among the Chiricahuas. All in all, the treaty had a fair chance at success, for both sides had eliminated many troublesome concerns. Yet they could not resolve overnight the one issue Monterde most feared: a mutual distrust and enmity of one another. Both peoples included high-strung individuals who had experienced tragedy and loss of life at the hands of the other. Only time could heal those wounds and lead to better relations.[45]

In truth, Lieutenant Vergara deserved enormous credit for his accomplishments. Assembling these Indians, many of them hostile, most of them highly suspicious of Mexicans, was quite an achievement, and a result almost entirely of his yeoman efforts. His peace mission bears some similarity to that carried out by American frontiersman Tom Jeffords to Cochise thirty years later. Both parties went in search of a chief who wanted peace after a decade of war. Both groups, because of their Apache guides, had good ideas on where to find the hostile Apaches. Each proved successful: Vergara in 1842 convinced Mangas Coloradas to journey to Janos to meet Chihuahua's Governor and Commanding General José Mariano Monterde, and Jeffords in 1872 brought American Brigadier General Oliver O. Howard to Cochise's camp and concluded a treaty. The similarities do not end there, however. Mangas Coloradas and General Monterde immediately developed a profound respect and fondness for each other. These same feelings developed between Cochise and General Howard. For Mangas Coloradas, who typically despised and distrusted Mexicans, this was an unexpected and astonishing development. Monterde recognized that the Apache-Mexican war was a two-way street; he was one of the few Mexican military men to understand this equation. Each side had committed acts of barbarity, and it was time for them to stop.

Mangas Coloradas had every intention of giving the treaty his best efforts. From the beginning he had cooperated with Mexican military officials at Janos, trying to make the treaty work and honor his word. On April 17 he returned to the presidio and conversed with Madrigal. Yet ominous signs were on the horizon. Within a few weeks of the agreement, a Chihenne raiding party under Delgadito, an emerging leader of Itán's local group, raided El Paso, killing several people and making off with several animals. Delgadito's trail led to Carrizalillo Springs. Captain Madrigal sent word to Mangas requesting that he investigate the raid and turn over the culpable parties. Mangas agreed to do so, but in the end took no action because several raiders were members of his band, and possibly even one of his sons was implicated. Moreover, they may have committed the depredation without knowing that Mangas had signed a treaty.[46]

A month later Mangas Coloradas backed up his commitment to Monterde with action. Like Pisago Cabezón, he had remained encamped in the mountains north of Janos (near Alamo Hueco), uncomfortable with the prospect of bringing his people to Janos,

where potential conflicts between restless Apaches and troublesome citizens might follow. In early May he informed Captain
Madrigal at Janos that a group of twelve Apaches (eight from
Fronteras and four from Janos) had left on a raid against Janos. At
noon of the same day, a traveler from Sonora appeared at the
presidio, telling Madrigal that Apaches had jumped him a few
miles away and had stolen nineteen head of stock. At once Captain
Madrigal sent Ensign José Baltazar Padilla with thirteen soldiers,
nine citizens, and seven Apaches to follow the trail. Padilla's party
had an interesting encounter with Mangas Coloradas, whose quick
response averted a general melee and saved the tenuous peace for
the time being. Captain Madrigal described the encounter to
Chihuahua's commanding general:

> Padilla's party did not lose a moment, making forced marches until it
> overtook the Sonorans' aggressors at the place called Agua Hueca,[47]
> which is thirty-six leagues distant from this garrison. There present
> were the general of the Mogollon Apaches, Mangas Coloradas, plus
> Pisago Cabezón, Teboca, and other leaders. The aggressors, perhaps
> encouraged by the presence of those Indians, prepared to defend
> themselves rather than hand over the stolen property. But the general
> Mangas Coloradas immediately took sides with Padilla's forces.
> Addressing himself to the aggressors, he warned them that unless
> they handed over immediately what they had stolen he would attack
> them with his band of Indians. He added that he had made peace
> treaties and was prepared to maintain them under all circumstances.
> Pisago, who also joined Padilla's forces, gave them a similar warning,
> and, in addition, called for the death of his son, who was one of them.
> This because he insisted that such a deed made his son an evil
> person, of whom he was ashamed. The other Indians that I have
> named likewise threw their support at this time to our side.
>   The stolen property which I have mentioned was immediately
> handed over to Padilla. The aggressors promised to mend their ways
> in the future and were pardoned by the Indians whom I have
> mentioned. . . . The one exception was Mangas Coloradas, who, after
> having called to their attention the seriousness of the offense, told
> them that as a consequence they should not hereafter set foot on any
> land where he had a ranchería.[48]

Padilla also lauded the efforts and loyalties of his seven
Chiricahua scouts, who included both the important Nednhi
warrior Cochi and Chino, a Chokonen. They had threatened to use

force unless the hostiles returned the stolen animals. Padilla returned to Janos with the confiscated stock on May 16. The next day Mangas Coloradas came into Janos and held a parley with Captain Madrigal. The chief "came to me at this garrison to inform you that he considers the peace treaties to be still in effect unaltered and that he holds his life and interests ready to be sacrificed at any time that the friendship which he has for you may require it." Monterde awarded ten pesos to the Indian scouts and twenty to Mangas Coloradas, but before Mangas could collect it, a deplorable event occurred to muddy the waters.[49]

One could almost have predicted that problems would develop during the Chiricahuas' attempt to make peace with Sonora. Shortly after Mangas had agreed to terms, the Chiricahua contingent of Marcelo, Matías, and Negrito left for Sonora with Lieutenant Vergara. On June 2, 1843, they met Governor Urrea at Guaymas and consented to an armistice with Sonora. In essence, if the Apaches left the Sonorans alone, Sonora would reciprocate.[50]

This tense period of good relations had a short-lived and precarious future. Ironically, the truce's fate had been decided even before Urrea and the Chiricahuas held their powwow. While the Mexican-Apache peace party was en route to meet Urrea, troops at Fronteras had murdered six Chokonen men for no apparent reason. Although details are sparse, the incident, symptomatic of the volatility in relations between the two races, rankled in the Apaches' breast. On May 26, 1843, Western Apaches killed two citizens and wounded a soldier while running off stock near Fronteras. Seven Chiricahuas happened to be at the presidio at the time of the raid and volunteered to help the soldiers. After a short pursuit they succeeded in recovering most of the stock. At that point, for some unknown reason, the Mexicans decided to retaliate against the Chokonens, although they had not had a hand in the recent foray. Without warning the soldiers inexplicably turned their weapons on their Chiricahua scouts, killing six of the seven unsuspecting Indians. One escaped to tell the story, which spread like wildfire to the Apache camps in New Mexico and Chihuahua and laid the foundation for war, because the Apaches had to avenge all their losses.[51]

This was the beginning of a chain of events that culminated in the renewal of hostilities between the Chiricahua bellicose faction, led by Mangas Coloradas, and Mexico, especially Sonora, which would bear the brunt of the new depredations. As a result, several of Fronteras's citizens would pay with their lives in the bloody cycle of revenge and violence that continued to be a way of life for the mortal enemies.

On May 31, a few days after the massacre at Fronteras, Mangas Coloradas, Manuelito, and four other Chiricahua leaders met with Madrigal at Janos. They wanted justice, but Chihuahua could do nothing but file a grievance with Sonora. Besides these concerns, Captain Madrigal faced other problems. The large number of Apaches had depleted his supply of rations and had left his small force vulnerable in the event the Indians resumed hostilities. Meanwhile, the massacre at Fronteras dispelled any notions the Chiricahuas had entertained for peace and led to the organization of sanguinary war parties that devastated Sonora's northern frontier. Although many Chiricahua groups continued to live quietly at Janos, some of their younger warriors joined the militant faction for raids into Sonora.[52]

This festering animosity surfaced in the summer of 1843. First, Relles, a moderate and generally peaceful Chokonen leader, complained to Mexican authorities about citizens spreading rumors of Mexican campaigns and ill will toward Apaches. Furthermore, he protested that the soldiers at Janos deliberately took target practice on the days that the Apaches showed up to receive their rations, which greatly aroused the restive Indians.[53] As for Mangas Coloradas, with relatives among the slain Chokonens, the incident at Fronteras was enough fodder to ignite his distrust and influence his hatred of Mexico, particularly Sonora. In mid-July Mexicans traced stolen stock to Mangas and Pisago's camp; this time the two chiefs declined to force those guilty to return the stock. According to José Mentisa, the Chiricahua scout who followed the trail, Mangas ordered the culprits to relinquish the stock but refused to enforce the command.[54]

Mangas and Pisago were not in a hospitable mood. Though they would not resume hostilities with Chihuahua, keeping their agreement made with Monterde, Sonora would be another issue. Beginning in late 1843, the Chiricahuas launched several war parties against Sonora (many led by Mangas Coloradas and the venerable Pisago Cabezón) which increased in severity almost monthly through early 1845. This gruesome cycle of revenge and retaliation characterized the mid-1840s. Many innocent people would fall on both sides, victims of an Apache arrow or lance, a Mexican machete or musket ball. Mangas Coloradas would never again consider making peace with Sonora, and it would be seven long years before he would even contemplate another agreement with Chihuahua. Many years later he expressed how he felt at that time about relations between his people and Mexico: "It would be war to the knife."[55]

Judging by future events, Mangas's characterization was right on the mark.

Chapter 6

MANGAS SETTLES THE SCORE

BY the late summer of 1843, Mangas had decided to end his brief truce with Mexico, and particularly with Sonora, which had shown repeatedly that neither its unstable government nor its frontier residents truly wanted pacific relations with his people. From that time forward, indeed for the remainder of his life, he would fiercely reject any peaceful contact with that state. His position was nonnegotiable; his opposition was inflexible. This antipathy for Sonora had its roots in relations preceding the end of the so-called presidio system in 1831, when the war officially began. After that year, Sonora time after time excited Mangas to anger with treacherous acts that required vengeance. Plagued by anarchy and governed by a series of leaders who subscribed to militant policies as the panacea to their Apache problems, Sonora would see its fortunes wane through the 1840s and into the early 1850s. Mangas Coloradas had a great deal to do with that situation. He led the warlike Chiricahuas—the Bedonkohes, Cochise's Chokonens, and the Santa Lucía local group. Even the Nednhis, living primarily in Mexico, occasionally joined him to even the score against their common enemies.

Beginning in 1844, Mangas's large war parties laid waste to several of Sonora's haciendas and smaller settlements. But Sonora's military would not go down without a fight, and with Urrea back in control, his cousin José María Elías González again became active in its armed forces. A no-nonsense commander, Elías González would inflict a serious drubbing on Apaches encamped near Janos and Corralitos in the summer of 1844. Yet in reality he destroyed primarily members of the peace bloc, the moderate factions of the

Chokonens and Nednhis, and his justice produced a result opposite
the one he had planned. In response to Elías González's attack,
Mangas Coloradas called a tribal council in late 1844 to develop a
Chiricahua strategy that led to the organization of another foray
against Sonora. The legacy for the remainder of the 1840s would be
written in Apache and Sonoran blood.

The Chiricahua hostilities against Sonora began in the late
summer of 1843. Pisago Cabezón and Mangas Coloradas left Alamo
Hueco for the Burro Mountains and refrained from raiding then.
Mangas would continue to honor his pact with Chihuahua's
Governor Monterde. His war parties ignored that state until the
mid-1840s, when Chihuahua recalled James Kirker's scalp hunters.
Instead, the Chokonens carried out the initial assaults to avenge
their men murdered at Fronteras. What really antagonized Sonoran
authorities, especially Colonel Elías González, was that the evidence linked these raiders to the rancherías near Janos, where they
continued to draw rations from Chihuahua's government. From the
Chiricahua point of view, they had kept their part of the bargain,
because they had considered themselves at war with Sonora since
the incident at Fronteras in late May 1843. Moreover, local officials
at Janos and Corralitos understood the situation and were perfectly
content to trade goods to the Apaches for the booty taken from
Sonora. It was a reciprocal trust, and the Chiricahuas played it to
the hilt. Beginning in late 1843 and throughout 1844, as their war
parties devastated Sonora, many of these raiders retreated to safe
havens near Janos and Corralitos; others returned to their remote
mountain homes in southern New Mexico. In contrast, Chihuahua,
with whom the Indians considered themselves at peace, was
virtually immune from the resurgence in hostilities. Whereas in
1842 there were one hundred separate reports of Apache raids in
Chihuahua, in 1843 there were but eleven and in 1844 only ten.[1]

The animosity against Sonora finally burst forth in earnest in
August 1843. Yaque, a recalcitrant Chokonen leader who may
have lost kinfolk in the massacre at Fronteras in May, led a group
of warriors on a raid into Sonora. Returning toward Janos with a
string of stolen mules and horses, he captured a Mexican and some
stock near the Carretas hacienda. Soon after, he held a parley with
a few citizens and agreed to sell his captive for a jug of whiskey. He
then returned to Janos. A few weeks later Yaque organized another
foray into Sonora. On September 9, 1843, Apaches in "considerable
numbers" attacked a party of eleven men near Cuchuta, some ten
miles south of Fronteras, and killed seven of them. The other four

men escaped to Fronteras and claimed that they recognized the Chokonen leaders Yaque, Posito Moraga, and Chepillo, all thought to be living near Janos. These two incidents served as eerie harbingers of things to come.[2]

Many Chiricahuas, mainly Nednhis and Chokonens, continued to draw rations at Janos and Corralitos. Others did so at Galeana, south of Corralitos, but during the fall of 1843, with smallpox manifesting itself at Galeana, groups of Chiricahuas migrated north to Janos. The Chokonen band leader Yrigóllen and several important Nednhi leaders of the Janeros local group, including the influential Coleto Amarillo, began drawing weekly rations. Janos authorities now rationed some eight hundred Chiricahuas. Many men left their dependents at Janos, where Mexican authorities provided protection and rations while they were raiding and killing in Sonora. This influx of new arrivals strained the supply of rations, which inevitably led to conflicts between local citizens and Apaches. In addition, the Indians could not outrun the small-pox epidemic that had crept insidiously north to the Janos area by late 1843. Combine these conditions with the fact that the true hostiles under Mangas Coloradas and Pisago Cabezón were living in southwestern New Mexico, biding their time for a foray against Sonora, and it becomes clear that Mexico's frontier was vulnerable to disaster.[3]

Besides their Apache problem, Governor Urrea and his cousin José María Elías González, recently appointed second chief of the commanding general, had other critical issues to contend with. They had hoped to launch a campaign against the Apaches in early 1843, but Urrea's ongoing struggle with Manuel María Gándara forced its postponement. Meanwhile, their war had paralyzed the state and destroyed Sonora's economy, not to mention the enormous loss in life and property. Urrea traveled to Guaymas to unravel a monopoly held on the export trade by a longtime supporter of his political opponent, Gándara. After resolving that crisis, he decided to take care of the Papagos, allies of the Gándaras. By May his forces had soundly whipped them. That summer Governor Urrea's forces also fought several clashes with Gándara's followers, who included the fierce Yaqui Indians, before he finally defeated his long-standing adversary in November, compelling Gándara to lie low for the next year.[4]

While this civil war continued to brew in Sonora, Monterde's peace at Janos was beginning to disintegrate. For Sonora, the conse-quences would prove to be dire.

The presence of over eight hundred Chiricahuas at Janos had placed enormous strains on the shoulders of Captain Madrigal. To begin with, his supply of rations had dwindled, and he had no idea how to provide for these newcomers who had moved north from Galeana to avoid the smallpox epidemic. Six months before, Madrigal had informed his superiors that he had distributed most of his provisions. He was at a loss about what he should do. In desperation he requested contributions from local citizens, but they could not raise enough. The hungry Indians became restless, and several clashes between them and the people of Janos occurred, any one of which could have led to war. Governor Monterde was an easy target. His political enemies and the press denounced him for negligence, especially regarding the Apaches in the northern frontier. They roundly criticized him for not ensuring that Chihuahua provide the Apaches with ample rations. During the summer of 1843 he had marched to Santa Fe to aid New Mexico's Governor Armijo thwart an expected invasion from Texas which never appeared. Since the Apache situation had deteriorated while he was out of the state, frustrated officials pointed their fingers at him, although he adamantly defended his actions and policy.[5]

Apart from the significant problems of rations, the straw that broke the camel's back was the lethal arrival of smallpox. It manifested itself at Janos in late December 1843. Whereas some seven hundred Chiricahuas were present in December, by the end of January fewer than one hundred remained. Most left because of the epidemic, which eventually took the lives of several men and two leaders, Chinaca and Chato Pisago, son of Pisago Cabezón. Others fled in response to the summons of Mangas Coloradas, who had left New Mexico for the first of what would be three major war parties against Sonora in 1844.[6]

In late January 1844, Captain Madrigal, concerned about the Apaches' disappearance, sent out a small force under Lieutenant Antonio Sánchez Vergara, who had helped bring in Mangas Coloradas the previous winter. In early February, Vergara found a Chokonen camp. Although trusted by the Apaches, Relles forbade Vergara from entering his ranchería, located between Ramos and Casas Grandes, probably at the Pajarito Mountains. Relles asserted to Vergara that his followers had remained at peace and that the Indians wanted to avoid contact because of their fear of contracting smallpox. They also suspected the Mexicans of issuing contaminated rations, a legitimate concern of the Indians—a wretched act that Janos officials would be guilty of some thirteen years later. Yet

Relles's primary reason for refusing Vergara permission to enter his camp was that his local group of twenty-two men was ready to join forces with other Chiricahua groups, all under Mangas Coloradas, for a foray into Sonora.[7]

In fact, Relles's band had been raiding in Sonora, though Vergara did not realize it. Along with other Chokonen local groups, the previous December they had killed one man and wounded another near Oputo, which, like Fronteras, would be the object of almost every Chiricahua war party in 1844. Next they had raided Cuquiarachi, southwest of Fronteras, before returning to Janos and Corralitos. At the last spot Relles traded three burros, and another Chiricahua boasted of their plans to make another campaign against the towns situated on the Bavispe River, particularly Bacadehuachi, Huasabas, and Oputo.[8]

Mangas Coloradas's war party entered Sonora from New Mexico about January 27, 1844, enlisting warriors as it moved south. It consisted mainly of Chokonens and Bedonkohes, with a few Chihennes from Itán's local group, at least according to the individuals recognized by Sonoran officials during the talks that the two groups held in early February. The Chiricahuas struck first at Oputo, an old Opata settlement about fifteen miles north of Huasabas. A fertile farming community in a mountainous region along the Bavispe River, Oputo had been a favorite target of Apache raiders since the late seventeenth century. On February 4, 1844, an estimated two hundred Chiricahuas jumped five men and two women within a mile of Oputo. They quickly killed the men and carried the women off into captivity. Three days later they showed up at Fronteras and wounded three men, captured two children, and stole most of its horses, some two hundred animals. Captain Teodoro López de Aros,[9] an experienced, Apache-wise officer, pursued the Indians with a mixed force of ten soldiers and thirty citizens, all on foot. De Aros estimated the Apaches at five hundred, undoubtedly an exaggeration. Despite their overpowering numbers the Indians decided to parley with de Aros, who identified Mangas Coloradas and the Chokonen leaders Esquinaline, Teboquita, and Delgado (not to be confused with the Chihenne leader Delgadito). After talking for several hours, Mangas ransomed the two children for supplies, likely tobacco and pinole. The release of the children was characteristic of Mangas Coloradas, for there is no case on record in which he harmed a captive child, Mexican or American, though his war parties routinely killed Mexican women and children. The war party moved east

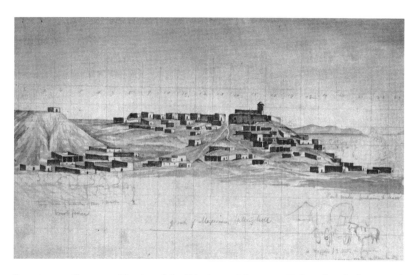

Fronteras, Sonora. During his lifetime, Mangas Coloradas led several assaults against this isolated presidio in northern Sonora. (Hine, *Bartlett's West*)

through the mountains for Batepito, where they split up. The Bedonkohes under Mangas Coloradas and Teboca, with a few Chihennes under Itán, headed for the Burro Mountains in New Mexico; meanwhile, the Chokonens under Yrigóllen, Relles, and Tapilá remained near Batepito, where they held yet another parley with a detachment of troops from Sonora.[10]

Rumors continued to fly in these turbulent days—some improbable, such as the one that Mangas Coloradas had enlisted the aid of the Coyoteros (Western Apaches) and Navajos in his war against Sonora. This was a frequent report during the 1840s and early 1850s, but in reality the Navajos never joined Mangas to wage war against Mexico. In contrast, the Western Apaches, notably the two White Mountain bands, did occasionally join him on incursions into Sonora. Yet his relationship with these two tribes was more of an economic alliance based on a reciprocal trade and social visits. Tayachil, a son of José Mentira, a Chiricahua who had continued to live in peace at Janos, furnished this information to Captain Madrigal. Mangas with Teboca, Cuchillo Negro, Itán, and the venerable Pisago Cabezón had made plans for another campaign against Sonora. Meanwhile, the leaders of the Chokonen band had come to a consensus: another revenge raid against Fronteras.[11]

This undertaking was solely a Chokonen venture. On March 5, 1844, at 8:00 A.M. Chiricahuas "in great numbers" ambushed several of Fronteras's citizens as they tilled their crops only three hundred yards from sentries. The Apaches killed one man and seriously wounded another. Captain de Aros courageously left in pursuit with twenty-nine men, all on foot (the Apaches had stolen their mounts the previous month), and overtook the Indians "where they were waiting for me behind the rocks" in the foothills east of the presidio. These Chokonens had no intention of talking, for this was a war party intent on exacting revenge, and that meant blood. The Apaches settled down to a sniping duel with the whites. For five hours both sides exchanged insults and gunfire until the skirmish abruptly ended when an Apache sharpshooter wounded de Aros and the Mexicans withdrew. In all, the Apaches killed one soldier and wounded two others. De Aros failed to mention any Indian casualties, but later reports revealed that his soldiers had wounded Yrigóllen and Posito Moraga, two important Chokonen band leaders.[12]

Later that month the Chokonens struck at Moctezuma, Bacerac, and Bavispe. During an encounter at Moctezuma, their outright disdain of Sonorans surfaced when they declared that "they [Apaches] really know how to fight while Sonorans went only to kill women and children." Soon after, a band under Tapilá raided Bacerac, killing Antonio Pisano, and then assaulted Bavispe, where one Apache contemptuously claimed that the Sonorans "are all wicked but we [Apaches] are men to rob and kill in Sonora, just like we do every time that we feel like it."[13]

This Apache later may have regretted his disparaging remarks. For soon after Tapilá's raid, Captain Eusebio Samaniego mobilized national guard troops from Bacadehuachi and Bacerac. Samaniego, a member of a prominent Bavispe family, was known for his courage, drive, fighting ability, and endurance unequaled by any officer on the frontier, American or Mexican. He was arguably the most effective adversary that the Chiricahuas had to confront in the mid-eighteenth century. The Chiricahuas called him "Chato," or "Flat Nose," and respected him. He followed the Apaches' trail to the Carcay Mountains in Chihuahua. There he attacked a small camp, killing Collante, wounding two other men (who escaped to Janos), and capturing three women and two children. Samaniego justified his crossing into Chihuahua without permission because his scouts had cut a fresh trail of hostiles. Moreover, the Indians' testimony clearly pointed out that the Chiricahuas customarily disposed of their stolen plunder at Janos and Corralitos, a disputed matter destined to become a truly significant issue. In any event, Samaniego's success was music to the ears of Sonora's military commander, Colonel Elías González, who had contemplated mounting an offensive against the Apaches living near Janos.[14]

In April the Chiricahuas returned to Sonora in force. Again, Mangas Coloradas, like an architect, drew up the plans for this war party, which featured warriors from each of the four Chiricahua bands. It was an extraordinary development, one that came about because of the reputation of Mangas Coloradas and the prestige of Pisago Cabezón, who had probably undertaken his last campaign. In all likelihood the easy victories and loot that Chiricahua raiders had taken over the last several months inspired and attracted many warriors to the fold. The principal leaders were for the Bedonkohes, Mangas Coloradas and Teboca; for the Chihennes, Cuchillo Negro; for the Chokonens, Yrigóllen, Esquinaline, and Posito Moraga; and for the Nednhis, Soquilla. They represented some three hundred fighting men.

The small villages along the lower Bavispe River would be their first targets. Entering northeastern Sonora, the Chiricahua war party penetrated deep into the interior, striking the district of Sahuaripa, killing at least nineteen men, women, and children. They returned north following the Bavispe River and on April 26, 1844, at Oputo they ambushed and killed three men and carried off many mules, burros, and horses. Soon after, Sonoran troops clashed with Mangas's war party, which routed the Sonorans in a hard fight, killing eight and wounding three more men. The Apaches later admitted they lost six men, but a rumor that the Mexicans had killed Cuchillo Negro proved false. From Oputo they duplicated their actions of the previous February and headed for the vulnerable town of Cuquiarachi, which they occupied much to the chagrin of its helpless residents. On April 28, 1844, at 8:00 A.M. they surrounded the town, killed or wounded several persons, and captured several others "at the point of a lance." They rode brazenly through the streets, boldly occupying the plaza in the middle of town, For the next three hours the Apaches maintained a constant fire, until they offered to ransom three of the children whom they had captured. Again, the chiefs who conversed with the Mexicans included Mangas Coloradas and Pisago Cabezón along with several Chokonen leaders, including Yrigóllen and Esquinaline, well known to the officials of Cuquiarachi. After the Indians returned their prisoners, they headed toward Fronteras, where they killed seven more people before splitting up. Mangas and Pisago Cabezón departed for Arizona and New Mexico; Soquilla's Nednhis with some Chokonens returned to Janos and Corralitos, Chihuahua. Among the dead they left behind was a servant of Colonel Antonio Narbona, a resident of Cuquiarachi, who would avenge this attack in the months to come.[15]

During the next few months the Chokonens and Bedonkohes remained in Arizona and New Mexico, where they were busy with perhaps the most important economic endeavor of the band: the mescal harvest. The warriors had returned to their local group camping areas, joining their families in the gathering of the sweet and juicy crowns of the agave. This activity was a local group venture. Usually several families would join up and travel to the mescal country, where they would establish temporary camps. The Bedonkohes and Chokonens exploited the slopes and foothills of the Dragoon and Chiricahua Mountains for the nutritious plant. The Chihennes gathered the mescal plant at several places—from extreme southwestern New Mexico in the Animas, Little and Big Hatchet Mountains as far north as the Black Mountains, north of Santa Rita del Cobre. Besides the eastern slopes of Chiricahuas, Mangas favored two other areas: the first, the place the Indians called Nadazai, meaning "Mescal Extends Upward," was in the rocky foothills located along the canyons and creeks below White-water Baldy in the Mogollon Mountains; the second, and probably his favorite, was Tceguna, meaning "Canyon Spreads Out," which encompasses the valley between the Mogollons and the Pinos Altos country. This large area was just north and northeast of Santa Lucía Springs, sometimes known as Mangas Springs, the place that in later years an American Indian agent would suggest as a possible reservation site for three of the Chiricahua bands.[16]

After the mescal harvest, Mangas Coloradas organized his third major war party of the year against Sonora. In early July, Captain Rey at Janos reported that the hostiles had moved their rancherías to the Burro and Mogollon Mountains, likely preparing for the fall harvest of piñon nuts and acorns.[17] Mangas departed with his men from one of these places and ventured into Chokonen territory, the route of most of his expeditions into Sonora. Again, as with the April campaign, members of each of the four Chiricahua bands likely participated. Unfortunately, the details about what happened are unknown, for there were no white survivors, and no testimony from the Apache side has been found. Yet one could speculate that no one other than Mangas Coloradas could have pulled off the next victory. In late July 1844, a large Apache group obliterated a Sonoran force of twenty-nine men under Ensign Manuel Villa near Santa Cruz. Mangas apparently led the Indians, who had successfully set up the timeworn decoy tactic. The Apaches had tried the same strategy at Fronteras in an earlier engagement, but the experienced Captain Teodoro de Aros had held his men in check. Evidently Villa and his men did not realize that they had run into a well-planned ambush, for the Indians wiped out him and his twenty-eight soldiers to a man. There is only circumstantial evidence to point to Mangas's involvement in the stunning victory. He had been recognized during his previous campaigns; this time there were no survivors to tell the tale. But only Mangas could have assembled such a large body of Chiricahuas. The locality and characteristics of the fight and the fact that Elías González found the spoils of this victory in Chiricahua rancherías near Janos a few months later point to a Chiricahua involvement. If so, in all probability Mangas Coloradas led the participants.[18]

In any case it was a staggering victory for the Apaches, a crowning blow, and a drubbing for the Mexicans so egregious that Elías González, who had been fuming for months over his belief that the Chiricahuas living near Janos had committed many atrocities against Sonora, decided to take matters into his own hands: he would lead an army into Chihuahua to strike the Apache camps so that the Indians could also feel the horrors of war. Only then would they lose their will to fight, or so he believed. In one way he was correct, for the Apaches respected force. They had agreed to peace treaties with Chihuahua in 1832 and 1842 because of the effective campaigns waged against them in their territory. They understood that defeat in battle was a hazard of war. An attack on a ranchería in which most of the victims were women and children was another matter altogether, even if the men of that camp had been committing hostile acts. Instead of whipping the Apaches into submission, such an assault only served to incense them further and thus provide them with fodder to avenge their losses. In a way the never-ending cycle of warfare between the Chiricahua Apaches and Sonora could have been resolved only by one culture's exterminating the other. Neither race, however, could accomplish that. There had been too much killing, too much hatred, too many individuals on both sides who yearned to avenge either a relative's or friend's death. During the 1840s and 1850s the Chiricahuas retained enough power to preserve their territory and in some cases to recapture part of their old range by forcing out their tenants or by making them live in tiny, isolated pockets of population. Even at the end of the Apache Wars, which culminated in the deportation of the Chiricahua tribe from Arizona in 1886, neither side trusted nor forgave the other, and the antipathy lived on into the twentieth century.

Elías González had pondered for at least a year the idea of striking the Chiricahuas in northwestern Chihuahua. He had previously written Chihuahua's Governor Monterde of his plans to mount an offensive against the Apaches who had been committing hostilities in Sonora. Monterde, the officer who had gained the respect of Mangas Coloradas, was deeply concerned that Sonora's troops would upset the skittish Apaches living peacefully along Chihuahua's northern frontier. He instructed Elías González not to bring troops into Chihuahua in search of Apaches, for that would introduce serious difficulties to the brittle peace.[19]

For a while Elías González respected Monterde's wishes, but he continued to receive reports that bespoke of the deteriorating conditions of the northern frontier. The Chiricahuas had launched several brutal raids against Sonora's settlements, after which they returned to Janos, where the town's officials rationed them and encouraged them to trade their Sonoran spoils to cooperative Mexicans. In late September 1843, Urrea had complained to Mexico City about the devastating raids, stating "that this has happened because of the protection which is given them" at Janos. He urged authorities at Mexico City to condemn this practice and "to issue a resolution that will control this evil." At the same time, a Fronteras civilian wrote the prefect of Arispe a despairing letter predicting that the citizens would abandon their homes because of the Apache terror. The letter, which Urrea also forwarded to the minister of war in Mexico City, charged that before Chihuahua's peace treaty in June 1842 the Apaches used to plunder the settlements of Sonora and Chihuahua and sell their loot in New Mexico. Now Sonora had absorbed the brunt of the resurgence in hostilities. "These barbarians come over to our towns and commit murders and robberies. Evading the vigilance of our troops, with the quickness of lightning they go back to their camps, where they are protected and defended from punishment by the Commander at Janos."[20]

The federal officials in Mexico City had demanded a response from Chihuahua's Governor Monterde on how he planned to correct this evil practice. Addressing the charges one at a time, Monterde had stressed that his Apache policy had succeeded because of his fair and honest treatment of the Indians. Even the "General of the Mogollons," Mangas Coloradas, had responded to Monterde's policies, acting with a "noble deportment" in keeping his word to retrieve stolen animals. In contrast, Monterde believed that Sonora's militant philosophy had failed miserably because Urrea was "imbued with the idea that without any need for treaties his forces would forcibly subdue these tribes." In fact, Monterde had tried to ward off Apache raiding into Sonora by sending an Apache peace party to Governor Urrea, who had not taken any overt actions to improve relations. Monterde tersely remarked that Sonora's problems had begun immediately after its troops had wantonly slain six Chokonens at Fronteras in the spring of 1843. Their kinfolk, exacting revenge, had committed the depredations and murders in Sonora, asserted Monterde. While he may have believed this because of reports he received from his subordinates, the truth was that every Chiricahua band waged war against Sonora by late 1843. This war, which had begun as a Chokonen venture, had evolved into a tribal enterprise. Some hostiles (some of the Chokonens and most of the Nednhis) returned to the Chihuahuan frontier, while others, under Mangas Coloradas and Pisago Cabezón (the warlike Chokonens, Chihennes, and Bedonkohes), retired to their homes in Arizona and New Mexico.[21] During 1844, Elías González had continued to get reports from his presidio commanders and local prefects about the Apaches at Janos. One common rumor reported by Sonoran travelers to Janos and Corralitos had it that Janos's citizens openly traded whiskey and ammunition to the Apaches in exchange for the loot stolen in Sonora. The Apaches would often crow about their victories and speak contemptuously about Sonorans. Several Chokonens boasted that they had killed citizens near Fronteras and Oputo.[22] The massacre of Villa's detachment near Santa Cruz proved to be the last straw. The energetic Elías González decided to put together a force to invade the Janos frontier, confident that he would catch the Chiricahuas unaware.

Elías González vowed to resolve the long-standing problem of the Chiricahuas' raiding Sonora from their safe havens inside Chihuahua. He had concluded that the Chiricahuas deserved to be punished, and he set to work marshaling troops and supplies for simultaneous operations both north and south of Janos to deprive the Indians from using these areas as sanctuary. He may have planned this operation before the loss of Villa's command at Santa Cruz. Details are scarce. His large army, consisting of both presidio troops and national guard soldiers, with perhaps six hundred men, departed Fronteras on August 16, 1844. Its quarry: the Chiricahuas living in northwest Chihuahua.

According to Elías González, his army followed the trail of the Indians who had wiped out Villa's command. He may have believed that or he may have added this argument as an afterthought because he knew it would be compelling justification for his illegal act of taking his troops across the border into Chihuahua without permission, which he knew would lead to controversy. Colonel Antonio Narbona, the commander of the Fronteras presidio, acted as his second in command. Narbona had seen the Indians kill one of his servants during the attack at Cuquiarachi the previous spring. A man of high repute among his contemporaries, Narbona was a staunch and lifelong adversary of the Indians. In any event, only four days before the command left Fronteras, Gervacio Valencia went to Janos with Luis García,[23] a native of Bacerac who traveled a great deal between there and Janos. While there, they conversed with some Apaches, who told the two Mexicans that they had just returned from a raid into Sonora; they had in their possession mules and cattle, which they offered for trade. In addition, Valencia learned that the Mogollons (Mangas Coloradas's Bedonkohes) had left for New Mexico, while the other Indians had returned to their camps in Chihuahua, unaware that Sonora's forces were en route to Chihuahua.[24]

Elías González's command reached the Carretas hacienda, the last settlement in Sonora, situated a few miles from the Chihuahua border, on August 20, 1844. There Sonora's military chief composed a letter to the commander of Janos, Captain Mariano Rodríguez Rey, in which he explained why he decided to cross the border. He began his message by declaring:

Charged by the General Commanding the Department of Sonora to direct the operations of the campaign against the savage Indians who are laying it to waste, and convinced by the evidence that the peaceful Indians living there [where you are] are the ones who at the presidio of Santa Cruz killed Second Lieutenant Don Manuel Villa along with 28 who were with him, including Father Alday, and also the same ones who twice have stolen the horses from Fronteras, and the ones who shamelessly have twice attacked that same presidio, and the ones who assaulted the defenseless town of Cuquiarachi, there killing several individuals, and the ones who very recently killed two persons at Tetuachic Canyon, subsequently bragging at that same place that one was Colonel Narbona . . . and the same ones who in the last few days robbed the wagons and animals that Don Cesario Corella was taking to Bavispe, and in short those who have caused Sonora every sort of harm that can be invented by the insatiable thirst for blood, revenge and plunder which possesses that hypocritical, lazy, and completely untrustworthy trash, I find myself compelled by the urgent need to cross the border of the Department of Chihuahua to punish them wherever I may find them.

Elías González deliberately fabricated his next statement. While he wrote that he had given Captain Rey advance warning, in reality he distrusted the people and the military at Janos and had taken great pains to ensure that the letter was not delivered until *after* he had attacked the Chiricahua camps. He concluded the message: "But so that at no time shall it be thought that the authority of your Department is being pushed aside, I have the honor of giving you this notice in advance. I trust that due secrecy will be kept and that, instead of protecting the Indians out of a mistaken understanding of the situation, you will put yourself on the side of justice and of Sonora. I want to take this opportunity to convey to you my esteem and regard."[25]

Once his army entered Chihuahua, he divided his force. He took one division and veered southeast toward Corralitos; the other division under Colonel Narbona headed east toward Janos. By the late evening of August 22, 1844, Narbona's detachment of some three hundred men had surrounded Janos, although no one there knew of his arrival until the sentry heard noises from the Apache village outside the presidio. According to Captain Rey, who seemed preoccupied with justifying his every move, Narbona's force acted with "all possible stealth, not firing a single shot instead attacking with bayonets so as to avoid any noise." They fell on the camp of José Mentira, an older headman of the Nednhis. The avenging Sonorans killed two men, nine women, and five children besides capturing five others, including José Mentira, whom the troops later executed. At daybreak on August 23, Captain Rey went out to the grisly scene, where a resident handed him Elías González's letter written three days before. Rey sadly predicted more bloodshed, for Elías González's command had taken the route "toward Ramos, Casas Grandes, Corralitos, and Barranco, for the purpose of attacking the Indians he will find there, something that will probably happen today or has already happened."[26]

Unfortunately for the Apaches, Rey's ominous warnings came too late for anyone to heed. That same day, Elías González's troops, joined later by Narbona's force, jumped several rancherías near Corralitos, including one in the Escondida Mountains. They destroyed the camps of Manuelito, a moderate Chokonen leader, and Soquilla, the principal chief of the Janeros group of the Nednhi band. The greatest carnage took place in their rancherías. All told, the army killed some sixty-five more Chiricahuas, the majority women and children, and captured another twenty-five. Thus, the Sonorans, in their two attacks near Janos and Corralitos, had killed some eighty Apaches and captured thirty more. Neither Elías González nor Narbona expressed any remorse over the number of women and children brutally slain by their unbridled men, who had turned into an uncontrolled mob feeding upon Indian blood. The Sonorans also confiscated an overwhelming amount of evidence linking these rancherías to depredations in Sonora. Even more important, they recovered two muskets that belonged to Villa's soldiers killed in the ambush at Santa Cruz. Elías González felt vindicated, for his troops had avenged the Chiricahua victories of 1844.[27]

Naturally the state of Chihuahua screamed foul play as it harshly denounced Sonora's actions in an outcry of unparalleled proportion. From Janos, Captain Rey protested that Elías González had not received permission to cross into Chihuahua. Moreover, as he correctly pointed out, Elías González had deliberately delivered his letter of August 20 after his command "had carried out their plans." Rey caustically declared that "the behavior of the commander of the Sonoran forces is very regrettable and surprising and flies in the face of all rights and respect which they must recognize as belonging to this Department and its authorities." But Rey decided not to get into a shouting match with the two Sonoran commanders because "it would be pointless and accomplish nothing more than becoming the object of one insult after another." Then he followed this with a dire warning, predicting that Elías González's justice would have the opposite of the intended effect. He opined, "I greatly fear that this unwise, imprudent, and unnecessary step will lead to this Department being once again drowned in a torrent of misfortunes, as it was until two years ago." He expected that even the peaceful Chiricahuas living in the Janos frontier would "probably attack there [Sonora] whenever they can."[28]

Chihuahua's press issued a scathing indictment of Elías González's unprecedented invasion. It charged Sonora's commanders

(Elías González and Narbona) of dereliction of duty "because they were either unaware of or have chosen to disregard the ironclad prohibition in the army's regulations forbidding, unless one has received orders from the highest authorities, crossing the borders of any of the territories which have been assigned to each military force." Instead, the editors of the Revista Oficial naïvely suggested that the Sonorans should have asked the Janos commander simply to turn over "those who should be prosecuted." In a document that includes more than a hint of hypocrisy, they went on to declare:

> The blow struck at Janos is inhumane, because it fell on defenseless people who had no reason to expect that they would be surprised in that place, where they were guaranteed protection by the peace treaty they had made. It is unjust, because it fell on the encampment of the chieftain José Mentira, who, as we guarantee and shall prove when we have a chance, has not left the presidio at Janos since he made peace. Finally, it is pointless, since Sonora will not gain any benefits from it. Rather the contrary, for it has given a motive for many bands to attack that Department, bands which have not done so since accepting the peace. . . .
>
> Moreover, we can contradict the assertion that the Indians from Janos are the perpetrators, since we are sure that the Indians who have died in their raids came from the Mogollon and Coyotero tribes, which belong to Sonora. Furthermore, on the Gila there is a sizeable gathering of Navajos, Mogollon, and Coyotero Indians who are doing a lot of damage to Sonora, and it seems that nothing would be more natural and appropriate than that the forces of that Department should direct their blows toward that gathering, thereby effectively punishing those who daily invade and attack the Department, instead of directing themselves against the bands which are living in this Department under the protection which should be provided by the peace treaty they have made.
>
> His Excellency, the Governor and General Commander of this Department . . . asks for the punishment of the person responsible for such an action. We implore the Supreme Command [President of Mexico] that the General Command will take salutary measures.[29]

This diatribe, made by individuals who had no idea what was happening along the Janos frontier, consisted of half-truths and misinformation. First of all, Rey was not about to turn over to Sonoran authorities any guilty Chiricahuas. His own welfare, and that of the citizens of northwestern Chihuahua, depended upon maintaining a peaceful coexistence with the Indians living in the frontier. The month before the attack he reported that his garrison consisted of thirty-three men: nine were in the guardhouse, four were sick, and seven were assigned to sentry duty for the fort and his herd, leaving just thirteen men available for other functions, including scout and patrol duties.[30] As to the innocence of the Chiricahuas at Janos, it is likely that some of these groups, in particular José Mentira's, abstained from raiding into Sonora. Yet throughout 1843, Captain Rey had rationed Yaque, Chepillo, and a host of other Chokonens after they returned from raiding and looting in Sonora. Mexican troops had recognized Soquilla, whose ranchería Elías González had attacked, as a participant in one of the parleys at Cuquiarachi after the Apaches had virtually laid siege to the town.[31]

By early 1844 every Chiricahua band had commenced hostilities against Sonora, although a few pacific local groups may have remained at peace. Still, the affair must be regarded as just as ugly as Apache war parties' slaughtering and capturing women and children during their raids. While the Bedonkohes, the Chihennes, and a number of Chokonens had retired north into present-day Arizona and New Mexico, the Nednhis and some Chokonens had remained encamped in northwestern Chihuahua. Elías González's decision to attack these groups, whom he considered at war with Sonora, made perfect sense to him. Why should he have tried to surprise the Apaches in the Mogollon country—Apaches who likely would easily have eluded his slow-moving army—when he had hostiles nearby in Chihuahua? To him there were no innocent Chiricahuas, which impression, as we have seen, echoed that of the militant Chiricahuas toward Sonorans.

The only prediction that came true was the newspaper's belief that Chihuahua now faced "the danger of an Indian uprising." This danger was real, for Elías González's campaign had effectively driven the Apaches from the Janos frontier and into the hands of Mangas Coloradas and the warlike faction of the Chiricahua tribe. Apache raids in Chihuahua would increase dramatically. Whereas in 1844 official military reports in Chihuahua reported only ten Apache raids, by the next year that figure had grown more than twenty-fold to 218, according to William Griffen's excellent study on Apache warfare in Chihuahua.[32]

Meanwhile, a satisfied Elías González returned to Sonora with his Chiricahua captives only to find himself embroiled in a storm

of controversy. His own investigation and analysis of the confiscated material gathered from the ransacked Chiricahua camps
convinced him that these Indians had waged war against Sonora.
The federal government in Mexico City demanded a response to
the charges made by Chihuahua about his clandestine attack.[33]
Anticipating this, he had prepared a report to justify his invasion.
He had probably talked to the leading military and civil officials
about preparing a report that would specifically identify the raiders
in Sonora as the "Janos" Apaches. Their accounts, he believed,
would justify his sortie into Chihuahua. Naturally the data that
they accumulated supported Elías González's version and left no
doubt that every evil Apache act that harmed Sonora originated at
Janos. Although their conclusions were oversimplified, their testimony was sufficient to exonerate Elías González.[34] The federal
government in Mexico City had no intention of censuring him for
killing Indians, especially Apaches.

In reality, Elías González's investigation pointed the finger at
some of northwestern Chihuahua's most prominent citizens. His
probe focused mainly on the stolen Sonoran livestock and loot that
his men had recovered from the Apache villages in Chihuahua. In
addition, his command had confiscated stolen Sonoran stock from
several prominent civil officials at Janos and Corralitos, therefore
implicating them in the lucrative yet nefarious trade between
Apaches and whites. For example, at Janos he found stolen animals
in the hands of Juan José Zozaya, an important citizen who would
serve as peace commissioner during the Chiricahua-Mexican
treaty of 1850. And at Barranco, a few miles northwest of Corralitos, his troops found Sonoran livestock in the possession of Robert
McKnight, former owner of the Santa Rita del Cobre mines. Even
worse, at Corralitos, José María Zuloaga,[35] the economic and political czar of northwestern Chihuahua, had to admit to mules and
horses bearing Sonoran brands. That these civil leaders would participate in such a vile activity both astonished and disgusted the
highly principled Elías González.[36]

At the time of the attack Mangas Coloradas had gone into camp
near the Gila, where Anglo-American traders were plying their
practice in trading arms and ammunition for mules and horses.[37]
Details of the massacre spread quickly throughout Apachería.
Unfortunately, Mangas Coloradas left behind no recorded thoughts
of Elías González's campaign. Nonetheless, because of his reaction
to the treacherous acts of whites against his people, we can imagine what he must have felt. The catastrophe had fallen on the

Chokonen and Nednhi bands, and undoubtedly many friends of his, and perhaps some kinfolk, were victims of the carnage. He was now the most respected and influential tribal war leader. He would rally his people. He would make Sonora pay.

Before Mangas could take action, however, the Chokonens under Yrigóllen, undoubtedly at the behest of Manuelito, the Chokonen local group leader whose ranchería Elías González had smashed, led a war party against Sonora. As with the forays of the previous spring, the Indians targeted the towns along the Bavispe River. It was apparently one large party that assaulted Bavispe, Huasabas, Oputo, and finally Moctezuma. All told, they killed five men and captured one person; in addition they made off with many mules and cattle from Oputo, where many disillusioned residents had come to the conclusion that they would desert the town rather than face another Apache war party.[38]

In late November, Francisco Narbona led a contingent of some one hundred national guard troops from Moctezuma in pursuit of the Apaches north to the Enmedio Mountains and then toward Janos. Without batting an eye he crossed into Chihuahua and some six miles southwest of Janos came across an old Nednhi named Negisle, who was at El Picacho gathering mescal with the permission of Janos authorities. After Narbona found in Negisle's possession a horse that Apaches had stolen from Sonora, he placed the old man in custody. Captain Mariano Rodríguez Rey tried to persuade Narbona that Negisle, "who scarcely can walk" (although such a disability did not prevent the Chihenne leader Nana from raiding in the early 1880s), had not obtained the horse from raiding in Sonora. It was likely, he insisted, that another Apache had given it or traded it to him. Instead of bothering the few Apaches left in the Janos neighborhood, Rey argued, the Sonorans should wage war against the hostiles living in southern New Mexico at Alamo Hueco. Convinced of Rey's argument, Captain Francisco Narbona released Negisle and then returned to Sonora.[39]

As for Mangas, he apparently had spent the fall of 1844 near his beloved Santa Lucía Springs and along the Gila south of the Mogollons. Elías González understood that it was only a matter of time before the Chiricahuas would respond to their bloody defeat at Janos and Corralitos. The relatives of the victims demanded revenge. The two bands that had lost the most members—Chokonens and Nednhis—likely originated a movement to organize a war party. It was only natural that they would ask Mangas Coloradas, the tribal war leader with ties to the Chokonens, Bedonkohes, and Chihennes, to participate. The Nednhi leaders Soquilla, Láceres, and Coleto Amarillo could also be expected to align themselves closely with the bellicose faction for the remainder of the 1840s. It therefore came as no surprise to Elías González when he received a message from his friend Antonio Narbona on December 27, 1844, which gave him ominous news. Narbona had received information that a large Chiricahua war party under Mangas Coloradas had united in the Chiricahuas and at Sarampión in the lower Peloncillo Mountains, directly opposite the lower Chiricahuas. Sarampeon had long been a favorite camping area of Cochise's Chokonens, especially during the winter. According to rumors, Mangas's war party intended to capture as many Sonorans as possible, undoubtedly to trade for their people captured by Elías González. Sonora's commander, learning of the threat, hoped to organize a campaign to strike the Chiricahuas before they entered Sonora.[40]

Surprisingly, there are no reports indicating the presence of a Chiricahua war party ravaging Sonora in early 1845. Yet the raid likely went off as planned, though the details are unavailable. The primary documentation for this period is sparse perhaps because of the ongoing political instability that resulted from the resurgence of intense fighting between Urrea's and Gándara's forces. Yet this portentous report of Mangas's intentions certainly compelled Governor Urrea and his subordinate, Elías González, to take action to keep the hostiles out of Sonora. Urrea, who had carried out important reforms in Sonora—improving schools, hospitals, and the judicial system—laid out a grandiose plan to pacify the Apaches once and for all.[41] In an unlikely move, in early February 1845 he asked the governors of New Mexico, Chihuahua, and Durango to cooperate in an all-out war against the Apaches, who "were killing indiscriminately citizens in Sonora, Chihuahua, and Durango." He asked that each state send out punitive expeditions against the Apaches, who would be certain to sue for peace once they understood the joint resolve. Urrea believed that the old presidio system, in which the Indians "did not have to work and were supported by the public treasury," was anachronistic. Once Sonora's forces subjugated the Apaches, the reform-minded Urrea would have ready his own solution: he believed that Mexico should oblige the Apaches to earn their keep by working, presumably in farming; his troops would force them to abandon their traditional mountain homes. He asked each governor to hustle up a fighting force against the Apaches and recommended that they maintain constant patrols, thus keeping the Indians continually on the run until the troops wore them down and compelled them to capitulate. He received favorable responses from each governor.[42]

Circumstances would prevent him from carrying out his radical idea. But just the threat of a punitive Mexican campaign may have discouraged Apache depredations in Sonora. The Indians had a network of informants: Anglo and Mexican traders and friends at their trading centers in Janos and Corralitos, Chihuahua, and Socorro, on the Rio Grande in New Mexico, which had become for the Chihennes and Bedonkohes a favorite place of commerce, since they had abandoned Chihuahua's northwestern frontier.[43] Undoubtedly they heard about Urrea's and Elías González's intentions.

These rumors were intimidating ones, and they may have gained credibility in the eyes of Mangas Coloradas and his Chiricahuas because of Elías González's recent six-hundred-man expedition into Chihuahua. One account even suggested that the hostiles had considered making peace with Sonora.[44] In any event, what is clear is that Mangas avoided Sonora for most of 1845. He may have done some raiding in Mexico; he likely continued to cultivate peaceful relations with the small towns along the Rio Grande in New Mexico as he would when the Americans arrived a few years later. Reports and rumors continued to link the Apaches to Socorro, New Mexico,[45] as Mangas and his people kept their distance from Urrea's militaristic Sonora. Meanwhile, in early 1845 federal officials in Mexico City recalled Chihuahua's Governor Monterde, whom many state officials blamed for the Apache uprising.

In the meantime, Urrea's productive reign as governor was coming to a close in Sonora. Although he had achieved great popularity in Sonora, the central government in Mexico City had concluded that Sonora must have new leadership to ensure stability. It determined that both Gándara and Urrea had to go. Therefore, Mexico City replaced Urrea with an interim government run by General Francisco Duque. Urrea surrendered his powers on April 10, 1845, but declined to leave Sonora until his campaign against the Apaches was completed.[46] By mid-1845 authorities at Opodepe, Oputo, and Cocospera had informed the governor that their people were on the brink of deserting their homes because of the Apache raids.[47] Duque hoped to take countermeasures. He appointed Elías González to the position of adjutant inspector, and at once the imaginative commander offered his own strategy for defeating the Apaches. His plan centered on propping up the presidios so that they could take the offensive into Apachería. Once that was accomplished, he would recommend a campaign of six hundred infantry and three hundred cavalry that could wage war against the Apaches in their mountain homes. Unfortunately for Sonora's residents, his plan, like Urrea's innovative idea, never got off the ground, chiefly because of internal chaos.[48]

By the spring of 1845 the Chokonen band had returned to northern Sonora, but Mangas had remained in New Mexico. In late April, Negisle, the only Apache man still residing at Janos, had gone to the Chiricahua camps in search of his daughter, who had gone to live with the hostiles. The chiefs told him that they considered themselves at peace with Chihuahua and that they planned to request terms with Sonora. Likely he had talked to the Chokonens, who had established a large ranchería at the Espuelas Mountains, directly east of the Enmedio Mountains in northeast Sonora and south of the Animas range in southwestern New Mexico. The place where the Chiricahuas camped appears to have been on the east side, at a place that they knew as Tsesl-ja-si-kaat, meaning "Rocks Brown in a Bunch."[49] They had migrated south in anticipation of the spring harvest of the mescal plant. Mexican troops would have left them alone if their warriors had remained at peace.

On May 8, 1845, a small Chokonen raiding party pilfered 117 cattle from Corralitos; fifteen days later it ran off sixteen oxen from Corralitos and five days later (May 28) stole twenty-three mules from Barranco. Ensign José Baltazar Padilla left in pursuit with twenty-seven troops and fifty-two citizens. They followed the trail to the Espuelas Mountains and discovered a large Chokonen village of more than one hundred families, probably some five hundred to six hundred individuals in all. Padilla's tenacity and courage paid dividends: in hard fighting spread over three days, his force clashed repeatedly with the Chokonens. All told, he claimed his men had slain fourteen Indians and wounded many others. His troops also captured a woman and a child. Finally he left the battleground with a loss of four soldiers dead and nine wounded, five of whom were citizens. After the defeat, the Chokonens scattered and regrouped in the Chiricahua Mountains. About a month later their leaders, Manuelito, Matías, and Yrigóllen, dispatched messengers to Janos requesting a truce.[50]

The Chokonens' request brought a temporary lull to the hostilities. Chihuahua, hoping to make yet another treaty, dispatched their outstanding negotiator, Lieutenant Antonio Sánchez Vergara, to Chihenne and Bedonkohe territory in New Mexico to figure out what the Chiricahuas were thinking. He grimly reported that most of the hostiles had relocated to the Mogollon Mountains under a chief named José María María, an important Chihenne chief also known as Ponce, a moderate leader then coming into prominence. Vergara would have mentioned Mangas Coloradas if he had met him. According to the information that Vergara gathered, the Chihennes and Bedonkohes had committed several depredations near Doña Ana and El Paso. He also digressed to point out that he had heard that they had sent campaigns against Chihuahua. Consequently, he recommended that the Chihuahuan government organize an expedition against the Chiricahuas based in the Mogollons.[51]

The first specific reference to Mangas Coloradas in 1845 came in the early fall of that year. Again, Ensign Padilla, who would eventually become well acquainted with Mangas Coloradas, led a patrol that captured an Apache warrior in the Enmedio Mountains. The man grudgingly admitted that he belonged to Itán's local group and that he had come with other warriors on a campaign against Sonora. Itán had remained in the Mogollons with Mangas Coloradas. He also revealed that they had opened up a new market in which to trade: Socorro, New Mexico, where they exchanged their loot for arms and powder.[52] These revelations led to a formal investigation by New Mexican authorities at Santa Fe, where several citizens testified to the illicit activities that they had observed at Socorro, which place would soon see a lot of Mangas Coloradas.[53] Before they could react to Vergara's advice and recommendations for an expedition against the Chiricahuas, Chihuahua's new governor, Angel Trias, and his commanding general, Pedro García Conde, had first to address serious Indian problems in their state. First, the Carrizaleño local group of Nednhis raided with impunity the northwest and central part of the state; second, the Comanches ravaged the countryside in its eastern section. Conde definitely "favored a bad peace over a good war" approach. Nonetheless, with the state's presidio soldiers unable to cope with this tremendous resurgence in the scope of Indian raids, frontier communities began to organize their own local militia to deal with the Apaches. In addition, these deplorable conditions along its frontier forced the state to consider the recall of Jim Kirker and his mercenaries, and he proved to be receptive to the idea.[54] Chihuahua's revised militaristic policy did not directly affect Mangas, who spent most of his time in the Mogollons and Burro Mountains, where it was almost impossible for the Mexican troops to inflict any damage. Yet the Nednhis and Chokonens living along Chihuahua's northwestern fringes would lie in the path of Kirker's mercenaries, whose objective was to exterminate Apaches.

The next incident of war did not involve either Mangas Coloradas or his Bedonkohe or Chihenne followers, but it exemplified the joint resolve that characterized relations in the mid-1840s between the residents of northeastern Sonora and northwestern Chihuahua who were caught in the middle of the Apache onslaught. This new determination set the tone for relations with the Chiricahuas for the remainder of the decade, as neither side, Apache nor Mexican, wanted peaceful relations.

On September 19, 1845, Luis García, fast earning a reputation as a dogged and fearless commander, sallied out from Bacerac with ninety men from the surrounding towns. Passing through Bavispe, he enlisted another fourteen men. During the next ten days he patrolled northeastern Sonora and then northwestern Chihuahua, carefully examining the Espuelas and Enmedio ranges in Sonora. Finding no fresh signs, he decided to cross into Chihuahua. As García's business frequently led him to Janos and Casas Grandes, he was well known and highly respected along the frontier. Even so, he requested permission from the "political and military authorities" of Casas Grandes to "go to them and discuss Apache matters." What a difference a year had made. The frontier residents of Chihuahua, having felt firsthand the wrath of the Chiricahua war parties, now eagerly wished to cooperate with Sonora. The untarnished reputation of Luis García did not hurt matters, either.

On September 27, García rode into Casas Grandes to hold a council with local officials. They furnished seven men "who knew the mountains" to act as guides. The next day he started marching southeast toward Galeana. En route, his scouts discovered fresh signs; he immediately dispatched Lieutenant Lauriano May with a small party of eighteen men, including Casas Grandes native Antonio Ortiz, who acted as guide. At Angostura, about thirty miles southeast of Casas Grandes, they surprised a small group of Indians, dispassionately killed five men and six women, and captured a "nursing child," whom they gave to a resident of Galeana. They also managed to capture two men, whom they brought to Luis García along with the "scalps and ears" of the dead males. García interrogated the prisoners. One man had in his possession a horse that he had apparently stolen from Sonora, a mount which, in fact, had belonged to a soldier serving with García. This sealed their fate. They defiantly refused to say anything except to reiterate that they were at peace with Galeana. García's "entire command asked that these Indians be put to death." They of course carried out the executions, but only after García considerately had them baptized. The baptism they "accepted willingly," but one wonders whether they truly appreciated García's concerns about saving their souls. After administering the sacrament, the Sonorans summarily executed the two Chiricahua men.[55]

Before the execution, one Apache conceded that he had recently been on a campaign into Sonora. Could he have been referring to the Apache expedition against Santa Cruz that had overwhelmed the town at 9:00 A.M., September 13, 1845, and had remained there for some six hours? That war party, mounted and on foot, had numbered three hundred, according to one eyewitness. The Indians cleaned out the town of its stock, killed ten persons, and captured thirteen more, including twelve-year-old Concepción Mejías, who would remain a captive for two years before he made his way back to his people. Many of the remaining residents now considered emigrating to California. Unfortunately, there is no evidence to pinpoint which Apaches were involved; however, recent activities, the number of Indians reported, and the large number of killed and captured all suggest a Chiricahua war party, though it was possible that the Western Apaches were responsible.[56]

In late 1845 the moderate blocs of the Chokonen and Nednhi bands opened negotiations with Chihuahua, claiming that they wished to make peace. Relles led the peaceful faction of the Chokonens, while Cristóbal and Francisquillo led the Carrizaleños. According to some reports, these two bands boasted three hundred warriors, though this figure seems a bit high. They had been raiding with the hostiles, whom they called Mogolloneros, but had decided to mend their ways and live in peace. Yet they failed to come into Carrizal for a scheduled conference, which perturbed Mexican officials. In response, military and civil officials organized a force of 340 men, including James Kirker and thirty of his mercenaries. They fell upon Chiricahua camps at the Sierra de Terrenate, northwest of Encinillas, had a brief skirmish, and killed a few Indians before the Apaches scattered into the mountains.[57]

Despite the conflict, as 1846 dawned those Chiricahua bands living in Chihuahua still yearned to work out an armistice. Mangas Coloradas and his followers remained in New Mexico, at war with both Sonora and Chihuahua. Perhaps the rumor that Chihuahua was going to recall Kirker's army and unleash it against hostile Apaches was reason enough to persuade the Chokonens and Nednhis to contemplate peace. Many older leaders had lived peacefully and even somewhat prosperously under the presidio system. The Chiricahuas were not an agricultural people, and the many years of close Mexican contact had left them dependent on the frontier towns for trade. For their own self-preservation those bands whose local group territory was in northwestern Chihuahua had to become pragmatic and accommodating in order to coexist with their enemies. Unfortunately for them, Kirker's mercenaries did not share this moderate approach. As a result, many Chiricahuas of the Chokonen and Nednhi bands would shed their blood for a false peace. What followed would outrank Johnson's perfidious act and Elías González's massacre at Janos and Corralitos. It would also have an impact on Mangas Coloradas, who, though not present, would bitterly recall the hideous atrocities that Kirker carried out against the unsuspecting Chiricahuas.

In May and June of 1846 the Chokonens under Relles, Yrigóllen, and Carro, and the Nednhis under Francisco and Láceres held a series of parleys with Ensign Carlos Cásares at San Buenaventura, about ten miles south of Galeana. Cásares was an unusual Mexican officer who actually sympathized with the Indians. He wished to forget the conflicts of the past, recognizing that both sides shared equally the blame. His sincerity and understanding imbued the Apaches with trust. He held out the carrot—rations— which he refused to issue until the Chiricahuas released every one of their captives. By the third week in June the Indians had returned several captives; Cásares's uncompromising policy had paid dividends.[58]

Although Cásares had set in motion the machinery for a promising peace, his honorable plans would remain unfulfilled. James Kirker would see to that. With the permission of Chihuahua's Governor José María Irigóyen, on June 26, 1846, the scalp hunter led a sundry crew of twenty-five men out of Chihuahua City in search of Indians—preferably hostiles, but he would kill any Apaches he could lay his hands on. The governor had informed his commanding general, Maurico Ugarte, who had received promising reports from Ensign Cásares concerning the prospects for peace, about Kirker's campaign. Ugarte supported the notion of volunteer troops because he faced a shortage of regular troops. Yet he hoped that Kirker's unconventional group would follow the letter of the law and not kill peaceful Indians. By the time Kirker received this communique, if indeed he ever got it at all, irreparable harm had already been done.[59]

After a ten-day march Kirker found himself at the home of José de la Riva, the subprefect of Galeana. Early in the morning of July 6, 1846, José Ponce, a citizen of Galeana, arrived at de la Riva's home with the news that Kirker's party had killed eighteen Chiricahuas at San Buenaventura, thus breaking the truce. Knowing that the Chiricahuas had a large village near Galeana, Kirker, with some citizens from Janos and Galeana led by José María Zuloaga (a frequent trading partner of the Chiricahuas), assembled his forces and set out to kill as many Indians as possible. The details of what happened next are sparse. Kirker's dispassionate report was general and vague, as was that prepared by Cásares shortly after the massacre. But George Ruxton, an English traveler and writer who visited Chihuahua City shortly after the affair, left behind an account which corroborated the Apache recollections of the Chokonen leader Yrigóllen, Jason Betzinez, and Mangas Coloradas. Yrigóllen was likely present, or in the vicinity, while Betzinez recorded Chiricahua history as he heard it from his elders. Mangas was preparing an expedition into Sonora, but he heard the grim details from the Chokonen and Nednhi survivors.[60]

The Chiricahuas would come to know Kirker's massacre as the time when the Mexicans were "lying in wait to double-cross them." The Indians' versions, as well as Ruxton's account, all agree that the Mexicans had invited the Apaches to a feast. They came to Galeana under the protection of a treaty. Mescal or whiskey flowed so freely that night that by the early morning "nearly everyone was lying in a drunken stupor," according to Apache accounts. Then Kirker's party appeared. They were also in a stupor, but it was one brought on by an insatiable appetite for Indian blood and for the money that Chihuahua continued to pay in bounties for Apache scalps. In the early morning of July 7, 1846, Kirker's barbaric party massacred the inebriated Chiricahuas in their sleep. The mercenaries ruthlessly slaughtered some 130 Chiricahuas, consisting of Chokonens and Nednhis. Age and sex were irrelevant; Kirker's crew systematically cut down and butchered any Indians in their path. In referring to the incident, Mangas Coloradas said that "my people were invited to a feast; aguardiente or whiskey was there; my people drank and became intoxicated, and were lying asleep, when a party of Mexicans came in and beat out their brains with clubs." Kirker's party slaughtered everyone they laid their hands on, including one pregnant woman whose child was "torn alive from the yet palpitating body of its mother, first plunged into the holy water to be baptized, and immediately its brains were dashed against a wall." After their deed, Kirker's party marched to the city of Chihuahua, "the scalps carried on poles . . . in procession, headed by the Governor and priests, with bands of music escorting them in triumph to the town."[61]

It was not a victory for those moderates living along the frontier. Ensign Cásares disputed Kirker's version that he had followed the trail of hostile Apaches to Galeana. Angrily, he warned that the affair would have "far reaching ramifications. All hope for peace is gone."[62] The Apaches would take revenge.

Kirker's despicable act, perhaps the greatest disaster to befall the Chiricahuas, provided a tragic climax to a decade and a half of hostilities between the Chiricahuas and Mexico. Most of the victims belonged to the moderate and pacific elements of the Chokonen band, which included the groups of Yrigóllen (who lost family members), Carro, Manuelito, Torres, and Relles—the last two victims of the slaughter. The Nednhi band, consisting of Láceres's local group of Janeros and Francisquillo's Carrizaleños, also suffered heavy losses. Kirker's slaughter united the moderates and the hostiles. For the rest of the 1840s every Chiricahua band went to war with Mexico. Over one hundred years later, Jason Betzinez referred to the massacre as the "ghastly butchering of our families."[63] Mangas Coloradas would remember it forever; its aftermath was predictable. For the next several years he would fiercely reject all relations with Mexico and cling to his traditional way of life in New Mexico. More challenges were on the horizon, and he would soon have another important consideration—the Americans.

Chapter 7

ETERNAL FRIENDSHIP TO AMERICANS

CHIRICAHUA-Mexican relations had declined to their lowest ebb of the nineteenth century by the time U.S. forces arrived in the Southwest in the fall of 1846. They came because war between the United States and Mexico had erupted earlier on April 25, 1846. Once there, they discovered an Indian culture that was wary of Americans because of recent experiences with Anglo-American scalp hunters and traders. Yet once the Indians learned that these troops had come to fight Mexicans and had no intention of staying on in Apachería, they welcomed them with open arms. The Chiricahuas, including Mangas Coloradas, perceived these newcomers as allies and thus were willing to aid them in any way possible.

From these travelers we get helpful impressions of Mangas Coloradas and the Chiricahuas at mid-century. His reputation as the most prominent and powerful Chiricahua leader in the Southwest was solidly in place by the time the Americans arrived in the region. He was approaching his late fifties, an age when he should have been slowing down and leaving the fighting to the younger men. His role should by now have evolved into that of advisor and honored patriarch. Yet, as with many great Chiricahua leaders of the nineteenth century—before him Pisago Cabezón and after him Cochise and Victorio—he would not enjoy that luxury. These were demanding and difficult times for his people.

Mangas continued to make his home in New Mexico near the Burro Mountains, occasionally moving further north to the rugged Mogollons while usually spending the winter at Santa Lucía Springs and other tributaries of the Gila. But his activities in 1847 and 1848 are difficult to track. Documents from northern Mexico, both Sonora and Chihuahua, are virtually nonexistent for that period. Those that have survived contain only a few scattered references to the Chiricahuas, because the expansionist Yankees from the north concerned Mexicans more than did the Indians. Yet we do know that in Sonora the Chokonens continued to wage war during this period. After the Kirker massacre the militant faction of the band, under Miguel Narbona and a daredevil leader by the name of Cochise, pushed the band to respond militarily. Yrigóllen, until this time a moderate leader, heartily endorsed the band's warlike philosophy, as he had lost family members in the Kirker massacre in 1846 and again to a Sonoran campaign in the fall of 1847. The Chokonens would discover that Sonora's northern communities were vulnerable, which probably surprised even their most vocal and most militant leaders.

Beginning in late 1847 and for the remainder of the decade, the Chiricahuas absolutely dominated Sonora's northern frontier, with little or no resistance from its armed forces. During this crucial time Gándara returned to power, and Sonora's government became more concerned about the threat of an American invasion. The Sonorans lived also in fear of an Apache-American alliance, though this was an illusory threat steeped in their own imagination. The Americans needed no assistance from the Apaches, whom they viewed with contempt, and never did invade Sonora. Instead, they chose Chihuahua as a launching point into Mexico.

Mangas Coloradas, normally associated with the Chokonen militants, was noticeably absent during most of 1847 and 1848. Because of his forceful personality, warlike reputation, and close family ties to Cochise, he had gained many recruits and allies from the Chokonen band in his war against Mexico, both before and after that time. Despite this, for some unexplained reason he did not join the Chokonens in Sonora until the fall of 1848. This would suggest that he had been in New Mexico for most of 1847–48. It was almost inconceivable that he was not active in these events. Yet if he were present, Sonora's military and civil officials would have mentioned him, because he was the most notorious Apache leader in Mexico, although the merciless Chokonen leader Miguel Narbona, fearless to the point of folly, had earned a gruesome reputation for himself in Sonora.

As mentioned earlier, reports from Sonora identified Mangas Coloradas as the leader of a band raiding south of Tepache shortly after Kirker's massacre of July 7, 1846. This foray had nothing to do with the war party that the Chiricahuas had organized to avenge Kirker's massacre—a tribal event, according to Jason Betzinez. Instead, Mangas's party struck deep into Sonora, bypassing many of the normal targets (perhaps they were out of mules, horses, and cattle), and had several clashes with Mexicans. On July 26, 1846, a group of five people left Batuc, a small village on the east bank of the Moctezuma River about forty miles south of Moctezuma, bound for Tepache, some thirty miles to the north. The trail during the first half of the trip traversed canyons and arroyos, with the Sierra Madre to the east and west. The travelers evidently made it to a hacienda called La Ranchería, where they found a grisly scene. Earlier that day the Apaches had taken possession of the ranch, owned by Francisco Blanco, and had killed the mayordomo, his wife and two children, and the six vaqueros. Before leaving, they lanced seventy head of cattle, just for devilment, and stole the rest of the mules and horses. The party from Batuc decided to go on toward Tepache, but they never made it. En route the Indians ambushed them and killed two more men, one woman, and a child. Ignacio Salvatierra somehow made his escape to Suaqui, where he brought the grim news.

Later that day a party of militia troops limped into Suaqui with the news that Mangas Coloradas's war party had attacked them and had killed their commander and six other men. Meanwhile, national guard troops from Batuc had followed the Apaches into the mountains and while attacking their temporary camp succeeded in rescuing four captives and recovering part of the stolen stock. The former captives revealed that Mangas Coloradas was in the vicinity, although they were not certain that he was at the ranchería that the Sonoran troops had surprised, which contained twenty-four warriors. The Bedonkohes and Chihennes eventually returned to New Mexico, where they heard additional details about Kirker's attack at Galeana.[1]

It would be several months before the Indians organized a war party to avenge the murders at Galeana. Meanwhile, Sonoran and Chihuahuan frontier citizens living at Moctezuma and Galeana, their confidence buoyed by Kirker's success, met in a joint council of war. A force from Sonora under José V. Barrios had left Moctezuma on July 23, 1846. Unaware of Kirker's massacre, he headed for Galeana "to plan with the Subprefect the measures that would be suitable under the circumstances by the Departments of Sonora and Chihuahua to be taken against the savages." Barrios became

ecstatic when told of Kirker's slaughter, for the scalp hunter's
actions showed a new, militant resourcefulness on Chihuahua's
part. He wrote:

> Since I learned the desire of the towns of the Department of
> Chihuahua that I visited, the enthusiasm which they showed to
> shake off the savage yoke that oppresses them, and since they had
> already taken the first step by opening hostilities against the Apaches
> at Galeana, when they killed 182 [other reports said 148] of both
> sexes and all ages. Because of this act I then believed them to be
> committed to both Departments, so I decided to lend my support to
> the campaign plan, which we agreed to there in Galeana on the 8th of
> this month [August].

He concluded his report by recommending that Sonora emulate
Chihuahua's bounty system, "since it would be a good help against
the savages."[2]

Moctezuma's military and political leaders formulated plans to
carry out this almost unprecedented spirit of cooperation between
the two states. The agreement, which contained twelve articles,
called for a one-year campaign "to pursue relentlessly" the Chiricahuas. The residents of Moctezuma, Janos, and Galeana agreed to a
progressive tax to finance the expedition. Each state would furnish
fifty men, acting in unison and stationed at Janos as long as the
Apaches remained along the northern frontier. If the Chiricahuas
moved to the Mogollons, the special force would relocate its base of
operations to Santa Rita del Cobre. It would "in all cases operate in
conjunction with the party of Don Santiago Kirker." The two
parties adopted many of the provisions of Kirker's agreement with
the governor of Chihuahua (in fact, some were exact copies). For
example, the arrangement permitted the force to divide up any
unbranded stock and other property confiscated from the Apaches.
Moreover, the participants would also "be entitled to a share of the
prize according to the scalps that they present." In Moctezuma,
public officials, including the influential José Terán y Tato, elected
José Barrios to "go in person to the higher government [governor]
and indicate to them what is needed to protect the security of these
towns, and in light of everything, and since the resources of these
towns have been absolutely exhausted, he should ask the higher
government for help with ammunition and supplies."[3]

Yet a more pressing issue soon replaced this enthusiasm to
exterminate Apaches. War had erupted between the United States

and Mexico, and that event soon brought a shifting of power and influence to Mexico's northern frontier. Sonora's and Chihuahua's priorities changed; the threat of an American military invasion concerned them more than the Apaches. Therefore, they shelved their plans of genocide, putting them temporarily on hold.

In recent years tensions had mounted between the two countries, and on April 25, 1846, when sixteen hundred Mexicans attacked a small group of U.S. citizens along a disputed region separating Texas from Mexico, open hostilities began. Mexico's troops killed three and captured several others. News of this act reached Washington on May 9, 1846; President James Knox Polk, a firm believer in manifest destiny, immediately delivered a war message to Congress, which overwhelmingly approved his decision and declared war on May 13, 1846. While General Zachary Taylor invaded Mexico from Texas, President Polk instructed Colonel (soon to be Brigadier General) Stephen Watts Kearny to organize an invasion force from Fort Leavenworth, Kansas.[4] Kearny's superiors ordered him to occupy New Mexico, then a Department of Mexico, and, once that was accomplished, to follow with an invasion of California, which the United States had in vain been trying to purchase from Mexico.[5]

Kearny had been a veteran of the frontier since 1819. Now in his early fifties, he was a highly respected officer noted for his exceptional intelligence, strict discipline, and energetic temperament. He left Kansas on June 30, 1846, with 1,568 men bound for New Mexico. Two other detachments followed him: Colonel Sterling Price with a force of 1,200 men recruited from Missouri,[6] and a unit of 500 Mormons who had volunteered at Council Bluffs, Iowa. Kearny's "Army of the West" reached Santa Fe on August 18, 1846, and promptly established a temporary government, appointing civilians to key positions. On September 25, 1846, he left for California with 300 men, guided by the mountain-wise old frontiersman Thomas "Broken Hand" Fitzpatrick.[7] He left Santa Fe to the command of Colonel Doniphan.[8]

Kearny's march followed the Rio Grande as it snaked its way south into Apachería. On October 6, 1846, about ten miles south of Socorro, the northeastern limit of Mangas's country, Kearny's command fortunately came upon the celebrated Kit Carson. The mountain man was leading a sixteen-man force on a transcontinental voyage bound for Washington with dispatches "bearing intelligence of the conquest" of California by John C. Frémont's command. Ten miles west of Santa Rita del Cobre, Carson's small

Stephen Watts Kearny, the American general who met Mangas Coloradas
in October 1846. (Courtesy Museum of New Mexico, neg. no. 7605)

party had come upon an Apache village near the future site of
Silver City. Since American soldiers were to meet Mangas near
there a few weeks later, this was certainly his camp, and he was
likely present. Carson revealed that the Chihennes "were somewhat frightened to see us. We said we were friends, were en route
to New Mexico, and wished to trade animals. They appeared
friendly . . . visited us and we commenced trading and procured of
them a remount, which was much required, our animals all having
nearly given out."[9]

Carson had no idea that American troops had occupied New
Mexico until he met Mangas's people near the copper mines. The

Chiricahuas informed him that "an American general had possession of the Territory." Carson was no stranger to that part of the
country. He had worked as a teamster for Robert McKnight at the
diggings in 1828, so he may have known Mangas Coloradas as
Fuerte. In any event, the Chihennes' friendly reception pleasantly
surprised Carson. They were "very anxious to be friendly with the
Americans and received them very cordially." On the heels of Kirker's massacre and the joint declaration of war that Moctezuma's
and Galeana's citizens had declared, the prospect of a U.S. invasion
of Mexico was music to the Indians' ears—particularly because the
Chiricahuas were planning their own expedition to avenge Kirker's
perfidious deed.[10]

Because of Carson's intelligence, Kearny decreased his force by
two-thirds, sending two hundred men back with Major Sumner,
and continued on toward California. He also rewarded Carson's
Herculean efforts by drafting him into service to retrace his steps
west to California, because he knew the country better than
Fitzpatrick did. Kearny sent "Broken Hand" to Washington with
Carson's dispatches. Hoping to meet the Indians at the Mimbres
River, the general sent Captain Henry Turner and a small force to
meet Mangas's people and assure them that the Americans were
"friendly and that they must not be alarmed."[11] They did not see
any Indians but saw many abandoned "Apache lodges scattered
about through the prairie," according to one account.[12] On October
18 they passed the deserted Santa Rita del Cobre and camped two
miles west. That evening Mangas Coloradas, "the principal chief
of the Apaches," came into camp, bringing with him one other
warrior, and met Brigadier General Kearny.[13]

This was Mangas's first recorded meeting with Americans—a
race that Mangas would come to respect and trust, people who
could inspire feelings very different from the contempt and hatred
he had toward Mexicans. The troops' discipline and order impressed
him. It became evident to him that these men were better armed,
more determined, and better fighters than their adversaries below
the border. According to eyewitnesses, he "was quite friendly" and
pledged "good faith and friendship to all Americans." After Brigadier General Kearny presented him with a few presents, Mangas
left, promising to bring in members of his band to trade mules to
Kearny's force. The next day the Americans camped at Santa Lucía,
or Mangas Springs, in a "beautiful valley, surrounded at a distance
of ten or fifteen miles, with high mountains." Mangas sent word
that he would appear the next morning with mules to trade.

He came in near mid-morning of October 20, 1846, with about thirty of his people. Mangas pledged once again "eternal friendship to the whites [who] might now pass in safety through their country." Moreover, he reiterated his abhorrence of the people to the south, declaring the Apaches' "everlasting hatred to the Mexicans." The Indians' business acumen surprised some Americans. These Apaches did not readily respond to the whites' offer of needles, thread, red shirts, and knives in exchange for their mules. The Americans quickly learned that this was not Manhattan and that they were not dealing with awestruck savages. Mangas's people were accomplished and sagacious traders in consequence of their many years of interaction with Mexican and Anglo-American traders. Thus, a surprised Captain Turner was moved to remark that "they exhibit more shrewdness in trade than we expected, and have the same provoking way of asking more when you offer what is first demanded." Nonetheless, the Apaches in exchange for goods did produce a few mules for Kearny's men.[14]

Captain Abraham Robinson Johnston mentioned that the three "principal" Chiricahua Apache chiefs west of the Rio Grande were Mangas Coloradas, Cuchillo Negro, and Lásada, who may have been Láceres, the important Nednhi leader. He also furnished a good description of Mangas's followers; undoubtedly many were Mangas's extended family group: "They ride small but fine horses. . . . They are partly clothed like the Spaniards, with wide drawers, moccasins and leggings to the knee; they carry a knife frequently in the right leggings on the outside; their moccasins have turned up square toes; their hair is long, and mostly they have no headdress; some have hats, some have fantastic helmets; they have some guns, but are mostly armed with lances and bows and arrows."[15]

Lieutenant Emory admired the Apaches' dexterity and horsemanship. Their manner of dress reminded him of "antique Grecian warriors." Most of the warriors possessed "the Mexican cartridge box, which consists of a strap round the waist, with cylinders inserted for cartridges." Before Kearny's command left Mangas's country, one chief, "eyeing the general with apparent great admiration, broke out in a vehement manner: You have taken New Mexico, and will soon take California; go then and take Chihuahua, Durango and Sonora. We will help you. . . . The Mexicans are rascals; we hate and will kill them all."[16] Kearny's army continued over the Gila Trail, bypassed Tucson and its detachment of Mexican troops, and went on to California.

Lieutenant Colonel Philip St. George Cooke and his famous "Mormon Battalion" came on Kearny's heels. Mangas had promised Kearny that he would show this command another route to take, but this proved unnecessary, as two experienced scouts, Pauline Weaver and Antoine Leroux,[17] guided Cooke's command. His army forged a new route, one that many overland travelers would follow in the late 1840s and early 1850s until the more direct route west via Apache Pass became known. His command did not encounter any Apaches as he made his way through the Chihennes' country; however, he may have met Mangas in Chokonen country. On December 2, 1846, Cooke's command encamped at the deserted San Bernardino hacienda, south of the Chiricahua Mountains. He had a few days before met the Chokonen chief Manuelito, who had promised to return with mules to trade. He kept his promise, bringing with him "a superior chief and several others." This superior chief could have been Yrigóllen, then the Chokonen band leader, or it may have been Mangas Coloradas, for five years later he told Boundary Commissioner John Russell Bartlett that he remembered Kearny and "Cooke, when they passed through this country a few years before."[18] If he did meet Cooke, likely it was immediately after or before the tribal foray against Chihuahua that had gone to avenge Kirker's massacre.[19]

Jason Betzinez, a Chiricahua Apache of the Chihenne band, wrote one of the more important books that see things from the Apache perspective. According to the eminent historian Dan Thrapp, Betzinez's book "is a prime source for the latter Apache wars, quite reliable."[20] In his remarkable account he readily conceded that his people had "little remembrance" of the Johnson massacre of 1837, and the "affair at Janos is noted mainly because my cousin Geronimo's family were killed there."[21] Yet he notes that the most serious incident recalled by his people was the massacre at Galeana (which he incorrectly placed at the Ramos hacienda). Betzinez wrote that "so far as we are concerned the ghastly butchery of our families at Ramos [Galeana] and the terrific revenge raid which followed constitute the greatest and bloodiest conflict in which Apaches were ever involved."

According to the way he heard it, some of his Chihennes had fallen victim to the slaughter. It was possible that one or more extended family groups had ventured south to Galeana to do some trading, "as had been their custom in the past." None of the Chihennes, however, were involved in the peace discussions with Ensign Cásares, for he had not identified any Chihenne leaders.

Betzinez's father may have been a son of Delgadito, a Chihenne leader who frequented northwestern Chihuahua regularly. So it was possible that he or some of his followers were present and therefore passed along the gory details as part of their oral history.[22]

In any event, shortly after the attack the survivors "straggled into the main camps of the Indians near Warm Springs." From these survivors we have a good idea of what happened:

> For many days and nights continuous wailing could be heard in the tepees and on top of the surrounding hills at daybreak each day. There was scarcely a family group that had not lost one or more of its members. The chiefs considered for a long time the action which they should take to pay back the Mexicans of Ramos [Galeana]. The problem was too serious to be decided without consultation and deliberation. But the desire for vengeance burned more fiercely as the days and weeks passed. Finally Baishan [Cuchillo Negro] the principal chief of the Warm Springs Apaches [Chihennes], called a council of the chiefs of several bands. Among those who responded were Cochise, Chief of the Chiricahuas [Chokonens], . . . Mangas Coloradas, chief of the Mimbreños, who lived near Santa Rita, and others whose names I do not recall.

As one of the Chihennes' principal band leaders, Cuchillo Negro was responsible for the organization of the war party. Mangas Coloradas was definitely involved, and so was Cochise, although he was not to be the Chokonen band leader for another decade. Miguel Narbona was then the fighting leader of the Chokonens. The war party departed from southern New Mexico. Before they left, "the chiefs announced that a great war dance would be held. Everyone in camp was invited to witness this exciting spectacle, whose purpose was to recruit volunteers for the expedition and to stir up a fighting spirit." Although this event had actually occurred before Betzinez's birth, he faithfully recorded the episode as he heard it from his elders:

> A bonfire was built at night in the center of a large cleared circle around which were gathered the onlookers. Ten paces west of the fire sat four or five men who thumped tom-toms and pounded a sheet of stiff rawhide, meanwhile singing a highpitched weird chant which may remind white people of bagpipe music—being both martial and stimulating. From time to time they would call out the name of some prominent warrior, who would then step forth from the crowd

and walk around the fire while the singers praised his bravery and deeds in battle. This was the signal for other Indians who wished to take the warpath to join this man in the promenade and later to serve under his leadership during the raid.

Finally when it seemed likely that all brave and eligible fighters had joined the war party, the men would form a line on the opposite side of the circle from the drummers then advance toward the latter in a succession of leaps, zig-zagging as if in a real assault. Brandishing their weapons they would approach the musicians then stop, yell, and shoot their guns or bows and arrows over the heads of the singers. It was realistic and exhilarating, especially to young boys who, just as today's children, loved to stage sham battles in imitation of their elders.

Following the dance the warriors commenced preparing for the invasion of Mexico. New bows and arrows were made, ammunition procured for the few available firearms, and extra moccasins and food supplies prepared.

"Several months elapsed" before the warriors departed for Chihuahua in, according to Betzinez, the fall after the massacre, thus placing it in the fall of 1846. If he is right, it must have been in November, because Mangas Coloradas met various American officials in October in New Mexico. It took the war party, which numbered 175 men and several novices, only a few days to get into position to attack the town. Cuchillo Negro planned the attack, assigning to each band specific targets on which to make their assault. As they made their charge, "thoughts of dead kinfolk" were in the minds of the men, and in the excitement they forgot the "plans and orders." These men wanted revenge, and that meant Mexican blood. The warriors swarmed out like angry hornets to do battle, occupying the town and its plaza. Yet the much maligned Mexican troops gave them a hot reception, killing several Indians early in the battle. Despite this unexpected opposition, the Apaches fought like "tigers." Finally the troops broke and ran, and the mounted Indians "galloped after them and impaled them in the back with lances."

The Chiricahua victory was complete, and despite the Apaches' fatalities (Betzinez incorrectly believed that Mexican gunfire had killed Cuchillo Negro during the battle), the men returned to New Mexico, "their spirits high."[23] The informants of Morris Opler described the Chiricahuas' victory celebration: "When the men come into sight, all the women gather and give their call of applause." The chiefs distributed the horses and cattle to "everyone who took part" in the foray. Then, a victory dance and feast was held, which could last for four days and nights. The leader called upon his men to reenact their feats during the battle. Then the entire camp celebrated with a dance called the round or victory dance, which they called "they come in with the enemy." It was a time for great celebration and rejoicing, especially if the warriors of the camp had returned victorious without sustaining casualties.[24]

Betzinez declared that "the men who took part in this battle, especially those who were my kinsmen, later told me that everyone agreed that this was the greatest of Apache victories. . . . The whole tribe were tremendously proud of their fighting men and for years thereafter loved to hear the stories of the battle retold." Mangas Coloradas, Cochise, and Delgadito, three of the primary war chiefs, much enhanced their reputation among their people in the battle, although it would have been difficult for Mangas's prestige to have risen any higher in 1846, for he was already the most influential leader in the tribe.[25]

Unfortunately, Chihuahuan sources during 1846–48 contain no information about this "revenge raid." The Janos records also are sparse for this period, and the official newspaper of the state devoted its coverage almost exclusively to political events or the war against the United States. Yet we may have a hint of the battle from an American officer whose journey took him through Galeana. First Lieutenant Cave Johnson Couts of the First United States Dragoons visited Galeana in September 1848 and observed that it "had been quite a town, but now much dilapidated. The inhabitants very white, [were] deadly hostile with the surrounding Indians. They boast upon killing some one hundred and fifty Indians about two years since at one time, but it was twenty-five Americans, who happened here at the time, and who did all the killing and fighting." He may have heard a reference to the Chiricahua war party. He heard that "the Great men of Galeana and the Great men of Chihuahua in concourse assembled were dispersed and chased to their homes by the Indians." According to his information, this incident took place in the fall of 1847, but he does not mention significant casualties on either side.[26] In May 1849, Thomas Durivage, a correspondent for the *New Orleans Daily Picayune*, passed through Galeana, which he described as "once a flourishing spot but the Indians have been its ruin and impoverished its wealthiest citizens."[27] It would appear that some major Chiricahua attack occurred between the summer of 1846 and early 1848. Some of Betzinez's facts were vague; still, his story, as he heard it from his elders, was an honest reconstruction of an event that undoubtedly occurred and had become etched in the oral traditions of the Chiricahuas.

For the next two years the activities of Mangas Coloradas are difficult to trace. In early March 1847 a large Chiricahua war party, composed primarily of Chokonens under Miguel Narbona, Yrigóllen, and Esquinaline allied with some Nednhis under Láceres and the Bedonkohes led by Teboca, killed twenty-five persons near Fronteras and Bacoachi. The presence of Teboca, at times called Mangas Coloradas's *segundo* (second in command), merits discussion. Why was Mangas not with the Bedonkohes? For years he had led them on virtually every expedition into Sonora. Yrigóllen may have unwittingly answered this question a few weeks later when he appeared at Fronteras carrying a white flag to indicate that he wished to parley.[28]

Three of Fronteras's most important men—Deciderio Escalante, the justice of the peace; Antonio Narbona, a retired military officer; and presidio commander Captain Mateo Calvo y Muro—bravely left the safety of the fort to converse with the Indians, who just a few weeks before had killed fourteen citizens from their town. Every leader wanted peace, claimed Yrigóllen, who spoke for his Chokonen band, Láceres's Janeros group of Nednhis, and Teboca's Bedonkohes. In light of the recent murders, Escalante favored military action, but Elías González, ever concerned about an Apache-American alliance, agreed to an armistice. As Sonora's commander of the northern frontier, he hastened to Fronteras and soon deduced why it was the Apaches seemed so anxious to make a truce.[29]

Illness and disease plagued the U.S. occupation force of New Mexico. These conditions had overextended the capacity of the military hospital at Santa Fe. Many deaths had occurred because of scurvy and measles. One American who visited the post cemetery in May 1847 noted that measles was the cause of most of the fatalities.[30] In any event, from their contact with Americans, the Chiricahuas had contracted measles, and the disease had infested the band. Moreover, the mescal harvest was approaching. The last thing they wanted to worry about was a Sonoran campaign at the very time they were occupied in gathering mescal, a time when their women and children were exposed to danger. Therefore, they solicited peace with Sonora. If the Chokonens, who had less con-tact with Americans and Mexicans than Mangas's Chihennes, suffered the effects of these contagious diseases, it was surely the case that Mangas's followers had likewise become infected.[31]

Mangas may have raided Sonora during the summer of 1847. In July a war party of one hundred Bedonkohes established a base camp in the Oposura Mountains, from where they dispatched several raiding parties in search of horses. According to the testimony of Francisco Acuña, who escaped after a captivity of almost five years, these Apaches had come from the Mogollon Mountains in New Mexico. Furthermore, they were friends of the Americans, with whom they had recently traded mules and other items. Unfortunately, because Acuña failed to mention the specific leaders, it cannot be definitely determined whether Mangas was present or not.[32]

In September, Antonio Narbona led an expedition into the Chiricahua Mountains that succeeded in capturing and then executing an old woman near Cave Creek. Colonel Narbona talked with Miguel Narbona and Esquinaline, who offered to meet the next day and make peace. The Indians reneged on their promise, however. The Mexican colonel's senseless execution of the old woman should never have occurred; the Chokonens would not forget this incident. That fall a campaign from Moctezuma captured members of Yrigóllen's family and further incensed the Chokonen band leader. Less than three months later, on December 23, 1847, the Chokonens would assault Antonio Narbona's hometown of Cuquiarachi, a few miles southwest of Fronteras, killing thirteen people, including the popular commander on the porch of his house, and capturing six children. According to local lore, as told to James Box, who heard the story in 1854 at Fronteras, the colonel had been "decoyed" by an Apache whom his family had adopted as a boy, a clear reference to Miguel Narbona. The remaining citizens abandoned the town, which the Spanish had established in 1654.[33]

In early 1848 the Chokonens organized another foray into Sonora, with members of the Bedonkohes, Chihennes, and some White Mountain Apaches from the Western Apache tribe uniting for the expedition. Again, they had vengeance on their minds, for they were "all stirred up" by the Galeana massacre and "would find a way to get revenge." There was no mention of Mangas Coloradas; indeed, the only reason we know anything about which Apaches were involved is because of the testimony of Manuel Bernal, a resident of Chinapa, whom the Indians had captured but who soon escaped from his captors. Bernal furnished many fascinating details of the Chiricahuas' frame of mind, all emanating from the mouth of the incorrigible Miguel Narbona, an erstwhile ally of Mangas Coloradas.

The Apache war party struck the small village of Chinapa, an old mission settlement established in 1648 on the Sonora River midway between Arispe and Bacoachi. Although Chinapa had been a frequent target of Indian raids, no one in Sonora could have anticipated the size and results of this incursion. Again, the Indians' primary objective was captives; they planned to use them to exchange for their people held in Sonora and Chihuahua. The Apaches, all on foot, "attacked the town in great numbers and by surprise" at 11:00 A.M. on February 18, 1848. The Indians killed twelve persons, wounded six, and captured an astonishing forty-two persons. Before leaving, they burned most of the town. Manuel Bernal claimed that the Apaches did not kill him because he showed no fear; instead, they "made him walk with his hands bound." After seven days of walking, he found himself near San Bernardino, south of the Chiricahua Mountains. During the night, while his guards slept, "he managed to untie himself and with greatest possible stealth, he left the camp without being heard." He somehow made his way to Fronteras. Captain Calvo y Muro sent him to Bacoachi, where local officials interviewed him. It seemed incredible that the Apaches would not kill an adult male and that a prisoner could escape his warrior captors.

Bernal did reveal important information about the Chiricahuas. He apparently knew the Chokonen war leader Miguel Narbona, who had spoken freely and haughtily about their recent campaigns and their plans. Miguel boasted that their next targets would be Bacoachi, and after that Ures and Sinoquipe. The Chokonens were "in alliance with the Janeros and Sierra Blanca band," meaning the Nednhis and the White Mountain Western Apaches. They also wanted to avenge a recent campaign from Moctezuma that had captured members of Yrigóllen's family. Yrigóllen had tucked his camp away in the Chiricahua Mountains. He had sent out the war party with instructions to "carry off captives in order to trade for his family." After they reached Yrigóllen's camp, one part of the war party (Bedonkohes) headed for the Mogollons and another part (Western Apaches) for the White Mountains in Arizona. It would appear that the Bedonkohes were with the Chokonens, who had even summoned the White Mountain band of Western Apaches to join them in their foray. Still there was no mention of Mangas Coloradas, although the Bedonkohes, whom he led during times of war, seem to have been involved.[34]

In 1847 and 1848, Sonora became even more vulnerable to Apaches. The return of Santa Anna to power in late 1846 marked the return of the federalist system to Mexico and Sonora. In January 1847, Luis Redondo, a relative of Manuel María Gándara, was picked to act as governor until the state could hold new elections. In February 1847, American troops invaded Chihuahua, a move which greatly alarmed Sonoran officials. Its legislature conferred unprecedented authority on Acting Governor Redondo, and one of his first moves was to reinstate the ubiquitous Elías González as commander in charge of defending Sonora from an invasion by the United States. The election of Manuel María Gándara as governor ended Redondo's tenure in May 1847. A U.S. blockade of Guaymas that began in the fall of 1847 and lasted until June 1848 soon became a big problem for Gándara. The siege was an economic disaster for Sonora. Deprived of hard currency and income because it was unable to collect import or export taxes and duties, the state faced impending bankruptcy. Furthermore, the fiscal chaos seriously affected its armed forces, especially its northern presidios, and forced the government to eliminate the wheat ration. And of course the state government had to hold back paychecks to its soldiers. For most of 1848, the garrisons at Tucson, Santa Cruz, and Fronteras threatened mass desertions or mutiny.[35]

In March 1848, after receiving the news about Cuquiarachi and Chinapa, Governor Gándara requested the state militia at Moctezuma and other towns to cooperate with Elías González's presidio soldiers. The governor, nearly frantic, noted that his state "finds itself exasperated because it is unable to attend with the quickness that we would like to the wars against the barbarians because of the shortage of resources in which we have been placed by the blockade at Guaymas." Yet because the war with the United States was ending, he was optimistic that the Americans would soon lift the siege. Then he vowed that "I shall be able to organize the forces and personally go to these places in order to plan the campaigns . . . until the enemy surrenders and promises obedience."[36] A few months later Manuel Gándara wrote the minister of war in Mexico City that the northern presidios, if fully staffed and equipped, could defeat the Apaches in three months, provided they did not find refuge on the northern side of the Gila, which was now United States territory.[37]

Still later, Gándara was forced to admit that the Apaches had extended their raids to the suburbs of Hermosillo; moreover, the Apaches had recently murdered José Victor Barrios and Juan

Campoy, two of Moctezuma's leading citizens who had helped organize the Moctezuma-Galeana compact of August 1846. Like an astute politician, Gándara wrote a scathing letter to Mexico City absolving himself of responsibility for the resurgence in hostilities. Instead, he attributed Sonora's plight to the policies in effect during Urrea's administration.[38] Little did he realize that the Chiricahua domination of Sonora was just beginning to take hold. If affairs in Sonora were bad in the spring of 1848, conditions would further deteriorate that summer and into 1849 and 1850, despite the ending of hostilities with the United States.

In the summer of 1848, Mangas Coloradas left the Gila country for northeastern Sonora. Why did he jettison his plans and move from New Mexico to Sonora? A dramatic incident certainly had something to do with that decision. On June 21, 1848, during a skirmish at Fronteras, Mexicans had inexplicably captured Cochise, his son-in-law, who was immediately "put in irons and shackled." Next they placed him in the calaboose, in actuality a man-made cave about twenty feet long that Mexicans had excavated from the side of the hill underneath the presidio.[39] Cochise remained a prisoner for about six weeks. Naturally the Chokonens wanted their important leader returned; consequently, during the summer of 1848 they laid siege to the town. Citizens feared to work their fields, and small parties dared not venture out from the safety of the fort. In late July the Chokonen chiefs, looking for prisoners, turned the screws even tighter, moving their large camp to within a mile of Fronteras. No supplies or parties were entering or leaving the fort. By August 7, 1848, the inhabitants were reduced to eating tortillas, the only food available. Finally, Captain Calvo y Muro allowed a group of twenty-three soldiers and citizens to leave the presidio to bring provisions. They had gone about ten miles when the Chiricahuas ambushed them at Cuchuta, killing or capturing the entire party except Jesús Escalante, who escaped to Fronteras after the Indians wounded him.

In response, Captain Calvo y Muro dispatched a relief party to Cuchuta. The Indians were waiting; they had killed eleven men in their ambush but had captured eleven men, including five soldiers, whom they offered to trade for Cochise. José Yescas, a soldier whom the Chiricahuas trusted, conversed with Chino and Posito Moraga, who offered to bring in their hostages for Cochise. The deal was consummated on August 11, 1848. Some ten days later the residents of Fronteras abandoned their homes and crops for Bacoachi. Many of its soldiers were absent on a scout with Ensign

Cochise. A recently discovered painting which is purportedly of Cochise, Chokonen band leader and son-in-law of Mangas Coloradas. (Photo courtesy Charles Parker)

Saturnino Limón.[40] Limón discovered that the famished soldiers had little stomach for the expedition, which had so far accomplished nothing but exhaust supplies and wear out the horses. By the time they returned to Fronteras, Sonora's oldest presidio had become a virtual ghost town. The presidio troops followed the citizens to Bacoachi, which would become their homes for the next two years.[41]

At no time had any report mentioned Mangas Coloradas during the negotiations for his son-in-law; he was ostensibly en route from New Mexico to Sonora. Once there, he did not return to his local

Prison at Fronteras, Sonora. Still visible today, this is most likely the place where Cochise was imprisoned for six weeks in the summer of 1848. (Author's photo)

group territory until the summer of 1849. Apparently he had developed some apprehensions of Americans, although not because of any recorded hostile encounters. For one thing, Anglo and Mexican traders in New Mexico exercised a tremendous amount of influence over their partners in commerce. They were consummate propaganda agents, frequently passing along either misleading or untrue information designed to further their own self-interests. Their conduct had sown hostility and distrust when Kearny's efforts had encouraged friendship. These men "go where they please without being subject to the slightest risk," remarked James S. Calhoun, recently appointed Indian agent of New Mexico. He wondered, "Why is it that these traders have no fears, no apprehensions, and pass in every direction through the country roamed over by the Comanches, Apaches, Navahos and Utahs unharmed in person and property . . . ?"[42] According to some reports, these merchants had warned the Apaches that the Americans, now that they had conquered New Mexico, were going to snap the whip at the Apaches. Mangas had undoubtedly noticed their presence in the Socorro area, and there were rumors that a garrison might be placed near Santa Rita del Cobre. These reports must have perplexed him, for Kearny had not mentioned the placing of American posts in his country.

Another rumor more disturbing to the Apaches, which turned out to be true, was that the terms of the Treaty of Guadalupe Hidalgo,[43] by which Mexico formally ceded New Mexico and California to the United States, had also obliged U.S. troops to prevent hostile Indians from entering Mexico to commit depredations. Most well-meaning American officials would ignore this requirement, realizing that it was a condition impossible to enforce. In addition, the U.S. government agreed to indemnify Mexican citizens for Indian depredations that originated from the United States, a condition that Agent Calhoun correctly pointed out could cost "millions, on account of the doings of the Mexican Apaches whose deeds will be charged to those on our side."[44] The treaty also compelled U.S. officials to return any Mexican captives in the hands of Indians. Yet the few times Americans enforced this article, it became a stumbling block in relations, for the Apaches could not comprehend why they had to return their captives, whom they had obtained during legitimate warfare, according to a treaty that they had not agreed to when Mexico continued to hold hostage many of their people.

Finally, Mangas Coloradas may have been disinclined to meet Americans, whether friendly or not, especially if they had brought contagious diseases to his people. Once in Mexico, his followers joined other bands at Alisos Canyon,[45] twenty-five miles south of the Enmedio range, where an extraordinarily large Chiricahua village was later found to contain three separate rancherías and several hundred wickiups, according to one eyewitness. These factors probably formed his decision to leave Santa Lucía Springs and Santa Rita del Cobre for Sonora, but the crowning blow was likely the plight of his son-in-law Cochise.[46]

Two Apaches, apparently members of his band, furnished another possible explanation. On September 10, 1848, a Sonoran patrol from Bavispe under Captain Sebastián Reyes captured two Apaches, a man and a woman, in the Espuelas Mountains. The couple had left their camp on the Gila eight days earlier in search of Mangas Coloradas, because they had heard that Shawnee and Delaware Indians who were members of Kirker's scalp hunters had come to Apachería with an American group seeking Apache blood.[47] Whatever Mangas's motives, he and his followers would remain with Miguel Narbona and Cochise's Chokonens and Teboca's Bedonkohes for much of the next two years.

For the duration of 1848 the Chiricahuas remained along the border. In September the Apaches broke up their large ranchería at Alisos Canyon. Some Indians moved north into the Animas and Hatchet Mountains in extreme southwestern New Mexico. Others, likely the Nednhis, moved into the Boca Grande range in northwest Chihuahua. The Chokonens also split up: some moved north into the Chiricahua Mountains; others moved west to Turicachi, from where they sent Chino, a brother of Posito Moraga, to Bacoachi to solicit peace. Captain Calvo y Muro requested instructions from his superiors on whether he should "enter into peace with them or . . . wage a formal campaign in the area where Chino said the encampments were located." When Chino failed to return, Calvo y Muro organized a scout to Turicachi, but he found that the Indians had moved north toward the Peloncillo and Chiricahua Mountains. In reality, the Chokonens had no intentions of returning or making peace; Chino's visit was mainly to gather intelligence and trade for whiskey.[48]

The Apaches would deal Sonora one final blow before the end of 1848. A war party hit Tubac, "a collection of dilapidated buildings and huts,"[49] and killed nine people and spread so much terror that the remaining residents abandoned the town. Most moved to San Xavier, some went to Tucson, and some returned to Sonora, while others opted for the gold fields of California, which were fast becoming an attractive place to many of Sonora's frontier residents. The redoubtable Elías González, whom Mexico City had recently named the military inspector of Sonora, became livid when he heard the news. He immediately ordered Captain Comadurán at Tucson to send twenty soldiers to reoccupy Tubac. Comadurán diplomatically demurred; other problems occupied his thoughts. Besides, he reasoned that his cousin's order made little military or practical sense, because Tubac's inhabitants had fled in horror. Those still in the vicinity had no intention of returning. Anyway, his own troops at Tucson were threatening to desert rather than reoccupy the abandoned town.[50]

Elías González did not know whether Tubac's attackers were Western Apaches, Chiricahua Apaches, or perhaps a combination of both tribes. It was an area raided frequently by both groups. But it mattered little from his point of view. By the end of 1848 the Chiricahua Apaches dominated Sonora's northern frontier. Large war parties roamed the state with impunity, systematically striking

Tubac, Arizona. A frequent target of both Western and Chiricahua Apache war parties, Tubac was finally abandoned in December 1848 but was resettled a few years later. (Browne, *Adventures in the Apache Country*)

the settlements and presidios along the frontier. Their siege had forced the citizens of Fronteras to desert that presidio, which had been a fixture in Apachería for over 250 years. With their spirits and confidence high, the Chiricahuas planned to continue their offensive in 1849. Even the intractable Mangas Coloradas had joined the militant Chokonens, led by Miguel Narbona and Cochise. Elías González was uneasy, awaiting the next explosion. The Chiricahuas happily obliged him. The first six months of 1849 would provide more of the same. He and other Sonoran militia or national guard commanders, like José Terán y Tato from Moctezuma and Eusebio Samaniego from Bavispe, would retaliate. Chihuahua, lacking presidio soldiers, reverted to its long-standing experiment of hiring mercenaries. For Mangas, who had avoided Mexico for much of 1847–48, the next two years would mean more war activity than he had experienced at any time since the conflict between the Chiricahuas and Sonora had erupted at Fronteras in June 1843.

Chapter 8

MANGAS COLORADAS
MUST BE KILLED

IN early 1849, Mangas Coloradas's Santa Lucía local group and Delgadito's Mimbres local group of Chihennes, Teboca's Bedonkohes, and the Chokonens under a host of capable war chiefs, with Miguel Narbona the most bellicose and most vocal, began a six-month reign of terror against Sonora. It mattered little whether the settlement was a small village, large city, or even a presidio—none was immune from the war parties, whose intrepidity and courage mounted with each success. In the spring of 1849, Chiricahua war parties would attack the three remaining presidios of northern Sonora: Bacoachi, Santa Cruz, and Bavispe. Despite these victories, part of the Chiricahua tribe, the peace bloc, notably the Nednhis under Coleto Amarillo, some Chihennes under Ponce and Cigarrito, and a few Chokonens under Manuelito, resumed negotiations at Janos with Lieutenant Baltazar Padilla. Besides their apprehension of Americans who were coming in greater numbers into their country, they claimed that bad blood existed between them and the hostile element, especially Mangas Coloradas. Manuelito insisted that Mangas Coloradas and Delgadito were the major obstacles to peace. In a startling announcement, he suggested that if Chihuahua truly wanted a stable peace, its forces would have to murder these two leaders, something Manuelito claimed that he had tried to do in the past without success.[1] His remarks seem self-serving, for his fellow Chokonens Miguel Narbona and Cochise were just as militant as Mangas Coloradas and he was not critical of them.

These Chiricahuas at Janos also expressed what had become a tribal sentiment: they had become apprehensive of Americans, many of them adventurers traveling through Chiricahua country bound for the California gold fields.[2] The initial feelings of goodwill between Kearny and Mangas Coloradas had turned sour. Apaches and Americans had shared a common enemy in Mexico, but now, with that war ended, the Americans and Mexicans were friends. Thus, to the Apaches the Americans must logically be their enemies, and they now perceived these newcomers as intruders into Apachería. Some Americans had even dared to prospect at Santa Rita del Cobre, which had lain abandoned for over a decade, although the Chihenne and Bedonkohe leaders had forbidden whites from attempting this practice. Yet the Chiricahuas also feared and respected American troops, who in 1849 began to make their presence felt at Santa Rita del Cobre and Doña Ana, a Mexican village situated on the Rio Grande five miles north of Las Cruces.

In January 1849 the Chiricahuas launched a major expedition against Sonora. In the two weeks between January 10 and January 23, they would kill virtually everyone in their path, some ninety-eight Sonorans, wound many others, and take many captives. They followed the vast Sierra Madre almost 150 miles into Sonora before striking southwest toward Alamos, which they bypassed in favor of a ranch named Duraznilla, located about midway between Hermosillo and Sahuaripa, about fifteen miles west of Nacori and thirty-five miles southeast of Sonora's state capital, Ures. At dawn on January 10, 1849, a war party of one hundred warriors, most on foot, attacked and burned the smaller structures of the hacienda. Before they left, they killed two children, four women, and ten men, most of whom were Opata and Yaqui Indians serving as vaqueros on the ranch. The survivors took refuge in the main hacienda while the Apaches systematically looted the ranch of its stock before heading northeast with their plunder toward the Mazatan Mountains.[3]

At Alamos, two men had seen the immense war party as it had maneuvered its way around the town toward Duraznilla. With most of the Indians on foot, the two mounted men easily eluded the Apaches. Reaching Alamos, they reported to Luis Tánori, an Opata Indian from a prominent Alamos family who was the commander of the national guard militia. He rounded up a force and went to the mountains, where he remained in ambush for two days before returning to Alamos. He arrived there the same day the Indians hit Duraznilla. Receiving news of the raid, Tánori at once left with thirty-six men to lay a trap along the "route which the

Apaches were to come by." The Apaches approached about mid-morning on January 11, 1849. Tánori's party could see them coming some four or five miles away from where he had set his ambush. His men "took the time to entrench and fortify themselves." Tánori, bound by "honor and duty," opted to engage the enemy despite their "superiority in numbers." Unbeknownst to him, the Apaches were well-armed, well-provisioned, and equipped with many rifles. They were driving some eight hundred to one thousand horses and mules when Tánori unveiled his ambuscade. After Tánori's first volley, the Indians abandoned their booty, regrouped, and poured a withering fire into Tánori's force, compelling him to retire to a more secure position on higher ground, but not before he left behind seven dead and seven wounded, four seriously. Two of these would later succumb to their wounds. Tánori believed that he had done some damage to the Apaches but did not know how much until after the battle. His discovery horrified him, though it had its equals in barbarity and savagery in outrages committed earlier by Mexicans on helpless Apaches. In the deserted Apache positions he found the corpses of nine Mexicans, whom the Indians had brutally murdered after the attack. According to Apache custom, the Indians had avenged their losses, executing nine of their captives.[4]

The next day, on January 12, 1849, this war party encountered a group of national guard troops from Ures at a place called Cecoral. Details are sparse, but we do know that during the fierce battle the Indians, incensed at their casualties in the Tánori fight, succeeded in killing another twenty-three soldiers and wounded sixteen others.[5]

The victorious Apaches continued their march northeast, heading toward the Moctezuma River, killing and raiding as they worked their way back to their base camps in northeast Sonora. After lying low for about a week, on January 22 they assaulted the Casas Grandes ranch, outside Tepachi, and killed three women, three men, and one child. They also captured five women and two children. Soon after, the remaining citizens evacuated the hacienda. As the Apaches continued their retreat north, their war party now swelled to two hundred, national guard troops from Cumpas ambushed them; another thirty-four men lost their lives to the Apache lance, bow, and rifle. Among the dead was Francisco Terán y Tato, the brother of José Terán y Tato, the important military commander from Moctezuma.[6]

All told, this war party, undoubtedly Chiricahuas, although no one in Sonora had identified any particular group or leader, killed ninety-eight people, wounded twenty-two, and captured seven women and children between January 9 and January 24, and these numbers include only the victims reported to the governor.[7] If they were Chiricahuas, their war leaders were Miguel Narbona, who seemed to have an insatiable desire for Sonoran blood, and Mangas Coloradas. These two men, with Cochise as a rising war chief, would be fixtures in northern Sonora for much of 1849 and 1850.

Sonora's Acting Governor Juan Gándara was furious at the disaster, lashing out at Elías González. Besides Fronteras and Tubac, Cocospera and Oputo (long a favorite Chiricahua target) had also been abandoned by their residents.[8] Juan Gándara implored Sonora's military commander to take action. Elías González responded by blaming the administration of Manuel María Gándara for not addressing the problems of the frontier, especially for ignoring the presidios. He challenged Acting Governor Gándara to provide adequate resources so that he could mount a major offensive against the Apaches. They had another significant dilemma to confront: many residents of the northern frontier were leaving for the California gold fields, thus further depleting the frontier of men and arms.[9]

Apache raids continued through February. Bands of warriors hit Arispe, Huepac, Baviacora, and Huasabas, killing another twelve persons.[10] When Acting Governor Gándara received information that the citizens of Cumpas were contemplating deserting their town, he immediately requested that Elías González dispatch troops to Cumpas. He suggested that Sonora's commanding general order the troops formerly stationed at Fronteras (now garrisoned at Bacoachi) to Cumpas to afford it protection. Elías González, never a bootlicker, summarily refused this recommendation. In a well-reasoned explanation, he wrote:

With sadness I have learned . . . of the sad situation in which the well-deserving town of Cumpas finds itself, and it is with even greater regret that I must explain to you in response that it is not in my power to comply with your wish that I should have the garrison's company from Fronteras move to occupy that place until it is in position to return to its natural location. . . . When there will be resources to supply it, it will be more just and better for the whole state that it occupy its abandoned garrison, by which means Cumpas will also be protected. [Furthermore] the Company of Fronteras, even if it were redeployed, is too poor to move to another post, since they do not have horses or saddles, or especially the necessary resources to feed themselves, and would leave their families in the same situation at Bacoachi.[11]

About this time Elías González wrote the secretary of war in Mexico City asking for economic assistance. On March 26, 1849, the federal government sent him a draft for eleven thousand pesos, instructing him to supply the presidios and mount and feed its soldiers. On May 2, soon after receiving these funds, the astute commander announced his intention to reoccupy Fronteras and Tubac.[12]

By then matters in Sonora could not have been much worse, it seemed, but they continued to deteriorate. First, in early March a Chokonen-Bedonkohe war party led by Miguel Narbona and Mangas Coloradas pillaged the settlements along the Sonora River south of Arispe. Both men had established their rancherías that spring in the Chiricahua Mountains, a secure base from which to raid into Sonora. Their primary target was Bacachi, a small Opata settlement located a few miles east of the mining town of Bana-michi. Whether by design or not, they chose an opportune time to attack. Only a few days earlier thirty men had left the area for the California gold mines. Eight of them were from Bacachi, the target of Mangas Coloradas's and Miguel Narbona's war party. The first assault saw the Indians cutting down everyone in their path; the Apaches killed seven men and five women and wounded five other men. They captured four men, ten women, and several children, including Merejildo Grijalva,[13] who during the 1860s and 1870s would become a famous army scout against the Chiricahuas, and a young girl named Marijenia Figueira. Before they left, they burned the town. At Banamichi, a few miles away, authorities were too afraid to send out a rescue party, though they could see the smoke from the burning haciendas. Instead, a party of national guard troops from Huepac and Aconchi rushed to the scene and dis-covered an appalling picture. The buildings were smoldering and corpses were scattered around the ranch. They buried the bodies and followed the Apache trail north to Sinoquipe, at which point they turned back and returned home.[14]

Fortunately, we have the accounts of two captives whom the Apaches took during this raid: Merejildo Grijalva and Marijenia Figueira, both children then who would remain with the Apaches for ten and fifteen years, respectively. The Chokonens adopted Grijalva into the band of Miguel Narbona; the Bedonkohes took Figueira, and she would become a member of Louis's family. Louis was likely a son of Mangas Coloradas. Fifteen years later Figueira would recall that during her years in captivity she had "been treated well." According to Grijalva, one division of the war party returned to Miguel Narbona's village in the Chiricahua Mountains. The other probably went to Pitaicache, where Mexican officials believed that Mangas Coloradas had located his base camp. About a month later Mangas would join his Chokonen relatives and move his camp to the Chiricahuas.[15]

Sonora's troubles mounted during the spring of 1849. The allied Chiricahuas had made plans to attack its three remaining presidios in Chiricahua country: Bavispe, Santa Cruz, and Bacoachi. Mangas Coloradas was probably involved in the affair at Bavispe on April 8, 1849, when two parties, each containing about fifty warriors, assaulted the presidio, killing two old men, one woman, and one child while capturing four children. Ten days later one captive appeared at Bavispe, saying that the Apache ranchería was at Pitaicache, which the Nednhi leader Coleto Amarillo had told Lieutenant Padilla at Janos was the site of Mangas Coloradas's ranchería.[16]

Their next target was Santa Cruz, which they surprised on April 29, but the arrival of troops and citizens prevented any damage. The next day two parties of courageous men left the presidio to work in their fields, each a few miles away—one to the north and the other to the south. That morning the Indians jumped one group, and within minutes seven citizens lay dead. The raiders also took most of the presidio's stock. Their audacity compelled eighteen families to emigrate for the interior, and the commander, Ensign Saturnino Limón,[17] predicted that many more could follow. The only Apache identified was Teboquita, a minor Chokonen local group leader. Later reports suggested that this raid had been a Bedonkohe-Chokonen venture with Mangas Coloradas, Miguel Narbona, and Yrigóllen likely involved.[18]

Less than a month later the Chokonens set their sights on Bacoachi, which they stormed "in great numbers" on May 24, 1849. Mangas was apparently not with them, for he had left the large Apache village at Pitaicache to harvest mescal in the Chiricahuas. In their first sweep, they seriously wounded two men and carried off a great deal of stock. Captain Teodoro López de Aros quickly gathered a party of thirty troops and citizens and pursued the fleeing Indians west, but the Indians abruptly halted and launched a counterattack. Outnumbering the Mexicans by a three-to-one margin, the Apaches in a sudden attack forced de Aros's men to flee, but not before the warriors had killed two soldiers and two citizens and had captured two men, a presidio soldier named Julian Romero and a citizen named Félix Montoya. The inevitable parley occurred shortly after, with Yrigóllen, Chino, and Casimiro representing the Chokonens, who inexplicably claimed that they would return in twenty days with their families to make a peace treaty, though de Aros did not believe their yarn.[19]

Little did the Apaches realize, as they returned to their camps in northeast Sonora, that Sonoran troops from the district of Moctezuma, led by an indefatigable officer, José Terán y Tato, had challenged the Chiricahuas' eighteen-month reign of victory after victory and total supremacy of Sonora's northern frontier. Like the Chiricahuas, Terán y Tato also had revenge on his mind; Apaches had killed his brother Francisco in combat near Cumpas during the January onslaught. His second-in-command was Eusebio Samaniego.

Terán y Tato had set to work marshaling troops and supplies for the expedition after the Apache assault of Bavispe on April 8, 1849. Luis García had taken a patrol to the Pitaicache Mountains in mid-April but felt his small force insufficient to penetrate the mountains, where he believed several Apache rancherías were situated. The presidio commander at Bavispe, Captain Sebastián Reyes, had concluded that the Chiricahuas who were living near Teras, Pitaicache, and Batepito had moved their camps near the deserted presidio of Fronteras.[20] Other groups, including Mangas Coloradas, had apparently moved north toward Arizona and New Mexico. García notified Terán y Tato, commander of Sonora's national guard, and the latter decided to take action.

On May 5, 1849, Terán y Tato left Moctezuma with 118 men and a small piece of artillery, planning to scout Pitaicache and Batepito, "where I have been informed that the Indian rancherías can be found." He enlisted recruits en route to Bavispe, which he left on May 14, his army swelled to 188 men. In the early morning of May 18 his scouts struck a fresh trail, which they followed along the Yaqui River toward Batepito, located about four miles northwest of today's Colonia Morelos. At 6:00 A.M. they found the "ranchería of San Juan," actually an extended family camp, which was one of several base camps for the Chokonen war party that had headed for Bacoachi. Therefore, at the time of the attack there were few men in camp, a condition which disappointed Terán y Tato, who was itching for a good fight. During the first volley the Mexican fire killed several Chiricahuas, all women and children. The few men in camp fought a stubborn rear-guard action to cover the withdrawal of their loved ones, who were heading for the woods and higher ground. San Juan, a noted fighter, mounted his horse and charged the Mexicans, but he met his match in the equally courageous Eusebio Samaniego, who thrust his lance through his adversary's body. Samaniego also shot another warrior in the fight. All told, the Mexicans killed three men and seven women and children; they also captured nine Indians, one man and eight women and children; one of the women was the wife of the Chokonen war leader Demos. Although in the words of Terán y Tato it was only a "small victory," it was nevertheless one of the few military setbacks that the Chokonens had suffered in recent years.[21]

Terán y Tato gathered important information from his prisoners about the Chiricahuas' movements, in particular those of Mangas Coloradas. They revealed that Mangas had indeed moved his camp to the Chiricahua Mountains in Arizona. The Apache captives also admitted that they had recently returned from a trading expedition at Janos and were planning to return there shortly. A few weeks later another former captive, Francisco Durán, would testify to Captain Sebastián Reyes at Bavispe that the Indians had gathered in the Animas and Hatchet Mountains in New Mexico a large war party that was on an eight-day binge from whiskey that they had received from Janos officials and New Mexican traders. They planned to launch a foray against the villages along the Sonora and Moctezuma Rivers.[22]

While the warlike factions had been raiding Sonora during the winter and spring of 1849, the moderate groups of the Chokonen, Chihenne, and Nednhi bands had been negotiating at Janos with Lieutenant Baltazar Padilla. Their statements clearly showed that the two factions, the militant and pacific blocs, had quarreled. Clearly, Mangas Coloradas and Delgadito led the former faction; Coleto Amarillo and Manuelito led the latter. (Padilla did not bother mentioning the inveterately hostile Miguel Narbona, because he was unequivocally opposed to peace.)

It was also clear that some Chiricahuas who had appeared at Janos requesting a truce had recently arrived from New Mexico very apprehensive of Americans. Padilla greeted the Indians' initial offerings with cautious approval. Even José María Zuloaga, sometimes scalp hunter, sometimes politician, but always the consummate pragmatist and businessman, was willing to consider their proposal. On February 20, 1849, a group of six Nednhis of the Janeros group, led by Cochi (not the Chokonen Cochise) and a warrior named Anselemo, approached the presidio insisting that they wanted to parley. Padilla went out with a few citizens and held a short conference in which the Indians claimed they wanted to make peace. The officer tried to learn their motive for requesting peace and concluded that they were probably acting in good faith. The Chiricahuas revealed that they had been living north of the presidio, likely near Boca Grande and Lake Guzmán, since the previous August and had not committed any raids near Janos. Moreover, they claimed that their Nednhi local group had not been in New Mexico and therefore had had no contact with Americans. The Apaches also ransomed a captive, who corroborated what Cochi told Padilla.[23]

Zuloaga, at Corralitos, told Padilla that if he had misgivings about the Apaches' behavior, he should seize them and send them to Corralitos, where Zuloaga would imprison them. To his credit, Padilla disagreed with Zuloaga's less than distinguished scheme.[24]

During the next month Chiricahua messengers returned to Janos three times and requested peace. The emissaries represented leaders of the four bands, including prominent men such as the Chihenne Ponce, the Nednhis Láceres and Coleto Amarillo, the Chokonen Yrigóllen, and the Bedonkohe Teboca. The presence of the last two chiefs was puzzling, for both were actively raiding in Sonora. Likely they were looking for a safe place in which to dispose of their Sonoran booty. According to Negrito de Carretas, a warrior then living at peace at Janos, the peaceful Chiricahuas would have to assassinate Mangas Coloradas and Delgadito to ensure stable relations. It was the only way for peace to work, for those two leaders defiantly opposed talks about peace. The Chokonen Manuelito, who had lost many followers in the Elías González and Kirker massacres, insisted that not until Captain Padilla obtained reinforcements at Janos would the peaceful Apaches consider killing Mangas Coloradas.[25]

Manuelito declared that he had attempted to murder Mangas before, but without success. No Apache would attempt the endeavor until the Mexican force at Janos was strong enough to provide protection. The origin of this disagreement was not known; perhaps these acrimonious feelings resulted from the times that Manuelito had led troops to recover stolen stock against Pisago Cabezón and Mangas Coloradas in 1842 and 1843. Perhaps the two had a long-standing feud which, because their leadership positions required each to seek peaceful solutions to problems, had gone unresolved and still smoldered in their minds, or at least in that of Manuelito.[26] For Delgadito, his hatred of Mexicans emanated from the Kirker affair in which he had lost kinfolk, according to Jason Betzinez. Manuelito's position paralleled Juan José Compá's standing of the mid-1830s. Both were "generals" in the eyes of Mexican officials, but they were paper generals, and Manuelito's following had decreased significantly by the late 1840s. He may have paid dearly for his audacious plot to murder Mangas Coloradas, for within a year he would die under mysterious circumstances.[27]

Meanwhile, on March 29 the Nednhi chief Coleto Amarillo came in with ten men and several women and formally requested an armistice with Mexico. Coleto Amarillo had left Santa Rita del Cobre because of the arrival of Americans in his country. His followers may have recently spilled American blood in New Mexico. In March, Chiricahuas battled Americans in the Mimbres Mountains and reportedly killed several Texans, including a Captain Schoomaker and six others during the hard-fought contest.[28] They apparently had also stolen some stock near Socorro, and an American patrol under First Lieutenant Abraham Buford had pursued them into Chihenne country but had failed to over-take them. This hardly discouraged Buford, however, and he drew up plans for a formidable campaign of one hundred American troops with fifty New Mexican volunteers to punish the Apaches. Buford's intentions became known by the Chiricahuas, whose net-work of Mexican traders undoubtedly warned them of the cam-paign. Coleto Amarillo asserted that many Chiricahuas had left New Mexico because of the Americans' hostile intentions. He wanted peace with Chihuahua, as did Ponce and Cigarrito; mean-while, some Chihennes (likely Delgadito's followers) had gone to Sonora and joined forces with Mangas Coloradas, then at Pitaicache with the Chokonens.[29]

Although official American policy toward the Chiricahuas had not changed, relations between the two peoples certainly had. With the end of the Mexican War and the discovery of gold in California, many whites were traveling through Apachería bound for the gold fields. These excursions inevitably led to encounters—some peaceful, some not—for these trespassers, as the Indians perceived them, had nothing but contempt for Indians. The pre-carious peace that had existed between Americans and Chiri-cahuas became even more fragile. Now the Chiricahuas had decided to fight the intruders if they liked the odds. The lure of plunder and munitions, for the Apaches knew that the Americans were generally well-stocked and well-armed, excited the Indians, whether in New Mexico or Mexico. In late February or early March 1849 the legendary explorer John C. Frémont led through Apachería a group of adventurers who captured two Chiricahuas near Santa Rita del Cobre after they had shot the horse of an American. Soon after, an Apache chief came in and held a powwow with Frémont, who assured the leader that the Americans were en route to California and had no intention of mining in Apache country. The Indians inspected the Americans' packs and let them go unmolested, satisfied that they had told the truth.[30]

More serious were other reported encounters in the spring of 1849 in which the Chiricahuas spilled blood of Americans. In mid-April, near Huasabas, Sonora, Apaches, likely Chiricahuas, jumped another group of Americans under a Captain McMullen, "an old Texas ranger." During the ambush, which took place on the west side of the Sierra Madre, the Apaches killed seven Americans. Two escaped to local villages; one who reached Huasabas said that the Indians had killed his companions, seven Americans and a Mexican. More encounters would follow during 1849, both above and below the border.[31]

Mangas himself may have participated in several encounters. In 1849 an American named Ferguson claimed he had had an engagement with Mangas Coloradas and one hundred warriors near Corralitos. Mangas was indeed in that area during the winter and spring of 1849. Ferguson embellished his story, but his description of Mangas Coloradas, whom he regarded as "haughty and insolent," seemed characteristic of the Apache chieftain at that time. And Ferguson resented the chief's insistence that tribute in the form of "a mule, five sacks of corn and cigars enough for all his warriors" be paid. His story seemed plausible to this point, at least until Ferguson claimed that he refused Mangas's demand. According to the story, the Apaches "surrounded [them] for four days," and then the whites fought their way through the Indians' lines, with Ferguson killing Mangas in hand-to-hand combat.[32]

Throughout April and May, while Mangas and the Chokonens were assaulting Sonora's presidios, the pacific elements of the Chiricahuas continued to arrive at Janos. On April 5, 1849, Manuelito came in, and Coleto Amarillo followed him in a week later. During May several American parties stopped at Janos on their way to California. They viewed the Apaches with scorn, and with good reason. During the night of May 10, 1849, one band of

Chiricahuas, after trading mules to the alcalde, became "intoxicated with aguardiente" and roamed the streets of Janos. A few days later another American party stopped at Janos en route to California. Upon his arrival there, Harvey Wood found "the town in possession of six Apache Indians who were amusing themselves by riding from store to store and making the proprietors furnish liquor or anything else they demanded." Thomas Durivage must have just missed this spectacle, for he arrived on May 12, 1849, and remarked that the "Apaches had been in town trading and playing monte before our arrival."³³

Meanwhile, the Carrizaleño local group, under Francisquillo, with a few Chokonens, had agreed to a treaty with Captain Antonio Rey at San Buenaventura. Chihuahua's Commanding General and Governor Angel Trias forwarded to Padilla copies of the agreement, instructing him to tell the Apaches about the conditions. On May 26, 1849, Padilla wrote Trias that he still hoped to consummate a treaty with the Chokonen leaders Yrigóllen, Posito, and Carro; the Chihenne Itán; and the Nednhi chiefs Coleto Amarillo and Poncito.³⁴

But his efforts would go for naught. On May 25, 1849, the state legislature of Chihuahua passed a law, called the Fifth Law or "Contracts of Blood," which authorized the government to pay bounties for Apache scalps and prisoners very much in the manner of the agreement with Kirker a few years before. Chihuahua's Governor and Commander Angel Trias had originally vetoed the law, believing that it was immoral and unconstitutional. The legislature, however, mustered the votes to override his veto and passed the bill. This act permitted anyone to hunt Apaches and receive rewards for scalps. The state would also pay for Apache captives: 250 pesos for a warrior and 150 pesos for a woman or child under fourteen years of age. To certify its humane intent, Chihuahua would pay only two hundred pesos for the scalp of a warrior. For a few months there was an open market on Apache scalps and prisoners. True to his character, the opportunistic José María Zuloaga at Corralitos became actively involved in this unsavory practice. Although the military at Janos was under the authority of Trias, the state's commander and chief, Zuloaga, the leading civilian official of the district, still exerted a great deal of influence over affairs at that presidio. On the other hand, at Janos the pragmatic Lieutenant Padilla had usually worked toward realistic solutions. Once the Chiricahuas learned about the policy, and saw firsthand its impact, they understandably had no desire to continue negotiations. The outcome was predictable: after a brief flurry of mercenary activity (with the Nednhi local group of Carrizaleños being the hardest hit),[35] the Chiricahuas retaliated against Chihuahua before eventually retiring to southern New Mexico, out of harm's way. According to Solomon Sublette, an American frontiersman and businessman living in Chihuahua, the new policy served to exacerbate relations. The Apaches had continued their "stealing and killing on all sides" because of the scalp hunters.[36]

In June 1849, Mangas Coloradas with a large body of warriors was lurking in northeastern Sonora near Janos. The Chokonens had appeared at Bavispe on June 4 and again on June 22, 1849, when one hundred warriors stormed the town, retaliating for Terán y Tato's victory a month earlier. Mangas Coloradas was not with them; he had moved to Janos, where an explosive situation threatened to erupt. Throughout June a few Chiricahuas had continued to show up at Janos to do some trading and drinking and to discuss terms with Padilla. On June 11, Zuloaga, incensed that the Nednhis under Arvizu had killed two men at San Buenaventura six days earlier, ordered Padilla to imprison any Apaches who came in to discuss terms. The next day he instructed the commander to hold Coleto Amarillo as hostage if he came in to parley. Zuloaga had also heard about an enormous Apache war party of four hundred men (which included Mangas Coloradas) that planned to invade Sonora and Chihuahua. He believed that these threats justified his duplicity, although Chihuahua's new bounty of 250 pesos for a captured warrior made his decision easier.[37]

On June 15, 1849, three Nednhi men—Negrito, Ratón, and Gervacio (a son of Juan José Compá)—arrived at Janos, unaware of Chihuahua's new law and Zuloaga's deceitful orders to Padilla. Captain Padilla had a long talk with them. They openly admitted that they had recently raided Bavispe and Bacerac and revealed that three days before they had battled Sonoran troops,[38] an encounter that had resulted in the deaths of four Apaches and several soldiers. Furthermore, enraged at the Apache fatalities, Candelario, another son of Juan José Compá, had executed his prisoner, a youth taken from Bavispe in one of their recent raids. After they foolishly revealed that a war party intended to raid Galeana, Casas Grandes, and Corralitos, Padilla decided that he had heard enough. He ordered the three men held as prisoners.[39]

Naturally, the Indians became concerned when the warriors did not return to camp. The next day members of Negrito's family came to Janos and inquired about his status; Padilla explained why he had detained the three. Concerned about the large number of Apaches in the area, early the next morning he sent his prisoners to José María Zuloaga at Corralitos. That day (June 17), Bartolo and a few other Apaches came in, followed by a sullen and morose Láceres with a group of twenty-five warriors on June 20, 1849. They were well mounted, well armed, and suspicious, prepared for war if necessary. Láceres boasted that his followers planned to raid the settlements south of Casas Grandes. Other Indians, including Mangas Coloradas, were waiting in the hills prepared to join Láceres if fighting broke out. Since Padilla was unable to produce the Apaches, Láceres believed that the Mexicans had killed his people. Padilla promised the Nednhi chief that he could see Negrito the next day, which temporarily eased tensions. Láceres and his warriors left, but Tonina, a younger brother of Galindo, a leading man of the Nednhis, stayed behind in a drunken stupor. The next day Zuloaga ordered Padilla to imprison him. Meanwhile, with his options fast dwindling, Padilla sent a messenger to Zuloaga asking for reinforcements and the return of Negrito's party. Zuloaga with seventy troops left for Janos that evening, bringing the three Chiricahua prisoners with them.[40]

In an ironic twist of fate, it seems that both the Chiricahuas and the Mexicans, unbeknownst to the other side, had made plans to massacre each other. The Chiricahuas had assembled a large force of warriors for a foray into Chihuahua. From their perspective the imprisonment of Negrito's party was unjust; after all, they had left the Janos area alone and had been involved in peaceful negotiations with Padilla during the last several months. Padilla's actions rankled the moderate faction, and they turned to Mangas Coloradas and the bellicose Chokonens for help, which the latter were all too eager to provide. Zuloaga's motives were simple: as an old ally of James Kirker, the logical politician believed that he had the best of both worlds. He could exterminate Apaches and, even better, get paid for it. En route to Janos, Zuloaga, who had enlisted the services of the infamous John Johnson as "interpreter and adviser," encountered an American group from Texas known as the Duval party, bound for California by way of Janos. Johnson's fingerprints were all over Zuloaga's treacherous scheme. The Mexican political leader told the Americans that once the Apaches came into Janos and let down their guard, he would issue a "signal" to his men, who would be hidden in the houses surrounding the plaza, to begin the carnage.

Zuloaga hospitably invited the Americans to "participate upon the promise of being allowed the captured horses." Yet ambushing men, even Indians, "from cover" was something to which the Americans would not stoop, so Zuloaga consented to allow them to "fight with exposed persons [once] the row began." Half the Americans, about twenty-seven men, "ever anxious and spoiling for a fight," joined Zuloaga. Neither Padilla's nor Zuloaga's reports mention what happened next. But Benjamin Butler Harris, a member of the Duval group, who had joined Zuloaga, wrote that the mixed Mexican-American party reached Janos "before daybreak" on June 21, 1849. Zuloaga "introduced his men, with the prisoners, into Janos, stationing them in houses facing the plaza." That morning the Indians "in small squads came in, suspectingly, each squad stopping at saloons for draughts of native brew and looking for signs of treachery." About one hundred warriors had collected on the plaza, waiting to negotiate for the release of Negrito'a party. Other Chiricahuas were in the hills waiting to rush in at the first sign of trouble. Mangas had remained outside the town, for he was too suspicious of Mexicans. A few days later he admitted to Duval's party that the Apaches also had a clever scheme, perhaps not as ingenious as the one devised by the Mexicans. According to him, the Apaches planned to turn the tables on Zuloaga and massacre "every Mexican under the pretense of making a treaty." Fortunately for both sides, the untimely arrival of the second half of Duval's party, whom the Apaches mistook for reinforcements of Mexican troops, abruptly spoiled the dishonorable intentions of both races. The skittish Indians bolted from the plaza, thus foiling the "treaty and exchange of prisoners—or rather the murder of Indians under pretext of a treaty," in the words of Benjamin Harris.[41]

Meanwhile, Mangas Coloradas retired to his base camps in the Enmedio and Espuellas Mountains, perhaps knowing that the American party would likely traverse Cooke's route through Guadalupe Canyon. At Janos, Zuloaga and Lieutenant Padilla had sharp words before the former took his "Apache hunters," as the Janos residents contemptuously referred to them, to Corralitos and filed a claim on behalf of five soldiers from Janos and citizens of Barranco and Corralitos to receive the bounties for capturing Negrito, Ratón, and Gervacio. Soon after, he left on a patrol, taking Negrito as guide, and on June 30 attacked a small ranchería, killing the Chokonen leader (Nachul) and recapturing two young children taken from Bavispe the previous spring.[42]

The Duval party, after a few days of feasts and celebrations, left Janos about June 26. Traveling along a "grassy, well-watered country," they marched about twelve miles before going into camp at what Benjamin Harris later identified as "Petotaha," which was La Palatoda, a few miles east of the Enmedio Mountains. Most of the party halted for lunch, but a group of some eighteen men "proceeded in advance . . . going through a gap in the Sierra Madre Mountains." They were yet in the Enmedio Mountains when a cry of "the Apaches are surrounding us" was sounded. Harris's party formed a "hollow square around the pack animals and bullets were sent after the advancing Indians, who returned the fire." The Texans fought their way to a creek and dug in to face the Apache attack, which they believed was imminent. The Apaches, however, kept up an intermittent fire, not daring to attack an entrenched force.[43]

Hollywood would have loved what happened next. Tom Edwards, a thirteen-year-old boy from Saint Augustine County, Texas, "thinking of my grandfather who was scalped and killed by Indians," mounted his mule and approached to within one hundred yards of the Apaches' position. "Deliberately aiming, he fired," but the ball struck the ground near the horse of none other than Mangas Coloradas. Mangas returned fire, missing the boy, who put spurs to his mule and emptied his six-shooter at Mangas, missing him each time. Mangas directed a few more volleys at Tom Edwards but also missed. Finally, seven or eight Americans left their positions and rescued the brave but foolhardy boy. A few hours later, the rest of the command arrived and went into camp.

The Americans were concerned, for they could see some two hundred Apaches "armed some with bows and arrows, some with lances and others with guns all mounted upon fiery steeds and charging to and fro just ready to make an attack." Instead of fighting, however, the Apaches, realizing that they had lost the element of surprise, advanced toward the Americans carrying a white flag, saying that they wished to talk. As usual, it was Mangas Coloradas who approached to within one hundred yards of the Americans; Elisha L. Davis represented the whites. It was an interesting interview. Mangas said that he was a friend of Americans and that he and his men would like to come into camp and talk. Some one hundred Apaches approached, all "well mounted and equipped with lances, bows, shields and some with guns." After meeting Captain Duval, Mangas asked to meet the boy who "rode out and shot at him." Duval introduced Tom

Edwards to Mangas, who, after "rigidly inspecting him from toe to toe," said "muy malo muchacho," though whether he was gently scolding the boy or complimenting him on his courage was unclear. Mangas declared that "he loved Americans. Until about five years before he had never seen one. About that time he got acquainted with an American who was his dearest friend." Whom Mangas was referring to was not clear, but one could make a case for Jack Gordon. Gordon, whose real name was Peter Worthington, was an American fugitive who had found a home with the Apaches.[44] In October 1849, while employed by Texan John Coffee Hays, a celebrated former Texas Ranger, to contact the Chiricahuas, he told an American at El Paso that he had been living with the Apaches for four years. When the Indians met an African American, likely "the first black man they had seen, several scrutinized his skin very closely." As he had with Kearny, Mangas proposed that the two groups unite to fight the Mexicans, who "were damned Christians." He admitted that the Americans' arrival had thwarted the Apaches' plans to obliterate Janos, yet they still planned "to wipe out Janos and the Mexicans from existence."[45]

Mangas did not carry out his threat. Instead, with Chihuahua's Fifth Law encouraging American and Mexican mercenaries, and rumors that Elías González was planning to launch an enormous campaign from Sonora against the Chiricahuas, nearly every group, including Mangas Coloradas's, retired north into Arizona and New Mexico. According to Apache testimony, the Indians had moved north to the Mogollon Mountains and the Gila River country to meet the Americans, who were offering them friendship and trade. Yet in reality there was little, if any, official contact between American officials and Mangas's people. Likely this citation referred to the association between New Mexican traders and the Apaches, one that was generally amicable, as both sides had material that the other wanted. Only the local group of Chokonens under two noted war chiefs, Tapilá and Triqueño, remained in Sonora. They had stayed because a Sonoran patrol had captured four members of Tapilá's family, and he hoped to take steps to obtain their release.[46]

Elías González lamented that his troops had no Chiricahuas to fight now that they had left for New Mexico. Still trying to make hay, he ordered Captain Teodoro de Aros with some 118 men to conduct a search-and-destroy mission for Tapilá's group. The troops encountered Apaches in the Pinito Mountains, but the Indians detected the command, which consisted mainly of infantry, and de Aros returned empty-handed. About a month later, Tapilá led a war party that ambushed a mixed force of citizens and soldiers between Bacoachi and Arispe, killing five men, including Corporal Serapio Olguin, whom the Apaches had captured the year before and had subsequently exchanged for Cochise. They also wounded two others and captured an astonishing thirty-four persons, thirty-one of whom they promptly exchanged for Tapilá's four relatives.[47]

Meanwhile, by early July 1849, Mangas Coloradas had returned to his Chihenne country at Santa Lucía Springs and the Burro Mountains. There he renewed his business association with New Mexican traders, who had little affection for the newly organized American government and American soldiers. Moreover, he observed a seemingly endless parade of American emigrants journeying through the heart of his country, bound for California and the gold fields. These pioneers, most of whom openly despised Indians, were a different breed of men from Carson and Kearny. Their attitudes, perspective, and objectives differed from those of trappers and military men who wanted to maintain harmonious relations with the Chiricahuas because they preferred peace to fighting. In contrast, these emigrants, obsessed with reaching the gold fields and California, had arrived with preconceived notions of the Apaches, whom they viewed with disdain. As one party after another made their way west, beginning in the spring of 1849, they eventually wore out their welcome with their Chiricahua hosts by the late summer of 1849. Just as ominous to Mangas Coloradas, some of these groups brought their own mining tools and were more than prepared to begin digging at the first sign of valuable ore, which was abundant in Chihenne and Bedonkohe country. Fortunately for Mangas, at this time his people were strong enough to intimidate any American party that dared to prospect in their country. Of course skirmishes and expressions of hostility broke out from time to time, because there were no American troops in Chiricahua country, nor were there any agents to oversee their activities.

This evolution from a precarious trust to one of open distrust was a gradual one that had begun in the late winter of 1849 and had continued to evolve shortly after Mangas returned to his country from Mexico that summer. Because Americans misunderstood the political organization of the Chiricahuas, they could not appreciate why one local group of Chihennes east of the Mimbres River country under Ponce might be friendly, while fifty miles west near Santa Rita del Cobre and Santa Lucía Springs another group under Delgadito and Mangas Coloradas might be hostile. The Mexican military and civil leaders along the frontier, who had the benefit of years of experience with the Chiricahuas, knew and understood which groups or bands were usually militant and which were normally pacific. In general, relations between Americans and Apaches were friendly during the early summer of 1849. In early June a report from Doña Ana indicated that "all is quiet" in Chihenne country. "Parties arrive almost daily from Texas on their way to California."[48] Next month, on July 22, 1849, one party of Americans traded with a large group of Chihennes near the Mimbres but did not encounter any Indians as they made their way west. In early August another group from Texas saw Apaches near Santa Rita del Cobre and Santa Lucía Springs, whose water had "a slight-sulphury smell but is clear, very cold and good tasting." Some Apaches seemed "frank and friendly—others were skulking about and made off when discovered." About the same time another group from Arkansas enjoyed amicable relations with Apaches near the Mimbres River. This was either Cuchillo Negro's or Ponce's local group, usually more pacific toward Americans than other Chihenne local groups.[49]

In contrast to these cordial meetings, subsequent developments would prove less than friendly as several hostile encounters occurred between the two races beginning in mid-August 1849. Mangas and his followers were involved in the fighting. On August 16, 1849, Captain Enoch Steen,[50] who was stationed at Doña Ana with one company of the First Dragoons, had a hard skirmish with Apaches near Santa Rita del Cobre. A native of Kentucky, Steen was commissioned a second lieutenant in the Mounted Rangers in 1832 before transferring to the First Dragoons the following year. A respected and well-liked officer in the Southwest, Steen, as one contemporary observer described him, was "a man of splendid physique, of the most temperate habits, and he had the endurance of Daniel Boone." He would become a fixture in Chihenne country for the next several years, becoming well acquainted with Mangas Coloradas and other Chihenne leaders. During the sharp encounter, the troops drove the Apaches into the hills, but not before the hostiles wounded Steen, shot though the body by a white man who was leading the Apaches. This white man was "Apache Jack" Gordon, who later admitted that he was in the fight and had fired the shot.[51]

Gordon was one of those border figures whose life touched briefly on several of New Mexico's important characters—red and white. Fleeing from white civilization after he had killed a man, he somehow became acquainted with the Chiricahuas and married a Chihenne woman, possibly of Mangas's band. As mentioned before, he may have been the white man referred to by Mangas as his "good friend" during the latter's meeting with Duval's party in Mexico. In any event, on August 22, 1849, six days after the fight with Steen's dragoons, the Chihennes ambushed an emigrant party near Santa Rita del Cobre and killed one man and wounded two others. According to a letter written by a Captain Bunches, the Americans succeeded in killing or wounding eight Indians. If so, this set the stage for further fighting, for the relatives of the slain would have demanded revenge. Fifteen days later, another group of travelers saw Apaches eyeing their movements, likely near the Burro Mountains. Whether Mangas was involved in these two fights is not known. The fact that these two encounters occurred in the heart of his country while he was in the neighborhood strongly suggests his participation. By the fall of 1849 he had become disenchanted with all whites, Mexican and American. While there may remain questions about his participation in the Steen and Bunches fights, we know that he was involved in the next incident, which occurred near the site of the two earlier fights.[52]

During the late summer of 1849 several groups of adventurers were roaming the Southwest in search of treasure. Among these explorers was a Frenchman named M. Ronde, whose party arrived at Corralitos in late August. Zuloaga proudly showed his Apache prisoners (Negrito's party) to Ronde, who left behind detailed descriptions of the Chiricahua men and their daily life working as slaves at the smelters. The prisoners were kept in leg irons and fed like peons,[53] although Zuloaga magnanimously allowed them to indulge in an Apache warrior's favorite pastime: gambling. Frequently disputes would occur, and Zuloaga would intervene and punish the guilty parties by locking them up in a dark room, a dreaded form of punishment to a race that loved the freedom of the mountains and desert. Negrito impressed Ronde, who described him as a "wiseman of the tribe with a kindly countenance." Gervacio, a son of Juan José Compá, was "perfectly proportioned . . . with a voice as sweet as that of a young girl." Tonina, a brother of the Nednhi leader Galindo, "had a timid countenance and passed his time howling when he was not crying." The youngest and most fierce looking warrior was Ratón, "a savage type with a stern manner who never smiled."[54]

About the time that Ronde's party was at Corralitos, a Nednhi raiding party from the band of Soquilla, an old ally of Mangas Coloradas, stole every horse from the presidio of Janos on August 31, 1849. Lieutenant Padilla, with thirty-six soldiers and seventeen citizen volunteers, all on foot, followed the Apaches' trail the next day. The Indians evidently did not count on any pursuit, for they had cleaned out the presidio of all its mounts. Yet the tenacious Padilla pushed his men forward, and the yeoman efforts of his men produced results. On September 9, 1849, his force jumped the Apache ranchería north of Palomas, near the Florida Mountains according to one account, and succeeded in killing five men, including Soquilla, and seven women and children while capturing nineteen.[55] Meanwhile, Ronde's party, which had left Janos bound for Santa Rita del Cobre, encountered Padilla with his captives near Boca Grande. He saw the Apaches' scalps, though he reported there were nineteen when there were only twelve casualties. He also picked up some interesting gossip about the fight. One young woman, probably the daughter of Soquilla, became "so violent in her counterattack on the Mexican soldiers at the time of the assault that one of the men was forced to shoot her with his pistol." Stories of Apache women warriors were not uncommon during times of crisis, especially when their village was under attack.[56]

Ronde's expedition continued north and finally reached Santa Rita del Cobre about September 18. The next day they reached the Gila, where the Chiricahuas opened fire, forcing the party to circle the wagons for defense. After a few days of intermittent exchanging of gunfire, finally on September 22, 1849, Mangas Coloradas arrived and characteristically agreed to a conference with Ronde. He consented to let the whites leave in peace under the condition that they abstain from prospecting and immediately withdraw from his country. Ronde accepted the proposal and returned to Janos, arriving on September 27, 1849.[57]

The Chiricahuas faced other considerations as the summer of 1849 came to a close. One matter that concerned them deeply was the highly publicized campaign from Sonora, financed by federal and state funds, which Elías González had organized during the spring and summer of 1849. Just as importantly, they had become preoccupied with the fate of the twenty-five Nednhis held in captivity by Chihuahua at Janos and Corralitos. On September 14, two days after Padilla had returned with his nineteen prisoners, a group of thirty-two Chokonens under Yrigóllen stole some stock from several citizens at Janos. Padilla and some sixty soldiers and citizens dutifully pursued the Indians, overtaking them at Galera, a few miles north of the presidio. There Yrigóllen raised a white flag, and he and Padilla had a talk. The Chokonen band chief claimed that he wanted peace, and to prove his sincerity he was willing to return the stock that they had just stolen. Yet in reality, this was a war party seeking blood to avenge Padilla's destruction of Soquilla's camp. Yrigóllen had ten of his warriors begin herding the stock toward Padilla's lines, when suddenly they switched directions and raced away from the Mexicans. Padilla and his twelve mounted men overtook the Indians at El Cerro Largo and recaptured the stolen livestock. Yrigóllen, bent on revenge, led thirty warriors in a counterattack and killed six men and wounded another.[58]

In October the Chiricahua bands united for a council in the Burro Mountains, after which the leaders decided to send a war party against Janos. They wanted hostages and loot, which they would use to exchange for their people held by Zuloaga and Padilla. This was primarily a Chokonen-Nednhi collaboration, with a few of Itán's Chihennes. Mangas Coloradas, though undoubtedly present, decided to remain in his country, perhaps anticipating the long-rumored campaign from Sonora, which would have to penetrate Apachería, for most of the bands were in New Mexico.

Elías González finally launched his campaign from Bacoachi on September 23, 1849. Organizing his force into three divisions, he took a command of 191 men (presidio troops and national guard militia) and headed north to present-day Cochise County, Arizona. He sent another detachment of 130 troops under the capable national guard leader José Terán y Tato to reconnoiter northeast Sonora to flush out any Apaches there. He ordered the third detachment, under Captain Agustín Moreno, with 80 men and the supply train, to establish a base camp at Sarampion in the lower Peloncillos, where Elías González's and Terán y Tato's commands would rendezvous at the end of September.[59]

On September 24, 1849, Captain Antonio Comadurán and some sixty soldiers from Tucson joined Elías González's command, which really needed these recruits, for within the first week several men, including the "tame" Apaches, or Apaches *mansos*, scouts from Tucson, had deserted his command. Because of sickness, Elías González was forced to leave behind at Santa Cruz fourteen men who were too ill to continue. During the march to the Chiricahua Mountains his men experienced several heavy thunderstorms, but these did not deter him. He dispatched scouting parties into the

Chokonens' home turf, but they were unable to find any recent signs. One command penetrated Rucker Canyon, which they called Colorado Canyon and today is known as Red Rock Canyon, a normal camping area of the Chokonens. After thoroughly scouting the Chiricahuas as far north as Apache Pass and finding no Indians, Elías González headed for the rendezvous point at Sarampion, only to discover, much to his chagrin, that his pack train had not arrived. As a result, he marched south and at San Bernardino encountered an American party en route to California who told him that they had seen Apaches on the Mimbres River, but none since then. Finally, on October 5, Elías González's command crossed the present-day boundary into Sonora and stumbled upon Captain Moreno's supply train near Caguillona, a group of small hills with a dependable water supply some fifteen miles north of Fronteras.[60]

Illness had also plagued Moreno's command; more than half his eighty men were sick. Consequently, the next day Elías González dispatched an escort to take fifty-two men to Bacoachi. Despite this inauspicious start, the desertions, the illness, the rainy weather, and rough terrain, the undaunted commander resumed his march north toward the Chiricahuas. He had too much at stake to return empty-handed. On October 7 a scouting party near San Bernardino captured an Apache who revealed that every Chiricahua local group and band, except Triqueño's group of Chokonens, had retired to the Burro Mountains because of an epidemic.

With his force of almost four hundred men Elías González headed straight for the Burro Mountains, marching into southwestern New Mexico and north through the Animas Valley. On October 8 they came across two Mexicans who had escaped from the Apache camps in the Burro Mountains. Tapilá's war party had captured one of them, Ramón Aguirre, at Berrendos the previous August. By October 12, 1849, the large Sonoran army had reached the foothills of the Burro Mountains, apparently undetected by the Apaches.[61]

Camped in the vicinity were local groups of three of the four Chiricahua bands (the Bedonkohes were in the Mogollons). As previously mentioned, one war party of perhaps 150 warriors had left for Janos. Those who remained behind, including Mangas Coloradas, were more concerned about an American party of one hundred men under John Coffee Hays,[62] recently named subagent for the Río Gila Apaches, who was attempting to establish contact with the Chiricahuas. When at El Paso, Hays contracted with the ubiquitous "Apache Jack" Gordon to guide his command into Mangas's country and set up an interview with the Chiricahua leaders. The alliance with the notorious Gordon disturbed Hays until he met Major Enoch Steen at Doña Ana. The commander, wounded by Gordon a few months before, told Hays that Gordon "would steal, lie and kill, but he was true to you" once he gave his word.[63] This comforted Hays. He embarked for Santa Rita del Cobre, where he hoped to meet the Chiricahuas. Gordon's efforts were successful, for, according to Robert Eccleston, the son of the chief, probably Mangas, sent word that the Americans "would not be disturbed," and the prospects looked promising for a meeting.[64] One wonders if it was Mangas Coloradas who sent word, for he was in the vicinity and was usually open to talking with American officials. In any event, subsequent developments were to force a change in that plan. For just as the Apaches were contemplating a parley with Hays, Elías González's campaign struck them from the rear and foiled any thoughts they had about meeting the Americans.

On the morning of October 13 a Mexican scouting party discovered two Apaches in the lower Burro Mountains. Elías González dispatched Captain Terán y Tato with his cavalry, and they followed the two to a secluded Chokonen camp in the Burro Mountains, which the Mexicans surprised, killing three warriors and one boy, capturing several others (including Yrinco, a brother of Manuelito, who escaped during the night), and confiscating stock, weapons, and other material. The Indians killed two Mexican soldiers and wounded another. Immediately after the skirmish, Elías González again dispatched Terán y Tato, this time with 140 infantry and fourteen cavalry to hunt for other rancherías. The Apache prisoners had admitted to Elías González that most of the warriors of this village had left on the expedition against Janos. After thoroughly scouting the Burro Mountains, Elías González concluded from the deserted rancherías that some three hundred families were in the vicinity; many obviously had left for the Gila. Two days later the Sonoran army again fought Mangas Coloradas and his men. In a running battle, which included a couple of howitzer rounds, the Sonorans killed seven more Apaches and put the rest to flight. They also recovered at least four young Mexican captives.[65] Jack Gordon, who was bringing in the Apaches to parley with Hays, joined the Apaches and fought the Mexicans. He came in later that night and informed Hays that there was "no longer any hope of inducing" the Apaches in to talk. The Indians "had been handsomely drubbed, were in ill humor," and had no desire to talk peace with either Mexicans or Americans. In fact, they may even have blamed the Americans for the disaster, as they had been on their way to meet them when Elías González's troops surprised them. According to Gordon, the Apaches had left for "their eastern strongholds," meaning either the Gila or the Mogollon Mountains.[66]

After the victory, the Sonorans met Hays's party near Santa Lucía. They had taken "3 or 4 children prisoners & had some scalps, & hanging to their field piece were several ears cut from the bodies of the Indians."[67] Elías González advised Hays of a route west through Puerto del Dado (Apache Pass) that would be more direct than Cooke's route into Mexico. Leaving two men behind to help guide the Americans, the Sonoran commander headed toward Janos in the hope of encountering the Chiricahua war party. Yet by the time he arrived, the Chiricahuas had left the area. Consequently, he decided to return to Sonora. His grand offensive was hardly an overwhelming success: his troops had killed eleven warriors, had taken five prisoners, and had recovered a few Mexican captives at a cost of five soldiers killed and five more wounded. It was not a decisive blow, nor was it significant in terms of casualties. Yet it forced the Chiricahuas to consider Sonora a formidable enemy. Although the Apaches could not have realized it, this was Elías González's first step in recapturing control of Sonora's northern frontier.[68]

Meanwhile, the Chiricahua war party at Janos had dropped everything and frantically hurried back to their camps in New Mexico immediately upon receiving news of Sonora's campaign. They had stolen every horse from Janos in the early morning of October 11. A heavy fog enveloped the area, and all the soldiers saw were groups of Apaches making off with their stock. As the fog lifted, a warrior approached with a white flag asking for a parley with Padilla in the name of the Chokonens Yrigóllen, Posito, and Manuelito; the Nednhis Coleto Amarillo, Láceres, and Arvizu; and the Chihenne Itán. The leaders refused to enter the fort and conversed with Padilla from outside the walls while many of their men, clearly intoxicated, roamed outside the presidio brandishing their arms. It was an explosive situation. Arvizu, whose sister Gertrudis was among the prisoners, spoke for the Indians. He demanded that Padilla release their people taken a month earlier (Soquilla's group) and the five warriors held at Corralitos by Zuloaga. In exchange they offered to return the presidio's horse herd.

As Padilla pondered the Indians' demands, the Apaches soon possessed another bargaining chip. A party of Americans, Frenchmen, and Germans, some twenty-six in number, had just arrived at the outskirts of Janos. They were bound for California and had been at Santa Rita del Cobre several weeks earlier until Mangas Coloradas's Apaches had run them out. Within five hundred yards of the presidio the Chiricahuas surrounded them, pretending friendly relations, then suddenly turned on the American party, captured them, and marched them off to the hills. The Indians stripped the Americans, cut open their packs, and stole their horses. Later that day Arvizu arrived at Janos, offering the Americans to Padilla for his Apache captives. Unfortunately for the Americans, while Arvizu was absent the Chiricahuas received news of Sonora's campaign in the Burro Mountains. A quarrel arose among them, with Coleto Amarillo counseling against killing their American prisoners. Because of his intervention and "the mercy of God and the darkness of night," most of the American party, naked and bruised, escaped to Janos. But the Chokonens, whose camp Elías González had struck, took their revenge. Seven men (three Americans, two Germans, one Frenchman, and one Mexican) were not so fortunate; the next day they were found lanced to death.[69]

The Apaches' capture and killing of the Americans at Janos created quite a stir. Zuloaga sent reinforcements from Casas Grandes and Corralitos, and American scalp hunter John Joel Glanton,[70] who was near Paso del Norte, rushed to the area, hoping to earn some quick cash by exterminating Apaches. Even Lieutenant Padilla, who normally preferred peaceful relations with the Chiricahuas, joined forces with Glanton for a few scouts. One patrol examined the Chiricahua Mountains but found no recent signs.[71] All of the Chiricahua bands had remained in New Mexico in the region extending from the Gila River country north to the Mogollons and east toward Santa Rita del Cobre.

By the end of 1849 the Chiricahuas were clearly a frustrated and confused people, not knowing where to turn. They distrusted Americans, who seemed to consist of three groups: the emigrant travelers bound for California, who had only contempt for the Indians; the miners and prospectors, who wished to exploit Apachería's valuable mineral resources and had adopted a laissez-faire relationship with the Apaches, tolerating them as long as the Indians did not get in their way; and finally the U.S. military, who so far had not been influential in Apachería but were beginning to make their presence felt and were destined to become an important factor in the months and years to come. At about this time at Lemitar, six miles north of Socorro, the already bad relations intensified further when American troops seized fifteen intoxicated Apaches, including two chiefs, and brought them to Socorro, where they were placed in confinement. They soon escaped, but this affair left an indelible impression on the skittish Chiricahuas, who now began to perceive the American military on the same basis as the unscrupulous Mexicans whom they despised and distrusted.[72]

As for Mexico, the Chiricahuas hated Sonorans, but Elías González's campaign plus the fact that they held Chiricahua prisoners had changed the equation. Chihuahua, the architect of the inhumane "Contracts of Blood," also continued to hold Apache prisoners. Its official policy toward the Apaches changed in late 1849 from one of extermination to one of accommodation. It repealed the law authorizing the "Contracts of Blood," supposedly on humanitarian grounds, but in reality this extreme position had served only to provoke more hostilities between the two races.

As for Mangas, as things turned out, he must have felt hemmed in by late 1849. He had become wary of Americans, hated Sonorans, and disliked Chihuahuans. John Hays summed up the feelings of Mangas and the Chiricahuas in his letter of resignation written to the secretary of the interior once he reached California. His report, dated January 3, 1850, provides a good analysis of relations between Mangas's people and the Americans:

> I sought to have an interview with [Mangas's people] but I failed in every effort to see them. They were shy and hostile, with feelings aroused against the whites by an attack recently made on them by some Americans employed by the Gov. of Chihuahua expressly to fight Indians. . . . I went into the country of the Gila Apaches, and sought by every means to establish a friendly intercourse with them without success. I deemed it folly to attempt to effect any good with these Indians. . . . [They] need severe chastisement before they can be made to know the policy of observing good faith with the white people.[73]

The coming year would see its share of hostilities. The peace faction of the Chiricahuas, deeply concerned about their families held captive in Sonora and Chihuahua, would open negotiations with those two states. Mangas Coloradas, with the Bedonkohes, his Santa Lucía local group of Bedonkohes and Chihennes, and the bellicose Chokonens under Cochise and Miguel Narbona, would do all in their power to pay back Elías González for daring to bring a large army into their land.

Chapter 9

A CRUEL WAR ON SONORA

BY now we have seen that Mangas Coloradas, like his contemporary the Chokonen band leader Miguel Narbona and his son-in-law Cochise, carried an intense and lifelong hatred for Sonora to his grave. Most of his raiding and war parties were directed against this very real enemy. But he did not harbor that kind of enmity toward Chihuahua, and in fact occasionally entered into very friendly relations with the people there. The reasons were twofold. First, it was a matter of simple economics. The remote frontier towns of northwestern Chihuahua offered sanctuaries in which the Indians could dispose of their loot and booty taken during their raids in Sonora. These towns lay on their return route to New Mexico. In exchange, unscrupulous Chihuahuans gave the Apaches guns, ammunition, liquor, and corn and other foods. The second reason, and likely more important, was that Mangas tolerated Chihuahua because that state's official Apache policy was usually more moderate than that of Sonora.

Generally speaking, Mexico's two northern states had different ideas about the Apaches. Chihuahua usually favored a course based on accommodation and peace, unlike its sister state to the west, which maintained a militant and hawkish stance in controlling the Apaches. There were exceptions to this distinction. Occasionally the pendulum would shift and Chihuahua's government would adopt such extreme positions as hiring mercenaries and adopting scalp laws; yet these policies were temporary, and sooner or later Chihuahuan officials recognized the error of their ways and removed from office those politicians who favored those controversial measures. Then it would return to its old method of handling its Apache problem, one that was based on peace treaties and rations.

Although these extreme policies, which spawned Kirker's scalp hunters and the 1849 "Contracts in Blood" law, embittered Mangas Coloradas, he did not hold the resolute enmity toward Chihuahua that he did against Sonora. He vividly remembered Sonora's execution of Tutije in 1834; Johnson's massacre in 1837, which claimed the lives of two of his wives; the premeditated murders of six warriors by the troops at Fronteras in May 1843; and Elías González's assault at Janos and Corralitos in 1844. During the early 1850s there would be more incidents of what the Chiricahuas considered Sonoran chicanery but what the Mexicans considered acceptable behavior under their rules of warfare against savages, or *los bárbaros*, as they called the Apaches. Sonora's military leaders were hawks in their own right. They advocated policies based on subjugating the Chiricahuas by force; nothing else was acceptable. Consequently, the Apaches resisted with vigor, and Sonora, plagued by internal strife for most of the 1840s, was vulnerable. The Chiricahuas capitalized on this chaos and exploited to the hilt their advantages along the northern frontier.

Despite the Chiricahuas' victories of the late 1840s, Sonora and Chihuahua each held one trump card as 1850 rolled around. Terán y Tato's victory at Batepito in May 1849 and Padilla's surprise of Soquilla's camp the following September, together with the imprisonment of Negrito's party at Janos, had left Mexico with at least thirty-three Chiricahua prisoners. Sonora held nine Chokonens, whom Terán y Tato had taken in his attack on San Juan's camp. Among the hostages were the mother and mother-in-law of Demos, an important war leader. Chihuahua held in captivity some twenty-four Nednhis of the Janeros group, including relatives of Arvizu and Galindo, two important leaders. Lieutenant Padilla had sent most, if not all, of the prisoners to José María Zuloaga at Corralitos. These captives had concerned relatives and friends who wanted to negotiate for their release.

In early 1850 the Bedonkohes and three of the four Chokonen local groups (Posito Moraga's, Esquinaline's, and Yrigóllen's) had decided to consummate a temporary truce with Sonora. The participation of the Chokonen band leader Yrigóllen was intriguing, for he had been an erstwhile ally of Mangas Coloradas during the 1840s. Still, he had been fighting Sonora for almost twenty years and had grown weary of the prolonged conflict. He chose Sonora for two reasons: first, nine of his band remained in captivity there, and second, he had led two war parties against Janos the previous fall, and he probably did not believe that Lieutenant Padilla would receive him with open arms. Furthermore, as he would reveal to Elías González, he feared Chihuahuan treachery because of Kirker's massacre at Galeana in July 1846 and Chihuahua's recent law that permitted scalp hunting. Meanwhile, as the Chokonen and Bedonkohe leaders migrated south to Sonora, about half the Nednhis and many Chihennes decided to relocate to northwestern Chihuahua from the Gila and Burro Mountains, hoping to make a formal treaty of peace at Janos. Therefore, by February 1850 the only hostile Chiricahuas were Mangas Coloradas's Santa Lucía local group of mixed Chihennes and Bedonkohes and the Chokonen local group headed by Miguel Narbona and Cochise. These leaders opposed any permanent truce with Sonora and Chihuahua, though they understood why their brethren were willing to discuss terms to secure the release of their people held in captivity.

As some Chiricahua local groups began to move south from Chihenne country into Mexico in early 1850, the militant Chokonens and some Chihennes decided to make peaceful overtures toward Americans. Thanks to the testimony of Teófilo and Mateo Jaramillo,[1] two boys whom the Chihennes had captured from Doña Ana on December 27, 1849, we get a glimpse of what was happening in the hostile camp. In January 1850 the leaders decided to send Itán to open negotiations with the Americans. Itán's party left Santa Rita del Cobre for Doña Ana, where they hoped to discuss terms with Captain Enoch Steen. En route to the Rio Grande, they ran into Americans, perhaps civilians, as no official report of an engagement with troops has been found. In any event, the whites defeated Itán's party, killing several, according to Jaramillo's story. In response, early in the morning of February 2, 1850, Miguel Narbona directed a war party of fifty-six men that raided Doña Ana and killed one man, wounded three others, and drove off every head of stock. The Apaches' audacity surprised the Americans, for the Indians had come so close that the troops caught sight of them from their quarters. Steen quickly rounded up a force. He took one detachment and crossed the Jornada del Muerto;[2] Second Lieutenant Laurence W. O'Bannon with twenty-five men marched northwest to intercept the Indians before they reached the Mimbres Mountains. North of San Diego Crossing, O'Bannon's party overtook the Apaches and in a brisk fight wounded at least three warriors and possibly more, as the Indians later told the Jaramillos that they had sustained heavy losses. The Indians

wounded one soldier. Meanwhile, Captain Steen's party encountered thirty to forty Apaches, "all mounted and dashing about on
their horses and cursing us in bad Spanish." Although Steen's
force, which had dwindled to seven men (many of his mounts had
given out), was too few to pose any real threat to the mobile
Apaches, the latter, respecting the Americans' firepower, rode
away to avoid a senseless encounter.[3]

After the fight, Steen suggested to his superiors that they consider establishing a depot in the middle of Chihenne country, at
Santa Rita del Cobre. Moreover, he planned to carry out a scout
into Mangas's country, expressing his "earnest desire to chastise
the Apaches." In mid-March Steen's command spent thirteen days
examining the country around Santa Rita del Cobre. Most of the
Chiricahuas, including Mangas Coloradas, had by then departed for
Mexico, so Steen saw only a few Apaches, and they were too
suspicious to come in even though the Americans displayed white
flags. During his long reconnoiter Steen, an avid outdoorsman who
preferred to have his troops stationed away from settlements,
became convinced that Santa Rita del Cobre would be an ideal
location for a military post. His rationale was convincing: "It is
about the center of the Indian [Chihenne] nation; there are quarters
sufficient for at least three companies that can be put in complete
repairs in less than a month at a very small cost; timber for
building and other purposes is abundant and easily procured. Water
and grazing is good if not better than can be found in any portion of
New Mexico I have seen." In addition, he added two compelling
arguments that he knew would catch the attention of his superiors:
he believed that relocating the garrison from Doña Ana to Santa
Rita del Cobre would convince the Apaches to make peace. Moreover, it would also save the government fifteen thousand dollars
annually.[4]

These hostile encounters with Americans in the last half of 1849
and the first few months of 1850 left the followers of Mangas
Coloradas disinclined to stay in New Mexico. When Miguel
Narbona's war party returned with casualties to its home base,
most of the Chiricahuas decided to leave immediately for Sonora
and join the Chokonens and Bedonkohes who had already opened
negotiations with their inveterate enemy, Elías González. With
spring approaching, and the mescal harvest near, by early March
1850, Mangas Coloradas also left his country near Santa Lucía and
brought his people into the mountains of northeastern Sonora and
southeastern Arizona. Once in Sonora, the war faction—the

Bedonkohes, some Chokonens, and Mangas's Chihennes—would resume raiding. From May 1850 through January 1851, Mangas led three war parties, each containing from two hundred to three hundred warriors, and struck with impunity Sonora's settlements. In part he was avenging Elías González's campaign into his country during the fall of 1849. Yet he also had another distinct motive, or, as we would term it today, an agenda. Much to his dismay, shortly after he left New Mexico, Teboca, the normally recalcitrant Bedonkohe leader, had appeared at Santa Cruz and solicited peace. The Chokonens were at Bacoachi, Sonora, talking with Elías González himself. Mangas Coloradas, Miguel Narbona, and Cochise were not going to let Elías González believe that his campaign of the previous fall had forced them to come in and beg for peace. Furthermore, this was the same Sonoran leader who had advocated extremist policies for almost two decades—the man whose forces had massacred some one hundred Chiricahuas at Janos and Corralitos in August 1844. Therefore, when Mangas arrived in Sonora, his people began raiding, which effectively disrupted the brittle negotiations between the moderate Chokonens and Elías González.

The Chokonens had first appeared at Bacoachi in early February 1850. A few years later one American, Captain James Box, described the presidio as "situated on a small elevated plain on the west side [of which] runs the Sonora River." Despite a well-irrigated land, the town was losing its population because of the Apaches, who had left them with only three milk cows and three horses when Box visited the town in 1854.[5] Whether the Indians sincerely wanted peace with Sonora or just wanted to exchange their prisoners for those taken by Terán y Tato the previous spring is unclear. Likely they did not expect Elías González to embrace their solicitations, and they viewed any truce as a short-term armistice. On February 7, 1850, a small group of Chokonens appeared at Bacoachi saying that they wished to discuss a truce. They represented most of the Chokonens and part of the Bedonkohes. Yrigóllen, Tapilá, Posito Moraga, and Triqueño Tito had established their camps at Cuchuta and Turicachi, south of Fronteras; Esquinaline and Teboca were at Caguillona, north of Fronteras; and other Chiricahua rancherías were at Cerro Prieto and Alisos, in northeastern Sonora. Miguel Narbona, Cochise, and Mangas Coloradas were conspicuously absent, still in New Mexico at that time. Captain Manuel Martínez detained two warriors, Antonio and Nestor, who was a brother of Demos, the Chokonen

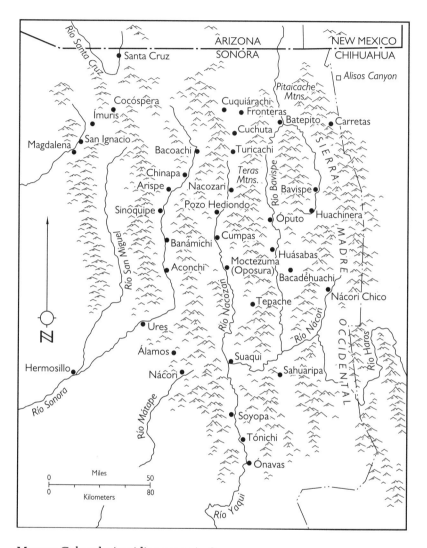

Mangas Coloradas's raiding range in Sonora

war leader whose relatives remained in confinement at Hermosillo. Three weeks later, on February 27, another Chokonen contingent approached Bacoachi bringing messages of peace. This time Chino (a brother of the Chokonen group leader Posito Moraga), Demos, three warriors, and several women came in and offered a prisoner exchange for those "taken the previous year by Terán y Tato."[6]

In response to Martínez's report, Elías González left Arispe for Bacoachi to discuss terms with the Chokonens. He agreed to the Apaches' proposal to exchange captives and on March 6, 1850, met Posito Moraga at Bacoachi. The skittish chief claimed that he truly wanted peace and agreed to return on March 10 to continue the talks. An interested observer during the powwow was Demos, whose relatives were in confinement at Hermosillo. He had remained at Bacoachi visiting with his brother and hoping that Elías González would turn over his kinfolk. Despite the parley, an aura of distrust produced a volatile atmosphere. Consequently, Posito Moraga failed to return on March 10, evidently fearing treachery. At this crucial stage, Demos, disgusted at "Posito Moraga's lack of attention," decided to go in person to the Chiricahua camps and forcibly take every Mexican captive held there. Accompanied by José Yescas, the drummer from the Fronteras garrison then stationed at Bacoachi, they went to the Chiricahua ranchería at Cuchuta and demanded that Posito's group turn over the six Mexican captives in their possession. When his own people resisted this request, Demos, displaying his arms, announced that he had given his word to Elías González that he would return the captives and that he would do so "even if it costs him his life." Finally the owners of the captives acquiesced and turned them over to Demos, who immediately went to Bacoachi and turned them over to Elías González.

He told the Sonoran commander, "I have kept my word so that you, too, will keep your word." Demos's work was not finished, however, for the newly released captives told Elías González that Yrigóllen held other captives in his camp. Immediately Elías González dispatched Demos, who talked to Yrigóllen and convinced him to come in to Bacoachi with his two captives and to discuss a permanent armistice with Sonora's commander. On March 19, 1850, the principal Chokonen band leader came in, returned his two captives, and informed Elías González that his followers truly wanted peace but that they had to "overcome the fear that [the Sonorans] are lying in wait to double-cross them as happened at Galeana [Kirker's massacre.]" Elías González was dubious but excited about the possibility of peace. He drew up a list of five conditions and hoped that this truce might provide Sonora with a respite from the devastating Apache raids. The main points of the treaty "accorded to the chieftains Yrigóllen and Posito Moraga" stipulated that the Apaches should live in designated areas, make war on the Coyoteros (Western Apaches), and help Mexican troops against hostile raiding parties. Elías González failed to address one important consideration—the issuance of rations and other economic assistance—because Sonora still faced a fiscal crisis. Instead, the treaty mandated that the Apaches sustain themselves by harvesting the mescal plant and by planting crops. At the least, as Elías González explained to his superiors in Mexico City, a truce could buy him time to marshal his troops. Finally, in honoring his commitment to Demos, the commander marched south to Arispe with the Chokonen leader and on March 31, 1850, released to Demos's custody his wife and mother-in-law.[7]

When Elías González returned to Arispe, he found that a dispatch had arrived from Santa Cruz with news that the Bedonkohe leader Teboca had come in to that presidio and requested peace. This was astonishing news to Elías González, for he knew Teboca's bellicose reputation. He characterized Teboca as "one of the Indians who most resist pacification, although very trustworthy when it comes to any agreement he makes." After a two-hour discussion Teboca and his twelve warriors left, declaring that "within fifteen or twenty days he would return to see what answer would be given him, and that he was going to advise Mangas Coloradas, since he is his general."[8] Another report said that the Apaches wanted to live in peace in the Chiricahua Mountains.[9] Teboca, Yrigóllen, and Posito Moraga had grown weary of the constant fighting and were honestly seeking a cease-fire; however, Mangas Coloradas and Miguel Narbona did not share these feelings. As it turned out, Mangas summarily vetoed Teboca's proposal. By late March, Mangas had decided to renew his favorite pastime of raiding Sonora.

Mangas's followers first struck along the Magdalena River. On April 1 a large group of warriors, well mounted, killed a herder outside San Ignacio. Soon after, they attacked travelers near San Ignacio, killed two women, wounded a man, and captured a ten-year-old girl. From there they continued to Magdalena and killed several more persons. A few days later they admitted to a group of Americans that they were from Mangas Coloradas's band, though

Santa Cruz, Sonora. Chiricahua war parties struck this presidio and its soldiers several times during the 1840s and early 1850s. (Browne, *Adventures in the Apache Country*)

it was unclear whether he was actually present.[10] Another unconfirmed report, perhaps apocryphal, placed him near Tucson at this time, where he held a powwow with several Americans, including John Glanton.[11] About three weeks later another band of Chiricahuas, likely Bedonkohes, assaulted a party of eleven Mexicans at Tulito, between Banamichi and Cumpas. At the first volley, six of the whites escaped; the Indians captured the five others and disarmed and stripped them. Instead of torturing them to death, as they normally would have done, the Apaches conversed with them. They claimed that they were Mogollons (Bedonkohes) and that they had no desire to make peace. Then, inexplicably, the Indians set them free, although they stole all of their property.[12] Perhaps the Bedonkohes had second thoughts about alienating those who truly wanted peace, or perhaps they spared them for future considerations. For, as Mangas had recently explained to an American party, "If we kill off all the Mexicans, who will raise cattle and horses for us?"[13]

By this time Elías González had begun to express some doubts about the fragile armistice he had worked out with Yrigóllen and Posito Moraga. On April 10, Chiricahuas ransomed José María Mejias, a twelve-year-old boy whose testimony suggested that he had been a prisoner of the war faction, probably Miguel Narbona's band. Mejias said that the Apaches had set their sights on Bacoachi, hoping to drive out the citizens there as they had those of Fronteras and Tubac. Furthermore, according to Mejias, they had solicited peace only to obtain corn and other food from the Mexicans. In reality, many Apaches were then "preparing their weapons so as to carry out their [raids] within ten days." Yet Elías González remained cautiously sanguine about the prospects for peace, dismissing Mejias's claims, since the boy "doesn't know the Indians' language" and therefore might have misunderstood the Apaches, "or he may have been put up to this by someone opposed to the peace." Moreover, he argued, Bacoachi is "the best defended place in the state, having 135 troops plus an artillery piece with its garrison." As late as April 24, 1850, he instructed Captain Manuel Martínez, "Do not miss the slightest chance to firm it [the peace treaty] up."[14]

Despite his idealism, by mid-April Sonora's commanding general had begun to receive reports that bespoke of deteriorating conditions along the northern frontier. Local civilian and military authorities reported Apache depredations at Bacoachi, Moctezuma, and Granadas. The Bedonkohe chief Teboca had not returned to Santa Cruz as promised, and it became apparent to Elías González that the war bloc, led by Mangas Coloradas and Miguel Narbona, had entered Sonora prepared to disrupt Yrigóllen's and Posito Moraga's plans for peace. Despite these incidents Elías González continued to wax optimistic. José Yescas, his reliable informant whom the Chiricahuas liked and respected, had recently returned from a visit to the rancherías of Yrigóllen and Posito Moraga "for the specific purpose of observing the behavior and conversations of the Indians." He saw only positive signs that the Chokonens sincerely wanted peace if Sonora would provide "assistance so as to live in peace, as was done under the Spanish government." Elías González concluded that the Western Apaches, or the Coyoteros, as he called them, had committed these recent hostilities. Believing that this was an opportune time to work out an agreement, he decided to take the initiative. He therefore proposed to Yrigóllen and Posito Moraga a new treaty, with rations the cornerstone of the agreement. On April 15, 1850, he wrote the governor of his plan, which took into account his twenty-five years' experience in dealing with the Chiricahua Apaches. Once Sonora's most hawkish and militant leader, who had asked no quarter and had given none, the perspicacious and pragmatic commander clearly was prepared to modify his steadfast position that extermination and complete subjugation were the only solutions to Sonora's Apache problem:

> Summing up, I have taken the precautionary measures which are the only thing, at the present time, I can do, considering not only that the situation of the troops has failed to improve but also I fear that if the delay in their pay continues, as so many times in the past I have reported to you, they may desert. That could make the complete ruin of the state certain. It is highly embarrassing for me to say such a thing, but duty and my own honor oblige me to repeat it daily to your excellency to comply with my responsibility. The principal purpose of this note was to explain to your excellency that I was suspicious of the first peace talks that I held with the chieftains [Posito] Moraga and Yrigóllen. I knew that their goal was that they should be given rations, as was formerly done, so that they would be able to live without their being obliged to steal. But I avoided the topic because since the system of presidio companies has been reorganized into military settlements, I questioned whether or not the regulations and accompanying instructions for the garrisons would be in force, and therefore I doubted whether I could make that decision, and I doubted even more whether there would be enough resources to put it in effect, since the allowance given to the settlements for feeding the Indians is not enough, nor is it paid. But in view of the fact that without this measure it is impossible to obtain a lasting peace, since likewise the Indians cannot exist with just hunting and [gathering] mescal, which are the resources they have at hand [and] in view of the fact that without supplying them with what they need to exist, it is not possible to oblige them to live at fixed places. While they are wanderers in the desert, it is very difficult to make them recognize the advantages of a social life or to make them take a liking to work. In view of the fact that no effort or expense should be spared to build a dike against the flow of blood that is drowning us in a wave of savages, and since it is absolutely impossible to set up a town or settlement for them, I am taking the liberty of requesting your excellency to intercede with the supreme government [Mexico City] in order to obtain: first, authorization to establish, according to the instructions that it may see fit to give, one or more settlements for those Apache Indians who will want to accept a peace treaty on . . . lands that are unused on the frontier. Second, that they should be provided free of charge the tools and implements needed for working the land, and that they should be accorded all the privileges which the laws provide for settlers. Third, that until they harvest their first

crops they should be provided with enough grain to maintain themselves, this at the expense of the National Treasury. Fourth, should
this project be agreed to, that the settlement or settlements which
may be established shall be subject to the military authorities for
only as long as is necessary for them to get organized and consoli-
dated. As I see it, this will be the only way to get humane results. . . .
Meanwhile, and so as not to lose what little progress has been made,
I am going to give instructions that this be offered to the Indians to
gain their confidence, telling them that starting with the very next
harvest they will be provided with rations provided that they accept
it [the peace] and devote themselves to working.[15]

Elías González sent this proposal to the military commander at
Bacoachi, who discussed it with Yrigóllen and Posito Moraga. On
April 23, 1850, Chino left for Arispe with an escort to discuss the
terms with Sonora's military commander. Several Chiricahua
emissaries remained at Bacoachi, including Yrigóllen, Yaque,
Yrinco, and a son of Esquinaline named Cavanillo. The presence of
the last three men is of interest because Yrinco was a brother of
Manuelito, the same man who suggested a year before to Captain
Padilla at Janos that they plot to kill Mangas Coloradas. Manuelito
had recently perished, supposedly from natural causes. Yaque was
an inveterate raider and in later years a contemporary of Cochise.
At this time Esquinaline was normally associated with Mangas
Coloradas's and Miguel Narbona's groups.

Meanwhile, on April 23, 1850, Chino reached Arispe and held a
parley with Elías González, who agreed to issue rations beginning
July 1, 1850, to those Apaches who settled at either Bacoachi,
Bavispe, or Santa Cruz. In exchange, these Indians must agree to
aid the troops against the "broncos," as he termed the hostile
faction. To avoid any misunderstanding, Elías González ordered
Captain Martínez at Bacoachi to repeat these terms to "Lucia,
Soledad, Carro, and other Indians who speak Spanish, and to José
Yescas, who, as I told you, should go to the Apache encampments
for this and other purposes already agreed on and to inform me
promptly and completely of the results." In closing his letter, the
hardbitten, steel-fisted, veteran warrior flung a parting admonition
to the governor: "In spite of what has already been reported, the
outcome cannot be foreseen with complete certainty, due to the
audacity, double-crossing, and unreliability of the Indians." Mangas Coloradas would have undoubtedly echoed these sentiments
about Sonorans if someone had asked for his opinion.[16]

The main fault of the treaty was Sonora's inability to provide rations until July 1, 1850.

Elías González soon learned that he had underestimated Mangas Coloradas's inflexible opposition to Sonorans and his unrivaled credibility among the Chiricahua bands. The Chokonen leaders Triqueño, Posito Moraga, and Yrigóllen could not do a thing to prevent Apache depredations in Sonora once Miguel Narbona, Cochise, and Mangas Coloradas brought their followers into Sonora. Furthermore, despite the terms of the treaty, they were averse to campaigning for the Mexicans against their relatives, no matter what Elías González had hoped would happen.

In fact, about the middle of May, Mangas Coloradas organized an expedition destined to strike deep into Sonora at the settlements along the Yaqui River. This was a Bedonkohe-Chokonen alliance, with some Chihennes from Mangas Coloradas's local group and perhaps a few Western Apaches. In late April, near the Gila River in Arizona, American traders met Apaches (likely White Mountain Western Apaches) who said that they were going to Sonora. In northeastern Sonora they joined forces with Mangas's war party and headed south, bypassing Bavispe into the Sierra Madre. About May 10 soldiers saw a trail of a large group of Apaches heading south, a fact corroborated by Yrigóllen, who sent a warning to the commander of Bavispe that Mangas Coloradas was in the vicinity.[17]

Their targets were Soyopa, a small mining and agricultural village located on a mesa on the west bank of the Yaqui River about ninety miles south of Moctezuma and some thirty miles southwest of Sahuaripa, and Onavas, about thirty miles south of Soyopa. They attacked Onavas on May 19, causing "a horrible carnage," but the number of casualties is unknown. At Soyopa, which they devastated on May 23, the war party killed sixteen people, wounded six others, and captured nine.[18] This may have been the time when Mangas Coloradas assaulted the great-grandfather of Manuel Valenzuela a few miles north of Tacupeto, which was some thirty miles east of Soyopa. According to Valenzuela, his great-grandfather, Jesús García, a man over six feet in height, was returning home from the California gold mines about 1850 when an Apache ambushed him with an arrow to the back. The Indian approached him, "jumped off his horse and knocked him down, stripping him of everything of value." The Apache, who was even taller than García, identified himself as Mangas Coloradas. Speaking in Spanish, he told García, "You people owe me much." A few residents of Bamori found García before he died, and he related the story of his encounter with the famous Apache.[19]

After these engagements, the Chiricahuas victoriously marched north, accumulating more stock as they retired toward their home bases along the border. In early June they stopped at Yrigóllen's and Posito Moraga's camps in northeastern Sonora, and there, according to some accounts, the two factions quarreled as Mangas Coloradas tried to convince the Chokonens to join him and break off their discussions with Elías González.[20]

Naturally Elías González became incensed when news of the sanguinary raids reached his headquarters. As the Apaches retired north, he ordered Captain Martínez at Bacoachi to take out his presidio forces and try to intercept the war party. He added that "you are to dedicate all your concern and determination to the punishment of that trash, knowing that you will be held responsible for any oversight or negligence." Regarding the Chiricahuas, Martínez was "to obtain exhaustive information about . . . the encampments of Triqueño, Posito Moraga, and Yrigóllen, who are said to be at peace, as well as Mangas Coloradas, and those who follow him, because there is news that they are waging a cruel war against us." Finally, trying to motivate Captain Martínez, he urged him to find out whether the rumors that the two factions had argued were true. Yet, true or not, he was to "move against Mangas Coloradas's Indians with or without Posito Moraga's consent."[21]

Elías González believed that Mangas had organized this expedition to undermine his armistice with Yrigóllen and Posito Moraga, who were usually Mangas's allies in the war against Sonora. Their ongoing negotiations with Sonora after the prisoner exchange had confounded and incensed Mangas, for these discussions ran contrary to their original plans. After the war party returned, Mangas's followers and those of Posito Moraga had a meeting, and a quarrel broke out, probably initiated by hot-headed followers of Mangas Coloradas and the bellicose Miguel Narbona, in which several Apaches were reportedly killed or wounded. In the end, Mangas's war party had served its design. The armistice with Sonora was over, and Elías González's ill-fated peace treaty never became a reality.

Meanwhile, after the reported disagreement with Posito Moraga, Mangas Coloradas, Miguel Narbona, and Cochise moved east toward Carretas, where in mid-June 1850 they held a council with a band of Western Apaches under Quericueryes, the war leader. The allies made plans for upcoming raids before they split up:

Mangas went toward Carrizalillo Springs along the New Mexico–Chihuahua border; Yrigóllen took his Chokonens to Pilares in the Sierra Madre; and Quericueryes, with Casimiro and a few Chokonens, left for a raid into the interior.[22] The alliance between the Western Apaches and Mangas Coloradas was a surprising union until one considers that his influence extended to other Apache tribes, particularly the White Mountain band of Western Apaches and the Mescaleros, because two of his daughters had married leaders of those groups.

Mangas Coloradas had presented another important subject to consider during this conference. The Chihennes and Nednhis were negotiating at Janos to make peace and thus secure the release of their people held as prisoners. Yrigóllen, anxious for an armistice now that his truce with Elías González had failed, decided to send his brother Aguirre to Janos to represent him during the peace talks. Before the meeting at Carretas broke up, Mangas asked Aguirre to act as his representative, saying that he "would agree to the outcome of the deliberations of the council" between the Chiricahua leaders and Chihuahuan officials. This concession by Mangas suggests that he was keeping his options open with Chihuahua in case he encountered problems with Americans upon his return to New Mexico.[23]

In late June, Captain Manuel Martínez left Bacoachi to intercept a band of hostiles near Turicachi. Much to his surprise, he overtook Quericueryes's raiders near Turicachi; the Apaches threw up a white flag, and Martínez, José Yescas, and a small escort met the Apaches between the two lines. Martínez asked them what they were doing there and inquired about the stolen stock. The Indians, entrenched on a hill, told him that they wanted peace, so Martínez alone met Casimiro, a moderate Chokonen leader, halfway up the hill. The two men talked and agreed to meet the next day. Casimiro and Captain Martínez did hold another parley the next day. Martínez told the Chokonen if he really wanted peace to tell Yrigóllen to bring his people to Bacoachi to live. Meanwhile, Martínez granted permission to Quericueryes to trade with several Opatas who belonged to his command. It was a curious arrangement, because the Apaches had stolen plunder and Martínez, true to his character, preferred to negotiate with Indians than fight. If this action did not disturb his superior, his next decision seemed to defy explanation and doubtless enraged Elías González.[24]

A month later, July 20, 1850, three Chokonen leaders (Carro, Casimiro, and Esquinaline) entered Bacoachi to talk with Captain

Martínez. They began their bullying tactics with Martínez, thus revealing that they respected only force. They wanted rations, as Elías González had promised, though they conceded that they had committed depredations in the interior of Sonora. Yet, since they had not done any mischief near Bacoachi, in their minds they "were worthy of rations." They claimed that their permanent homes were usually in the Chiricahua Mountains, although presently their rancherías were near Cuquiarachi. Captain Martínez had nothing to give them, so Carro, the leader of the group, asked for a peso for himself and four reales for Casimiro, Esquinaline, and Negro Gato (Black Cat). In addition the Indians demanded that Martínez release Antonio, who had remained a prisoner at Bacoachi since the previous February. Martínez told them he could not do so without orders. Carro and Esquinaline returned the next day and threatened to raid Bacoachi if Captain Martínez failed to release Antonio. Martínez, after discussing the situation with the civilian authorities at Bacoachi, turned Antonio loose. The Chokonens' blackmail had worked.[25]

Sonora would enjoy a much needed respite from Chiricahua raids until the fall of 1850. Mangas, an interested bystander to the negotiations that were unfolding at Janos, had retired to southern New Mexico by July 1850. As previously mentioned, Captain Padilla and José María Zuloaga at Corralitos continued to hold some twenty Nednhis of the Janeros local group (Soquilla's local group). Mexicans had murdered Negrito, the Nednhi leader who had scouted for Elías González during the fall of 1849, during a gambling and drinking bout. Another Indian woman, probably Gertrudis, the sister of Arvizu, had escaped in late January 1850. On April 30, 1850, she reluctantly returned to Janos with a proposal for an armistice. She represented Chiricahua leaders of the Nednhi and Chihenne bands who wanted to make peace now that they had heard that Zuloaga was no longer the political chief of the district. Padilla wrote his superiors for instructions.[26]

Chihuahua's Governor Angel Trias immediately accepted the Indians' proposal, rationalizing that it was more economical for the state to feed Apaches than incur the expense of costly campaigns that frequently accomplished nothing except to wear out men and mounts. Therefore, on May 11, 1850, he appointed as peace commissioners Antonio Guaspe, a retired captain, and Alejo García Conde. The latter was a brother of Francisco García Conde, the former governor who had made peace with the Chiricahuas in 1842 and had recently fallen victim to the cholera epidemic of

1849, which had taken the lives of more than six thousand Mexicans. They left for the northern frontier two days later.[27] Meanwhile, Captain Padilla instructed Gertrudis to return to the Apache camps and tell the chiefs that Chihuahua's government was interested in an armistice and would send a peace commission to Janos. Gertrudis sent word that the leaders would be in about May 9, but for some reason they did not make their appearance until May 22, when a contingent of some one hundred Apaches, including seven chiefs and about fifty warriors, came into Janos.[28]

The Indians waited for the commissioners for two days. On May 25, 1850, the commissioners arrived at Janos from Corralitos, but with an escort of fifty soldiers, which greatly disturbed the high-strung Apaches, many of whom were in a sullen and morose mood after a two-day drinking binge. They also undoubtedly recalled Zuloaga's attempt to trap them at Janos the year before. Only Arvizu remained. Like the Chokonen Demos, he wanted a treaty to get his relatives released from confinement. His persistence paid off, as did the efforts of Antonio Guaspe and Alejo García Conde. After spending a week at Janos, the latter wrote to Governor Trias about affairs there. García Conde believed that the Apaches remained highly suspicious of Mexicans and had requested peace "because their market from New Mexico, which had always been lucrative, has been shut down by American authorities." The Americans, he incorrectly believed, had "disarmed and whipped" the Chiricahuas. He recommended that Governor Trias take the initiative and provide the Apaches with weekly rations, noting that the treaty of 1833 had failed because the government had not provided any rations. He was correct in this regard, but he failed to understand that the Apaches' primary motive was to liberate their people held by Padilla and Zuloaga. Trias, who despised Americans, seized this opportunity to attract the Chiricahuas away from the Americans to Mexican soil. He promptly agreed to issue rations to the Apaches.[29]

On the day before, Alejo García Conde had written Governor Trias that the Chihenne Itán; the Nednhi leader of the Janeros local group, Láceres; and Ortiz, a Nednhi leader of the Carrizaleño local group, had come into Janos to resume discussions.[30] Over the next three weeks the two commissioners met with the Chiricahua chiefs, gradually convincing them that Chihuahua sincerely wanted peace. During this period they ironed out the details of the treaty, which contained nine articles, and gained the confidence of the leaders. One Indian who impressed them was Babosa, who admitted that the Indians, at war for the last eighteen years, had fled when they saw the troops that the escort had brought. Alejo García Conde considered Babosa "the most intelligent" Apache, for he was literate, educated during the years of the presidio system, and a man of "natural talents." The peace commissioners' efforts at gaining the Apaches' confidence impressed Janos official Juan José Zozaya, who knew the Apaches well. On June 18, 1850, the commissioners issued rations to the Indians, and six days later they consummated a formal armistice at Janos with the Chihenne and Nednhi bands.[31]

On June 24, 1850, six Chiricahua local group leaders—Ponce, Delgadito, and Itán of the Chihenne band and Coleto Amarillo, Láceres, and Arvizu for the Nednhis—agreed to nine articles of peace, one of which named Coleto Amarillo "general." The other articles were typical of past agreements: the Indians would aid the Mexicans against other hostiles, brand their stock, and comply with several other points that pertained to the administration of the peace. The other important issue that concerned the Apaches related to the exchange of prisoners. The Indians had returned two prisoners, claiming that many of their hostages had recently escaped to the New Mexican settlements on the Rio Grande. These statements were disingenuous, of course, as they continued to hold many captives in their power, and Mexican officials had not insisted upon inspecting their camps. In exchange, the commissioners released their twenty-two Chiricahua captives. As for Mangas Coloradas, Alejo García Conde first suspected that he had boycotted the proceedings because he had recently committed depredations in Sonora. Yet in a letter written to Elías González, he reported that Mangas had authorized the Chokonen chief Aguirre to act as his delegate and that he "would agree to the outcome of the deliberations of the council, which he asked to excuse his absence, both because of the distance from where he is and in order not to interrupt his sowing and other forms of field work in which he is engaged."[32] No one knows how much planting of crops Mangas Coloradas was doing at that time. Still, it was true that he had returned to New Mexico by the early summer of 1850. Throughout the 1850s his people did cultivate some areas, especially with American aid, so it was possible that he had planted corn at Santa Lucía, as he would in later years. Still, it was hardly the reason why he did not attend the conference. Likely he was just keeping his options open in case the Americans moved militarily against his people.

Although none of the Chokonens had signed the treaty, Yrigóllen had sent his brother Aguirre to observe the proceedings. It had become apparent to Sonoran authorities that peace no longer interested either Yrigóllen or Posito Moraga. In August two Chokonens from Piase's camp appeared at Bacoachi and solicited peace. They informed Captain Martínez that Yrigóllen, Carro, and Posito Moraga had now decided to make war against Sonora, planning to raid Bacoachi and Bavispe. In late August a Sonoran command encountered the Chokonens under Miguel Narbona, Triqueño, and Posito Moraga in force at Cuchuta. About this time Yrigóllen, anxious for a truce, knowing that he had to distance himself from the warlike Chokonen local groups, took his followers to Janos and made peace there, a decision that was destined to cost him his life.[33]

When Elías González received the letter from the peace commissioners at Janos, he immediately wrote to warn them of Mangas Coloradas's duplicity. Blaming Mangas Coloradas for the breakdown of talks between Sonora and the Chiricahuas, Elías González launched a personal vendetta against the Chiricahua chief. He cited the incident at Santa Cruz, when Mangas had sent "Teboca, his segundo," in to negotiate and then instead of returning launched a vicious campaign against Soyopa and Onavas, which caused a "horrible carnage." Mangas Coloradas is a man "who behaves in bad faith," wrote Elías González to the peace commissioners. This scathing attack on the character of Mangas would create problems for both the Apache chieftain and Juan José Zozaya, the man at Janos who was responsible for administering the treaty.[34]

Meanwhile, while Sonoran and Chihuahuan officials discussed Mangas's character, or lack of it, the Apache leader established his camp at Santa Lucía. Between forays against Sonora, Mangas met Captain Enoch Steen at Santa Rita del Cobre in mid-August. The energetic Steen had left Doña Ana on August 4, 1850, with a command of sixty dragoons "with the intention of visiting the Copper Mines and the vicinity of the Rio Gila and if possible to have a talk with some of the Gileño band of Apaches that I might negotiate a treaty with them and more especially might obtain from them two boys [Teófilo and Mateo Jaramillo] who were stolen from this place in the month of January 1850 [December 1849]."

The hard-working, zealous officer achieved his objective. Reaching Santa Rita del Cobre about August 9, his command six days later "induced to come into camp . . . Mangas Coloradas, the Head Chief of the Gileños and José Cito, the Chief who Commands over the country lying between the Mimbres and Rio Grande with about twenty warriors and a few women came in." Steen's conversation with these two chiefs, especially Mangas Coloradas, provides us with an excellent description of Mangas's view of his universe. Mangas's perceptions of Americans are of particular interest, because his expression, on the surface simple and honest, duplicated those statements that he had made to Kearny four years earlier. Furthermore, for the next decade, or essentially the entire 1850s, his actions and perceptions of Americans reflected what he here told Captain Steen. Steen reported the conference:

> I had quite a long talk with them in which I explained to them as clearly as possible the views and wishes of our Government with regard to them and the course which we wished them to adopt; they replied that they were very desirous of being and remaining at peace with the Americans—but at the same time would swear eternal hatred to the Mexicans; that while the Americans could pass where they wished through their country, and could eat and sleep with them as safely as if he was by his own friends; with the Mexicans it was and ever would be "War to the Knife."

Of interest here are the Jaramillo boys, whom Delgadito had captured, according to Mangas Coloradas and Josécito, and had subsequently sold in Sonora. On this score they were dissembling, or at least Josécito was, for he was the one who had brought the two captives to Bacoachi and had sold them to a citizen there. It was easy to blame Delgadito, who, until the mid-1850s, demonstrated markedly anti-American sentiments. He had remained near Janos to comply with the peace treaty of June 24, 1850. Without Delgadito in the area to defend himself, a little white lie would do no harm.

Steen returned to Doña Ana on August 21. On September 2, 1850, José María Ponce, "the Speaker of the tribe," came in to Doña Ana accompanied by Itán and Cuchillo Negro, followed soon after by Josécito and some thirty men and women. They renewed their vows of friendship to Americans. Steen believed that an agent with a "few thousand dollars worth of presents" could obtain "a lasting peace with this powerful band who have . . . given us so much trouble."[35] Steen may have wondered about Mangas Coloradas, who was conspicuously absent. He had gone to the Chokonens to enlist their help for another incursion against Sonora and Elías González, who had reoccupied Fronteras in September 1850 in an attempt to regain a foothold in his northern frontier.

This war party, led by Mangas Coloradas, Teboca, Esquinaline, and Miguel Narbona, contained an estimated three hundred warriors, which means that Mangas must have drawn his strength from sources other than his Chiricahuas. Later reports suggested that Mangas Coloradas had attracted many warriors from the Coyoteros, or Western Apaches. If so, he was again using his vast influence based on alliances forged because of his reputation and relationships with leaders of the Western Apaches. In addition, the Chokonens had close ties with the two White Mountain bands, and Miguel Narbona, Cochise, and Esquinaline were prominent leaders of this war party. In any event, the Apaches first struck the Santa Cruz–San Ignacio area, cleaning out ranches of their stock. Near Imuris they murdered eight citizens before returning toward Arizona in early October. Mangas's raid infuriated Elías González, who ordered José Terán y Tato to gather a force and pursue the hostiles.[36]

Terán y Tato's force, which consisted of 272 men, left Fronteras on October 14, 1850, and followed the trail of Mangas Coloradas's war party to Apache Pass in the Chiricahua Mountains. From there the trail led to San Simón and north to the Gila River, which was now U.S. territory, so Terán y Tato turned back toward Sonora. He believed his troops had cut the trail of hostiles under Miguel Narbona and Teboca. Returning south, he split his force, sending one hundred men under the command of Captain Reyes Cruz to scout Embudos and Pitaicache while he took the remainder to the deserted Cuchuverachi hacienda, where he had left his supplies. From there Terán y Tato continued his patrol to Pilares, where on October 30, 1850, his command jumped the ranchería of Posito Moraga and Triqueño Tito and killed two men, five women, and one child and captured ten others.[37] The prisoners admitted that Posito Moraga had just returned from visiting Janos. Four months later Triqueño avenged Terán y Tato's attack and assaulted his hacienda at Pibipa, seven miles south of Moctezuma, killing four people and stealing some stock.[38]

While Elías González was at Fronteras, on October 12 he received a patronizing letter dated September 25, 1850, from Juan José Zozaya at Janos. Zozaya, who had succeeded Antonio Guaspe as the peace commissioner upon the latter's death, was responding to Elías González's communication of the previous July in which the commander had pointed out that Mangas Coloradas had intentionally disrupted his agreement with Yrigóllen's and Posito Moraga's Chokonens. Zozaya wanted Elías González to know that

Yrigóllen had come into the fold at Janos, had camped near the presidio, and considered himself at peace with Sonora. The Chokonen chief promised to "keep the good faith that he pledged to you." Zozaya also wished to separate his peaceful Indians from the hostiles, pointing out to Elías González that "since Mangas Coloradas, Teboca, and Esquinaline have not come forward to sign the treaties that I have mentioned, they, together with the Coyoteros, have committed the raids in Sonora, according to reports given me by the Indians themselves." Zozaya, aware that Elías González had invaded Janos and massacred over one hundred Apaches in the summer of 1844, closed his letter by assuring Sonora's commander that he would not allow any raiding into Sonora by the Indians whom he was rationing. This was a difficult task. Yet his diligent efforts and consistent policies almost eliminated this fraudulent practice.[39]

Elías González appreciated Zozaya's letter. He responded that "indeed during the same days when you were kind enough to communicate this warning to me, the said Indians were busy attacking us at Santa Cruz and the San Ignacio River, where they [committed] another thousand atrocities." The no-nonsense officer bluntly declared that Terán y Tato was following the trail of the hostiles, and if it led to Janos, "you will have the unpleasant experience of seeing them punished there as they deserve and natural law permits." Meanwhile, Elías González gratefully accepted Zozaya's offer to keep an eye on the activities of the peaceful Apaches at Janos.[40]

Subsequent events showed that Zozaya carefully heeded the advice of Sonora's legendary military commander. Chihuahuan officials desperately wanted the peace to work. They put into practice policies to prevent the Chiricahuas from using Janos as a base from which to raid into Sonora, as had happened in 1843 and 1844. Elías González had clearly explained what actions he would take if he believed this was happening. Zozaya, as peace commissioner, found himself in a delicate position. He recognized that Elías González would unflinchingly invade Janos if he felt the Apaches were raiding Sonora from Janos; yet any such action from Sonora would waste his efforts to keep peace in Chihuahua.

In December he faced two significant challenges. Two Chokonens from the Pitaicache Mountains in Sonora, likely from Posito Moraga and Triqueño's local group, tried to sell at Janos eight head of stock stolen in Sonora. Zozaya refused permission and confiscated the stock, planning to return the animals to their rightful owners. Sonora's governor applauded his action. Then, in mid-December the peace commissioner had to address another important issue. Mangas Coloradas, after leaving the Burro Mountains for northern Mexico, had dispatched an emissary to Zozaya to request peace, undoubtedly hoping that the commissioner would invite him in and ration his people for the winter. Zozaya, however, told Mangas's messenger that before he could open negotiations, the chief first had to make peace with Sonora.[41] Mangas undoubtedly scoffed at that idea.

Meanwhile, in Mexico City federal officials had responded to the pleas of Sonora's able and ambitious Governor José de Aguilar, who had replaced Gándara as the latter's coalition began to lose power. During the summer of 1850 Aguilar had written several letters about the Apache problem in Sonora.[42] The federal government took steps to remedy the problem by replacing José María Elías González with an officer who thought himself omniscient: Colonel José María Carrasco.[43] He arrived with an impressive title (commanding general and inspector of the military colonies) but with only forty federal troops. Believing that he was Sonora's savior, Carrasco exhibited an arrogance and driving temperament that effortlessly offended anyone who annoyed or inconvenienced him. The minister of war in Mexico City had unceremoniously booted out Elías González even though his Herculean efforts to stem the tide in the last two years had slowly begun to show progress in the fight against the Apaches.[44]

Before Carrasco had arrived in Sonora, in early January two Apache war parties invaded Sonora. One consisted of warriors from the Chokonen band led by Posito Moraga, Triqueño, and Yrigóllen, perhaps with some Nednhis from those rancherías at Janos. Mangas Coloradas led the second group, which included Ponce's Chihennes, Teboca's Bedonkohes, the Chokonens under Miguel Narbona, Esquinaline, undoubtedly Mangas's son-in-law Cochise, and reportedly some Western Apaches. According to official reports, each group contained at least 150 warriors.

One war party, apparently Mangas Coloradas and Cochise's, penetrated deep into Sonora and struck the outskirts of Hermosillo before it eventually turned back for its homeward march. The second group concentrated its efforts on the settlements along the Sierra Madre, hitting ranches and villages in the district of Sahuaripa. Details concerning the extent of the Apaches' activities are sparse. These two immense war parties boldly ravaged the countryside and struck widespread terror as they went, with little resistance from Sonora's national guard troops, who appeared awe-struck at the Indians' audacity. Mangas's people met with feeble resistance, which probably surprised him, as he was unaware that Colonel José María Carrasco had replaced their inveterate adversary, Elías González. Carrasco had not yet reached Sonora, thus leaving a vacuum in leadership.

In any event, as the Indians moved north Sonora's governor ordered Captain Ignacio Pesqueira to enlist a force of fifty national guard troops at Arispe and march northeast to rendezvous with a similar force from Bacoachi,[45] which was under the command of Captain Manuel Martínez, the same officer whom the Chokonens had intimidated into releasing Antonio the previous summer. On January 16, 1851, Pesqueira's command united with Martínez at Cerro Colorado, a small group of hills about twelve miles east of Pozo Hediondo ("Smelly Springs" or "Stinking Springs"). The next day Pesqueira moved the command about twelve miles northeast to another range called Sierra del Cobre; there he concealed his troops in ambush to await the Apaches as they moved north toward their villages. Pesqueira sent out a patrol which returned early January 20 with the news that they had seen a cloud of dust in the valley to the south, which, they believed, was caused by Indians retiring north with their booty. Although unaware of the Apaches' numbers, the two captains dutifully moved their force into position at Pozo Hediondo to trap the unsuspecting Indians.

Pozo Hediondo, today known as Gran Esperanza, was located in a beautiful valley surrounded by hills to the east and south. Today the Agua Caliente ranch lies at the foot of the hills where the main battle took place.[46] As the vanguard of Apaches approached, the Mexican force, which outnumbered their enemy two to one, attacked and routed them, forcing the Indians to abandon about three hundred head of stock and flee for higher ground. Pesqueira's force "succeeded in dislodging them from a very advantageous position." As the Indians withdrew, the Mexicans continued to pursue, believing that they had the small force on the run. What Pesqueira failed to realize was that the main body of some 150 warriors under Mangas Coloradas was coming up the valley driving before them some one thousand horses. The Apaches, surprised at the Mexican attack, had turned the tables on their adversaries and had decoyed them into the jaws of a trap.

For the next three hours the Apaches and Mexicans fought a pitched battle—"war to the knife," as Mangas had phrased it to Captain Steen only a few months before—much of it hand-to-hand

Pozo Hediondo (Ojo Hediondo), Sonora. This was where Mangas Coloradas led the allied Chiricahua bands that routed Captain Ignacio Pesqueira's troops. (Author's Photo)

combat, as the two sides were so close that the Indians could use their deadly lances and accurate bows. Geronimo, who was in the fight, recalled that the Chiricahuas struck the Mexicans from the front and rear. Like many young warriors, he enhanced his reputation in this battle. He "fought with fury" and "many Mexicans fell by my hand." The Apache assault systematically forced the Mexicans to retire from one hill to another, so by 4:00 P.M. their deadly fire had killed or wounded every Mexican officer. During the fight the Apaches killed Captain Manuel Martínez of Bacoachi and wounded Pesqueira and his assistant, Rafael Angel Corella (an unabashed Apache-hater).[47] About this time Yrigóllen and Posito Moraga arrived with another group of warriors, perhaps one hundred or more. The two sides skirmished until dark, when a welcome lull in the fighting occurred. Pesqueira could report but fifteen men able to fight. The Apaches had killed twenty-six and wounded forty-six of Pesqueira's one hundred men. According to one Mexican eyewitness, Pesqueira's force had killed or wounded some seventy Apaches, undoubtedly an exaggeration.

According to Mexican reports the Apache force consisted of some 400 to 700 warriors in the battle. Of course no one knows for sure how many Indians were in the fight, and white accounts usually exaggerated Indian numbers and fatalities. There were not 700 warriors, and even 400 would have been an extremely large number for the Chiricahuas, considering that some Chihennes had remained in New Mexico and that most of the Nednhis were at Janos. A possible scenario was this: the Chihennes, led by Ponce, 50 men; the Bedonkohes under Teboca, 50 men; virtually the entire Chokonen band under Miguel Narbona, Cochise, Esquinaline, Carro, Posito Moraga, Triqueño, Tapilá, and Yrigóllen, 175 men; some 25 Nednhis under Juh; and a band of Western Apaches, 50 men. This total of 350 warriors was split between the two war parties, with Mangas as the overall commander.

Although we do not know for certain what Mangas's role was in the actual fight, we could speculate that he, as would befit any Chiricahua war chief, was actively involved in the battle, urging his men forward and leading by example. He did not own the reputation as a fighter that his son-in-law Cochise did, but as a leader of the Chiricahuas, even at the age of sixty, he still assumed an active role—for no Apache chief stood in the background while his men fought. Never had the Chiricahuas fought so spectacularly in battle; this was a testament to Mangas's single-mindedness and leadership abilities. His importance at Pozo Hediondo rested on his ability to draw together the coalition of bands and to infuse them with a confidence—perhaps bordering on arrogance—that they were invincible to Sonoran firepower, which resulted in the rout and annihilation of Pesqueira's command. Mangas hardly could have realized it then, but this victory at Pozo Hediondo marked the climax of the Chiricahua five-year reign of undisputed domination of northern Sonora. Sonora's new commander, Colonel José María Carrasco, would use this defeat to rally the citizens of northern Sonora to his cause and renew that state's militaristic philosophy as the only solution to the Apache problem.[48]

After the defeat, Pesqueira sent a messenger to Cumpas for reinforcements. The next day one hundred men arrived and discovered the grisly picture of fresh corpses strewn about the battlefield, and the scene of carnage so horrified the Mexicans that they refused to follow the Apaches' trail. By this time it was too late, anyhow, for Mangas's war party had continued to Bacoachi, probably realizing the presidio was short of manpower because many of its men had fallen during the fight at Pozo Hediondo.[49] At 9:00 A.M. January 21, 1851, the Apaches surprised eleven people outside the presidio. They killed six, including Teodoro Bustamante

Ignacio Pesqueira, a future governor of Sonora. He led the troops at Pozo Hediondo, who were nearly annihilated in January 1851 by Mangas Coloradas's war party. (Courtesy Arizona Historical Society, no. 7452)

(the alcalde, or mayor), and captured the other five. Soon after, the Indians "as such is their custom," asked for a parley to trade their prisoners. After a lengthy powwow with Mangas Coloradas and other Apaches whom the Mexicans recognized, the townspeople ransomed a few people, leaving at least three in the hands of the Apaches, including two boys, Saverro Heradia (whom we will hear of again) and Jesús Arvizu,[50] who would become a member of Mangas Coloradas's extended family group until he was traded to the Navajos a year later. The war party headed east toward the Pitaicache Mountains, where the bands split up; most of the Chokonens remained there, Yrigóllen's Chokonens and Juh's Nednhis returned to the vicinity of Janos, and Mangas Coloradas and his Bedonkohes and Chihennes left for New Mexico.[51]

Mangas reached his ranchería located near the Burro Mountains, probably at Santa Lucía, by the end of January. Before leaving Mexico, he had sent another messenger to Janos to ask about making peace there. Again, Zozaya rebuffed his emissary, insisting that the hostiles first make peace with Sonora before he would consider negotiating. Teboca and Esquinaline requested that Zozaya sign a pass for them to return to Sonora and open negotiations. They must have had second thoughts, or maybe no intentions at all, for to request peace with Sonora after the Pozo Hediondo fight would have been tantamount to suicide. Meanwhile, immediately upon Mangas's return to U.S. soil, Delgadito informed him that an American officer wished to meet him for a talk.[52]

This man was Captain Louis S. Craig,[53] who commanded an escort of eighty-five men of the U.S. Boundary Commission under John R. Bartlett. Craig had arrived at Santa Rita del Cobre to establish a depot for the commission on January 25, 1851. The day before, he had met several Apaches, "among them a subchief (Delgadito)." Craig had a friendly talk with Delgadito and told him that he was "very anxious to see his chief Mangas Coloradas, that I understood that he was very friendly disposed towards the Americans." Mangas had entered New Mexico about the day that Craig had met Delgadito, and on February 2, 1851, he visited Craig at Santa Rita del Cobre. About the meeting, Craig wrote:

> I expressed great pleasure on meeting with him, and informed him that I had always understood that he was a friend to the Americans; that the country which he and his people resided on had lately been purchased from the Mexican Government by the Americans, and that he and his people so long as they conducted themselves in a

proper manner would meet with the kindest treatment from the American Government; that we were now about to run the line between the two countries, and expected to be among his people for some eighteen months or more and that I hoped that he would see that his young men did not interfere with our animals while grazing in the neighborhood of the Cantonment.

Mangas characteristically replied that "he had a great hatred for the Mexicans but that he looked upon Americans as his friends, and that instead of interfering with our animals should any go astray, he would see that they were brought in to us."[54] In the Apache view of his universe, Americans had not yet committed any egregious acts to warrant open hostilities. Yet they were still newcomers who were encroaching on Mangas's country, so he must have harbored some resentment of them. For the interim, Mangas would continue to send representatives to Janos, hoping that they would invite him in and issue rations to his people until they could harvest the mescal plant in the spring.

Meanwhile, in Sonora the new commanding general, Colonel José María Carrasco, arrived in late January to find the northern frontier in turmoil after the Chiricahuas' drubbing of Pesqueira's force at Pozo Hediondo. Although the Apaches had killed 111 Sonorans in 1850, which was down from the 187 killed in 1849,[55] the situation was not getting any better. To compound matters, the discovery of gold in California had depleted the frontier of manpower, as many able-bodied men from Sonora's settlements had rushed to the gold fields.[56] Carrasco was determined to take control. He promptly announced that his main objective was to punish the Apaches. In Sonora, knowledgeable persons believed that many hostiles were living at Janos under the peace agreement of 1850, from where they raided into Sonora. Indeed, some Chiricahuas from Janos had fought in the Pozo Hediondo fight, but most of that large war party consisted of warriors from the bands that had not made peace at Janos. Two months before the Pozo Hediondo battle, Elías González, who understood the Apache political structure as well as anybody, had credited Juan José Zozaya, the peace commissioner at Janos, for doing all in his power to ensure that the Indians at Janos were not raiding in Sonora.[57]

Hoping to find explanations to this controversy, on January 28, 1851, eight days after the disaster at Pozo Hediondo, Terán y Tato appointed Bacerac resident Luis García, a veteran national guard commander, to the post of special commissioner to go to Janos and investigate conditions there. García's contemporaries regarded him as a man of integrity and character. Terán y Tato ordered García to find out whether the Chiricahuas at Janos were responsible for any of the raiding in Sonora. He correctly pointed out that the massive war parties were not just Western Apaches, but also included many Chiricahuas whom the citizens of Bacoachi and the survivors of Pozo Hediondo had recognized. Terán y Tato wrote García: "Therefore, so that we may be sure about this, and so that we can know whether or not the peace is being observed in good faith, it is necessary to be certain which are the Indians who report for review and rations every eight days. . . . It is possible that there may be good faith in this matter in the state of Chihuahua, but here up to the present, there does not seem to be anything except war to the death for everyone."[58]

García reached Janos on February 18, 1851, and immediately conferred with authorities. After remaining at Janos for the next ten days, he wrote a report that supported Zozaya's contentions that the Chiricahuas living at Janos had not participated in any of the recent campaigns. He concluded that the 180 families living in five rancherías near Janos were keeping their agreement with Chihuahua, which, in turn, issued rations to them. He had seen no evidence of any raiding into Sonora. Instead, he concurred with Zozaya's findings that the culprits were the Western Apaches along with the Chokonens at Pitaicache, who were under Posito Moraga, Triqueño, Miguel Narbona and Cochise, and Mangas Coloradas's followers in New Mexico. In conclusion, García termed the treaty at Janos between Apaches and Mexicans "a model base."

Juan Zozaya, the peace commissioner, was quite familiar with the contraband trade that had been a way of life at Janos for the past ten years. Elías González had named him as one of the principals involved in this practice after the commander's invasion in 1844. Zozaya apparently tried to control this illicit practice and definitely tried to keep the hostiles from coming to Janos and tainting the treaty, thus subjecting Janos to a possible invasion from Sonora. Since he could not be everywhere at once, undoubtedly some illicit trading continued and the more militant Chiricahuas carried on some unsanctioned raiding into Sonora. Unfortunately for García and Zozaya, by the time the scrupulously honest García had written his official report, Colonel José María Carrasco was already en route to Janos with a large Sonoran army to strike at the Chiricahuas, most of whom were innocent of the crimes laid at their wickiup's door.

In any event, García's report would not have affected Carrasco's course of action. Reaching Ures by January 19, 1851, the colonel immediately ordered all deserters to return to their commands within eight days or face a firing squad. He planned to convene a council of war that would include both military and civilian officials. His zeal impressed Sonora's Governor José de Aguilar, who wrote that Carrasco has brought a formal plan to defend the state from Apache incursions. In mid-February Carrasco reached Bacoachi. By then he had assimilated everything he needed to know. He concluded that the Chiricahuas at Janos deserved to be punished and that he would lead a force there and see to their punishment.[59]

While at Bacoachi, Carrasco made his Apache policy public knowledge. He declared a "war to the death, except females of all ages and males under the age of fifteen." His forces were forbidden to negotiate with the Apaches when on campaigns against them. In his new edict, which he sent to the governor, he also disparaged the efforts and integrity of his predecessors, José María Elías González and José Terán y Tato. Among other things, he charged them with neglecting to train their soldiers and with submitting to the governor erroneous reports about victorious campaigns. Carrasco could not have expected that El Sonorense would publish his private but scathing letter to the governor, which was how Elías González and Terán y Tato discovered the accusations.[60] These unfounded allegations incensed Elías González, who was already upset at his abrupt dismissal, and his explosion point was then attached to a very short fuse. Carrasco's charges equally enraged Terán y Tato. Both men wrote to the governor vehement letters defending their honor and refuting the specious charges.[61]

Meanwhile, as Carrasco was preparing to march his four-hundred-man force from Fronteras to Janos, there was a flurry of activity at Janos. To begin with, toward the end of February Coleto Amarillo, the Nednhi chief who was the "general" of the Apaches at Janos, informed Zozaya that they had heard rumors of a campaign from Sonora against the Apaches at Janos. Zozaya tried to calm the jittery leader, probably hoping that Luis García's report on conditions at Janos would deter any Sonoran invasion. Despite Zozaya's sincere intentions, the rumor proved to be an eerie harbinger of things to come. Next, Zozaya said that he had heard again from Mangas Coloradas, who had left the Burro Mountains and claimed that he wanted to join the peace treaty at Janos. According to his messengers, Mangas wished to live in extreme southwestern New Mexico at either Santo Domingo Playa, Alamo Hueco, or the Animas Mountains.[62] Significantly, none of these locations was close enough to Janos that Mexican troops could easily surprise his people. His motives were unclear, but it was likely that he expected a Sonoran response to his victory at Pozo Hediondo. As the Sonorans' last campaign had penetrated the Chihenne and Bedonkohe strongholds of the Burro Mountains, he may have expected that Carrasco's army might take the same approach. Finally, on the last day of February 1851, five Chiricahua leaders came into Janos to talk to Zozaya. Unfortunately their names were not reported, but Geronimo recalled that he was present with the Bedonkohes under Mangas Coloradas. In addition, we could speculate that the other three were the Chokonens of Esquinaline, Posito Moraga, and one of their leading war chiefs, Tapilá, who was at Janos in early March trying to barter Pesqueira's saddle that he had taken at Pozo Hediondo.[63]

On Monday, March 3, 1851, Zozaya issued rations to some 180 families, representing over six hundred Indians, and he expected some 200 more Indians for the next ration.[64] According to what the Apache prisoners later told Carrasco, all of the Indians were present. In other words, there were no Chiricahuas raiding in Sonora. Two days later, in the early morning of March 5, 1851, Carrasco's force was near Janos, undetected by either Apaches or Mexicans. He later justified his attack by noting that he was in pursuit of stolen stock taken at Bacerac, which mission, he felt, gave legitimacy to his invasion. Regardless of stolen stock or not, his army, thirsty for revenge and Apache blood, was going to invade Janos. Carrasco split his army up near Janos. He dispatched one division under Lieutenant Colonel Prudencio Romero, guided by a soldier from Janos, to jump a ranchería a few miles southeast of Janos. Romero found the camp, but the Indians had recently abandoned it, so he continued to Janos. En route he encountered seven Apaches, killed two, and captured the other five. Then he went to Janos and surrounded the town, arriving shortly after a group of Chiricahuas had entered the town in flight from Carrasco's command.

Carrasco's army had discovered and attacked Yrigóllen's ranchería a few miles west of Janos. Most of Yrigóllen's people, including Tapilá, escaped upriver, but when Yrigóllen with three men and four women tried to stop the assault, signaling a desire to parley, Carrasco's men cut them down instantly. The Sonorans undoubtedly destroyed the village, and perhaps others, before going on to Janos, where they found Romero's force outside the presidio's walls. Carrasco entered Janos, where he killed several more men, although the details are unclear. Among the dead was Arvizu, the Nednhi leader of the Janeros local group who was second in command to Coleto Amarillo. Arvizu had not left Janos since he had signed the treaty, according to José María Aguirre, the political chief of Galeana. All told, the Sonoran mob claimed to have killed sixteen men and five women and captured sixty-two, of whom fifty-six were women and children. Most of the casualties were Chokonens and Nednhis, although it seems likely that Carrasco's army murdered more women and children than the commanding general reported, at least if we can believe Geronimo. In his auto-biography Geronimo recalled that he lost his mother, wife, and three children in the attack. His chronology is wrong, however, as he placed the Carrasco massacre before the Pozo Hediondo fight.[65]

In any event, according to contemporary reports and Geronimo's recollections, Mangas Coloradas was in the vicinity at the time of Carrasco's attack. When the warriors returned to their camp and found it destroyed, they "assembled at our appointed place of rendezvous." At a council convened by Mangas Coloradas "it was decided that as there were only eighty warriors left, and [as we] were furthermore surrounded by the Mexicans far inside their own territory, we could not hope to fight successfully. So our chief, Mangas Coloradas, gave the order to start for home in Arizona, leaving the dead upon the field."[66]

Over the next few months the Chiricahuas would not imme-diately respond to this attack, as the authorities in Chihuahua had predicted, because Carrasco had escorted his sixty-two prisoners to Ures and Guaymas. Throughout the following summer the Choko-nens attempted to obtain the release of their people, but they were unable to recover most of them. As for Mangas Coloradas, Sonora's militancy had compelled him to return to his home in New Mexico. There he discovered that American troops and civilians with John Russell Bartlett's boundary commission had occupied Santa Rita del Cobre. Mangas would have his first period of normal relations with Americans. Naturally, because the two cultures differed so profoundly from each other, and neither race com-pletely understood the values of the other, this period of peace would be short in nature.

Chapter 10

AMERICANS OCCUPY
SANTA RITA DEL COBRE

MANGAS Coloradas's emotions must have swung from one extreme to the other during the months following Carrasco's clandestine attack at Janos, which served to reinforce his perception of Sonorans. Against those people his hatred boiled over; it was truly a war "to the knife." Carrasco's abduction of sixty-two Chiricahuas, including fifty-two children, to Sonora forced the Indians to bide their time and delay any massive revenge raid. That could come later. Instead, in the coming months the Chokonens and Nednhis, whose people Carrasco had captured, tried to arrange a treaty with the expectation that Carrasco would release his hostages. Although Mangas was not directly involved in these negotiations, he was clearly in Sonora during the spring of 1851. Hoping that he would not launch any war party until their efforts had run their course, the Chokonens kept him informed of their discussions with Carrasco.

As this saga unfolded, Mangas Coloradas faced new and potentially menacing challenges of his own in New Mexico. John Russell Bartlett's Boundary Commission, sent from Washington to survey the border between Mexico and the United States, had set up headquarters at the unoccupied adobe presidio at Santa Rita del Cobre. With him rode an escort of American troops under Captain Louis S. Craig. For several weeks the Chiricahuas remained about the mines, coming in to trade and to receive gifts from the Americans, who wanted to complete their task without conflict with the Apaches. But that would prove to be an impossible task. Minor disputes occurred, and whites spilled Apache blood; both races gradually wore out their welcome with the other. In late

1851 and early 1852 the Chihennes did engage in some raiding and skirmishing with Americans, especially after the latter established a fort at Santa Rita del Cobre five months after Bartlett's commission had moved further west. Yet throughout all of this, Mangas's thoughts and actions always seemed to turn toward Sonora, which, during 1851 and the first six months of 1852, continued aggressively to make war on the Chiricahuas. When Mangas returned home from his annual spring sojourn in 1852, Cuchillo Negro informed him that the Americans wanted to make a treaty with him, one that he would gladly embrace.

Meanwhile, Carrasco's army had remained at Janos for several days, hearing testimony from their Apache prisoners and from several of Janos's citizens. Sonora's commanding general recognized that his actions and conduct would generate much controversy, at least in the eyes of Chihuahuan officials, who had immediately condemned his actions and had lodged a formal complaint to the federal government in Mexico City. Yet a cocksure Carrasco was not concerned, for he knew that he had the support of the federal government, which, after all, had sent him to Sonora to resolve its Apache problem. Although he was an egotistical and arrogant man, Carrasco impressed those Americans he met with his hospitality and his affable nature, which, however, masked an unflinching ruthlessness to his Apache enemies.

On March 6, 1851, the day following his assault, Carrasco wrote José Aguirre at Galeana to justify his occupation at Janos. To begin with, he said that his army had followed the trail of those Apaches who had recently annihilated Pesqueira's command at Pozo Hediondo. In fact, he had recovered Pesqueira's horse, which had a bullet wound in its right foot, and his saddle from a chief (Tapilá) who had fled upriver during the attack on Yrigóllen's camp. His men killed Arvizu because "he tried to escape," a frontier euphemism for murder in cold blood. Witnesses reported that the Sonorans had executed the Nednhi chief in his tracks, just as had been Yrigóllen's fate. Finally, to turn the screw tighter, Carrasco closed his letter of self-congratulation with a charge that indicted several citizens of Janos and Corralitos in the contraband trade, which served to encourage the Apaches already raiding in Sonora.[1]

Aguirre at once responded to Carrasco's missive. He disputed the charge that the Indians who had fought Pesqueira were living at Janos. He pointed out that Tapilá and Pealche (or Piase) had come to Janos the day before Carrasco's attack and noted that authorities had prohibited them from entering the presidio. Then they visited

Yrigóllen's ranchería, where they spent the night, and were present by coincidence when Carrasco attacked the camp the next morning. He concluded his response by denying that these Indians were involved in any of the raiding into Sonora.[2]

Sonora's army remained at Janos until March 10. Carrasco investigated conditions there, interviewing local residents and the adult Apaches whom he had captured. His main informant turned out to be Tinaja, a man well acquainted with Mangas Coloradas. Tinaja conceded that the Indians went to Sonora every three or four moons to raid, after which they returned to Janos to dispose of their stolen stock. He implicated several Janos citizens in this illicit traffic plus several Chiricahuas, including Candelario, Yaque, and Piase—none of whom was a member of his group. Surprisingly, he revealed that these citizens acted as brokers for an organized network that moved the booty to Paso del Norte. One woman, Sisgalle, likely a wife of the Chokonen chief Chagaray, confirmed what Tinaja told Carrasco; another woman, Rita, declared that the Indians sold the mules and horses openly to the citizens. After Carrasco recovered over three hundred head of stock, including thirty-eight horses and mules that had belonged to Sonoran soldiers and citizens, he decided to leave Janos. He had heard and seen enough.[3]

He left the presidio on March 10, 1851, taking with him sixty-two prisoners: six men, four women, and fifty-two children. That afternoon a group of "very frightened" Apaches cautiously filtered into Janos, hoping in vain that Carrasco had not taken their people back to Sonora. They did not hold Chihuahua responsible for the fiasco; instead, they endeavored to convince Carrasco to return their kinfolk. This turn of events clearly anguished those parents who had lost children to Carrasco's invasion. Military and civil officials at Janos conceded that the Indians, who left in a dispirited and melancholy mood, were threatening to avenge the assault. Although one band under Chinito, a Nednhi leader of the Janeros band, did resume hostilities, undoubtedly to avenge Arvizu's death, about two-thirds of the Chiricahuas who were receiving rations before Carrasco's attack (ninety-five families and four hundred individuals) returned to receive rations in early April. At this time Mangas Coloradas had joined the Chokonens in northeastern Sonora, uncertain about their next move until they knew what Carrasco intended to do with their people.[4]

Meanwhile, Chihuahua's governor sent a cogent and forceful protest to federal officials at Mexico City, expecting that they would censure Carrasco and uphold the sovereignty of Chihuahua. He believed that Sonora's commanding general should have attacked the Coyoteros and warlike Chiricahuas from the Gila. After all, according to his subordinates, they were the Indians responsible for the depredations in Sonora, not the Apaches living at Janos. He pointed out that the distinguished Luis García of Sonora had investigated affairs there and had concluded that the Indians were complying with the terms of their agreement. The governor argued that Carrasco had no legal authority to invade Chihuahua. He had violated military laws that prohibited commanding generals of one state from crossing into another without permission. Furthermore, once he entered Chihuahua he was subject to the jurisdiction of its commanding general, according to articles three and four of Treaty Number Six. His operation has destroyed "in a moment the fruits and the hopes of our sacrifices. . . . His conduct has been harmful and offensive to the state of Chihuahua."

In truth, the versions of Colonel Carrasco and Chihuahua's governor were neither duplicitous nor hypocritical. If anything, they were guilty only of emphasizing their own subjective viewpoints. On the one hand, Carrasco did find evidence that linked these Indians to raids in Sonora, although his justification that he followed a trail of hostiles to Janos was hogwash. On the other hand, Chihuahuan authorities in the state capital at Chihuahua City were ignorant of what was going on at Janos, basing their arguments on what public officials from Galeana and Janos told them. With this mountain of information, and the fact that Carrasco had trespassed into their sovereign state without permission, they felt certain that Mexico City would recall Carrasco and censure him.[5]

Meanwhile, as Carrasco countermarched to Ures, Sonora, he received a hero's welcome at each town that he passed through. At Moctezuma, residents celebrated his arrival in a manner similar to that by which Rome had greeted its victorious legions. El Sonorense, Sonora's official newspaper, a partisan advocate for genocide, was ecstatic about his feat, hoping that it was a forerunner "for the success of his second expedition, which he will undertake." After reaching the capital on March 26, 1851, he placed the Chiricahua prisoners in the hands of Captain Teodoro López de Aros, who immediately escorted them to Guaymas. The Apaches never heard of most of their relatives again.[6]

Two days after he arrived in Ures, Carrasco penned his version to his superior, the minister of war and navy at Mexico City, justifying his actions while also adding several arguments that he knew would prove to be compelling:

The government of Chihuahua spends a considerable sum every month buying sugar, wheat, corn, cigarettes, and sheep to provide rations for the Apaches who live in the countryside and only come on Mondays to get the ration. Moreover, it is given to their families when they themselves are on a campaign in Sonora. The people who sell grain have a vested interest in the peace treaties in that after supplying it to the commissioner and after he has distributed it, they buy it back for a little liquor and some cotton goods which are smuggled in through El Paso. In this way they make a big profit, in addition to the fact that it produces the hunger which leads the Indian men to go to Sonora to steal horses and cattle. They then sell the part of this which they do not consume. Your excellency will see that all of this is well proved by the indictment that I had made at that settlement [Janos], a document which contains testimony given by the Indians and the residents. Even more conclusive is the gathering which I had assembled in the town, of the beasts of burden and the riding animals which belong to residents and men in the military. They are all from Sonora and have been stolen in recent days. In short, your excellency, all along the Chihuahuan border from Janos to El Paso . . . no cattle are eaten and no animals are saddled except those from Sonora. Can his excellency, the governor of the state of Chihuahua, the General Commander, and the Inspector of the Military Colonies all tolerate something which has not been permitted by independent nations even in more savage times? What would Christianity have done? What would Europe have said if a state had opened its doors to the blond beards when they were controlling the Mediterranean taking devastation to the coasts and captivity to the inhabitants? What would it have said, I repeat, if one of the small states in Italy had, through cowardice or greed, opened a market for resale of the fruits of piracy and of the Christian slaves sold there by Turks and Algerians? Anathema would have been pronounced, such a people would have been struck from the list of the nations, and its name would have become only a synonym for savagery. . . . Let the free state of Chihuahua, Excellent Sir, imitate the free countries; let it make war on the barbarians. If it succumbs it will at least have the consolation of having done its duty. For its part, the General Command of Sonora will not rest until it has civilized or destroyed the enemies of the State.[7]

In the end, Carrasco's arguments carried the day, just as he knew they would. Federal officials in Mexico City had no intention of censuring him for doing his job—killing Apaches. In a document that includes more than a hint of hypocrisy, on April 4, 1851, they issued Circular Number Five, from the office of the minister of war and navy, which laid out the grounds when a military commander of one state could cross the borders of another. It explained that the border should not be an obstacle for frontier officers when they were in pursuit of hostile Indians. It did require, however, these forces to notify the "respective civil and military authorities so that they can take the necessary steps to cooperate and punish said Indians." In Mexico's eyes, this edict would circumvent the problems that Carrasco's invasion had caused. Yet it was hardly an answer. As long as one hostile Chiricahua raided Sonora while there were Apaches at peace at Janos, Sonoran officials, with genocide as their political solution, would finger those Indians living near Janos.[8]

Frontier civil and military officials anticipated that the Chiricahuas would immediately avenge Carrasco's attack. A report from Bavispe in mid-April suggested that a large war party had united north of there, but it seems they caused few problems at that time. The mayor of Bacoachi expected an assault, requesting the governor to send arms and ammunition for fear his "town may fall into the hands of the enemy."[9] These rumors tend to support the impression that Mangas Coloradas had arrived in northeastern Sonora, which usually meant the Indians would be spilling Sonoran blood. While most bided their time, hoping to open talks to secure the release of their captives, some Chiricahuas started out to avenge this wanton attack.

Miguel Narbona and the war faction of the Chokonens did not need a reason to satisfy their voracious desire for Sonoran blood. On March 9, five days after Carrasco's clandestine assault, Miguel Narbona had led a Chokonen war party that killed several individuals at Bamori and Sinoquipe. At the first place, one Mexican inflicted a head wound on Miguel. When the Apache leader attacked Sinoquipe the next day, he had a bandage on his head and admitted to Justo Calderón, shortly before he ran his lance through him, that Mexicans at Bamori had wounded him during the prior attack.[10] At Janos, El Chinito, a Nednhi leader of a Janeros local group, also began raiding in Chihuahua to avenge the death of Arvizu. With twenty other warriors he ambushed a party south of Janos, killing two men, wounding others, and burning several wagons. Ponce and Coleto Amarillo denounced this attack and declared that the hostiles had gone to the Mimbres River; at least this is the report we have from Delgadito, who was also in northern Mexico with Mangas Coloradas.[11]

Meanwhile, by the third week in May, Carrasco had returned to Fronteras, from which he would launch his vaunted second campaign. While he was making final preparations, on May 23, 1851, John Russell Bartlett arrived at the presidio with a small escort, including Colonel Craig. The adventurous boundary commissioner was traveling to Arispe in search of supplies. Carrasco's four-hundred-man army (three companies of infantry and one company of cavalry) failed to inspire the aristocratic and stodgy New England bookseller. The soldiers were dressed "in every variety of costume" with "scarcely a pair of shoes among them." The officers impressed Bartlett, for they were "well dressed and exhibited a striking contrast with the privates." The presence of an Apache Indian with the rank of sergeant among Carrasco's noncommissioned officers surprised Bartlett. This man, probably Mariano Arista, "had long been in the Mexican service, where he was well treated [and] familiar with the haunts of his people." Bartlett pointed out that Carrasco "has determined . . . to make it [a war] of extermination."[12]

This campaign left Fronteras in late May. At Alamo Hueco, in New Mexico's panhandle, Carrasco's forces jumped the ranchería of Láceres, leader of the Janeros Nednhis. There his men captured one old man, who later died, and recovered some twenty-three animals. Next they went to Janos, where they met several Chokonen and Nednhi leaders, who expressed concerns about their relatives whom Carrasco had taken to Sonora. With Yrigóllen dead, Chepillo and Chagaray, who had kinfolk among the hostages held by Carrasco, represented the Chokonens. Gervacio (a son of Juan José Compá) and Calderón represented the Nednhis. Carrasco held the trump card and played it for all it was worth. He agreed to return his prisoners if the Chiricahuas would make peace and settle at either Fronteras, Bavispe, or Bacoachi. His terms, which contained twenty-eight articles, were not negotiable. The Apaches, desperate to see their loved ones, agreed to everything and promised to send word of Carrasco's proposal to the Chokonens at Pitaicache and to Mangas Coloradas.[13]

Carrasco returned to Fronteras in mid-June. After a short stay he began his march south for Arispe. Unfortunately for the Chiricahuas, he came down with cholera and died on July 21, 1851, leaving relations with the Indians up in the air. Despite this, by late July some four hundred Chokonens had complied with his terms and had gone into camp near Fronteras. In August, Chepillo and Chagaray traveled to Ures to visit their relatives, among whom was Chagaray's wife. Finally, when the two sides failed to reach a solution, the two leaders returned to Fronteras, gathered up their followers, and bolted for the mountains.[14]

As for Mangas, that spring of 1851 he was in northern Sonora with the bellicose Chokonens under Miguel Narbona, Carro, and Cochise. While Carrasco was marching his ponderous army here and there, the Chiricahuas began to retaliate against Sonora. One party went as far south as Tepache, where it attacked several ranches. Soon after, this band, or another one, assaulted Granadas and killed seven men. In early June an American named Antonio Hicks arrived at Janos with a party of four Americans, one English-man, one Frenchman, and one Mexican. They were bound for California. The citizens warned them that the Apaches would attack his small party, but Hicks's group decided to go on, his numbers swelled to ten men. At Guadalupe Canyon on June 8, 1851, fifty Indians (although eyewitness accounts report that two hundred Apaches were present) ambushed them, killing one American and wounding three others. Bartlett, whose party met half of Carrasco's command there about a week after the attack, later questioned Mangas Coloradas about the incident. The chief replied that it was done by a band "over whom he had no authority." Mangas may have been dissembling on this point, for he was not about to admit that his people had killed an American, even if it was in Sonora. He was indeed present and probably participated in the attack on Hicks's party in conjunction with Cochise's and Miguel Narbona's Chokonens.[15]

John Russell Bartlett's Boundary Commission had reached Santa Rita del Cobre in early May 1851. Bartlett, born in Providence, Rhode Island, in 1805, was educated in Montreal with accounting as his emphasis. To this point in his life he had held a variety of positions: banker, bookseller, writer, and artist. A tall man with a long beard and dark brown hair, the erudite Bartlett was sincerely interested in the American Indian, whom he viewed as the "noble Redman" of the James Fenimore Cooper novels. His background gave no indication that he was suited for this role. In fact, he had longed for an appointment as minister to Denmark. When that did not pan put, the secretary of the interior offered him the job as boundary commissioner at three thousand dollars per year plus

John R. Bartlett, United States Boundary Commissioner. He left behind important recollections of his meetings with Mangas Coloradas and the Chihenne leaders at Santa Rita del Cobre in 1851. (Courtesy Arizona Historical Society, no. 28,103)

expenses. This position was attractive to Bartlett because it offered an opportunity to travel west and learn more about the American Indians whom he was certain to meet. A man of integrity and diplomacy, Bartlett, however, accepted a position for which, according to one historian, "he had no qualification except political connections."[16]

Bartlett felt compelled to use patronage as the basis for filling many of the 111 positions on the commission staff. Some of his personnel decisions were good ones. For example, he named John Cremony, a former reporter with the Boston Herald and a Mexican War veteran, as interpreter, and his good friend Dr. Thomas Webb as surgeon. The capable Captain Louis S. Craig, with eighty-five men of the Third Infantry, provided the escort and protection for Bartlett's surveying party. Bartlett met his Mexican counterpart, Commissioner Alejo García Conde (who had just negotiated the June 1850 peace treaty with the Chihennes and Nednhis) at El Paso in early December 1850. The two men, who developed an instant rapport and an excellent working relationship, were to decide the line for the boundary between the two countries. By the time he occupied Santa Rita del Cobre, his party contained almost three hundred whites, which included soldiers, members of his surveying party, and civilians hired on from El Paso and southern New Mexico. Typical of his new employees was Santiago Brito, a thirty-one-year-old native of Sonora. Brito, who had enlisted as a soldier at Janos in 1840, had recently received his discharge from the Mexican army. He would eventually settle at Pinos Altos, undoubtedly becoming well acquainted with Mangas Coloradas.[17]

This invasion of Americans and their Mexican hired hands naturally displeased the Chiricahuas. They were openly hostile to any group of whites—Mexican or American—who had dared to work the mines at Santa Rita del Cobre since its abandonment in 1838. In late January 1851 near Cooke's Canyon the Chihenne chief Cuchillo Negro met John Cremony, whom Bartlett had sent with Dr. Webb, James Thurber, and Captain Craig to examine Santa Rita del Cobre as possible headquarters for the commission. Cuchillo Negro advised Cremony that "for many years no white man has penetrated these regions, and we do not permit people to enter our country without knowing their purpose." Cremony explained their plans and said that a large body of troops was only a day behind him. Cremony's explanation failed to impress Cuchillo Negro until he saw that the American had told the truth. Shortly after, as previously mentioned, on February 2, 1851,

Santiago Brito. He was acquainted with many Chiricahuas, including Mangas Coloradas. A former presidio soldier at Janos, shortly after his discharge in 1850 Brito found employment with Bartlett's Boundary Commission. He later settled at Pinos Altos, where this picture was taken in the late 1870s. He son, Frank, became one of Teddy Roosevelt's famed Rough Riders; his grandson Santiago (Jimmy) Brito continued this heritage with five years of service in Europe in World War II, including the D-Day invasion at Normandy. (Courtesy Santiago P. Brito)

Captain Craig had a friendly meeting with Mangas Coloradas at Santa Rita del Cobre. Meanwhile, Bartlett's good friend Dr. Webb advised him that Santa Rita del Cobre would be a suitable site for the commission's headquarters.[18]

Cuchillo Negro and Mangas Coloradas had few options, since they had no wish to fight American troops, whom they respected. Besides, these troops had not harmed them in any way except in legitimate battles. They were neither scalp hunters nor mercenaries and to this point had not committed any acts of aggression to provoke the Chiricahuas. The Chihennes and Bedonkohes had previously intimidated other parties, which were small in numbers when compared to Bartlett's civilian and military entourage. It was Craig's detachment of troops that tilted the equation and convinced the Indians that accommodation was preferable to fighting. They had no reason to risk needless casualties when the Americans would be moving on. Moreover, as did the Butterfield Overland Stage Company of the late 1850s, Bartlett armed his workers to the teeth with the best weapons then available.

Yet the arrival of Bartlett's commission and its occupation of Santa Rita del Cobre disturbed the Apaches. For the previous three years Mangas had heard that his country now belonged to the Americans, yet for the past two centuries the Chiricahuas had heard the same argument—that their country belonged to the Spanish and in recent years the Mexicans. To Mangas this was just another phase, another cycle, that he would have to confront. His people had driven out the Mexicans and, if necessary, would do the same to the Americans if they attempted to settle in his country. When Captain Craig and Bartlett told them that the party was there solely to survey the country, had no intention of working the mines or prospecting, and would be moving on after it completed its work, Mangas Coloradas and his people had no choice but to find a middle ground until the Americans moved west.

Bartlett reached Santa Rita del Cobre on May 2, 1851, shortly after a mule had thrown him and kicked his shoulder, an injury that would incapacitate him for two weeks. There he found excellent resources: water, grazing, lumber, shelter in the form of fifty abandoned adobe houses, and a deserted triangular presidio. These structures, with a little work, would prove more than adequate for his needs. He also renewed his friendship with Captain Craig, a veteran officer with a fine reputation earned during the Mexican War, who, with his command, had set up quarters there some three months before. Mangas Coloradas and many Chihennes and

Bedonkohes were in Sonora at the time of Bartlett's arrival. On May 16, Bartlett left for Sonora to procure supplies. He returned to Santa Rita del Cobre on June 23, 1851, and later that day finally met the legendary Chiricahua chief, whom he had heard so much about. As it turned out, Mangas Coloradas had followed Bartlett's party from Sonora back to New Mexico.[19]

As the principal leader of the Bedonkohe and Chihenne bands, Mangas Coloradas had concluded that peace and moderation were "the better part of valor," at least according to John Cremony.[20] He came in with "twelve or fifteen of his tribe" and declared that he was a friend of Americans. Bartlett was honest but simplistic and naïve in his discussion with him about relations with Mexico. During the next few months Bartlett would hold several parleys with Mangas, who referred to himself as "the head chief of all the Apaches," obviously meaning the Chihennes, Bedonkohes, and Janeros local group of Nednhis (the Chokonens had remained in Arizona). Mangas impressed the New Englander as a man "of strong common sense and discriminating judgement . . . [who] for the welfare of his tribe . . . would be willing to make sacrifices." To this point Bartlett had been disappointed with the Indians whom he had met, for none had fit his image of Cooper's "noble savage." Mangas Coloradas, however, affirmed his regard for Cooper's portrayal. A good relationship developed between the two men, and Bartlett even learned a limited vocabulary of Apache words from Mangas. Bartlett advised Mangas to "raise his own corn, mules, horses, etc. instead of stealing them from the Mexicans." Mangas listened respectfully but demurred, simply replying that he was "too old to begin to raise corn or to cultivate the soil and that he must leave these things to his young people to do."[21] In subsequent years he would heed Bartlett's advice.

The commissioner informed Mangas that the Treaty of Guadalupe Hidalgo had bound Americans to protect Mexicans and to prevent the Apaches from raiding into Mexico. The chief did assure Bartlett, however, that he would not harm the Mexican Boundary Commission under García Conde, which would be working jointly with Bartlett's group. To promote this goodwill, Bartlett issued presents and gifts to the leaders, including a "suit of blue broadcloth" to Mangas Coloradas and many other articles of clothing and food to the chief's immediate family. Bartlett described the outfit:

[It was] a frock coat lined with scarlet and ornamented with gilt buttons. His pantaloons, at his request, were open from the knee downwards, after the fashion of the Mexicans, with a row of small fancy buttons on one side, and a broad strip of scarlet cloth on the other side from the hip downwards. A white shirt and red silk sash completed the dress. While the tailor had it in hand, he visited him daily to watch its progress, and a child might have envied him his delight.[22]

Mangas wore the suit proudly for a week until he lost it to another Indian while gambling, a favorite pastime for Chiricahuas of all ages and sexes.[23]

Several incidents that rankled in the Apache breast almost nullified this auspicious beginning. The relationship between the Chiricahuas and Mexicans would prove to be the root of the problems. The conscientious and honest Bartlett, who had no idea of the intensity and magnitude of the hatred between the two races, faced the monumental task of appeasing the Indians while also abiding by his responsibilities to Mexico as set out in the Treaty of Guadalupe Hidalgo. His decisions, based upon his objective interpretations and his common sense, were acts of humanity rather than duplicity. Yet they inevitably agitated the Apaches, who had not been participants in the Treaty of Guadalupe Hidalgo. From their perspective, their mores and values were equal to those of Bartlett, and he had imposed decisions upon them that were unacceptable to their universe.

Within two weeks of Bartlett's and Mangas Coloradas's first meeting, three incidents occurred with results that may very easily be imagined. The first was minor, at least as far as Mangas Coloradas was concerned. The second, which impaired relations, served to establish further the ground rules to the Apaches. The final incident resulted in the spilling of Apache blood. Since the Apache victim was not a member of Mangas's band, Mangas restrained his immediate followers. Yet he could do little to control the aggrieved members of Ponce's and Delgadito's local groups, whom Bartlett's decisions directly affected.

On June 27 a group of New Mexicans arrived at Santa Rita del Cobre with a beautiful Mexican girl whom they had recently obtained by trade from the Indians. Her name was Inez González, and she was from Santa Cruz, Sonora. The Pinal Apaches (a Western Apache band) had captured her at Cocospera Canyon on September 30, 1850, during the ambush that claimed the lives of Lieutenant Santurnino Limón and several others. The New Mexicans had not anticipated Bartlett's response. When he heard of her

Mangas Coloradas's new outfit, an artist's rendition of the new outfit that Bartlett provided Mangas Coloradas. A few days later Mangas lost it to another Apache while gambling. (Cremony, *Life Among the Apaches*)

plight, Bartlett requested that Captain Craig immediately demand that the traders turn the girl over to the Boundary Commission. They complied without resistance. Three months later Bartlett, in an emotional and heart-warming venture, personally delivered the girl to her parents at Santa Cruz, Sonora.[24]

The next day (June 28, 1851), Mangas Coloradas and Delgadito had just arrived with many of their people when two Mexican boys ran into the tent of John Cremony, which he had pitched on the outskirts of Santa Rita del Cobre, and begged for his protection. Their names were José Trinfan and Saverro Heradia. The Apaches had captured Trinfan, who was ten or twelve years old, at Fronteras six years before; they had taken the thirteen-year-old Heradia from Bacoachi the day after their victory at Pozo Hediondo a little more than five months before. Cremony at once decided to take the boys to Bartlett's tent, where they would find protection. In dramatic fashion he described the gauntlet of Apaches that he and the two boys went through, with his servant, José, bringing up the rear, to reach Bartlett's tent. When Mangas and Delgadito learned of the incident, they asked Bartlett to make restitution to the owner of the two boys. The commissioner diplomatically refused, hoping to convince the two chiefs that his actions were mandated by the Treaty of Guadalupe Hidalgo. He seemed disappointed that they "did not, or would not understand, and left our camp evidently much offended." He asked Mangas to return the next day when "I would endeavor to satisfy him." Instead, Mangas stayed away, likely because he knew that Bartlett had sent the two boys under a strong guard to García Conde, who subsequently returned them to their families.[25]

The Chiricahua leaders had gathered in council to decide a course of action. "After the lapse of several days, the chiefs with their people, including the owner of one of the boys, again made their appearance." According to Bartlett's personal journal, on July 4, 1851, the Chiricahuas, including four chiefs—Mangas Coloradas, Delgadito, Ponce, and the Nednhi band leader Coleto Amarillo— came in for a conference. "Nothing was decided, and they returned to their camps." The next day they came back; this time they had a long powwow that one American recorded verbatim. As the head chief, Mangas Coloradas spoke first:

Mangas Coloradas,—Why did you take our captives from us?
Commissioner,—Your captives came to us and demanded our protection.

Mangas Coloradas,—You came to our country. You were well
received by us. Your lives, your property, your animals, were safe.
You passed by ones, by twos, and by threes, through our country; you
went and came in peace. Your strayed animals were always brought
home to you again. Our wives, our children, and women came here
and visited your houses. We were friends! We were brothers!
Believing this, we came amongst you and brought our captives,
relying on it that we were brothers, and that you would feel as we
feel. We concealed nothing. We came not here secretly or in the
night. We came in open day and before your faces, and we showed
our captives to you. We believed your assurances of friendship and we
trusted them. Why did you take our captives from us?
Commissioner,—What we have said to you is true and reliable. We
do not tell lies. The greatness and dignity of our nation forbids our
doing so mean a thing. What our great brother has said is true, and
good also. I will now tell him why we took his captives from him.
Four years ago, we, too, were at war with Mexico. We know that the
Apaches make a distinction between Chihuahua and Sonora. They
are at peace with Chihuahua, but always fighting against Sonora. We
in our war did not make that distinction. . . . Well, when that war
was over, in which we conquered, we made peace with them. They
are now our friends, and by the terms of the peace we are bound to
protect them. We told you this when we came to this place, and we
requested you to cease your hostilities against Mexico. . . . We mean
to show you that we cannot lie. We promised protection to the
Mexicans, and we gave it to them. We promise friendship and
protection to you, and we will give it to you. . .

Bartlett's unyielding logic failed to mollify Ponce, usually one of
the more moderate Chihenne leaders, and almost caused a quarrel
to break out. Ponce argued vociferously that "you took our captives
from us without beforehand cautioning us." The Indians had taken
these prisoners "in lawful warfare." What about Apaches held in
Mexico? The Apaches were foolish to have trusted Bartlett, Ponce
declared. Bartlett, his integrity questioned, accused Ponce of acting
like a child and a woman because he spoke "angrily and without
due reflection." Bartlett's insult was too much for Ponce, who,
before he told Bartlett not to "speak any more," defended his honor
and correctly pointed out that the commissioner was ignorant
about "the wrongs that we have suffered." Bartlett ordered Ponce to
"sit down. I will hear no more talk with you." He then selected
Delgadito to "speak for your nation."

Delgadito admitted that the Apaches recognized that "the Americans are braves; we know it." Then he set out on another course, emphasizing that to the Apaches this was a matter of right and wrong. They wanted justice, for the warrior who took these captives did so "at the risk of his life and purchased [them] with the blood of his relatives." In response, Bartlett advised Delgadito that as a matter of principle he could not purchase the captives. Yet, he agreed to allow a willing Mexican to provide compensation to the Indian for his loss. After some bickering, on July 7, 1851, the Apache man reluctantly agreed to sell his captives for merchandise worth two hundred and twelve dollars. All in all, it had been a messy business, and potentially explosive. Bartlett's lack of patience and tact had earned him an enemy in Ponce and other Chihennes.[26]

On the day before this crisis reached its shaky conclusion, still another had erupted into a volatile situation. On July 6, 1851, a Mexican teamster named Jesús López critically wounded an Apache man in a dispute over a whip owned by the Indian. Bartlett, then in his tent, immediately ran to the door and saw pandemonium in the camp. Apaches and whites were running in all directions. Undoubtedly recalling the Johnson massacre, Mangas Coloradas, Delgadito, and Coleto Amarillo, who were in camp at the time of the shooting, "seized their arms, and, mounting animals, retreated to a small hill a few hundred yards from the fort." Most of their followers huddled around their chiefs for protection. At this crucial juncture, Captain Craig stepped in and restored some semblance of order. Undaunted, he went alone to the Apaches' position and persuaded the chiefs to come in to observe white man's justice. Craig's soldiers brought López "with his feet in chains" before the Apaches. López admitted that he had shot the Indian "in a private quarrel." Mangas Coloradas and the other chiefs realized that the Americans had had nothing to do with the unfortunate affair and the "conference ended in good feeling."

The Indians demanded justice, however. That day they agreed that "if the man died, they should require punishment of the murderer. If he lived the Mexican should be compelled to labor, and the proceeds of it be given to the family of the wounded man, as a remuneration for the loss of his services." Tensions eased until the wounded man died on Saturday, July 19, thirteen days after López had shot him.[27] The Indians demanded that the Americans turn over López to them for punishment. Instead, Bartlett offered to send him to Santa Fe, where the governor would put him on trial. This hardly appeased the Chiricahuas, and on July 21, 1851, a large group arrived to hold a powwow with Bartlett.

This time Mangas came in. As early as July 10 he had informed Bartlett that he was going "to remove his camp to a hunting ground where he could procure deer." He planned to return to Santa Rita del Cobre at the end of the month. Likely he had gone to Santa Lucía Springs. During the council Bartlett carefully explained that he had no choice but to turn over the murderer to the authorities at Santa Fe for trial. If found guilty, the man would be punished, according to American law. That evening Mangas had dinner with Bartlett in his tent before returning to his camp at Santa Lucía.[28]

Two days later the Chiricahuas returned, led by Ponce, Delgadito, Coleto Amarillo, and Nachesoa, along with the mother of the murdered Apache.[29] They protested Bartlett's proposal. Ponce articulated their thoughts in a heart-wrenching speech recorded by John Cremony: "But the Apaches will not be satisfied to know that the murderer is punished in Santa Fe. They want him punished here, at the Copper Mines, where the band of the dead brave may see him put to death—where all the Apaches may see him put to death (making the sign of being suspended by the neck). Then the Apaches will see and know that their American Brothers will do justice to them."

In response Bartlett offered "to keep the murderer in chains, as you now see him; to make him work, and to give all he earns to the wife and family of your dead brave." Again, the Indians rejected Bartlett's pragmatic white-man's solution, for their culture demanded the blood of the murderer. Ponce again responded in an impassioned yet common-sense manner:

> You speak well. Your promises are fair. But money will not satisfy an Apache for the murder of a brave! No! thousands would not drown out the grief of this poor woman for the loss of her son. Would money satisfy an American for the murder of his people? Would money pay you, Señor Commissioner, for the loss of your child? No! money will not bury your grief. It will not bury ours. The mother of this brave demands the life of the murderer. She wants no goods, She wants no corn. Would money satisfy me, *Ponce* (at the same time striking his breast), for the death of my son? No! I would demand the blood of the murderer. Then I would be satisfied. Then would I be willing to die myself. I would not wish to live and bear the grief which the loss of my son would cause me.

The mother of the murdered Apache finally agreed to accept a thirty-dollar payment (the amount due the murderer Jesús López) plus a twenty-dollar payment each month.[30] Although Bartlett believed that he had avoided a catastrophe, in reality relations between the Americans and the Chiricahua Apaches had begun to deteriorate. It would be almost a year until they began to improve.

The Indians, now suspicious and distrustful of Bartlett and his men, no longer made daily visits to the Americans. On July 27, Bartlett noted in his journal that "only three Indians came in today." The next day several mules belonging to Captain Craig were discovered missing; Bartlett and Craig assumed that the Apaches had taken them. Accordingly, on July 29, Captain Craig gathered a force of thirty men and visited Delgadito's camp on the Mimbres River about eight to ten miles east of Santa Rita del Cobre. Craig's arrival "alarmed" the Apaches, but he diplomatically alleviated their concerns and talked with their leaders, who assured him that they had not taken the mules. Cremony, who always distrusted Apaches, believed that they had begun to raid the Americans' stock solely because they could claim a reward by recovering it and returning it to the Boundary Commission.[31]

As for Mangas Coloradas, after his appearance on July 21 to discuss the status of Jesús López, he had left the area for his country at Santa Lucía Springs. According to Cremony, he invited his son-in-law, a chief among the Navajos, to bring his followers to Chiricahua country "to assist him to get rid of his unwelcome intruders." Mangas's emissaries told the Navajos that the Americans were "rich in horses, mules, cotton cloth, beads, knives, pistols, rifles, and ammunition." While this was all true, one must question the reliability of Cremony's statement that the Navajos had come with hostile intentions to aid Mangas in a war against the Americans. They appeared with one thing in mind—trade. Cremony implied that Mangas Coloradas and the Navajos had entered a covert conspiracy to attack the Americans at the opportune time. Instead, about August 18, Mangas came in with a large band of Navajos and traded with the Americans. Bartlett believed that they were spies to size up the Americans' strength. Yet the Navajos, like the Chiricahuas, were not about to engage in any open conflict, though they would steal a few horses or mules if they could get away without detection.[32]

During the visit, Captain Craig informed Mangas Coloradas that he distrusted the Navajos, having heard that they were dishonest and inveterate raiders. To assuage Craig's skepticism, Mangas "agreed to hold himself responsible for any animal lost." Mangas probably made this commitment in good faith, but his pledge would backfire. In late August, Chiricahuas, primarily Ponce and Delgadito's followers, and a few Navajos committed several stock raids at Santa Rita del Cobre. The Navajos fled north into their country, and the Chiricahuas retired south toward Janos and Corralitos. On September 4, 1851, an enervated and frustrated Captain Craig, who had been in the saddle for much of the prior two weeks chasing hostiles, recommended a militant course of action to Major General Winfield Scott, commander in chief of the army in Washington:

> These Indians must be well-flogged, and be made to return all the property which they have stolen or this country can never be settled. . . . My opinion is that the Government ought to send two mounted Regiments to this country independent of the troops now here or they ought to withdraw what they have here and let the Indians have the country. The Apaches have droves of horses. Mangas Coloradas, I think, has some of the finest horses as I have ever seen since I have been in this country. If we could rid them of their horses, I have no doubt that they could soon be persuaded to turn their attention to agriculture.[33]

By late August, Bartlett had decided to abandon Santa Rita del Cobre and move his base of operations further west. Captain Craig informed his superiors that Bartlett's commission "will no longer require this point to be kept up as a depot." Yet Craig recommended, since Santa Rita del Cobre was "in the heart of Apache country," that Colonel Sumner place a permanent garrison of troops there. If not, the Apaches would force the fifteen or twenty citizens engaged in mining near Santa Rita del Cobre to leave the area.[34] The Chihennes and Nednhis, meanwhile, led by Mangas Coloradas himself, disillusioned with Americans, sent peace emissaries to Juan José Zozaya at Janos in late August. Zozaya, who was chagrined when he heard that the Chiricahuas had made peace with the Americans at Santa Rita del Cobre, invited the Chiricahuas in for talks.[35]

Once in Chihuahua, they faced a revitalized military led by Angel Trias, the anti-American governor who also despised Apaches. Yet, like most Mexican officials, Trias much preferred having the Indians under his thumb in Mexico as opposed to under American influence in New Mexico. Trias had spent much of the summer of 1851 campaigning against Cojinillín, Francisco, and Felipe, the leaders of Carrizaleño local group of Nednhis. Trias met Coleto Amarillo at Corralitos about August 26, 1851. The Nednhi chief convinced Trias that the Indians wanted to make peace. Two days later Trias went to Janos and met several Chiricahua leaders, who assured him that they were trustworthy. He also conferred with Juan José Zozaya, the peace commissioner, who told Trias that the Indians sincerely wished peace. Trias informed the Chiricahuas that he had come to reward the Apaches for maintaining the peace after Carrasco's unjust attack.[36]

Trias was uncertain why the Apaches had left Santa Rita del Cobre, but one citizen who came to Janos from there mentioned that Jesús López's killing of the Apache was one reason. During the first few weeks of September, Trias met the Nednhi leaders Láceres and Coleto Amarillo and then Delgadito, Ponce, and finally Mangas Coloradas with their followers. All agreed to abide with the terms of the treaty that had been in effect before Carrasco's attack. Nonetheless, when ration day came on Monday, September 22, the Chiricahuas failed to come in, undoubtedly fearing treachery, since Trias had arrived with many soldiers. The Indians' actions confounded Zozaya and Trias, who now speculated that they had gone either to Fronteras, where the Chokonens were negotiating for their captives taken by Carrasco, or back to Santa Rita del Cobre, since Bartlett's commission had broken camp and moved out of their country. As it turned out, Mangas had retired to the Burro and Mogollon Mountains, where his followers began the fall harvest of piñon nuts, acorns, mesquite beans, walnuts, berries, and datil (or yucca fruit) to carry them through the winter.[37]

The breakdown in talks between Sonora and the Chokonens, who suddenly realized that the former had no intentions of returning their captives, led to a resumption of the long-standing conflict. After Apaches, many likely Cochise and Miguel Narbona's Chokonens, killed an astounding fifty-nine Sonorans in August 1851, Sonora announced that it would retaliate. Lieutenant Colonel José María Flores, a veteran of the Mexican War and the fighting in California, succeeded Carrasco and at once adopted the hawkish policy of his predecessor toward the Apaches. By October 1851 he had gathered a force of more than 300 men. He directed one division, which consisted of 172 presidio troops and two pieces of artillery. The competent José Terán y Tato, back in the fold now that a new regime had replaced his outspoken critic Carrasco, headed the second division of 150 national guard troops. They planned to establish a base camp at San Simón, some fifteen miles northeast of Apache Pass.

En route to San Simón, Terán y Tato sent out a patrol under his indefatigable aide Captain Eusebio Samaniego. On October 13, Samaniego's force jumped Posito Moraga's and Triqueño's Chokonen ranchería near Carretas and killed four warriors, two women, and one boy and captured six women and three children. Samaniego united with Terán y Tato's command near the Chiricahua Mountains before they continued to San Simón, which they reached on October 21, 1851. There Flores split his force. He headed to the Gila and Western Apache country, where he encountered Apaches, killing five men and capturing four others. Terán y Tato, emulating Elías González's strategy of two years before, headed for Mangas's country in the Burro Mountains. Mangas easily eluded the Sonorans, likely moving further north to the Mogollon country.

Meanwhile, Terán y Tato returned south to Mexico and in late October surprised the Pilares Mountains ranchería of the Chokonen war chief Tapilá, "a most terrible Apache," and killed eight warriors and captured five others. An astute Terán y Tato predicted that the Chiricahuas would soon solicit peace to orchestrate a prisoner exchange. Tapilá proved that Terán y Tato was a good prognosticator, for a few weeks later he appeared at Bavispe with a large group of Chokonens to discuss an exchange of hostages. According to the Mexican reports, the Indians arrived already drunk and in an obstreperous mood. Naturally, fighting erupted, and the Mexicans were forced to kill Tapilá and thirteen other men. They also captured twenty-seven women and children—in self-defense, of course. There was obviously more to this story than what the Mexicans had reported. These were significant losses to the Chiricahuas, for Tapilá was, with Miguel Narbona, the leading war chief of the Chokonen band.[38]

News of the tragedy spread north to Mangas Coloradas, who, soon after, gave the Chiricahuas' version of these events to Indian Agent John Greiner in New Mexico. Naturally, his story contradicted the official report written by Bavispe's commander, declaring that the Sonorans had trapped and slaughtered his people:

> Are we to stand by with our arms folded while our women and children are being murdered in cold blood as they were the other day in Sonora? [Those] people invited my people to a feast. They

manifested every show of friendship towards us. We were lulled into security by this happening [when] at the close of the feast a barrel of aguardiente [whiskey] was brought to the ground. My people drank and got drunk and then the Sonoronians beat out the brains of fifteen of them with clubs. Are we to be the victims of such treachery and not be revenged? Are we not to have the privilege of protecting ourselves?[39]

Perhaps in response to Tapilá's death, in December 1851 an enormous Apache war party of some two hundred men invaded Sonora and struck the district of Moctezuma and the outskirts of Hermosillo and Ures, killing some thirty men in one encounter. Whether Mangas Coloradas or the Chiricahuas had anything to do with this incursion is not known, for the victims did not live long enough to identify their attackers. Nonetheless, since Mangas Coloradas was not in his local group territory in early 1852 it seems probable that he had responded to the Chokonens' invitation to lead an avenging war party into Sonora.[40]

The recollections of José Miguel Castañeda might offer further proof that Mangas Coloradas had brought his people into Chokonen country. A young teenager in 1851, Castenada had accompanied John Able's expedition from Chihuahua to California. In late 1851, Able had ten thousand head of sheep that he intended to drive to California. It was probably about this time that he encamped at the deserted San Bernardino ranch northeast of Douglas. There they met Mangas Coloradas and three hundred of his band, men, women, and children. Able gave ten sheep to the Indians, who "after a feast departed with every indication of friendship." A few days later the Apaches returned, and after receiving only two sheep, left in an angry mood. Soon after, they stole several horses but were unable to run off any sheep.[41]

While Mangas was absent from New Mexico, military affairs in his country had undergone dramatic changes. The War Department in Washington had instructed New Mexico's new department commander, Colonel Edwin Vose Sumner,[42] to carry out a different policy to "revise the whole system of defence."[43] Sumner, who had replaced Colonel John Monroe, a heavy drinker who despised his service in the Southwest, arrived in New Mexico with the same omniscient attitude that Carrasco had displayed when he had reached Sonora. A classic martinet in the military sense, Sumner effortlessly offended virtually everyone whom he met, particularly nonmilitary people. Sumner decided to relocate the garrisons from the settlements to the frontier, where they could better control the Indians and better protect the Mexican border. This new philosophy would also reduce operating costs at each fort, as the troops, in theory, could build their own quarters, plant their own crops, and gather their own wood and forage when they were not campaigning against hostiles. He carried out the orders of his superiors. Despite his arrogance, autocratic rule, intolerance of state officials, and disdain for Washington-appointed Indian agents and civilian officials (for whom he made life miserable), Sumner, in the words of eminent historian Robert Utley, "sketched the broad outlines of a defense system that endured without basic change for forty years."[44]

Sumner's policies would have a profound impact on the Mescaleros east of the Rio Grande and the Chiricahuas to the west. He withdrew garrisons from El Paso, Doña Ana, and Socorro and established new forts at Fort Conrad (on September 8, 1851), twenty-four miles south of Socorro at the northern tip of the Jornada del Muerto; Fort Fillmore (on September 23, 1851), six miles southeast of Mesilla; and Fort Webster, at Santa Rita del Cobre, recently abandoned by Bartlett's commission. Undoubtedly the recommendations of Captains Steen and Craig were the primary reasons that Fort Webster, named for Secretary of State Daniel Webster, was placed at Santa Rita del Cobre. Captain Israel Bush Richardson led one company of the Third Infantry and established the new fort about January 23, 1852.[45] Either that day or the next, a group of one hundred Apaches under Delgadito and Ponce visited the post.

They wanted peace, but because several ugly confrontations had occurred during the last few months, the Americans were disinclined to grant it. In late 1851, Apaches, believed to have been Chiricahuas, and, if so, from the local groups of Cuchillo Negro, Delgadito, and Ponce, killed several men along the Rio Grande. In one attack, which Ponce later blamed on Mangas Coloradas, in the region between El Paso and Fort Fillmore the Indians killed a teamster and captured fifty-one mules. About six weeks later, on January 25, 1852, Apaches attacked American troops at Laguna, north of the Jornado del Muerto, and killed five soldiers of the Second Dragoons and wounded three others. According to New Mexico's Governor James S. Calhoun, the guilty parties were the Gila Apaches, which was a generic term used for the Chiricahuas. Although the Mescaleros possibly committed some of these depredations, little doubt remains that the Chihennes and Bedonkohes considered themselves at war with Americans.[46]

Thus, when the Apaches approached Fort Webster on the morning of January 23, 1852, Captain Richardson did not roll out the red carpet. He knew that these Indians had raided Bartlett's Boundary Commission late the previous summer, and he believed that they had recently depredated along the Rio Grande. Richardson immediately called the garrison to arms and began preparations to "attack and pursue them." This stopped the Indians in their tracks. They sent one woman to the post with a white flag of truce. She told the officers that the Apaches wanted to make a peace treaty. Captain Richardson sent her back with a message that he would talk only if the whole band came in. Finally, after a conference, two Chihenne leaders came in. One was Ponce and the other was probably Delgadito. Richardson asked them about the raid of the previous month near Fort Fillmore. They blamed it on a band living "on the other side of the mountains in Mexico under Mangas Coloradas," therefore suggesting that Mangas was probably still with the Chokonens in either southwest New Mexico or southeast Arizona. Richardson, who was itching for a fight, told the two Chihenne leaders to "vamoose," then declared that "if he caught any of them prowling around the vicinity, he and his soldiers would make quick time in sending them to their happy hunting grounds." As soon as they returned to their lines, "they showed signs of preparing for a fight so we opened fire on the Apaches first with our muskets and soon after with our old brass howitzer." The soldiers' withering volley dispersed the Indians in all directions. They wounded several Indians and captured two wounded women, whom the Apaches had left on the battleground.[47]

Major Richardson's aggressive response had been a show of force to the Chihennes—a warning to the Apaches that the Americans were there to stay. Yet Richardson's unprovoked attack (for the Apaches were not about to attack the post) did bring further tragedy to his own troops. He had spilled Apache blood; in the Apache view, they had no choice but to avenge this wanton assault. Richardson anticipated a response, and he prepared his garrison for an Apache siege. The day after the fight, he began efforts to strengthen the fort. First he built a platform "inside of our triangular enclosure" so that the howitzer "would be able to project over the wall." Then he sent out a detachment to cut wood for the fort's fuel supply.

There would be no siege, for it was in the middle of winter and it was not the Apaches' mode of warfare, although they had occasionally surrounded Mexican forts and towns for short periods.

Fort Webster (first site), New Mexico. Located in the heart of Chihenne band territory, this was the former location of Santa Rita del Cobre. Bartlett's Boundary Commission occupied these buildings in 1851, and United States troops occupied them in January 1852. (Courtesy National Archives, no. 111-SC-91059)

The Chihennes would have needed to enlist the aid of Mangas Coloradas and the bellicose Chokonens to carry out that strategy. Instead, they returned on January 26, 1852, three days after the first confrontation, with revenge on their minds. They executed their plan well. First, Apaches opened the fight by swooping down on the oxen and cattle herd, drawing the soldiers away from the security of the fort. While the women and young warriors drove off the herd, "the older warriors guarded their retreat and decoyed us off into a different direction." Then the Chihennes, who numbered about fifty fighting men, counterattacked, their arrows swishing "very close to our ears." An intrepid Captain Richardson with a small force got separated from the command, and many soldiers feared that the Apaches had killed him, but he later turned up safely. The Indians did succeed in avenging the earlier attack, for they killed three, two sergeants (Bernard O'Daugherty and Nicholas Wade) and one private (John Croty). The Apaches had evidently captured Wade, whom they tortured to death and "horribly mutilated."

Supposedly they also scalped him, "probably because he had red hair, scalps of which they seem to have a strong desire for."

Actually, the Chiricahuas normally did not practice scalping, although whites often reported it because the Indians had mutilated the corpse to the point that the victim was not recognizable. Yet for the Chiricahuas to have removed the scalp as a trophy of war was an unusual, if not unheard of, practice. They had disfigured Wade's body to avenge the killings of January 23. The Apaches' losses were not known, but the Americans believed that they had wounded several Indians, and later reports suggested that Delgadito was among them. Private Matson described the somber funeral of the three soldiers, who "were popular and brave." He wrote in his diary: "The triple funeral was a sad ceremony. No funeral is a pleasant one. But a funeral at a lonely frontier military fort after a skirmish in which the comrades who are buried have been killed and one tortured by savages is a sorrowful affair."[48]

Shortly after, the Chihennes stole the entire train that belonged to a man named Constante, a Mexican resident of Doña Ana, at Cooke's Spring. Constante had delivered eight wagons of corn to Fort Webster and on his return home had stopped at Cooke's Spring for the night. Not expecting danger, he turned out his stock to graze. When he awoke the next morning he discovered that the Apaches had taken every head. That morning five warriors came into camp and offered to return his oxen in exchange for "powder, lead, tobacco, blankets and calico." Their blackmail worked. Constante gave them everything, but the Apaches returned in force, threatening to attack his small party. He and his men abandoned their wagons and walked to Doña Ana.[49]

In late February 1852, when Governor Calhoun at Santa Fe received news of these Apache hostilities and a petition from Socorro citizens requesting protection from the Apaches, he immediately blamed Colonel Sumner. Bad blood between the two had existed almost from the moment that Sumner had arrived in New Mexico the year before. Calhoun had hoped to make a treaty with Mangas Coloradas and other Apache leaders at Santa Rita del Cobre the previous summer. Yet Sumner had for some unclear reason refused his request for an escort of troops to the mines. Perhaps he was just being difficult. Still seething from Sumner's imperious rebuke, Calhoun took this opportunity to criticize the military commander by suggesting that his penurious policies had impeded the troops and in some cases had left them unable to perform their duties. On February 29, 1852, he informed Daniel

James S. Calhoun, Territorial Governor of New Mexico. (Courtesy Museum of New Mexico, neg. no. 9835)

Webster, secretary of state at Washington, that "not one single act of the Indians has been chastised." That same day he flung another arrow at Sumner in a letter to Luke Lea, the commissioner of Indian affairs, insisting that he could have averted the present troubles with the Apaches if Colonel Sumner had furnished him with the arms necessary to equip the militia. Once provisioned, Calhoun proposed to "take the field in person and see for myself that the Indians were chastised into obedience or have them entirely exterminated." In closing, he informed Luke Lea that he had hired Charles Overman as special agent for the Apaches of southern New Mexico.[50]

Meanwhile, even before Calhoun was espousing his views, on February 3, 1852, Colonel Sumner had already ordered Major Marshall Saxe Howe to launch a one-month campaign into Chihenne and Bedonkohe country, hoping to strike Mangas Coloradas, when he heard from Captain William Helmsley Emory that the "Indians along the line [border] . . . are for all practical purposes in an actual state of war." He hoped that the campaign, which numbered over three hundred troops, would deal a decisive blow to the hostile Chiricahuas.[51]

The base of operations for the campaign was Fort Conrad on the Rio Grande some twenty-four miles south of Socorro. Here Sumner had assembled a large army of infantry and dragoons commanded by Major Howe of the Second Dragoons. On February 25, as they neared the Mimbres River, a few Apaches ambushed Howe's guide, a Pawnee Indian, wounding him through the left hip. The troops observed fifteen Apaches positioned in an impregnable spot. The soldiers wanted to go "around them and if possible kill them," but Major Howe vetoed their plans, much to the dismay of the troops. As it turned out, his caution was a harbinger of how he would respond throughout this campaign.

On February 27, 1852, they reached Fort Webster at Santa Rita del Cobre. One eyewitness said that "there are 50 men here, all frightened out of their wits" since the earlier encounters with the Chihennes. To stave off an Indian attack, they had "old wagons, logs, barrels, rocks, and other articles . . . piled around their fort, making it almost impossible to get to it." On March 1, 1852, the command left for the Gila and Santa Lucía Springs country "in quest of Mangas Coloradas." The second day out they found "fresh signs of Indians," but according to the diary of Private James Bennett, a dragoon with the expedition, Major Howe "concluded to go the other way!" Despite having almost three hundred men, Howe ostensibly had no stomach for fighting. Instead, when he stumbled on fresh signs, he sent a courier back to Fort Webster requesting reinforcements from Major Gouverneur Morris.[52]

This request incensed Morris, who believed that Howe's three-hundred-man army was on a wild goose chase. Yet he could not refuse Howe's appeal without good reason, although he was concerned that he would be stripping his post of half its force. He curtly responded to Howe that "I am bound to suppose that some contingency has happened to your command or you would have given this order before you left Fort Webster." He complied with the request and sent Captain Richardson with two noncommissioned officers, thirty privates, including Private Matson, and a howitzer. Major Morris, however, clearly had little respect for his fellow officer. The next day he wrote headquarters at Santa Fe that Howe's request had left the post vulnerable to an Apache attack.[53]

In reality, nothing had happened to Howe except that he had panicked when he came across fresh signs. Yet Mangas Coloradas, who had gathered a force of ninety warriors, had no intention of confronting an American force of over three hundred men. Howe's command reached Santa Lucía Springs and then the Gila River on March 5. There they climbed a hill and, taking out their field glasses, saw "smoke curling up in one or two places," according to Private Bennett, and "a fresh trail of Indians and cattle," according to Private Matson. Both would have been in the vast valley that lay between the Gila and the Mogollon Mountains. Major Howe, however, set out in the opposite direction, heading south along the Gila. Private Bennett bemoaned the decision: "Oh! What feelings arose within the breast of each soldier that had a spark of courage in him! To endure a long journey, get in sight of the Indians, have a spirited action in anticipation, and then our cowardly old Major from mere personal fear orders a 'Countermarch!' The shouts of the men should have caused his cheek to have flushed with shame." Private Matson was equally incredulous, but he placed more of the blame on the guide, who had led them "on a wild goose chase." After a cursory scout in the Burro Mountains, the command returned empty-handed to Santa Rita del Cobre on March 12, 1852. Private Matson termed the experience "the greatest piece of humbuggery I have encountered since I joined the army."[54]

Major Morris heard similar complaints when the expedition returned from its "fatiguing, useless, and fruitless march." He unequivocally criticized Major Howe, calling the campaign "a total failure." He earnestly requested that Colonel Sumner provide him with a similar force or authorize him to muster into service for thirty days a group of sixty miners led by prominent men such as Captain Dodge, Mr. Love, and Mr. King of Socorro. If allowed, he would "bring the Indians to terms if it is possible to do so."[55]

As for the Chihennes and Bedonkohes, the former had left Santa Rita del Cobre after the January fight. Delgadito had taken his band and hightailed it to northern Sonora. On March 6, 1852, troops from Fronteras under Captain Miguel Lozada, guided by Mariano Arista, found his camp an hour before daybreak on the brow of a very rugged hill in the Caguillona Mountains, about fifteen miles north of Fronteras. Lozada divided his command into three detachments, and at sunrise he charged the camp. It was a complete surprise. His men killed five warriors, two women, and one child. They also captured five women and one child besides fifty-four horses and mules and the entire camp. His soldiers wounded many others, including Delgadito, whose injuries supposedly were serious. The remnants of Delgadito's camp fled north to the Chiricahua Mountains and united with the Chokonens under Miguel Narbona and Cochise.[56]

Meanwhile, a party of miners had come into Fort Webster about mid-March reporting that Mangas Coloradas and a body of ninety warriors were encamped west of the Burro Mountains, prepared to ambush the soldiers. Mangas's warriors were actually en route to Arizona to join with the Chokonens, Bedonkohes, and Delgadito's Chihennes for their annual spring incursion into Sonora.

In Sonora, meanwhile, its new military commander, Miguel Blanco de Estrada, began preparations for a systematic campaign against the Chiricahuas that he would launch from Bavispe, Fronteras, Santa Cruz, and Tucson. The first two presidios would operate together, while the soldiers from Santa Cruz and Tucson would conduct joint operations. A total of 520 men, 130 from each presidio, would take the field.[57]

While Sonora's military was on the move, Mangas Coloradas and his party of more than one hundred warriors had reached the west side of the Chiricahua Mountains opposite the Swisshelm Mountains shortly after noon on March 20, 1852. There he was surprised to find some 180 Chokonens, Bedonkohes, and Chihennes in parley with a force of Sonorans under Terán y Tato, Captain Miguel Escalante, and Captain Teodoro de Aros. One of Mangas's sons, probably Cascos, had joined in the powwow, along with Miguel Narbona, Esquinaline, and several of Teboca's sons. The Sonorans, fearing treachery, ended the conference when they caught sight of Mangas's group. Soon after, Delgadito reappeared and talked with Ensign Manuel Gallegos about recovering his people taken two weeks before at Caguillona.[58] Delgadito offered to return his Mexican prisoners for those held at Fronteras.

Because Gallegos had no authority to agree to anything, the two sides adjourned the council. The next day the Sonorans went into camp at Bonita Canyon in the Chiricahua Mountains. At daybreak on March 22, 1852, the massive Chiricahua war party, estimated at some three hundred warriors, attacked the Sonorans. They came from all directions, most of them mounted, and wounded Captain de Aros in their first charge. But Escalante and de Aros rallied their men, who poured an effective fire on the rampaging Indians. With the element of surprise gone, the Chiricahuas withdrew, although they maintained a steady fire for the next two hours. The battle lasted two hours and thirty-six minutes. The Chiricahuas had killed three men and wounded ten, six seriously. De Aros estimated the Indians' loss at twelve dead and thirty wounded. Soon after, the fight ended, and the Mexicans moved north to Apache Pass while some Apaches moved south into Sonora.[59]

A week after the battle Delgadito and possibly Mangas Coloradas showed up at Fronteras in force. On March 30, 1852, the Indians surprised fourteen men who were working their fields outside Fronteras. Most of the soldiers were off on a campaign against the Nednhis in southern New Mexico and northern Chihuahua. The Indians killed two men and captured six others, several of whom they had wounded. Next they came to the hills east of the presidio and appeared with white flags. They wanted to exchange their prisoners for the ones taken on March 6 at Caguillona. Sonora's military commander at Arispe authorized the deal on April 2. He was not happy about Captain Gabriel García's actions, but the prisoner exchange went off as agreed and the Apaches left for the interior.[60]

This was but a minor setback for Sonora, for even before it had occurred the joint campaign from Bavispe and Fronteras had dealt the Janeros band of Nednhis a crushing blow. On March 16, 1852, Captain Eusebio Samaniego surprised Láceres's ranchería near the Carcay Mountains and killed three women and captured five others, whom he dispatched to Bavispe for safekeeping. From there, Samaniego went to Janos and enlisted as guides two Apaches (Gerbacio and Josécito) and a few citizens from Janos. On March 24, Samaniego's command united with Captain Miguel Lozada's detachment at Boca Grande, which brought the combined force to 230 men. They sent out the scouts to ferret out the trail, which they picked up in southern New Mexico. It led from the Florida Mountains to the south toward Lake Guzmán in Chihuahua. By early morning of March 27, 1852, the large Sonoran army was in place to surprise the village, which numbered eighty wickiups. After opening fire from two hundred yards, the Mexicans stormed the village, catching the Nednhis and a few Chihennes by complete surprise. When it was all over, some twenty-eight Apaches, including Coleto Amarillo and El Chinito, five other warriors, and twenty-one women and children, lay dead on the battlefield. The Mexicans also captured four adult Apaches and twelve children and recovered a captive from El Paso and sixty-three head of stock. The citizens from Janos took three scalps, including that of the "famous chief Coleto Amarillo." The only chief who escaped was Itán, normally closely associated with Mangas Coloradas.[61]

Details of Mangas Coloradas's activities from April and May of 1852 are unclear. Yet we know from his own statements that he was in Chokonen country, which he used as a base from which to raid Mexico, thus avenging the Sonoran campaigns against the Nednhis and Delgadito's Chihennes. One thing appears clear: as the Chihennes and Bedonkohes returned to their ancestral homes in New Mexico in the late spring, they understood that they must make peace with the Americans. Cuchillo Negro, camped on the Mimbres River, met with Major Morris at Fort Webster in early June and requested peace with Americans. The old chief claimed that every Chihenne leader wanted peace and that he would "send runners to Mangas Coloradas and the other principal chiefs" asking that they come in to Fort Webster for a conference. The Chihenne leader said that the chiefs were "some distance off and scattered over the country and it might take 9 or 10 days to communicate with them," thus implying that Mangas was probably still in Chokonen country, perhaps gathering mescal until it was time for his people to move to his northern camps near the Gila wilderness country.[62] Cuchillo Negro left no doubt that Mangas was still their most important leader. Private Matson in his diary corroborated what Cuchillo Negro had said: "They have told us no treaty they might make would be effective unless sanctioned by Mangas Coloradas. Some of the young chiefs are therefore sent after Mangas and told to instruct him to come in and attend a peace council."[63] After the rough treatment his people were receiving in Sonora, Mangas would prove to be receptive to good relations with Americans.

Chapter 11

A TREATY AT ÁCOMA

MANGAS, his people having recently suffered from a lethal dose of Sonoran firepower and treachery, would prove receptive to making peace with Americans when he returned to New Mexico from Sonora in late spring 1852. In fact, he wasted no time in journeying north through Navajo country to the pueblo of Ácoma to meet New Mexico's colorful military commander, Colonel Edwin Vose Sumner, and New Mexico's Acting Superintendent of Indian Affairs John Greiner.[1] On July 11, 1852, the two most powerful military leaders in New Mexico, one white, one red, formally met. That day Mangas Coloradas signed a treaty—the only one he would sign with Americans in his lifetime. He would keep his part of the bargain except the condition that prohibited him from raiding into Mexico. According to some accounts, he had clearly voiced his objection to Colonel Sumner about that article of the agreement. If so, the military commander probably would not have raised an eyebrow. But because his customary haunts of Santa Lucía and the Gila wilderness country were remote from whites, Mangas's life changed little after the treaty.

After the fall harvest of acorns and piñon nuts, in early 1853 he took his followers on their customary jaunt through Doubtful Canyon and Apache Pass to join his son-in-law Cochise for their winter sojourn against Sonora. This foray would prove to be a memorable one for Mangas. His war party avenged Sonora's triumphs of 1851 and 1852 by killing a close relative of their former adversary, José María Elías González. Furthermore, in the Chiricahua Mountains in the spring of 1853 Mangas held a parley with Mexican troops led by a future governor of Sonora—the same man whose force he had annihilated at Pozo Hediondo in January 1851, Ignacio Pesqueira. After that meeting, he returned to New Mexico, where he found that a new governor with yet another Indian policy wished to meet him and make yet another treaty with the Chiricahuas.

In mid-1852, Mexican reports suggested that the Sonoran campaigns had driven Mangas Coloradas out of Sonora and into the hands of Americans.[2] In part these reports were true. Yet it was also the time of the year when Mangas's people, after gathering and harvesting mescal in Chokonen country, normally returned to Santa Lucía. Mangas's contemporaries, including Ponce, who spoke "pure Castilian Spanish," along with Itán, Josécito, and Cuchillo Negro, appeared at Fort Webster on June 15, 1852. They told Major Gouverneur Morris that "all the Apaches [wished] to make a permanent treaty with the Americans." Ponce indicated that it might take three weeks to find Mangas Coloradas; to hasten matters, he offered to "go in person" after his chief and bring him to Santa Fe for the treaty. Major Morris apparently harbored the same scathing contempt for civilian authorities as did his superior, Colonel Sumner. "If I am not interfered with by subordinate agents of the Indian Department . . . [I] trust that I will be able to conduct this business to the satisfaction of the Colonel Commanding." Mangas had other ideas, however. On July 1, 1852, Delgadito and Itán appeared at Fort Webster with tidings from him. Though the text of the message is unknown, Delgadito likely notified Major Morris that Mangas had already headed north into Navajo country to meet the Americans.[3]

Just the thought of the great Chiricahua leader coming in to make peace excited New Mexico's Acting Superintendent of Indian Affairs Greiner. He had replaced Governor James S. Calhoun,[4] who had also acted as the Superintendent of Indian Affairs before he had left New Mexico on May 29, 1852, for Washington, D.C., after becoming critically ill from the effects of jaundice and scurvy. The autocratic Sumner promptly behaved in a way that would have made a Mexican revolutionary leader proud by summarily declaring himself acting governor. Ironically, only two days before Calhoun's departure, Sumner had written a provocative letter to the secretary of war in Washington in which he recommended that the government abandon New Mexico and return it to the Indians and Mexicans. After all, he reasoned, why should the Americans inhabit a country whose people were "idle and worthless"? He predicted that the territory, essentially a welfare state in his eyes, would be "precisely the same as it is now" in twenty-five years. He proposed a simple solution: withdraw the troops and civil officials. This would allow the two remaining parties—the Mexicans and the Indians—to defend themselves as they had before American arrival.

Almost as an afterthought, Sumner closed his letter by noting that the Apaches had sent word that they wished to make peace. Acting Superintendent Greiner had recently received word that the Chihennes and Bedonkohes were "desirous of being on friendly terms."[5]

Meanwhile, at Santa Fe on June 30, 1852, Greiner received a party of Pueblo Indians from Ácoma who told him that the Apaches, meaning the Chihennes and Bedonkohes, would come to their pueblo Sunday, July 11, 1852, to conclude a peace treaty. This news elated Greiner, for he probably learned that the celebrated Mangas Coloradas himself would be in. Charles Overman, special Indian agent appointed by Calhoun, was in Santa Fe at the time preparing to travel to Santa Rita del Cobre to bring in three Chiricahua leaders. Overman scrapped his travel plans when the Pueblo Indians brought Mangas's message. After consummating a treaty with the Mescaleros on July 1, 1852, Greiner began making plans for a trip to Ácoma to meet with the Chiricahaus.

On July 3, Greiner asked Colonel Sumner for an escort of troops to go to Ácoma, where "a large body of Indians is expected to be in attendance." Signing his letter with the title acting superintendent of Indian affairs, Greiner knew that he would incur the wrath of Sumner, who had previously declared that he was in charge of Indian affairs until Calhoun returned to New Mexico. In characteristic fashion, Sumner responded in an overbearing manner: "I am going myself to meet and treat with the Gila Apaches at Ácoma on the 11th inst. in conjunction (if he chooses to accompany me) with the senior Indian agent in this territory." Greiner laconically responded that the "agents appointed by the President of the United States, for the Indians in New Mexico will 'choose' (as suggested) to accompany Col. Sumner to treat with the Apaches at Ácoma. No unwarrantable assumption of arbitrary power, on the part of a military commander will for a moment, cause them to swerve from their official duties." Hoping to turn the screw tighter, Greiner closed by reminding Sumner that he would submit his complaint to the authorities in Washington to decide who were "the proper officers to negotiate Indian treaties in N[ew] Mexico." Petty disputes aside, on July 11, 1852 the American representatives reached Ácoma.[6]

Edwin Vose Sumner, New Mexico's independent and autocratic military commander of the early 1850s. He feuded constantly with civil officials but also found time to make a peace treaty with Mangas Coloradas at Ácoma. (Courtesy, National Archives, no. 111-B-6272)

A large band of Chiricahuas was nearby, but they feared to enter the town, and with good reason. The Pueblo Indians had built Ácoma on a high tableland about 350 to 400 feet above the plain,[7] with only one way to enter and leave the pueblo. Why did Mangas choose Ácoma, located some fifty miles north of Datil, normally the northern point of his range? His association with the Navajos was perhaps one reason, and he reportedly had traded at Ácoma in the past. En route he had visited his relatives and friends among the Navajos and had done some trading. It was about this time, or perhaps earlier, that he and the Navajo leaders had established a boundary that separated Apache country from Navajo land. Years later, George Martine, son of the famous Chiricahua scout Martine,[8] told Americans that the two tribes established this line at Gallup in northwest New Mexico.[9] However, this does not agree with the historical evidence. More likely they agreed to a boundary from the Arizona border east to Quemado, Datil, and Magdalena and culminating at Socorro on the Rio Grande. About this time Mangas also exchanged a Mexican captive, a thirteen-year-old boy named Jesús Arvisu, to the Navajos for a horse. He had taken Arvisu during the attack at Bacoachi on January 21, 1851, the day after the Pozo Hediondo fight. The bargain devastated Arvisu, but he grew accustomed to the more sedentary life as a Navajo and became an important interpreter in the years to come. After the difficulties with Bartlett regarding Mexican prisoners, perhaps Mangas had traded the boy knowing that the Americans would insist upon the liberation of their Mexican captives as a condition of the treaty. In any event, Mangas was encamped near Ácoma by the time the American peace contingent arrived.[10]

Greiner became alarmed when he learned that the Apaches had second thoughts about coming in. Describing them as "wild as hawks," the agent turned to the Navajos for advice. They suggested that he dispatch a messenger with presents to invite Mangas Coloradas to the peace council. Accordingly, he sent Charles Overman with some twenty dollars' worth of gifts to convince Mangas to meet the Americans. The Navajos had given Greiner sound advice. If Mangas accepted the gift, and a refusal would be an act of disrespect, then he would feel bound to reciprocate for the agent's generosity.[11]

Soon after, the chief arrived and made his way along the only trail that led to the pueblo. Mangas Coloradas often showed his willingness to parley with Americans, for he usually trusted them (being one of the few Chiricahua leaders who did), even if it meant

Ácoma, New Mexico. Mangas Coloradas walked these steps to meet Colonel Edwin Sumner and sign a peace treaty with Americans. (Author's collection)

endangering his own safety. It must have been quite a meeting between the venerable and powerful Chiricahua Apache chief and the martinet from New England. Accompanied by a few of his people, the chief audaciously entered Colonel Sumner's tent, "made himself very much at home," and in a matter-of-fact manner acceded to Sumner: "You are chief of the white men. I am chief of the red men. Now let us have a talk and treat."[12] Although he was now in his early sixties, Mangas very much impressed John Greiner, who described Mangas as "a magnificent looking Indian. . . . He is undoubtedly the master spirit of his tribe."[13] Mangas, who boasted that his "will and word are law to [my] people," admitted that his people had grown weary of war and now desired peace with Americans. The Mexicans, however, were another story.[14]

The treaty, which contained eleven articles, called for the Chihennes and Bedonkohes to recognize the jurisdiction of the United States, to establish friendly relations between the two races, and to allow the government to establish military posts and agencies in their country. It also required the Indians to return their Mexican captives and prohibited Mangas's people from raiding into Mexico. In return, the Americans pledged to issue presents and other supplemental items, but the pact provided no regular timetable for the issuance of these gifts. Mangas agreed to each condition until the Americans addressed and further explained the one relating to raiding into Mexico.[15]

All at once the great chief's eyes widened and his expression changed. He had come to Ácoma to make peace with Americans, not Mexicans. He reasoned: "Are we to stand by with our arms folded while our women and children are being murdered in cold blood as they were the other day in Sonora? . . . Are we to be the victims of such treachery and not be revenged? Are we not to have the privilege of protecting ourselves?"[16] Sumner and Greiner heard his passionate appeal for justice. The sincere agent grimly added later that "it will be extremely difficult to keep these Indians at peace with the people of Mexico." The autocratic Sumner, who had no sympathy for either Mexicans or Indians, may have publicly stated the government's case, but privately he apparently gave Mangas Coloradas tacit permission to continue his incursions into Mexico, at least according to what the chief later told an American officer.[17]

From Mangas Coloradas's perspective, the treaty contained several significant points. First, it ceded no land to Americans, who had neither the leverage nor any compelling reason to make this demand then. If they had, Mangas would not have consented. Though Mexico had always claimed New Mexico, the Apaches never recognized that position, for they ruled Apachería. Furthermore, throughout his life Mangas never agreed to any treaty that forfeited his rights to his country. He was the only Chiricahua leader to sign the treaty at Ácoma; no other chiefs had had the courage to come in. Yet he clearly represented five other Chihenne leaders, whose names adorned the treaty, but not as signers at that time: Ponce, Itán, Sergento, Dosientos, and José Nuevo. By making this agreement and securing peace, Mangas could concentrate on his despised enemies to his south in Sonora; he would not have to concern himself with American campaigns from the north or east. His people could live without the rations; they had done so for decades. Therefore, when the presents were infrequent and the rations were spartan, he probably was not as much disturbed as were other Chihenne local groups who lived near Santa Rita del Cobre and the Mimbres River. These groups may have expected rations such as those the Mexicans had furnished them, and when they were not forthcoming they did not usually take the agreement seriously, at least in the view of historian Robert Utley.[18] According to Apache oral history, Mangas declared to his people: "We will show them [Americans] the importance of our word. If we say we will keep peace, we will do so. We keep our agreements."[19] And he did.

While Mangas Coloradas was at Ácoma, many Chihennes had come into Fort Webster. In the first week of July a large group encamped near the post, where Second Lieutenant Nathan George Evans, a future brigadier general for the Confederacy, and others furnished them whiskey, which resulted in several days of precarious relations. On July 4 and again on July 5, Private Matson recorded in his diary that "every Indian in camp is drunk." When an inebriated soldier fired at an Apache, they all fled to the hills, apprehending treachery. The next day Americans convinced the Indians to return, and about a week later Ponce arrived with the news that Mangas had made peace with Colonel Sumner and had started for Fort Webster to meet the officers. A dubious Private Matson wrote, "I don't believe the tricky old scoundrel will come here." But the chief proved his skeptics wrong, for on July 23, 1852, he entered the fort, announcing with much bravado that he had made peace with Colonel Sumner.[20]

According to Private Matson, Mangas was "dressed in the uniform of a Mexican General of artillery," a garb which likely he had lifted from the body of a slain Mexican officer. Matson further recorded in his diary:

There is a reward of $10,000 for old Mangas offered by the Mexican Government, dead or alive, but this sum has not been sufficient to secure his capture by that Government. Mangas speaks Spanish well. He possesses supreme power over his Apache people and thinks a great deal of himself. He called up one of his subjects and showed him to us. This one had his nose cut off, and pieces of both of his ears sliced off permanently disfiguring him. Mangas told our officer he had done this to perpetually disgrace him because the man had killed a Mexican [and] taken his horse and rifle, without permission from Mangas.[21]

This paragraph contains some elements of truth, for rumors had it that Mexico had placed a large bounty—five thousand pesos, according to some accounts—for Mangas's scalp. Yet the story that Mangas had disfigured a member of his own local group for killing a Mexican stretches credibility; clearly such punishment is inconsistent with ethnological data and atypical of his personality. Apache leaders did not practice cruelty on their own people.

Mangas arrived shortly after a Chiricahua war party, under Delgadito, Ponce, Cuchillo Negro, and Láceres, had departed for a foray into Mexico, probably against Sonora, leaving their women and children camped near the fort. Mexican troops had recently slain several members of Poncito's group, and the Chiricahuas had set out to avenge these deaths. The incident that Poncito alluded to probably occurred in Sonora, in either the Pitaicache Mountains on June 19 or the Teras Mountains on July 9, 1852. The Mexicans claimed they killed several warriors in the first engagement near Pitaicache and perhaps others in the second fight in the Teras Mountains. Several women from Poncito's group had appeared at Fort Webster with their hair cropped short, a Chiricahua custom during their mourning period.[22]

Mangas may have joined his brethren, for on August 3, Private Matson reported that two Navajo warriors and several women had come into the fort and requested provisions. They had probably come south with Mangas and were preparing to return to their country now that his followers had headed south to catch up with the war party that had left two weeks before. Mangas Coloradas's absence during an important peace council at Fort Webster in mid-August suggests that he may have gone to Mexico.

Acting Superintendent Greiner arrived at Fort Webster on August 12, 1852, "for the purpose of meeting the other chiefs" who had not accompanied Mangas Coloradas to Ácoma. But when he did not meet any Indians, Greiner sent out runners to bring them in. Three days later Ponce and Itán, just back from their foray into Mexico, brought in a contingent of two hundred Apaches and agreed to abide by the terms of the treaty recently signed by Mangas. But, like their chief, they vigorously protested the idea of making peace with Mexico. Unlike Mangas, however, they consented to cease raiding Mexico if the government would protect them and their families—a declaration difficult to believe. Finally, Greiner reported a surprising statement (if true): The Apaches would consider selling parts of their country if they received appropriate compensation.[23]

If nothing else, the conscientious Greiner, who had just received an appointment as secretary for the territory, provided some insight into the breakdown of the Chihenne band. He made revealing comments because they fit precisely into the Chihenne local group designations used by contemporary authorities. He called them Gila Apaches, a generic term that sometimes encompassed the Chokonen, Chihenne, and Bedonkohe bands, though he was referring to the Chihennes. The "Gila Apaches appear to be under the control of three chiefs: Mangas Coloradas, Ponce and Llatana [Itán]." Mangas's country was "along the Gila River running westward from the Burro Mountains." Ponce claimed an extensive area—from the Burro Mountains "east to the Rio Grande and north to Santa Barbara." Itán was the leader of the group living near Santa Rita del Cobre. Greiner failed to mention Delgadito, for that leader had not come in to formally make peace, or the Janeros band of Nednhis under Láceres and Eligio that had moved into Chihenne country after defeats at the hands of Eusebio Samaniego the previous spring.

About the time that Greiner arrived at Fort Webster, Colonel Sumner issued orders instructing Major Morris to abandon the post at Santa Rita del Cobre and relocate it to the Mimbres Valley.[24] The directive must have satisfied Morris, for he had recommended this course of action to Sumner in a letter dated May 31, 1852. He furnished Sumner with a variety of reasons why he should move the post to another location. The new site offered better water and improved communications with Forts Conrad and Fillmore, and it enhanced the troops' ability to control the Apaches who lived along the Mimbres. Perhaps Morris's most compelling argument (though it was disingenuous on his part) was the one he believed would persuade Sumner to approve his suggestion. On the one hand he correctly pointed out that the new site on the Mimbres would prove to be a fertile area for cultivation, implying that his soldiers would take out their hoes and begin tilling the earth. On the other hand, he failed to mention that it was too late in the year to begin farming and that he had no intention of placing the same emphasis on this issue as did his superior.[25]

Morris had pushed the right button. To comply with the orders of the secretary of war to reduce operating costs in New Mexico, Sumner's pet project throughout his tenure (besides usurping the authority of civil officials) was the one that had the soldiers plant their own crops to reduce overhead at each post. Most officers failed to embrace Sumner's enthusiasm for this project. Colonel Joseph King Fenno Mansfield, who in 1853 completed an inspection of the forts in Sumner's department, labeled it "a failure generally." Captain Enoch Steen reasoned that soldiers made "bad farmers at best," a statement that Major Morris would have endorsed.[26] Perhaps Major Morris's most compelling reason to evacuate Fort

Webster was the perception of American military officers that the isolated post in the middle of Chihenne country lay vulnerable to an Apache siege. This belief remained a common misconception among American military men, who grouped all Indians in the same light, not understanding that guerilla warfare was the Apaches' fighting style. Unlike the more powerful Plains Indians, they lacked the patience and the manpower to sustain a prolonged siege.

Mangas Coloradas must have reacted jubilantly when he heard the news that Major Morris had abandoned the Spanish presidio at Santa Rita del Cobre on September 2, 1852, and had led his command fourteen miles east to its new site on the west bank of the Mimbres River about one mile west of present-day San Lorenzo. About a week later a Mexican soldier arrived at the new post with the tidings that his force, perhaps operating from the district of Galeana, had recently defeated a band of Apaches, probably a Chihenne war party returning from an incursion into Mexico.[27]

While Morris and his soldiers began the task of constructing new quarters, it soon became apparent that a few Apaches ("vagabonds . . . whom the chiefs can't control") had resumed raiding near Fort Webster. Their depredations consisted primarily of minor stock raids. In August they took thirty of Judge Hopping's mules near Mesilla and fled toward Lake Guzmán in Chihuahua, though some reportedly found their way to Fort Webster, where the judge later recognized them. On September 17 another band stole some fifteen mules and five or six horses from the post. As it turned out, two of the mules belonged to Lieutenant Evans and another to Major Morris, who asked Colonel Sumner what economic "measures he would be justified in taking." The major recommended a simple solution: the army should unilaterally deduct any funds allocated to the Apaches by the treaty "to compensate for the loss sustained by the officers and citizens."[28]

This empty request from Major Morris seemed to confirm rumors Sumner had heard that something was awry at Fort Webster. This travesty had become apparent to Lieutenant Colonel Dixon Stansbury Miles,[29] commander of Fort Fillmore. Miles, though known for such eccentric behavior as "wearing two hats at the same time," had acquired a fine reputation among his contemporaries. Though a martinet to some, for most he had the "energy and willingness to assume any responsibility."[30] He had written Sumner a month before from Fillmore, noting that a "matter of exceeding vexation and mortification is occurring that requires the interposition of the Colonel commanding the department." Miles had obviously heard the scuttlebutt that several officers at Fort Webster, including the commanding officer, had become involved in trading contraband with the Indians. He did not mention what they gave the Apaches in exchange for their stock (all stolen of course), but Private Matson, in his diary, clearly stated that on several occasions the officers had supplied whiskey to the Indians in exchange for their mules. Ponce had come to Fort Webster on September 22 and had returned most of the mules and horses taken five days before. He claimed that Navajos had taken the stock. Major Morris neglected to mention in his official correspondence that he had dutifully given Ponce a reward for returning the animals. According to Private Matson, Morris compensated Ponce and his party with whiskey, which "made them yell and [kept] the whole garrison awake all night." What had become evident to Colonel Sumner was that the major was the wrong commander for Fort Webster; his independent policies and outrageous conduct had sown drunkenness and distrust among the restive Apaches when a sensible officer could have promoted friendship and goodwill.[31]

Meanwhile, in the fall of 1852, Mangas Coloradas had established his village in the Burro Mountains and Mogollon country, where his people hunted and gathered the fall crop of piñon nuts, acorns, and walnuts. He also made at least one trip to Socorro and Lemitar on the Rio Grande and renewed trading acquaintances there, telling the citizens of the region that he would cooperate in recovering any stock taken by Apaches.[32] Mangas had distanced himself from his former ally, Delgadito, the one Chihenne leader who had spurned the treaty of 1852. On September 22, 1852, Delgadito had led a party of forty-five Apaches that stole 132 head of cattle and four horses from Alexander Degas near Doña Ana. Sumner allowed that Delgadito was "sour and suspicious" but declared that he expected him to "soon come into the treaty."[33]

Meanwhile, New Mexico's new governor, William Carr Lane,[34] had reached Santa Fe in September and had taken the oath of office there on September 13, 1852. Lane, in his early sixties, was a tall redhead who could boast of a diversified and successful career in public life: a medical doctor, former army surgeon, and onetime mayor of Saint Louis who had fought against the legendary Shawnee leader Tecumseh in the early 1800s. A universally respected man revered for his scruples and ethics, Lane, from the time of his arrival, clashed with the irascible and egocentric Colonel Sumner, who did all in his power to make life as miserable for the new governor as he had for the previous one. Finally, after a series of petty insults, an exasperated Lane, also self-centered and a man not inclined to back down from a fight, challenged Sumner to a duel. For once even the supercilious Sumner, never concerned with doing what was politically correct, rejected Lane's proposal. Even he realized that he could not get away with killing the governor in a duel without repercussions to his military career.[35]

About six weeks after taking office, on October 27, 1852, Governor Lane appointed Indian Agent Edward H. Wingfield, a Georgia native, to replace Special Indian Agent Charles Overman, whom the acting commissioner of Indian affairs in Washington had discharged on August 29, 1852.[36] In the words of one historian, Overman "had proven inept."[37] Whether he was an accomplice of Major Morris and others in the contraband trade was questionable. Nonetheless, he had done something, either real or imagined, to incur the wrath of his superiors.

Finding an honest and diligent Indian agent was a difficult task. The position guaranteed tremendous challenges and promised few rewards (the Indian department in New Mexico received inadequate funding) and was one particularly wrought with danger. Before he left office, Acting Superintendent of Indian Affairs Greiner had suggested that a governmental policy based on treating the Indians with "a proper spirit of kindness toward them is the best mode of governing them."[38] His humane suggestions, of course, were correct. If the government had allocated the proper resources in money and people and had followed up with competent and conscientious agents, it may well have averted much of the trouble that developed in the years to come.

Mangas Coloradas did sincerely want peace with Americans, and throughout the 1850s he adopted policies likely to lead to a long-term armistice. Even with the increasing American presence, by late 1852 he probably had not yet seen any significant changes to his way of life. His people continued to live free and unencumbered as they always had in the remote Gila wilderness, hunting, gathering, and raiding into Mexico. The warlike faction of the Chihennes and Bedonkohes had not relinquished its right to raid Mexico. Many of their problems with Americans resulted from this custom, particularly when they returned to New Mexico with their Mexican captives, who they believed were legitimate spoils of war. In fact, one could make the case that Americans failed to exercise any control over the Chiricahua bands until Indian officials

William Carr Lane, Territorial Governor of New Mexico, 1852–1853.
(Courtesy Museum of New Mexico, neg. no. 9999)

permanently appointed the competent and conscientious Michael Steck agent in 1854. Until that time Mangas would deal with four agents, some better than others, most quickly disillusioned, and all hamstrung by a lack of funds with which to provide assistance to the Chiricahuas.

Lane instructed Agent Wingfield to proceed to Fort Webster and establish his quarters there or at the "trading post of Mr. Sherman and Duval, located about eight miles from Fort Webster." The governor soothingly assured Wingfield that he would find "comfortable quarters and agreeable companions" at the latter place, apparently believing that Colonel Sumner's tentacles had reached out and poisoned the minds of the officers at Fort Webster, still under command of Major Morris.[39] On November 6, 1852, Wingfield, mounted on a mule provided by Lane, left Santa Fe for Chiricahua Apache country. Along the way he heard that the Apaches (perhaps including Mangas himself) had recently visited Lemitar and Socorro, undoubtedly trading with the locals. Passing Socorro, he stopped for several days at Fort Conrad, twenty-four miles south of the town, where he unexpectedly met Itán and three other Apaches. Wingfield informed Itán that he wanted to meet the Chihenne leaders at Fort Webster. The chief promised to bring his people in within twenty days and to send messengers to Mangas Coloradas and Ponce, who apparently had established their winter camps in their local group territory.[40]

After leaving Fort Conrad, Wingfield encountered a Mexican expedition of one hundred men, probably a force from Paso del Norte under Mariano Varelo,[41] about twenty miles south of Fort Webster. Governor Angel Trias had ordered Varelo to hunt Apaches in accordance with Chihuahua's new militaristic policy. Wingfield was unimpressed with the Mexican force, calling them "suspicious looking," and was relieved when they returned to their country without molesting either the Apaches or the citizens of southern New Mexico. After a ten day tedious trip from Fort Conrad," Wingfield finally reached Fort Webster on the Mimbres River on December 7, 1852.[42] There he found half the soldiers lodged in tents while the rest were cramped in buildings made of logs and mud. He must have heaved a sigh of relief when he found that the veteran dragoon officer, Captain Enoch Steen, who had been east on recruiting duty for most of 1852, had replaced Major Morris as post commander (Sumner had transferred the controversial Morris to Fort Union). After Steen received his orders in November, he immediately proposed that the army contract its farming efforts at

Fort Webster to civilians. This suggestion struck a raw nerve with Colonel Sumner, and, predictably, fell flat on its face. The department commander tersely reminded Steen of his priorities: ensure discipline of his troops, keep the Apaches quiet, and farm, farm, farm.[43]

The likeable and competent Steen made Wingfield feel welcome at the post. Surprisingly, Sumner had already issued orders authorizing Steen to provide two rations a day for the agent, for which, wrote Wingfield, "I am very much obliged." The agent selected a spot about three-fourths of a mile from the fort, where he planned to build quarters with the expectation that Lane would reimburse him for legitimate expenses. Throughout December the agent waited in vain for the Chihennes to appear. Finally, toward the end of the month, he sent out a messenger inviting "some of the chiefs to visit me." On January 7, 1853, two Chihennes from the peace faction, Ponce and Negrito, came in and reiterated their desires to live in peace. They said they would return within twenty days with their followers but did not mention Mangas Coloradas, who had gone to Chokonen country for his annual winter foray against Sonora.[44]

A few days later Captain Steen reminded Governor Lane that the Apaches lacked the bare necessities ("very poor and badly clad"), and he correctly predicted that they "must steal or starve."[45] A few weeks later the well-meaning Steen penned another letter to Lane, recommending that a site on the east bank of the Gila be reserved for the Apaches to farm. Once established, the Americans could entice the Indians in and teach them "how to support themselves by growing grain and vegetables, and breeding livestock." Yet, until then, the government would have to ration the Apaches to prevent their raiding the settlements, especially those in Mexico. Steen's ideas appealed to the governor, who was eager to try out the captain's pragmatic plan.[46]

Winter frequently meant hard times for the Indians, for they were between the fall and spring harvests and hunting was not always a profitable venture. With the food supply nearly depleted, and the warriors having some free time after helping the women with the fall harvest, winter was also the time when the Chiricahuas traditionally launched raids to supplement their gathering and hunting. Though Mangas had kept his bargain made with Sumner, a few Chihenne groups continued to commit minor stock raids in New Mexico. It was likely a few young warriors from Ponce's group who, on January 8, 1853, robbed some stock from a corral at Los Lunas, situated on the west bank of the Rio Grande about twenty miles south of Albuquerque. Captain Richard Stoddert Ewell,[47] known affectionately as "Old Baldy," took thirty men and a few Mexicans and pursued the nimble Apaches. The Indians had made a beeline south toward Mesilla; before reaching there, however, they turned abruptly west and slipped into the Mimbres Mountains. Ewell halted his pursuit, remembering that the Mexicans had informed him that "they had been assured by the Apache Chief Mangas Coloradas that he would recover the property in case he was advised." Besides, the raiders had committed this theft "for the sake of food [since] the Apaches [are] said to be in a starving condition." A perspicacious Ewell, like Steen, also revealed that he understood the distinction between what the Chiricahuas termed war and raiding, a difference that most Americans never understood: these "are thefts rather than displays of hostility."[48]

A few weeks later Apaches ran off some cattle from San Antonito, south of Socorro. Captain William Steele followed the Indians to the Mimbres River, where he surprised their camp, killing one and wounding two others, before destroying the ranchería of seventeen wickiups. Among the wounded was Ponce, peppered with buckshot in the forehead, according to what Private Matson heard later at Fort Fillmore. Shortly after, relatives and friends of the slain Chihennes avenged this attack and attacked the mail escort near Fort Webster, killing two soldiers and taking their mules and horses.[49]

By mid-February several Chihennes came into Fort Webster, held a parley with Captain Steen and Agent Wingfield, and expressed remorse for the recent raids. They promised not to commit any more depredations. During the next month virtually every important Chihenne band leader except Mangas Coloradas, who was still with the Chokonens, appeared at Fort Webster. Even Delgadito, formerly the most recalcitrant of all Chihenne leaders, had come in looking for assistance and assuring the Americans that he wanted peace. The combination of Steen's integrity and persuasive powers with Wingfield's lure of rations imbued them with confidence. Steen noted that in their first visits the Indians were nearly destitute of food and clothing. They had become "well satisfied" after the Americans had given them food and other presents. The veteran cavalryman closed his report by requesting twenty horses so that he could take a trip down the Gila to find Mangas Coloradas.[50]

Meanwhile, at Santa Fe, reports of recent Apache depredations in southern New Mexico reached Governor William Carr Lane, who, impressed with Captain Steen's proposal, decided to investigate matters for himself. At this time he also became embroiled in a controversy regarding the "Disputed District," basically the area in New Mexico "thirty-four miles wide and 170 miles long" that the United States would purchase as part of the Gadsden Treaty. With these two situations on his mind, he decided to journey south. On February 28, 1853, his entourage left Santa Fe bound for Mesilla. En route he stopped at Fort Conrad for four days, picked up thirty dragoons, and left on March 11 for Doña Ana. Upon arriving there, Lane took it upon himself to issue a proclamation taking control of the "Disputed District" until the government properly resolved the matter with Mexico through negotiations. Fortunately for all concerned, Colonel Sumner judiciously refused to support Lane's impetuous and unauthorized scheme, which nearly caused war to erupt between the United States and Mexico. In response to Lane, Chihuahua's Governor Trias brought a force of eight hundred men to near El Paso, prepared to fight Americans, if necessary. Consequently, Lane modified his belligerent position and retired to Doña Ana, where he hoped to make a treaty with the Mescaleros before heading west to Fort Webster.[51]

On March 31, Lane arrived at Doña Ana, hoping to meet the Mescaleros, who were up in arms over recent events. It should be noted that the previous October, Colonel Miles at Fort Fillmore had reported that a rift had occurred between the Mescaleros and the Chihennes. Although Ponce's and Cuchillo Negro's local groups historically had maintained close relations with the Mescaleros, the two tribes were culturally and politically independent of each other. The Mescaleros had told Miles that they were "afraid" of the Chihennes, because the latter had recently killed one of their leaders. Miles revealed his misconception of Apache political organization by remarking that this discord "was news to me. I ever thought they acted harmoniously with each other."[52] This was typical of most Americans in southern New Mexico of the 1850s: an Apache was an Apache; most saw only insignificant differences between bands, when in reality profound cultural differences remained between the Chiricahuas and the Mescaleros. Next, it should be understood that in early February a group of Mexicans known as the Mesilla Guard slaughtered fourteen or fifteen Mescaleros near Doña Ana. The Indians had come in peaceably when, for no apparent reason other than sheer naked savagery, the bloodthirsty Mexicans turned on the Apaches and massacred them. This pernicious attack would prove to be a foreshadowing of relations between the inhabitants of Mesilla and Doña Ana and the Apaches in the years to come. It was one of the most fearful atrocities in the history of southern New Mexican relations between Apaches and whites. Governor Lane waited at Doña Ana for a week, but the Mescaleros stayed away.[53]

On March 29, 1853, Lane left Doña Ana for Fort Webster. In case the Mescaleros came in during his absence, he left blankets, tobacco, and corn in the care of Pablo Melendres,[54] the prefect of Doña Ana County. Reaching Fort Webster on April 2, the governor's party received a warm welcome from Captain Steen, who invited Lane to share his quarters. During the next three days Lane held several important talks with the chiefs of the different groups (some three hundred Chihennes were present), carefully explained the articles of the compact, and presented "medals as emblems of authority" to José Nuevo and Cuchillo Negro, leaving one with Agent Wingfield for Ponce, who arrived on April 7. Lane's entry in his diary on April 7 was brief and to the point: "Treaty, or Compact signed with Mimbres & Helah [Gila] Apaches, by wh[ich] they agree to become Stationary, to cease to live by plunder &c."[55]

Governor Lane's intentions were honorable and just, but it was obvious that the author of this visionary compact had no proper conception of Apache society and culture. Several conditions were ill-conceived and undoubtedly ridiculed by the Apaches. These included the stipulations that the Indians must abandon their predatory way of life, build permanent dwellings, begin cultivating the earth, make laws (though they had their own laws that dictated appropriate behavior) that would specifically prohibit "the ancient custom of retaliation," choose a head chief who could speak for the tribe, and return all stolen property. In exchange Lane agreed to provide the bands with corn and beef for two years and a "reasonable amount of food" for three more years. To encourage the Indians' conversion from warriors to ranchers, Lane's compact committed the government to furnish the Apaches with breeding stock and farming implements. The eminent Apache historian Dan Thrapp put it best: "One might as well covenant with the wind to still or the tide to cease. . . . These provisions went against the whole fabric of Apache custom and social organization."[56]

Six Chihenne leaders—Ponce, Cuchillo Negro, José Nuevo,[57] Veinte Realles, Riñón,[58] and Corrosero—signed the compact. The articles invited Mangas Coloradas, Victorio, Itán, Delgadito,

Victorio, Chihenne leader who tried to live in peace with Americans.
(Courtesy National Archives)

Laceris, and Losho (perhaps Loco), all absent on the Gila, to join in
the accord. Some of these chiefs were off gathering mescal, while
others, notably Mangas Coloradas, were on an incursion against
Sonora.[59]

Two days after the parties consummated the treaty, Governor
Lane, with his escort, accompanied by Captain Steen and sixteen
dragoons, set out to examine Santa Lucía Springs and the Gila
River, which the governor had concluded would be a fine spot for
an Apache reservation. He returned to Fort Webster on April 17,
again met the Chihenne chiefs, and left the next day for the Rio

Grande. Before going, he gave Agent Wingfield a check for two thousand dollars for agency expenses as well as seven medals to distribute to the Apache chiefs as they came in. Lane also told Wingfield that conditions at the agency greatly disturbed him. He was particularly dismayed to have discovered upon his arrival that the Apaches were "perfectly idle" instead of "raising crops of corn." It seems that Captain Steen had allocated to Wingfield's interpreter, Francis Fletcher,[60] all the vacant land not currently under the plow. This appalled Governor Lane, who tried to correct the situation by hiring Fletcher to teach the Apaches basic farming "so that each band may enjoy the fruits of its own industry."[61]

Lane had no way of knowing while he was absent from Santa Fe that President Franklin Pierce had replaced Commissioner of Indian Affairs Luke Lea with George Manypenny. Lea had helped to conceive and draw up the Indian Appropriation Act of February 27, 1851, which recognized that the government had a moral obligation to take care of the Indians. Lea advocated that the administration set aside reservations for each tribe with "well-defined boundaries." He also suggested that until the Indians became economically independent, authorities in Washington should allow the agents to issue stock, agricultural tools, and clothing. Furthermore, the administration should permit the Indian agent to help the Indians "in the erection of comfortable dwellings, and secure to them the means and facilities of education, intellectual, moral, and religious." Clearly, Lane had adopted some of Lea's ideas. George W. Manypenny assumed office on March 30, 1853, and ten days later he ordered Lane "to cease and desist" the agricultural program at Fort Webster. He also vetoed Lane's provisional compact, though it would be some time until Lane officially received the news. Four months later Manypenny admitted that he had made his decision in haste, without understanding the merits of what Lane was trying to accomplish.[62]

As previously mentioned, Mangas Coloradas had left Chihenne country in early 1853 for Chokonen country. From there he joined his allies on a foray against Sonora, whose militia or national guard troops in the northern region, especially at Bavispe, had continued to carry the fight to the Chokonens whenever possible. Captain Eusebio Samaniego, the experienced, Apache-wise commander, had continued to wage war against the Chokonens that winter. In January his command killed five Chiricahuas at Sierra Larga in northeast Sonora, and it skirmished with the Chokonen leaders Triqueño, Carro, and Yaque in the Teras Mountains in mid-

February.[63] Yet the French Intervention in late 1852 and early 1853 had compelled Sonora's leaders to concentrate troops to repel the invasion, thus leaving the interior vulnerable to the Apaches.[64] By February two large bands had penetrated deep into the Sierra Madre. On February 19, 1853, one party attacked a ranch in the district of Sahuaripa and stole many mules and horses. That same day another band attacked Milpillas, a hacienda near Bacanora, and killed nine people and stole all of its stock. One week later another Apache war party, estimated at seventy warriors, assaulted a ranch near Tonichi, situated on the Yaqui River some twenty miles south of Soyopa, and killed five persons and captured several others.[65]

The Chiricahaus continued their raiding throughout March, attacking ranches and travelers at several places in the districts of Arispe, Bavispe, and Sahuaripa. Toward the end of the month reports from Sonora suggested that raiding parties of Chiricahuas were retiring north from the interior and had moved to the Teras Mountains, where "many bands of Apaches" had united.[66]

In early April an incident brought Mangas into contact with two of his old enemies—José María Elías González and Ignacio Pesqueira of Pozo Hediondo fame. In mid-March a raiding party stole twenty-five burros and two horses from Bacanuchi, about ten miles west of Bacoachi. The next morning Abundio Elías González, twenty-two-year-old nephew of José María, gathered a force of twenty-two men and pursued the trail for four days but failed to overtake the Indians. On the afternoon of April 3 the Apaches returned with lightning speed, audaciously stealing every mule of the hacienda. Abundio Elías immediately gathered a force of eighteen men and followed the trail; soon after, another nine men left with orders to unite with Elías. Before they could effect that merger, however, Elías's small group came upon the Apaches. The daredevil leader ordered his men to attack the Indians, much to the dismay of most of his followers. He led the charge, but his men lacked their leader's nerve. During the battle Abundio Elías discovered that "in the middle of the fight he was cowardly abandoned by the men he led." The Indians killed one man, wounded three others, and captured the youthful Abundio Elías.[67]

The Apaches' capture of Abundio Elías immediately received statewide attention. The prefect of Arispe dispatched troops to ferret out the trail, which seemed to lead toward Fronteras. Sonora's Governor Manuel María Gándara (again back in power after dictator Santa Anna restored himself to power in Mexico City), placed thirty federal troops under Captain Ignacio Pesqueira, who enlisted another fifty national guard troops from Banamichi and Bacachi, to "obtain the freedom" of Abundio Elías. On April 10, Pesqueira left Banamichi for Arispe, where he received reinforcements of fifty soldiers. He was all set to leave for Fronteras on April 12, but early that morning Apaches stole some of his horses, temporarily slowing him down. Yet he persevered, requesting Elías González at Bacoachi to send to him all the available mules and burros in the city. On April 13, Pesqueira's command reached Turicachi, south of Fronteras, knowing that it had cut the trail of a large war party. Pesqueira promptly sent a courier to the commander at Fronteras to warn him, but it was a day too late.[68]

Mangas Coloradas's war party had one last object before it returned to Arizona and New Mexico: Fronteras. The presidio had become a traditional, almost obligatory target for the Apaches—easy pickings, as far as they were concerned. They also knew that its troops had participated in many of the bloody campaigns of the previous year. Naturally, the Chiricahuas had to avenge these campaigns. The raiding parties had united at a rendezvous site south of Fronteras. Now a formidable war party, they planned to sweep through the area, kill anyone in their path, take every head of stock, and then retire to their secluded rancherías in the mountains of southern Arizona and New Mexico. This time, however, the Chiricahuas faced stiff opposition. At 10:00 A.M. on April 12, without warning, an estimated three hundred Apaches assaulted the presidio from the south. They slaughtered five boys who were tending their flocks of sheep and swept away most of the oxen, horses, and mules of the fort. For the next five hours they swarmed around the presidio like angry hornets. Finally, late in the day, the Apaches broke off the engagement, taking their dead and wounded with them. According to their own accounts, Mexican marksmen had killed eight Apaches and wounded many others.[69]

A month later Mangas conceded to American officials that his people had suffered heavy casualties.[70] Despite the bloodshed, it was a typically indecisive fight that would have little impact on future relations, but neither party probably realized all of that then. Yet the battle may have sealed the fate of the indomitable Abundio Elías, if in fact he was still alive. The Sonorans had spilled plenty of Apache blood; the Chiricahuas undoubtedly retaliated. Elías had probably revealed to the Apaches that he was a nephew of José María Elías González, the officer whose command had butchered over one hundred Indians near Janos almost a decade before. They may have considered using him to exchange prisoners, for he would have brought several Indians in return. It was also possible that the Indians may have preserved Elías's life until they returned to their rancherías in the Chiricahua Mountains. If so, they surely ritualistically tortured him to death in a public event for band members to celebrate. One Chiricahua described their treatment of Mexican male prisoners to Morris Opler:

> The Chiricahuas treated Mexicans in a rough way when they were captured. . . . These Chiricahuas were more the enemies of the Mexicans than of any other people on earth, because the Mexicans treated these Chiricahuas in a nasty way.
> They say they used to tie Mexicans with their hands behind their backs. They then turned the women loose with axes and knives to kill the Mexican prisoner. The man could hardly run, and the women would chase him around until they killed him. . . . Usually the people whose relatives had been killed wanted it to be done. They wanted to have their way about it.[71]

Because it occurred so long ago, we will probably never know how the brave Abundio Elías González met his death. His body was never found.

Meanwhile, Captain Pesqueira, who seemed preoccupied with justifying his every move, reached Fronteras, remained there inexplicably for a week, and then departed on April 24 to scout the "Chiricahua Mountains." Along the way he reconnoitered the Animas and Sarampeon (Peloncillos) Mountains before heading to the northeast part of the Chiricahuas, which he entered through "Cañon de las Paces," known today as Cave Creek Canyon.[72] On May 1, 1853, his troops captured an Apache lurking near his lines. Pesqueira interrogated the Indian, who admitted that his village lay within a few miles of the Mexicans' camp. At once the Sonoran commander prepared a force of ninety men under Rafael Corella, a confirmed Apache hater whom the Chiricahuas had wounded at Pozo Hediondo. As they approached the camp, the captured Indian cried out a shrill warning, thus affording his group members the opportunity to escape uninjured. After observing smoke signals from all directions, Pesqueira decided that he "would have to suspend the campaign" and return empty-handed to Fronteras.

The Sonoran commander had not realized that his command was in the midst of several hundred Apaches led by the redoubtable Mangas himself. The Apache chieftain and his band, with women and children, had encamped in the Chiricahuas, waiting for their men to return from their incursion into Sonora. They were also there because it was the time of the year to harvest and bake the mescal plant, which always grew in abundance along the eastern slopes of the Chiricahuas from the Apache Pass area south to Cave Creek. At 6:00 P.M. on May 1, the sentry reported that he now had in view two Apaches with white bandanas a short distance from camp. Pesqueira responded with one of his own, hoping "to talk to them about ransoming Abundio Elías and others whom they had taken." He sent Loreto Surdo, a citizen of Fronteras, to ask the Apaches what they wanted and to propose an exchange of captives. One Indian was Mangas, as usual always willing to parley. He consented to a prisoner exchange and agreed to search "every ranchería for Abundio Elías." Mangas sent Surdo back to Pesqueira to ask when and where the prisoner exchange should take place. Pesqueira responded, "Fronteras, in eight days." The chief demurred, saying that it was not enough time and instead offered to meet Pesqueira in twenty days at Fronteras.

Mangas's pledge was disingenuous. Pesqueira retraced his steps to Fronteras; en route his men shot and murdered their Apache prisoner while in the act of "trying to escape," the ever convenient frontier euphemism. Once there, he waited for Mangas to come in, but the chief had no intention of doing so.[73] Instead, as Mangas later put it, because of his indelible distrust of Sonorans "he doubted their sincerity" and decided to leave the Chiricahua Mountains and "get his people off in the night."[74] He returned to New Mexico with his people, along with several Chokonens, their horses and mules loaded down with Sonoran booty and their recently harvested mescal.

Meanwhile, after Governor Lane's council with the Chihennes at Fort Webster, Agent Wingfield eagerly awaited Mangas's arrival. On April 17 he had advised Lane that he expected to ration some three hundred Chihennes, a figure that would increase when Mangas Coloradas, Delgadito, and Itán arrived with their groups from their Sonoran foray. Ponce's and Cuchillo Negro's Chihennes had quickly revealed that Wingfield's mission of making them self-sufficient farmers would be a difficult task. On April 27 he informed Lane that the Chihennes had begun cultivating their fields near the fort. Yet in the next breath he conceded that the Indians were using their corn ration differently from what he had intended. Wingfield tersely growled that "yesterday I found many of the Indians drunk from a miserable beer they make from corn."

The next day he warned the culpable parties that he would stop the rations if their drinking continued. But a week later he once again exuded optimism, reporting that "our farming experiment succeeds admirably." The Apaches had planted fifty acres of corn, pumpkins, and melons, according to Captain Steen. Of course one might regard any Apache farming activity, on any scale, as a success. It was also possible that Wingfield was applauding a program that he knew had little chance to bear fruit. After all, it was his superior's idea, and a little white lie or some unsolicited flattery may have gained him the goodwill of the governor, for he knew that during his visit Lane was disappointed at the state of affairs.[75]

About the time Wingfield was writing his rosy report on the farming efforts, two women from Mangas Coloradas's band arrived, fresh from the Chiricahua Mountains. They must have started a week before Mangas's parley with Pesqueira in the Chiricahuas, for they arrived on May 2, one day after the meeting between the two foes. They brought favorable news. Mangas, they said, was "glad to hear that all the Rio Mimbres Apaches want a good peace and are settled to planting corn." Surprisingly, they neglected to mention the Chiricahuas' fight at Fronteras, but instead told Wingfield that Mexicans had "badly whipped" a band near Lake Guzmán. They were referring to a campaign from Janos under Captain Baltazar Padilla that had attacked Poncito's band near the Florida range in southern New Mexico. On April 26, the sixty-nine soldiers, guided by two Chiricahuas (one was Gervacio Compá, a son of Juan José Compá), discovered the Apaches gathering mescal, attacked them, and killed a man, evidently a relative of Poncito, and captured another young woman. Padilla's force occupied the camp, burned their "jacales" or wickiups, and confiscated twenty-five horses. The defeated Apaches, who had walked to the agency, had "lost all their clothes, mescal, and came in nearly naked and nearly starved." Clearly, they had come in "for protection and to plant."[76]

In mid-May Mangas sent an envoy to inform Captain Enoch Steen that he was coming in for a talk. The messenger told Steen that the Sonorans had "badly whipped" the Indians. "His women and children barely escaped" with their lives. Steen, who had previously expressed his desire that the Sonorans "would catch Mangas and give him a good drubbing," now anticipated that Mangas would soon "pay me a visit."[77]

On May 18, 1853, Mangas finally came in to Fort Webster (the Apache chieftain's first visit to the post since its relocation to the

Mimbres River) and met with Agent Wingfield and Captain Steen. Wingfield was awestruck to meet the chief whom he had heard so much about during the past six months. Despite his advanced age of about sixty-three, Mangas in his physical appearance and mental acumen was imposing and impressive by any standards. Elated over this fortunate development, Wingfield in a letter to Governor Lane glowingly described the chief:

> Mangas Coloradas came in today. I assure you that he is a noble specimen of the genus homo. He comes up nearer to the poetic ideal of a chieftain, such as Homer in his Iliad would describe than any person that I have ever seen. No feudal Lord in the paltry days of Chivalry ever had his vassals under better subjection. His manners are stern, dignified and reserved, seldom speaks but when he does it is to the point and with great good sense. You may be assured that he is the master spirit among the Apaches. The Indians are to hold a junta or council tonight and let us know the result on tomorrow.[78]

The following day Mangas and several other chiefs met Wingfield and Captain Steen and gave their "cordial consent to the articles of the treaty." Mangas may have wondered why another agreement was necessary since in his mind he had abided by the terms of the Ácoma treaty with Colonel Sumner. When Wingfield explained his compact to him, the chief must have realized that he had nothing to lose and everything to gain. Lane's offer of regular rations and breeding stock certainly pleased him. Mangas, who had met Steen three years before at Santa Rita del Cobre, asked the captain to establish a fort on the Gila "to have a post between him and the Mexicans." He proposed to gather his people there and to comply with the terms of the treaty. He even offered to accompany Steen to point out the best site for a post. Steen estimated that Mangas's followers could amount "to over 1000 souls." As Mangas's own local group totaled about one hundred souls, Steen must have included the Bedonkohe band along with Itán's and Delgadito's Chihennes, with perhaps a few Chokonens who had come in from Arizona. The chief also admitted that the troops at Fronteras had killed three of his men during the assault there. Steen summarized the conference by declaring that "Mangas has more sense than all the rest of them put together."[79]

But just one week after Steen outlined this optimistic scenario, relations began to turn sour. Again, as it had with Bartlett and other American civil and military authorities, the subject of the

Indians' Mexican prisoners became a problem. A Chihenne chief named Losio or Losho, a leader in Ponce's group, brought in four Mexican girls, aged six through eleven, undoubtedly expecting the Americans to offer a ransom. He had not reckoned with the indomitable will of Captain Steen. Like Bartlett before him, Steen seized the girls from the Apache. Instead of paying the presents, Steen and Wingfield issued Losho rations. Upon leaving, the Chihennes "appeared much dissatisfied, displaying signs of belligerent nature."[80]

Another unexpected problem that required a prompt response from Agent Wingfield was the perplexing arrival of some two hundred Chiricahuas. These Indians were probably Bedonkohes, but if not were surely Chokonens, who had never before been at the agency. Though far removed from their band territory, they wanted rations. Their arrival alarmed Steen, who believed that they would cause trouble. Accordingly, he requested reinforcements of either one company of dragoons or one of infantry, because he had "so few men at the Post available for duty." He pointed out that after "taking out of the present command for the cultivation of the farm and those for the quartermaster department, I have but thirty-five men for duty, including the daily guard."[81]

Steen's concerns were well founded, for, as early as June, Delgadito's band returned from its raid into Mexico. The chief contemptuously ignored Wingfield and clearly wanted nothing to do with the agent at all. Delgadito, sullen and morose, had rejected all relations with Americans, trying to remain as distant from whites as possible. His band contained many younger, bellicose warriors who had deserted Itán, Ponce, and Cuchillo Negro's groups after they had made peace with the Americans. Private Matson reported in his diary that Steen's troops at Fort Webster had launched a campaign against Delgadito's band near the Mimbres, killing at least two warriors and wounding several others.[82]

Governor Lane, always ready to erupt with any matters concerning Agent Wingfield, did just that soon after he received Wingfield's report about Mangas's appearance at Fort Webster. After receiving Manypenny's edict, Lane had contracted a case of cold feet about the financial liability of feeding so many Apaches. Concerned about the possibility of sustaining upwards of a thousand Apaches, he took his frustration out on Agent Wingfield, whom he blamed for the current state of affairs. His anger was further compounded with the arrival in Santa Fe on May 29 of Mr. Duvall, the post sutler at Fort Webster. Duvall told Lane that Mangas had applied for permission to bring all of his people to the Mimbres to "cultivate the soil." The governor jumped to conclusions and accepted Duval's version without investigating the facts. This development incensed Lane, who wanted to tear Wingfield's hide off, because the additional expense of feeding Mangas's followers was not in his budget and he believed that the lands along the Mimbres could not support more Apaches. Lane, inferring that Wingfield had agreed to this, placed the blame squarely on the agent's shoulders.

Yet neither Mangas nor Wingfield had proposed such a move. Mangas was not about to encroach on the group territory of Ponce and Cuchillo Negro, not when he was much more comfortable living at Santa Lucía along the Gila. If anything, it was Wingfield's idealistic perception of Indians that got him into trouble; he had the interests of his charges at heart. Wingfield had not learned that Washington had rejected Lane's treaty until June 15. By that time, however, Governor Lane had decided to replace Wingfield with another agent. In any event, whether Duval's misconception was deliberate or unintentional was not known. Yet it was the straw that broke the camel's back, as far as Lane was concerned. Dr. Michael Steck, agent for the Utes and Jicarillas, happened to be at Santa Fe. On June 3, Lane relieved him of all responsibilities there and reassigned him as temporary agent for the Gila and Mescalero Apaches, replacing Wingfield.[83]

The appointment of the sincere and capable Dr. Steck would mark the beginning of a long and beneficial relationship between the Americans and the Chihennes. Mangas's world was beginning to change, though he may not have recognized it then. More Americans were coming to his country, and the Chiricahuas' on-going war with Mexico had taken a toll on the Apaches, especially the Chokonens and Nednhis. Mangas and his chief lieutenants, Delgadito, Cuchillo Negro, Ponce, and Itán, were aging. The arrival of Agent Steck would eventually bring stability to the Chihenne world. They had finally found a man whom they could trust, although it was a faith which had to evolve over time. His steadying influence and indisputable integrity would prove to be responsible for one of the better developments in the annals of American–Chiricahua Apache history.

Unfortunately, Steck's first assignment with the Chiricahuas was a temporary one. His successor, newly appointed Indian agent

James Smith, would perform his duties competently, but like his predecessor he lacked the funds to provide anything but meager assistance to the Apaches. The positive steps implemented by Wingfield and Lane came to a halt. Mangas Coloradas, dissatisfied with the bad faith of the government, would become even more aloof toward Americans in the following year of 1854.

Chapter 12

AMERICANS BREAK
THEIR PROMISES

WE will never know for sure whether Mangas believed the new agreement with Wingfield would take effect and that the Americans would issue regular rations to his people. He probably was not too concerned, for he had lived his life thus far as a free Apache, not relying on assistance from either Mexicans or Americans. He would take rations if the distribution site was convenient to him. Yet at least two Chihenne local groups, those of Ponce and Cuchillo Negro, were becoming much dependent on rations. Thus, their life-style began to change as they moved closer to the agency and began farming on a small scale to keep in the good graces of their agents, who had become difficult to keep track of. The Apache agency began to look like a revolving door as Washington assigned four agents to the Chihennes in a period of one year, partly because of a change in national politics from the Whig administration of President Millard Fillmore to the Democratic administration of Franklin Pierce and partly because of the unfortunate death of a promising agent. These bewildering shifts hardly inspired confidence among the more militant and aloof bands, of which Mangas Coloradas remained the undisputed leader. Historian Robert M. Utley believes that in the early 1850s Mangas "pursued an ambiguous course" toward Americans.[1] Certainly he was not averse to attacking Americans in Mexico—for the Apaches considered travelers in northern Mexico fair game and he knew he was safe from American troop reprisals. Yet after agreeing to terms at Ácoma, Mangas refrained from raiding in New Mexico, with which he was at peace.

Meanwhile, from Santa Fe, Agent Michael Steck journeyed to

the Ute and Jicarilla agency at Taos, wrapped up matters there, and returned to Santa Fe on June 23.[2] Two weeks later, on July 8, Steck, mounted on a government mule and furnished with a "saddle, bridle, and gun," departed for Fort Webster. But along the trail he became acutely ill, which forced him to remain at Socorro for a few days.[3] There he managed to pick up the latest Apache news, writing Governor Lane that the Apaches of the Gila region were at Santa Rita del Cobre "engaged in planting."[4] But Steck did not know the country that well, and his report erroneously implied that Mangas Coloradas's followers had moved from the Gila to Santa Rita del Cobre to begin farming operations.

Steck reached Fort Webster at the end of July. En route a Mr. Anselmo, the express rider, overtook him and delivered a letter from Governor Lane, written on July 11, which was a stinging indictment of Wingfield. Clearly, from Lane's insulting tone, he had already tried and convicted Wingfield without a thorough investigation of the facts. The governor's outrage mounted like a snowball rolling downhill as he wrote his instructions to Steck. After first slapping Wingfield's hand for improper completion of paperwork, and implying he may have been involved in unethical business conduct, Lane launched his first missile at the former agent. Why had he "collected so many of the wandering Apaches at his agency and offered food to them? . . . His mismanagement will cause great embarrassment, not only to me, but to you also, and to my successor, by creating expectations amongst the Indians that must be disappointed, they exhausting the appropriation for Indian service in New Mexico for the current year." In the next paragraph Lane brusquely questioned Wingfield's emotional health. "Why did Agent Wingfield encourage Mangas to bring his own and other bands from their homes on the Gila, to the Mimbres? Has the agent been insane? The lands of the Mimbres will not accommodate the bands of Ponce and other chiefs who are actually there." Finally, having found a loophole in the treaty, he admonished Steck that "the Indians will reproach you, with the bad faith of government, but there will be no just ground for the reproach. The conditional bargain has not yet been approved, and may be rejected. Agent Wingfield has issued food, without discrimination."[5]

Lane's missive was egregiously unfair to Wingfield. It was not the agent's fault that the governor's superiors had disapproved his visionary provisional compact of April 7, 1853, in which Lane, representing Washington, D.C., had committed the government to issue rations to those Indians involved in planting. Lane's agreement had also invited the bands of the Gila wilderness, Mangas Coloradas, Itán, and Delgadito, to embrace its conditions in return for food and breeding stock. In today's world of instantaneous communications, the commissioner of Indian affairs would have immediately informed Lane and Wingfield that he had rejected the agreement. Logistics and communications were much different in 1853, however, and Lane did not receive word until at least a month later, and Wingfield not until June 15.[6] Shortly after, Wingfield informed those Apaches who were following the letter of the treaty, and dutifully trying to farm, that some nebulous institution in Washington had vetoed Lane's agreement, primarily because the budget was spent. The Apaches had no conception of American political structure—that the official government policies toward Indians were subject to change every time a new administration assumed power. Ironically, Lane's compact was an enlightened first step toward bringing the Apaches into the American sphere of influence. He wanted to alter the behavior of the Indians, turn them from raiders to farmers, and furnish them with enough economic assistance to obviate their incursions into Mexico. Unfortunately, until the early 1870s Congress failed to appropriate enough money to support the Chiricahua Apaches. Consequently, raiding (especially in Sonora), the third element of their economy, continued throughout the 1850s.

Alert to a portending crisis with the Chihennes, Lane feared that he would be held responsible for having spent his budget on Indian affairs for the current fiscal year. His disparaging remarks concerning Wingfield's sanity and his rationalization to Steck that the Apaches had no reason to be upset with the government's decision tended to support this conclusion.

Steck investigated affairs at Fort Webster, and his findings must have chagrined the governor. In fact, a copy of Steck's analysis was not found among the official records of the New Mexico superintendency but instead in Lane's personal papers in the Missouri Historical Society. Could Lane have intentionally removed this letter because it provided information that contradicted his indictment of Wingfield? After examining Wingfield's accounts, Steck exonerated him of any dereliction of duties concerning feeding the Indians:

> There is no doubt that the articles mentioned in the above accounts have been furnished and what I think will surprise you more is they have all been fed to the Indians except the 14 head of beef cattle and

126 fanegas of corn. Those who came regularly to the post for their rations numbered about 300. In my interviews with the chiefs I have told them that the Great Father was angry with them as they had not complied with that part of the treaty that required them to work, and that they had also wasted their corn in making tiswin, to get drunk upon.[7]

By this time Wingfield, who apparently never saw Lane's accusatory letter, had officially written his closing report to Lane. Clearly he was proud of his contributions:

On the eve of leaving this post of duty I am disposed to review my course since I have been here and I assure you that I have everything to be proud of when I see what has been accomplished. When I arrived here it was not considered safe for a man to go over two hundred yards from this post without being armed to the teeth, now, everything is quiet, no such danger is feared by anyone, peace is restored to our frontier, and in a good degree to that of Mexico. I do not claim all the honor in bringing about this state of things. I wish to be considered only as an auxiliary or coefficient in the good work.[8]

Soon after Steck's August 3 letter to Lane, Wingfield left for Santa Fe, arriving there on August 12. Meanwhile, the temporary agent began the task of organizing the agency. Governor Lane had ordered Steck to take the four Mexican girls seized from the Apaches to Pablo Melendres, the prefect of Doña Ana, so that Melendres could deliver them to Mexican officials. Governor Trias of Chihuahua had written Wingfield that he would arrange for their return, and Steck decided that since they were safe at the fort at little cost to the government, he would keep the girls there until he heard from Trias. Steck talked to them, and their story touched his heart: "Their ranch was attacked; their fathers and mothers killed; their younger brothers and sisters taken by the feet and their brains dashed out against the walls in their presence." In coming years the honest and objective Steck would come to realize that this brutal and stark picture of relations between Mexicans and Chiricahua Apaches went both ways. Neither group had a monopoly on savage and barbaric behavior toward the other. Neither party could recall who began the bloody warfare. Violence begot more violence, and the never-ending cycle seemed destined to continue with no end in sight.[9]

Dr. Michael Steck. Sincere, honest, and competent, Steck was one of the earliest Apache ethnographers and perhaps their best agent. (Keleher, *Turmoil in New Mexico*)

During the second week of August, Steck traveled to each ranchería along the Mimbres River. On August 12 he killed the last beef and issued his reduced rations to the Indians. Although "a few of the Indians were dissatisfied," they took the ration. The conditions of the Chihenne band surprised him. White encroachment on their lands and their long war with Mexico had significantly affected their numbers and their ability to make a living. He found each man to have "two to five wives" and reported that "often from ten to fifteen are dependent on a single hunter." Yet the lack of game in their country had made it impossible for them to live without raiding. The government had two options: "It is plain as the light of day that they must be rationed or a war of extermination commenced if we wish to prevent these depredations. They must steal or starve." Steck concluded by declaring his intent to visit Itán, Delgadito, and Mangas Coloradas's bands on the Gila and the Bedonkohes in the Mogollon Mountains.[10]

Yet Steck's itinerary becomes unclear at this point. According to his "Abstract of Provisions Issued to Apache Indians for the Quarter Ending September 30, 1853," he rationed 150 Gila Apaches and 175 Mogollon Apaches on August 14, and another 300, primarily Mimbres, on August 24. He apparently did not meet Mangas Coloradas, who normally would have moved his people to the Mogollons and Gila wilderness country for the fall harvest of acorns, walnuts, piñon nuts, and berries. Between these two ration dates, Steck settled the accounts of Pablo Melendres at Doña Ana. He left the agency about August 27, 1853, and reached Santa Fe on September 2.[11]

Even before Steck left, on August 21, two Chihenne local groups under Cuchillo Negro and Josécito came into Mesilla, requesting a treaty to "trade with the citizens of the town." They claimed that they had come from the fort on the Mimbres (Fort Webster) and that they wanted to remain for ten days—that is, until the trading was done. Domingo Cubero, the prefect, posted notices that he would fine any individual twenty-five pesos for violating the law that prohibited the selling of liquor to the Apaches. A few days later the Chihennes returned, and Cubero again rebuffed them. Finally, on August 24, Cuchillo Negro crossed the Rio Grande with Francis Fletcher and "swore by all the saints and their sons that they had come in peace and wished only to trade in a friendly fashion." For the third time in four days Cubero turned them away.[12] Yet Fletcher, who was supposed to be teaching the Indians how to farm, had no problem acting as a broker for the Indians. In exchange for the Apaches' mules he obtained whiskey for a warrior named Ratón,[13] a member of Delgadito's local group, who promptly got drunk and then killed his two wives and brother-in-law.[14]

Meanwhile, the new Apache agent, James Smith, whose brother had once served as governor of Virginia, had arrived at Fort Webster about August 26 and conferred with Michael Steck ("the more I see of [him] the more I like him"). Smith conceded that he had "never seen a wild Indian." His education began immediately. Within days of his arrival, he met Delgadito, "a powerful man and a warlike leader of great influence second only to the great Mangas Coloradas," and promised the chief that he would punish Fletcher. Despite his inexperience, in the short time he was the agent he proved to be a keen observer and fair-minded man who might have developed into a good agent if he had not met a premature death three months later. He diligently took a crash course on the Southern Apaches, carefully itemizing each band from information that he received from local frontiersmen, traders, and military men. The Chiricahuas living in New Mexico were the Mimbres (Chihennes), 100 lodges; the Mogollons (Bedonkohes), 125 lodges; and the Gila Apaches (probably Mangas Coloradas's band and the Chokonens), 150 lodges. The Chiricahuas living in Mexico were the Janeros (one Nednhi local group), 100 lodges, and the Carisals, or the Carrizaleños (another Nednhi local group), 80 lodges. Since according to his estimates each lodge contained about five people, the total tribal population in 1853 would have been about 2,775 individuals.[15] It was a good guess, but probably about 10 to 15 percent high. In 1840 the four Chiricahua bands may have totaled 2,800 to 3,000 individuals, but their numbers had decreased significantly in the 1840s, a result of their vengeful and fierce war with Sonora and the efforts of James Kirker, José María Elías González, José María Carrasco, and Eusebio Samaniego, among others.

As a new agent, Smith did not wink at the plight of the Chihennes but saw them as they were. "The Indians were poor, miserable and filthy. They live on game when they can get it, on the mescal, the piñon [nuts], the cedar and other berries. . . . When pressed by hunger they eat mules and horses of their own, and if they have none, infest the roads and settlements for the purpose of stealing them." Like Steck, he concluded that the government had two choices: either feed the Indians or exterminate them. There was no middle ground. The Chihenne chiefs gave Smith an earful about the integrity of the government. They wanted rations and provisions of corn, meat, powder, and lead. They caustically complained to Smith that the government had not fulfilled its treaty obligations. They had no understanding why Washington had not approved the treaty. Smith requested that Governor Meriwether allow him to issue regular rations. Otherwise, he insisted, the Indians will begin raiding. "A small amount of money will prevent this but millions will be necessary to whip and exterminate them." Perhaps a visit to the Great White Father in Washington would prove beneficial to all concerned. In addition, the agency headquarters, a stopgap facility, consisted of "one room built with sticks and mud," a storeroom, and a kitchen "almost in a state of dilapidation."[16]

All summer no one at the agency had heard from Mangas Coloradas, which meant that he had likely gone south on a foray against Sonora. In one period of three weeks from July 10 through the end of the month, Chiricahua war parties had laid waste to central Sonora, killing over 150 Sonorans in twenty days. The Chokonens had several large groups involved—one under Posito Moraga, Triqueño, and Teboquita and the other led by Carro and Yaque. Likely Miguel Narbona, Esquinaline, and Cochise formed a third band, with perhaps Mangas Coloradas and some Bedonkohes. There were so many war parties in Sonora that the official state newspaper, *El Nacional*, editorialized that "numerous parties of Indians are actually roaming over the central part of our state." The Apaches "are a cancerous wound which threatens the existence of the state. The desperate struggle leaves us powerless and breathless. . . . There is no remedy; meanwhile, the savages trample on our country. We have no other prospect but misery and death because prosperity and progress are impossible for a people who every day lose their fortunes and their lives."[17]

In any event, on September 8, 1853, Mangas suddenly made his first appearance at the agency since late May or early June. He arrived with Itán and Delgadito to get rations and meet the new agent. Lacking rations, Smith was "compelled to buy two beeves and some 50 to 75 bushels of corn to appease the Indians and keep them friendly." Mangas obviously impressed Smith:

Mangas Coloradas is the head chief of all the tribes and comes down here from the Gila with his warriors and some women for corn and beef. He refused the little I offered him at first, but on explanation and throwing in a beef he took it and has since behaved well. . . . He is the most dignified and noble looking Indian I ever saw. [He is] a man of large frame and great muscular power. They say that he is a truthful and honest man in all he says and if properly conciliated can control all the bands.[18]

Agent James Smith had come west with New Mexico's new Governor David Meriwether, an experienced administrator and politician, who had succeeded William Carr Lane. Meriwether had come to Santa Fe in 1820 as a representative for a mercantile company when Mexican officials arrested and placed him in jail. New Mexican authorities soon released him but admonished him that he would be shot if he ever returned.[19] A hearty and robust man, Meriwether was descended from the stock of independent and hard-fighting Kentucky frontiersmen. He had hunted and trapped in the West since his early twenties and had also been a successful politician in Kentucky. On his return to New Mexico thirty years later he also became the superintendent of Indian affairs; for these two duties the government paid him twenty-five hundred dollars per year.

Besides those civilian changes, the War Department had finally replaced Colonel Edwin Sumner with Colonel John Garland,[20] a sixty-one-year-old officer whose military career had begun during the War of 1812. The new commander, an unpretentious and accommodating individual, would prove a breath of fresh air for New Mexico. Harmony now existed between the two leading officials of the territory.

Garland believed in delegating responsibilities; in contrast, Sumner had micromanaged the department. An old friend of Sumner, Garland had no desire or intent to disparage the efforts or results of his predecessor. Nonetheless, when he realized that he had inherited a department in shambles and that Sumner had made decisions solely on controlling or reducing costs as the main criterion, he conceded that some of his old friend's decisions and philosophies were "misapplied" and that "his economy ran into parsimony." Colonel Sumner had established nine posts during his regime; after both Garland and Colonel Joseph King Fenno Mansfield inspected these posts in the late summer and early fall of 1853, Mansfield recommended that Garland abandon and relocate three of them and partially rebuild two others. Mansfield lauded the efforts of Major Steen, an "experienced and gallant officer," and was gratified "to learn that most of the men of his [Steen's] company had joined the Temperance Society." Mansfield concluded that Fort Webster was improperly located and therefore too expensive to supply. Thus, he recommended that Garland consider a site on the Gila, near Santa Lucía, to aid travelers on the thoroughfare to California and "overawe" the Apaches. Instead, in November Garland ordered Steen to abandon Webster and relocate the garrison to the west bank of the Rio Grande. The troops evacuated the post on December 20, 1853, and moved to the new site at Santa Barbara, which would become known as Fort Thorn, on the Rio Grande near present-day Hatch. Agent James Smith, justifiably thinking it "unsafe to remain" after the military left, convinced Governor Meriwether to allow him to move to the Rio Grande with Steen.[21] Victorio's biographer, Dan Thrapp, believes this move had "profound effects" upon the political unity of the two eastern bands, the Bedonkohes and Chihennes. Half the Chihennes, essentially Cuchillo Negro's and Ponce's local groups, moved their rancherías to the eastern face of the Mimbres Mountains to be closer to the agency. These local groups thus separated themselves from the groups led by Delgadito and Mangas Coloradas. Delgadito remained along the Mimbres for much of the time; Mangas, when not in Chokonen country, remained in his traditional headquarters at Santa Lucía, the middle man between the Chihennes and the Bedonkohes.[22]

Garland did not explain why he had opted to ignore Mansfield's recommendation and move the garrison to the Rio Grande. His reasons, however, in order of importance, must have been as follows: He could supply the post more efficiently and economically at its new location. In addition, the Mescaleros were acting up, and he could deploy Steen's command to cover the western limits of their territory. The move also removed the Indians from the pernicious influence of unscrupulous traders and opportunistic men like Francis Fletcher. Finally, it removed the command from Chihenne country and away from a controversial subject that had become embarrassing to American civil and military authorities: the travesty of the Chiricahuas' Mexican captives. This issue had endangered James Gadsden's negotiations with Santa Anna. The Treaty of Guadalupe Hidalgo obligated American representatives to liberate these captives. Each time this happened, however, a minor crisis resulted that threatened to explode into violence.

The outcries from Sonora had heated up during the summer of 1853. As Americans made their way west, following Cooke's route, they usually stopped at Fort Webster and traded with the Apaches. Many of these parties also halted at Santa Cruz and Tucson. A main topic of conversation was invariably the Apaches. In addition, Mexican campaigns in northern Sonora, especially those led by Captain Eusebio Samaniego, inevitably met with these emigrant parties. Often the common theme was that the Apaches living along the Mimbres River were receiving protection

Fort Thorn, New Mexico. Agent Michael Steck's Indian agency was
located near here. (Courtesy National Archives)

and rations from the Americans. This camp of six hundred Chihennes, supposedly led by Mangas Coloradas, allegedly contained
between fifty and seventy Mexican captives.

The rumblings grew louder in early August 1853 when, near
Batepito, Captain Eusebio Samaniego, guided by the Apache scout
Sergeant Mariano Arista, captured the sixteen-year-old son of a
Chokonen leader named Pascualito. Accompanied by two prominent Chokonen chiefs (Carro and Yaque), Pascualito tried to arrange
for an exchange of prisoners. Yet the Apaches were too wary to
approach Samaniego, who had the reputation of being their most
formidable adversary in northern Sonora. The young Apache man
confirmed two rumors: the Chokonens had recently been in touch
with Mangas Coloradas, and the Apaches residing along the
Mimbres River were holding many Mexican captives.[23]

Samaniego's report drew the attention of Governor Manuel
Gándara, who immediately became enraged about American
involvement. He wrote to the minister of relations in Mexico City
repeating Samaniego's version and specifically mentioning the
culpability of Americans and the role of Mangas Coloradas in this
fraudulent practice. Gándara suggested that Governor Trias of
Chihuahua investigate, since he was closer to New Mexico, or that
the federal government send a secret commission to find out the
facts. Mexican authorities raised the issue with James Gadsden,

then in Mexico City bargaining with Santa Anna to siphon off as much of northern Mexico as the cash-hungry dictator would be willing to sell.[24]

Gadsden, involved in sensitive negotiations with Santa Anna, wrote four letters to Colonel Garland during a two-week period "with respect to the purchase of Mexican prisoners by the garrison of Fort Webster." Garland asked his commanding officers at Fort Webster and Fort Fillmore to respond; in the meantime, he wrote Gadsden on Christmas Day, 1853, to inform the minister of what he had observed during his visit to Fort Webster two months before. He pointed out that he had seen several liberated Mexican captives whom Americans had "not purchased but forcibly taken from the Apaches."[25] Major Richardson at Fort Webster agreed with Garland, writing that "after a thorough investigation of the subject I can see no cause of complaint whatsoever by the Government of Mexico." In fact, Major Steen had adopted a resolute position regarding any captives: he took them "by force . . . without any compensation whatsoever." The only exceptions were a few captives who had found protection with the Americans after fleeing from their captors and two captives whom Estevan Ochoa,[26] a prominent citizen of southern New Mexico, had purchased from the Apaches.[27] Ochoa did so at the request of Agent James Smith after Governor Meriwether had denied the agent permission to buy the captives. The governor clearly informed Smith that "such a traffic can never be tolerated, as this would be to offer a premium to the Indians to capture others."[28]

Private Matson, in his diary entry of July 8, 1853, corroborated their accounts: "The wife of Ponce's son, a medicine woman, is a Mexican who was stolen seven years before. Her father is here and demands her. He was taken at the same time she was. He still bears the scars of the knives of Indians who tortured him. He was destined for the stake but escaped. Until now he never got tidings of his daughter. Major Steen ordered Ponce to either bring her in or fight and said we would get into his camp and take her away from them. She was brought to us."[29]

In truth, Major Steen and Indian agents Wingfield, Steck, and Smith had done all in their power to resolve this difference. The Chihennes had learned their lesson from dealing with Bartlett two years before and understood they could not bring their captives when they visited the post for rations. They also knew enough to remove them to safe havens when Americans were going to visit their rancherías. The American military was not yet powerful enough to unilaterally demand these prisoners from the more militant bands, with whom they were trying to maintain peaceful relations. They might get away with such an imperious order to Ponce, who with Cuchillo Negro was the most moderate of the Chihenne chiefs. What would have resulted with Mangas Coloradas, Delgadito, or the Bedonkohes was an entirely different question. Such an action might have driven the Apaches off into the hinterlands and created unwanted tensions. All in all, the American garrison at Fort Webster, under the direction of the competent Major Steen, handled the situation with both diplomacy and veiled coercion, offering the olive branch first, and only when necessary resorting to rattling the saber.

Mangas was unaware of this controversy and of the military and civilian changes occurring in New Mexico. Regardless, shortly after meeting Agent Smith in September, a large Chiricahua war party convened in the Burro Mountains for a foray into Mexico. From this point forward there is no record of Mangas's coming into the agency either at Fort Webster or at its new location at Fort Thorn until the fall of 1854. Why did he not come? Perhaps one factor was the refusal of the Americans to issue regular rations. Perhaps he did not care for Smith or did not want to go all the way to the Rio Grande, where the agency would be relocated, to receive inadequate rations. Just as importantly, the successes of Chiricahua war parties in Sonora during the summer and fall of 1853, which had avenged Carrasco's and Samaniego's campaigns of 1851 and 1852, seemed to reinvigorate his desire to fight Mexicans. Whatever the reason, he would spend much of the next year with the Chokonens. He joined his son-in-law Cochise for incursions against Sonora before finally returning to New Mexico in the fall of 1854 after an absence of almost a year.

In October 1853 Mangas made another foray into Sonora and upon his return ran into a staggering New Mexican herd of fifty thousand head of sheep en route to its California market. One of the owners, Judge Miguel Antonio Otero, who had met Mangas during the treaty at Ácoma in July 1852, talked with "Mangas Coloradas and three hundred warriors" at either Cow Springs in southwestern New Mexico or near the San Pedro River in Chokonen country. According to Dr. Thomas E. Massie, who participated in the drive, Mangas "had become restive and hungry" after Washington had stopped its rationing policy and thus made "a terrible and destructive" foray into Mexico. "On his return with his rich plunder" he came to the camp of Judge Otero. The chief gave the judge the same reception that he had given Kearny seven years before. He "relieved the judge of all apprehensions by assuring him that as they were both captains and countrymen (Americans) the Judge might pass without fear of molestation throughout that country, which belonged to him." At Tucson they learned that Mangas had just returned from Sonora. He had haughtily ordered the vaqueros at Gándara's hacienda at Calabasas to place the stock "in good order by the time he returned upon another incursion."[30]

In January 1854 a captured Chokonen admitted to Sonoran military officials that Mangas Coloradas and Delgadito had joined the Chokonens in the Chiricahua Mountains and were planning to attack settlements in Sonora. The dogged Eusebio Samaniego picked up additional information when his patrol captured three Indians (two women and one old man named Naguile) in the Pitaicache Mountains. Soon after, he discovered a ranchería near Batepito, captured five others (one a daughter of the Chokonen leader Casimiro), and killed a respected warrior named Taleluz, "distinguished among the Indians by his bravery." Taleluz wounded one soldier before Samaniego's men cut him down with a volley of bullets. The prisoners admitted they were en route to the Teras and Pilares Mountains to meet other groups. Samaniego immediately marched to Pilares, saw a ranchería "through his eyeglass," and prepared to attack it at first light. Although the rugged terrain proved to be a real obstacle for his troops, he succeeded in capturing four women, one the wife of Teboquita, and recovering a captive, whom the Apaches had wounded during the attack. The Chokonens, led by Triqueño, had taken her during a January 3, 1854, raid at Tepache. Samaniego burned the camp and a great deal of mescal besides recovering thirty head of stock, two hundred bullets, and a quantity of powder.[31]

Captain Samaniego picked up more intelligence when sixty-three Chokonens appeared near Bavispe in late January, hoping to exchange their captives for the nine he had taken earlier that month. Their first response clearly showed that Samaniego's recent scout had enraged them. This was a true war party, which they had hastily organized, for in typical Chiricahua fashion they took revenge directly against Samaniego. One Chiricahua informant told Morris Opler that a war party would sometimes go after "the same enemy who killed their people."[32] This time, since they knew who had captured their people and their objective was to ransom their relatives, they decided to give Eusebio Samaniego a little payback. Early on the morning of January 28, 1854, they

assaulted the Samaniego ranch south of Bavispe, but the inhabitants escaped to the safety of the hacienda. The Indians broke off
the attack and headed south toward Bacerac. Before reaching there
they swept by the Teramochic hacienda, killed a man and a child,
captured four others, and soon after had a running fight with
eighteen soldiers from Bacerac, in which they killed three more
Mexicans. Meanwhile, Captain Sebastián Reyes and national guard
commander Eusebio Samaniego arrived on the scene with a large
force of men, including Sergeant Mariano Arista, their capable
Apache scout.

That afternoon Casimiro released one captive, the child taken
from Teramochic, and proposed a prisoner exchange. The next
morning, January 29, the first trade occurred—Casimiro's daughter
for one Mexican—followed soon after by another one-for-one
exchange. The Chokonens agreed to return the next day and
ransom two more captives from Bacerac and the stock that they
had pilfered in exchange for the rest of the Indians held at Bavispe.
That trade did not go as well, for one Chokonen, a man named
Chirumpe, apparently arrived intoxicated, and Casimiro and
Chrisotomo soon approached the presidio to inquire about his
status. From there the facts become garbled as the reports of
presidio Captain Sebastián Reyes and Captain Eusebio Samaniego
vary. Apparently Captain Reyes had left the Mexican lines to talk
to Casimiro and a few others when Captain Samaniego, noticing a
six-shooter in Casimiro's belt, and suspecting treachery, launched
an attack on the Chokonens, killing Casimiro, Chrisotomo, and
Chirumpe and possibly others. Meanwhile, the rest of the band,
under Carro and Yaque, disappeared into the Sierra Madre, but not
before they killed their two prisoners from Bacerac. This was
another significant loss to the Chokonen band. We will never
know whether Samaniego had become trigger-happy or had opened
fire in calculation.[33] In April, Samaniego sent the Apache captives
to Moctezuma. In the middle of May, Terán y Tato forwarded
them, except one baby who was ill and remained at Moctezuma, to
Ures.[34]

During the two days of talks between Samaniego and Casimiro,
the latter had told the Sonorans of a council in the Chiricahua
Mountains between the Chokonen band, under Miguel Narbona,
Cochise, and Taces, and the Bedonkohes and Chihennes under
Mangas Coloradas and Delgadito. The Indians decided on a foray
and chose the towns and ranches between Sahuaripa and Ures as
potential targets.[35] About January 10 they entered Sonora by the

Peloncillo Mountains and Guadalupe Pass and began making their way south at a leisurely pace through the vast Sierra Madre. Bypassing Bacadehuachi, they moved east to the Moctezuma River, which they followed southward. (Samaniego's scout of early January must have just missed them.) At some point the large war party, numbering two hundred to three hundred warriors, split into several bands of thirty to fifty warriors.

Exactly which group Mangas was with is impossible to say. When news of the various depredations reached the governor at Ures, *El Nacional,* the official state newspaper, lamented in its issue of February 17, 1854, that "numerous parties of Apaches have appeared in the state in recent days, all armed with carbines and rifles that they have recently acquired." It then went on to explain that the Indians had obtained many of their weapons from the nefarious commerce with Americans along the Mimbres, which account was clearly an oversimplification. According to Luis Tánori, an Opata commander who was in charge of national guard troops of his district, these same Apaches had committed the infamous sanguinary raids of the previous summer.[36]

Sonoran reports stated that Mangas led a group that was raiding southeast of Ures. As he swept north with its plunder, his band attacked Agua Caliente ranch and continued by Rancho Viejo and Alamos. Governor Gándara, expecting the war party to continue north toward Cumpas and Moctezuma, ordered troops to waylay it near Pozo Hediondo.[37] This time, however, Mangas, perhaps recalling the bloody encounter of three years before, decided to ignore these settlements. The pragmatic Apaches also had another reason, at least according to Captain James Box, who visited Bacoachi and Fronteras about this time: "The Apaches know there is nothing left to steal, now they go to richer places." Therefore, instead of continuing north the Indians went east into the Sierra Madre near Oputo and followed the range north toward Arizona.[38]

It was unlikely that Mangas had reached his ranchería in the Chiricahuas in time to meet Second Lieutenant John Grubb Parke, who was investigating a possible railroad route through southern Arizona and had camped for a few days at Apache Pass. For two days, on March 1 and March 2, Apaches had come into Parke's camp. On the second day they sold some mules. Parke did not mention the names of any of the leaders who came into camp (and if Mangas was near he would have met Parke), so probably he had not yet returned to the Chiricahuas. A month later, A. B. Gray's surveying party, which consisted of thirteen "well-armed and well-mounted whites," also visited the Chiricahuas, crossing the mountain through its southern pass, today known as Tex Canyon. At the western side of the Chiricahuas, near Rucker Canyon, they came across fresh Indian signs with trails "running in every direction."[39]

In May another war party, numbering two hundred warriors, entered Sonora. On May 11, 1854, an escaped captive, a native of Sahuaripa, arrived at Huasabas. He informed authorities that he had fled from a band led by Delgadito and Costales,[40] who "were very cruel to their captives" even though Costales was himself a Mexican by birth. The former prisoner failed to mention Mangas Coloradas, but he was probably present, for Delgadito usually took his cue from him, and the war party, according to eyewitnesses, numbered about two hundred men, split among Chihennes, Bedonkohes, and Chokonens. Duplicating their march of the previous February, they returned to Alamos, where they decoyed a group of twenty-two men under the courageous Opata leader Luis Tánori, "who had dedicated his efforts to fighting Apaches." Tánori and eleven of his men perished; the remainder escaped to Alamos with the Apaches on their heels. The Indians audaciously surrounded Alamos, killing two women and one man, and burned a hacienda and its seven buildings nearby. From there they went north with their plunder, driving horses and cattle with them. Near Mazocahui they assassinated two miners, and later, in a sharp engagement, they killed five militiamen near Baviacora.

Hoping to cut them off before they retired to their secluded rancherías, Governor Gándara rounded up a company of presidio troops from Fronteras, whom he had withdrawn from the frontier post and stationed near Ures because of the threat of another French invasion. A veteran sergeant, José Yescas, a soldier known and trusted by many Chiricahuas because of his long service at Fronteras, led this detachment but could not overtake the Apaches. In the past the Chiricahuas had located their base camps in the Teras, Pilares, or Pitaicache Mountains. But the tenacious patrols of Captain Eusebio Samaniego had compelled them to move these temporary campsites away from his jurisdiction. Consequently, the Chihennes had situated their home camp in the Oputo Mountains south of Teras, and the Chokonens had established their rancherías at two places: Miguel Narbona and Cochise near Turicachi, and Posito Moraga, Triqueño, Carro, and Yaque at the Ajo Mountains between Fronteras and Bacoachi, where they were safe because neither place could then have mounted an offensive. By late May the warriors had returned to their base camps. As they moved north, Mangas led nineteen warriors on a lightning raid against Janos, killed three citizens, and stole some stock. The Chokonens under Miguel Narbona raided Fronteras, stole sixteen mules and horses, and captured one boy. With summer approaching, the confederated bands migrated north to present-day Arizona and New Mexico. Mangas, instead of moving to his usual summer headquarters at Santa Lucía and the Gila wilderness country, apparently remained in Arizona, though no one knew for sure.[41]

The personal war between Captain Eusebio Samaniego and the Chiricahuas dragged on through the summer of 1854. Samaniego seemed to have become obsessed with defeating the Chokonens, whose local groups customarily lived a part of every year in north-eastern Sonora. To subjugate Apaches, as history has proven, whites employed a formula that combined two independent variables: competent military leaders with common sense and the tenacity of bulldogs, and resourceful guides who could ferret out a trail. The equation became unbalanced if only one was present; a successful campaign required both, as American commanders such as Reuben F. Bernard in the 1860s and George Crook in the 1870s and 1880s would discover. To campaign against Cochise, Bernard had the consummate guide of the 1860s—Merejildo Grijalva, who knew well the habits and territory of the Chokonens, since he had lived with them for a decade after they had captured him as a youth. Crook had men such as Al Sieber,[42] who knew Apaches and the country of central Arizona as well as did the Apache scouts— many of them Chiricahuas—who were willing to scout (some say betray) their own relatives. At Bavispe, Samaniego had three men—two Apaches and one Opata—who served him well during the early 1850s. His best was Mariano Arista, probably a Chiri-cahua, who for some unknown reason had decided to adopt Mexican life; he regularly provided the most important knowledge and service. According to Samaniego, Arista knew the "practices of the Apaches and was knowledgeable about their country."[43]

In late June 1854, Samaniego sallied out of Bavispe with a large force guided by Arista and the Opata Indian Alverto Guaymuri. They headed for the Animas Mountains in southwestern New Mexico, where an extended family group of either Chokonens or Nednhis was living. The Animas included several good springs and were historically an important center for hunting and gathering. There Samaniego's scouts jumped an encampment and captured fourteen people, including an old warrior named Guillen. Most of the men were not in camp. Afterwards, Samaniego marched to Teras and captured a Bedonkohe warrior named Severiano, an old associate of Mangas from the days at Santa Rita del Cobre when Mangas was still known as Fuerte; Severiano's presence thus suggests the presence of the Chiricahua tribal leader in Chokonen country. Samaniego also liberated a child taken from Fronteras during Miguel Narbona's recent raid and learned that a group of Chokonens had gone toward Turicachi. Severiano, "one of the worst in his tribe," suffered the fate of most adult men captured by either Apaches or Mexicans: death. As Samaniego put it, Severiano was killed, naturally, "while trying to escape," although execution would probably be a more accurate description of his death. Samaniego magnanimously credited his two scouts, Arista and Guaymuri, for "their energy and bravery" as well as presidio Captain Sebastián Reyes, who also distinguished himself.[44]

Reyes and Samaniego would pay a price for their relentless campaigns. Toward the end of August, Chokonens ambushed five men along the trail between Bavispe and Oputo. They killed a man and captured Tulgencio Samaniego, a relative of Eusebio, and directed him to write a note offering the exchange of himself and another man for Guillen and the others captured in the Animas Mountains in June. Terán y Tato had sent these hostages to Ures, where they did not remain long. Soon after, they escaped—an event that must have surprised Terán y Tato. He assumed they would find their way back to their people and the Chokonens would then no longer need their bargaining chips. He was right; Tulgencio Samaniego, like Abundio Elías, was never heard of again. The news of the Apaches' escape from Ures must have distressed Eusebio Samaniego. About the same time, Apaches had ambushed and wiped out a party of five men between Bavispe and Huasabas; one was a son of Captain Sebastián Reyes. In their mind the Chiricahuas had retaliated against those responsible for the deaths of Casimiro and other men the previous winter.[45]

About the time of this incident, Mangas Coloradas raided near Santa Cruz. He apparently attacked two groups of American emigrants along the route between San Bernardino and Santa Cruz, though whether he knew they were Americans is not known. He did not bother to investigate their nationality before attacking parties in northern Sonora. They were fair game. The first was Beck's train, from which James Houston was killed, and the other was that of Fairchild, whose brother was killed east of Santa Cruz, Sonora. Both parties lost several head of cattle. According to J. G.

Bell, who was a drover with a Texas cattle herd bound for California, Mexicans at Santa Cruz told him that Mangas Coloradas was in the neighborhood and had committed the depredations.[46]

If so, Mangas did not remain too long, for a group of thirty-six Americans under a man named Callahan, accompanied by some twenty-five Mexican volunteers from Santa Cruz, followed a band of hostiles into the Huachucas, attacked them, killed twenty-one Apaches, and recovered a captive taken from Tucson some four years earlier. Given the location, one might conclude that they had attacked a Chiricahua group. But the Western Apaches were active in southern Arizona that summer, and it was unlikely that any Chiricahua band had a captive from Tucson unless that person was obtained by trade.[47]

In any event, soon after the hostilities near Santa Cruz, Mangas took his people back to New Mexico. Much had changed during his absence. The troops had evacuated Fort Webster the previous December, and the Chihennes promptly burned it. Agent James Smith had died of natural causes at Doña Ana on December 15, 1853. Edmund Graves, the son-in-law of Governor Meriwether, had replaced Smith, arriving at Doña Ana on January 23, 1854, but Graves experienced negligible contact with the Indians under his charge.[49] Without an agent present, the progress in farming and the trust established by Wingfield and Steck had ground to a halt. Graves, from Doña Ana on June 8, 1854, conceded that the suspension of these efforts had impaired relations.[50] Add to this deterioration in relations the Americans' suspension of rations, and one understands why even the moderate faction of the Chihenne band had become suspicious and distrustful of Americans.

Fortunately, President Franklin Pierce reappointed Michael Steck Indian agent for New Mexico. Ironically, Steck had received the endorsements of several military officers and had apparently won the job over Moses Carson, the half-brother of the celebrated Kit Carson. Commissioner of Indian Affairs George Manypenny informed Steck of his reappointment as agent on May 9, 1854. Steck came west with Governor Meriwether (who had been east on personal business), who at once ordered him to the Chihenne and Mescalero agency at Doña Ana to succeed Agent Graves, who had resigned. On July 23, 1854, Meriwether instructed Steck to move the agency to Fort Thorn and to "apprise the Indians of your agency of your arrival and location."[51]

By then Steck, whom today we would call a self-starter, had already begun collecting news and information about his Indians.

He arrived at Doña Ana on July 6 and just two days later reported that "the Gila Apaches have been behaving well." In his next sentence he threw out a bombshell, announcing that the leader of the peace bloc, Ponce, had been "killed by one of his own people in a drunken frolic." In a later report Steck revealed that one cornfield "was destroyed . . . when the Indians' own horses trampled it during [the] drunken frolic." Within a few weeks he completed the business of moving the agency's records to Fort Thorn. He arrived there on August 8 and set up headquarters at the abandoned town of Santa Barbara, where he rented its buildings and warehouse from Pinckney R. Tully.[52] Mainly because he wanted this challenging assignment, he would have a profound influence on Mangas Coloradas and the Chihennes. They needed an agent of principle who could provide the right mixture of sympathy with an occasional harsh dose of reality. With his medical training he was a meticulous observer with a curious nature and an insatiable desire to learn about his charges, thus becoming one of the early Apache ethnologists.[53]

On August 12, 1854, Cuchillo Negro and Josécito paid Steck a visit and made "strong protestations of friendship" to the agent.[54] The next day he left the agency with two men, bound for the Apache villages on the Mimbres "to ascertain the feeling of the Apache chiefs toward our Government, and to see to what extent they were cultivating the soil on that stream." After a six-day trip in which he met several Chihennes, but none of the "principal chiefs," a few Mexicans told Steck that the Chihenne leaders had intentionally avoided him. Mexicans had intimated to the Apaches that Steck was a spy for American troops, who were planning a campaign against them. The lack of farming disappointed Steck, and he advised the Apaches to make the most of the fall gathering season ("acorns, berries, and mescal") because he had so few presents to offer them.[55]

In truth, the Chihenne leaders had not purposely avoided Steck. They were unable to see him because they had gone to Mesilla, where they hoped to receive permission to come in and trade. The list of leaders at Mesilla was a virtual *Who's Who* of early 1850s Chihenne chiefs. All of their important leaders were present except Mangas Coloradas, who was in Arizona with the Chokonens. On August 13, Crisanto, accompanied by a man and three women, all from Delgadito's group, appeared at Mesilla. They told Domingo Cubero that their "capitancillo," Delgadito, wanted to make a peace treaty and receive a license to trade with the people of Mesilla.[56]

Five days later Itán came in, accompanied by Cuchillo Negro, Josécito, Poncito, Riñón, Costales (their interpreter), and fifty women and children. Itán did most of the talking. He told Cubero that Delgadito had developed an unexpected illness and was too ill to travel. A more possible scenario was that Delgadito, the most bellicose of these Chihenne chiefs, had decided not to come in because he distrusted Cubero, known for his inflexible opposition to Apaches.[57] The Apaches wanted a solid and strong peace. They had proven this by refraining from depredations near Mesilla. Itán emphasized that the Mescaleros were responsible for any recent raids near there, and Domingo Cubero, the prefect, so informed his superiors at Paso del Norte. The Mesillans refused to grant the Apaches a license to trade and told Cubero to send the Indians away.[58]

After this rebuke, the Apaches decided to visit Steck at Fort Thorn, but not before some members of Delgadito's band stole some horses at Mesilla. On September 13, Cubero informed his superiors that Delgadito and Itán with their people had gone to Fort Thorn and visited Steck. In October the diligent agent took another sojourn into Chihenne country and conferred with most of the important chiefs. He did not say whether he met Mangas, though the chief had finally returned from Arizona. He found the Indians peaceful but nearly destitute. Steck cautioned Meriwether that "much has been promised them" and if the government failed to fulfil its commitments, the Apaches would have to begin raiding. Steck urged the governor that "cultivation of the soil is the surest road to civilization. . . . No time should be lost in the accomplishment of an object that promises so much good."

Steck recognized that hunting, gathering, and raiding comprised the economy of the Chiricahuas. Yet game was becoming scarce, and to dissuade the Indians from raiding, Americans were attempting to turn them from warriors into farmers, thus leaving them with half their former food supply. He believed the government had to furnish the other half "if we wish to maintain peace." This policy, he declared is "the only means of preventing depredations. Reverse our positions, place the white man in a starving condition and I doubt whether he would consult the right to property more than the Indian. He to [sic] would steal and justify himself by declaring that self preservation is the first law of Nature." Dan Thrapp put it best: "His [Steck's] appeal was strong and well reasoned. Only a very small amount of money might save the Southwest from disaster. Yet for many years such a calamity hovered on the horizon simply because the dollars applied were so paltry, given so grudgingly by a penny-pinching Washington, and came forth so belatedly."[59]

Toward the end of October the Chihenne chiefs began arriving at Fort Thorn to receive Steck's rations. Cuchillo Negro, Josécito, and Sergento arrived on October 25 with about sixty of their people; two days later Mangas finally came in, with Delgadito, Itán and ninety of their followers. This may have been the first meeting between Agent Steck and the powerful Chiricahua tribal chief, who would return on the eleventh of the following month for rations.[60] It would be the beginning of a long and fruitful relationship—one that would endure for the remainder of the decade. Steck's influence with Mangas Coloradas would steadily increase over the next few years. The two men from vastly different worlds would come to respect each other.

Chapter 13

THE GOOD AGENT STECK

MANGAS Coloradas could not have realized how much his life would change after his meeting Indian agent Michael Steck at the Apache agency located near Fort Thorn in late October 1854. The evidence is equivocal about whether he had met the agent before; suffice it to say that whenever and wherever their first meeting occurred, the two men developed a mutual respect that would endure until 1860. Once the Indian bureau in New Mexico provided funding for the Apache agency, the paternal Steck would discover that many Indians were receptive to his idea of farming. Among these, surprisingly, Steck could include Mangas. Receiving regular monthly rations from Steck, the Apache leader began to rely on the assistance. The chief's life-style also began to change. For the first time in years, and maybe decades, illness and perhaps advancing age had prevented Mangas from making his annual migration into Chokonen country and, from there, the foray against Sonora during the winter of 1855. Now in his mid-sixties, Mangas would not be organizing large war parties against Sonora with the same regularity as he once had.

His influence among the Bedonkohes also began to wane. One reason was the site of Steck's Apache agency. Mangas's favorite area to camp had historically been Santa Lucía Springs, situated between Bedonkohe and Chihenne territory. Now, with Steck's reserve on the Rio Grande, during the farming season of 1855 he may have relocated his camp from Santa Lucía Springs to the valley along the Mimbres. This would have separated him from the more militant Bedonkohes and Chokonens, whom he had led during times of war. His son Cascos and his brother Phalios

Palacio, however, continued to lead and inspire the Bedonkohes, who would continue to raid without fear the small towns and settlements of the Rio Grande. Mangas's sickness in 1855 had drained the vigor from his powerful body; the malady had definitely sapped his strength. For eighteen months he lived in a kind of semiretirement, apparently no longer capable of the energy and passion necessary to lead the warlike factions of the Chiricahuas. But the spring of 1856 found his health improved, and Mangas reasserted his claim to leadership. He was clearly still the dominant Chiricahua chief.

Through these years great territorial changes were also occurring. In mid-1854 the United States expanded the region known as New Mexico with the Gadsden Purchase from Mexico. By the terms of James Gadsden's treaty, negotiated in late 1853 and ratified by Congress in June 1854, America acquired from Mexico title to the Mesilla Valley and all the country south of the Gila for ten million dollars. The United States bought this tract of land because of the gold rush to California and the future need for a railroad south of the Gila. Santa Anna, politically vulnerable, desperately required money. The United States understood his predicament and, holding the trump card, used this leverage to abrogate a thorny condition of the former treaty of Guadalupe Hidalgo—the one that required the government to control Apache raiding into Mexico and to liberate the Apaches' Mexican captives. In truth, however, the United States had expended little effort and money toward either of those ends.[1]

Initially, according to Hubert Howe Bancroft, the sale of their northern frontier hardly bothered the residents of northern Mexico, because the Apaches inhabited much of the land sold to the United States.[2] This ambivalence did not last long. Implicit threats of Yankee expansionism and explicit threats from American and French filibusters, coupled with the incessant Apache raids from north of the line, left Sonorans increasingly apprehensive toward most Americans. Although Apache raids into Mexico eventually diminished, the Chiricahuas continued to raid Mexico, even after the treaty, with impunity. These assaults exasperated Mexican officials, who accused American settlers and governmental officials of trading arms and ammunition to Apaches in return for stolen Mexican livestock, a charge that undoubtedly had some validity and was repeated countless times during the next decade.[3]

Congress had allocated money for the care of the Indians in New Mexico after the ratification of the Gadsden Treaty. Consequently, in November 1854, Governor Meriwether journeyed to Fort Thorn and met the "Gila Apaches" on November 11. He declared in his succinct report that "the interview was satisfactory." Steck provided about one thousand dollars' worth of presents to about three hundred Chiricahuas. The governor encountered Mangas Coloradas and other chiefs. Yet, unlike most Americans who met Mangas, Meriwether did not mention him. He also talked with the Janeros local group of Nednhis under Láceres, José Nuevo, and Delgadito Janeros (so called to distinguish him from Delgadito the Chihenne leader). Besides Mangas, the other Chihenne local group leaders were Delgadito, Itán, Losho (probably Loco),[4] and Josécito. Meriwether promised them assistance, but whether the Indians took him seriously or not was another issue. In mid-December Steck rationed the Chihennes, but the local groups of Nednhis and Mangas failed to come into Fort Thorn. Except for Cuchillo Negro's local group that lived east of the Mimbres Mountains, most Chiricahuas found the new location an inconvenient site to receive rations. Therefore, in the years to come, Steck would frequently bring the rations to a central point, such as Santa Rita del Cobre, for distribution.[5]

The competent Steck continued to do all in his power to bring stability to the Chiricahua world in early 1855. In January he issued rations of corn, mutton, and beef to every Chihenne leader, including Mangas Coloradas, who came to the agency at Fort Thorn on January 20. The Indians preferred beef to any other meat (except mule), but Steck did not have adequate funds to distribute more than a few head. For example, during the quarter ending March 31, 1855, he gave the Indians five head of cattle to slaughter. Yet this program of monthly rations served a beneficial purpose, especially because winter, known as Ghost Face to the Chiricahuas,[6] traditionally the most difficult time for the Apaches to obtain food, was normally when they raided Sonora. Mangas launched no foray into Mexico that winter. Steck's rations probably had not convinced him to stay put, but they did help to discourage the raids, and other conditions were of influence, too.

Agent Steck's monthly report for February 1855 addressed several important issues that were endemic in the annals of Chiricahua-American relations. He began his report by insisting that the "most friendly feeling towards our Govt. seems to exist." Yet, in the next breath Steck cautiously warned Meriwether that "all that will be necessary to maintain the same kind feelings will be for the Govt. to fulfill its promises from us in planting in the coming spring." He then turned his attention to the sensitive matter of Mexican captives, which remained an important subject, yet one that would eventually diminish in scope over the next decade as the Chihennes and Bedonkohes came under the control of American agents. During February the Americans had liberated four captives "from among these Indians." Two had escaped from the Apaches and had requested protection from the Americans at Fort Thorn; the other two "were delivered by the Indians for a trifling consideration." But what Steck considered "trifling" may not have been insignificant to the Indians. During the next year Chiricahuas told Mexicans that the objective of their war party was to take captives to trade them to the Americans at Fort Thorn. Finally, Steck discussed the hostile Bedonkohes, who numbered about four hundred and lived in the Mogollons. They had continued to pilfer stock from the settlements along the Rio Grande. He felt that a visit by him, with a few hundred dollars' worth of presents, would prove sufficient to "conciliate" this band.[7]

As spring approached without specific news from Meriwether, Steck and the Chiricahuas began to get nervous. The agent clearly believed that he must convert the Apaches from warriors into farmers if they were to survive as a race. On March 5, 1855, he asked the governor about the prospects "of holding a treaty with the Apaches." He also wondered about the presents that Meriwether had promised during his November visit. After all, the Apaches "have been promised assistance now for three years. To put them off again another year would be to destroy confidence and add new difficulties in the management of the tribe. They recollect the promises you gave them and are confidently looking for it." Even Mangas Coloradas was receptive to planting, but he had little faith in the promises of the Americans. He had signed a treaty three years earlier and had agreed to Lane's provisional compact two years before, and now Steck and Meriwether were contemplating yet another treaty. He must have pondered why Americans felt compelled to make another pact without regard for their prior unfulfilled commitments. This uncertainty, this lack of confidence in the Americans, was the chief reason that Mangas and many Chihennes considered a move to Janos to make a treaty with Captain Baltazar Padilla and José María Zuloaga, whom they normally distrusted.[8]

Meriwether curtly informed Steck that the commissioner of Indian affairs at Washington had forwarded neither instructions nor the authorization to make a treaty. Yet Commissioner George

Manypenny, sincerely interested in the welfare of the American Indian, had advocated in his annual report for 1854 that the government had a moral responsibility to aid and to educate Indians. He also concurred with Steck's position that the government must transform the Apaches from raiders to farmers.⁹ It was not only a humane policy, but also a pragmatic and cost-efficient one. The agent took the rebuff in stride and told the governor that he had just returned from a visit to Cuchillo Negro's camp on the Animas River, "an excellent place for planting [where] his band had cleared three acres of land." After a rest of two days, he intended to return to Cuchillo Negro's camp "to assist him in planting." Then he planned to go on to the Mimbres to teach Delgadito, Mangas Coloradas, and Ponce's extended family group how to raise a crop.¹⁰

Finally, in late April the president appointed Governor Meriwether special commissioner to make treaties with the Indians of New Mexico. Accordingly, on April 28, 1855, Meriwether instructed Steck to assemble the Mescaleros and Chiricahuas at Fort Thorn on June 7. The governor selected this date because it "will be the day of the full moon, which will enable you to designate the time so that the Indians will understand and recollect it." Agent Steck was away from his agency, helping the local groups of Delgadito, Itán, and Mangas Coloradas plant on the Mimbres. He therefore did not receive Meriwether's instructions until he returned to Fort Thorn on May 9. The prospect of a formal treaty excited Steck, and in mid-May he assured the governor that all the "chiefs will be present except Mangas Coloradas, who will probably be unable to attend. He is still very sick but promises to be there if well enough to attend."¹¹ We do not know what malady had afflicted Mangas, and unfortunately Steck, himself a medical doctor, neglected to mention let alone describe it.

Yet by the time Steck received word of Meriwether's plans, a war party had already set forth on a foray into Mexico under the Chihenne chiefs Itán, Josécito, and Costales. With some Bedonkohes, they traveled west to Apache Pass and joined the Chokonens for an expedition into Mexico. Delgadito remained along the Mimbres, not leaving until early June, when he set out for Fort Thorn to receive rations and to make a treaty with Governor Meriwether. Mangas authorized Delgadito to represent his interests and speak for him.¹²

About the time that this was happening, Governor David Meriwether departed from Santa Fe for Fort Thorn to consummate the treaty with the Chihennes and Mescaleros. En route, he stopped at

Los Lunas, where he enlisted the services of Captain Richard S. Ewell to escort him to Fort Thorn. He arrived about June 7, 1855, amid a sultry and oppressive heat wave. The thermometer hit readings over one hundred degrees every day during the week that Meriwether remained at the post. Meriwether reported that "there was a very full attendance of the bands treated," while another account estimated that 250 Apaches were present. On June 9 the governor concluded the treaty with the Mescaleros and Chihennes but not with the Gila Apaches (he was referring to the Bedon-kohes), for they had undertaken an expedition into Mexico. Fifteen Chihenne and Janeros Nednhi leaders put their marks on the treaty. The three principal Chihenne local group leaders of the 1840s and 1850s—Cuchillo Negro, Itan, and Delgadito—agreed to terms, as did two important Nednhi leaders, Laceres and Jose Nuevo. Also signing were Loco and Riñón, two leaders coming into prominence among the Chihennes. Interestingly, two Chiri-cahua women, Monica and Refugia, were also listed on the treaty, having acted as interpreters during the proceedings. In his contem-porary report, Meriwether casually dismissed Mangas's absence, labeling him of "minor importance."[13] The governor's recollec-tions, written thirty years later, were somewhat confusing, but he did mention Cuchillo Negro's presence as well as that of Monica, a Chihenne woman who served as interpreter during the powwow and whose name appears from time to time in other negotiations.

Monica, who Meriwether believed was seventy or seventy-five years of age (which would place her birth in the early 1780s), acted as the interpreter from Spanish to Apache. Her competency impressed the governor, who called her "the best [interpreter] I ever had." He asked how she had become so proficient at Spanish. She replied: "When I was a little girl, about half grown, my mother gave me to some Catholic sisters, who had taught me to read in a book, and sing and pray. But after my mother's death, my father took me away from the sisters and carried me back to the tribe, at which time I was fully grown. I have forgotten all about books and singing and praying, and still live with my tribe, acting as inter-preter for the Mexican traders, who come to trade with my people."[14]

By the terms of Meriwether's one-sided treaty the Chiricahuas for the first time agreed to cede land to the government in exchange for regular rations, tools, and annuities. The Chihennes and Nednhis agreed to live on a tract of land bordered to the west by the Mimbres River and to the east by the Mimbres Mountains

Loco, an important Chihenne leader who signed the June 1855 peace treaty at Fort Thorn. (Courtesy National Archives)

and the Black Range. Yet, if valuable mineral deposits were discovered in this area, the government had the right to reclaim this
land and relocate the Indians to another region. The last article of
the pact prohibited the Apaches from raiding in to Mexico. Likely
the Chihenne leaders were unaware of the conditions until they
arrived at Fort Thorn, and one has to wonder even then if they
understood what they were signing. Meriwether reported that "no
objection was made to any provision of the treaties." In all, the
Mescaleros and Chihennes, each of whom Meriwether estimated
at "six to seven hundred souls," agreed to cede some twelve
thousand to fifteen thousand square miles to the government.
Each reservation contained between two thousand and twenty-five
hundred square miles. Governor Meriwether had negotiated six
treaties with Indians in 1855 as part of the government's plan to
place hostile Indians on reservations. Complying with the terms of
the treaty, the Apaches returned forty stolen horses and four
Mexican children. The Mescaleros refused, however, to relocate
west of the Rio Grande because such a move would place them
near the Chihennes. Meriwether was initially dubious, but after a
Mescalero killed a Chihenne during a quarrel, he concluded that
the two tribes should have separate reservations.[15] In the end, Congress refused to ratify any of the six treaties that Meriwether had
negotiated, primarily because it felt the government should not
have to pay the Indians for land lawfully acquired from Mexico, at
least by white man's logic and law.

Mangas did not endorse the treaty, appearing, in the words of
Dan Thrapp, "strangely reluctant to sign it. Statesman that he was,
he saw more clearly the restrictions it placed upon the Indians
than the illusory benefits it promised them and decided he would
never be a party to it." Perhaps he understood that he would forfeit
his rights to Santa Lucía and the Burro Mountains. He initially
consented to accompany Steck to Santa Fe to complete the pact,
but he later had second thoughts about journeying that distance
from Chiricahua country. Instead, he reneged on his offer, telling
the agent that the oppressive summer temperatures prevented him
from going. Besides, he had heard that diseases were rampant
there. Though he agreed to comply with whatever Delgadito and
Itán had signed, he would not formally "acknowledge this fact by
touching pen to the document," according to Thrapp.[16]

Meanwhile, in Sonora, the military officials had commented on
the absence of Apaches in northeastern Sonora, the habitual haunts
of the Chokonens and Nednhis. Governor Gándara had placed

Captain Andrés Zenteno in charge of the garrisons at Santa Cruz, Tucson, and Tubac, which had become a military colony in 1851.[17] In March Zenteno led one command of eighty men and reconnoitered the mountains between Fronteras and Bavispe. "During that time no trace was found of Apaches in the places almost always inhabited by the Indians called Janeros [Chiricahuas]." Soon after, Captain Bernabé Gómez dispatched another force of eighty men into Western Apache country. Near the Gila in Arizona, his men battled two hundred Western Apaches ("Coyoteros and Tontos") who were heading south for a campaign against Sonora. In a two-hour fight they drove the Indians north of the Gila, killing four Apaches and recovering twenty-five quivers with their bows, three carbines, three lances, several moccasins, and a large quantity of mescal. Shortly after, Gómez sent another campaign of 120 men under Captain Zenteno to the Chiricahua Mountains. A Western Apache woman from the Pinal band, who had fled to Tucson to escape an abusive husband, told Captain Gómez that Apaches were harvesting mescal in the Chiricahua Mountains. She also made another disclosure disturbing to Sonoran military officials: The Western Apache bands had contemplated making a treaty at Tucson until they "had received information from the mouths of American traders to the effect the Mexicans were unable to cross the Gila. Therefore they have not returned to conclude the peace but are continuing the war." This revelation confirmed the worst fears of Sonorans—that the Apaches would find refuge north of the Gila. Meanwhile, in northeastern Sonora, Terán y Tato, after pursuing a war party into the Sierra Madre, concluded that the Indians had taken Sonora's mules to Chihuahua.[18]

At about this time Terán y Tato voiced his displeasure about a subject that he felt was impeding the efforts of military commanders in northern Sonora: the lack of cooperation and communication between the presidio commanders and national guard troops. He implied that he believed this development was a deliberate attempt by the governor to keep opposition forces from uniting against him. And indeed, Governor Gándara's conservative coalition had begun to show signs of unraveling, especially since the Plan of Ayutla in March 1854 had advocated the removal of dictator Santa Anna from the presidency of Mexico. The movement had spread throughout Mexico, and Gándara, a onetime supporter of Santa Anna, found his regime threatened by the opposing liberal party. Gándara had virtually ignored the garrisons

and towns of northeastern Sonora; he had never been much concerned about that region, especially when it came to fighting
Apaches. His political base lay to the south and central part of the
state. He had, however, ordered a small detachment of soldiers to
garrison his ranch at Calabasas to protect it from Apache raids. By
the spring of 1855, Gándara's sole concern had become, simply,
survival, as the regime of his former benefactor Santa Anna was
ending. Terán y Tato clearly blamed Gándara for the inertia and
chaos that seemed to dominate the frontier's military forces. He
lamented:

Much harm is done by a lack of communications; the garrisons do
not work in contact with each other nor with the towns of the
interior. When this band of Indians came into the area the trail was
discovered at Tinaja del Maromero on the road between Bavispe and
Fronteras. Both commanders found out about it because the soldiers
made the report to them, but no one wanted to communicate it to
the towns in the interior, nor do they even give warning. I do not
think your excellency should have changed the orders given by your
predecessors in this matter, for it is very clear that through indolence
harm is being done that could have been avoided, at least as far as is
possible, if not completely.

Terán y Tato had carried out a greater number of successful campaigns than any other commander of northern Sonora except
Eusebio Samaniego from Bavispe. Clearly exasperated, he continued:

In this instance a good result could have been achieved if I had
received information about the mission that was leaving Fronteras
for the Chiricahua [Mountains]. There is no question that I would
have marched with my company, even though it was dead from
hunger, until I had overtaken their trail. But having not received any
information, how could I continue on in the condition I found myself
in? . . . You can imagine the anger and vexation which this caused
me. By chance Don Luis García passed by that day from Bavispe, and
through him I learned that troops from that garrison had left on the
21st to join forces at Fronteras and begin a campaign in the
Chiricahuas. Had I received that information we would have joined
them at Fronteras, and perhaps the final result would have been
different. I am fully aware that neither the Inspector nor the commanders are under any obligation to inform me regarding their
operations. However it would seem that a sense of humanity and the

duty to maintain a harmonious reciprocity should lead us to provide at least some hint of what may develop. That was the earlier method, and now that it is not followed it has become needed.[19]

Meanwhile, in Chihuahua, a small foraging party of thirty warriors under Costales had entered northwestern Chihuahua and had engaged in several raids near Janos on May 24, 1855. In response, Captain Padilla rounded up a force of civilians and soldiers and cut the trail to the abandoned hacienda at Ramos, where he spent the night. The next morning his scouts followed the tracks of twenty Apaches that led into the Pajarito Mountains, about eight miles south of Ramos. Eventually they overtook two Apaches, promptly killing one and capturing the other, a young warrior named Nalze. He turned out to be quite a prize—a nephew of Itán and the son of Monteras, a prominent Chihenne warrior. Nalze told Captain Padilla that the raiding party had departed from Santa Rita del Cobre to join the Chokonens at Dos Cabezas (probably at Apache Pass), picking up additional warriors in the Peloncillos before splitting up (some went to Sonora and some into Chihuahua).

Nalze also told Captain Padilla that many Apache leaders, including Mangas Coloradas, had expressed sentiments intimating a desire to make peace with Chihuahua. According to him, the chief contemplated coming to Janos to discuss terms, perhaps because he had heard that Captain Antonio Sánchez Vergara (whom he had met in early 1843 and had come to trust) was involved in negotiations. In fact, one Chokonen group under Yrinco had gone to El Carmen to meet the respected officer to learn if they could join in the treaty made with the Carrizaleño local group of Nednhis. Chihuahuan campaigns had systematically reduced the fighting power of this group in the last decade, as they had that of the Chihennes, whose numbers had decreased dramatically in recent years. In late April or early May the chiefs ratified the terms of the treaty. In return they wanted the rations they were accustomed to receiving during Spanish times and permission to brand their stock. This band, which totaled 289 individuals, consisted of fifty-seven warriors with seven leaders (including Cojinillín and Felipe), one hundred women (forty-four were widows), and 133 children. This unit of the Nednhi band thus contained 20 percent adult men, 35 percent adult women, and 45 percent children, clearly defining the impact of the recent hostilities, primarily in Chihuahua. Interestingly enough, Agent Steck at about the same time prepared a list of Chihennes and Bedonkohes who were under his care. His numbers were surprisingly similar: 20 percent adult men, 33 percent adult women, and 47 percent children. Both bands had suffered equally from warfare and disease.[20]

Shortly after capturing Nalze, Captain Padilla held a parley with the Chihenne leader Costales and a warrior named Crisanto at Cerros Colorado, a small group of hills east of Janos. Costales reiterated what Nalze had told Padilla: the Apaches would return to make a treaty. When Padilla and Zuloaga discovered that Nalze was not only the son of the prominent warrior Monteras but also a nephew of Itán, they predicted that the Chiricahuas would soon open negotiations.[21]

We can only speculate on what truly motivated the Apaches to consider another treaty with Mexicans. It likely suggested the Indians' disillusionment with Americans, whose Indian agents could not keep the promises made in their treaties. Steck's rations of corn and an occasional supply of beef were also inadequate for the Apaches' needs and paled in comparison to what they had previously received at Janos in 1842–44 and 1850–51. We cannot overlook another possibility: that Nalze admitted to Captain Padilla that it was time for the mescal harvest (when the Apaches were vulnerable to enemy actions), while Alamo Hueco, Carrizalillo Springs, and Boca Grande were within striking distance of Padilla's troops. This talk among the Apaches' headmen may have been a ploy to forestall any planned campaign so that they could harvest their mescal in safety before returning to the Gila and Mimbres country.[22]

The peace treaty at El Carmen was short-lived; within a few months the Nednhis began raiding and authorities at Carrizal and Galeana received orders to commence offensive actions against the Indians. About mid-July, Josécito's Chihennes, with a group of Bedonkohes, killed fourteen miners at Corralitos and seriously wounded two other men. This party also raided Galeana and captured two boys, one being Refugio Corrales. Corrales remained a hostage of the Bedonkohes for sixteen months. He later testified that after the raid the Chiricahuas returned to Santa Rita del Cobre, where they divided; Josécito went into camp near there, while the Bedonkohes took Corrales north into the Mogollons.[23]

A few months later, Mangas, after receiving rations from Steck during the summer of 1855, must have begun to feel better, for he decided to retaliate against Padilla at Janos for capturing Itán's nephew. To what can we attribute his improving health? Mangas

may have participated in a series of sweat baths, ceremonies conducted by a shaman which were used to ensure "good health, . . .
long life, and to cure sickness." Another plausible explanation is
that Mangas may have been the victim of witchcraft, for the
Chiricahuas believed "there is little sickness which cannot be
attributed ultimately to sorcery." If Mangas's followers discovered
the individual who bewitched their leader, they would have burned
the witch and his or her paraphernalia.[24] In any case by mid-August
1855 he led a small raiding party against Janos that killed one man
and wounded another.[25] Mangas then returned to New Mexico.

Meanwhile, troops from Sonora had hotly pursued several
Chiricahua war parties as they retired to New Mexico with their
booty and captives. Three separate bands brought a total of forty-
two captives, according to what Steck heard. The agent had sent a
trader to Mangas's camp at Santa Lucía to convince him to come to
the agency. Mangas demurred, saying that he "could not leave his
people at this time" because of a campaign from Sonora that had
penetrated the Peloncillos. He was concerned that the Sonorans
might move north to the Burros and the Gila wilderness country.
The particulars about this expedition are vague, but one could
make a good case that either Captain Ignacio Pesqueira or Captain
Eusebio Samaniego was involved, or both. In any event, the threatened battle failed to take place.[26]

As Steck's first year as agent for the Southern Apaches came to a
close, several issues touched the compassionate man. To begin
with, the Apaches' numbers were declining. In the census he
turned in with his annual report dated July 30, 1855, he placed the
Chiricahuas under his jurisdiction (which included the Chihennes,
a group of Bedonkohes under Mangas Coloradas's brother Phalios
Palacio, and perhaps the Nednhis under Láceres and Eligio),[27] at
178 men and 893 persons in all. His report sounded alarming,
however, because of the disparity between the numbers of men
and women. He attributed this to the warfare of the previous
century. The constant hostilities in the last twenty-five years had
reduced the Chihennes' fighting strength to half. He grimly
reported that just within the last six months twelve men had
perished, nine from sickness and disease and three in battle.[28]

The Bedonkohes' raiding in New Mexico, especially along the
Rio Grande, concerned Steck. They had raided a small village south
of Fort Fillmore in February. Two months later Steck reported that
the "unruly" Mogollons continued to raid. In June they ran off
some mules from Fort Craig; during the last six months of 1855

they stole several hundred head of stock, according to Agent Steck, who conceded that they had no compelling reason to stop raiding.[29] Until the army could prevent these incursions, Steck realized that precarious relations would prevail. It was often difficult to figure out which Apaches continued to commit these depredations. Steck, unable to visit them in their rugged Mogollon country and unsuccessful in convincing them to come into Fort Thorn, reluctantly concluded that the troops should snap the whip at the independent and haughty Bedonkohes. According to the disclosures of a captive then living with them, they "have nothing and must steal or starve."[30]

The Bedonkohes, whom whites called the "Gila" or "Mogollon" band, must have felt invincible. Yet just as the Americans misunderstood the Apaches, the Indians misinterpreted and underestimated American troops. To this point they had conducted raids for stock and booty. In October and November 1855 two small raiding parties left their strongholds in the Mogollon country for the Rio Grande; one group stole 150 mules from José Chávez in Bernalillo county, but troops recovered 120 of them.[31] Another band, under the principal Bedonkohe leader Chaynee, stole stock from Ramón Luna, likely near Socorro or Lemitar. Late Sunday, November 25, or early the next morning, a second group of eight Indians murdered a man and wounded two others west of Mesilla. The party consisted of two relatives of Sergento (a son-in-law and a nephew), a brother of Ronquillo, and a brother and a son of Delgadito Janeros.

About the time this raid occurred, Delgadito Janeros was at Fort Thorn for his rations. Before leaving, he admitted to Steck that some of his people had stolen some cattle at Mesilla, which confession led Lieutenant Colonel Miles to infer "of course they done the killing likewise."[32] This was frustrating to Americans because the Apaches' loose political structure, with authority vested in the hands of extended family and group leaders instead of prominent band chiefs, went counter to what Americans arrogantly believed the Apaches' political organization should be. This confusion inevitably led American military men to arrive at solutions based on broad generalizations or incorrect assumptions. To them an Apache was an Apache, a simplistic notion that would lead time and again to further violence and bloodshed, with innocent victims on both sides.

Yet Miles proved that he understood one feature of Apache warfare: the cause-and-effect relationship. Killing was usually in response to a previous insult or murder. That these fatalities occurred at Mesilla came as no surprise to him, for the townspeople and the Apaches (Mescaleros and Chihennes) had been inveterate trading partners. In a matter-of-fact manner, Miles concluded his report by stating, "I am inclined to the belief that the Indians in their assault on [the] people of Mesilla designed it as avenging wrongs done to them by the men they killed."[33]

Meanwhile, at Fort Thorn, Captain Joseph Horace Eaton, an 1831 graduate of West Point and a veteran of the Mexican War, decided to take action "at least to show the Indians a determination on our part to take signal notice of their atrocities." He rounded up a mixed force of thirty infantry and thirty-one dragoons and set out from San Diego Crossing on December 5, 1855, with twenty-one days' rations. He had tried to "conceal" his plans from the Chihennes and Mescaleros who "congregate about the agency," but his efforts were in vain. Believing the Apaches to be living in the Florida Mountains, Eaton marched his command west toward Cooke's Spring in the heart of Mangas Coloradas's country. After his forces pursued the Indians for two days, a messenger overtook Eaton with a note from Agent Steck. Steck advised Eaton that Costales, Delgadito's second-in-command, had brought definite news concerning the Apaches involved in the raid at Mesilla. Noting that these Indians resided in Mexico, thus making them Nednhis, Steck informed Eaton that none of the Chihennes or Bedonkohes were responsible. Therefore, he recommended that Eaton pick up the trail at Cooke's Spring, confident the track would then bend south to the Florida Mountains and continue to Janos.[34]

Eaton took Steck's advice but found no signs leading from Cooke's Spring to the Florida Mountains; accordingly, the captain, finding it necessary to make a statement, or at least to present a show of force to the Indians, decided to march his soldiers over the trail as long as his provisions and men could hold out. Eaton was not aware that he was pursuing a band that had not committed the raid at Mesilla; he did not realize that this party was a distinctly different group, one that had stolen stock, probably near Socorro. By mid-December he had reached San Vincente Spring, about ten miles south of today's Silver City, when the guides reported that the trail led north toward the Gila River. With that news, and because his provisions were running low and one of his officers was "seriously ill" with an undiagnosed sickness, Eaton grudgingly abandoned the pursuit.

Happily, after Captain Eaton encamped near San Vincente his detachment enjoyed a surprise visit from a party of warriors including two of Mangas's kinfolk—his son Cascos and his brother José Mangas—who had abruptly appeared in the hills overlooking Eaton's camp. The officer invited them into camp; Cascos, José Mangas, and one or two others fearlessly came in because they had "done no wrong." The two men provided seemingly accurate information about their village and the hostile Bedonkohes, which was perplexing because Cascos was an important leader among them. They "pointed out to me the direction" of Mangas's camp "about a day's march over the San Vincente Mountains to the north," undoubtedly Santa Lucía Springs. They revealed to Eaton that his command had cut the trail of a band of Apaches led by Chaynee, whose village was on the Gila. Although Eaton felt Mangas's band was innocent of any wrongdoing, he candidly informed the Indians that "the tracks of the cattle entering Mangas Coloradas's country would throw suspicion upon him [Mangas] in the minds of the Commanding General & the Indian Agent & that it would be well for Mangas to visit Dr. Steck, the Indian Agent, and clear himself of any suspicion." José Mangas and Cascos promised to pass these concerns along to Mangas, who, they asserted, planned to visit the agency within the next eight days.[35]

Instead of coming in, however, Mangas remained aloof, secure in his own country. Steck told Eaton that he planned to assemble the chiefs to demand the surrender of the warrior who had killed the Mexican and restitution for the property stolen at Mesilla and Socorro. If the Indians refused and continued to "show an uncompromising spirit," Eaton would be ready with a simple solution: "I do not hesitate to say war with the whole Apache nation west of the river should be declared, and they should be made to understand that it will never end." Although historians would consider Eaton's blunt plan extreme, it was typical of the manner in which nineteenth-century whites perceived the Apache problem. It mattered little to him that 95 percent of the Chihennes and Nednhis in southern New Mexico had remained at peace with Americans. Because of a few stock raids and an unfortunate killing, Eaton was prepared to pummel the Indians into submission. He suggested that troops establish a depot at either Santa Lucía or San Vincente, where soldiers could launch a campaign into the Mogollon Mountains. In concluding his report, which he based on information received from José Mangas and Cascos, Eaton identified the Bedonkohe leaders as Miguel, El Carro, Juan Apache, El

Fresco, and Capitan Chaynee. In reality, however, Eaton had named two of the primary Chokonen leaders (Miguel Narbona and Carro), who may have been in Bedonkohe country at that time.[36]

Steck faced immediate obstacles in bringing the Apaches in, for Eaton's scout into their country had left them nervous and jittery. About December 20, Apaches raided Socorro, stealing over thirty horses, mules, and cattle. Steck conceded that civilians had followed the trail into "the camp of some of the chiefs who signed the treaty of June 9, 1855," and he immediately informed the Apaches that he would withhold rations until they returned the stock. This was a serious threat, for it was early winter, the Apaches' most difficult period to get food, and Steck's meager rations were vital to survival. The agent sent two Mexicans to the Apaches' villages in the foothills of the Mimbres range, but the two could not convince the skittish Indians to come in. Finally, in late December, Steck with an escort of two men left to visit the Chihenne rancherías at Tierra Blanca, some fifty miles northwest of Fort Thorn and five miles southeast of today's Kingston.[37] There he met the Chihenne local group leaders (Delgadito, Itán, Cuchillo Negro, Riñón, and Pajarito) and two Nednhi leaders of the Janeros (Láceres and José Nuevo). With Costales and Monica acting as interpreters, the leaders denied that their people had participated in any of the recent raiding except the one at Mesilla, in which a son of Negrito and a brother of Ronquillo were involved. They claimed that the Bedonkohes and Mescaleros had committed most of the stock raids in Socorro and Valencia counties. Cuchillo Negro admitted that the stolen stock the citizens had trailed into his camp was the work of a small band of Mescaleros under a bellicose leader named Showano. This explanation was believable, for Showano, known as "the greatest thief and villain in the tribe," reveled in his reputation, crowing that he had personally killed fourteen white men and that he would continue hostilities even after the June treaty with Meriwether.

Meanwhile, Steck, actively conducting his own investigation, concluded that the chiefs were honest in their protestations, because he had detected only a few bones of cattle near the Indian camps. The Bedonkohes' activities frustrated Itán and Delgadito, who blamed that band for most of the depredations along the Rio Grande. In fact, they suggested to Steck that the military send troops "into their country as that would stop their stealing a great deal which was laid to them." They confirmed what José Mangas had told Eaton: the Mogollon Mountains were "exceedingly rough—high mountains and narrow canyons." They proposed two approaches: one from the Gila going north into the Mogollons and the other from the Tularosa River, located north of the Mogollons, which would proceed south toward the Gila. Troops could reach there from either Lemitar or Socorro by heading west on a crude wagon road. Steck did not mention Mangas Coloradas, who apparently remained in his winter headquarters at Santa Lucía Springs.[38]

In Santa Fe, William Watts Hart Davis, secretary to Governor Meriwether, had assumed temporary charge of Indian affairs because Meriwether had gone east on business. Steck's arguments failed to persuade Davis that the Chihennes had done all in their power to punish the malefactors. On January 29, 1856, in his response to Steck, Davis suggested that the Chihenne leaders make plain their sincerity for peace by exerting efforts "to control their bad men, or in case they cannot do so, they must report them to you, and assist you in having them punished." Again, as Dan Thrapp succinctly points out in his *Victorio and the Mimbres Apaches*, Davis's response "revealed the official's woeful ignorance of Apache social organization and the limitations it set upon chiefs and head men."[39]

In mid-February Steck replied to Davis, hoping that an example of Chihenne cooperation would convince his superior of their peaceable intentions. About January 20, 1856, Delgadito had sent word to Steck that Cigarrito's son and a few other raiders intended to repeat their success of the past November and again depredate near Mesilla. This time the Apaches underestimated the fortitude and resolve of the Mesilla Guard, a local militia organized to fight Indians. The small raiding party of five men stole four oxen and drove them west. Twelve men from Mesilla responded to the alarm, overtook the Indians eight miles west of town, and attacked them, killing and scalping three warriors, including the son of Cigarrito. According to Steck, these raiders had also stolen a few horses from the Chihennes, who followed them and killed two more men. Though the intertribal shedding of blood was an infrequent event, it would happen when one group or band felt threatened by another.[40]

During the first three months of 1856, Mangas Coloradas spent some time at Santa Lucía Springs. He may have accompanied a large Chiricahua war party that had gone to Sonora in February to avenge the deaths of two warriors killed near Fronteras in late December 1855. Returning from a foray in the interior, on February

17, 1856, the Chiricahuas attacked their favorite target, Fronteras, killed and captured several people, and ran off every head of stock. That night the Indians ransomed Juan José Granillo. The Apaches had told Granillo that their objective was to seize captives and trade them to the Americans for ammunition.[41]

Whether Mangas was involved in the attack on Fronteras or not, by spring 1856 he definitely had returned to his own country. Now brewing were developments that would affect him and his people, and he would have to confront them. First, his health had clearly improved, for he had made plans to join Cochise's Chokonens for an incursion into Sonora. Second, and perhaps more important, the U.S. military had begun preparations for an expedition into Mogollon country, which they would have to reach by marching through Mangas's range. The events that followed had little direct influence on Mangas, yet the injudicious actions by the American commander produced a volatile atmosphere which gave the Chihennes and Mangas second thoughts about the integrity of Americans, especially the military.

On February 24, 1856, Colonel Garland issued orders directing an expedition against the Gila and Mogollon Apaches (the Bedon-kohes). It was to be a two-pronged assault. One command under Captain Daniel T. Chandler, guided by Blas Lucero, a respected scout from Albuquerque, and fifteen Mexicans, was to march from Fort Craig to the Tularosa, north of the Mogollons, and then head south to the lower Mogollons. There they would unite with a detachment from Fort Thorn under Lieutenant Alexander Early Steen, son of Enoch Steen. Agent Steck, who planned to accompany the division from Fort Thorn, had heard from Mangas Coloradas shortly before leaving the fort. The chief admitted that his "own people had been of the number engaged in committing robberies above the [Rio Grande] and that he could not restrain them." Perhaps some of this activity had taken place when Mangas was in Arizona and Mexico with the Chokonens, or perhaps here was further evidence that his influence and prestige were waning.[42]

By March 12, Steen's command was encamped at a site twelve miles west of Santa Rita del Cobre. There Steck penned a quick note which Riñón, likely a son of Cuchillo Negro, delivered to Captain Eaton at Fort Thorn. The agent revealed that Delgadito and Itán had provided intelligence about the location of the villages of the warlike Bedonkohes. According to the Chihennes, the hostiles had over two hundred mules, horses, and cattle plus a large herd of sheep that they had recently stolen from a settlement on the Rio Grande. Lieutenant Steen's command continued in a northwest direction for Santa Lucía, struck the Gila near present-day Cliff, crossed it, and marched for two days to rendezvous with Captain Chandler's detachment, which had come from Tularosa and marched south along the western slopes of the Mogollons. They united several miles above present-day Buckhorn. There the scouts cut the trail of a large sheep herd, just as the Chihennes had told Steck they would, and Blas Lucero's scouts followed it like bloodhounds in a southwesterly direction into the Almagre Mountains, probably the range we know today as Black Mountain, west of present-day Redrock. They attacked the camp, killing one man, wounding three or four, and capturing some 350 sheep and thirty-one horses and mules. This was either a Bedonkohe or Chokonen village under a particularly warlike leader named El Cautívo (the Captive), a close associate of both Cochise and Mangas Coloradas. According to Refugio Corrales, a Mexican captive in the Apache village, many families of this ranchería had just returned from the Chiricahua Mountains, where they had been gathering mescal and a raiding party had just arrived with a herd of sheep that they had stolen on the Rio Grande.[43]

According to Corrales, Chandler's attack caught the Indians completely by surprise: "They had no notice of Colonel Chandler's expedition until he was in their camp." He said that besides the one Indian whom the soldiers had killed in camp, two other warriors had later succumbed from their wounds. The Bedonkohes would remember this attack and would in the coming months ruthlessly avenge these deaths.[44]

Meanwhile, after the attack the united command marched south to the Gila, which they followed northeast toward Santa Lucía. En route they discovered and destroyed several recently abandoned rancherías, including one that belonged to Mangas Coloradas's brother, Phalios Palacio.[45] At Santa Lucía the command turned east to return to their home bases, Fort Craig and Fort Thorn. Unfortunately, Chandler's command was a few miles in front of Lieutenant Steen's command. When approaching the Mimbres River, where the Chihennes were waiting to see Steck, Chandler inexplicably opened fire on the Apache camp "without knowing or stopping to inquire who it was he was firing upon." After several volleys, Costales approached the Americans and convinced them to stop shooting. Chandler told Delgadito and the other chiefs he had "fired upon them supposing them to be Mogollons." At the first fire the Apaches had deserted their camp, but not before the soldiers' volleys had killed one woman and wounded four others— a woman and three children. Still another child was never found.

Steck was livid, charging Chandler with misconduct. At the least, Chandler certainly revealed a lack of sensitivity to the Apaches when he cavalierly offered to make amends by paying them for their losses. He later defended his actions by claiming that his scouts had captured a horse that had the same brand as those recovered in the attack on El Cautívo's camp. Stationed at Fort Craig, Chandler knew little about the Chihennes or their country. His error may have been an honest, if careless, blunder. To be fair to him, he did order a halt to the firing when Costales approached and indicated a desire to parley. It was also possible that his men did capture a horse that had the same brand as those recovered at the hostile camp. Refugio Corrales mentioned the close relationship that the Bedonkohes and Chihennes enjoyed. They "intermarry with each other, and join together to celebrate their feasts; they mingle a great deal with each other." In fact, the night before Chandler's attack some Chihennes had left El Cautívo's camp to return to their country.[46]

Steck lamented: "To manage our Indians he must have confidence in your kind intentions and how can he confide in you when . . . you greet him with musketry and the shrieks of dying and wounded women and children?"[47] Three weeks later the agent issued presents worth $108 to compensate the relatives of the women and children whom Chandler's troops had killed or wounded in the unfortunate affair.[48] Except for this overture, Chandler's attack did not have any immediate consequences; it alone did not lead to an immediate deterioration in relations with the Chihennes. Delgadito and Itán trusted Steck, and by now they had concluded that they must remain at peace with Americans. Their alternative was to improve relations with Mexico, hardly an attractive option. The Bedonkohes, however, did eventually retaliate—a response that eventually led to a total breakdown in relations between the Chiricahuas and the Americans.

As for Mangas Coloradas, Refugio Corrales declared that he was "opposed to these war parties," at least in New Mexico. The chief and his followers had horses and food, while the Bedonkohes "have nothing and must steal or starve."[49] Mangas was likely in either southwestern New Mexico or the Chiricahua Mountains in Arizona when the troops were traversing his country. He publicly had not made any comments regarding Chandler's campaign;

apparently those activities had no immediate bearing on his relations with Americans.

A few weeks after his return to the agency, Steck left for the Mimbres River to meet the Chihennes, issue rations, and begin planting. On April 18, Mangas arrived at the Mimbres. Steck reported that he "is friendly, he is alone, his people have deserted him." Mangas and Delgadito cautioned Steck that a few Bedonkohes were in the area, probably heading to the Rio Grande to raid. Three days before (April 15, 1856), they had visited Mangas's ranchería at Santa Lucía and killed a horse for him—a form of tribute to the venerable leader (as long as it was not Mangas's property). On April 20, Steck rationed the entire Chihenne band, some five hundred individuals in all. Many Chihennes began planting along the Mimbres; a few months later Steck would report that some two hundred acres were under cultivation— enough to subsist many of the Chihennes for six months. Steck furnished Mangas with seed and hoes to begin cultivating at Santa Lucía.[50]

After receiving rations, Mangas returned to his village at Santa Lucía. His stay was short, however, for he soon left for Mexico with the Bedonkohes under his son Cascos; some Chihennes under Victorio, Monteras, and Negrito; and the Chokonens under his son-in-law Cochise. Using the mountains east and south of Bavispe as their base, they sent raiding parties east to Chihuahua and west into Sonora. The Chihenne contingent, which numbered about thirty warriors, concentrated its efforts in northwestern Chihuahua at Janos, Barranco, Corralitos, and Casas Grandes. Victorio's raiders engaged in several raids near Casas Grandes, killing a man and stealing much stock before breaking off and heading north toward Carrizalillo Springs and New Mexico. Captain Baltazar Padilla immediately gathered a force composed of presidio troops and citizens from Janos, Barranco, and José María Zuloaga's mines at Corralitos—fifty-two men, all mounted. For three days he followed the Indians, who had herded their stolen stock to the Vado de Piedra, a small mountain north of Lake Guzmán some fifteen miles east of Boca Grande. There they divided: the main body left toward Carrizalillo Springs, and a group of four warriors under the Chihenne leader Negrito, with their stolen stock, headed north toward present-day Columbus in southern New Mexico.

They had let their guard down, however, not expecting Mexican troops to have followed them so close to refuge north of the border. The tenacious Padilla cut their trail near the Casas Grandes River, overtook the raiders on open ground, and killed three men (whom they scalped to redeem the bounty) and captured the other. Among the dead was the prominent Chihenne chief Negrito, a successor to Ponce as leader of a Mimbres local group of Chihennes. The prisoner revealed to Padilla that this raiding party had come from the Mimbres River and that a large band of Chiricahuas, composed of Bedonkohes and Chihennes, which included many from Mangas Coloradas's band, had headed to Sonora on a campaign.[51]

Still, we do not know the extent of Mangas's involvement in this incursion into Sonora. Steck's next reference to Mangas Coloradas was not until June 29, 1856, over two months after the two had met on April 18, 1856. Padilla's prisoner did mention Cascos, probably Mangas's eldest son, as the leader of the Bedonkohe contingent raiding Sonora, undoubtedly with the Chokonens. Cascos had begun to take the mantle of Bedonkohe war leader from his father and apparently had developed into a very successful war chief. Mangas had regained his health and remained vigorous despite his advancing age. A few months later American traveler John C. Reid would describe Mangas as "large, erect, and of powerful mould."[52] He must have accompanied Cascos and his son-in-law Cochise into Sonora, for he missed few chances to strike his hated enemies below the border.

The month of May in the year of 1856 was not a good one for several of Sonora's northern settlements. The state's political hierarchy was in shambles. Liberals who had opposed Gándara's rule of Sonora since the Plan of Ayutla in March 1854 had advocated the ouster of dictator Antonio López de Santa Anna, who was unpopular in Sonora for selling its northern frontier in the Gadsden Treaty. Gándara had once been a loyal supporter of the dictator, but he eventually saw the end coming and decided to champion the Plan of Ayutla. The mounting pressure finally forced Santa Anna in August 1855 to flee Mexico City for Venezuela. Despite Gándara's conservative ties, the new federal government unexpectedly appointed him governor and commanding general in the fall of 1855. This announcement shocked Sonora's liberals, who were led by José de Aguilar, who just happened to be Gándara's brother-in-law. Yet Gándara's regime lasted only a few months, for in early 1856, Mexico's liberal President Comonfort removed him from power and appointed José de Aguilar provisional governor and Colonel Pedro Espejo commanding general.

Gándara relinquished control of the government but refused to step down as the state's commanding general. He formally censured

Espejo, claiming that the colonel had supported the former dictator. In March, Gándara brazenly deported Espejo from Sonora. Shortly after, he turned over the governorship to Aguilar. Yet he defiantly refused to relinquish control of the state's armed forces. Gándara then retired to his hacienda and became a do-nothing commander, though all along he made preparations for another showdown with the liberal forces.

Aguilar very well understood his brother-in-law, appreciating that he would not rest until he had regained the governorship. Thus Aguilar wisely began to court influential civil and military leaders who ascribed to the liberal philosophy. Among them was Ignacio Pesqueira, an ardent nationalist and the hero of Pozo Hediondo, who was then adjutant inspector of the presidios. Pesqueira, trying to defend the frontier from the Apaches, complained that Commanding General Gándara had neglected his duty by feigning illness. Moreover, the inspector insisted, the commander had ignored his requests for assistance and joint action. In truth, Gándara was marshaling his own forces and resources for a showdown with Pesqueira to take control of Sonora. Gándara's threat forced Pesqueira to relocate some of his presidio troops from the north into the interior to counteract Gándara's forces. A battle was imminent. Such was Sonora's plight when the Chiricahua war party selected the mountains near Bavispe as its home base in May 1856.[53]

Throughout May the Apaches harassed Bavispe and Bacerac, killing and capturing a few citizens and leaving the inhabitants too frightened to work their crops. Military authorities had ordered Bavispe's commander to send out patrols to Batepito and Carretas to ambush any Apaches retiring north with their plunder. Furthermore, at Bavispe, their best scout, a Chiricahua Apache named El Negro, had recently died. He had been a reassuring presence and seemed to inspire the citizens of Bavispe with confidence. Without him the residents of that town seemed paralyzed with fear.[54]

On May 25 a group of citizens arrived at Bavispe from Janos with information undoubtedly received from the captive whom Padilla's forces had taken during the fight with Negrito's party. They brought news that the campaign had originated from the Chihenne rancherías along the Mimbres River, where Costales, Delgadito, and Mangas Coloradas were planting corn with the assistance of the Americans. The Apache prisoner revealed that the chiefs' goal was to accumulate horses for an extended foray into the interior of Sonora. According to the captive, the Apaches understood that

Chihuahua's governor was offering a bounty of two hundred pesos for the scalp of a warrior, one thousand pesos for that of Costales, and a whopping five thousand pesos for that of Delgadito or Mangas Coloradas.[55]

A few days before Sonoran authorities received this intelligence, the Chokonens, with probably some Bedonkohes, virtually destroyed Chinapa, located on the Sonora River below Bacoachi. This small hamlet had had a pathetic history of being hit by Chiricahua war parties; in 1848, for example, one had attacked the town and killed or captured many of its citizens. On this occasion in the early morning of May 21, 1856, the Indians stormed the town, killing or capturing everyone in their path. One of Chinapa's citizens raced into Arispe later that afternoon to deliver the gory details to the prefect, Rafael Angel Corella: "Today the town of Chinapa does not exist. . . . The Apaches have finished; they have captured Chinapa." Corella immediately gathered a force of eighty-five national guard troops and sped to Chinapa's relief. They arrived there at 11:00 P.M. and discovered a most dreadful silence. After the soldiers had stumbled over several corpses, a barking dog drew Corella's attention to a stone house where the town's survivors (ten men and many women and children) had taken refuge. Its exit was smoldering, but only the door was burned. Corella placed the blame on Gándara for removing many of the frontier's troops to the interior. Within months he would join with Pesqueira's forces to battle Gándara's followers and drive Gándara from Sonora.[56]

Mangas spent the summer of 1856 about the Mimbres River, Santa Rita del Cobre, and Santa Lucía, where he had begun to plant corn. Steck issued rations on June 29 to his small local group of fifty individuals. About a month later, Steck, accompanied by American capitalist Charles Poston and five other Americans, left Fort Thorn with several wagonloads of corn. They went to Santa Rita del Cobre, where on July 25, Steck rationed the entire Chihenne band. Three days later Mangas came in from Santa Lucía with sixty-five of his people and received rations. Poston observed that the Apaches made *tiswin* from Steck's corn issue. The Apaches' marksmanship also impressed Poston, who noted that they "always cut the bullets out of the trees, as they are economists in ammunition if nothing else."

Poston correctly recalled that he met about 350 Apaches at Santa Rita del Cobre, "the most noted being Mangas Coloradas, a fine looking chief." Steck and Poston's party camped at the old triangular fort; the Apaches remained outside. Poston had many

Charles Poston, an early Arizona mining entrepreneur. He met Mangas
Coloradas at Santa Rita del Cobre in the summer of 1856. (Courtesy
Arizona Historical Society, no. 60,594)

talks during the week in which he stayed with Steck and the Chiricahuas. Mangas and the other chiefs declared that they wanted peace with Americans but "that the Spanish and Mexicans had treated them badly and that they would kill them and rob them as long as they lived." The atmosphere resembled that of an old-time rendezvous. The Americans "exhibited our new firearms which were then Sharp's rifles and Colt's revolvers, shot at marks, and drank tiz-win, roasted venison and made the Indians some presents. What they appreciated most was some matches which they wrapped carefully in buckskin." The chiefs assured Poston that "they would not disturb" the Americans providing the Americans did not interfere with their incursions into Mexico. When the Americans returned to the Mimbres River, they discovered that one mule was missing. Poston "complained to the chief," perhaps Mangas or, if not, Delgadito, who admitted that "some of the boys had stolen it and he would have it sent back." The chief returned the mule.[57]

That August, Steck completed his annual report concerning the conditions of the Indians under his care. The perceptive and compassionate man had come to know his wards, their life-style, and their culture. Even today we can easily discern his strong feeling and his great concern for the Chihennes' plight. Throughout his report he emphasized that the government must fulfill a moral commitment to the Apaches in terms of issuing sufficient food and assistance to change their behavior, namely their raiding. He also praised the efforts of his Chihennes to become farmers. "They have evinced a deep interest and a very considerable zeal" for farming, he stated. Steck had recently visited Santa Lucía and the Gila country. He proposed to assemble the Bedonkohes and Chihennes there because he believed that it would make an excellent site for an Apache reservation. His rationale made sense. This location would save money, isolate the Apaches from settlements, and allow him to manage the Indians more easily. Again, he urged that the Americans make a formal treaty; Mangas Coloradas had stressed the need for such a pact with Steck several times since Chandler's expedition.

Despite the agent's optimistic views about turning the Apaches into farmers and his conclusion that the Apaches' efforts have "surpassed our expectations," Steck conceded that the Chihennes required more assistance than the government was providing. This was a sore subject with Governor Meriwether, who honestly felt that Steck favored the Chihennes at the Mescaleros' expense. Yet because the government had not significantly increased its assistance, Steck persisted in a pessimistic view of the Apaches' future. Their numbers had decreased dramatically because of their long war with Mexico, their fighting among themselves (usually when they were drunk), and the lack of strong central leadership. Interestingly enough, Steck believed that Mangas still led the Bedonkohes during times of war; otherwise, the leaders exerted little influence outside their own groups.

The perspicacious agent insisted that if the government had heeded his advice, many lives and hundreds of thousands of dollars would be saved in the years to come. He was confident that "if they [Chihennes] are given appropriate assistance, no trouble need ever be feared from this band." But the frugal policies of the government toward Mangas Coloradas's people remained in place. The Bedonkohes continued to be a source of problems, for they remembered Chandler's attack on El Cautívo's camp. As Steck aptly pointed out in his annual report, the government should treat the Bedonkohes, Chihennes, and Mangas Coloradas's group as one people, with a thoughtful and pragmatic policy to turn them from warriors into farmers to make them self-sufficient.[58] Instead, over the next year the Bedonkohes' hostilities forced the military to organize an expedition to punish the recalcitrants. To avoid getting caught in the crossfire, most of the Chihennes, Nednhis, and Chokonens, including Mangas Coloradas and Cochise, would reluctantly take their followers into Mexico.

Chapter 14

ALL TRAILS LEAD TO JANOS

IN the summer of 1856 the Chihennes and Chokonens sent peace envoys to Janos, where they met Captain Baltazar Padilla. One could question their sincerity, especially that of the Chihennes, because it may be they solely wanted to secure the release of Monteras's son Nalze. Yet this decision also signaled a growing disenchantment with Americans by some bands, mainly because of a paucity of assistance and a belief that the government had not lived up to the treaty of 1855, at least in terms of rations and subsistence.[1] The Indians had no conception of American democracy—that Congress had to ratify treaties before they became law. Furthermore, they had a profound fear that the American military would not discriminate between them and the hostile Bedonkohes. Padilla and José María Zuloaga encouraged these solicitations, for the Mexicans perceived in them an opportunity to entice the Indians to their frontier away from American control. As for Mangas, he had no sympathy for those local groups who had requested peace; his actions proved unequivocally that he opposed their course of action and disclosed also that he would do all in his power to disrupt the fragile armistice as he had in years past. Ironically, by early 1857 relations between Americans and Chihennes had become so impaired that most of the Chiricahuas, including Mangas Coloradas, did seek refuge in northern Mexico. Many would rue the day that they had embraced the Mexicans at Janos, especially because they had placed trust in José María Zuloaga, onetime accomplice of James Kirker and now the virtual political and economic czar of northwestern Chihuahua.

The negotiations at Janos had begun on July 30, 1856, when Itán, Láceres, and Monteras, with seven warriors, nine women, and a few children, arrived at the presidio and requested a truce. Though disenchanted with American treatment, they mainly intended to exchange one of their prisoners for Nalze, the son of Monteras, who had been in captivity at Janos for over a year. The Indians offered Prudencio Aralos, a Janos resident whom they had captured three months earlier. Zuloaga, concluding that the governor and commanding general would approve, agreed to the swap of prisoners. Although the Chihennes soon returned to the Mimbres, the negotiations had convinced some of them, especially the Nednhi leader Láceres, whose local group territory was traditionally in northwestern Chihuahua, that they might receive a better deal at Janos than Steck could currently provide.[2]

At least two of the Chokonen local groups had also renewed relations at Janos. They had also grown weary of war, having been fighting the Mexicans since Carrasco's attack on Yrigóllen's camp at Janos in March 1851. Aguirre (Yrigóllen's brother), Yrinco (Manuelito's brother), and a relatively unknown chief named Parte had dispatched emissaries to Janos.[3] During the summer of 1856 a second Chokonen local group, living in the Chiricahua Mountains under Chepillo and Esquinaline, also sent envoys. A third Chokonen local group—and the most warlike—wanted no part in the negotiations. Its leader, Miguel Narbona, had died about 1856, apparently of natural causes. Cochise, who had succeeded him, had so far shown no interest in resuming relations with either Captain Padilla or José María Zuloaga. Meanwhile, by mid-August some thirty-six Apaches resided near Corralitos, from where they would accompany Commissioner Zuloaga to Chihuahua City to make a normal peace with the governor.[4]

Yet two independent but ever-present concerns derailed the Chiricahua representatives who were to meet the governor. In late August, veteran Sonoran national guard commander Luis García pursued across the border into Chihuahua some hostiles who had conducted raids in his state. Only through the intervention of the people at Janos were hostilities averted. Naturally this affair ruffled the Indians, who vividly recalled Carrasco's and Elías González's attacks. Chihuahuan officials labeled García's actions "criminal, and against the dignity and interests of this state."[5] The second event, which occurred lightning-quick and without warning, was characteristic of both Mangas Coloradas and Cochise, whose objective was to disrupt the brief armistice at Janos. On September 2,

1856, at the siesta hour, Mangas Coloradas and thirty to forty warriors defiantly raided Janos's horse herd, galloping off with over one hundred head of stock. Mexicans recognized with Mangas several Indians, whom Captain Padilla at Janos called "broncos," meaning he felt them to be incorrigible hostiles. Among them were leading warriors of the Chokonens, Bedonkohes, and Nednhis. Apparently none of the Chihennes participated. Besides Mangas Coloradas, the Janos soldiers recognized Cascos and El Cautívo for the Bedonkohes; Barboncito, Galindo, and Perea for the Janeros local group of Nednhis; and Durasnillo and other Chokonens whom Padilla had not mentioned, likely including Cochise.[6]

Mangas knew that a small group of Nednhis, which included a brother (Esquiriba) and a nephew of Láceres, had entered the presidio of Janos under terms of a preliminary peace agreement. A few members of this band, which included an influential woman named Jusepa, had actually arrived at Chihuahua City the day before Mangas's foray at Janos to confer with the governor about a treaty. The raid embarrassed Padilla; he immediately placed under guard Esquiriba's group of thirteen people, including four men, until further notice. Eyewitnesses had recognized several warriors involved in the raid, among them a few, including Barboncito, who had recently spoken with Padilla about peace. These identifications incensed Padilla, who felt betrayed. In a rage, he and the crafty José María Zuloaga opted on a strategy that had worked in 1850. They decided to use the captives as ransom to force Mangas to return the stock and to lure other Chiricahuas to Janos away from American control.[7] According to one report, the detained Apaches believed that Mangas Coloradas might offer to return the livestock as a bargaining chip to get the prisoners released.[8] Yet Padilla acknowledged that the Indians had already taken the stock to New Mexico, and he believed that they had no intention of returning it. Fearing that the Indians might respond with force to free their people, the captain requested civilian reinforcements from Zuloaga.[9]

After nearly two weeks of inactivity, Captain Padilla dispatched one Apache woman, Carlota, with ten soldiers from Janos to visit Láceres's ranchería, located on the Mimbres River. After a brief conference, Láceres sent Baquerón, who had received rations at Janos in late 1843 as a member of Coleto Amarillo's band, to offer restitution in either stock or captives. Baquerón and Carlota also carried a letter written by Phalios Palacio, Mangas's brother, to Captain Padilla. They reached Janos on September 24 and remained there for six days, when Baquerón left for the Chiricahua rancherías on the Mimbres. He carried Padilla's response to Phalios Palacio, the Bedonkohe chief who had migrated from his country in the Mogollons to receive rations from Agent Michael Steck and Governor Meriwether.[10]

Padilla had written the following:

> Carlota gave me the letter you sent me. Baquerón was treated well here and is returning to take this letter to you in which you will see, and he will tell you, how well the men, women, and children who are detained here are treated. They are not prisoners as you maintain. [They will be detained here] until Láceres, Itán, and Delgadito, with all of the Janeros Apaches, and all the others who want to, come to ratify the peace they have requested with Commissioner Don José María Zuloaga. We must never lose our friendship because what we want is that all those who desire a good, big peace, come here to live with us. You must tell this to all the Apaches in order that, without fear, they will come to this presidio to receive their rations. Tell Jusepa not to be afraid. She should come and she will see how well the people here will treat her. Everyone knows that she is not to blame and that what they want is peace with everybody. Tell Yrinco the same thing, and [tell] Láceres that we are waiting for him, as he has offered to come, with the whole theft that Mangas Coloradas took off, and to see if he can bring in the latter's head because we will pay as much as he wants. . . .[11]

Padilla's letter requires analysis. His statement concerning Esquiriba's party was disingenuous; they remained in confinement at Janos even if the Mexicans were treating them well. Clearly, Padilla and Zuloaga perceived this to be an excellent opportunity to entice the Apaches to return to Janos, where they would be under Mexican control. To bring them in, they played their ace in the hole: an offer to issue regular rations, something the Americans had never done, despite having made such pledges in three treaties in the last four years. But perhaps the most interesting comment was Padilla's proposition to Láceres that he should bring in the head (or scalp) of Mangas Coloradas. The Mexicans offered to pay a liberal sum to the person who could accomplish this, the same offer made to Manuelito seven years before. Yet not one Apache took Padilla up on his offer for a reward, for to do so meant probable death to the assassin and his family. This suggestion was also interesting because Phalios Palacio was a brother of Mangas Coloradas. Padilla and Zuloaga, who had more experience with the Chiricahuas than any other whites on the North American continent, either Anglo or Mexican, must have understood the relationship between the two men. Perhaps they may have heard of bad blood between the two brothers, or perhaps they hoped Mangas's actions had so enraged Láceres that he would take action. Yet, whatever they thought, no Chiricahua would have considered such a treasonous venture, knowing that Mangas held close ties to the bellicose Bedonkohes and to Cochise's Chokonens, who would certainly avenge such a perfidious and traitorous act.

A few weeks after Baquerón returned to the Mimbres River with Padilla's letter, the Indians showed it to Agent Steck and Governor David Meriwether, who had journeyed to the Mimbres River to issue annual presents. On September 20, 1856, Steck issued rations to Mangas and his immediate followers, fifty persons in all.[12] About that time the agent also reported that Mangas had expressed dissatisfaction about the inadequate rations that Steck distributed. He complained that Steck had shown favoritism to the Chihennes of Delgadito, Cuchillo Negro, and Itán at the expense of his people.[13] In October, Steck rode with the governor to the Mimbres River, which they reached on October 14, and proudly showed him the fields under cultivation. Meriwether had hoped to continue to Santa Lucía, "where Mangas Coloradas is planting." Instead, pressed for time because he had to council with the Mescaleros at Fort Thorn, he remained at the Mimbres for two days to meet the principal chiefs. One whom he met because it is known he was present was Phalios Palacio, whose band Meriwether reported "occupied a country at the head of the Mimbres River," though he probably meant the Gila. Meriwether described him as a man "who spoke the Spanish language quite well. On my asking him how he came to speak that language, he said that after the death of his father and mother, while he was a boy, he was adopted by a Catholic priest and had been raised by him and educated to manhood, when he returned to his tribe again." The governor also distributed "presents" in the form of blankets, butcher knives, hickory shirts, axes, brass kettles, tin cups, tobacco, hoes, spades, and a few head of cattle. The Indians showed Meriwether and Steck the letter from Padilla that clearly stated he would not release Esquiriba's party until Mangas Coloradas and the "broncos" returned the stolen stock. Both officials encouraged Mangas to comply with the request, but by then the Apaches had dispersed the stock in several rancherías and had undoubtedly slaughtered most of it for food.[14]

After Steck and Meriwether returned to Fort Thorn, at the request of the Apaches they wrote Padilla, asking him to set free Esquiriba's party because his band had nothing to do with those who had committed the raid. It pained the agent to see his Chihennes lumped in with Mangas Coloradas and the Bedonkohes. Steck argued that the Indians on the Mimbres were innocent bystanders; Padilla and Zuloaga should place the responsibility for the raid squarely on the shoulders of Mangas Coloradas and the Bedonkohes. Although he knew that the Chihennes had continued to raid Mexico, he assured Padilla that they "had manifested for the past years a desire to be at peace" with both the United States and Mexico. Furthermore, Steck conceded to Padilla that "Mangas Coloradas and his people have committed many depredations against the property of both governments." He pointed out that Esquiriba's party were innocent victims; they differed from Mangas Coloradas's Bedonkohe and Chihenne followers of the Gila wilderness country. The concerned agent admitted that Esquiriba's friends could not recover the stock, though they had done all in their power to comply with Padilla's demands. Therefore, he pleaded with Captain Padilla to use his influence with José María Zuloaga to "free those captives." Obviously the Apaches had told Steck that they trusted Padilla more than the hard-line Zuloaga, whom they had always feared and were wary of.[15]

On October 24, 1856, Captain Padilla reported that Monica, the trustworthy Chihenne interpreter, had arrived from Fort Thorn with letters from Steck and Meriwether. Although Steck had told a few white lies in his passionate appeal to Captain Padilla, we can forgive him, for he was operating out of sincere intentions and honorable motives. In particular, the agent knew that his "innocent" Chihennes had for years made systematic incursions into Mexico, especially Sonora, with Mangas Coloradas and Delgadito. Although their forays had diminished sharply in numbers over the last few years, he realized that the raids did continue, for there was the death of Negrito, which he had reported in a letter to his superiors earlier that spring. Captain Padilla, a Hispanic gentleman, carefully responded to Steck's missive, cataloging testimony that he had obtained from Apaches whom he had captured during the last eighteen months. He began by naming several warriors who had participated in the September raid with Mangas Coloradas, including a few who belonged to Láceres's band. Padilla had referred the matter to Zuloaga, and both concluded from the testimony they had gathered from Apaches and escaped Mexican prisoners that many of these forays (and they cited specific cases of raids led by Victorio, Costales, and Negrito) had "undoubtedly" originated from the Apache camps on the Mimbres. Padilla politely ended his communication by thanking Steck for his efforts to return the stolen animals to their rightful owners.[16]

Meanwhile, a review of the correspondence between Governor Meriwether and Agent Steck, and the governor's reports to Washington, suggests that a minor rift had developed between the two men. As governor and superintendent of Indian affairs, Meriwether had to assume an enormous number of responsibilities in New Mexico. He seemed to chafe under Steck's reminders, diplomatic though they were, that his Indians needed assistance and that the government had not fulfilled its agreements. One can see a gradual erosion in their relationship as the governor came to the conclusion that Steck's benevolent policies with the Chihennes (whom he believed Steck was "inclined to pet") favored them at the expense of the Mescaleros. Peace and war factions divided the Mescaleros. Though the majority seemed to favor peace, the actions of the hostile faction affected the entire tribe. Unfortunately, the age-old dilemma faced Americans: How can we distinguish between hostile and pacific Mescaleros?

Meriwether simplistically believed that Steck's disenchantment with the Mescaleros was occasioned by the Indians' theft of a horse from him.[17] It was, however, much more serious than that. In early 1856 one small group of bellicose Mescaleros under the defiant leader Showano (whom we have met before), who liked to boast about the number of Americans he had killed, had taken refuge west of the Rio Grande in Chihenne country.[18] In April and May, after committing depredations, Showano sought shelter with Cuchillo Negro's local group, which had friendly relations with the Mescaleros because their territories adjoined each other. About mid-May, Captain Eaton sent a detachment from Fort Thorn to attack Showano's followers, who were in Cuchillo Negro's camp some five to seven miles west of the Rio Grande. The Apaches detected the command, however, and escaped. Eaton became suspicious and believed that Costales may have warned the Mescaleros.[19] Shortly after, Cuchillo Negro came into the fort with Steck; Eaton summarily ordered him to leave—and unequivocally told the chief that he would seize and imprison his people if they remained at the post for another forty-five minutes. The captain growled to Cuchillo Negro that he would consider his band enemies since they had provided sanctuary to the Mescaleros. They must drive Showano's group across to the east side of the Rio Grande.[20]

Steck had already taken it upon himself to stop the Mescaleros' rations. They had made his decision easier when most of the tribe remained in the mountains of southeastern New Mexico to avoid controversy with the people of Mesilla, with whom they seemed to have the same love/hate relationship that the Chiricahuas maintained with the people of Janos. In early March 1856 a band of Mescaleros had visited Fort Stanton on the Bonito River nine miles west of today's Lincoln. The commander, Captain Jefferson Van Horne, handed out a few rations.[21] Two months later Meriwether urged Commissioner of Indian Affairs George W. Manypenny to appoint a separate agent for the Mescaleros because one man could not "attend in a proper manner to the Gila Apaches, Mimbres Apaches, and the Mescaleros." He recommended that Manypenny authorize the establishment of the agency's headquarters at Fort Stanton.[22] By the end of the year the army, with food and presents provided by Steck, assumed responsibility to feed the Mescaleros at Fort Stanton. In early December they rationed some 300, including 106 warriors.[23]

In reality, Meriwether's absence in the east on personal business in late 1855 and early 1856 had left him out of touch with Apache affairs in southern New Mexico. After receiving Steck's monthly report for May 1856, he apparently discovered that the agent had stopped rationing the Mescaleros. The governor became indignant, for if Steck had ceased the Mescaleros' rations, then, Meriwether logically but uncharitably concluded, he must be furnishing a "liberal supply" to the Chihennes. Furthermore, not only had the agent the temerity to request an additional one thousand dollars for the Chihennes, but he had also asked the status of the June 1855 treaty that Congress had not ratified, a touchy subject to Meriwether. (Congress in fact never ratified the treaty.) Meriwether curtly told Steck to "feed the Mescaleros if they are peaceably disposed." He implied to Steck that the agent devoted too much of his time to overseeing the Chiricahua farms on the Mimbres, although Meriwether knew nothing firsthand. He explicitly reminded the agent: "You are not expected to cultivate the lands of the Indians entirely for them, but merely to assist them to a limited extent and give them such instructions as may be necessary to enable them to do most of the work themselves."[24]

Meriwether toned down his rhetoric after his October visit to the Chiricahuas on the Mimbres River. Not only had he seemed miffed at the agent, but he also refused to give him any credit for his efforts. He grudgingly acknowledged to Commissioner of Indian Affairs Manypenny that "though much gratified at their success at farming, I am certain that Agent Steck overestimates the success of their efforts. . . . My opinion is that these Indians have not cultivated more than one-half of the amount stated by him." Yet in reality, Steck had accomplished much. Almost single-handedly he had altered the habits of at least two Chihenne local groups—those of Cuchillo Negro and Delgadito. The latter's conversion from raider to farmer was indeed a tremendous achievement, for just a few years before, Delgadito's bellicosity toward Mexicans ranked on a par with that of Mangas Coloradas and the Bedonkohes. Even worse, he was probably the most hostile Chihenne leader that the Americans faced. Steck had gained Delgadito's confidence, convincing him that for his people to survive he must make peace. He had also sold the chief on the absolute necessity of farming, and, as a result, Delgadito's followers had cultivated a substantial corn crop in 1855 and 1856. Instead of minimizing Steck's accomplishments, Meriwether, it now seems, should have given the agent a hearty commendation for these important steps.[25]

About a month after Steck and Meriwether gave the Indians presents, a major controversy erupted involving Navajo Agent Henry Lafayette (Linn) Dodge.[26] At the forefront were the Bedonkohes under El Cautívo, whom Chandler had attacked the previous spring. Although Mangas played no direct role in the affair, he diligently responded to requests to use his influence to free Dodge, whom the Indians had captured. El Cautívo happened to have accompanied Mangas during the September attack at Janos. The ramifications from this incident were truly significant. The Apaches' captivity of Agent Dodge marked the beginning of a chain of events that culminated in the famous Bonneville campaign of 1857, which saw the largest concentration of troops ever placed on Mangas Coloradas's home territory. After the Dodge incident, the American military decided to send an enormous campaign to the Gila River and Mogollon Mountains to punish the incorrigible Bedonkohes. Naturally, the presence of American troops in Apachería greatly disturbed the Chiricahuas. To the delight of Mexican officials, most of the bands simply moved south to Fronteras and Janos to avoid the Americans' retaliation. It would prove to be a no-win situation for the Chiricahuas. Those who went to Mexico would eventually return to the United States, their numbers greatly reduced from again having trusted José María Zuloaga at Corralitos. The few who had remained in Apachería paid the price in blood.

On November 16, 1856, Navajo Agent Henry L. Dodge, an eccentric but competent agent from a prominent Missouri family, accompanied a patrol led by Captain Henry Lane Kendrick,[27] a highly regarded officer who had done much to gain the trust of the Navajos. They left Fort Defiance bound for Zuñi, which the Apaches had raided the previous month. A few Navajos also accompanied Kendrick's troops as guides. At Zuñi a few days later, the Zuñi "war captain," Salvador, joined the command. On November 19, while the detachment was bivouacked about thirty miles south of Zuñi, Dodge and Armijo, a Navajo chief, decided to go hunting before breakfast. Early that morning Dodge shot a deer; Armijo remained to dress the carcass while the agent went in search of more game. Later that day Armijo joined the command near Salt Lake; Dodge failed to come in, which did not concern Kendrick too much because the agent was "a good woodsman" and the troops had not seen any signs of hostile Apaches. But later that evening Kendrick directed a search, ordering twelve men to climb the adjacent hills and "fire off their rifles." Still, Dodge failed to respond.[28]

Although Dodge could not hear the shots, a group of Bedonkohes, who were gathering salt before beginning a campaign, panicked when they did. The Indians had also reached Salt Lake that day, but upon perceiving the Americans approaching they "fell back behind the hills to wait until night." That evening they returned, and "while they and their horses were drinking, they heard much firing." This proved to be Kendrick's search party discharging their weapons to get Dodge's attention, but the Apaches believed that the troops had discovered them. As a result, the Indian party, which consisted of four or five warriors, a woman, and three captives, scattered to the winds. During the confusion, Refugio Corrales, a fifteen-year-old boy from Galeana whom the Indians had captured sixteen months before, made his escape. The next morning he joined one of Kendrick's patrols searching for stock stolen by the Apaches near Salt Lake.[29]

The youth had not heard of Dodge's capture, yet he suspected the "foot party who had gone in advance" was responsible. It turned out that during the night the Apaches had stolen several animals belonging to the command. That morning Kendrick, now alarmed for Dodge's safety, sent the Navajo and Zuñi scouts to search for the agent. They picked up his trail easily enough and then followed it to the place where the Apaches had captured Dodge, but apparently had not killed him, or so they believed. From the signs, both Armijo and Salvador concluded that Dodge's captors were Gila and Mogollon Apaches (Bedonkohes) rather than Coyoteros (Western Apaches of the White Mountain groups).[30] This war party had come to strike the Zuñis or Navajos, with whom they had been at war in the last few years. Why and when these hostilities developed are still not clear. Remarkably, not since 1853 had the Navajos ventured south of Ácoma. Now at least two independent sources reported that an Apache expedition composed of Western White Mountain Apaches and Bedonkohes had gone on a campaign into Navajo country. Agent Steck reported such from his agency at Fort Thorn; Major Steen, from Fort Buchanan in Arizona, declared that he had heard from an escaped prisoner the same thing.[31]

Refugio Corrales thought it likely that the Indians had captured Dodge but had not killed him. Three days after the agent's capture, Kendrick's command returned to Zuñi. The captain sent a special dispatch with the details of the affair to Captain Van Horne at Albuquerque. In his brief note, he asked Van Horn to forward details to Colonel Garland and Governor Meriwether. More important, he suggested that his superiors get word quickly to Agent Steck at Fort Thorn; Steck could pass these details along to Mangas Coloradas or to his brother (Phalios Palacio), for they certainly had sufficient influence among the Bedonkohes to open negotiations to ransom Dodge. Kendrick reported additional information when he reached Fort Defiance on November 26. He remained optimistic about Dodge's fate because Refugio Corrales and others told him that Dodge and Mangas Coloradas were personally "acquainted." Surely the chief would "send for him" when he found out the details.[32]

Governor Meriwether also notified Steck and ordered him "without delay [to] send out one or more parties of Mimbres Apaches, or Mangas Coloradas's people, to communicate with the Mogollon and Gila Apaches, and if possible to procure the release of Agent Dodge."[33] Steck had recently left for Fort Stanton with presents for the Mescaleros and thus was not present when Meriwether's message arrived; fortunately, Captain Thomas Claiborne, post commander of Fort Thorn, took the initiative. On December 4, 1856, he sent Ammon (or Ammin) Barnes with two Chihennes, Costales and

Rattón, to the village of Mangas Coloradas. Steck returned from Mescalero country on December 5 and discussed the situation with Delgadito, who agreed to send Tinaja, a prominent man with ties to the Chokonens and Bedonkohes, to the Almagre and Mogollon Mountains, where he believed the Bedonkohes had located their winter villages.[34]

Delgadito returned on December 17 with more information. Mangas Coloradas had "directed" him to tell Steck that the Bedonkohes and White Mountain Apaches from Arizona, probably the eastern band of the latter, had sent a war party into Navajo country, where they had stolen horses, mules, and sheep while also capturing two wagonloads of goods. He thought the depredations occurred near Ácoma, though, as it turned out, the war party had divided into two bands, one raiding near Ácoma and Zuñi while the other foraged near Los Lunas and the Puerco River. Because Mangas as yet knew nothing about the fate of Agent Dodge, he decided to send his brother José Mangas into Bedonkohe and Chokonen country to find out what he could.[35]

The next day, December 18, Captain Claiborne provided additional information to department headquarters in Santa Fe. His short note was of interest because it provided concrete information about Mangas's activities. At the time of Dodge's capture, the chief had just arrived at Lemitar on the Rio Grande, undoubtedly to trade. Claiborne wrote:

> I have the honor to forward by express to you, what has just been brought to my knowledge by Dr. Steck and Delgadito, chief of the Mimbres Apaches. Mangas Coloradas sends in word here for "the information of the whites in the valley, that the Mogollon and Coyoteros have joined in making war upon the Whites. . . . They are resolved not to make peace."
>
> Mangas sent his brother [José Mangas] to ascertain the fate of Capt. Dodge, the Indian Agent, and we may expect news in a few days of his fate. Mangas was in Lemitar at the time of the capture of Dodge and knows nothing of his capture, and will not side with the revolted Indians. His conduct in this timely information seems to be altogether fair; Delgadito & the Mimbres Indians are very friendly & wish to be so considered. He and Tenacher [Tinaja] came with Dr. Steck to see me & give information.[36]

On January 2, 1857, José Mangas and Tinaja returned with the sad news that the Apaches had "shot dead" an American whom they had captured while hunting about a "day's ride" from Los Lunas. Steck concluded there was "little doubt that Agent Dodge is the American killed. They further state that no American is or has been a prisoner among these Indians." The Apaches had carried out the cold-blooded murder strictly for revenge. About a month before, a party of White Mountain Apaches had raided Zuñi, were pursued, and were forced to leave behind their booty. In addition, the Zuñi warriors had killed a man; the brother of the dead man had helped to organize this war party of White Mountain Apaches and Bedonkohes. When the Indians captured Dodge, this man exercised his rights, under Apache law, to avenge his brother's death, and therefore killed Dodge. After this, the war party divided into two groups: the Western Apaches went toward Zuñi and Ácoma; the Bedonkohes continued east to Los Lunas and the Puerco River, where they committed depredations. Troops from Los Lunas followed the Bedonkohes into what was likely the western face of the Black Mountains, opposite the Mogollons, and overtook the raiders, killing at least one and recovering part of the theft.[37]

José Mangas and Tinaja evidently spoke to a small group of Bedonkohes or Chokonens at either the Peloncillo or the Dos Cabezas Mountains. They were under El Cautívo and Lsana,[38] the leaders of the village "that Colonel Chandler attacked last spring." From them José Mangas and Tinaja learned the details of Dodge's death.[39]

In mid-February a party from Fort Defiance returned to the site of Dodge's capture and discovered his remains, which they removed to Fort Defiance for burial.[40] Colonel Benjamin L. E. Bonneville, temporarily in charge of the Department of New Mexico while Garland was east on leave, vowed to punish the Bedonkohes. These "depredations committed are of too outrageous a character to be passed over. They must be punished." Bonneville was already beginning to lay the seeds for a massive campaign against the hostiles—one that would affect the Chiricahua bands and at least one group of the Western Apaches.[41]

While the Chihennes and Steck focused much of their attention on the fate of Captain Dodge, another development arose which threatened to sow more hostility and distrust where there had been healthy friendship. The long-standing enmity between Apaches and Mexicans surfaced again. In the late evening of December 29, 1856, two Mexicans from El Paso, Manuel Meztas and Dolores Sánches, stole sixteen horses from Delgadito's camp;

Indians recovered twelve of them the next day. Steck sent Costales and Rattón to follow the trail toward Mesilla, but they decided to return to San Diego Crossing and spend the night. It turned out to be a fateful decision, for sometime that night two Mexicans who worked at the ferry house brutally murdered them in their sleep. They split Costales's head "with a blow from an axe," cut his throat, and scalped him. Rattón suffered a similar death. The Mexicans dumped both bodies into the river. When the Apaches did not return, the commander at Fort Thorn sent Second Lieutenant Alexander Early Steen to investigate. On January 1, 1857, Steen discovered the ghastly scene and fished Costales's corpse from the river. Rattón's body was never found.[42]

Upon examination, the two Mexicans who committed these murders revealed that they had done so for the same reason that the Apaches had killed Navajo Agent Dodge. Almost unbelievably, the two unfortunate affairs had a common thread, for one of the Mexicans who had committed the murders was Martín Corrales of Galeana, brother of Refugio, the same individual who had escaped from the Apaches the day after Dodge's capture. In fact, on the day before Martín Corrales killed the two Apaches, the Assistant Adjutant General, Department of New Mexico, had instructed Major Gouverneur Morris at Fort Fillmore to advise Martín Corrales of his brother's escape from the Apaches and safe arrival at Santa Fe. Unfortunately, before Corrales heard the news, he literally took matters into his own hands, butchering Costales and Rattón. Corrales and his accomplice fled to Chihuahua beyond extradition, despite the efforts of the U.S. consul at El Paso.[43]

Meanwhile, Delgadito assured Steck that the Chihennes would not seek to avenge Costales's death. Perhaps because he was a Mexican by birth, the Indians felt less inclined to retaliate. Yet Rattón was Apache by birth and of considerable influence, and yet there is no record of any action taken because of his murder. In any event, the Chihennes would have retaliated against Mexicans and not Americans, despite Steck's and Meriwether's concerns. The Apaches were not holding the Americans responsible for the bloody atrocities at San Diego Crossing.[44]

Unexpectedly, by early 1857 most of the Chihennes decided to leave their homelands. Undoubtedly the rumors of the impending retaliatory campaign against the Bedonkohes and White Mountain groups of Western Apaches helped to mold their decision. They had also grown weary of American promises to feed them; typically, the rations consisted of corn only, with beef an infrequent luxury. Although distrusting Mexicans, they were forced to admit that the rations at Janos came regularly and consisted of more than just corn. In addition, the Nednhis under Láceres had resumed negotiations there (primarily to get Esquiriba's party released), and the Mexicans were treating the Indians well. About this time another significant development occurred: the Chihenne band, which Mangas Coloradas had dominated for the last quarter of a century, had begun to split into smaller factions under four local group leaders—Delgadito, Itán, Josécito, and Cuchillo Negro, with Delgadito the most influential. Itán apparently died sometime in late 1856 or early 1857. Cuchillo Negro was aging, and Delgadito, perhaps Steck's biggest supporter, had become a moderate leader. Thus, the band became splintered, and younger leaders such as Victorio, Riñón, and Loco began to emerge. As for Mangas Coloradas, who had traditionally led the Chihennes with the support of Itán, Delgadito, and others, he had begun to ally himself with the great Chokonen Cochise, his son-in-law, who by 1857 had emerged as the dominant Chokonen local group leader.

Steck could sense in early 1857 that relations had begun to unravel. That winter he had gone to Santa Fe for a visit; his absence upset Meriwether (who continued to second-guess the agent whenever he had the chance), because the governor felt that Steck should have remained with his Indians during this critical period. During February not one Chihenne had come to the agency.[45] In March, Steck admitted to Colonel Bonneville that the Chihennes had "some bad men among the band." Suddenly, after years of traveling in Chihenne country, usually with one or two assistants, Steck felt uncomfortable, even fearing for his own life. He asked Bonneville to furnish him with "an escort of twenty-five men and an officer to remain with me while planting (probably thirty days)."[46] Meriwether informed Steck that Bonneville "doubts that he can provide you with an escort."[47] Steck's request was academic, however, for by then hostilities had erupted, though the Chihennes had initiated them. In mid-January a small raiding party stole some stock at Mesilla. About forty members of the Mesilla Guard doggedly followed the trail to the Florida Mountains, where on or about January 21, 1857, they overtook the Apaches and killed a prominent man named Flacón and his two sons.[48]

In March the troops from Fort Fillmore got into the act. Again they were responding to a band of Chihennes who had been lurking along the Rio Grande between Fort Thorn and Mesilla.

The Indians had stolen the horses of a Mr. Garretson, deputy surveyor of the territory. On March 8, 1957, First Lieutenant Alfred Gibbs of the Mounted Rifles, with sixteen men and two civilian guides (Garretson and a man named Dickens), followed the trail that crossed the Rio Grande about ten miles north of Doña Ana. By noon the next day they discovered the spot where the Indians had rested; there were seven in all, four mounted and three on foot. Though Gibbs feared that the Indians had escaped his grasp, since they were close to the Mimbres Mountains, he tenaciously continued his pursuit. About 1:30 that afternoon Gibbs's soldiers spotted the Indians. A script writer could not have written a better story. The leaders of the two sides, the Apache chief and Lieutenant Gibbs, personally led their men into battle. The spirited engagement was climaxed by a duel between the two stalwart and courageous men. Both were doing their duty as they had been trained: one an Apache chief trying to bring home stock to feed his hungry people and the other a military officer seeking to recover stock stolen by Indians. In the words of Lieutenant Gibbs, this is what happened:

Ascending a little rise, we saw an Indian about fifty yards off coming to meet us, and at the same moment we saw the mules at the bottom of a little arroyo and six Indians looking at us then beginning to run. The men were immediately dismounted and we commenced on them with rifles. As fast as the rifles were discharged, the men loaded and mounted, and followed at a gallop the Indians, who ran like wild turkeys. It was evident that the game was up. Three were badly wounded though running still, and there was a mile before they could get to the mountains. The men were urged to be steady and to keep their revolvers till the last. As we rode on, the chief who was badly wounded, kept encouraging his men, whenever he did this they turned and charged us furiously. As I passed near him, he was making at one of the men on foot, whose horse had been shot, and I stopped and shot him a fifth shot with my revolver. He turned on me, and as my horse reared, he passed his lance into me although parried with my pistol. One of the men then brought him down. Riding forward then about a quarter of a mile, beyond, I came upon the rest of my party close up with the Indians, and the shot telling continually. Here, becoming very faint from loss of blood, I dismounted to prevent from falling off, and giving my horse to Corporal Collins, whose horse had been shot from under him, directed him to keep up with the party, until he killed all the Indians, or until pursuit was hopeless, and then to rally and return to where his horse fell where he would find me. I found the chief dead with ten balls in him, and the five men left behind with the animals reported they had one horse, five mules, bows and arrows, knives, blankets, etc. of the Indians. In about a half an hour Corporal Collins returned with his party, and reported six Indians dead, and the other one severely wounded [and likely dead].[49]

By this time the Chihennes had stopped visiting the agency, and Steck was concerned. In early March he sent a man to the Mimbres to "ascertain the course of their strange conduct." The man returned and told Steck that he had seen only one camp, which contained five warriors and some one hundred women and children.[50] Thus, it seems probable that the warriors whom Gibbs's patrol had overtaken and killed were heading back to this camp near the Mimbres. If so, Gibbs's men might have killed Itán, because no further references to him have been found. If not he, Monteras, a prominent war leader, was another possibility. Both men were known to raid the settlements along the Rio Grande.

By this time it had become clear to Steck that part of the Mimbres local group of Chihennes had left for either Janos or the Chiricahua Mountains in Chokonen country, where Mangas Coloradas had gone to harvest mescal. Meanwhile, on March 14, only five days after Gibbs's fight, a few women and children coming in from Cuchillo Negro's camp told Colonel Miles that Mangas Coloradas, Delgadito, and most of the Indians had left the Mimbres for Janos and would not return until "next moon."[51] A band of Chihennes, at the site where Delgadito normally camped, skirmished with American troops on the Mimbres. The soldiers killed one Apache and wounded another. If Delgadito had not yet reached Janos, he probably left for there shortly after this engagement. The troops had punished his people every time they met in battle, and by this time all the Apaches had heard that the Americans were planning a massive campaign into the Gila and Mogollon country.[52]

Most of the Nednhis had opened negotiations with Captain Padilla at Janos. Undoubtedly the release of their kinfolk was their main objective, but the increasing tensions north of the border and lack of dependable rations there proved to be other factors in their decision. On December 22, 1856, Láceres dispatched Bartolo to talk to Captain Padilla about making a treaty. The commander discussed the Apaches' solicitations with José María Zuloaga, now the peace commissioner, who believed they could settle the matter diplomatically. Zuloaga agreed to overlook the animals that Mangas Coloradas had stolen the previous summer. Besides, by now he knew the Indians had undoubtedly slaughtered them for food. Instead, he invited Láceres in for more talks.[53]

On January 2, 1857, Láceres came in with Poncito, Felipe, and Pascolo. The last two belonged to the Carrizaleño local group of Nednhis, whom Chihuahuan troops had kept on the run in late 1856. Soon after, Láceres went to Corralitos to conclude the armistice with Zuloaga; on January 19 they traveled to Chihuahua City to ratify the treaty. A few weeks later, Láceres and Poncito brought their followers to Janos and encamped near the presidio. Láceres's group totaled 150 people; Poncito's small group numbered 34. By April 1, Delgadito brought in his Chihenne group of 51 persons, and Felipe came in with 98 Nednhis. If the Indians behaved well, and if they proved their sincerity, the commanding general, José Merino, would authorize Padilla to free Esquiriba's party. In early May, Steck wrote Acting Governor Davis (Meriwether had left New Mexico for good) that the Chihennes had gone to Janos, where Mexican officials issued rations every eight days. The Indians went there to "obtain the release of their captives" with the understanding that they would also receive more "liberal provisions." Yet Steck expected that they would return to the agency after the troops (the Bonneville expedition) left their country.[54]

As for Mangas Coloradas, he had stayed with Cochise's Chokonens in the Chiricahuas, uncertain about his next course of action. In February the Chokonen Yaque, an inveterate raider, arrived at Janos from the Chiricahua Mountains with several hundred stolen sheep from New Mexico. Zuloaga denied him rations; Yaque, however, found a ready market to dispose of his sheep. In March, Steck heard from two citizens from Janos that the Apaches were "carrying on a brisk trade of mules and horses and [had] sold 600 sheep." Later that spring Zuloaga realized that many Chiricahuas—Chokonens, Bedonkohes, and the followers of Mangas Coloradas—were living at Alamo Hueco and other ranges just north of the border. Zuloaga admitted that he had sent envoys to them, but he insisted that they had refused his overtures. Mangas Coloradas and Cochise had adopted a wait-and-see approach.[55]

Meanwhile, in New Mexico, Colonel Benjamin Louis Eulalie Bonneville launched his campaign,[56] which, he hoped, would punish primarily the Bedonkohes and, to a lesser extent, the Eastern band of the White Mountain Apaches. Bonneville had organized a big Indian hunt, using a depot on the east bank of the Gila River a few miles southeast of Cliff near Greenwood Canyon, according to the renowned authority on southern New Mexico's military posts, Lee Myers.[57] On May 1, 1857, the northern column, under one-armed Colonel William Wing Loring of the Mounted Rifles, a North Carolina native who would become a major general in the Confederate Army, left Albuquerque for the rendezvous site. Loring's command consisted of three companies of his own regiment, two companies of the Third Infantry, and several Pueblo Indians as guides. The last leg of his journey paralleled the route taken by Captain Chandler the previous year. They marched south along the western base of the Mogollons but failed to flush out any Apaches. Loring's wing reached the Gila depot on May 18. The southern column from Fort Thorn, under Lieutenant Colonel Dixon S. Miles, left Fort Thorn on May 1, one day after Colonel Bonneville had left there with the pack train. Bonneville reached the rendezvous site on May 11 and at once made plans to keep the Bedonkohes on the run until his troops killed them, compelled them to surrender, or drove them from their strongholds. A third command came east from Fort Buchanan under Captain Richard S. Ewell, who was filling in for Major Enoch Steen because of the latter's illness. All told, each wing contained some 350–400 men, and Ewell's command about 120. Thus, the expedition totaled over 900 men, a number unsurpassed in the annals of Apache warfare; one officer sarcastically suggested that 50 men would have been adequate. He may have been right.[58]

Because of its objective as well as its ostentatious display of troops and firepower, the campaign was the object of scorn and the butt of jokes by several of its officers, who were forced to endure oppressive heat, long periods of thirst, and much hardship while pursuing an enemy whose mode of fighting was guerrilla warfare.[59] The Bedonkohes had already left their country, moving into southeast Arizona and slipping south below the border. Yet after coming across an Indian trail, Bonneville dispatched Loring's command to scout the Pinos Altos and Mimbres range. Loring cut the trail of two thousand sheep which led northeast into the Mimbres range and then further north to the Black Mountains, actually the northern portion of the Mimbres range. There on May 24, 1857, his command attacked the camp of Cuchillo Negro; killed him, five other men, and one woman; and captured nine woman and children, including the wife of Cuchillo Negro. They also recovered one thousand sheep and other stock.[60] Meanwhile, on June 27, 1857, the other arm of the expedition, under Colonel Miles, accompanied by Colonel Bonneville, struck the White Mountain Apaches thirty-five miles northwest of the Graham Mountains in Arizona and mowed down thirty-eight warriors and four women while capturing forty-five, primarily women and children. The Indians wounded two officers and seven enlisted men.[61] It mattered little to Bonneville that these Indians had committed only a few depredations in New Mexico and were definitely not as warlike as the Bedonkohes. They were Apaches, and he had corpses and prisoners to certify his stunning victory. But justice was done in one respect. The Eastern White Mountain Apache who had shot Dodge in cold blood lay dead on the field, a victim of Captain Ewell's dragoons.[62]

In mid-July, Bonneville broke up his depot some six miles north of Santa Lucía. The few Chiricahuas who had seen the troops at their home base must have come away impressed, if not overwhelmed. The grand campaign was the first and the last of its kind in Apache warfare; the premise may have worked well in the open country against the northern Plains Indians, but not against the guerrilla warfare of the Apaches. If anything, one could say that Bonneville's enormous entourage had accomplished one thing: it displayed to the Chiricahuas the potential of American firepower. It had been a tremendous show of force—an ominous reminder to the Indians that would keep the Bedonkohes and Chihennes in check for the remainder of the decade. Colonel Garland wrote his superior in Washington that the "chastisement they have received will be long remembered by them. The effect produced upon contiguous bands will doubtless prove most salutary."[63]

It also had ramifications on Cochise's Chokonens. In mid-May, as Captain Ewell made his way to the rendezvous site on the Gila, he established a temporary camp in the Chiricahua Mountains, probably near Apache Pass. From there he took sixty-five men on a patrol that apparently encircled the mountains and returned to its base after a week of scouting. After a day of rest, Ewell decided to make another scout "on a somewhat different route." One day later he recovered twenty-one horses, possibly near Cave Creek in the northeastern part of the range. Soon after, the Chiricahuas, probably under Cochise, displayed a "white flag" and sent in "a captive Mexican boy to talk." In all likelihood this boy was Merejildo Grijalva, Cochise's interpreter, who in later life recalled having met Captain Ewell. Ewell tried to convince the boy to

Benjamin Louis Eulalie de Bonneville, Commander of the Department of New Mexico and organizer of the Bonneville campaign of 1857 against the Western and Chiricahua Apaches. (Courtesy U.S. Army Military History Institute, Roger D. Hunt Collection)

desert Cochise, but the Mexican "feared that the Apaches would retake & kill him, that they were numerous & brave & would take hold of a grizzly bear, etc. & that they treated him kindly, especially the women." When Ewell moved his men in position to attack the Apaches, the interpreter returned to the Apaches. That night the Indians fired shots into the camp, trying to stampede the stock, but Ewell had taken the precaution of picketing his horses. The Indians did, however, apparently succeed in retaking their stock that Ewell had previously captured. The troops responded with several volleys, which Ewell believed had taken effect because of the screams and wails that he had heard from the Indians' positions.[64]

Ewell's patrol had undoubtedly compelled some Chokonens, perhaps with Mangas, to move south of the border and to consider relations with Mexico. Within the next month the Chokonens sent emissaries to Fronteras. Mangas could not consider such a step, for he still despised Sonorans, but many Chihennes, including his old friend Delgadito, were content at Janos, where Padilla and Zuloaga were providing rations weekly.

In early June military authorities at Bavispe received news of Mangas's exact whereabouts. A Chokonen raiding party attacked Miguel Samaniego's ranch on May 31, 1857, capturing two boys. Two days later another band stole twelve mules and horses from Agustín Acuña. Captain Reyes Cruz with a small detachment went out in pursuit of the Indians. On June 4 at Sierra Larga his soldiers captured one Indian, a young woman about fifteen, and killed a warrior in hand-to-hand combat. From the woman Captain Cruz learned that the raiders belonged to Carro's and Parte's groups; furthermore, they had just left along the border a large Chiricahua band that had refused to make peace at Janos. These hostiles consisted of Bedonkohes and Chihennes under Cascos and Mangas Coloradas and a large group of Chokonens under Cochise, Esquinaline, Carro, and Parte. According to the Apache prisoner, they had repudiated the peace treaty at Janos and had no intention of agreeing to terms.[65]

Captain Cruz immediately wrote José María Zuloaga at Janos, hoping that he might discover the status of the two boys captured from Samaniego's ranch. The peace commissioner was sympathetic and assured Cruz that "I will make every determined effort to recover the stolen animals and the two young men." Zuloaga unequivocally blamed the hostilities on Mangas Coloradas. He informed Cruz: "Although I have made the most determined effort to cause certain chieftains and their bands to accept pacification, namely Mangas Coloradas, Cascos, Esquinaline, Parte and others of the broncos, I have been unsuccessful, and they are still gathered at Alamo Hueco and the surrounding area, land which is on the other side of the American border." In the next breath Zuloaga, who had a keen understanding of the Chiricahuas, showed that Mangas Coloradas, despite approaching seventy years of age, still exerted a tremendous amount of influence with the Chokonen and Bedonkohe militants:

> Since Mangas Coloradas has always opposed peace, it would not surprise me that since he was at the said council, he would try to prevent the Indians from accepting the peace and even cause them to disturb those who live near said places [Janos]. I believe that for this reason he has attacked those places and taken captives so as to ransom the Indians who are held prisoner at the presidio of Janos. I will go there next Sunday to see whether it can be discovered which Indians have committed the thefts, and then take prisoner those Indians who come down from their encampments.[66]

A week later Monica, the erstwhile interpreter of Delgadito's band, sent her son to Janos to warn Padilla that Cascos planned to raid that presidio.[67] Yet for some unknown reason, the raid never took place. Instead, the Chokonens, Chihennes, and Bedonkohes, probably influenced by Bonneville's nine-hundred-man army in the heart of Mangas's country, decided to make peace with Mexico. In early July the Chokonen Pablo, a son of the old Chokonen chief Matías of the 1830s, entered Fronteras to parley with Captain Gabriel García. Pablo represented the entire Chokonen band, about seven hundred individuals under Cochise, Chepillo, and Esquinaline. In addition, the notorious El Cautívo, either a Bedonkohe or Chokonen chief, was with Cochise. García promised rations, a plan that both the state and federal government endorsed. But later that month the skittish Chokonens failed to come in, apparently having had second thoughts about trusting Sonora.[68]

Mangas Coloradas's next move must have shocked Captain Padilla and José María Zuloaga. Toward the end of June he arrived at Janos with several other Chihenne group leaders, including Victorio, Sergento, and Veinte Reales, and joined their kinfolk under Delgadito and Riñón (a son-in-law of Delgadito). Mangas's local group totaled sixty-five individuals—twenty men, thirty women, and fifteen children. A few months later another thirty women and children came in, bringing his immediate following to ninety-five persons. Eventually some Chihennes and Nednhis opted to camp near Zuloaga at Corralitos. Mangas Coloradas would not go that far; he clearly distrusted Zuloaga. Early that summer Chihuahuan authorities claimed that these newcomers swelled the Indian population to more than one thousand, although official Janos records indicated there were only about six hundred.[69]

In August and September, Cochise's Chokonens visited Janos to receive rations and whiskey and to dispose of stolen stock. These wilder Chiricahuas, especially the Chokonens and Bedonkohes, were usually an unsettling influence. That Mangas Coloradas even considered trusting Zuloaga only indicated how desperate he must have felt his situation was in New Mexico, where he feared to return because of Bonneville's offensive. Zuloaga and Padilla called them "broncos"—in other words, incorrigibles. Perhaps the two Mexicans still smarted over Mangas's raid of the previous September, which had disrupted promising negotiations and left the presidio short of horses. They perceived this as an irresistible opportunity to eliminate as many "broncos" as possible, including the one man whom they had been trying to kill for the past decade— Mangas Coloradas. Again, details are sparse, but the evidence suggests that by late August or early September, Zuloaga had deliberately issued poisoned rations to the Apaches, probably mixing arsenic or strychnine with their whiskey allowance.[70]

By early September many Chokonens, having come down with high fevers, left Janos and subsequently appeared at Fronteras. On September 22, the commander there, Captain Gabriel García, issued rations to 680 Chiricahuas, primarily Chokonens with some Bedonkohes. Cochise was there, but Mangas had remained at Janos, at least according to the records of that presidio. García pleaded for funds to feed the Apaches, which would prevent them from retiring across the border into the United States. But Sonora's new governor, Ignacio Pesqueira, occupied in the south suppressing a Yaqui rebellion and Gándara's forces, his treasury depleted, could offer little assistance. The best he could do was to appoint as peace commissioner Rafael Angel Corella, a battle-hardened officer who preferred punishing the enemy instead of appeasing them. Corella was dubious of the Apaches' solicitations; in his view, "these savages do not have any good will."[71]

On October 9, 1857, Cochise sent in a messenger to Fronteras. The man revealed that Cochise and El Cautívo had gone into camp near Guadalupe Canyon, where many of their people had become seriously ill with fever, victims of either malaria or food poisoning at Janos. The emissary admitted that "while at Janos they were always very sick. Several women and children had died and at least ten men." The healthy members had moved north into the Chiricahua Mountains to gather acorns. Cochise wanted peace, claimed the warrior, who may have been his brother, Coyuntura. The next month another Chokonen woman appeared at Fronteras as a representative of three local groups—those of Cochise, Esquinaline, and Colchón. She acknowledged that several Apaches remained seriously ill and that ten Chokonen men had died, including Carro, Tinaja (who had acted as Steck's emissary to the hostiles during Agent Dodge's disappearance), and Chabila, and several women and children (probably forty to fifty individuals in all). Furthermore, she told García that the Americans had sent word to them, probably a message received from Dr. Steck, who had invited the Chihennes to return to New Mexico. That statement alone got the attention of the Sonorans. Venerable José María Elías González, though officially retired, urged the state to provide rations before the Indians slipped north to make peace with the Americans.[72]

According to a letter written by Sylvester Mowry, former military officer turned mining capitalist, Mangas Coloradas had moved to Fronteras, but this was not true.[73] He may have considered peace with Chihuahua, but he never would have contemplated such with Sonora. Instead, by early September he had undoubtedly become suspicious of Zuloaga when his people began to get ill from their rations. He probably relocated to the Chiricahua Mountains for the fall harvest of acorns and other nuts and berries. Apparently, Zuloaga's scheme was a selective poisoning of Mangas's followers, the Bedonkohes, and the Chokonens, for some groups, including that of Victorio and other Chihennes, remained until the end of 1857. But when Mangas realized what Zuloaga had done, he decided to return to New Mexico, where he arrived by early November, promptly sending word to Steck.[74]

Throughout the preceding spring and summer Steck had urged the Chihennes to remain in Mexico until the troops had left Apachería and returned to their home forts. In May 1857 the agent finally got Meriwether off his back when the governor resigned and returned to his native Kentucky. Soon after, federal officials appointed James Collins, a staunch Steck supporter, as superintendent of Indian affairs for the Department of New Mexico. Collins immediately recommended that Steck be reappointed Indian agent when his term expired, for "his place really cannot be supplied by another. He has had much experience with Indians and has the confidence of those under his charges to a degree that any other could not acquire by years of his service." In September, Steck finally sent word to the Chihenne chiefs at Janos that he wanted to see them. Some 150 Chihennes came in on October 15, 1857, and received rations, but these may have been from Cuchillo Negro's local group, which had never left New Mexico.[75]

When the Chihennes returned to their country, they immediately made their presence known at Santa Rita del Cobre. During their absence a man named Leonardo Siquieros had begun mining operations there, evidently with a promise from Colonel Garland that "in case of necessity he should be furnished with a sufficient guard for protection." Siquieros, who would later serve as an interpreter for Agent Steck, had a violent confrontation with a brother of Mangas Coloradas. On November 13, José Mangas arrived at the mines, clearly intoxicated after several days of drinking tiswin. He "began abusing Mr. Sequero [Siquieros] in a shameful manner saying to him that he had no business at the mines [and] that part of the country belonged to his tribe, and that he would drive them away from there immediately." Siquieros told José Mangas to leave and return when he sobered up so that he would "make everything right with him." Instead, an intoxicated José Mangas became belligerent toward Siquieros. From Mesilla, a Mr. Leonard described what happened next:

> The Indian José Mangas had his rifle in his saddle which he immediately grabbed and was making ready to fire upon Sequero [sic] when one of Sequero's [sic] sons arrived and ran into the house for his father's rifle by his father's order. He fired, hoping to dismount the Indian who by this time was on his horse. Sequero's [sic] son did not aim at the Indian as he did not wish to kill him. However, the first shot he missed his mark; the second shot he hit the horse, the ball passing through him and killed an old Indian woman that was in range with the horse, which of course infuriated the Indians and they immediately declared war upon us and all the country, and that not one of us should be left to tell the tale.

The Chihennes had uttered this timeworn threat throughout the 1850s. Usually the presence of a large band of menacing Apaches would have caused the whites to pull up stakes and leave for safer places. Not Siquieros, however, for the military had promised him protection, and he intended to remain; he gave the Apache chiefs three or four hundred dollars' worth of goods, "which seemed to satisfy them for the present."[76]

Siquieros did not mention whether Mangas Coloradas was one of the "chiefs" whom he had compensated for the death of the woman. Yet he was near Santa Rita del Cobre, probably on his way to meet Steck at Fort Thorn. Four days later he and 350 Apaches showed up there to confer with Agent Steck, who had just returned from Mescalero country.[77] The next day he held a long conference with Mangas and other chiefs, but not Delgadito, who, perhaps thinking that Steck was still in Mescalero country, appeared at Fort Stanton, where its commander ordered him to return to his country.[78] His Indians' plight touched the compassionate agent, who wrote his superior, James Collins in Santa Fe, of their ordeal:

> They are exceedingly poor, almost naked, and actually in a starving condition. Since May last when I directed them to go south to avoid the troops sent against the Mogollons [Bedonkohes] they have been living at Janos and occasionally received rations from the Govt. of Mexico. They have suffered much from disease and many of them have died. From their own story the mortality has been very great. Scarcely a family has returned that doesn't have their hair cropped short, the badge of mourning for some near relative. They believe they have been poisoned and I have little doubt that many of them have as reports reached me from the citizens of Janos that many of them had been poisoned and the symptoms as described by the Indians resemble those of poisoning by arsenic—probably administered with whiskey as that formed a part of their rations.[79]

Mangas Coloradas revealed to Steck that several Bedonkohes had "contracted diseases and many of them have died." Steck later told John Greiner that sixty Chihennes had perished from the poisoned rations, losses similar to those suffered by Cochise's Chokonens.[80] Steck's training as a medical doctor and the testimony he heard from citizens of Janos provided sufficient evidence to validate the suspicion that Zuloaga had poisoned the Chiricahuas, although the next year Steck suggested that some Indians may have died of malaria. Historian Dan Thrapp pointed out in his *Victorio and the Mimbres Apaches* that civilized societies had historically used arsenic or strychnine to decimate not only the American Indians but also the aborigines in Australia and the Bushmen in South Africa. Outraged by the fruits of his research, Thrapp declared, "Lack of conscience knows no societal bounds."[81]

We will never know exactly how many of Mangas's followers fell victims to this perfidious scheme. Like Cochise in his later years, who refused to eat rations provided by Americans, Mangas may have been too suspicious of Zuloaga to consume the whiskey. He was not a heavy drinker anyway, though he enjoyed the Apache native brew of tiswin. Before leaving Steck's agency, he told the agent that the Bedonkohes wanted "to bury the hatchet." Steck encouraged Collins to make a treaty with these two bands. If this could be done, he said, he would recommend that Collins reserve adequate funding to provide for the Indians during the interim period between the actual treaty and its ratification by Congress. This had been the downfall of Meriwether's treaty of 1855. "You might as well talk Greek to them as try to explain the delays and that Congress must appropriate the money," admonished Steck.[82]

For Mangas, his life would settle down for the remainder of the 1850s. In fact, two important beneficial relationships grew steadily stronger from 1858 until 1860. The first was with Agent Steck, who continued his visionary program of converting the Apaches from raiders into farmers. Mangas resumed planting at Santa Lucía and encouraged his younger people to do so also. The second was with Cochise, who by now had emerged into the principal Chokonen band leader. With their ties by marriage, their common hatred of Sonora, and their mutual desire to coexist with Americans, the two leaders discovered that their bands had similar goals and purposes. For the rest of Mangas's life, his story and Cochise's story ran a parallel course—one frequently immersed in Mexican blood and later that of Americans.

Chapter 15

CALM BEFORE THE STORM

IN late 1857, Mangas Coloradas, after returning from Janos, established his village at Santa Lucía north of the Burro Mountains. Undoubtedly he hoped to mend relations with Agent Steck and the American military and live in peace. He resumed planting and even contemplated living in a house if Steck would have one built for him. Yet for the rest of the decade Americans would come to his country in record numbers: farmers and ranchers settling along the Mimbres River; hardy frontiersman working for the Butterfield Overland Mail Company, which had constructed stage stations at intervals through Apachería; and soldiers who had established a temporary fort at the Burro Mountains. Although he may not have endorsed each infringement into his country, he tolerated them as part of the changing times.

Besides these interlopers, Mangas faced the one element of men whom his people had banned from settling or working in his country: miners. In contrast, he had a difficult time accepting their invasion, first at Santa Rita del Cobre and later at Pinos Altos when Americans discovered gold there, inevitably triggering a minor gold rush to the area. Though their presence sickened him, he could do little to drive them out. Chiricahua bands remembered Bonneville's massive offensive, which, although more image than substance, remained a frightening illustration of the potential use of American firepower. The Chihennes continued to decrease in numbers, and with Delgadito aging, they lacked a strong central leader. As for Mangas Coloradas, he continued a trend that he had adopted in early 1857. He frequently looked west to his son-in-law Cochise and allied his Chihenne-Bedonkohe local group, along with the Bedonkohe band, to a common cause. When trouble arose, it was Cochise to whom he would turn, especially if that difficulty was with Sonora. And of course these last few years of the 1850s were far from idyllic. With the whites steadily increasing in numbers, and a tragedy or two in Sonora, Mangas confronted challenges that a man his age should not have had to face. Usually when a chief approached the age of seventy, his position by then had evolved into one of a patriarchal leader, or "he who commands for the home," as the Chiricahuas were wont to put it.[1] Mangas, like Victorio and to a lesser extent Cochise, did not enjoy that luxury. Instead, with the help of Cochise, perhaps the greatest fighting Chiricahua chief, he continued with vigor to lead his people against his enemies, especially in Sonora.

In early 1858, Steck resumed issuing regular rations to Mangas Coloradas's local group and to the Chihenne band. During the first quarter of 1858 he provided corn to 450 Chihennes and Mangas's following of 75–100 individuals.[2] But the Indians could not subsist on these inadequate rations, which amounted to a monthly subsidy of eleven pounds of corn per adult and half that for a child. Steck likely made his distribution to the Apaches at Santa Rita del Cobre, which Leonardo Siquieros had continued to work despite growing opposition from the Indians. When American military or civil officials were not around, the Indians tried to bully and intimidate the miners, who were primarily Mexican laborers from Chihuahua. This combination of several hundred Mexican miners, most of whom lived in fear of Apaches, and the Chiricahuas planting along the Mimbres and the Gila, who loathed Mexicans, and especially miners, left everyone uneasy, awaiting the inevitable explosion.[3]

According to Steck, the Indians liked "Don Leonardo" and were "on friendly terms with him."[4] Apparently relations went well for several months, because Steck had resumed his planting program with Delgadito and other chiefs on the Mimbres and with Cuchillo Negro's old local group. That group, "the poorer portion of the band" without much stock, now under Riñón, Chabnocito, and probably Loco, resided on Palomas and Animas Creeks, both about thirty-five to forty miles northwest of the agency. Before he left Mesilla, on May 3, 1858, Steck had conceived a plan "to commence a farm on the Gila" near Santa Lucía for Mangas Coloradas, the Bedonkohes, and the Chihennes "that I have induced to go there and plant." Nonetheless, the Chiricahuas forced him to alter this arrangement. Evidently they feared an imminent outbreak of hostilities with the White Mountain Apaches; moreover, as we shall soon see, Mangas Coloradas had already moved west to Cochise's territory, where he remained for a few months. On his return he and the Bedonkohes began planting near the Gila and Santa Lucía Springs.[5]

Steck experienced other problems in early 1858. The Mescaleros had come in and made peace, and a band of some thirty had gone into camp near his agency, undoubtedly feeling secure. After all, Fort Thorn lay within a mile of Steck's headquarters, and their enemies at Mesilla resided thirty miles south of them. At daybreak on April 17, 1858, however, another senseless tragedy occurred. The Mesilla Guard, consisting of thirty-six men, surprised the sleepy camp at Steck's agency and "butchered indiscriminately men, women, and children." Before the troops from Fort Thorn could respond, the raiders had slaughtered seven Apaches and wounded three others. First Lieutenant William Henry Wood rushed forward with infantry and captured the entire party of Mexicans "as they were retreating with a number of little children whom they had made captive." Steck was absent, but several whites living near the agency, including Pinckney R. Tully, provided shelter for the fleeing Mescaleros. Garland ordered Wood to send the prisoners to Socorro for trial. They made bail, and a jury later exonerated them for their actions, as most thought it would. None of their peers was going to find them guilty of killing Apaches. A little over a year later the governor of New Mexico applauded their accomplishments "as worthy of imitation" even though, referring to this unprovoked act, "upon one occasion they may have carried their retaliation too far."[6]

About a month later Lieutenant Wood sent a sergeant and twenty-one men to Santa Rita del Cobre to "render [Leonardo Siquieros] all the assistance possible in protecting the Mexicans there engaged, should the Indians attempt to retaliate for the recent massacre at the Indian agency." Yet surprisingly, the vicious massacre of the Mescaleros did not interest the Chihennes. Moreover, Mangas Coloradas had a crisis of his own to resolve. In the first few months of 1858, Sonoran troops from Cucurpe had overtaken a band of raiding Chiricahuas and had killed two of his sons, probably including Cascos. He would make them pay.[7]

Consequently, in early May 1858, Mangas Coloradas led the Bedonkohes into Chokonen country via Stein's Peak, enlisted Cochise (whose wife Dos-teh-seh had lost two brothers) and many of his followers, and headed into Sonora. They again found it virtually defenseless, although prefects of several districts had in vain begged the governor for assistance. According to Sonoran reports, more than five hundred Apaches plundered the state "under the pretext of avenging the deaths of Mangas Coloradas's sons." This account suggests that Mangas had vowed to continue killing until he had exacted his revenge in Sonoran blood—in this case three hundred victims. Perhaps one could question the source of this anonymous statement, but it appears consistent with other manifestos uttered by Mangas and Cochise, especially regarding Sonora. Either an escaped Mexican captive or a Chiricahua captive was likely the source of this proclamation. In any event, Mangas's followers struck with impunity the districts of Moctezuma and Sahuaripa. On their return north, they symbolically raided the ranch of peace commissioner Rafael Corella before stealing almost every head of stock from Fronteras.[8]

By the first week of June, Mangas had returned to U.S. soil, where he apparently met an overland party at Stein's Peak. The Americans, members of Charles Poston's Santa Rita Mining Company, hailed from Cincinnati and were en route to the mining region of southern Arizona. Their group consisted of twelve Americans, well armed with Sharps rifles and revolvers. One man, Phocion Way, recorded his impressions in his diary. From El Paso they followed the primitive trail established by the San Antonio–San Diego Mail Company, also known as James Birch's "Jackass Mail," the forerunner to the Butterfield Overland Mail Company. While they were encamped at Soldier's Farewell, twelve miles west of Cooke's Canyon, three men came into camp to report to the Americans that seventy Apaches were at Stein's Peak, which Way's party would reach the next day. The confident Americans believed that their arsenal would overwhelm the Indians, because "very few of them have rifles and we would be a match for the whole 70." Way failed to mention whether he changed his mind after traveling through the narrow canyon, appropriately called Doubtful Canyon. It was such an ideal site for an ambush that in later years Cochise thought nothing of attacking U.S. troops in this canyon. But the Apaches had made peace with Americans, and Mangas Coloradas, lately returned from Sonora, rode out to meet the Americans.

Shortly after daybreak on June 9, 1858, Way's party "saw numbers of Indians coming down from the mountains. At first they looked like specks in the distance, but they approached very rapidly. Most of them were mounted on horseback. There were

Ruins of Stein's Peak Stage Station, New Mexico. (Courtesy Dan Thrapp)

probably between 60 and 100 in this vicinity—men, women and children—and they appeared to be all coming toward us." Immediately the leader of the Americans ordered his men to "hitch up and leave as soon as possible." Way's group started before the Apaches arrived, meeting many of them on the road. He furnished an excellent description of what was likely Mangas's local group:

> They were truly a wild and fierce looking race. The men were almost entirely naked and the women not much better. They looked very much disappointed when they found we were not going to stop. They grinned at us, spoke to us in Spanish as we passed (nearly all of them talk Spanish). . . . A number of them stood along side of the road and stared at us as we passed. The old chief came after our wagon on his horse with his long lance in his hand. He shook hands with some of our party and appeared to be very friendly. He told us where we could get water and rode along side of our wagon some distance. He only asked for a little sugar for his sick child. We gave him fine loaf sugar, and he bade us goodbye and turned back. He is a very old man and

was dressed some better than his people. He looked very important, and told us that he was a colonel. . . .[9]

The description of the "old chief," the location where the encounter took place, the size of the group, and the fact that Mangas was known to be in the vicinity all suggest that the Apache chief whom Way's party met was indeed the venerable Mangas Coloradas.

Once in Arizona, Mangas Coloradas realized that Cochise's Chokonens were encountering challenges similar to what he was experiencing in southern New Mexico.

In late 1856, American troops arrived in Arizona to replace Mexican troops from Tucson who had returned to Sonora. Veteran southwestern officer Major Enoch Steen had marched west from Fort Thorn on October 19, 1856, with four companies of the First Regiment of Dragoons, almost three hundred men and officers, as well as blacksmiths, carpenters, other civilians, and six months' supply of stores. Although he had orders to locate a post at Tucson, where the Mexican garrison had quartered, Steen had left New Mexico with a preconceived bias against establishing any fort there or at any other "town or Mexican village."[10] The son of a Kentucky backwoodsman, Steen had expressed these sentiments in years past. Not surprisingly, after visiting Tucson and inspecting these quarters, he immediately pronounced them "miserable" and unfit for human habitation. He promptly moved his command some sixty miles south to Calabasas, eight miles above the border. Naturally his autonomous decision incurred the wrath of every American living in Tucson, but this did not concern the unflappable officer. In fact, he was not much moved even when these citizens forwarded a petition to Colonel Garland at Santa Fe alleging that Steen selected his site based on "private interests." Actually, economics had prompted their complaint, for Steen's decision had denied employment and business opportunities to Americans living in Tucson. What was not appreciated sufficiently was the fact that his presence in southern Arizona had helped to stimulate the growth of ranching and mining in that area. It also led to an ephemeral period of better relations with Sonora, at least until an American band of filibusters, under Henry Crabb,[11] invaded northern Sonora, where Pesqueira's troops defeated and subsequently executed them.The following spring Steen agreed with Captain Ewell's recommendation to establish the post at the head of the Sonoita Valley, which would become known as Fort Buchanan.[12]

About the time that Major Steen had established Fort Buchanan, James E. Birch had won a contract to carry the mail between San Antonio and San Diego, with stops at El Paso, Tucson, and Yuma Crossing. The trail followed known waterholes through southern New Mexico and southern Arizona. The company completed some forty trips from July 1857 through September 1858 without problems from the Chiricahuas. The stations between Mesilla and Tucson were resting spots, as Birch's operation had not bothered building any stations. After Birch's death, his heirs transferred the contract to George Giddings and R. E. Doyle, but they, like Birch, also lacked the necessary capital. In the fall of 1858 the Butterfield Overland Mail Company replaced the San Antonio–San Diego Mail Company.[13]

In contrast, the Butterfield Company, armed with a contract valued at six hundred thousand dollars for four years, had sufficient resources to establish 141 stations over the twenty-eight-hundred-mile route between Saint Louis and San Francisco. The mail company usually placed these stations about twenty miles apart. By the end of 1859 it had added more stations, and now had some 200, including several in Chokonen and Chihenne country in southern Arizona and New Mexico. The mail company, which employed two thousand people at the peak of operations, instructed its employees to keep their distance from the Indians and to avoid trouble as much as possible. At the same time, it admonished them to be prepared for Indian attacks and treachery. Consequently, each stage station had a small arsenal of Sharps rifles and experienced men who knew how to use them. In September 1858, one year after the company received the contract, the Butterfield Overland Mail route was operational.[14]

One of the more dangerous sections along the route lay between Mesilla and Tucson in the heart of Cochise's and Mangas Coloradas's country. Nine stage stations threaded this isolated stretch, giving employment to one hundred men and costing about one hundred thousand dollars a year to operate. Giles Hawley provided competent direction. In Mangas's country, the mail company initially built five stations from the Arizona–New Mexico border to the Mimbres River. With water the primary consideration, Butterfield's personnel located stage stations at Stein's Peak, Soldier's Farewell, Ojo de Vaca (Cow Springs), the Mimbres River, and Cooke's Spring. In 1859 the company added Barney's Station between Stein's Peak and Soldier's Farewell. The stage employees would see their share of Apaches in the next few years. Like

Cochise, Mangas Coloradas wanted to maintain amicable relations with the Americans at each station. He knew that the military would punish any hostile act; besides, these rugged frontiersmen, living along the overland route, were not direct threats either to him or to his way of life.[15]

Meanwhile, Mangas Coloradas, after the foray into Sonora, had split from Cochise's Chokonens and had made his way back to the Mimbres River, where Steck and many Chihennes had planted crops. Most of the Bedonkohes accompanied him, which further convinced Steck that he could eventually unite the two bands on a common reservation, either at Santa Lucía or a few miles north along the Gila. Mangas did not stay long in his country, however, because Cochise had requested his help against the Sonorans. The Chokonens, concerned about the increase of whites in their country, and feeling that Americans might hold them responsible for the fight with Captain Ewell's detachment and the killing of two men at Apache Pass the previous year, had decided to move south to Fronteras and solicit peace. They chose to deal with a known commodity, the Sonorans, instead of opening relations with an unknown commodity, the Americans. They should have known better than to trust Sonorans—especially those at Fronteras, whom they had been systematically plundering for the past twenty-five years.

In early July 1858, Soledad, a Chokonen woman, showed up at Fronteras and requested peace for the entire band. The Chokonens had tried to make a treaty the previous fall, when the entire band of almost seven hundred had received rations. They had also sent emissaries during the spring of 1858, but the two longtime foes could not resolve their differences. On July 11, Soledad returned; in addition to the Chokonen chiefs Colchón, Chepillo, and Esquinaline, she had heard from Cochise, who indicated that he wanted to come in. Besides their very real fear of Americans, other apprehensions may have contributed to this decision. Governor Ignacio Pesqueira, having suppressed Gándara's forces, had issued a manifesto on May 14, 1858, naming the Apaches as public enemy number one and announcing his plans to "undertake a war desired by all Sonorans" against them. Cochise's people no longer had Janos to turn to, for they had been poisoned there the previous fall, and Captain Padilla had relocated the garrison to San Elizario. With Padilla gone, any future negotiations would be with José María Zuloaga, whom they distrusted. The small Apache party left the next day, promising to return within four days to consummate the agreement.

They fulfilled their promise and returned on July 14, 1858. As usual, there are the inevitable discrepancies between white and Indian accounts of the affair. According to their own accounts, Mexicans had no choice but to defend themselves when the Chiricahuas arrived, intoxicated and truculent, looking for trouble. This does not make any sense and seems to defy explanation, at least if one gives equal weight to the Apaches' version. They did not arrive drunk; instead, the Sonorans liberally furnished them with mescal and then turned their weapons on the unsuspecting Indians. At or near the presidio, the Sonorans killed some twenty-three men (including three leaders—Colchón, Lucas, and Carlos) and nine women. One man escaped on horseback, heading to the Apache camp at Cuchuta, south of Fronteras. A force from Fronteras followed and killed three more men and another woman near the camp. This Sonoran chicanery had inflicted a tremendous loss for one Chokonen local group, evidently the one formerly headed by Posito Moraga and Triqueño Tito. After the Sonorans' initial euphoria had subsided, the justice of the peace, Cayetano Escalante, realized that the Apaches would return "to avenge this and attack us in great numbers." Thus, he requested reinforcements.[16]

Ironically for the Sonorans, the premeditated massacre at Fronteras forced the Chokonens into the hands of Americans, the one thing knowledgeable Sonorans, including José María Elías González, had feared. After the slaughter, Cochise, who had moved his camp to a site near Fronteras and was waiting to hear about the peace treaty, returned to Arizona and sent runners to Mangas Coloradas and the Bedonkohes. Together they would avenge the massacre at Fronteras.

The war party began to come together in early September 1858, some six weeks after the catastrophe at Fronteras. Responding to Cochise's call, Mangas Coloradas had assembled three hundred Chiricahuas (seventy warriors) near the Burro Mountains. This group consisted primarily of Bedonkohes and included his two brothers, José Mangas and Phalios Palacio, among the leaders.[17] According to one report, a band of Chihennes also joined them. By September 10 they had moved west to Stein's Peak, where they met Cochise's Chokonens and made plans for their reprisal against Fronteras. This was a major war party, probably totaling 150 to 200 warriors, with vengeance on their mind. Sylvester Mowry reported that at Stein's Peak he met José Mangas, who boasted that the warriors were going to Fronteras "to wipe out the town." Mowry added that "all the men had collected at Stein's Peak when I passed."[18]

As previously mentioned, the Chiricahuas normally organized a war party to avenge deaths. Its objective and scope differed from those of a raiding party in one major element: the revenge factor, which meant that the Indians were out for blood. The objectives of a raiding party were both economic and political, with the stolen stock and plunder serving as a necessary part of their subsistence and giving the warrior many opportunities to enhance his prestige. A war party set out to punish a specific ranch, town, district, or state—normally those very parties that had prompted the organization of the war party. While a raiding party could include as few as five warriors and usually no more than twenty, the number in a war party could range from thirty or forty to two or three hundred.

By the evening of September 15 the Chiricahuas had safely reached the mountains east of Fronteras and were actively preparing for the attack that would take place next morning. They had chosen an opportune time for the assault. Of the seventy soldiers at Fronteras, only twenty remained at the post. The other troops had left on a patrol or had set out for Bacoachi for supplies. Of the twenty soldiers who remained, several served only as guards or sentries for the citizens working their crops. Once their prey had left the protection of the presidio and had begun tilling their crops, at 9:00 A.M. the Chiricahuas, generously estimated at three hundred by the commander at Fronteras, thundered down from the mountains and assaulted the Mexicans at the *cienega*. Yet their attack was poorly coordinated. All the Mexicans except one were able to flee to the security of the presidio; an older man, Sergeant Simón, was caught and killed by the Apaches. Mangas Coloradas and Cochise led the warriors and pursued the fleeing Mexicans up the slopes of the hill on which the presidio was located, attacking it from all sides. But the citizens and soldiers repulsed their furious assault, fighting "them off with rifles and spades and [firing] three cannon balls to disperse them."[19] Cochise and Mangas retired to the hills, content to wait for another opportunity to strike Fronteras. Their losses are unknown. The Indians, especially Cochise, respected the cannon perched on top of Fronteras's walls. With the element of surprise gone, finally they left the area and headed south to find another target.[20]

Yet Cochise remained in the general area of Sonora, looting and plundering. And a few weeks later an angry Mangas Coloradas returned to Stein's Peak with a band of seventy warriors. He had to curtail his incursion into Sonora to return to Santa Lucía, where he was to meet Agent Steck and James Collins, superintendent of Indian affairs for the Department of New Mexico. Near the stage station Mangas Coloradas stopped and "demanded of the conductor, an old Indian fighter," some corn. The man denied that he had any, which seemed to satisfy the chief. But one Indian, on a close inspection of the wagon, noticed several sacks of corn and reported to his chief. Mangas, perturbed at the conductor's dishonesty, walked over to him and in a paternalistic way placed his hand on the American's shoulder and snarled, "Want twelve sacas [*sic*] corn damn quick." Though his English was poor, the stage employee understood Mangas's stern demand and complied with his wishes. By early October the chief had returned to New Mexico, where, at Soldier's Farewell, stage passengers saw a large band of four hundred Apaches. This was undoubtedly Mangas's band on its way to Santa Lucía to meet Agent Steck and James Collins. Yet he had no plans to remain there for the winter.[21]

About mid-October, Mangas met the two agents of the Indian Department on the headwaters of the Gila, north of Santa Lucía, where they distributed annual annuities to the Bedonkohes, whom Steck estimated at 125 men and 500 women and children, and to the Chihennes, reduced to 70 men and 450 women and children.[22] Steck and Collins discussed with Mangas and the other chiefs their idea about setting aside a reservation at Santa Lucía. As early as the previous February, Collins, based on Steck's endorsement, had recommended to Commissioner of Indian Affairs Charles E. Mix that the government establish an agency near the Gila to accommodate the Chiricahua bands, the Mescaleros, and the White Mountain Coyoteros. In May 1858, Steck continued to believe that he could locate the Chiricahuas and Mescaleros "at any point that may be selected for them." Yet, he emphasized, the government must maintain its policy of liberal rations. Commissioner Mix, in Washington, concurred with Collins, informing him in July that the government would continue to feed the Apaches, but that the government wanted to make them a "self-sustaining population." To achieve this, he authorized Collins to issue agricultural tools and seed until they are "able to support themselves."[23]

Collins's support of Steck's policies must have been a great relief to the agent. His relationship with Meriwether had soured to the point that the governor had questioned or tried to nitpick everything he did. Collins and Steck thought much alike. They agreed that the government should develop a reservation at Santa

Lucía for several reasons: it would remove the Indians from the settlements on the Mimbres and Santa Rita del Cobre (where Steck had recently gone to break up a bootlegging operation that was trading whiskey to the Apaches);[24] the valleys offered excellent grazing; the nearby mountains afforded good timber; and fertile land existed along the river. To keep pernicious and opportunistic whites from meddling with the Apaches, Collins recommended that the military establish a post near the proposed reservation. Furthermore, he and Steck felt that the Apache chiefs seemed disposed to move there and begin planting. Mangas Coloradas convinced James Collins that he was anxious "to have the facilities afforded his people to settle as proposed and he assures me that whenever that was done his people would not only remain quiet themselves, but they would aid us in giving protection to the settlements from other less obedient bands."[25]

Before leaving, Steck told Mangas that he would return in the spring to help him plant. Meanwhile, Mangas took his portion of the annuity goods and returned west to Cochise's country near Apache Pass, where he planned to spend the winter. From there he could live in safety and make another incursion into Sonora, which might atone for the disappointing showing the previous September. A Bedonkohe warrior in his mid- to late thirties, a man who never needed any encouragement to raid Sonora, accompanied Mangas to Apache Pass. Known among his people as Goyahkla (He Who Yawns), he was called Geronimo by the Mexicans. According to Geronimo himself, by this date he had emerged as an influential man among the Bedonkohes. He had joined Mangas on many incursions into Sonora, at times sharing leadership with him. At this late date it is difficult of course to evaluate everything that Geronimo claimed in his autobiography. Still, even today we can verify that many incidents described by him did take place. His biographer, Angie Debo, in her critically acclaimed book *Geronimo: The Man, His Time, His Place,* accepts Geronimo's recollections while allowing that they contain some discrepancies. These inconsistencies, she points out, are to be expected when we remember that he recorded his story when he was past eighty years of age from the "memories of a long life remote from calendars and written records."[26]

About a week after Collins and Steck had distributed the annual annuities to the Chiricahuas, Mangas Coloradas with his immediate followers had returned to Apache Pass. One traveler mentioned that when he spoke to Mangas, the Apache chieftain admitted that he had come to spend the winter at Apache Pass. Clearly he was echoing what José Mangas had told Sylvester Mowry the previous month. José Mangas promised that his people would not attack the stagecoaches because he knew the authorities would dispatch troops to castigate his people. His brother José Mangas had also revealed to Mowry that the Apaches would protect the route that ran through their part of the country.[27]

Mangas was still at Apache Pass in mid-November when Mowry arrived there as a passenger on the stagecoach. Recently elected as delegate to Congress from Arizona, he would take the stage to Saint Louis and from there would book transportation to Washington. Mowry, who hated Apaches and regularly compared them to rattlesnakes, had an informative conversation with Mangas Coloradas at Apache Pass about November 17, 1858. He observed: "The name of their head chief is Mangas Coloradas. He is a man of large and powerful frame, and a disposition for any mischief. He stands in awe of Americans, but holds the Mexicans in extreme contempt. The former, he says, always carry their guns before them and loaded while the Mexicans have theirs slung at their backs and very often unloaded. The consequence of the chief's opinion is that his followers will attack Americans only when they can take them in ambush and without fear of loss to themselves."[28]

This last statement was clearly Mowry's opinion, and the available evidence does not support it. Mangas's followers for reasons other than fear abstained from depredations against Americans, although below the border Americans were fair game because the Indians did not always stop to determine the identity of their victims. In Arizona and New Mexico, however, the Chiricahuas, including Cochise, definitely desired peaceful relations with Americans.[29]

While Mangas was preparing for an expedition into Sonora, Agent Steck had decided to pay Cochise's Chokonens a visit. It would be his first visit to the Apaches who lived in Arizona. Collins had encouraged him to meet and try to make peace with these elusive bands, mainly to protect the stagecoaches and travelers along the Butterfield Overland Mail route. The station personnel at Apache Pass had likely sent word to Steck of Cochise's presence. The previous summer Steck had written James Collins about a band that lived in the Chiricahua and Peloncillo Mountains which he believed numbered 150 warriors and 600 women and children. As it turned out, his estimate was on target. He probably learned a great deal more about the Chokonens when

Sylvester Mowry, military officer and mining capitalist. He met Mangas
Coloradas at Apache Pass in late 1858. (Browne, *Adventures in the
Apache Country*)

he met Mangas Coloradas near Santa Lucía. Before coming, he wrote James Tevis,[30] station-keeper at Apache Pass, and asked him to notify the Chokonens that he would arrive with presents.[31]

About December 1, 1858, Mangas and Cochise with some one hundred Bedonkohes and Chokonens left on a raid against Sonora. Leaving only "the sick and disabled" warriors at Apache Pass with the women and children, they invaded Sonora from two points: Cochise entered near present-day Douglas and headed for the Sierra Madre; Mangas Coloradas, with Geronimo, crossed into Sonora from the Huachuca Mountains.[32]

They encountered unexpected and very tough resistance, for the previous fall Governor Pesqueira had reinforced Sonora's northern frontier because of rising tensions with Americans and to discourage Apache hostilities. During the fall of 1858, Lieutenant Colonel José Juan Elías had left Ures with additional troops and a piece of artillery bound for Fronteras. En route, he stopped at towns and ranches to receive contributions and volunteers. His march provided him with a vivid picture of the deplorable state of the frontier. He passed Chinapa, now deserted, and Bacaochi, which was almost a ghost town. He pledged that the government would provide security and protection to any hardy citizens who dared to settle at Chinapa; in addition, the prefect of Arispe promised seed, tools, and stock. When Elías finally reached Fronteras about November 10, 1858, he immediately appointed Captain Cayetano Escalante as commander of the national guard there. Escalante at once adopted plans to keep continual patrols in the field. On December 13, in the Otates Mountains southeast of the Teras Mountains and a few miles west of Bacerac, Escalante's command surprised a ranchería, killed eighteen Indians, sixteen being women and children, and captured four. The prisoners revealed to Escalante that they had just arrived in Sonora, apparently from New Mexico, on a campaign. Given that the Indians told Steck about this affair and that rumors had reached Bavispe that the Chiricahuas at Santa Rita del Cobre were planning to attack Fronteras, this might have been a Chihenne operation, perhaps even from Delgadito's camp, as he had occasionally made his winter headquarters in Sonora in the past. Likely Escalante had attacked the base camp while the warriors were out raiding.[33]

The details of Cochise's and Mangas Coloradas's activities in Sonora are not at all clear. We do know that Cochise's incursion was a brief one, for by the end of December he had returned to Apache Pass, where he met Agent Michael Steck for the first time.[34] Steck issued presents to the Chiricahuas, who included many of Mangas's women and children awaiting the return of their men from Sonora. Meanwhile, Mangas's war party had plundered ranches and attacked travelers near Cocospera and Bacanuche, secreting their stolen stock in their mountain ranchería. By early February, after a two-months absence, his small bands of raiders began to drift back to Arizona. Sonorans trailed one party into the Dragoon Mountains but could not overtake them. Another patrol did surprise Apaches near Cuchuverachi, a few miles southeast of present-day Douglas, Arizona, and killed one Indian and captured a child, thirty-one mules, fourteen horses, and twenty-six cattle.[35] This apparently was not Mangas's group, for when he arrived at Apache Pass about February 18, 1859, he brought with him many mules, horses, and other booty.[36] He did not remain with the Cho-konens for long. Within days he gathered his people and returned to New Mexico to keep his appointment to plant with Steck.

In March, Steck arrived at Santa Lucía to begin planting. It would be the dawn of a new era for Mangas, who, pushing seventy years of age, now seemed content and prepared to spend the rest of his days learning to farm and live in peace. The next year and a half would be a tranquil period of his life as the once fierce war chief settled into a more sedentary life-style, planting corn and other vegetables and seemingly enjoying the new change of pace. On June 15, Steck wrote Collins that our "farming operations have been successful." The enlightened agent, undoubtedly pointing out to the headmen that farming might ensure the survival of their race, had convinced every Bedonkohe and Chihenne leader to plant. Steck gave personal attention to Mangas, who made an astonishing concession to the ways of the white men. The chief asked the agent to build him a house, a sure sign that he under-stood that his days of wandering were ending.[37]

About this time Colonel Bonneville had embarked on an inspection tour of the Department of New Mexico, which included Fort Buchanan and Tucson. With Fort Thorn's abandonment the previous February, Bonneville decided to search for an alternate site on which to locate a post in Apachería, with the Burro Moun-tains, Santa Lucía, Santa Rita del Cobre, and the Mimbres River under consideration. Steck wrote Bonneville, hoping to meet him in mid-May at the Mimbres River. Following Steck's wishes, Bonneville journeyed to the Mimbres and met the agent on May 14, 1859. They had a long conference about Apache and military affairs as well as the influx of new settlers and miners on the

Mimbres and at Santa Rita del Cobre, respectively, and the potential site for the location of the next military post in Mangas's country. Bonneville remarked:

> In my two interviews with Doctor Steck, agent for the Apaches, he informed me that he had assembled the Indians on the Gila, near the old depot of the Gila expedition, was living alone among them, and instructing them how to plant. That from their exertions and industry he had much to hope, and that although there might be some few rogues amongst them, the mass of them were desirous of being at peace, so much so that they would not allow him to travel about for hunting or other purposes without sending two of their people with him for fear some accident might happen and suspicion be thrown upon them. . . .
>
> [Steck also stated] that the Copper Mines [were] being worked and employed one hundred and eighty men and the proprietors were desirous of working four hundred. That the laborers etc. were chiefly Mexicans from Chihuahua and were viewed by the Indians as enemies of old standing, and that already one Indian had been killed, and a Mexican by way of retaliation. He urged me to send an officer and twenty men to the mines to prevent further difficulties, which I did at once from Fort Fillmore. The valley of the Mimbres is beginning to be settled and we together believed that a post located southeast of the Burro Mountains eight or ten miles north of the Overland Mail station, . . . overlooking the valley would have a moral influence over the surrounding Indians, and would also cover the country laid open by the abandonment of Fort Thorn. . . .
>
> Agreeing with the Doctor, I immediately ordered Company "C" Rifles commanded by Lieut. Howland, together with one hundred men under Major Gordon, to locate the company at that point. I gave directions after performing this duty that Major Gordon and the hundred men should show his command to the Indians on the Gila and at the copper mines and then return to his station.[38]

Although neither man realized it at the time, Steck's casual statements regarding the settlement along the Mimbres and the difficulties at Santa Rita del Cobre proved to be a foreshadowing of things to come.

Following Bonneville's orders, Captain William Hamilton Gordon left Fort Fillmore on June 27, 1859, with some 130 men— 48 dragoons, 52 infantry, and about 30 Mounted Rifles. Before departing, he had complied with Bonneville's orders and had sent a lieutenant and twenty-one men to Santa Rita del Cobre. After scouting the valley of the Gila, on July 10 Gordon's command, guided by Philippe Gonzales, a leading scout, reached "Ojo de Lucero," a spring about twelve to thirteen miles south of present-day Tyrone. There he decided to establish a "permanent encampment" because of the availability of wood, water, and grass. By this time Steck had come into camp with Mangas Coloradas. Leaving Lieutenant Howland at Lucero Springs with his infantry and Mounted Rifles, Captain Gordon took fifty men, along with Philippe, Steck, and Mangas Coloradas, and marched to Santa Lucía, where Steck had gathered some four hundred Bedonkohes and Chihennes. The next morning (July 13), Steck and Mangas proudly showed off their cornfields and crops, which "extended some three miles in length and are in fine condition." The Indians' accomplishments impressed Gordon, who knew many of the Apaches because of his stint at Fort Thorn. He soothingly pointed out that "the Indians were peaceably disposed . . . were glad to see us, visited our camp, and all went on well." Mangas went one step further and personally gave the officer a tour of "his fields, and said this was his home, and he could be found here at any future time, and that he wanted peace."[39]

On July 17, 1859, leaving Lieutenant Howland at "his permanent encampment," Captain Gordon left for Santa Rita del Cobre and the Mimbres River. The troops must have allayed tensions between the Chihennes and the Mexicans at Santa Rita del Cobre, for Gordon withdrew the escort and took them back to Fort Fillmore. In an ominous note, the captain reported that he found Americans at the Mimbres River "who wanted to get my command into difficulties with the Indians whom I knew to be entirely well-disposed."[40]

Gordon's comments reveal the challenges that army officers faced during these changing times. Local citizens and the partisan press frequently criticized the army for inactivity and incompetency. Today it not only has become fashionable but also politically correct to denounce the army for exhibiting a lack of understanding and compassion for the Indians whom they were charged with either controlling or subjugating. Of course neither generalization is correct. Nothing was all black or all white; there were always shades of gray. Ironically, in southern New Mexico, Mangas Coloradas's people probably trusted the military far more than they did the civilians and miners who had swallowed up their territory. These newcomers had only contempt for the people whom they were displacing. Likewise, those farmers and ranchers who settled along the Mimbres were occupying land that for centuries had been the hunting, camping, and, more recently, planting grounds for the Chihenne band, which had declined in numbers at an alarming rate during the 1850s. Although many of these outsiders were honest and hard-working men, this influx, especially at Santa Rita del Cobre, attracted the rogue element that was endemic to a virgin and sometimes lawless frontier. Traders, bootleggers, gamblers, thieves, and murderers came to Mangas's country. Just as ominously, many of these interlopers were Mexicans, for whom the Apaches had only contempt and hatred. Thus, the American and Mexican presence, especially along the Mimbres River and at Santa Rita del Cobre, distressed the Indians, who were no longer powerful enough to intimidate or forcibly evict the interlopers.

That did not prevent them from trying, however. The previous spring a large party of Chihennes had appeared at the mines and had ordered the Mexicans to leave.[41] Shortly after, a detachment under First Lieutenant John Porter Hatch from Fort Craig happened to be in the area, scouting for a possible wagon route. His fortunate arrival temporarily allayed tensions between the Indians and the proprietors at Santa Rita del Cobre. Likely at the request of Leonardo Siquieros, Hatch held a powwow with the "principal chiefs" of the Chihennes. He concluded that "they appear friendly and promised not to disturb the miners."[42] This minor emergency, if that is what it was, dissipated. But the presence of the miners at Santa Rita del Cobre would prove a most unpredictable arrangement at best. Soon after (though details are sparse), a Mexican killed an Apache there. It was only a matter of time before the Chihennes would avenge this act.

In truth, Mangas Coloradas seemed to distance himself from much of the controversy at Santa Rita del Cobre and along the Mimbres River. At least two Chihenne local groups had traditionally lived in these territories. Mangas had gravitated more and more to his own people, the Bedonkohes, since returning from Cochise's country. During July and August of 1859 he visited Lieutenant Howland's camp near the Burro Mountains. Howland recommended this location as a suitable site for a military post and suggested that he could commence building quarters. He had gained much knowledge of the Apaches and of their "camping grounds." The Bedonkohes visited his camp daily and seemed gratified that the government cared about their welfare. Unfortunately, relations between Howland's command and Mangas's

people came to an abrupt halt. On September 19, Colonel Bonneville ordered that the temporary post be abandoned and the men
return to Fort Fillmore.[43]

Steck understood clearly the inevitability of conflict between
the Chihennes and the new settlers along the Mimbres and the
miners at Santa Rita del Cobre. In his annual report, dated August
1859, he reiterated his solution to the problem—the Santa Lucía
reservation. Steck believed that the Chihennes and Bedonkohes
"never will recover from the shock" of Bonneville's campaign that
had compelled them to move south into Mexico, where many had
perished from malaria. (Surprisingly he did not refer to the food
poisoning at Janos.) He reported that disease and sickness had
reduced these two bands from 400 to 150 families, though this
observation seems exaggerated. He again proposed just as he had in
his last two annual reports that the government set aside a reservation at Santa Lucía for the Chiricahuas. The valley could easily
hold the Chihennes, Bedonkohes and Cochise's Chokonens, "the
most warlike band," from the Chiricahua Mountains. Furthermore, if the government wanted to remove the Mescaleros east of
the Rio Grande, they could be placed there, although the Chiricahua bands and the Mescaleros had no desire to live in close prox-
imity to one another. He concluded by praising Colonel Bonneville
for his support and cooperation and by recommending that the War
Department establish a permanent post at Lucero Springs.[44]

That fall of 1859, Steck set out from the Rio Grande to visit the
Chiricahua bands. On October 29, 1859, he rationed eight hundred
Chihennes and Bedonkohes at the Burro Mountains. Steck found
the Indians content, and "nothing occurred to give rise to a suspicion that anything but the best of feelings prevailed." Afterwards,
the agent continued west to San Simón, where he gave food and
presents to Cochise and his Chokonens, who were "friendly and
grateful." Learning more about this band, he became convinced
that he could consolidate them with Mangas Coloradas at Santa
Lucía.[45]

This contentment did not last for long. The Bedonkohes, living
near Santa Lucía, were unaffected by the encroaching whites along
the Mimbres and at Santa Rita del Cobre. That soon changed, however, for the fates of the two bands were intermingled, primarily
because of their decreasing population and the fact that both bands
still looked to Mangas Coloradas for direction in times of crisis.

Despite these foreboding times, Steck made plans to leave his
agency. Before doing so, he rationed the two bands at Santa Rita del

Cobre at the end of January 1860 and again in February. He had requested from Collins a two-months leave of absence to visit friends and to attend to pressing personal business. Collins was unenthusiastic, but when Steck assured him that he had capable men who could handle the agency's affairs in his absence, the superintendent acquiesced.[46] The agent had originally scheduled his departure for February 20, but New Mexico's new military commander, Colonel Thomas T. Fauntleroy, had asked him to query the Apaches about acting as guides in a campaign the colonel planned to send from the Gila country against the Navajos. On February 26, Steck met the "Apache chiefs near the Copper-mines." They claimed much knowledge of Navajo country and "were not only willing but anxious to accompany the troops." Because Mangas Coloradas had traditionally held close ties to the Navajos, Steck likely was referring to the Chihennes and perhaps to a few of the younger Bedonkohe chiefs. In any event, the military did not call into play their services.[47]

On March 10, 1860, Steck wrote Collins about the conditions of the Apaches under his care. The Indians living near Santa Rita del Cobre were "behaving well as usual," but the Americans' insatiable appetite for their land, which contained gold, silver, and copper, distressed them. The whites were grabbing the best country along the Mimbres and driving off their game. Furthermore, many new-comers near Santa Rita del Cobre were "irresponsible" Americans who were itching for trouble. This ongoing illicit traffic between Apaches and whites, specifically the whiskey peddlers, greatly concerned and distressed Steck. The combination of the Americans' invasion and the two-months absence of their competent agent disturbed both Collins and the Apaches. The departure of Steck would lead to precarious relations, an unpredictable arrangement at best, with all the ingredients for a calamity present.[48]

A week later the agent sent Estavan Ochoa, a Mesilla resident and later a noted southwestern merchant, to assist Mangas Coloradas and any other Apaches who wanted to plant at Santa Lucía. Steck thought highly of Ochoa, describing him on March 20, 1860, as "a responsible man [who is] well acquainted with Indians and I have confidence in his doing as well as though I were myself present." He also mentioned that a band of Apaches had just killed a man and stolen some stock near Mesilla. The Mesilla Guard had pursued them to the Florida Mountains and then south toward Lake Guzmán, in Chihuahua, where they found a large Nednhi camp but turned back in the face of overwhelming odds,

As for Steck, finally, on March 22, he boarded the eastbound stage for Saint Louis and headed home.[49]

After several weeks at home in Pennsylvania, Steck traveled to Washington to meet the commissioner of Indian affairs, Alfred Burton Greenwood. James Collins had written Greenwood a laudatory letter of introduction for Steck, who, he believed, "understands thoroughly everything" about Indian affairs in New Mexico. On May 11, 1860, Steck and Greenwood conferred and agreed upon a fifteen-square-mile reservation for three of the four Chiricahua bands (the Nednhis having remained in Mexico), with Santa Lucía its headquarters. Steck estimated the three Chiricahua bands at three hundred men and eighteen hundred women and children. The reservation would "include a rich and fertile valley watered by the Gila River [and was] large enough to accommodate" the Chokonens, Chihennes, and Bedonkohes. Steck, elated over this happy outcome, set out on his journey to New Mexico.[50]

At that same moment, in southern New Mexico, still another episode occurred which affected the drama. It was the beginning of a chain of events that culminated in Mangas's taking up arms against Americans, although he could hardly have realized it then. The Chihennes had probably thought that matters between them and the encroaching whites could not have gotten much worse. Unfortunately for Mangas's people, American prospectors struck gold in the mountains northwest of Santa Rita del Cobre. This discovery, at a place to become known as Pinos Altos, soon inspired a minor gold rush as a new horde of Americans and Mexicans swarmed into Chihenne country. Life would never again be the same for Mangas Coloradas or the Chihennes.[51]

Mangas apparently tried to keep his people away from the Americans and Mexicans in the Mimbres country. It was probably about February or early March of 1860 that he happened to be camped near Ojo de Vaca, or Cow Springs, a stop on the Butterfield Mail Route, where he met Henry (Hank) Smith, who was driving a herd of cattle across southern New Mexico toward the Rio Grande. Smith's chronology is confusing and ambiguous; this encounter could have occurred during the previous fall of 1859, but the winter of 1860 seems more probable. No matter when, the incident testifies to Mangas's characteristically friendly attitude toward Americans.

With an American named Jack Pennington and eleven Mexicans, Hank Smith left Fort Buchanan in southern Arizona with twelve hundred head of cattle bound for Fort Bliss, at El Paso,

Texas. Driving the herd east, Smith ingeniously decided to hire Apaches as herders, compensating them with a few head of cattle, to ensure that he would get the cattle to their destination. After employing this strategy successfully at Apache Pass, Smith opted to try it again as he approached Cow Springs, for he found a band of Apaches under Mangas Coloradas camped near the spring, which was about thirty feet square. Mangas agreed to assign a few of his young men the responsibility of driving the herd to the next water, at Warm Springs, located about twenty miles to the northeast on the way to the Mimbres station and about ten or twelve miles southeast of present-day Hurley. That night Mangas Coloradas slept near Smith, who shrewdly gave a blanket to Mangas's wife and hired ten Indians at a dollar each to serve as night sentries for the herd. The next day the Apaches helped Smith drive the herd to Warm Springs, where he found good water and grass and decided to lie over and rest for a few days. This pleased the Apaches. The next few days "were spent feasting, resting, and running foot races."[52]

The Chiricahuas enjoyed foot races during their leisure time in camp. Undoubtedly the physical aspect of the contest and the gambling associated with it aroused much excitement for this competition. Usually the course was about one hundred yards long, but in some cases they laid out a cross-country course for longer distances.[53] Hank Smith won several buckskins by racing against the Indians. The only disturbance occurred when Smith's "Indian boss herder" defeated a young chief named Kajo,[54] who became agitated after the Indian women made fun of him for losing to an older man. Violence threatened to erupt, but Smith and Mangas "stopped the fuss" and restored harmony.[55]

According to Smith, after delivering the herd he joined a party of eleven Americans and three Mexicans who were embarking on a prospecting expedition into the Pinos Altos Mountains to find an old mine. Traveling up the Mimbres, Smith's party found the "placer," but after prospecting for three weeks they decided to leave, for it "was worked out." They next moved into the Pinos Altos Mountains, where on May 18, 1860, three of the party—a veteran prospector named Jacob Snively and two men named Hicks and Birch—made the first strike of gold, The miners originally called the site Birchville, but soon after renamed it Pinos Altos for the tall ponderosa pines that adorned the country. Within days news of the discovery had spread like wildfire, and a boomtown developed almost overnight as gold-crazy men swarmed in from California, Texas, Arizona, and Mexico.

Hank Smith, an early settler of Pinos Altos. He met Mangas Coloradas in both peace and war. (Courtesy Crosby County Pioneer Memorial Library)

On June 11 the rosy reports of gold had reduced the personnel at some stage stations to but one man. During June one traveler came across over two hundred people between the Mimbres River and Mesilla, all "anxious to get there [Pinos Altos] first." On June 24, 1860, a little over one month later, one observer wrote: "All wild with the gold fever—everything that can leave has gone out. The Overland stages have lost many of their men." A report from the Mimbres River corroborated this seemingly extravagant account: "All the Overland Mail Company employees have left to go to the mines." Within one month, according to Hank Smith, some five hundred miners had arrived at Pinos Altos.[56]

While this was happening, Mangas Coloradas and many of his followers were at Santa Lucía, where Ochoa had helped them to plant their crops. It is unclear whether the Chihennes, whose territory had been wrung out by the settlements at Santa Rita del Cobre, the Mimbres River, and now Pinos Altos, had joined their Bedonkohe relatives to plant there. At any rate, it would appear that the smoldering tensions that existed before Steck's trip to Washington had finally erupted. The Chihennes, frustrated and hungry and their patience exhausted, decided to take action against the settlement along the Mimbres, sometimes called Mowry City after Arizona's enthusiastic public relations man of the late 1850s, Sylvester Mowry. In retrospect, who could have blamed them? As for Mangas, it does not appear that he had any direct role in the events that followed along the Mimbres River.

Some raiding had begun in southern New Mexico as early as January 1860, though no one knows for sure whether the Mescaleros or Chiricahuas were responsible. On January 31 a correspondent from Mesilla informed the readers of the *Missouri Republican* that the Apaches had committed "depredations against settlers" near the Mimbres settlement, but he neglected to provide specifics. Likely the Apaches had warned the settlers to leave the country, and such a threat would seem sufficient cause to claim "Indian raids." Moreover, many miners at Santa Rita del Cobre and a few settlers from the Mimbres had sent their families to the Rio Grande for protection, a sure sign that hostilities were imminent. At Amoles, fifteen miles from Mesilla, the Indians had killed four Mexicans and stolen some stock; the correspondent could not identify which Apaches had committed these killings. The Mescaleros are better candidates than the Chihennes, although we cannot discount the Nednhis from Mexico.[57]

In March 1860, Nednhis raided near Mesilla, killing three Americans and stealing a large quantity of stock. Thirty men of the Mesilla Guard mounted a hot pursuit, following the trail west to the Florida Mountains and then due south into Chihuahua and Lake Guzmán. There they found a large Chiricahua village of 380 Indians, about the strength of the Janeros and Carrizaleño local groups of Nednhis, who had remained in northern Chihuahua since early 1857, when Láceres made peace at Janos. Because the Indians were "well armed and far exceeded the Mesilla party in numbers, they returned to Mesilla for reinforcements." They could not secure any, however, because Colonel Fauntleroy had ordered many of Fillmore's troops north on a campaign against the Navajos.[58] It was a prudent decision, for these Apaches consisted of more than just the kind of unarmed women and children whom the Mesilla Guard had slaughtered at Doña Ana and Fort Thorn. Among these Indians was probably the Nednhi chief Juh,[59] the daredevil Chiricahua leader who despised Americans as much, if not more, than he did Mexicans. Ranking with Cochise in fighting ability, he had the reputation as one of the boldest and most warlike Chiricahua leaders of the second half of the nineteenth century.

In mid-April Apaches pilfered six mules from an unidentified stage station near Mesilla, and on April 13 they stole twenty head of stock near La Mesa, about fifteen miles south of Mesilla.[60] The Chihennes apparently got into the act in late April, stealing some stock because they were hungry. They also hoped their actions would frighten the whites living along the Mimbres and encourage them to leave. They had complained to Steck that Americans had taken the choicest parts of their country and had driven out their game. If the government permitted this to continue, they would have "no country left."[61]

From the settlements on the Mimbres, Sherod Hunter, a Tennessee merchant who had come west in 1857 after the death of his wife and child, wrote a letter requesting aid from Lewis S. Owings, recently voted governor of the "Provisional Government of Arizona" by thirty prominent delegates from Arizona and southern New Mexico at Tucson. Owings, who had come to Mesilla in 1858 from Texas, had already enjoyed a colorful career. At the age of sixteen he reportedly had fought in the decisive Battle of San Jacinto, in which Sam Houston's army had captured Mexico's dictator Santa Anna, and later he had become a prominent San Antonio merchant and politician.[62] On May 6, 1860, Hunter informed Owings that within the past few days the Apaches, undoubtedly Chihennes, "have committed a number of thefts . . . from three different farms." Echoing the pleas usually heard from isolated Sonoran villages, Hunter stated that farmers were unable to work their crops and insisted that if Owings could not provide assistance, the ranchers would have to abandon their farms. He suggested that a militia company of well-armed and well-mounted men "could in a short time . . . scour their mountain haunts and [effectively] drive them out."[63] Owings endorsed Hunter's urgent appeal, describing the Mimbres settlement as one "of vast importance" to the development of southern New Mexico. But the commanding officer at Fort Fillmore had to refuse Owings's request, as most of his garrison had been moved north for the Navajo campaign. Ironically, the Chihennes shared Owings's concerns about the Mimbres settlement, but obviously for different reasons.[64]

A few weeks later a war party returned in force. It is difficult to conceive of a Chiricahua war party in Chihenne country that did not contain Mangas Coloradas, or even the traditionally more bellicose Bedonkohes with their Chokonen allies, but this one might have been strictly a Chihenne affair, with perhaps some Nednhis from Mexico. On May 20, 1860, Apaches attacked near Santa Rita del Cobre a Mexican mule train of twenty-four mules loaded with sugar. They killed five Mexicans and took all the mules. Less than a week later they returned to the Mimbres and assaulted another party and stole nine mules, which prompted the men to send the women and children to the Rio Grande. It was good they did, for on the morning of May 29, 1860, soon after the thirty Mexican and American ranchers rose to tend their crops, a large band of Apaches (generously estimated by Hunter at four hundred), well armed with rifles and revolvers, some mounted and some on foot, made good on their threats and swarmed out like angry hornets to do battle with the ranchers. If the report is accurate, the fight was a classic, full of heroism on both sides. Before the ranchers could repel the Indians' assault, the Apaches had succeeded in killing six Americans and five Mexicans and had wounded another eight, some seriously. Hunter believed that his men had killed or wounded between twenty and thirty Indians. After the battle he sent a man for help, and although the Apaches hit the messenger with two arrows, he made his way to the stage station at Cooke's Canyon, from where a man rode into Mesilla with the news. Owings requested help from Fort Fillmore, but Lieutenent Lazelle had no mounts and but ten men available for

duty. Thus, he could furnish no reinforcements. Consequently
Samuel S. Jones, a former proslavery sheriff from Kansas, had to
lead a group of fifteen men, "all who could procure horses," to
relieve the settlement. The settlement apparently survived unti
1861, for that summer, on August 13, the census taker reported
fifty persons living there, including twenty-four males over the age
of sixteen.[65]

With this turmoil in southern New Mexico, the Chihennes
evidently disappeared after the fight on the Mimbres. Some, under
their once powerful chief Delgadito, bolted south to northern
Mexico and joined their Chokonen and Nednhi relatives who had
solicited peace at Janos and Corralitos. Ever the opportunist,
Zuloaga gloated to Governor Pesqueira in Sonora about Mexico's
good fortune in drawing the Chiricahuas away from American
influence. He predicted that the armistice might attract fifteen
hundred Chiricahuas.[66] Later that summer, Chokonen chief
Esquinaline sent a woman into Fronteras to open negotiations. She
readily admitted that she represented several headmen living near
Janos, including the Chokonen Parte and the Chihenne Delgadito.
They had left the United States, she explained, because they no
longer wished to live among the Americans. Other Chiricahuas,
including Cochise himself, the powerful war chief of the Chokonens, had also become disillusioned with American treatment.[67]
Surprisingly, we hear nothing of Mangas Coloradas during this
time. Although many of his old allies, including Delgadito,
Esquinaline, and Cochise, had turned their attention to Mexico, he
apparently had remained at Santa Lucía. We do know that there in
August 1860 he renewed his friendship with Agent Michael Steck,
just in from Washington, D.C., to establish the Chiricahua reservation at Santa Lucía.

Steck would find storm clouds on the horizon. The presence of
American miners, who had trespassed into Mangas's country with
no regard for the rights of the Indians, and the events that
subsequently occurred between Cochise and American troops at
Apache Pass made war inevitable. Once again the Chihennes and
Bedonkohes would look to Mangas for leadership. Allied with the
Chokonens, for the first time in the past quarter-century he would
share with his son-in-law Cochise the mantle of tribal leadership.
Ultimately, of course, all would pass to the younger man, the most
celebrated of all Apache fighting men, whose perception of
Americans would be molded by these conflicts.

Chapter 16

MANGAS COLORADAS DECLARES WAR ON AMERICANS

IN August 1860 the last thing Mangas Coloradas had on his mind was going to war with Americans. Not that relations had gotten any better, however. The American presence in his country had proven to be a major source of problems—especially since the strike at Pinos Altos a few months before. This major intrusion into the heart of Mangas's country not only destroyed the Apache land but also psychologically devastated the Indians. The miners carved up the earth, cut down trees, and drove out game to build a makeshift town that seemed to sprout up overnight. Of course this insidious invasion appalled the Indians, for they had never seen such an influx of Americans in their country. Furthermore, these newcomers were rugged frontiersmen, usually well armed, and openly contemptuous of Apaches. According to Chiricahua oral history, Mangas occasionally went into Pinos Altos, alone or with a few of his people, to trade or perhaps to affirm his desire for peace.[1] If so, this befitted his character and personality—he had never been afraid to talk peace, especially to Americans, whom he had come to respect.

Yet a profound sense of despair must have gripped the once powerful bands of Chihennes and Bedonkohes. Just a decade before, they would have intimidated these interlopers into leaving, or evicted by force this intrusion. But the Americans shocked the Apaches, responding to the discovery of gold by arriving in numbers that simply overwhelmed the Indians, who had never seen such a wave of people coming into their country with intentions of remaining. With the memory of Bonneville's campaign fresh in their minds and the overwhelming crowd of miners in

their country, some Chihennes, including most notably Mangas
Coloradas's onetime fighting ally Delgadito, resolved to forsake
their lands for Mexico. There Delgadito found that many
Chokonens, who had left Arizona because they were apprehensive
about the American presence in their territory, had resumed relations below the border. Others, including Victorio, sought refuge in
the mountains along the border with Chihuahua in such regions as
Tres Hermanas, Alamo Hueco, and other ranges in which they felt
they would be safe from Americans. Yet Mangas, with many
Chihennes and Bedonkohes, remained in the area, awaiting the
return of Agent Michael Steck from Washington and praying to
Yusen, their god, that the whites would somehow vanish from
their country.[2]

This unchecked encroachment into Chihenne territory must
have astonished Steck when he returned to southern New Mexico
from Washington, D.C., that summer. He at once began working
to realize his dream of establishing an agency for the Chiricahua
bands. On August 12, 1860, he informed Captain Ewell at Fort
Buchanan of his plans to lay out the Santa Lucía Reservation.
Until he could officially establish the reservation, he would need
help, and he therefore requested an escort from Ewell, perhaps
believing that it would be difficult to remove the Chokonens from
Apache Pass to Santa Lucía. He would definitely have needed aid,
for there is no record of Cochise's ever consenting to move to Santa
Lucía, which was extremely distant from his Chokonen territory.
Ewell, known affectionately as Old Baldy by his men, heartily
endorsed Steck's proposal, though he recognized that the government must feed the Indians until they raised their first crop. In
closing his letter, Ewell flung a parting admonition to Steck.

He warned the agent that the Southwest had several correspondents writing to newspapers, particularly in Saint Louis and San
Francisco, who habitually censored government officials, not
excepting army officers and Indian agents, for their coddling of
Apaches. Just a few weeks before, several letters had appeared that
had denounced Ewell for using diplomacy to recover stolen stock
from Cochise's Chokonens at Apache Pass. These "amateurs," as
Ewell liked to refer to them, believed he should have attacked the
Indians once he learned of their guilt, even though he would have
violated a flag of truce. Instead, by employing peaceful means the
captain incurred the wrath of these correspondents, who believed
that the government's policies were too lenient and benevolent.
Captain Ewell, always touchy to criticism, warned Steck that "you

must be prepared to hear the dogs howl when you make the presents as there are several here who are paid by the newspapers for their howls." He assured the agent that he would join him whenever Steck called.[3]

Meanwhile, in late August or early September, Steck journeyed to Santa Lucía to begin laying out the reservation. It would be fifteen miles square, with Santa Lucía its southeastern boundary. Immediately he ran into difficulties. Upon hearing of Steck's mission, a group of indignant miners from Pinos Altos, including two of the men who had discovered gold there, met the agent near Santa Lucía with a petition to remove the agency even before he had officially established it. Their actions left Steck incredulous; their impudence and brass revealed that their greed knew no bounds. As far as they were concerned, they had every right but the Apaches had none. Their perceptions of Indians typified the extreme positions held by a core of Americans who believed that genocide or imprisonment was the only solution to the American Indian problem. The petition, specious and untrue, showed that they were greedy bigots who wanted to swallow up the rest of the Chihenne and Bedonkohe land. After all, they must have reasoned, what if this proposed reservation contained valuable minerals? Would those not go to waste in the domain of the barbaric Apaches?[4]

The miners' audacity incensed Steck. Upon returning to the agency in early October, he fired off a letter to Collins refuting their claims. The sensible agent systematically dismantled their assertions. He pointed out to Collins that these individuals claimed to have "taken possession of these lands" in August 1860 but had "not made any improvements." Steck noted that the federal commissioner of Indian affairs had instructed him to survey the reservation the previous May, thus predating the miners' complaints by at least three months. Besides, he succinctly stated, this "is the only place now left in their country they occupy that is not already in the possession of the white man." Collins requested instructions from his superior, Commissioner of Indian Affairs Alfred B. Greenwood, and on January 5, 1861, Greenwood recommended that Steck take legal action to "remove the intruders."[5]

Unfortunately, by the time Greenwood's response arrived, his solution was immaterial. In October, Steck, perhaps disgusted with affairs, decided to become a candidate for Arizona's delegate to Congress to replace Sylvester Mowry, who had recently resigned. What prompted the agent's decision to enter politics is unclear. Maybe he had grown weary of the lonely and unrewarding life in

Site of Santa Lucía Reservation, New Mexico, as seen when looking
northeast from Buckhorn, with the Mogollon Mountains in the distance.
This valley would have been part of Steck's Santa Lucía Reservation.
(Photo by Kathi Plauster)

New Mexico as Indian agent, maybe his visit east had left him
with a desire to return there, or maybe he could sense that
hostilities were imminent and that his conception of a reservation
at Santa Lucía would never become a reality. In fact, one report in
October stated that Apaches had run off some of his mules near
Santa Lucía.[6] In today's terms, Steck may have been a victim of job
burnout.

On November 4, 1860, Steck rationed the Chihennes and
Bedonkohes at Santa Lucía, and while there he promised to meet
them again in early December on the Mimbres River. He went on
to the Chokonens, probably at San Simón or Apache Pass, on
November 10. While he was absent, voters elected him delegate to
Congress by a wide margin. Consequently, when he returned to
Mesilla, he informed Collins that he intended "to leave as soon as
possible" for Washington. In his place he planned to enlist the ser-
vices of a "responsible man," either Ammon Barnes or Pinckney R.
Tully.[7]

Steck's announcement troubled James Collins, who seemed
clairvoyant on December 2, 1860, when he wrote his subordinate

of his concerns that in the agent's absence the miners "will cause trouble" with the Indians. He expected the agent to "take responsibility in regards to [his] agency" before he left for Washington.[8] By the time Steck received this letter, however, the die was cast. A group of miners at Pinos Altos, under Cochise's former adversary James Tevis, launched an unprovoked attack against the Chihennes living along the Mimbres, who had gathered there to meet Steck. Steck, however, for some unexplained reason, had failed to keep the appointment or to send a representative in his place. The Apaches, including Mangas Coloradas, blamed him for the tragedy that followed. To be fair to Steck, we should note that while his presence may have prevented this unfortunate affair, which contributed to the outbreak in hostilities, in time surely such an incident was inevitable.

At daybreak on a crisp Tuesday morning, December 4, 1860, a group of some thirty well-armed miners, most of them frontiersmen from Texas, anxiously straddled their horses, awaiting James Tevis's order to charge the Indian camp. The ranchería, located on the west bank of the Mimbres near the site of the second Fort Webster, was a Chihenne camp of Elías and Chabnocito, leaders of the local group formerly headed by Cuchillo Negro. Tevis claimed that his party had followed the trail of Indians who had killed a mule near Pinos Altos; other accounts say that these Apaches had been raiding stock. It was possible that they had pilfered some stock, but the actual extent of their raids has never been clear. In any event, once Tevis found the camp, he gave orders for his men to charge the unsuspecting ranchería at first light. Screaming Texas war whoops, Tevis and his followers struck the sleepy village; fortunately for the Indians, many of the Americans' horses were skittish mustangs that had just been broken, and the men had trouble getting them under control. The Indians, evidently short on firearms, responded with a shower of arrows, which hit a few horses and slightly wounded a few men. Before it was all over, Tevis's men had killed four Indians, including Chief Elías, wounded others, and captured thirteen women and children.[9]

The bravado displayed by the miners soon gave way to fear, for after the battle a large group of furious Indians, perhaps including Mangas Coloradas, bent on revenge, surrounded the Americans. Two ranchers on the Mimbres sent a courier to Major Isaac Lynde at Fort Floyd, soon to be renamed Fort McLane, at a site that the Apaches called Apache Tejo.[10]

Following the reorganization of the Military Department of New Mexico, Colonel Fauntleroy had ordered Lynde to establish a post near the Mimbres River. Lynde, with four companies of the Seventh Infantry, had spent some three weeks examining the country. Finally, on September 16, 1860, he had settled on a site about fifteen miles south of Santa Rita del Cobre, twenty miles southeast of Pinos Altos, and twelve miles west of where the overland mail route crossed the Mimbres. His men lived in crude jacals until they could build permanent dwellings in the spring. Lynde reported that water, timber, and grazing were available in sufficient amounts to sustain the post. It was to this place that the courier came with the account of the miners' plight.[11]

As soon as Lynde heard the news, he sent reinforcements under Second Lieutenant John Sappington Marmaduke, a future governor of Missouri, to "protect the settlement there, and to take the prisoners from the party that had captured them."[12] On December 7, Lynde also dispatched a messenger to Steck at Mesilla, described the events as he then understood them, and asked the agent to assure the chiefs that "this is the act of individuals and not of the authorit[ies]." Lynde declared that the "Indians have stolen large numbers of stock from the inhabitants lately, which has led to this difficulty."[13] For some undetermined reason Steck did not report the incident to James Collins until the day before he was to leave for Washington. The agent denied any responsibility for what had happened, conveniently ignoring the fact that he had reneged on his appointment with the Chihennes; instead, implying that some of the trouble was the Apaches' own doing, he suggested that the miners' assault did not surprise him. He had warned them "of the danger of having any intercourse with the miners but I could not prevent it. They were in the almost daily habit of trading with them." His next statement suggested that he had talked with the Apaches, but this was not true. He probably had sent someone to investigate Tevis's assault while he remained at Mesilla making preparations for his trip to Washington, D.C. The chiefs "have promised that they will not go to war [and] that the settlements will not be disturbed." They vowed, however, to make the miners at Pinos Altos "pay dearly." If war broke out, he feared that the Indians would flee south to Janos and Corralitos, Chihuahua, where he knew that Delgadito's small local group of Chihennes was already living. The next morning Steck departed for the East; he would discover conditions in southern New Mexico much changed when he returned the next summer.[14]

Meanwhile, Lieutenant Marmaduke reached the Mimbres River and met Tevis and his party. Tevis turned over the Indian prisoners but refused to restore the stock that his men had confiscated from the Indians. The miners returned, unpunished, to Pinos Altos; Lieutenant Marmaduke retraced his steps to Fort Floyd with eleven of the Indian captives (he had released two children to Chabnocito before leaving). Before Marmaduke's detachment arrived at Fort Floyd, Major Lynde sent Captain Matthew Rider Stevenson to seek out the Chihennes and hold talks with them. He apparently met Marmaduke's command along the trail and took the Indian prisoners with him to the Mimbres. On December 12, 1860, Mangas Coloradas, "the principal Apache chief," came in and held a pow-wow with Stevenson. The tone of the Apache response was somber. What about the Apaches murdered and the women and children captured? the chiefs wondered. The captain reiterated what Marmaduke had told Chabnocito before he had left for Fort Floyd with the Apache prisoners. He also asked Mangas to return the next day with Chabnocito, and they would talk further. They appeared as requested the next day, and Stevenson told them that they must come in to the post with José Mangas, Victorio, and Riñón "with all the stock and arms which the Apaches had stolen from the whites during the past month." Mangas, who denied that any stolen stock was in their possession, pointed the finger at Steck for their problems, insisting that the agent "had not kept his promises to meet them." Stevenson returned to the fort with eleven hostages.[15]

A short time later, Acting Agent Tully left Mesilla with corn to distribute to the Indians but could not find any near the Mimbres. He lamented that the miners had "shot dead" Elías, "the best Indian in the tribe," and had captured the wife and children of Chabnocito, "the head chief [of the Chihenne Warm Springs local group] and one of the bravest men in the tribe." From what Tully could learn, the Indians had left their usual haunts, "some say for Apache Pass, some say for Chihuahua." Yet, on an ominous note, before leaving they declared "that they did not want peace with Americans and said if the settlers on the Mimbres did not leave they would kill them all."[16]

Jason Betzinez, whose grandfather Delgadito had already relocated with his Chihenne followers to Mexico to escape the Americans' invasion, corroborated Tully's revealing insight about the Chihennes' state of mind. Referring to the miners' attack, he wrote that the Chihennes' war with Americans began "suddenly and for no reason at all as far as the Indians could tell." The whites had "attacked and killed quite a few of the Apaches. The reason was simply a greed for the gold which they thought was to be found in the Indian country."[17]

As for Mangas, he and the Chihennes had probably retired to a safe place in the Mogollons, where they held a council to figure out their next step. Mangas's local group, with some Bedonkohes, decided to head for Chokonen country and join Cochise; on their way west one group stole twelve mules from Americans near the Burro Mountains and apparently took them to Apache Pass.[18] Meanwhile, the Chihennes opted to return to Fort Floyd, renamed Fort McLane, on January 18, 1861, to negotiate the return of their people still held in confinement there. In mid-February, Chabnocito, Riñón, and Victorio appeared at Fort McLane and met with Major Lynde. The officer was eager to mend relations and avert hostilities, because headquarters had ordered him "to use every effort to dissuade and prevent the settlers from inflicting unnecessary outrages upon the Indians at the same time keeping the Indians from becoming hostile or aggressive." Convinced of their sincerity, Lynde released his hostages, pointing out that the chiefs "professed to be friendly to the Whites and promised to do all in their power to keep peace and prevent any depredations by the men of their bands." Chabnocito, thought to be the most important Chihenne chief in Delgadito's absence, assured Major Lynde that he would send for Mangas Coloradas "and thought he could induce him to come in and make peace."[19]

Chabnocito's assertion implied that Mangas Coloradas now considered himself at war with Americans. His comments are also revealing, because Chabnocito made them about a week after war erupted between the Bedonkohes and Chokonens and American troops at Apache Pass. Chabnocito did not mention the fighting at Apache Pass, though he had probably heard about the difficulties, given the Apaches' communication network. This was the infamous Bascom affair, which needs no in-depth treatment here. Suffice it to say that American troops treacherously captured Cochise and members of his family after he came in to confer with Second Lieutenant George N. Bascom about a boy captured by Western Apaches. Bascom, misunderstanding the political organization of the Apaches, had his troops surround the tent, planning to detain Cochise and his family until the chief returned the boy. But Cochise did not have the boy, and when he learned of Bascom's plans, he cut his way out of the tent and fled into the hills. His family was not so fortunate, however, and was unable to escape. Next followed an unfortunate chain of events that culminated in Cochise's attacking the whites, capturing and torching a Mexican freight train, and burning at the stake several Mexican captives. A few days later Cochise's people tortured to death their four white prisoners. Bascom responded by hanging six Apaches, three of whom were relatives of Cochise, including his beloved brother Coyuntura.[20]

According to Bascom, during the hostilities some five hundred to six hundred Apaches (an obvious exaggeration), now under Mangas Coloradas, had flocked to Apache Pass.[21] Other documentation supports Bascom's assertion of Mangas's presence. Geronimo confirmed that the Bedonkohes were there, but after the incident he said that Cochise took command of both bands, which would have been natural, considering Cochise's state of mind.[22] We have more evidence that Mangas had left New Mexico to join Cochise at this time. On February 8, 1861, while the Bascom affair was winding down, some one hundred miles south of Apache Pass a few citizens from Fronteras conversed with several Chiricahua warriors, who asked about the peace treaties at Fronteras. The Indians admitted that their party, who were setting out on a raid deep into the interior, consisted of twenty-two men from Cochise's and Mangas Coloradas's bands.[23] Many historians have documented Bascom's treachery at Apache Pass and have shown convincingly that it triggered a full-scale war between Cochise and the Americans. Its effect on Mangas is not as well known, but a message that he sent to Americans in September 1862 provides us with some insight into his reasons for going to war against Americans.

Although there was some raiding for stock (which the Apaches did not normally consider an act of war) before the Bascom affair, no reputable historian can dispute the impression that war between Cochise and Americans began after the affair.[24] In contrast, the events that drove Mangas Coloradas to war are not as clear-cut in the eyes of historians. We must examine and analyze Mangas Coloradas's own words and then scrutinize the legend that has surrounded him for so many years about why he began fighting Americans. Then, perhaps, we can attempt to view his motives in a new light. According to Mangas Coloradas's own words in September 1862, he was "at peace with the world until the troops attacked & killed many of his people." Finally, he declared, after the third assault he "armed himself in self defence" and went to war.[25] The first two assaults are clear: Tevis's attack on Elías's

ranchería and the Bascom affair at Apache Pass. What was the
third incident? Could Mangas Coloradas be referring to the time
that miners at Pinos Altos purportedly whipped him, which,
according to accepted history, became the compelling reason he
went to war?

According to John Cremony, this is what happened. Mangas
secretly went to the miners, one by one, and promised to show
each man where gold was "far more abundant and could be
obtained with less labor." The passages are vintage Cremony. He is
here supposedly quoting Mangas: "You good man. You stay here
long time and never hurt Apache. You want the 'yellow iron'; I
know where plenty is. Suppose you go with me. I show you; but
tell no one else. Mangas your friend, he want to do you good. You
like 'yellow iron'—good! Me no want 'yellow iron.' Him no good
for me—can no eat, can no drink, can no keepee out cold. Come, I
show you." Cremony continues: "For a while each person so
approached kept this offer to himself, but after a time they began
to compare notes, and found that Mangas had made promises to
each, under the ban of secrecy and the pretense of exclusive
personal friendship. Those who at first believed the old rascal, at
once comprehended that it was a trap set out to separate and
sacrifice the bolder and leading men by gaining their confidence
and killing them in detail, while their fates would remain
unknown to those left behind."

The next time that Mangas came into camp, the burly miners
seized him, strapped him to a tree, and "administered a dose of
'strap oil' well applied by lusty arms. His vengeance was more
keenly aroused by this deserved treatment, and from that time
forth every sort of annoyance was put into operation against the
miners. . . . Mangas desired their extirpation. He wanted their
blood; he was anxious for their annihilation."[26]

From these passages an embryo was born and subsequently took
on a life of its own. This story, probably apocryphal, has become
embedded as historical fact—a legend that writers and historians
have perpetuated into this century. In sorting out these legends
and myths, I have found that they frequently have some basis in
fact. Cremony's version, if credible, provides a simple equation
that explains why Mangas Coloradas went to war after almost
fifteen years at peace. It has both cause, the whipping, and effect,
war. While there is nothing inherently improbable about the story,
it is certainly open to question. We must accept Cremony's colorful writings with definite reservations, and then only if corrobor-

John C. Cremony, a former Boston journalist who acted as interpreter for Bartlett's Boundary Commission and later served as an officer with the California Volunteers in Arizona and New Mexico. Cremony's colorful recollections were not always reliable. (Courtesy Arizona Historical Society, no. 24,548)

ating evidence is available. In this case, as we shall soon see, there is no other primary source material that would validate Cremony's version.

Moreover, the window of time in which this alleged incident could have occurred was brief. On December 13, 1860, Mangas Coloradas and Chabnocito held a parley with Captain Stevenson near the Mimbres. Mangas clearly would not have come in if he had already declared war on Americans. But he did appear, and he held civil conversations with the captain, after which he set out for Cochise's country. Two months later Chabnocito told Major Lynde at Fort McLane that he would send for Mangas, who he believed would "come in and make peace." By this chronology, the betrayal at Pinos Altos would have taken place between mid-December 1860 (after the miners' attack on the Mimbres) and late January 1861, before Mangas Coloradas went to join Cochise, probably with the intent of making a campaign against Sonora. Yet that the great chief would stride into Pinos Altos after the miners had just wantonly murdered several of his people on the Mimbres was about as likely as the possibility that James Tevis, the leader of the hooligans, would appear at the Chihenne camp to beg forgiveness for his wanton attack.

Of course, if such an incident as the beating did actually occur, it could have taken place before December 1860, but then why would Steck have expended so much effort to set aside the Apache reservation at Santa Lucía if Mangas had already gone to war? And why would Mangas have come in to parley with Captain Stevenson on December 12 and 13 at the Mimbres River if he were at war with the miners for their ignominious "whipping" of him? John Russell Bartlett and John Cremony both wrote books to describe relations in the early 1850s between Mangas Coloradas's people and the boundary commission near Santa Rita del Cobre. Both men frequently described the same events—their councils and negotiations with the Chiricahuas and the recent period of warfare between Apaches and Mexicans. Bartlett recorded these stories carefully and honestly; Cremony recorded these same stories, but fictionalized many details, using his Yankee ingenuity to embellish them, particularly when it came to Indian and white fatalities. He probably thought he was doing a service for his readers, most of whom had never seen a live Indian. In fact, in 1872 Cremony wrote an article entitled "Some Savages" which was published in the *Overland Monthly*, in which he attempted to describe the very Apache leaders whom he had met during his years in the Southwest. He was very creative in his writing and clearly fabricated much of the piece—a product of his lively imagination. Surprisingly, in this article he neglected to mention the alleged whipping of Mangas Coloradas as he had in his book *Life among the Apaches*, published four years before. If Cremony did hear the story—and there is not one shred of evidence to suggest that he did, other than what he wrote himself—it must have been when he returned to the Southwest with the California Volunteers in 1862. For if Bartlett had heard this gossip, he likely would have mentioned it in his book.

If this story is indeed true, some of Cremony's contemporaries would surely have written about it, whether they were military officers, Indian agents, newspaper correspondents, or even the miners who were in the vicinity, for all of these were actively discussing Apache affairs in late 1860 and early 1861.

It should be noted that Captain Stevenson did not mention the incident after meeting Mangas Coloradas twice in December 1860, and neither did Major Lynde, who commanded Fort McLane from the fall of 1860 until its abandonment on July 3, 1861, and wrote several letters during that period in which he discussed relations with the Chihennes and Bedonkohes. The *Mesilla Times*, published in 1860 and 1861, contained a great deal of information about the Pinos Altos mines but nothing about the beating incident. One contemporary letter dispatched to the *Missouri Republican* in late November 1861 indeed attributed Mangas's outbreak to Bascom's indiscretions. After the incident at Apache Pass, Cochise went to war, as did Mangas, who threatened to exterminate "all whites within the limits of his range."[27]

Apache Agent Michael Steck wrote many letters in 1860 and was with Mangas in the late summer and fall of 1860, but he apparently never heard of the whipping affair or he would have reported it. It could have occurred, of course, after his departure, but that seems unlikely. In mid-December 1860 he left for Washington, D.C., at which time Pinckney Tully became acting agent. In a letter written on January 3, 1861, Tully emphatically attributed the Apaches' disappearance to the miners' assault on Elías's band on the Mimbres River.[28] Tully found a part of the Chihenne band in January, and from that month until May 8, 1861, he issued rations to them at Fort McLane.[29] Mangas was not near; by late May, Tully clearly believed that Mangas Coloradas had gone to war. In early June he admitted that the outbreak of war perplexed him, for he had issued rations regularly to the Chihennes, though not to the Bedonkohes, who, as Geronimo said, considered themselves at war with Americans after the Bascom affair.[30] Steck, Tully, and their superior at Santa Fe, James Collins, believed that war had resulted from the miners' attack at the Mimbres River and the infamous Bascom affair at Apache Pass, which impression accords with what Mangas alluded to.[31] We also have the previously mentioned accounts of Hank Smith and James Tevis, two of the miners at Pinos Altos, both well acquainted with Mangas Coloradas. Each mentioned difficulties at Pinos Altos, mainly stock raids, but nothing about the alleged whipping.[32]

What did the Chiricahuas in the nineteenth century have to say about all of this? The answer is simple: not one word. Jason Betzinez was born about the time that the Chihennes and Bedonkohes went to war. In his account, which is reliable and objective, he clearly says that the war began when American miners attacked the Chihennes. He did not mention anything about Mangas Coloradas's being whipped at Pinos Altos. But perhaps even more important than Betzinez's recollection is Geronimo's autobiography. A Bedonkohe, Geronimo spent a great deal of time with Mangas Coloradas in the late 1850s and early 1860s. His recollections are trustworthy on many issues—especially the Bascom affair and the treachery surrounding the death of Mangas Coloradas. If the miners at Pinos Altos had whipped Mangas Coloradas, Geronimo would have heard of it and mentioned it as a contributing cause for going to war. Yet he is altogether silent on this score. Most significantly, as mentioned before, Mangas never mentioned the alleged mistreatment at Pinos Altos, either in September 1862, when he solicited peace with Americans, or in 1863, when Americans captured him near Pinos Altos. Apaches, like most of us, have long memories when it comes to betrayal. It took Cochise over a decade to recover any trust in American troops after they ambushed him at Apache Pass. If the miners had whipped Mangas at Pinos Altos, why would he have returned to the scene of this treachery in the spring of 1862 and in January 1863?

Why then, have historians so readily accepted Cremony's version as history instead of relegating it to the realm of legend and folklore, where it deserves to be? Perhaps because it provided writers with a logical explanation about why Mangas went to war. Cremony's book *Life among the Apaches* has long been considered a classic in Apache history. Yet it has not been subjected to the critical analysis of historiography. Other historians of the Indian Wars who had few dependable Apache sources were forced to consult this book. Perhaps the first account of this period to perpetuate Cremony's version of the whipping at Pinos Altos was J. P. Dunn's *Massacre of the Mountains,* first published in 1886. In 1931, Will Levington Comfort published a critically acclaimed novel, *Apache,* which was a fictionalized biography of Mangas Coloradas. Though wonderfully told, with sensitivity and com-passion for the Apache people, it was a novel—a terrific story derived from Comfort's research. One of his primary sources was Cremony; he naturally accepted and enhanced—as a fictional work entitled him to do—Cremony's version of the whipping at Pinos Altos. In the mid-1930s Paul Wellman, another highly respected writer, wrote *The Indian Wars of the West,* which became one of the standard sources for Apache history. He employed Cremony as a source for the "flogging," as he called it, but added some color and details. About the same time that Wellman wrote his book, Woodworth Clum wrote *Apache Agent,* based on the reminis-cences of his father, John Philip Clum. Like Wellman, Clum added his interpretation, even identifying the miners who carried out the deed (probably gleaned from Comfort), but his book has no refer-ences and, as a source, must be used with caution.[33]

More recent historians have relied upon many of these sources, all having their origins with Cremony, to describe the calamity that allegedly befell Mangas. Even a recently published book from the Chiricahua point of view, *Apache Mothers and Daughters,* an oral history based on four generations of reminiscences beginning with the daughter of Victorio, discusses the whipping. Surprisingly, the author's source for this incident is not her own Apache infor-mants, nor Cremony directly, but John Upton Terrell's *Apache Chronicle.* And who were Terrell's sources? Cremony, Wellman, and Clum, naturally.[34]

Yet we must examine two more issues.

First, in the diary of Private Sylvester W. Matson, published in *The Journal of Arizona History,* appears an entry for July 8, 1853, noting that "gold diggers had caught and badly beaten" a son of Ponce, who had taken a Mexican captive for a wife.[35] Cremony and Bartlett had left the Southwest the year before, so neither reported the story. Yet someone might have told Cremony the anecdote when he returned with the California Volunteers in 1862. Could he have twisted this around and made Mangas the victim? Yes, according to the way many of Cremony's contemporaries perceived him.[36]

Second, Eve Ball, the remarkable woman who had gained the trust and confidence of the Chiricahuas in the mid-twentieth century, provides an impression in her book, *In the Days of Victorio: Recollections of a Warm Springs Apache*, which was based on many years of interviews with James Kaywaykla, a relative of Victorio. Apparently Kaywaykla had heard of the miners' whipping of Mangas at Pinos Altos, for Eve Ball wrote that they "had bound him to a tree and lashed him with ox goads until his back was striped with deep cuts." Kaywaykla, in his preface, "A Word from the Narrator," admits that he had "read widely and [was] familiar with the military reports about my people and with the records of historians."[37] Perhaps his knowledge of the incident came from Cremony, or perhaps he heard it from one of his people, but it is not clear. Ball does acknowledge Cremony as a source for material in the book. Surprisingly, in her later book, *Indeh*, she does not even mention the incident. This in no way impugns the veracity of Kaywaykla or Ball, for both of whom I have a tremendous amount of admiration and respect. Yet it would have been helpful to know Kaywaykla's source and whether he had heard this story from an Apache elder who might have provided an eyewitness account to him.

In summary, I doubt Cremony's veracity. I doubt that the miners at Pinos Altos ever whipped Mangas Coloradas. Whether someone told Cremony this story or he fabricated it himself does not make much difference. The fact is that there is not a shred of hard evidence to support his claim. Until I see conclusive evidence, I believe that Mangas Coloradas went to war because of the miners' assault at the Mimbres River and Bascom's actions at Apache Pass. Then, during the first half of 1861, several other developments occurred which imbued the Chiricahuas with a new-found confidence; they again believed they could drive the whites from their domain.

Unlike those of Cochise, whose trail we can easily follow in the months following the Bascom affair, Mangas Coloradas's activities are more difficult to trace. When threatened, Mangas usually headed toward the Gila country and the Mogollon Mountains. Typically, after the Bascom affair he headed north and probably, perhaps with Cochise, cleaned the San Simón station of stock.[38] Geronimo was with the Bedonkohes at this time, and he recalled that the Indians "disbanded and went into hiding in the mountains," and "after this trouble [the Bascom incident] all of the Indians agreed not to be friendly with the white men any more."[39] As for Cochise, he plunged south into northern Sonora to lick his wounds and plan his retaliation against Americans. He joined many Chiricahuas who had taken refuge near Fronteras, where they were receiving rations. They had moved south to avoid the Americans' invasion and now included members of three Chiricahua bands: Delgadito's Chihennes, Esquinaline's Chokonens, and the Nednhis under Galindo, who had succeeded Láceres as chief of the Janeros local group of that band.[40]

Meanwhile, at department headquarters in Santa Fe, civil and military leaders moved to quell the Apache outbreak before it became general. James L. Collins, his explosion point now at the end of a very short fuse, asked Commissioner of Indian Affairs David Greenwood to see what he could do about getting Steck to return to his agency. He felt that if Steck could not be persuaded, they should at once appoint a new agent for the Southern Apaches. He uncharitably placed the blame and responsibility for the recent difficulties squarely on Steck's shoulders, claiming that if the agent had been present to issue rations, the Apaches would have been content and "the present difficulty would have been, beyond question, prevented." Collins's view was simplistic and naïve. He had recently heard rumors that Steck was politicking for his job as superintendent of Indian affairs in New Mexico (which appointment Steck received in 1863). Therefore, Collins's outspoken criticism of Steck was inspired, in part at least, surely by his personal feelings.

Of course it was inevitable that hostilities between whites and the Chihennes would occur; after all, Americans were poaching and prospecting in some of the choicest regions of Apache country. Steck's presence would not have averted hostilities. Collins failed to articulate the real reason for his anger, which was legitimate. Steck's apathy, manifested in his quick and untimely departure from the territory, had incensed Collins, especially because it came at such a crucial time, only ten days after the miners' attack on the Mimbres. Collins, frustrated by Steck's uncharacteristic neglect of duties, felt powerless to do anything from Santa Fe. Thus, he lashed out at the agent. Over the next few months the superintendent repeatedly requested his superiors in Washington to order Steck back to New Mexico; meanwhile, in southern New Mexico and Arizona, hostilities slowly gained momentum, especially in the country of Cochise, where in late April the Apache chief began to wage an unmerciful war against Americans.[41]

In response to the news of Apache hostilities, Colonel Fauntleroy decided to launch punitive campaigns against the Mescaleros east of the Rio Grande and the Chiricahua bands west of the river.

The commander sent two companies of reinforcements and placed the troops at Fort Buchanan and Fort Breckenridge under Lynde's command. Lynde, however, had no stomach for the expedition, and his campaign did not get off the ground. According to him, "it would be useless to attempt to operate against these Indians." He may have been right, for he had no idea exactly who the hostiles were or where they were living. At that time (early April), Acting Agent Tully continued to ration part of the Chihenne band. Cochise had not yet returned in force to Arizona, and Mangas Coloradas had been quiet, likely living in the Mogollon country. Yet storm clouds were forming on the horizon—part the Apaches' doing and part because of the impending crisis facing the nation as civil war was about to erupt. When it did, it first affected military operations in the Southwest, and the resulting tremors inevitably trickled down into the civil sector. Not even a prophet could have foreseen how rapidly the Chiricahuas, led by two impassioned leaders, Cochise and Mangas Coloradas, both fighting to avenge wrongs inflicted against their people, would regain their territory.[42]

About a month after the Bascom affair, the first big blow to southwesterners came when the Butterfield Overland Mail Company shifted its route to the central part of the nation because Texas had seceded from the Union. Many experienced frontiersmen lost their jobs and left the area for either California or Texas. Cochise and Mangas, delighted over this opportune turn of events, believed that their menacing threats had compelled the stage company to shut down operations. In reality, the outbreak at Apache Pass had nothing to do with the decision. The Apaches had no idea of the political winds swirling about the country; they could only sit back with amazement as miners, ranchers, stage personnel, and finally the military left in droves, just as the Spaniards and Mexicans had in the past.

Meanwhile, Cochise and Mangas planned their course of action. Cochise, with his Chokonens, had returned to Apache Pass, seeking vengeance. In April he and Mangas held a council, deciding then to split their forces and make a campaign: Cochise was to take about sixty warriors and return to Arizona near Stein's Peak; Mangas Coloradas was to command a similar party of Bedonkohes and return to his old stomping grounds to attack the whites near Pinos Altos, Santa Rita del Cobre, and the Mimbres River.

Cochise's war party ambushed and killed nine men, most of them former Butterfield employees, near Stein's Peak. In the sharp fight the Americans wounded Cochise, but not seriously. Cochise's warriors captured two men, who had apparently attempted to parley with him. With vengeance in his heart, Cochise roasted them upside down with their heads suspended eighteen inches above the fire. Shortly after, on May 1, 1861, a band of Apaches arrived at Santa Rosa, just south of the unoccupied San Bernardino hacienda, with stock and booty taken from the massacre at the eastern mouth of Doubtful Canyon, which the Apaches called Tsisl-lnoi-bi-yi-tu ("Rock White in Water"). Cochise with about thirty warriors had remained, searching out new prey. They found it in an American freighter train at San Simón station heading for the Rio Grande. The Indians succeeded in running off seventeen head of stock. Cochise, as was customary, led his men into battle, boldly charging into the whites and discharging several rounds at Jud Jones, an American teamster who had tried to recover the stock.[43]

East of Chokonen country, in New Mexico, most of the Chihennes, under Victorio, Chabnocito, and Riñón, had tried to remain at peace, since Lynde had returned their people the previous February. We know that in late April, James Collins even clung to the hope that Tully could convince the Chihennes to begin planting at Lucero Springs (apparently the Chihennes did not want to plant at Santa Lucía, which they considered Mangas's area). Acting Agent Tully had continued to issue periodic rations through May 8 to these Chihennes, apparently most of the band "formerly under Dr. Steck." Collins opined to Tully that "we must try to keep them together and they will form a nucleus around which we may be able to unite all the friendly Indians of this tribe." The Chihennes had tried to remain neutral, but they could not resist the overtures of Mangas Coloradas and his Bedonkohes upon his arrival in Chihenne country in May 1861, after leaving his council of war with Cochise.[44]

The Chihennes had not participated in the raids committed by the followers of Mangas Coloradas who had stolen stock from Pinos Altos and Santa Rita del Cobre in late February and early March.[45] But soon after Mangas returned to the area, and perhaps emboldened by the abandonment of the mail route, the Chihennes under Victorio, Riñón, and Chabnocito went to war. On May 7, 1861, twenty Apaches assaulted Mexican freighters near Pinos Altos, killed one of them, and took their mules. About two weeks later, on May 22, Mangas's followers ran off every head of stock from Fort McLane. They must have also been active along the Mimbres River, for in early June the *Mesilla Times* reported that the ranchers had abandoned their crops and homes for Mesilla because of Apache hostilities.[46]

During the spring of 1861 reports identified the Chokonens and Western Apaches as the hostiles. The Chihennes' depredations surprised Acting Agent Tully, but it was not until his letter dated June 2, 1861, that he first accused the "Coppermine" Apaches, as the Chihennes were called, of raiding. He reported that Apaches had killed several people. Their hostilities bewildered the agent: "What has led to this outbreak I am at a loss to know. They have had their rations issued regularly to them." Tully, who now believed the Indians had opened negotiations with Mexico, made another interesting observation: "They have become emboldened since the withdrawal of the Overland Mail, for they believe that they have caused its withdrawal." He also reported that the miners had abandoned the Pinos Altos gold mines.[47] This news would have been cause for rejoicing among the Chiricahuas, if it had been true. Unfortunately for the Indians, it was not. Miners had deserted the area in droves, but the settlement, which once contained some five hundred men, still numbered about one hundred. What Tully had probably heard or seen was that many miners were leaving the country because gold was getting more difficult to find and the water supply was dwindling, which made it difficult to continue prospecting. The Apaches' presence may have frightened a few men out, but for the most part it was a matter of economics and nothing else. These tough individuals obsessed with gold fever would provide a good deal of southern New Mexico's protection for the next few months, especially because in July the military abandoned its posts in southern Arizona, Fort Buchanan and Fort Breckenridge, and in southern New Mexico, Fort McLane. Anticipating a Rebel invasion from Texas, the department commander at Santa Fe ordered the soldiers to the Rio Grande.[48]

In June the allied Chiricahuas had all but closed the road between Tucson and Mesilla. Agent Lorenzo Labadi arrived in Mesilla en route to Tucson, where he was to investigate the conditions of the Apaches mansos, or "tame" Apaches. He was unable to secure transportation to Tucson because reports of Apache raiding continued to reach Mesilla. On June 3 at Cooke's Peak the Indians killed two Mexicans and stole two mules belonging to Ellsburg and Ambery, two Mesilla merchants. In mid-June they raided Pinos Altos, and on June 18 they struck a hay camp, killing John Gillem and wounding another man. Meanwhile, in Arizona, Cochise had continued to create havoc, raiding relentlessly in May and June, including one assault on the herd at Fort Buchanan. Years later, Cochise made a statement that probably reflected accurately the feelings of both him and Mangas Coloradas. He characterized this white exodus from his country as follows: "At last your soldiers did me a very great wrong, and I and my whole people went to war with them. At first we were successful and your soldiers were driven away and your people killed and we again possessed our land." The informants of Eve Ball corroborated Cochise's statements, telling her that Mangas Coloradas and Cochise thought their actions had compelled the soldiers to withdraw.[49]

Early that summer of 1861, officials in Washington answered Superintendent James Collins's pleas when Agent Michael Steck arrived from the East. In mid-July the physician and Chiricahua agent went to Mesilla. Steck immediately determined that the conflict had become general, and he reluctantly concluded that "I am unable to do anything. . . . It may be many months before the presence of an Indian agent will be needed here."[50] He was right, except that it would be years, rather than months, before the Chihennes would meet another agent of the Indian department. Beginning in July 1861, the two greatest Chiricahua leaders of the mid-nineteenth century, emboldened by the withdrawal of the Butterfield Overland Mail and the evacuation of the military posts in their country, joined forces to drive the remaining Americans from their domain. Mangas Coloradas, now over seventy years of age, had no problem deferring to his younger son-in-law, who brought unrivaled passion, unsurpassed courage, and an unequaled charisma to the struggle. The natural leadership qualities of Cochise were inspiring, and he found it easy to attract members from the four Chiricahua bands and even some recruits from Western Apache bands. A new era had dawned for the Chiricahua tribe. The years to come would be charged with excitement, celebrated for heroic exploits, and crowned with success. Mangas, who had never wanted to go to war, must have had mixed feelings. Though he shared in the victories and was caught up in the initial euphoria, he soon realized that they were fighting a futile cause, especially when, in the next year, a large body of federal troops arrived from California and took possession of New Mexico. Their arrival proved to be a fateful consequence for Mangas Coloradas.

Chapter 17

WAR!

MANGAS Coloradas could not have relished going to war against Americans, at least not at this stage of his life. He had advocated accommodation and peace with them ever since Kearny's entrance into his country fifteen years before. But the affairs of late 1860 and early 1861 had given him no other choice but to take military action. His son-in-law Cochise had launched his self-prescribed mission of driving Americans from southern Arizona, a decision which happened to coincide with the whites' virtual abandonment of the territory. Like dominos, one Anglo institution after another fell as Americans withdrew from stage stations, ranches, forts, and mines in Chokonen country. Many of southern Arizona's citizens, now faced with a general Apache war, had to flee on the heels of the military to escape with their lives. In the eyes of the Chiricahuas, who had previously repelled Spanish and Mexican encroachment, this hasty evacuation, coming as it did immediately after Cochise opened hostilities, must have occurred in consequence of their efforts. In Cochise's world there was no other rational explanation. He naturally claimed responsibility, and in July 1861 he joined forces with Mangas Coloradas's Chihennes and Bedonkohes in New Mexico to try to emulate his success in southern Arizona. For the first time the two greatest Chiricahua chiefs of the middle of the nineteenth century united to fight Americans. Mangas, buoyed by Cochise's victories, the abandonment of Fort McLane, and the evacuation of the stage stations in his territory, now believed that he could drive the hated miners at Pinos Altos and Santa Rita del Cobre from his country. According to one report, "He threatened extermination to all whites in the limits of his range."[1]

In *Cochise: Chiricahua Apache Chief*, I covered in depth Cochise's and Mangas Coloradas's activities in New Mexico from July through September 1861.[2] Yet since many readers of *Mangas Coloradas* may not have read *Cochise*, it is necessary for me to repeat these events to the extent they involved Mangas.

At midsummer 1861 the two chiefs set up their temporary headquarters near Cooke's Peak, called by the Apaches Dziltanatal ("Mountain Holds Its Head Up Proudly"). There, as Americans left Arizona and southern New Mexico for the east, Mangas Coloradas and Cochise lay in ambush to kill as many whites as possible. Their presence there also further isolated the miners at Pinos Altos from the settlements along the Rio Grande, for most travelers used the mail route that traversed Cooke's Canyon going to and from Pinos Altos. Not only was this course the shortest route, but it also contained a dependable supply of water at Cooke's Spring. Those parties entering Cooke's Canyon from its western mouth encountered a broad canyon that gradually narrowed in several places, particularly as the road approached the mouth at the eastern entrance to the canyon. Naturally, the reliable water supply made it a mandatory place to stop for troops and travelers. Brigadier General James Carleton thought that Cooke's Canyon rivaled the infamous Apache Pass as the most dangerous point in southern New Mexico and Arizona.[3] Yet in terms of fatalities, it exceeded the two most dangerous passes in southeastern Arizona—Apache Pass and Doubtful Canyon—combined. One informed estimate claimed that between 1861 and 1863, Apaches ambushed and killed one hundred whites in Cooke's Canyon, a report which, for a change, seems not to have been much exaggerated. Shortly after the California Volunteers established Fort Cummings at the eastern mouth of Cooke's Canyon on October 2, 1863, their commander wrote that they discovered "the canyon sadly defaced with human bones and graves."[4] Travelers through here left behind grim and morbid descriptions of the area. One soldier, George Hand, noted in his diary that he "found many bones, skulls, & graves" upon arriving at Cooke's Canyon.[5] Another person observed: "Place all along is graves, broken wagons . . . piles of rocks denoting a grave . . . [and] a human skull."[6]

It was into Cooke's Canyon that a party of seven Americans rode early on the morning of July 20, 1861. They had apparently volunteered to take the San Antonio and San Diego Mail Company's coach from Mesilla to San Diego.[7] The seven men, many of whom were former Butterfield employees, had also decided to leave

Cooke's Canyon, New Mexico. The combined forces of Cochise and Mangas Coloradas ambushed several parties of whites in this canyon during the summer of 1861. (Photo by Kathi Plauster)

because they were northern sympathizers and feared imprisonment by the Confederate forces that had occupied El Paso. Known as the Free Thomas party, they consisted of Freeman Thomas, Joe Roescher, Mat Champion, Robert Aveline, Emmett Mills, John Wilson, and John Portell. They reached Cooke's abandoned stage station that evening and probably encamped there that night.[8] They left the next morning, July 21, 1861, and had traveled only about a mile or so when the combined forces of Mangas Coloradas and Cochise, ranging from one hundred to two hundred warriors, fell upon them. Unable to continue forward, they bolted into a side canyon and headed for higher ground.

According to William Oury's account, the attack completely surprised the Americans. Once up the canyon, they stripped the coach of guns (breech-loading Sharps rifles), ammunition, water, and other essentials and sent the team down the hill, hoping this would satisfy Mangas Coloradas and Cochise. It did not. The Indians surrounded the besieged party and throughout the day poured down from the hills a withering fire of arrows and musket balls into the ranks of the Americans, who had hastily built stone fortifications, about two feet high, at the top of a small hill.

At this point it becomes difficult to reconstruct the sequence of events. Various stories reflect the imagination of the writer who had available to him only a few facts of the grisly day. As none of the seven Americans survived the battle, and the Apaches never did provide many details, the account of the episode has been shaped primarily from the cursory survey conducted by the men who came upon the corpses a few days after the fight and reconstructed the affair. Alexandre Daguerre and J. J. Thibault, two freighters en route to Mesilla, were the first to come upon the remains. They have described the scene, a testimony to the firepower of the Americans, in this way: "All about this wall the ground was strewn with battered bullets. Every rock and stone within many yards, which could have partially secreted an Indian, had bullets lying near. One small tree, some 150 yards from the wall, had the marks of eleven balls in it."

The Apaches had killed four men within the breastworks. Two lay some fifty yards in the rear; and the other, presumably John Wilson, was found one hundred and fifty yards away. According to at least one account, Mangas Coloradas left before the battle had ended, but not before having taken heavy losses. The Americans may have wounded both Cochise and his eldest son Taza before the Chokonens and their allies finished off Thomas's party, probably on July 22, 1861. When Daguerre and Thibault came upon the horrifying scene a few days later, they discovered that the Apaches had stripped every body, broken the arms of most of the men, and riddled their heads with bullets—a gruesome testimony to the effective firepower of the seven Americans, whom the Apaches had mutilated to avenge their casualities in the fight. James Tevis, whose actions had so mightily contributed to the resumption of hostilities, had left Pinos Altos with a group, which probably included Daguerre and Thibault, for Mesilla. He helped inter the bodies, but not before the "buzzards had picked the eyes" out of them.[9]

Despite their casualties, Cochise and Mangas Coloradas reportedly bore witness to the courage of the seven Americans. Mangas allegedly admitted to Jack Swilling that Thomas's men had killed twenty-five warriors and crippled many more; moreover, according to Mangas, if the Apaches were as brave "as these few white men, he could whip the world."[10] W. W. Mills, whose brother was a victim of the fight, claimed that he heard the Apaches admitted to a loss of 40 warriors.[11] But William Oury's account is quite different from those of Mills and Swilling. Oury claimed that Cochise had confessed he lost 175 warriors, which, of course, is absurd, for there probably were not even that many Apaches in the engagement. Like Mangas, Cochise, who admired bravery even among his enemies, also paid homage to the bravery of the seven Americans, declaring that "with twenty-five such men he would undertake to whip the whole United States." Likely even Swilling's account overstated the Indians' losses. It was inconceivable that Apaches, even fighting for vengeance, would have so exposed themselves as to cause a loss of that size. They were renowned for their patience and stealth, and they had no compelling reason to take undue risk when they had the Americans under their thumb. We shall never know, of course, the exact number of Apache casualties, but a loss of five or six men seems about right.[12]

The Chiricahuas retired to Janos after the fight. Oury reports that Cochise told of his role in the fight at Corralitos. Keith Humphreys, a historian in the Las Cruces area, heard a story in the 1930s from Natividad Padilla that corroborated earlier reports of the Indians' visit to Janos. Padilla told him that he saw the Indians at Janos when they came in to seek treatment for a wounded son of Cochise, probably Taza, shortly after the Cooke's Canyon fight. He witnessed the Apaches trading the Americans' gold watches for ammunition.[13] W. W. Mills also heard that the Indians "sold [the Americans'] arms and watches in Mexico," though whether they actually sold the Sharps rifles and the revolvers would be open to question.[14] A report from Fronteras at this time also confirmed the Chiricahuas' presence in northern Chihuahua: "The Apaches have been trading their plunder taken from the Americans at Janos and Corralitos."[15] After a short rest, the allied Chiricahuas departed, their thirst satisfied, their bellies filled, and their ammunition restored, thanks to the generosity of their sometime friend, sometime enemy, José María Zuloaga. Cochise and Mangas Coloradas returned to New Mexico and assumed their temporary headquarters in the hills near Cooke's Canyon, awaiting the arrival of their next prey.

It came in the form of a group of American ranchers from southern Arizona who had decided to abandon their homes for more civilized parts. The recent attacks in Arizona by Cochise's Chokonens and the Western Apaches, and the abandonment of Fort Buchanan, had compelled these courageous individuals to leave while they still had their lives. Known as the Ake party (named for Felix Grundy Ake, a fifty-year-old farmer), the wagon train consisted of six double wagons, two buggies, and one single wagon when it reached Tucson. There Moses Carson, a half-brother of the more celebrated Kit Carson but an outstanding mountain man in his own right, joined Ake's party, as did several other people. They carried many of their possessions and herded several hundred head of cattle, sheep, goats, and horses. They were, in effect, an open invitation to Cochise and Mangas.[16]

Ake had planned to rendezvous with the soldiers who had evacuated Fort Buchanan, but when he arrived at the Cienega, about twenty miles east of Tucson, he discovered that the troops had already departed. Nonetheless, he decided to continue, believing that his party was large enough to discourage an attack. Indeed, Apaches normally did not attack companies of this size. Yet he had not counted on Cochise and Mangas Coloradas's allying their bands. Not only had the events of the last few months imbued them with confidence, but the spoils of their victories had provided them with more firepower—Sharps rifles and revolvers—than ever before.

The eastbound whites saw no Indians along the route, although at Apache Pass they observed "ropes and some bones and rags a-hanging" at the Bascom execution site. Forging on to the Mimbres, they encamped at the abandoned stage station. That evening they heard that some two hundred Apaches had wiped out a party of nine Mexicans at Cooke's Canyon, which they were to pass through the next day. Ake and several of his men expressed doubts about the report and actually discredited it. They had no way of knowing how true it was. The messenger, whom Ake took to be a "Frenchman," was Anton Brewer, a butcher at Pinos Altos, who had gone to Mesilla to buy some cattle for the starving citizens of the mining town. He had bought some forty head and employed eight or nine Mexicans to herd the cattle to Pinos Altos. They decided to return through Cooke's Canyon, and near the site of the Apaches' ambush of the Free Thomas party they halted to have dinner. This proved to be a fatal decision. Hank Smith later described what happened:

> As the Mexicans were huddled in a group eating their lunch the Indians had little trouble surrounding and killing all of them. Brewer, who was guarding the cattle as his men ate, heard the Indians and took out up the canyon, outrunning them on a good horse. Fifteen men, including Smith, went to Cooke's Canyon to bury the men. They were found in a close pile, horribly mutilated. We raked them together with poles as best we could and covered them with rocks as the ground was too rough and rocky to make any graves, and not having tools to make them with.[17]

Undaunted by this report, Ake's party left the Mimbres before sunrise.[18] Cochise and Mangas Coloradas, with close to two hundred warriors, had prepared an ambush at a narrow part of Cooke's Canyon not too distant from where they had wiped out Brewer's vaqueros and Thomas's party. About midmorning the stock, driven by several Americans and Mexicans, apparently entered the canyon first, followed by the wagons and a few stragglers. As they approached the narrow part of the canyon "where the hills were closing in," Thomas Farrell, escorting the lead wagon, almost tripped over the mutilated corpse of one of Brewer's Mexican vaqueros. He soon discovered another body some one hundred yards from the first. All the men gathered about the lead wagon when Farrell returned. Pointing to the narrow gap ahead, he proposed to send flankers out on both sides of the canyon. Then they could hold the area to ensure that the wagons and cattle could pass safely through to the springs.[19]

Only two men agreed with Farrell—Jack Pennington and Captain Nathaniel Sharp. The remainder, led by Ake and Wadsworth, entered the narrow trail.[20] When all the wagons had crawled into the trap, Cochise and Mangas gave the sign to attack. The eager and confident Apaches, some squatting and others lying down behind rocks, unleashed a tremendous volley of arrows and bullets, which instantly killed John St. Clair and James May, who were in the lead with the herd. They also shot one of the horses pulling Phillips's spring wagon, which had been leading the caravan, and thus blocked the way. Phillips and his wife abandoned their rig, took their infant son and their money sack, and fled to Ake's wagon, which, with a couple of other wagons, had formed a triangular fort behind which the party all took refuge. With the Americans in chaos, the Chiricahuas came "swarming" out of the rocks, some "dressed like soldiers [and] armed with cap guns." They stampeded the herd before several Americans regrouped under William Redding and charged into the Indians' ranks. Although additional Indians emerged from their concealed positions and wounded him in the leg, the valiant Redding continued to lead assaults. Eventually the Chiricahuas shot him down, his body remaining in the narrow pass of Cooke's Canyon.[21] Mangas and Cochise did not let their men mutilate Redding's corpse; later, one chief, probably Mangas, allegedly told an American at Pinos Altos that Redding was a "heap, brave man."[22]

Meanwhile, the fighting continued as the day dragged on. At the first firing a group of seven Americans with the rear wagon, which included Sam Houston, a nephew of the distinguished Texan, and several women and children promptly deserted their friends and turned back to the Mimbres. This left about seventeen Americans available to fight the Indians. But they were the bravest of the bunch. Several distinguished themselves. Among these were Jack Pennington of the famous Arizona family of pioneers; Moses Carson, who fought "like hell, brave as a lion and quick as a cat"; and Chickasaw Brown, a Chickasaw Indian who "jumped behind a rock and took off his hat and started shooting," reportedly killing several Apaches. Then there was sixty-year-old Nathaniel Sharp, whom the Apaches had shot through the ear and neck with an arrow. The veteran Indian fighter was merely annoyed. Without losing a beat he "busted off the shaft and pulled the head out through the back, with the barb still on it."

As the Indians began to round up the stock and drive it through to the opposite end of the canyon, Felix Grundy Ake and William Wadsworth decided to climb a small hill to gain a better vantage point on the retiring Indians. They thought they were out of range, but several Chiricahua snipers opened fire and pumped two bullets into Wadsworth, mortally wounding him. Ake at the time was in an opium-induced stupor, according to one account. His daughter frantically implored Tom Farrell to leave the American position to bring Ake to safety. Farrell rescued Ake and in the process shot "one of the biggest Indians I have ever seen." But while he was frantically trying to drag Ake to cover, Farrell was struck in the back by an Apache bullet and seriously wounded. The ungrateful Ake left him writhing in the dust, but Jack Pennington and Nathaniel Sharp rushed out from the corral and carried the courageous Farrell to safety, and eventually he recovered from his wounds.

From this point forward the battle gradually evolved into a sniping duel between the two adversaries. Cochise and Mangas had achieved their objective—they had the stock, their men had killed a few Americans, and there was no compelling reason to risk further casualties just to kill a few more whites who were leaving their country anyway. The fighting finally began to subside in the early afternoon when Mariano Madrid, a teamster, killed one last Apache. The Indians disengaged and withdrew with their plunder of perhaps four hundred cattle and nine hundred sheep. Cochise and Mangas split up. The younger chief decided to drive part of the herd into Chihuahua to sell; Mangas likely continued north into the Mimbres and the Black range. Though the Americans had killed several Apaches, the Indians' actual losses are not known; we can only guess that they probably equaled those of the beleaguered Americans. Having suffered a loss of four dead and between five and eight men wounded, the whites limped back to the Mimbres River. The lead wagon, containing many of the women and children, was pretty much unaffected; behind them, the other wagons followed as best they could.[23]

Meanwhile, Houston's group, which had deserted at the first volley, had reached the Mimbres stage station and had sent a messenger to Pinos Altos, where a company of Arizona Guards under Captain Thomas J. Mastin, Lieutenant Thomas Helm, and Lieutenant Jack Swilling was stationed. According to Hank Smith, who was at Pinos Altos with Captain Mastin, they did not ride to the rescue until the next day, but others remembered that Mastin's party met the survivors at the Mimbres. If so, Mastin might have mustered his company at Pinos Altos in response to the massacre of Brewer's Mexican herders the day before the attack on Ake's group, He could not otherwise have reached the Mimbres from Pinos Altos at the same time as Ake's party did. Smith's recollections were probably right, but he was thinking about the messenger who brought the news about the massacre of Brewer's party.[24]

Although Lieutenant Colonel John Baylor mustered the Arizona Guards into Confederate service, their immediate duty was to fight Apaches and "to reopen the road between Mesilla and Tucson, [and] especially to rout the savages from Apache Pass."[25] Many of these men knew the Apaches from their trading expeditions at Pinos Altos. Mastin, who knew Mangas Coloradas, had a great deal of respect for the chief, declaring that he was the Apaches' "ablest statesman" and the "most influential and sagacious of all the chiefs."[26] In any case, Mastin's Arizona Guards, numbering about thirty-five men, met Ake's survivors east of the Mimbres. Learning that the Apaches had already driven off the stock, Mastin correctly deduced that they would probably ride south toward northern Chihuahua. After enlisting several of Ake's party into the Arizona Guards, Mastin decided to make "a straight shoot for the Florida Mountains in the hope of catching up with the Indians, and knowing that they could not travel very fast with the sheep, we might have a chance to overtake them."[27]

After riding all night, the guards were rewarded with big dividends. Mastin had bought enough time to secrete his men in ambush as the Indians, who probably likewise had traveled all night, approached the barren foothills of the Florida Mountains. By this time they were surely tired and perhaps careless. Certainly the all-night march had fatigued their horses. As the guards saw the Apaches coming, the eager Americans could scarcely believe their good fortune. The prospect of turning the tables on the Apaches and fighting them on open ground was too good to be true. When the party had approached to within a quarter of a mile of the Americans, Mastin's men jumped "out of the draw" and charged the astonished Indians. They furiously drove into the Chiricahuas, whom they estimated at eighty men, retook the cattle and sheep, and killed eight warriors in the process, according to Hank Smith. Mastin's troops then doggedly pursued the confused survivors back to the foothills of Cooke's range before the Indians finally melted into the rocks and hills.[28]

Mastin's command had likely struck the division under Cochise. Cochise and Mangas Coloradas eventually discovered that these Americans had come from Pinos Altos; likely they had already considered attacking this last bastion of white settlement in Chihenne country but may have rejected the idea because of its size and strength. Yet they could not let Mastin's victory go without a response. The success of this ambush and the fatalities inflicted upon the Indians at the Florida Mountains may have made their decision easier. It was also conceivable that they believed Chihuahuan troops had engineered the ambush, given the location of the Florida Mountains. Agustín Acuña, a Bavispe citizen, had returned from Corralitos on September 11, 1861, with news about Cochise and an unconfirmed report that a Chihuahuan campaign had killed twelve Indians, though it was unclear whether these rumors applied to the Arizona Guards' battle or perhaps to a campaign by Joaquín Terrazas. According to some Chiricahaus who had just been at Corralitos, Cochise had summoned warriors to the Animas Mountains, from where he planned to attack Fronteras.[29]

Meanwhile, another puzzling report claimed that the Chiricahuas, and if so, Mangas Coloradas, had appeared at Pinos Altos in early September and had talked with a Confederate officer, likely Captain Thomas Mastin. Of all this Mastin dutifully informed Colonel Baylor at Mesilla, and Baylor gave him explicit instructions which were tantamount to genocide, if that was what Mastin wished. If Mangas's people came in, Baylor authorized Mastin "to kill them anyway he could." The colonel "did not care whether he made them drunk, poisoned them, or shot them on sight."[30]

Likely the Chiricahuas merely hoped to gather information and intelligence about the strength of the Americans who remained at

Pinos Altos; surely they had no intention of making peace there. Perhaps, after this reconnaissance, Mangas sent messengers to Cochise suggesting that their combined forces could successfully attack Pinos Altos and drive the miners from his country. In any event, Cochise promptly postponed his foray against Fronteras and returned to New Mexico. He and Mangas hoped to launch a final blow against the miners at Pinos Altos either to wipe them out or to frighten them into leaving once and for all.

Although the ambush by the Arizona Guards certainly surprised Mangas and Cochise, it could not have amazed them any more than the events that they had recently witnessed. Just a month before, they had watched in astonishment as the troops from Arizona and Fort McLane deserted their posts and marched east. They had no way of knowing that their hostilities had not compelled this withdrawal. They did not realize that departmental headquarters at Santa Fe had ordered the troops to Fort Fillmore to thwart the anticipated Confederate invasion of New Mexico from Texas. It was well known to the North that Jefferson Davis not only coveted the natural resources of the Southwest and California, but also desperately desired a sea outlet in southern California to counter the Union's blockade of southern port cities. A command led by Lieutenant Colonel John Baylor,[31] a lean, blue-eyed Indian fighter notorious for his hatred and contempt for Indians, had occupied Fort Bliss, which Federal troops had evacuated, on July 1, 1861.[32]

Major Lynde, after abandoning Fort McLane, took command of Fort Fillmore near Mesilla on July 5. New Mexico's federal commander, Colonel Edward Richard Sprigg Canby,[33] who believed that Fillmore was a key element in the defense of southern New Mexico, ordered additional muskets and ammunition transferred from Fort Craig to Fort Fillmore, which then contained a military force of almost seven hundred men. To augment Lynde's position even further, in mid-July Canby ordered the Arizona garrisons from Breckenridge and Buchanan to begin their trek west to join Major Lynde's command at Fort Fillmore. By the time this caravan of soldiers had reached Cooke's Canyon (about three weeks before Ake's party), Captain Moore received word that Major Lynde had abandoned Fort Fillmore and had headed east for Fort Stanton. En route, Lynde had unbelievably surrendered his force of seven hundred men to Baylor's army, which numbered fewer than two hundred, without firing a shot. On July 27, 1861, Baylor's command had overtaken Lynde's thirsty army east of the Organ

Mountains and had found them willing to capitulate for a cup of water. Baylor paroled the men at Mesilla.

In truth, morale of the federal forces in southern New Mexico had declined to an all-time low. Not only had the soldiers gone unpaid for six months, but they also had not received any recent news about the fighting in the East, and many of their officers had already resigned to join the secessionists. After Lynde's debacle, in early August the garrison at Fort Stanton abandoned its post for Fort Craig, thus leaving southern New Mexico completely in the hands of the Confederates and, of course, the Apaches. Meanwhile, after receiving Canby's dispatch, Captain Moore burned his wagons and supplies at Cooke's Canyon, changed directions, and struck out northeast through the desert to Fort Craig, the southern outpost of Federal forces. They therefore avoided certain disaster, for Baylor's command, with many Arizona Guards from Pinos Altos, had set up an ambush west of Mesilla.[34]

The sentiments of the Americans who populated Mesilla, the principal city in southern New Mexico, favored secession. After capturing Lynde's army, Baylor immediately proclaimed himself governor and established a provisional government for the territory of Arizona that began urging men to enlist into militia units, including, as previously mentioned, the formidable Arizona Guards of Pinos Altos. At Tucson the citizens adopted the Confederate cause, although most Americans had joined the exodus after the army moved out. The Apaches held the country between Mesilla and Tucson, and other than a few centers of mining activity in southern Arizona and at Pinos Altos, the remainder of southern New Mexico west of the Rio Grande was unoccupied. The Tucson *Arizonian* described the abysmal scene in southern Arizona: "Our prosperity has departed. The mail is withdrawn; the soldiers are gone and their garrisons burned to the ground; the miners murdered and the mines abandoned; the stockraisers and farmers have abandoned their crops and herds to the Indians, and the population generally have fled, panic struck and naked in search of refuge. From end to end of the territory, except in Tucson and its immediate vicinity, there is not a human habitation."[35]

About mid-September Cochise led his Chokonens and a few Nednhis north from the Animas Mountains to rendezvous with the Bedonkohes and Chihennes under Mangas Coloradas, probably in either the Burro or Mogollon Mountains. This expedition, a tribal venture, apparently contained more warriors than any of the war parties of the previous summer, since reports from Mexico were suggesting that some men from the groups receiving rations at Fronteras had joined Cochise. During the early morning of September 27, 1861, the Chiricahua chiefs assembled their followers around them in the outskirts of Pinos Altos, which consisted of several satellite camps. Cochise and Mangas Coloradas had assigned each cluster of warriors, under a local group war leader, a particular camp to strike.

Hank Smith and several of his Arizona Guards, under Captain Tom Mastin, had reached Pinos Altos before daybreak. Smith, having immediately bought provisions at Roy and Sam Bean's store, had started for his log cabin at Birch's Gulch when he heard firing erupt at Bear Creek Gulch about a mile away. The Indians' initial assault apparently surprised the miners, although local history has it that the Apaches had audaciously lined up shoulder to shoulder at the top of the hills overlooking the town. Then, at a signal from Cochise and Mangas Coloradas, in unison the horde of whooping warriors charged down the hill and attacked the settlement. Although Hollywood would now love such a scenario, Cochise and Mangas failed to take this ostentatious display into account. Actually, the two leaders had drawn up a carefully conceived plan—one that the two had carried out successfully against Mexican settlements. Early that morning, shortly after the first "peep of day," the Indians struck simultaneously at the mining camps spread out from the main town. The fight became general. The Indians' surprise assault had left many miners cornered in their diggings and either unable or too frightened to venture out and fight. Others fought from their log homes; some battled from behind trees. Hank Smith claimed that many miners did not participate in the fight because they were simply too frightened.

Smith, with three other men, rushed to his log cabin at Whiskey Gulch, where he and others eventually repulsed the Apaches. This accomplished, he sped off to the main camp. He found the Chiricahuas and whites "in a hand to hand fight." Early in the battle the Indians had tried to set fire to the log houses, but they were generally unsuccessful. Fierce fighting continued throughout the morning. By noon the battle was concentrated around Bean's and Roman's supply stores in the center of town. Here the Apaches mortally wounded Captain Tom Mastin and killed two other men at Roman's store. Finally, about noon, the Americans, with the help of several women at Bean's store, fired the small cannon loaded with nails and buckshot, which staggered the Apaches. In a furious counterattack, the miners then routed and drove off the Apaches.

Pinos Altos, New Mexico, site of the September 27, 1861, fight between the allied Chiricahuas, under Cochise and Mangas Coloradas, and American and Mexican miners. (Photo by Kathi Plauster)

Both sides suffered heavy casualties. According to Hank Smith, the Apaches left ten dead on the battleground, and he believed that they had carried off twenty more dead and wounded. The Apaches killed five men (Mastin and J. B. Corwin of the guards and three civilians) and wounded seven others. Though the numbers suggest a victory for the Americans, in the days that followed many miners deserted their diggings for either Santa Fe or Mesilla. Only seventy miners and a detachment of Arizona Guards remained at Pinos Altos.[36]

The encounter at Pinos Altos was yet another in a series of hard-fought engagements between the Chiricahua Apaches and the remaining whites in New Mexico. It had been a show of force, a warning to the whites. Mangas Coloradas and Cochise, the two greatest Chiricahua fighting chiefs of the mid-nineteenth century, had carried the offensive to their hated enemies. Yet the Americans and Mexicans had killed several of their warriors in these sharp engagements, including several prominent men. The hard fight at Pinos Altos had cost the Chiricahuas more warriors than any other engagement fought during the alliance between Cochise and Mangas Coloradas. The Chihenne leaders Chabnocito, a daredevil fighting man, and Delgadito, formerly a bellicose man, were apparently killed at either Cooke's Canyon or Pinos Altos. The Chokonen Esquinaline, a steadfast fighting ally of Mangas Coloradas in the 1840s and 1850s, also died at this time, likely in battle. The lifespan of a Chiricahua war chief was typically short, for he "would go before [his men] in battle and perform great feats to spur them on."[37] Both Cochise and Mangas Coloradas epitomized this behavior.

After the fight at Pinos Altos the war party attacked at least two freighter trains. One was Harney's train, which fought 150 Apaches for fourteen hours, suffering a loss of two men, and the second was Charles Hayden's train, which the Chiricahuas assaulted about twelve miles south of Santa Rita del Cobre. Hayden was transporting several Mexicans from Santa Rita del Cobre to the Rio Grande when the Apaches attacked and captured two young men. Having suffered losses in the Pinos Altos fight, the Apaches were in ill humor. They ruthlessly "made spread eagles of the men in sight of Hayden's camp and tortured them to death by shooting and lancing them." Eventually Lieutenant Jack Swilling and thirty-five Arizona Guards rescued the train and escorted it to the Mimbres settlement.[38]

Soon after the Chiricahuas left the area. Cochise plunged into northern Mexico, where he soon resumed relations at Fronteras. Several Indians appeared at Fronteras with a message from Cochise. They also happened to provide insightful information regarding his status within the Chiricahua tribe. From what they revealed, Cochise was "at the head of them all. . . . He has all the warriors from Mesilla to Sarampion [Peloncillos] waiting for the enemy [Americans] to come and make a campaign against him." Clearly, with Mangas aging, Cochise had become the dominant Chiricahua leader. Moreover, he expected the Americans to send a force into Apachería to chastise him. But he vowed to be prepared.[39]

While Cochise moved into Mexico, Mangas probably found sanctuary north of the Gila in the Mogollon Mountains, for it was the time of year to harvest acorns and piñon nuts. He soon heard more bad news. A campaign from Chihuahua had attacked a village near Lake Guzmán, killing seven Apaches and capturing sixteen. Among the dead was a brother of Mangas, in all likelihood Phalios Palacio.[40] There is no record of Mangas's avenging this attack; he probably remained that winter in the secluded canyons and valleys which dominated the lower Mogollons, out of range of the Confederate and Union troops who were fighting each other along the central and upper Rio Grande. Encamped there, he

fortunately avoided northern Mexico, where smallpox had manifested itself and was taking a heavy toll on the Chokonen and
Nednhi bands who had made peace at Fronteras and Janos.[41] That
winter and early spring of 1862, Cochise tried to consolidate a large
force to attack the Mowry mines in southern Arizona, but Mangas
remained in his country, seemingly weary of war.

That spring of 1862, Mangas Coloradas may have sent an emissary to Pinos Altos to request peace. According to William Fourr,
Mangas had moved to a site near Pinos Altos at that time. The
commander of the Arizona Guards asked instructions from Lieutenant Colonel Baylor at Mesilla. Baylor had just returned from a
scout into Chihenne and Nednhi country that had taken him as far
south as Corralitos, Chihuahua, where he had captured several
Chiricahuas and promptly practiced what he preached—executing
them.[42] Upon receiving this communication, he issued his infamous order that reeked of duplicity, brutality, and insensitivity. It
was a command born of ignorance, and it deservedly got him in
hot water with his superiors in Richmond, especially when Federal
forces began to use it as propaganda to convince Indian nations in
the South that Baylor's philosophy of genocide represented the
Confederacy's Indian policy. From Mesilla on March 20, 1862, he
instructed Captain Thomas Helm, commander of the Arizona
Guards at Pinos Altos:

> I learn from Lieutenant J. J. Jackson that the Indians have been in to
> your post [Pinos Altos] for the purpose of making a treaty. The
> Congress of the Confederate States has passed a law declaring
> extermination to all hostile Indians. You will therefore use all means
> to persuade the Apaches of any tribe to come in for the purpose of
> making peace, and when you get them together kill all the grown
> Indians and take the children prisoners and sell them to defray the
> expense of killing the Indians. Buy whiskey and such other goods as
> may be necessary for the Indians. . . . [I] look to you for success
> against these cursed pests who have already murdered over 100 men
> in this Territory.[43]

Fortunately for Mangas Coloradas, he decided to remain in the
Mogollon country, where he was safe from American troops, who
remained concentrated on the Rio Grande. But he and Cochise
soon had another American force to reckon with—a volunteer
force from California which, in the spring of 1862, had entered
western Arizona and had begun a systematic march across the

desert to unite with Canby's troops on the Rio Grande. Canby's troops had just defeated a large Rebel force under General Henry H. Sibley, who happened to be a brother-in-law of Canby. Sibley had won most of the battles but had lost the campaign when his supply lines became stretched and the Federal forces, aided by Colorado Volunteer troops, drove him back to Texas, where he had come from. About the same time, in the spring of 1862 the California Column began its arduous march from southern California to the Rio Grande, with a stop at Tucson, which a small force of rebels under Captain Sherod Hunter had occupied on February 28, 1862. Hunter stayed until early May, when he heard that the California Volunteers were en route to Tucson. Upon his retreat to Mesilla, he found the rebel forces in disarray; dispirited and disillusioned, many had left for Texas and Mexico and some for California. Baylor and Sibley had also vacated the region—the former for Richmond and the latter to San Antonio. The rebels' dream of a Confederate empire stretching west to California had dissipated.[44]

The California Column was organized to repel the Confederate invasion of New Mexico. Brigadier General James Henry Carleton led the volunteers, who numbered 2,350 infantry and cavalry troops. Carleton, an experienced and able officer—some would call him a martinet—had previously served in New Mexico. His objectives were to drive the Confederate forces from Tucson and the Mesilla Valley, to reoccupy the abandoned southwestern forts, and to reestablish Federal rule in Arizona and New Mexico. By the time he arrived, however, Canby's troops had already defeated the rebels. Besides guarding against a Confederate invasion, the role of Carleton's army for the remainder of the war was to make Arizona and New Mexico a safe place for travelers, to provide security for miners and ranchers, and to revitalize commerce. Naturally, the Apaches stood in Carleton's way as the major obstacle to the achievement of these goals. Carleton, like Baylor before him, felt that most Indians were animals and deserved killing. Thus, his policies eventually mirrored those of the Confederates, and Mangas Coloradas would eventually suffer the consequences.[45] In fact, one could say that the importance of the California men to the territory of New Mexico far transcended their role as soldiers during the military occupation in the Civil War. For after the war, some 340 soldiers remained in New Mexico and helped develop its mines, opened up farms and ranches, and became important leaders in law and politics.[46]

On May 20, 1862, Lieutenant Colonel Joseph Rodman West, a short, balding man who was generally popular with his men, with the first elements of the California Column occupied Tucson. Hunter's small detachment of Confederates had just left for New Mexico. On May 24, Carleton ordered that garrisons reoccupy Forts Buchanan and Breckenridge. By June 5, most of the column had reached Tucson. Carleton, disgusted at the anarchy there, declared martial law three days later. He arrested "nine cutthroats, gamblers and loafers who have infested this town to the great bodily fear of all good citizens." Tucson soon became a law-abiding town.[47]

Yet Carleton was woefully unaware of conditions along the Rio Grande. On June 15, 1862, he sent three men to carry a message to Brigadier General Canby in New Mexico. Cochise's men killed two of them in the San Simón Valley a few miles east of Apache Pass. The third man, John Jones, miraculously escaped and made his way to the Rio Grande, where rebel troops captured him. Yet he somehow got word to Canby that "the Column from California is really coming."[48]

A few days after he had sent these messengers, Carleton ordered Lieutenant Colonel Edward E. Eyre and a force of 140 men of Companies B and C, First California Cavalry, to make a scout between Tucson and Mesilla. At Apache Pass, Eyre's command ran into Cochise and about seventy-five Chokonens. Eyre, whose superiors had ordered him to avoid conflicts with the Indians if possible, held a parley with the haughty Chokonen chief even though his men had heard shots and reported three soldiers were missing. Mangas Coloradas was apparently not present. Eyre assured Cochise that the Americans had only friendly intentions: "We wished to be friendly with the Apaches; that at present I was only travelling through their country and desired [that] he [Cochise] would not interfere with my men and animals; that a great captain was at Tucson with a large number of soldiers; that he wished to have a talk with all the Apache Chiefs and to make peace with them and make them presents."

Eyre's naïveté must have amused Cochise, who undoubtedly believed that these troops intended to punish his people for their hostilities of the past year, especially since his men had already killed three of Eyre's soldiers. Soon after the powwow, the troops found the bodies, stripped and lanced in several places. Eyre prudently made camp outside the eastern mouth of Apache Pass.[49] For some unknown reason he did not send a warning to Carleton about the Chiricahuas' hostility at Apache Pass, which, as historian Larry Ludwig, ranger-in-charge at Fort Bowie, points out, was "one of the reasons Eyre was out there in the first place."[50]

Thanks to Eyre's candor, Cochise began preparations to ambush the next party of soldiers traveling through Apache Pass. According to Apache oral history, Cochise summoned help from the three other Chiricahua bands—the Bedonkohes under Mangas Coloradas, the Chihennes under Victorio and Nana, and the Nednhis under Juh.[51] In addition, Cochise's erstwhile ally Francisco, the warlike Western Apache leader of the Eastern White Mountain band, may also have participated. The two great chiefs would not be disappointed. Except for a small force left behind at Tucson, Carleton had prepared a systematic march to the Rio Grande.

On the hot, dry, and dusty streets of Tucson on July 4, 1862, Carleton ordered his soldiers to appear in dress parade to celebrate the nation's birthday. At this time he gave his men the happy tidings that the column would go on to the Mesilla Valley. On July 9, Lieutenant Colonel West ordered Captain Thomas L. Roberts, First Infantry, California Volunteers, to take command of a 126-man detachment made up of 72 men of Company E, First Infantry; 24 men of Company B, Second Cavalry, under none other than John Cremony; 20 men of Company E, First Infantry, under First Lieutenant William A. Thompson (his company manned the two howitzers); and 10 men of Company H, First Infantry, under First Lieutenant Alexander Bartholomew MacGowan. In addition, another 25 to 30 civilian teamsters were to accompany the command. Carleton had ordered Roberts, like Eyre, to avoid fighting Apaches unless attacked. Naturally, the twenty-two teams and 242 head of stock made an attractive target to Cochise and Mangas Coloradas.

Roberts's command left Tucson at 4:30 A.M. on July 10 and marched twenty miles to the Cienega, arriving there about 6:00 P.M. The next day his command rested. Early on the morning of July 12, he resumed his trek east and halted later that day at the San Pedro River, where he rested his men and horses. He had now entered Chokonen country. Here, as instructed, Roberts left MacGowan's detachment and three cavalrymen to guard the supplies that he was leaving for the next group of troops that were to follow him east. Roberts even further divided his command, taking eighty infantrymen with the howitzers, eight troopers, and three wagons with civilian teamsters to Dragoon Springs. Captain Cremony, with the rest of the command, twenty-five infantry and cavalry, and with some twenty civilian teamsters, remained with the train and cattle. Roberts allowed his command to rest a day at Dragoon Springs, remaining there until 5:00 p.m. on July 14, when he, with a force of about ninety-five men, which included five or six civilian teamsters, began their march to Apache Pass, which lay forty miles to the east.[52] Mangas Coloradas and Cochise watched the command from the time it left Dragoon Springs. The dust that the company kicked up would have been visible for miles. The two leaders had assembled at Apache Pass a body of warriors estimated to number anywhere from one hundred to a ridiculous eight hundred.[53]

Unfortunately, the Indians have left behind no detailed account of the fight from their point of view. In later years, Cochise allegedly told one American participant that when the soldiers came "straggling into the pass" after a march of forty miles in nineteen hours with only a cup of coffee to sustain them, he confidently believed that an easy victory was in the palms of his hands and that his men would easily kill every one of the soldiers.[54] Asa Daklugie, son of Juh, echoed Cochise's sentiments when he told Eve Ball that the Indians were sure of preventing the soldiers' attempt to reach the water at Apache Spring. The Indians had superior numbers, secure positions, and the element of surprise in their favor. Yet the California Volunteers prevailed, with both sides concurring that Lieutenant Thompson's howitzers, which fired forty shells into the Apaches' positions, proved to be one of the keys in averting a catastrophe.[55]

Roberts's detachment marched all night across Sulphur Springs Valley, which included the famous playa where his men sloshed through water and mud made six inches deep by recent July thunderstorms. Once this was crossed, the command had a twenty-mile march over a dry and dusty trail to the western mouth of Apache Pass. The march was trying and challenging to both man and beast. According to one participant, the ordeal "was one never forgotten by those who made it; all night long the burdened infantry marched over the forty miles of dusty road, the heat was oppressive and the pace fast enough to test the muscles of men who had become hardened by their march from the Pacific coast."[56] We must remember that even as his men approached the western summit of Apache Pass, Roberts had received no information about the difficulties that Eyre had experienced there three weeks before.

The soldiers followed the Butterfield Overland Mail route, which threaded its way through the ravines and canyons of the

pass toward the abandoned mail station. Having seen no signs of
Apaches, Roberts's command, though definitely in a state of alert
as it entered the notorious defile, may have begun to relax as it
approached the stage station. The infantry was strung out along
the road, and the cavalry that had arrived at the station had already
taken the saddles off their horses, another indication that the men
were unprepared for the Apaches' attack.[57]

Most accounts agree that the weary men reached the deserted
stage station about noon, although Private John Teal recalled it
was about 10:30 A.M. Cochise and Mangas Coloradas had prepared
a two-pronged ambush. Mangas, with his Bedonkohes and Chihennes, had positioned his men behind the rocks and boulders in
the steep hills on both sides of the trail to ambush Roberts's command once they reached the stage station. As his detachment
reached the unoccupied station, the Chiricahuas unleashed a
"murderous volley" into the rear guard of his command, probably
some twenty soldiers who manned the howitzers and another five
teamsters with one or two wagons. The Indians' first fire killed
Private Charles M. O'Brien "with a bullet through his brain,"
wounded a teamster named Andrew Sawyer, and wounded perhaps
one other man, said to have been a hospital steward. Then,
according to one account, the Apaches came out from their positions and charged the command. Furious hand-to-hand fighting
occurred until Roberts, with the rest of his command, rushed back
to relieve the soldiers and drove the Indians into the hills. Lieutenant Thompson's "jackass battery" also helped the cause by
launching a few well-placed shots at the Apaches' positions.
Roberts estimated the Indians' losses at four dead and several
wounded. The thirsty and weary soldiers returned to the stage
station shortly after midday, still six to seven hundred yards from
water.[58]

But the fighting had just begun. Cochise and Juh had posted their
Chokonens and Nednhis on the hills south and north of the spring
behind natural rock fortifications and breastworks that they had
constructed, according to what Asa Daklugie, son of Juh, told Eve
Ball. They also knew that they outnumbered Roberts's command
of some ninety-five soldiers and citizens by about two to one, and
they were firing from protected sites while the soldiers' march left
them exposed to the Indians' fire. The plucky Captain Roberts,
although a greenhorn at Indian fighting, acted decisively, and it
would be difficult to say how he could have inspired his men any
more than he did. According to Fountain's account, Roberts

Howitzer positions, Battle of Apache Pass. (Photo by Kathi Plauster)

declared, "Boys, there is the water, we must have it or die; I ask no man to do more than I shall try to do. I expect no man to do less. This is no place for cowards or skulkers; if I fail to do my duty men shoot me down for by God I will shoot down the first man who shows the white feather here today." His men, tired, thirsty, and angry, "responded with a cheer that shook the rocky ribs of the canyon" and announced to Cochise that more fighting lay ahead. Mangas had either remained in the hills near the western mouth of the pass or had gone around the soldiers to join Cochise in the fighting at the springs.

Thus, Roberts deployed his command into two platoons. He instructed Sergeant Albert Fountain to take one command of infantrymen to "deploy as skirmishers, make a dash for the spring and try to hold it until we [can] obtain sufficient water for our immediate necessities." Meanwhile, he directed the second platoon with the howitzers to lob shells over the heads of Fountain's men against the Apache positions above and on both sides of the springs. Fountain's men bravely "dashed forward" into the canyon toward the spring, with the Indians firing heavily but evidently overshooting because they were aiming at targets below them and had failed to gauge accurately their sights. When the soldiers were within fifty yards of the precious commodity, the Indians unleashed another tremendous volley, which killed Private John Barr. Roberts, sensing that his men were sitting ducks, at once ordered the bugler to sound retreat, and Fountain's patrol fell back, without water.[59]

Clark Stocking, a private in Company A, Fifth California Infantry, who marched through Apache Pass after the fight, obtained an interesting anecdote from one of the participants. He was apparently describing the events of the first day's fighting:

> One group [of Apaches] about 800 yards above us was especially troublesome, as they had several rifles of as long range as our own. The most troublesome of those occupied a lofty crotch of an oak-tree, whence a puff of smoke was seen to sift out through its foliage every time one of our men was hit. The gunners of the howitzer had been trying to get his range, but failed. Just then the hospital steward, an old discharged artilleryman who had grown grey in the service with General Scott, came along, pushed the gunners from the howitzer, elevated it to his satisfaction, took his sight, and pulled the lanyard. I certainly never saw or heard of such a shot. A sharpshooter with a rifle could not have beaten it. The shell struck the tree and exploded apparently in the centre, for nothing was left of it but a slivered stump.[60]

Meanwhile, as Roberts's soldiers regrouped and struggled to regain their composure and determination, the Chiricahuas brazenly yelled and taunted the men who had come so close to gaining control of the spring. The soldiers defiantly responded with "fierce and brutal curses from cracked lips and swollen tongues." They implored Roberts "to lead them to water—or death." Roberts, "cool as an icicle," confidently assured the men: "Keep cool boys, I will get you out of this scrape all right; we are going to whip those Indians and get that water." He vetoed the suggestion of another charge, preferring to wait until the howitzers could have another crack at the Indians. Yet "the trails of both pieces were broken," which prevented the gunners from attaining the elevation needed to shell the Indians' positions along the heights. Fort Bowie Ranger-in-Charge Larry Ludwig described what probably happened: "The part of the trail that was broken was where it attached to the axle. This was probably broken in an attempt to get needed elevation to shell the Apache positions high on the slopes. Once the elevation screw was at maximum elevation, the only way to get height would be by lowering the trail. This could be done by setting it upon a steeper slope or by putting the trail in a hole. By doing this the recoil would come straight back on the trail, splitting the wood."[61]

Roberts was forced to chose another plan. He ordered Fountain to ask for twenty volunteers to storm the highest hill to the left of the springs (today known as Overlook Ridge), where a large band of Chiricahuas had taken refuge behind breastworks—a circular formation about thirty feet in diameter. By gaining that height the Americans would occupy the highest position—the key point in the defense of the springs. Once they had taken that place the whites would command the ground north and west of the springs and thus be in position to flush out any Apaches east or above the springs. Every man volunteered, so Fountain took the first twenty in line. As the weary and thirsty soldiers began to climb the hill, ten men at a time would dash forward, lie down, and cover the other ten. A May 1996 archaeological survey of the top of the hill corroborated that "this position . . . came under heavy fire from troops below,"[62] undoubtedly the work of Fountain's men as they systematically climbed Overlook Ridge. The remaining soldiers stood poised to make a dash for the springs when Fountain's men gained the heights.[63]

Meanwhile, as Fountain neared the summit and raised his canteen, hoping for one last drop of water, an Apache fired from a loophole in the breastworks, sending a bullet that "passed through the canteen" an inch from his mouth. Once he realized that the bullet had missed him, his fright turned to relief and then to rage. Jumping up, he ordered his men to "fix bayonets and make one dash to the summit." As his men bravely raced for the summit, the Indians sent a volley toward them, but their aim was bad and once again they "overshot" the soldiers. Fountain kept on coming until his charge had succeeded in gaining the breastworks, right on the heels of some fifty Apaches, who ran down the hill on the other side. Fountain's glorious charge changed the course of the battle. His men now owned the high ground and with it the fate of the battle. His soldiers could fire upon the Apaches above the springs and those perched on the heights where Carleton would order the establishment of the first Fort Bowie a few weeks later. Once Fountain controlled the breastwork, the rest of the command raced to the springs with "camp kettles and canteens"; meanwhile, the infantrymen moved the howitzers to higher ground and immediately began lobbing shells at the last entrenchments east and south of the springs. According to the informants of Eve Ball and the recollections of Jason Betzinez, the Chiricahuas at this

Albert Fountain. As a sergeant in the California Volunteers, Fountain led a group of men that dislodged the Indians from breastworks on Overland Ridge. He was one of the many heroes of the Battle of Apache Pass. (Courtesy Rio Grande Historical Collections, New Mexico State University Library, no. RG95-57)

Indian positions, Battle of Apache Pass. Fountain led the charge up the ravine, which runs diagonally to the right, to dislodge the Apaches. Indian positions were scattered along these rugged ridges. (Photo by Kathi Plauster)

juncture abandoned their positions, taking their wounded with them. Yet, curiously, the artillery fire had not killed any Apaches, at least according to the Indians. Soon after, Fountain could see many Apaches "scampering to the hills to escape the bursting shells." During the fight an unlikely hero had emerged: a dog named Butch, who had joined the column at San Diego. He ran "around the brush & chaparral, barking and hunting Indians" before losing one toe during the fight, "shot off" by the Apaches. The courageous conduct of Fountain and his twenty men had won the day for the California Column.[64]

Captain Roberts, concerned that Captain Cremony might bring his command with the wagons into the pass, dispatched six cavalrymen under Sergeant Titus D. Mitchell to find Cremony's force and instruct him to remain until Roberts could rendezvous with him later that night. Sergeant Fountain, apparently equipped with binoculars, from his position high on Overlook Ridge could see Mitchell's troopers exit the western part of the pass, followed soon after by a band of mounted Chiricahuas. Fountain, feeling that the Indians had probably killed or captured Mitchell's men, immediately went to Captain Roberts to report what he had seen.[65]

A band of Chiricahuas, some forty to fifty in number, overtook Mitchell's troopers about four miles west of Apache Pass. At the first fire they wounded Private Jesse D. Maynard and two horses, but the cavalrymen succeeded in galloping off ahead of the Indians. Private John Teal, who had helped to man the howitzers during the hot fighting for the springs, had dismounted to rest his fatigued horse. During the Apaches' assault a group of fifteen or twenty Indians, led by Mangas Coloradas himself, cut Teal off from his companions. Teal described what happened next:

> The Indians then turned toward me. I had mounted & fired my carbine at them, they closed in around me, both mounted & on foot. The chief or commander of the Indians was armed with a citizen rifle but was unwilling to fire at me without a rest so, after rallying his warriors, he ran for a rest & I after him but, on looking over my shoulder, I saw the mounted Indians to[o] close on my rear for safety, so I turned on them & they scattered like birds. I turned again to tend to the old chief but I was to[o] late, he had got to a bunch of Gaita [Galleta] & was lying on his belly on the opposite side of the bunch pointed straight at me, which caused me to drop from the horse on the ground & the Indian shot the horse instead of me. The horse left & I laid low sending a bullet at them whenever I had a chance. We kept firing until it was dark when a lucky shot from me sent the chief off in the arms of his Indians.[66]

Although Teal had no idea which chief he had downed, it turned out that his victim was none other than Mangas Coloradas. Teal believed that the frequency of his shots had surprised the Indians, for he had a breech-loading rifle, likely a Sharps carbine, which far exceeded in rapidity of fire the infantry's regular cap-and-ball musket. Teal noted that the Indian leader was an "old chief," and Mangas's presence at the head of his men fits well with the typical conduct and actions of an Apache war chief. With Cochise directing the warriors at Apache Springs, it was only logical to conclude that Mangas, after the first attack, had likely remained with his warriors near the western mouth of the pass, hoping to cut off any stragglers trying to escape their ambush. It was also conceivable that he had joined Cochise near the springs and, seeing Mitchell's cavalry leave, decided to take a force through a back canyon to cut off the whites before they reached the open ground in Sulphur Springs valley. According to Apache tradition, and from what Cremony later learned, the

The ravine between these two hills is possibly the place from whence Mangas Coloradas and his men emerged to attack John Teal's party. Mangas was wounded a mile or two west of here in the Sulphur Springs Valley. (Photo by Kathi Plauster)

Chiricahuas took Mangas to Janos, Chihuahua, where a doctor nursed him back to health.[67]

Having walked eight miles with his saddle and gear, the brave Teal reached Cremony's camp near Ewell's Spring before midnight. A few hours later Captain Roberts with half his command rendezvoused with Cremony's detachment. After resting for a few hours, they left for Apache Pass at daybreak. As they entered the famous defile, Roberts deployed skirmishers on both sides of the canyon and reached the stage station without encountering any resistance. Leaving the wagons and teamsters at the stage station, Captain Roberts with his entire command of about 150 men prepared for another fight for the springs, which the Apaches had reoccupied. Placing his two howitzers in the center of the canyon, with the infantry deployed as skirmishers and the cavalry mounted in readiness behind the infantry, his command fearlessly began a slow but systematic march toward the Indians' positions with the howitzers shelling their breastworks and the infantry firing volley after volley "as if on drill." Cochise's Chokonens did not remain long; in minutes they abandoned their breastworks and hastened off to the south. By this time many Chihennes and Bedonkohes had already deserted the fight and had left for northern Chihuahua with the wounded Mangas Coloradas.[68]

The fight for the springs ended about 4:00 P.M. The official casualties for the whites in the two-day fight were two killed and two wounded; Roberts estimated that the Indians had suffered a loss of at least nine dead.[69] In contrast, Cremony, who had not participated in the fierce fighting during the first day, claimed that he learned from a "prominent Apache who was present in the engagement that sixty-three warriors were killed outright by the shells, while only three perished from musket fire."[70] Cremony's propensity to overstatement is evident here. Conversely, Apache versions understate the incident, claiming that the soldiers had killed few, if any, warriors.[71] In truth, the number of Apache casualties cannot be determined with accuracy any more than can the number of Indians engaged in the fight. Cochise and Mangas Coloradas likely perceived that the California Column had come to punish them for their hostilities of the past eighteen months. Yet their ambush was an opportunity for loot, and as Dan Thrapp writes, they were "very sure that they could break it off and get away when they chose; that was the nature of an Apache ambush."[72]

Cochise took his Chokonens to Sonora after the Battle of Apache Pass.[73] Mangas remained at Janos until time healed his wounds and then returned to his safe haven in the Mogollon Mountains. His alliance with his son-in-law Cochise had ended. Now, in his early seventies, his wounds recently healed and the bluecoats back in his country, he wanted to settle down again at Santa Lucía Springs and resume planting. Unfortunately for him, General James Carleton, whose march from Tucson east to the Rio Grande was marked by skeletons, skulls, graves, and charred wagons—all stark testimonials to the audacity and brutality of the Apaches—had no such thoughts. He wanted nothing to do with Mangas's proposal, which he believed insincere, and had come to advocate only one method of dealing with the Apaches: extermination.

Carleton would make Mangas Coloradas pay for having the nerve to defend himself from the miners and ranchers who had appropriated the best hunting grounds and farming lands of his people.

Chapter 18

THE GREATEST OF WRONGS

ALTHOUGH from the Chiricahua perspective the fight at Apache Pass ended in a virtual standoff, the events that followed had negative ramifications for both Cochise and Mangas Coloradas. Captain Thomas Roberts, whose courage had deservedly won him accolades from all quarters, wisely recommended that Carleton establish a post near the springs. "Otherwise every command will have to fight for the water, and . . . are almost certain to lose some lives." Carleton, who arrived at Apache Pass about July 27, heeded Roberts's advice and decided to place a permanent garrison there "because of the hostile attitude of the Chiricahua Indians." Accordingly, he issued General Order No. 12, which decreed that Major Theodore A. Coult and one hundred men of Companies A and G, Fifth California Infantry, occupy the new post at Apache Pass. The fort, named Fort Bowie, would remain a fixture at Apache Pass until 1894. Besides guarding the precious spring, its main responsibility was to keep communications open on both sides of the Chiricahua Mountains. Apparently Carleton had not yet formulated his extreme views toward the Apaches. These would develop during his march to the Rio Grande as he saw firsthand the remains of the victims slain since the beginning of the war. At Fort Bowie he issued orders "to attack all Apaches" unless they arrived with a flag of truce. A few months later his Apache policy had evolved to the point that he modified this directive and instructed his subordinates to reject any flags of truce and simply attack all Apaches. Carleton vowed that Cochise and Mangas Coloradas would pay the price for having had the temerity to attack his command. The general considered the Apache assault a personal affront, and he would not take it lying down.[1]

Carleton left Apache Pass in late July for the Rio Grande. Two miles east of the pass he found the remains of nine white men who had left Pinos Altos bound for California; he concluded that on July 13, as the parties approached the eastern mouth of the pass, the Chiricahuas had ambushed them from a gully "which cannot be seen from horseback until the rider is within fifty yards of the spot." From all appearances, death came quickly to most of the party. Yet the Indians captured at least one man and burned him at the stake; "the charred bones and the burnt ends of the rope" were still visible.[2]

In this startling way occurred the beginning of Carleton's journey through Chiricahua country. The devastation that he continued to come upon horrified the down-East Yankee from Maine, who usually exuded self-confidence. As he marched along the overland mail route east toward the Rio Grande, skeletons, skulls, graves, and charred wagons marred the landscape, all stark testimonials to the audacity and brutality of the Indians. Upon reaching Santa Fe to take command of the Department of New Mexico from Brigadier General Canby (who had been transferred to duty in Washington, D.C.), he received more reports from the superintendent of Indian affairs for the Department of New Mexico emphasizing the critical condition of the territory because of Apache raids. Furthermore, the Indians had gone unpunished, and this galled the stern officer. These frightening pictorials left Carleton with a vivid and compelling impression of Apache warfare. Moreover, with the Confederates no longer a threat, he had to find something else to occupy his men, who had volunteered to fight the rebels, not Indians. Thus he turned his attention, every bit of it, to the Indians because he knew no other way. Although his earliest orders had been to avoid conflict with the Indians, in the fall of 1862 he redirected his enormous energy and indefatigable zeal against the Apaches.

Carleton was a disciplinarian, a martinet, and a highly principled man who imposed his morality and devotion to duty on his subordinates. A devout Christian, a good family man, and a gentleman, he was intolerant of those who dissented from his views. His main problem was his focus, his perspective. The view from his lens was too narrow. Yet he carried out his duties with a zeal and energy which the Department of New Mexico had never before seen. During the Civil War he became the absolute ruler of New Mexico; his decisions, based on his morals and convictions, were,

Brigadier General James Henry Carleton. Carleton rejected Mangas's peace solicitations and instead ordered a campaign against him. (Courtesy Museum of New Mexico, neg. no. 22938)

of course, correct. He could not be dissuaded. Carleton inevitably offended many people.

We can explain Carleton's Apache philosophy in one word: extermination. He would give no quarter. A decade later Colonel George Crook waged constant war against the Apaches of Arizona to force their subjugation. He treated them with firmness but received them with compassion and dignity when they were ready to capitulate. In contrast, Carleton had no feelings for Indians. He demanded unconditional surrender. And even when some bands were prepared to lay down their arms, he either imposed conditions that were totally unacceptable to the Indians or refused their offers because in his estimation his troops had not sufficiently whipped them. Thus, when Mangas Coloradas requested an armistice, he unfortunately fell into the latter category. By that time Carleton had become obsessed with a psychopathic hatred of Apaches.

After the Battle of Apache Pass on July 15, 1862, the Chiricahuas committed few hostilities in southern Arizona and New Mexico during the summer of 1862. They had fled to northern Mexico after the fight—Cochise and many of his followers to Fronteras,[3] while Mangas sought treatment at Janos, where a doctor, under threats of death, extracted the ball from John Teal's carbine.[4] By mid-August, with Joaquín Terrazas patrolling northwest Chihuahua with a large body of troops seeking the Carrizaleño group of Nednhis,[5] Mangas opted to return to the Mogollon Mountains. Although Cochise harbored no thought of making peace with Americans, Mangas Coloradas believed it was the best course for him and his followers. Likely many Bedonkohes and Chihennes agreed with him. Mangas was past seventy years of age, but he continued to lead these two bands during times of crisis. It was not uncommon for a Chiricahua chief to maintain his status in his twilight years if he remained "clear of mind and commanding in manner despite advancing years."[6]

In mid-September Mangas Coloradas left the Mogollon Mountains and headed to Ácoma, where he had made the celebrated peace treaty with Colonel Sumner, the only compact he ever signed, a little more than a decade before. On September 19, 1862, when he arrived there, he asked Juanico Romero, "an Indian of some note from the Pueblo of Ácoma," to go to Cubero "and ascertain if he [Mangas] would be allowed to come in to treat for peace." What Romero reported to Captain Julius C. Shaw of the First New Mexico Cavalry Volunteers the officer included in a letter to Brigadier General Carleton:

> At present Mangas lives at Mogoyon [Mogollon Mountains], formerly lived at Cuero (not Cubero) [probably means Santa Lucía] where himself & people used to till the land and were at peace with the world until the troops attacked & killed many of his people. After the third assault he states that he armed himself in self-defense but is now anxious for peace & wishes to return to his former home and pursuits, and to live like a Christian. He would have come himself in person but was afraid of the Mexicans killing him—but will return in ten or twelve days to ascertain the results of his mission.

Shaw ended the letter by asking Carleton for instructions.[7]

Mangas Coloradas clearly wanted to return to Santa Lucía and resume planting. He characteristically trusted Americans, but not the Mexicans at Cubero. This distinction, we shall see, would prove to be his downfall.

Carleton paid no attention to Mangas's solicitations. He had recently received reports from Colonel Joseph Rodman West, the diminutive commander of the troops in the District of Arizona (whose boundaries were the Colorado River east to the Rio Grande south of the Gila and Fort Thorn, and southwestern Texas—essentially southern Arizona and southern New Mexico),[8] that his troops were unable to cover all the country over which the Indians depredated. West, following Carleton's orders, had previously sent troops and provisions to Pinos Altos to feed an estimated twenty families who remained there.[9] On October 3, 1862, perhaps a week after receiving Shaw's letter, Carleton, in a seemingly casual note to West, dismissed any consideration of Mangas's peace solicitations: "Mangas Coloradas sends me word he wants peace, but I have no faith in him."[10]

Carleton clearly arrived at this assumption in ignorance of the fact that before the outbreak of hostilities twenty-one months before, Mangas had always advocated peaceful policies with Americans. The aging chief had always favored diplomacy and tact with Americans. The Chiricahuas' oral history and Mangas's own actions bore this out. In a way, he was a victim of his own reputation—one, however, earned from his warlike activities below the border. In the Southwest, no other chief symbolized the practice of Apache warfare more than Mangas Coloradas, despite his record of peaceful coexistence with Anglos since Kearny's arrival in 1846. As it turned out, Carleton unequivocally refused to hear Mangas out; instead, he decided to launch a campaign against him, hoping either to exterminate the Apaches or to pummel them so unmercifully that he would force their unconditional surrender.

That fall Colonel West reported that the "Indians are troublesome" at Pinos Altos.[11] In response, General Carleton, who assumed that Mangas was responsible for any depredations near the mines, set the groundwork for operations against the venerable Apache chief. On October 14, 1862, he asked West to gather the intelligence necessary to support his plan: "It is desirable to make a campaign against Mangas Coloradas's band of Apaches which have committed so many outrages against travellers and the people of Pinos Altos. The winter is the best time to operate against these Indians. I wish you to do me the favor to gather up all the information you can on the haunts of Mangas's band, its probable numbers, the best guides for the country, etc. If Jack Swilling could be trusted, he would doubtless make a fine guide to a force operating in the Pinos Altos neighborhood."[12]

Three weeks later West responded to Carleton's suggestion:

The desire expressed by the general commanding to send an expedition against the Indians in the vicinity of the Pinos Altos Mines can be attained, and I think with successful results, if troops can be spared from the northern portion of the department. Jack Swilling is at the mines and is available for service. I have in Government employ here a Mexican boy stolen from Sonora, who was seven years a captive of Mangas Coloradas's band [probably Merejildo Grijalva]. With such guides and a good force a severe castigation could most likely be inflicted upon the Indians.[13]

Thus, West and Carleton had laid the foundation for a strike against Mangas Coloradas; simultaneously, the Chihennes and Bedonkohes, represented by Mangas Coloradas, rebuffed at Cubero, had shown up at Pinos Altos, wanting peace and food. According to Geronimo's recollections, at the mining settlement they held a parley with some citizens and a few soldiers, who agreed to issue beef, blankets, and provisions to the Indians. Mangas, desperately wanting peace, agreed to return within two weeks with his people. According to Billy Fourr, at this time Mangas visited Jack Swilling, who in drunkenness expressed the intent to kill Mangas after the chief admitted complicity in the Freeman Thomas fight at Cooke's Canyon.[14] Mangas clearly did not take Swilling seriously, for he soon returned to Bedonkohe country either in the Mogollons or perhaps the Peloncillos north of Stein's Peak and "assembled the whole tribe in council" (by this Geronimo surely meant the Bedonkohe band). His Chiricahuas faced a time of crisis, and Mangas, still the most influential leader of the Chihennes and Bedonkohes, offered his vision for the future—one that included an armistice with Americans and a return to planting at Santa Lucía. He had pointed the way, and now he would go in person and show them how to get there. Geronimo distrusted Americans, but the leaders decided that Mangas with half the band would go to Pinos Altos to test the peace. If the whites proved sincere, and the rations were plentiful, then the entire Bedonkohe band would come in. Accordingly, about half the band journeyed to New Mexico and Pinos Altos in early January 1863.[15]

Once in Chihenne country, Mangas apparently met with Victorio and other Chihenne local group leaders, including Nana. Though needing peace, they, like Geronimo, distrusted Americans. They attempted, but in vain, to dissuade Mangas from this risky venture.[16]

Since Kearny's arrival in New Mexico in 1846, Mangas Coloradas had held innumerable parleys and conferences with Americans, whom he had found honorable and trustworthy. He had no way of knowing that the two new military leaders in New Mexico, Brigadier General James Carleton, commanding the Department of New Mexico, and Joseph Rodman West, recently promoted to brigadier general, commanding the District of Arizona with headquarters at Mesilla, viewed him as public enemy number one. As far as they were concerned, the ends justified the means; they would employ whatever methods necessary (even the most unscrupulous) to accomplish his demise. They clearly believed that if they could capture or kill Mangas Coloradas, they could destroy the will and backbone of the Chihenne and Bedonkohe bands. They failed to understand that any act of treachery would only enrage the Chiricahuas and prolong the fighting, as it did with the execution of Cochise's brother Coyuntura at Apache Pass.

About the time that Mangas sat in council with the Bedonkohes and Chihennes, Carleton had issued General Order Number 1, which called for the establishment near the headwaters of the Gila (close to Mangas's beloved Santa Lucía) of a military post which would become known as Fort West. These orders also directed Brigadier General West to "immediately organize a suitable expedition to chastise what is known as Mangas Coloradas's Band of Gila Apaches. The campaign to be made by this expedition must be a vigorous one and the punishment of that band of murderers and robbers must be thorough and sharp."[17] West not only carried out these orders to the letter, but he also took them one step further, undoubtedly feeling that his superior officer would endorse any actions that he might take to eliminate Apaches, especially the men. He did remember that Carleton's previous orders, while insisting that all warriors be killed, had urged that women and children be spared.[18]

Brigadier General West left Mesilla about the second week of January with a force of 250 men bound for the unoccupied Fort McLane, where he planned to establish temporary headquarters for his operations against Mangas Coloradas. En route, after sundown on January 14, 1863, hearing that Mangas had returned to Pinos Altos, Captain William McLeave sent Captain Edmund D. Shirland with an advance guard of twenty soldiers "in pursuit of a

notorious Indian Chief, Mangas Coloradas." Guided by New
Mexico's best Apache scout, Juan Arroyo, they reached the deserted
Fort McLane the next day and unexpectedly encountered a group of
American prospectors under famous mountain man Captain Joseph
Reddeford Walker.[19] Walker's expedition had been traveling through
Apachería for the past few months. Jack Swilling, former Arizona
Guard officer, had recently joined Walker's party. Together they had
hatched a scheme to capture an Apache chief to ensure their party a
safe trip through Apachería. They discussed the plan with Shirland,
and several of Walker's party, under their chosen "captain," Jack
Swilling, decided to join Shirland's command and go on to Pinos
Altos, where Swilling had recently met with Mangas. Leaving early
in the morning of January 16, the mixed party of citizens and
soldiers reached Pinos Altos shortly after sunrise. At once they
"hoisted a white flag" and waited all day for the chief to appear
and walk into their trap, but he did not come in. Captain Shirland
believed that Mangas had seen the troops and was too wary to
come in.[20]

But he had not fled the area. The Chiricahua leaders were in fact
at that very time sitting in conference, with the consensus
suggesting that they forget any thoughts of making peace at Pinos
Altos. They undoubtedly knew that West's command was en route
from Mesilla, although they may have been unaware of Shirland's
small advance party at Pinos Altos. But even the efforts of the
influential Chihenne chiefs Victorio and Nana could not dissuade
Mangas Coloradas, who desperately wanted permission to return
to Santa Lucía, where he could live in peace and resume planting.
The Americans had never betrayed him, and, although he may not
have completely trusted the miners at Pinos Altos, he apparently
had some faith in Jack Swilling. His people, he felt, needed to
make peace, and Mangas had determined on this course over the
objections of his followers.[21]

Shortly before noon on January 17, 1863, Jack Swilling, who had
hidden Shirland's soldiers in the "chaparral and in the old shacks"
at Pinos Altos, noticed Indians in the distance. Daniel Ellis
Conner, a member of Swilling's party, has left behind two accounts
of the chicanery employed to capture Mangas Coloradas. In a letter
to Arizona historian James McClintock, he described what
happened next:

> Suddenly Swilling issued a war whoop that might have made an
> Apache ashamed of himself. There was only a short delay when

Nana, the Chihenne leader who tried to dissuade Mangas Coloradas from going to Pinos Altos to talk peace with the Americans. (Courtesy National Archives)

Mangas, a tremendously big man, with over a dozen Indians for a bodyguard following, was seen in the distance walking on an old mountain trail toward us, evidently observing us intently. A precipice broke down the mountain between the two parties and the trail bent up to cross it at a shallow place, probably 150 yards from us. Jack left us and walked to meet Mangas, who, with his bodyguard slowly but decisively crossed the ravine. Swilling, though six feet tall, looked like a boy beside Mangas.

They both could speak broken Spanish. We could not hear what was said, but Swilling looked back at us. We interpreted the look to mean that he wanted to be covered. When our squad suddenly leveled our guns upon the party, for the first time Mangas showed appreciation of his serious position. Swilling went up to him and laid his hand on the chief's shoulder and finally convinced him that resistance meant destruction of the whole party. They came walking toward us, bodyguard and all. When Swilling told Mangas that his bodyguard wasn't wanted, he stopped with some gutturals and finally instructed them in Spanish, "Tell my people to look for me when they see me!" When we passed back over the summit the soldiers came out of their concealment, disgusting Mangas beyond measure.[22]

Before dismissing his men, who included Victorio and at least one of his sons, Mangas warned them that they "were not fooling with Mexicans now." Swilling informed Mangas they would hold him as ransom to ensure that the Apaches did not harm Walker's party as it prospected in Apachería.

Conner's second version comes from a manuscript that he wrote and that was published in 1956 under the title *Joseph Reddeford Walker and the Arizona Adventure.* He described Mangas as follows:

His dress consisted of a broad-brimmed small-crowned chip or straw hat of Mexican manufacture—a check cotton shirt, breech cloth or clout, and a high pair of moccasins with legs to them like boots. . . . [He was] a large athletic man considerably over six feet in height, with a large broad head covered with a tremendously heavy growth of long hair that reached to his waist. His shoulders were broad and his chest full, and muscular. He stood erect and his step was proud and altogether he presented quite a model of physical manhood. If Mangas ever had any or many peers amongst his people in personal appearance, I never saw them during the five years experience in their country.[23]

Jack Swilling. After convincing Mangas Coloradas to come to Pinos Altos, he betrayed and helped capture the aging chief. (McClintock, *Arizona: The Youngest State*)

Daniel Ellis Conner. He witnessed the brutal slaying of Mangas
Coloradas. (McClintock, *Arizona: The Youngest State*)

From Conner's two versions we can readily see that the military had nothing to do with the capture of Mangas Coloradas, although Captain Shirland subsequently claimed credit in his report written on January 22, 1863. The next day, January 18, the soldiers with Swilling's party returned to Fort McLane.[24] During the trip from Pinos Altos to the fort one of Mangas's sons, probably either Seth-mooda or Salvador, overtook the command. Swilling permitted him to talk to his father. It was a poignant and moving scene. One eyewitness termed it "pathetic" as Mangas insisted that his son return to his people. It was an emotional farewell. The chief knew that his status was grave and must have wondered whether he would ever see his people again. We will never know if he thought the Americans would actually murder him; these thoughts, if they did creep into his mind, would come later. As the father and son parted company for what both sensed might be the last time, the younger man left with tears in his eyes.[25]

Upon reaching Fort McLane, Jack Swilling turned his prisoner over to Brigadier General Joseph Rodman West. The chief was mounted on a "wild . . . little sorrel pony [with] a frail shell of a saddle and stirrups so short that his knees were constantly jabbing at his chin." Clark Stocking remembered that "Mangas was the most magnificent specimen of savage manhood that I have ever seen. He was six foot five inches of stature, erect and haughty of pose, with a grimly severe expression of countenance, rigid as a face cut in stone."[26] Mangas towered over West, who "looked like a pygmy beside the old Chief." Mangas must now have recognized the desperation of his plight, for he defiantly now "refused to talk."[27] Whereas the day before he had proudly declared that he was the chief of the Bedonkohes and Chihennes, he now disa-vowed that title, probably realizing that these Americans had no comprehension of Apache political structure. He had expected that the whites would embrace his offers for peace and would forgive his former actions when he and his people had made war on the Americans—a war that the Apaches felt had been forced upon them by the whites. West, however, held Mangas accountable for every depredation in southern New Mexico, in particular a brutal raid against a government train the previous October in which Apaches had killed one man, wounded another, and captured seventeen mules. Mangas denied complicity and "protested his innocence," which turned out to be the truth, as subsequent events showed. It mattered little to Brigadier General West that Mangas probably had nothing to do with this depredation or that

Fort McLane, New Mexico. Though nothing of the fort remains today, this is close to the spot where Mangas Coloradas was executed. (Photo by Kathi Plauster)

the chief sincerely may have wanted peace. West contradicted the report of Shirland (who claimed that he had captured Mangas) and blatantly lied in his official report to Carleton by writing that Mangas "had voluntarily placed himself in my power." One supposes that would be so if he had requested protection from West, but that certainly was not the case. West thirsted for a shot at the Chiricahua giant, whom he wanted to cut down to size. By then, the chief's imperious demeanor and his refusal to admit responsibility for his actions during a state of war grated on the diminutive general. West had the imposing chief in his power; he, the military commander of the district, would decide his fate.[28]

West informed Mangas, "[You have] murdered your last white victim, you old scoundrel." He gestured to the east, where Cooke's Canyon lay, and remarked that it was covered with the "bleached bones" of Mangas's victims. Mangas, though disinclined to speak at all, responded that he had fought only in self-defense, only after "we were attacked by the white man who came digging up my hills for the yellow iron," a claim that was undeniably true from the chief's perception.[29] The general then told Mangas that he would not seek to avenge all the atrocities that Mangas had carried out against Americans. Instead, West magnanimously advised the chief that "the remainder of his days would be spent as a prisoner in the hands of United States authorities; that his family would be permitted to join him and they would be well treated." In view of his circumstances, this might have seemed to Mangas an attractive gesture, but the chief haughtily spurned it. West sternly warned Mangas that if he attempted to escape, the soldiers would kill him. Yet, what the general told the soldiers who were to guard Mangas that night was, it now seems clear, a totally different story. West consigned the chief to an open adobe room at Fort McLane, the only one still standing, inasmuch as the Indians had burned the post after its abandonment in 1861. The general posted a constant watch over Mangas.[30]

The evening of January 18, 1863, proved to be a bitterly cold and dreary night. West, who had ordained himself judge and jury, met with the guards later that evening and ordered them to execute the chief. His instructions, according to Clark Stocking, who claimed to have overheard them, were: "Men, that old murderer has got away from every soldier command and has left a trail of blood for 500 miles on the old stage line. I want him dead or alive tomorrow morning, do you understand? I want him dead."[31]

At midnight the sergeant of the guard replaced the two guards with four men (a sergeant and three privates) to take the next shift. This group included Sergeant Henry C. Foljaine, Private James Colyer, and Private Jonn V. Mead.[32] Stocking may have been the third private. They had every intention of obeying West's orders.

Captain Walker had agreed to split the sentry duties with West's command. That night one of his men patrolled half the perimeter, while a soldier took the other half. Daniel Ellis Conner happened to be on duty when the guard changed at midnight. It was a typically "cold and disagreeable night" in south central New Mexico. Soldiers and civilians alike had wrapped themselves in their blankets, and a "profound silence" gripped the camp. The only fire burning was the one kept by the soldiers guarding Mangas. Conner observed that the new guards who had come on duty at midnight began to taunt and tease Mangas Coloradas whenever Conner turned his back and began to march into the darkness out of their sight. At one point Conner noticed that while Mangas lay asleep with only a blanket for protection, he became fidgety and began tucking the lower end of the blanket "over one foot with the other." He soon realized the source of Mangas's restlessness. After walking to the far end of his beat, Conner turned around and

Brigadier General Joseph Rodman West. He told his sentries, "I want him dead," and they followed his orders and executed Mangas Coloradas. (Courtesy Library of Congress)

marched toward the fire. He noticed that the "soldiers were annoying Mangas in some way." As he approached the fire, they would cease their badgering of the chief, but Conner knew something was amiss.

When he was out of the other sentry's line of vision, he walked rapidly to the far end of his beat, then turned and "walked leisurely back and observed the sentinels' pranks. I could see them plainly by the firelight as they were engaged in heating their fixed bayonets in the fire and putting them to the feet and naked legs of Mangas, who from time to time would shield his limbs from the hot steel." They would repeat this cycle. As soon as Conner marched away, they resumed their sadistic torture of Mangas until Conner renewed his approach. Conner "didn't appreciate this conduct" but said nothing. Their intentions would have surprised the twenty-five-year-old Kentucky native. About 1:00 A.M. on January 19, 1863, as Conner returned about halfway to the open adobe building, he saw Mangas lift himself "upon his left elbow" and begin "to expostulate in a vigorous way by telling the sentinels in Spanish that he was no child to be playing with." These were his last words. The two privates, Mead and Colyer, "promptly brought down their minnie muskets to bear on him and fired, nearly at the same time through his body. The Chief fell back off of his elbow into the same position in which he had been lying." What happened next is not clear. Conner said that these two soldiers each fired two shots into Mangas's head; Clark Stocking claimed that Sergeant Henry Foljaine rushed in "and gave him a ball through the head with his pistol."[33] This second version finds corroboration in an account published by Orson Squire Fowler, a New York phrenologist who examined the skull of Mangas. Fowler, who received the skull from Surgeon David B. Sturgeon,[34] concluded that there is "an entering bullet hole on the right posterior parietal, with radiating cracks, and an exit wound removing part of the right forehead and frontal sinus area." Fowler noted only one wound in the back part of the head, which means that Sergeant Foljaine, or another guard, shot Mangas in the back of the head.[35]

The gunfire woke the entire camp, but all quickly returned to their blankets when they learned that the victim was only an Apache, shot "while trying to escape." The sergeant reported to West's tent and provided him the details. The general asked, "Is he dead?" Foljaine responded, "He is, sir." West laconically acknowledged the affair: "Very well, Sergeant, then let his guard go to sleep."[36] With their prized captive now dead, the guards calmly returned to the comfort of their blankets. Naturally, General West's official report to headquarters differed dramatically from the actual details. According to him, within one hour Mangas had "made three efforts to escape and was shot on the third attempt." The general had done all in his power to protect the chief: "I have thus dwelt at length upon this matter in order to show that even with a murderous Indian, whose life is clearly forfeited by all laws, either human or divine, wherever found, the good faith of the U.S. Military authorities was in no way compromised."[37]

West obviously hoped his duplicitous report would be the last word on the ignominious treatment and shameful death of Mangas Coloradas. And Carleton apparently accepted his version without question.[38] In fact, however, West's report contained several bald-faced lies, which he probably expected the public to accept. At this time Carleton remained concerned about a possible rebel invasion from Texas. With the Apaches having dominated southern Arizona and New Mexico until the California troops had restored order and stemmed the tide, he would likely have applauded West's orders to eliminate Mangas Coloradas, whom they viewed as the principal southern Apache, or Chiricahua, leader. Neither Carleton nor West expected that this "Black Flag" policy, as it later became known, only served to exacerbate further the distrust and hostilities between the two races. It left indelible impressions on Cochise, Victorio, and a "minor" Bedonkohe leader named Geronimo. If more moderate leaders had then headed the military instead of the hawkish Carleton and West, and if the Indian Department in New Mexico had enjoyed a real voice in Indian affairs, it is almost certain that the two sides could have come to a bloodless compromise, and probably peace.

In the years after the execution of Mangas Coloradas a great deal of evidence steadily surfaced which exposed the hypocrisy of West's report. Several California Volunteers later talked about the affair. Three accounts of soldiers present at Fort McLane (Clark Stocking, John S. Crouch, and John Martin) accused the guards of having startled Mangas by throwing adobes at him, or at the wall near him, causing him instinctively to jump up, at which point the guards shot him and, according to the last two accounts, bayonetted him. Another soldier, John Townsend, agreeing with Conner, declared that "hot coals were thrown upon him, causing him to rise, whereupon he was shot." It has been pointed out that while these men were apparently at Fort McLane that cold and gloomy night, they were likely asleep at the time of the incident. But word of the execution was bound to spread throughout the camp, and the actual circumstances surrounding Mangas's death soon became very well understood.[39]

Not surprisingly, of course, many of these soldiers, who had seen firsthand the results of Apache warfare, had neither empathy nor sympathy for the Indians. They did not understand just exactly why the Chiricahuas engaged in hostilities, and the remains of tortured victims did little to warm their feelings for the Indians. Thus, they could justify the execution, feeling that Mangas deserved this fate even though he had voluntarily come in to make peace. Clark B. Stocking expressed the sentiments of the whites: "He got what he deserved and no one in our command pitied him or cried about it."[40] Daniel Ellis Conner succinctly declared that none of the soldiers or civilians believed that Mangas had attempted to escape, "for they all knew better, officers and all."[41] Darlis A. Miller, in her definitive study *The California Column in New Mexico*, concluded that the prevailing attitude held by most California soldiers (indeed by most southwesterners) regarding the circumstances of Mangas's death was apathy. It mattered little to them whether the guards had shot Mangas while he was trying to escape or whether they had simply executed him. After all, he was only an Indian. What it boiled down to was that they now had one less Indian to kill.[42]

Arizona pioneer "Uncle" Billy Fourr, who came to New Mexico in 1861 from Missouri, heard the details of Mangas's death from Captain McCleave. According to Fourr, McCleave insisted that the sentries had orders to kill Mangas if he tried to escape. To encourage this, they decided not to tie him up or restrain him in any manner. Yet the chief refused to take the bait. Late one night the guard poked Mangas with a bayonet, which caused him to jump, at which point the guard shot and killed him. Fourr attested that he also heard this version from other soldiers who claimed to have been present.[43] In 1865, Judge Joseph G. Knapp accused the troops of arousing Mangas from his sleep, whereupon they "instantly perforated him with bullets and killed [him]."[44] About the same time, John Greiner, former Indian agent and acting superintendent of Indian affairs of New Mexico, who had met Mangas at Ácoma in July 1852, unequivocally declared that Mangas's guards had murdered him.[45] Charles Connell, who knew the Chihennes in the late 1870s, also had heard the story that the guards threw an adobe stone at Mangas while he was sleeping. As soon as the chief instinctively rose to his feet, the guards shot him down.[46]

In the morning after the murder, Conner had a chance to examine the body of the chief. He found "the old Indian's long hair in strands over his face." Several soldiers came over to view the corpse. One soldier, John T. Wright, borrowed a large bowie knife from a cook and efficiently removed Mangas's scalp. At noon the body was placed on a blanket, dumped in a gully, and covered up. But this was not the end of the mutilation. A few days later, after West had left for Mesilla, a group of soldiers with Surgeon Sturgeon exhumed Mangas's body and severed the head, which they boiled and prepared to send to a museum in New York.[47] About eighteen months later, Assistant Surgeon John Quincy Adams, nephew of the former president, while passing by Fort McLane with a detachment of troops, heard the story of Mangas's death. One soldier claimed to know where the soldiers had dumped Mangas's body, which was only a few yards from the place where he was shot. Adams, like Sturgeon, wanted his skull, but the best he could find "was a thigh-bone."[48]

An hour after the execution of Mangas Coloradas, Brigadier General West sent out two patrols, hoping to strike the Indians before they realized that his troops had killed their chief. Captain William McLeave took one command of twenty cavalrymen and rode to Pinos Altos. That same day Mangas's local group, ignorant of the chief's fate, peacefully approached the town. McCleave ordered his men "to attack them, which was done, killing eleven and wounding one, the latter proved to be a wife of the Chief [Mangas]. One of the killed being his son," probably Sethmooda. The civilians at Pinos Altos joined in the fight. McCleave searched for Apaches the following day (January 20) before returning to Fort McLane. Meanwhile, Captain Shirland had taken fifty cavalrymen toward the Mimbres River, where in the morning of January 20, 1863, he discovered a Chihenne ranchería, likely Victorio's camp, "located on one of the most rugged, high, and difficult mountains to ascend and pass I ever saw." Somehow his command surprised the Indians and killed nine "near their wigwams." Shirland also believed that his men had killed or wounded several others. He also recovered thirty-four head of stock, which included government mules taken the previous October 31 "on the Jornada."[49] Both patrols returned with scalps and other trophies of war "dangling from their saddles."[50] George Hand, at Mesilla when West's command returned on January 25, 1863, reported that some of the "boys brought in scalps."[51]

Captain William McCleave. He led a patrol that killed several of Mangas's followers near Pinos Altos. (Courtesy Rio Grande Historical Collections, New Mexico State University Library, photo no. RG95-57)

To the Apaches the execution of their legendary tribal leader and the subsequent mutilation of his corpse were the "greatest of wrongs."[52] Their chief had gone to the Americans, probably unarmed and with no intent of malice. His enemies had seized, murdered, and decapitated him and finally mutilated his corpse.

This appalling treatment of their unarmed chief, who sincerely desired peace and who had gone to war only reluctantly "in self-defense," was agonizing in itself. James Kaywaykla, a member of Victorio's Chihenne band expressed the sentiments of the Chiricahuas: "The killing of an unarmed man who has gone to an enemy under truce was an incomprehensible act, but infinitely worse was the mutilation of his body."[53]

Asa Daklugie declared: "To an Apache the mutilation of the body is much worse than death, because the body must go through eternity in the mutilated condition. Little did the White Eyes know what they were starting when they mutilated Mangas Coloradas. While there was little mutilation previously, it was nothing compared to what was to follow."[54]

A Chiricahua informant revealed to Morris Opler what the Apaches believe occurs when an individual dies: "We think of a dead person going on to another life—of his whole body, as it was on earth, going to the other world. He is really transferred to the other world." Another informant, who evidently had a near-death experience, declared that all remain as they were, "the same age as they were when they died. I saw people as they were when they went."[55]

Naturally, contemporary whites would have disagreed with the Apaches' perspective that little mutilation had occurred before Mangas's execution. Much of it may have been the work of Cochise's Chokonens in response to the death of his brother Coyuntura. Whether Mangas participated in the torturing and mutilating of Americans is unclear.

In Santa Fe, Carleton was ecstatic when he received the news. In dispatches to his superiors in Washington, he gloated over this accomplishment, though he provided no specific details. He declared: "Mangas Coloradas, doubtless the worst Indian within our boundaries and one who has been the cause of more murders and torturing and of burning at the stake in this country than all together—has been killed." He declined to explain just how the chief had been killed, and again he highly exaggerated the exploits of Mangas Coloradas—at least above the border. He was hardly the most bellicose Indian in the Southwest. That distinction had to go to Cochise, who passionately vented his hatred of Americans after they betrayed him at Apache Pass in February 1861. Mangas, ever the diplomat, had gone to war as a last resort. Carleton may not have realized that Mangas had lived in peace with Americans for sixteen of the eighteen years since Kearny's arrival in 1846. He clearly misunderstood Apaches and never seemed to appreciate that the Indians were driven to fight by the same principles—love of their land, defense of their way of life, and protection of their families—that the Union espoused in fighting against the rebels.

It is easy to understand why the death of Mangas Coloradas so enraged the Chiricahuas. If he had died in battle at the head of his men, the Indians would have responded differently, chalking it up to the hazards of warfare. But he had not. The Chiricahuas were accustomed to Mexican treachery, and many had become wary of Americans. Mangas Coloradas was the one leader who trusted the integrity and honor of Americans. This faith not only cost him his life, but also, many Chiricahuas believed, affected his spirit in the hereafter. My esteemed friend Dan Thrapp has put it best: "The greatest tragedy of the affair was less the death of the aging chieftain than the lasting distrust generated on the part of the Apaches toward white Americans and soldiers."[56]

Brigadier General West's decision to execute Mangas Coloradas failed either to defeat or to mollify the Chiricahuas. It had an effect opposite that West and Carleton had intended: it mobilized the Chiricahua bands. Normally the death of a leader would be avenged by the local group, and in some cases by the band. But Mangas's importance transcended the group and band level. Thus, avenging his death became a tribal matter. Cochise, Victorio, and Luis, a Bedonkohe chief who was probably one of Mangas's sons, organized a large war party during the summer of 1863 to avenge Mangas's death. They attacked several groups of Americans along the Rio Grande and at Cooke's Canyon. At San Diego Crossing on the Rio Grande, on June 17, 1863, they killed a brave officer named Lieutenant L. A. Bargie. They applied the same barbaric treatment to his body as the troops had to Mangas. He was found with "his head cut off, his breast open, and his heart taken out."[57]

The actions by West and Carleton only served to prolong the war with the Chiricahua Apaches in the Southwest. If they had responded honestly to Mangas's proposal, quite possibly the two sides could have worked out a long-term truce, thus saving hundreds of lives and thousands of dollars. Unfortunately, Carleton, the absolute ruler of New Mexico until after the Civil War, was the wrong person to deal with Apaches. He continued to advocate policies aimed at extermination and nothing else. During the summer of 1863 the Chiricahuas' former agent, the competent Michael Steck, returned to New Mexico as the superintendent of Indian affairs. But, like Sumner, who had clashed with a host of

Indian officials a decade before, Carleton allowed Steck no rapport at all. As in the case of Sumner, the blame could here be placed squarely on the general's shoulders. The war with the Chihenne and Bedonkohe bands of Chiricahua Apaches continued into the late 1860s in New Mexico and with Cochise's Chokonens until the early 1870s in Arizona.

Mangas Coloradas's life had spanned more than seventy years. He had fought the Spanish, made peace with them, vigorously fought Mexicans (especially in Sonora), with an occasional truce between hostilities, and generously embraced the Americans when they arrived in his country. Ironically, the ignominious circumstances surrounding his death had compelled his people to continue fighting for a cause that he had realized was hopeless. Without his leadership, the Bedonkohes began to follow Cochise's Chokonens and Juh's Nednhis; by the time of Geronimo's final surrender in 1886, they were no longer a distinct band. Meanwhile, the Chihennes, under the direction of capable local group leaders like Victorio, Loco, and Nana, endured a quarter of a century of mistreatment. The government shuffled them from one reservation to another and finally removed them from their beloved Chihenne country to the hated San Carlos Reservation in Arizona. Mangas Coloradas's people resisted the government's concentration policy. In the late 1870s and into the mid-1880s they fought Americans and Mexicans until their inevitable defeat at the hands of these overwhelming forces, before they were gathered up with the remnants of Cochise's and Juh's people and exiled to Florida in 1886. They remained prisoners of war in Florida and later in Alabama and Oklahoma until 1913, when two-thirds of the tribe elected to leave Oklahoma and return to the Mescalero Reservation in southern New Mexico.

Today the descendants of Mangas Coloradas live either in Oklahoma, as members of the Fort Sill Apache Tribe, or in southern New Mexico on the Mescalero Apache reservation. Although they have adapted to the white man's ways, they have retained the essence of their culture and remain a proud and dignified people. Mangas Coloradas personified this ability to adapt and accommodate to a new world as he viewed it. He would be proud of his people, who have somehow survived, who have been able to cope, all the while preserving their cultural identity.

The story of the Apache Indians of the Southwest has its beginnings in the most primitive form of the age-old struggle for survival. In the very beginning the adversary was merely nature in her extremes of weather, in disease, in famine. From the time of the white man's first experience in their land it becomes an ordeal, a story inclining to tragedy. Because of greed and arrogance, vengeance and misunderstanding, the narrative is fraught with terrible sufferings and deprivation, grisly horrors, and incredible wrongs. Perhaps the most climactic moment occurs in the murder of an aged but ever proud Apache chieftain, in the execution of Mangas Coloradas on that bitterly cold and dreary prairie night at Fort McLane in southern New Mexico, known to the Chiricahuas as Apache Tejo, when two very different civilizations collided in awful climax.

NOTES

INTRODUCTION

1. National Archives and Records Center, Record Group 94, Records of the Adjutant's General Office (AGO), 1780–1917, Letters Received, Main Series, Microcopy 619 (cited hereafter as NA, RG94, M619, with roll number), Roll 284, Mowry to West, June 28, 1862.

2. National Archives and Records Center, Record Group 75, Records of the Bureau of Indian Affairs, Letters Received, 1824–80, New Mexico Superintendency, 1849–80, Microcopy 234 (cited hereafter as NA, RG75, M234, with roll number), Roll 554, Hackney to Commissioner of Indian Affairs, January 31, 1867.

3. Manuel Valenzuela correspondence with author, January 28, 1993.

4. Robert M. Utley, *The Lance and the Shield: The Life and Times of Sitting Bull*, 11–13.

5. This discussion on leadership is taken from Morris E. Opler, *An Apache Life-Way*, 462–70; and Morris E. Opler, "An Outline of Chiricahua Apache Social Organization," in *Social Anthropology of North American Tribes: Essays in Social Organization, Law, and Religion*, ed. Fred Eggan, 233–36.

6. See Edwin R. Sweeney, *Cochise: Chiricahua Apache Chief*, for a biography of this fighting Apache leader.

7. Morris E. Opler, "An Interpretation of Ambivalence of Two American Indian Tribes," *Journal of Social Psychology* 7 (1936), 100.

8. NA, RG75, M234, R546, Bartlett to the Secretary of the Interior, February 19, 1852.

9. *Boston Evening Transcript*, February 4, 1873.

CHAPTER 1

1. Morris Opler, "A Chiricahua Apache's Account of the Geronimo

Campaign of 1886," *New Mexico Historical Review* 13 (October 1938), 369.

2. Ralph Hedrick Ogle, *Federal Control of the Western Apaches 1848–1886,* 5; Frederick Webb Hodge, ed., *Handbook of American Indians North of Mexico,* I, 63; Jack D. Forbes, *Apache, Navaho and Spaniard,* xi–xxiii; Richard J. Perry, *Western Apache Heritage: People of the Mountain Corridor,* 135–39.

3. Grenville Goodwin, *The Social Organization of the Western Apache,* 1.

4. Opler, "An Outline of Chiricahua Apache Organization," in Eggan, *Social Anthropology,* 176.

5. Morris E. Opler, *Myths and Tales of the Chiricahua Apache Indians,* 15; Perry, *Western Apache Heritage,* 151.

6. Anthropologist Morris Opler concluded that the Chiricahuas consisted of three bands: the Eastern Chiricahuas (Chihennes), Central Chiricahuas (Chokonens), and Southern Chiricahuas (Nednhis). The Chiricahuas recalled another band, the Bedonkohes, who were a distinct unit until the time of Mangas Coloradas's death in 1863, after which they assimilated into the other Chiricahua bands, some following Cochise and others Victorio and Juh. Geronimo was a Bedonkohe by birth. Opler, *Life-Way,* 1–2; Stephen M. Barrett, *Geronimo's Story of His Life,* 12–14; Eve Ball, with Nora Henn and Lynda Sánchez, *Indeh: An Apache Odyssey,* 22; Angie Debo, *Geronimo: The Man, His Time, His Place,* 71; Jason Betzinez, with Wilber S. Nye, *I Fought with Geronimo,* 14–15.

7. Opler, *Life-Way,* 1–2; John Gregory Bourke Diary, entry dated April 7, 1883, copy in Arizona Historical Society; Morris E. Opler, "Chiricahua Apache," in *Handbook of North American Indians,* ed. Alfonso Ortiz, X, 418.

8. Barrett, *Geronimo's Story,* 12–14; Ball, *Indeh,* 22; Debo, *Geronimo,* 71; Betzinez, *I Fought with Geronimo,* 14–15.

9. Opler, *Life-Way,* 2.

10. Opler, *Life-Way,* 462–64; Opler, "Chiricahua Apache," in *Handbook,* X, 410–11; Barrett, *Geronimo's Story,* 14.

11. Opler, "Chiricahua Apache," in *Handbook,* X, 411–12; Opler, *Life-Way,* 462–64; Harry W. Basehart, "Chiricahua Apache Subsistence and Socio-Political Organization," A Report of the Mescalero-Chiricahua Land Claims Project, Contract Research No. 290-154, University of New Mexico, 8–9; Opler, "Outline of Chiricahua Apache Organization," 235.

12. Opler, *Life-Way,* 181; Opler, "Chiricahua Apache," in *Handbook,* X, 411–12.

13. Betzinez, *I Fought with Geronimo,* 9; Gillett Griswold, "The Fort Sill Apaches: Their Vital Statistics, Tribal Origins, Antecedents," Field Artillery Museum, Fort Sill, Oklahoma, entry on Mangas Coloradas, 24–25; Sweeney, *Cochise,* 44–45.

14. John A. Murray, *The Gila Wilderness Area: A Hiking Guide,* 12.

15. Dan L. Thrapp, *The Conquest of Apachería,* 12–13; Manuel Valenzuela correspondence with author, July 1, 1992; Basehart, "Chiricahua Apache Subsistence," 80; Opler, Life-Way, 10.

16. Max L Moorhead, *The Apache Frontier: Jacobo Ugarte and Spanish-Indian Relations in Northern New Spain, 1769–1791,* 15–16.

17. William B. Griffen, *Apaches at War and Peace: The Janos Presidio, 1750–1858,* 22–23.

18. Ibid., 29–31.

19. Moorhead, *Apache Frontier,* 16–17.

20. See Dan L. Thrapp, *Encyclopedia of Frontier Biography,* II, 1072–73, for a biography of O'Conor.

21. Griffen, *Apaches at War and Peace,* 31–33.

22. Moorhead, *Apache Frontier,* 123–29; Max L. Moorhead, *The Presidio: Bastion of the Spanish Borderlands,* 95–114.

23. Moorhead, *Apache Frontier,* 170–72.

24. Ibid., 186–87; Griffen, *Apaches at War and Peace,* 55–56.

25. Griffen, *Apaches at War and Peace,* 57–59; Moorhead, *Apache Frontier,* 186–88.

26. Moorhead, *Apache Frontier,* 186–89.

27. Ibid., 198–99.

28. Moorhead, *Presidio,* 101; Moorhead, *Apache Frontier,* 126–28; Robert C. West, *Sonora: Its Geographical Personality,* 77.

29. Griffen, *Apaches at War and Peace,* 81–82; William B. Griffen, "The Chiricahua Apache Population Resident at the Janos Presidio, 1792 to 1858," *Journal of the Southwest* 33 (Summer 1991), 155–56, 160.

30. William B. Griffen, "Apache Indians and the Northern Mexican Peace Establishments," 189, in *Southwestern Culture Histories: Collected Papers in Honor of Albert H. Schroeder,* ed. Charles H. Lange, *Papers of the Archaeological Society of New Mexico* 10 (1985).

31. Opler, *Life-Way,* 7–8; Goodwin, *Social Organization,* 533–34; Opler letter to author, March 1, 1982; Ruth McDonald Boyer and Narcissus Duffy Gayton, *Apache Mothers and Daughters,* 25. For an excellent discussion of the derivation of Apache names, see Goodwin, *Social Organization,* 522–35.

32. Zimmerman Library, University of New Mexico, Michael Steck Papers (hereafter cited as Steck Papers), Steck's Annual Report dated August 1856.

33. Betzinez, *I Fought with Geronimo;* Barrett, *Geronimo's Story;* Opler, *Life-Way;* Daniel S. Matson and Albert H. Schroeder, eds., "Cordero's Description of the Apache—1796," *New Mexico Historical Review* 32 (October 1957), 335–56; José Cortés, *Views from the Apache Frontier: Report on the Northern Provinces of New Spain,* ed. Elizabeth A. H. John.

34. The source for the rest of this chapter, unless otherwise noted, is Opler, *Life-Way,* 10–18, 23–37, 67–75, 135–44, 464–70; Opler, "Chiricahua Apache," in *Handbook,* X, 401–18.

35. Betzinez, *I Fought with Geronimo*, 30–31; Opler, *Life-Way*, 318.

36. Barrett, *Geronimo's Story*, 31; Betzinez, *I Fought with Geronimo*, 33–34; Opler, *Life-Way*, 327; Bryan Hodgson, "Buffalo: Back Home on the Range," *National Geographic* 186 (November 1994), 70–71.

37. Cortés, *Views from the Apache Frontier*, 57–58.

38. Opler, *Life-Way*, 356–58.

39. Debo, *Geronimo*, 21.

40. Opler, *Life-Way*, 318.

41. Ibid., 67; Morris E. Opler and Harry Hoijer, "The Raid and War-Path Language of the Chiricahua Apache," *American Anthropologist* 42 (October–December 1942), 618–19.

42. Opler and Hoijer, "Raid and War-Path Language," 617–34, contains seventy-eight such words.

43. Oakah L Jones, Jr., *Nueva Vizcaya: Heartland of the Spanish Frontier*, 203, 215–17.

CHAPTER 2

1. Benjamin Wilson, "Observations of Early Days in California and New Mexico," Bancroft Library, University of California.

2. Griffen, *Apaches at War and Peace*, 192, 202; Sweeney, *Cochise*, 44–45; Eve Ball, correspondence with author. Most sources simply state that Mangas Coloradas was a large, well-built man over six feet tall. His height has been estimated at between six feet and six feet seven inches. John C. Reid, who met Mangas Coloradas in 1857, described him as "very large, erect, and of powerful mould." Two Apache agents in 1853 described Mangas Coloradas in a similar manner. One said that he was a "noble specimen of the genus homo," while the second wrote that he was a man of "large frame and great muscular power." John Cremony reported that Mangas was over six feet tall, while a surgeon who measured him a few hours after his death said that he was six feet, four inches—and this was when he was in his early seventies and might have lost an inch or two in stature. Clark Stocking, who saw Mangas Coloradas in January 1863, put him at six feet, five inches. Daniel Conner, who saw Mangas Coloradas hours before his execution, described him as a large, athletic man considerably over six feet in height. Charles Lummis heard that he stood six and a half feet tall, while some Chiricahuas today estimate him to have stood six feet, seven inches. John C. Reid, *Reid's Tramp*, 175; NA, RG75, M234, R546, Wingfield to Lane, May 29, 1853; Smith to Meriwether, September 8, 1853; John C. Cremony, "Some Savages," *Overland Monthly* 8 (March 1872), 202; *Boston Evening Transcript*, February 4, 1873; Edgar B. Bronson, *The Vanguard*, 99–100; Daniel Ellis Conner, *Joseph Reddeford Walker and the Arizona Adventure*, 36–37; Charles F. Lummis, *Land of Poco Tiempo*, 161; Boyer and Gayton, *Apache Mothers and Daughters*, 25.

3. David Meriwether, *My Life in the Mountains and on the Plains*, 259.

4. Opler, *Life-Way,* 144; Boyer and Gayton, *Apache Mothers and Daughters,* 4.

5. Griffen, "Chiricahua Apache Population," 163; Sweeney, *Cochise,* 401.

6. Betzinez, *I Fought with Geronimo,* 14–16; Barrett, Geronimo's Story, 35–36; Griswold, "Fort Sill Apaches," 24–25, 90–91.

7. Betzinez, *I Fought with Geronimo,* 14–16; Barrett, *Geronimo's Story,* 35–36; Griswold, "Fort Sill Apaches," 24–25, 90–91.

8. Benjamin Butler Harris, *The Gila Trail: The Texas Argonauts and the California Gold Rush,* 70.

9. See John C. Cremony, *Life among the Apaches;* Cremony, "Some Savages"; *Boston Evening Transcript,* February 4, 1873.

10. Cremony, *Life among the Apaches,* 47–48.

11. Opler, *Life-Way,* 351.

12. Boyer and Gayton, *Apache Mothers and Daughters,* 26–27.

13. *Boston Evening Transcript,* February 4, 1873.

14. Opler, *Life-Way,* 200–208.

15. Griffen, *Apaches at War and Peace,* 87–88.

16. Boyer and Gayton, *Apache Mothers and Daughters,* 26.

17. Dan L. Thrapp, *Victorio and the Mimbres Apaches,*18; *Mesilla Times,* October 18, 1860; Sweeney, *Cochise,* 403 n. 3; Griffen, *Apaches at War and Peace,* 87–88; University of Texas at El Paso, Janos Collection, Roll 15 (hereafter cited as JA with roll number), Salcedor to military commander of Janos, February 3, 1804.

18. Griffen, *Apaches at War and Peace,* 90–93.

19. Ibid.; JA, R2, Baca to Ronquillo, January 27, 1814; William B. Griffen, "Chiricahua Apaches," copy in author's possession, 237-244.

20. Griffen, "Chiricahua Apaches," 243–44; JA, R11, Bonavia y Zapata to military commander, Janos, August 12, 1813.

21. JA, R11, Bonavia y Zapata to military commander, Janos, August 13, 1814.

22. JA, R11, various census lists for 1815 and 1816; Griffen, "Chiricahua Apaches," 245–46.

23. JA, R3, various census reports for 1816 and 1817; Griffen, *Apaches at War and Peace,* 121–23. For two good accounts on conditions in northern Mexico at this time, see the two articles by Joseph F. Park, "Spanish Indian Policy in Northern Mexico, 1765–1810," *Arizona and the West* 4 (Winter 1962), 325–44; "The Apaches in Mexican-American Relations, 1848–1861," *Arizona and the West* 3 (Summer 1961), 129–46.

24. JA, R19, military commander of Janos to commanding general, November 5, 1817.

25. JA, R13, Conde to military commander of Janos, September 14, 1819; JA, R12, Conde to military commander of Janos, October 12, 1819.

26. Sweeney, *Cochise,* 15–16; James E. Officer, *Hispanic Arizona,* 1536–1856, 97–100, 110–15.

27. JA, R12, census dated April 28, 1819; JA, R12, R13, censuses for 1820 and 1821; Sweeney, *Cochise*, 15–16.

28. Griffen, *Apaches at War and Peace*, 120–22; William B. Griffen, *Utmost Good Faith: Patterns of Apache-Mexican Hostilities in Northern Chihuahua Border Warfare, 1821–1848*, 5.

29. Sweeney, *Cochise*, 16–17; Officer, *Hispanic Arizona*, 103–104.

30. Hermosillo, Archivo Histórico de Sonora (cited hereafter as AHSH), Folder 221, Ibarra to Elías González, March 17, 1850; Sweeney, *Cochise*, 16–17.

31. Sweeney, *Cochise*, 16–17; JA, R17, R18, various ration lists, 1825–30.

32. Sylvester Pattie was born in 1782 in Kentucky. In 1812 he moved to Saint Charles, Missouri, with his wife and family and established a sawmill in southern Missouri. In 1822, when his wife Polly died, a victim of tuberculosis, a depressed Pattie sent eight of his children to live with relatives and took his eldest son James to New Mexico. The Patties secured licenses to trap the Gila. They eventually arrived at Santa Rita del Cobre, where they took a lease on the mines, which proved to be quite profitable. In 1828, Pattie made his way to San Diego, where he was unjustly imprisoned by Mexican authorities. He died in jail on May 24, 1828. Thrapp, *Encyclopedia*, 1120–21.

33. Paul I. Wellman, *The Indian Wars of the West*, 250–51; James O. Pattie, *Personal Narrative of James O. Pattie of Kentucky*, ed. Timothy Flint, 116.

34. Pattie, *Personal Narrative*, 111–23.

35. Officer, *Hispanic Arizona*, 351 n. 38.

36. Florence C. Lister and Robert H. Lister, *Chihuahua: Storehouse of Storms*, 91–93.

37. Sweeney, *Cochise*, 17–18; Griffen, *Apaches at War and Peace*, 131–33.

38. Sweeney, *Cochise*, 17–19; Officer, *Hispanic Arizona*, 120–22.

CHAPTER 3

1. Calvo, born in Cuba, was named the commanding general for the states of Chihuahua and New Mexico in 1831. He declared war on the Apaches on October 16, 1831, and received much credit for improving military affairs in Chihuahua. In 1834 he temporarily assumed the position of governor along with his duties as commanding general. In 1835 he initiated an important treaty with the Comanches at El Paso. Bancroft wrote that he was a man who "had earned well-merited praise." He died on February 28, 1838. Francisco R. Almada, *Diccionario de historia, geografía, y biografía chihuahuenses*, 767–68; Lister and Lister, *Chihuahua*, 97–98; Hubert Howe Bancroft, *History of the North American States and Texas*, II, 593.

2. Arizona Historical Society, Sonoran State Archives (cited hereafter as SA with roll number), Roll 12, Simón Elías González to Governor, June

28, 1831; AHSH, Folder 36, Commanding General to Governor, June 23, 1831; Governor to Commanding General, July 5, 1831; Almada, *Diccionario chihuahuenses*, 38.

3. JA, R24, Commander of Janos to Zúñiga, January 22, 1832; Griffen, *Apaches at War and Peace*, 139–40; Griffen, "Chiricahua Apaches," 466–67.

4. Goodwin, *Social Organization*, 86.

5. SA, R12, Morales to Governor, February 23, 1832; Governor to Morales, February 26, 1832.

6. SA, R12, Morales to Governor, March 27, May 9, 1832; JA, R24, Calvo to Commander, Janos, May 7, 1832.

7. Officer, *Hispanic Arizona*, 123–25; Sweeney, *Cochise*, 20.

8. Morris E. Opler, ed., *Grenville Goodwin among the Western Apache*, 29; Basehart, "Chiricahua Apache Subsistence," 73–74; Opler, *Life-Way*, 453.

9. SA, R12, Governor of Chihuahua to Governor of Sonora, document entitled, "Triumph over the Apaches," June 7, 1832; Griffen, *Apaches at War and Peace*, 140–41; Sweeney, *Cochise*, 19–21.

10. SA, R12, Governor of Chihuahua to Governor of Sonora, "Triumph over the Apaches," June 7, 1832; Basehart, "Chiricahua Apache Subsistence," 86; Sweeney, *Cochise*, 20–21.

11. Cayetano Justiniani, born in Chihuahua, enjoyed a successful military and civil career. During his military service he held both administrative and field positions. He gained much experience with Apaches, who for the most part trusted him. In 1837 he became the prefect of El Paso del Norte before being summoned to return to the military in 1839, when he was appointed commanding general of Chihuahua. He fought against the Americans in the Mexican War. Chihuahuan historian Francisco Almada said "he was a model of integrity." He died on June 18, 1863. Almada, *Diccionario chihuahuenses*, 398.

12. Griffen, *Apaches at War and Peace*, 142; JA, R5, Conde to Justiniani, August 30, 1832; Almada, *Diccionario chihuahuenses*, 38. Unfortunately, no list of the twenty-nine leaders who agreed to the treaty has been located.

13. SA, R13, Elías González to Governor, July 6, 1834; JA, R6, Calvo to Ponce de León, December 15, 1835; *El Fanal de Chihuahua* (Supplement), November 4, 1834; David J. Weber, *The Taos Tappers: The Fur Trade in the Far Southwest, 1540–1846*, 221–22.

14. Robert McKnight was born in Virginia in 1790. He came west in 1809, living in Missouri before arriving in New Mexico in 1812. At Taos, Mexican officials arrested him as an American agent and imprisoned him for nine years in Mexico. Authorities finally released him in late 1820 or early 1821. He went to the United States for a few years before returning to New Mexico in 1824. In early 1828 he and a friend, Stephen Courcier, took over operating Santa Rita del Cobre. About that time he became a Mexican citizen and married a Mexican woman. He was a prominent

figure in the 1832 and 1835 treaties with the Chiricahuas and became a controversial man, despised by some Indians. Mexican officials accused him of conducting illegal trade with the Chiricahuas in 1837, a charge that could have been brought against many inhabitants of Santa Rita del Cobre and Janos. In 1838 he left Santa Rita and eventually surfaced at Corralitos, where he went to work for José María Zuloaga. He died there in early 1846. See Thrapp, *Encyclopedia*, II, 915–16; Sweeney, *Cochise*, 405 n. 33; JA, R28, Zuloaga to Military Commander at Janos, March 7, 1838; John Russell Bartlett, *Personal Narrative of Explorations and Incidents in Texas, New Mexico, California, Sonora, and Chihuahua*, I, 228–29; Leroy Hafen, *The Mountain Men and the Fur Trade of the Far West*, 9, 259–68.

James Kirker, infamous because of his occupation as a sometimes scalp hunter, was born in Northern Ireland in 1790. He came to New York in 1810 and migrated west to Saint Louis in 1817. In 1824 he came to Santa Fe and remained there for a while before leaving in the late 1820s for Apache country and Santa Rita del Cobre, where he became associated with the Chiricahuas. His movements were difficult to follow during the 1830s. At times he seems to have been closely involved with the Chiricahuas to the point that it was reported that he accompanied them on raids into Sonora. Despite his unsavory reputation, Chihuahua's governor hired him in the late 1830s to exterminate Apaches. He had several skirmishes with them, accumulating scalps and pesos in accordance with Chihuahua's bounty for scalps. His contract was canceled in 1840 but renewed in late 1845. The next year he and his mercenaries slaughtered 148 Chiricahuas at Galeana, an incident long remembered by the Indians. He died in California in 1853. See Sweeney, *Cochise*, 401 n. 26; Thrapp, *Encyclopedia*, II, 788. For a biography of Kirker, see William C. McGaw, *Savage Scene: The Life and Times of James Kirker, Frontier King*.

15. JA, R24, Calvo to Military Commander of Janos, September 16, 1832; October 9, 1832.

16. JA, R25, Ponce de León to Military Commander, Janos, February 27, 1833; Ponce de León to Military Commander, Janos, May 9, 1833.

17. Medrano, an Opata "general," was a sworn enemy of the Apaches. His force of Opatas was normally assigned to protect Sonora's northern frontier, with Bavispe usually his base of operations. An Apache war party killed him and his family in April 1835. Francisco R. Almada, *Diccionario de historia, geografía, y biografía sonorenses*, 407.

18. SA, R12, Medrano to Governor, May 3, 1833.

19. Ibid., Francisco Arregui to Vice-Governor of Sonora, April 15, 1833.

20. Ibid., Military Commander at Fronteras to López, May 15, 1833; JA, R25, Juan José Compá to Barela, April 25, 1833.

21. JA, R6, Saenz to Janos Alcalde, May 10, 1833; University of Texas at El Paso, Juarez Collection (hereafter cited as Juarez Archives with roll number), Roll 4, Revilla to Prefect del Paso, June 27, 1833.

22. SA, R12, Ruiz to commander of troops at Moctezuma, June 2, 1833.

23. Griffen, *Apaches at War and Peace*, 146–47; Griffen, "Chiricahua Apaches," 483; Robert C. Stevens, "The Apache Menace in Sonora, 1831–1849," *Arizona and the West* 6 (Autumn 1964), 215–16.

24. Officer, *Hispanic Arizona*, 126. José María Elías González was undoubtedly the most important military leader in Sonora from the early 1830s until the early 1850s. Born into the prominent Elías family at Arispe in 1793, he joined the military in 1809 as a cadet. He had an active role in Mexico's War for Independence, and in 1821 he was promoted to captain. Four years later he was named adjutant inspector for Sonora and Sinaloa. In 1834 he became Sonora's commanding general, succeeding Colonel Francisco Arregui, whose presidio troops were in a mutinous state. About that time he began to get well acquainted with the Chiricahuas. In 1836 he negotiated a treaty with them at his home in Arispe. In 1844 he led Sonoran troops against Chiricahuas, whom he believed had been raiding Sonora, and killed almost one hundred at Janos and Corralitos. In 1851 he retired amidst controversy. His successor, Colonel José María Carrasco, roundly criticized the condition of Sonora's armed forces, and Elías González took great exception to Carrasco's allegations. He was a thoughtful, pragmatic man who understood Apaches. He died in 1864 at Ures. Almada, *Diccionario sonorenses*, 213–14; Stuart F. Voss, *On the Periphery of Nineteenth-Century Mexico, Sonora and Sinaloa, 1810–1877*, 69, 85–86; Armando Elías Chomina, *Compendio de datos históricos de la familia Elías*, 115–18.

25. Josiah Gregg, *Commerce of the Prairies*, 207. Gregg heard a story of a battle between Apaches and Mexicans at Socorro in which the Mexicans lost thirty-three killed and many wounded, while the Apaches lost six or seven killed. He places the event about 1834.

26. SA, R13, Bustamante to Governor, January 8, 14, 1834; Narbona to Governor, January 13, 1834.

27. SA, R13, Bustamante to Governor, January 14, 1834.

28. SA, R13, Romero to Prefect of Arispe, January 12, 1834; F. Narbona to Governor, January 13, 1834; Compoy to Governor, January 14, 1834; Corella to Governor, January 20, 23, and 28, 1834.

29. SA, R13, Bustamante to Escalante y Arvizu, April 26, 1834; Juan González to Escalante y Arvizu, April 5, July 6, 1834; Juan Elías to Governor, April 3, 1834; Ramirez to Commander, Tubac, July 3, 1834; Elías González to Governor, July 6, 1834; Moraga to Governor, July 4, 1834; Sweeney, *Cochise*, 22–23.

The Babocómari ranch was located on the banks of Babocómari Creek on an old Spanish land grant, about twenty miles wide, located south of the Whetstone Mountains in today's Santa Cruz and Cochise Counties. The hacienda was owned by the influential Elías González family and during the 1830s and '40s was one of the largest cattle ranches in northern Sonora. In 1866, United States troops occupied the old ranch and established Camp Wallen, a fort designed to contain Cochise's Chokonens. It was abandoned in 1869. Jay J. Wagoner, *Early Arizona: Prehistory to Civil War*, 188–192.

30. SA, R13, Villasquez to Governor, July 14, 16, 1834; Officer, *Hispanic Arizona*, 127–28.

31. Juarez Archives, R9, Villa to municipal president, Paso del Norte, March 12, 1834; Governor of Chihuahua to Alejos, May 20, 1834.

32. SA, R13, Elías González to Governor, July 6, 1834; Griffen, *Apaches at War and Peace*, 148.

33. Griffen, *Apaches at War and Peace*, 148.

34. *El Fanal de Chihuahua*, November 4, 1834.

35. Cuchillo Negro (ca. 1785–May 24, 1857) was an important leader of the Warm Springs local group of the Chihenne band. According to Jason Betzinez, he was a major war leader during the 1840s and 1850s. Known as Baishan among his people, he commanded a range between the Rio Grande and the Mimbres Mountains, along with the area near Cañada Alamosa and Ojo Caliente. John Cremony, who knew and apparently liked him, was impressed with his character and described him as "a gigantic savage, fully six feet four inches in height . . . but for so huge a body, a deficiency of muscle in his arms and legs." In May 1835 he was listed on a census at Santa Rita del Cobre. In the early 1840s he usually followed the lead of Mangas Coloradas. In 1846 American artist John Mix Stanley painted him. During the 1850s he participated in several treaties with Americans in New Mexico and received rations from Indian agents throughout this period. He was killed by Pueblo Indian scouts during the Bonneville campaign on May 24, 1857. Betzinez, *I Fought with Geronimo*, 4, 7–8; Cremony, "Some Savages," 206–207; JA, R28, census taken at Santa Rita del Cobre, May 31, 1835; Thrapp, *Encyclopedia*, I, 352.

36. Itán was a prominent leader of a Chihenne local group closely associated with Mangas Coloradas and Delgadito. His local group territory was the vicinity of Santa Rita del Cobre, or the Copper Mines. He was listed as a chief in the census taken there on May 31, 1835, and the next year was negotiating there with Pisago Cabezón and other leaders. With Mangas Coloradas he agreed to terms at Janos in March 1843, but he never brought his followers in. The next year one of his men was captured near Janos, and he admitted that Itán's followers were at war with Sonora and Chihuahua but went to Socorro, New Mexico, regularly to trade. By the late 1840s Itán seemed to become a more moderate leader, distancing himself from Mangas Coloradas's policies and joining the more moderate Chihenne leader Delgadito and Coleto Amarillo and Láceres, leaders of the Janeros local group of Nednhis. With these leaders he made peace at Janos on May 24, 1850, one which he kept until the Carrasco massacre the following March 1851. He was with the Nednhi chiefs Coleto Amarillo and El Chinito at the time they were killed on March 27, 1852, during an attack by Sonoran troops near the Florida Mountains, south of Deming. After this he moved his group to U.S. territory and signed peace treaties in 1852 and 1855. He enjoyed

friendly relations with Americans until 1856, when he moved his people back to Janos and made peace during a prisoner exchange. He passes from the scene in 1857. Sweeney, *Cochise,* 90–91; Edwin R. Sweeney, "I Had Lost All: Geronimo and the Carrasco Massacre of 1851," *Journal of Arizona History* 27 (Spring 1986).

37. *El Fanal de Chihuahua,* November 25, 1834.

38. The "tame" Apaches, or Apaches mansos, were the remnants of Apaches who had remained at peace, living near Tucson and Tubac. They apparently were Chiricahuas; at least that is what the informants of Grenville Goodwin and Morris Opler reported. Goodwin, *Social Organization,* 86; Morris Opler, "The Identity of the Apache Mansos," *American Anthropologist* 44 (October–November 1942), 725. My thanks to G. Donald Kucera of Tucson for bringing this article to my attention.

39. Antonio Pascual Narbona, the son of an important Sonoran military leader by the same name, was born about 1800. He rose through the ranks and participated in many of the campaigns against the Chiricahuas in the 1830s and 1840s. It was his father who captured a young Chokonen boy who would become known as Miguel Narbona, the fiercest Chokonen war leader of the 1840s and early 1850s. Antonio Narbona was appointed commander of Sonora's northern frontier in 1841, establishing his home base at Fronteras. He joined Elías González in a surprise attack at Janos and Corralitos in August 1844, his command killing between twenty and thirty Apaches at Janos. In the fall of 1847 he led a campaign from Fronteras which killed an aged Chiricahua woman in the Chiricahua Mountains. The Chokonens threatened to retaliate, and they did, killing Narbona and seven others at Cuquiarachi, near Fronteras, on December 23, 1847. His widow and son moved to Ures after his death. See Sweeney, *Cochise,* 62–64, 407 n. 75; Thrapp, *Encyclopedia,* II, 1042; James Box, *Captain James Box's Adventures and Exploration in New and Old Mexico,* 56–57.

José Ignacio Terán y Tato was born in Bacoachi in the early 1800s. Educated in England, he spoke excellent English. By the 1840s he had become one of the wealthiest men in Sonora. Always a staunch foe of the Apaches, he became even more determined after they killed his brother Francisco in early 1849. In the early 1850s he personally directed and financed several campaigns from Moctezuma, acting in his capacity as the commander of Sonora's national guard. He died in France on January 26, 1868, and left the bulk of his wealth to civic institutions in Sonora. See Sweeney, *Cochise,* 408 n. 4; Almada, *Diccionario sonorenses,* 688–89.

40. Vivora, born in the 1790s, had a long and fascinating life. His father had been an important leader from the 1790s until his death in 1804. Vivora's actions usually paralleled those of his close associate and band leader Pisago Cabezón. Like Pisago, he made peace at Fronteras in 1836 and at Janos in 1842. He was present during the infamous Johnson massacre of Juan José Compá and a score of others in 1837 and eluded Kirker's scalp hunters in 1846, but he could not escape the white man's

lethal disease of smallpox, to which he succumbed at Fronteras in early 1862. *Estrella de Occidente*, March 7, 1862.

41. SA, R14, Escalante y Arvizu to Bustamante, November 2, 1834; Mora to Bustamante, November 21, 1834; Governor of Chihuahua to Bustamante, November 18, 1834; *El Fanal de Chihuahua*, November 25, 1834; Bancroft, *History of the North Mexican States and Texas*, I, 654; Opler, *Life-Way*, 335.

42. Griffen, *Apaches at War and Peace*, 163–64; William B. Griffen, "The Compás: A Chiricahua Apache Family of the Late 18th and Early 19th Centuries," *American Indian Quarterly* 7 (Spring 1983), 21–49.

43. Relles (Reyes) was an important Chokonen band leader from the early 1830s until his death in 1846. Possibly the father of the legendary Chokonen leader Cochise, Relles was born about 1790, likely in southeastern Arizona. He considered Fronteras as his peace establishment, spending much time there during the 1820s. He and his contemporary Matías were moderate leaders of the Chokonens, generally preferring peaceful relations to war. He participated in the peace treaties at Fronteras in 1836 and at Janos in 1842. He was the prime mover in the May 1846 truce at Galeana, Chihuahua, where he was murdered on July 7, 1846, a victim of James Kirker's scalp hunters.

Matías, born about 1790, was a Chokonen leader with generally pacific views. Like his contemporary Relles, he made his headquarters near Fronteras from the 1820s until his death in the mid-1840s. On several occasions he became actively involved in peace negotiations, even traveling to Guaymas, Ures, and Chihuahua City, His sons Pablo and Elías became Chokonen local group leaders under Cochise in the 1850s.

Tapilá, a Chokonen chief usually associated with the warlike faction, was born in the 1790s. He may have been related to Pisago Cabezón or may have married into the family of the latter, for he appears on ration lists from 1816 through 1819 as a member of Pisago Cabezón's local group. In the early 1820s Tapilá apparently married a woman of Cide's group. In 1835 he was mentioned in the census taken at Santa Rita del Cobre, again affiliated with Cide's group. Throughout the 1840s and early 1850s he was mentioned during several encounters with Mexican troops or as a leader of various war parties in Sonora. He played a prominent role in the Chiricahua victory at Pozo Hediondo on January 20, 1851. Sonoran troops killed him in November 1851 at Bavispe, where he had gone to exchange prisoners.

44. JA, R28, Calvo to Justiniani, no date but probably January 27, 1835, document entitled "Conditions for the Preliminary Peace with Juan José Compá"; Justiniani to Calvo, February 12, 1835; SA, R13, Rey to Escalante y Arvizu, May 9, 1835; Justiniani to Commanding General, Chihuahua, April 3, 1835.

45. Stevens, "Apache Menace," 217.

46. SA, R13, Elías González to Escalante y Arvizu, June 27, 1835; JA, R24, Justiniani to Military Commander, Janos, June 19, 1835; JA, R28,

Ponce de León to Justiniani, April 7, 1835; Griffen, *Apaches at War and Peace,* 159–60.

47. SA, R13, Elías González to Governor of Sonora, June 17, 1835; Elías González to Villascuna, June 1, 1835; JA, R26, Commanding General, Chihuahua to Ronquillo, May 31, 1835; Ronquillo to Justiniani, June 14, 1835.

48. *La Noticioso de Chihuahua,* August 7, 1835; SA, R13, Elías González to Governor, August 13, 1835; JA, R28, Ponce de León to Justiniani, August 13, 15, 1835; R6, Justiniani to Commanding General, Chihuahua, September 10, 1835; R26, Ronquillo to Justiniani July 20, 1835; Griffen, *Apaches at War and Peace,* 161.

49. *El Noticioso de Chihuahua,* December 4, 1835.

50. SA, R14, Elías González to Governor, February 10, 1836; *El Noticioso de Chihuahua,* April 22, 1836.

51. San Juan was a respected Chokonen man, a member of Pisago Cabezón's group and in the late 1840s an important warrior under Yrigóllen, a Chokonen band leader after the death of Pisago Cabezón. Terán y Tato's command killed him during a fight in the Pitaicache Mountains in northeast Sonora in May 1849. Edwin R. Sweeney, "One of Heaven's Heroes: A Mexican General Pays Tribute to the Honor and Courage of a Chiricahua Apache," *Journal of Arizona History* 36 (Autumn 1995), 219–20; Sweeney, *Cochise,* 72.

52. Griffen, *Apaches at War and Peace,* 166–68.

53. Miguel Narbona, born in the early 1800s, was a Chokonen captured by Sonoran troops under Antonio Narbona (Senior) about 1812. He remained with the Narbona family for some ten years before he returned to the Chiricahuas. His role in the peace treaty of 1836 with Sonora was a minor one; he probably acted as interpreter in the discussions. By the mid-1840s, however, he had become the single most feared Chokonen leader in Sonora, having developed a pathological hatred of Sonorans. He led numerous war parties into Sonora in the 1840s and 1850s, including one in March 1849 that captured Merejildo Grijalva, who would become a noted scout against the Chiricahuas in the 1860s and 1870s. Cochise was Miguel Narbona's segundo, or second in command, and succeeded him as a local group leader upon his death, apparently of natural causes, about 1856. Sweeney, *Cochise,* 60–64, 406–407; Edwin R. Sweeney, *Merejildo Grijalva, Apache Captive, Army Scout,* 3–4.

54. *El Noticioso de Chihuahua,* November 25, 1836; AHSH, Folder 74, Elías González to Governor, October 1, 1836.

55. Sweeney, *Cochise,* 29; Griffen, *Apaches at War and Peace,* 171.

56. SA, R14, Elías González to Governor, February 12, 1837.

CHAPTER 4

1. Arce was killed by Apaches at El Ojito, between Rosales and Chihuahua City on January 1, 1841. Almada, *Diccionario chihuahuenses,* 47.

2. Sweeney, *Cochise*, 29–30; Griffen, *Apaches at War and Peace*, 173.

3. JA, R27, Arce to Ponce de León, January 26, 1837; Sweeney, *Cochise*, 30.

4. AHSH, Folder 83, Justice of the Peace (Fronteras) to Governor of Sonora, January 19, 1837.

5. SA, R14, Elías González to Governor, February 12, 26, 1837; AHSH, Folder 102, Escalante to Governor, February 26, 1837.

6. SA, R14, Escalante y Arvizu Proclamation, March 5, 1837; AHSH, Folder 102, García to Governor, March 3, 1837; Escalante to Governor, February 22, 1837.

7. John Johnson, a hatter by trade, was born in Kentucky about 1805. He came to Missouri in the early 1820s and in 1827 went west to Santa Fe. In August he made his first trip to Sonora and by 1830 had acquired title to a hacienda at Moctezuma, Sonora. His numerous journeys and trading expeditions in New Mexico and Sonora left him well acquainted with the Chiricahuas. In 1835 he married a woman who was a native of Moctezuma. They had four sons. After gold was discovered in California, Johnson made several trips there before he died in 1852. His descendants have held a variety of prominent positions in Sonora's government. Rex W. Strickland, "The Birth and Death of a Legend: The Johnson Massacre of 1837," *Arizona and the West* 18 (Autumn 1976), 257–86; Thrapp, *Encyclopedia*, II, 731–32.

8. Basehart, "Chiricahua Apache Subsistence," 76; Arizona State Museum, Tucson, Grenville Goodwin Collection, "Place Names in the Territory of Chiricahua, Mogollon and Mimbres Apaches." According to Robert Julyan, author of *The Place Names of New Mexico*, these mountains received their name *animas*, meaning "souls . . . who have died . . . and may refer to the numerous people who lost their lives in the area," perhaps from Apache encounters. Robert Julyan, *The Place Names of New Mexico*, 17.

9. Strickland, "Birth and Death of a Legend," 257–86. See Sweeney, *Cochise*, 31–35, 407–408 n. 76, for a summary of the Johnson affair and the effect it had on Apache-Mexican relations.

10. Eve Ball, *In the Days of Victorio: Recollections of a Warm Springs Apache*, 46; Ball, *Indeh*, 22; Boyer and Gayton, *Apache Mothers and Daughters*, 25–26.

11. *Conditions of the Indian Tribes: Report of the Joint Special Commission*, 328.

12. Betzinez, *I Fought with Geronimo*, 1.

13. Sweeney, *Cochise*, 37.

14. Boyer and Gayton, *Apache Mothers and Daughters*, 26.

15. Goodwin, *Social Organization*, 533–34.

16. Wilson, "Observations of Early Days in California and New Mexico."

17. AHSH, Folder 102, Elías to Commanding General, July 21, 1837; Folder 83, Gallegos to Governor of Sonora, July 26, 1837; Folder 83, Escalante to Governor of Sonora, August 7, 1837.

18. Juarez Archives, R8, Prefect of Galeana to Prefect del Paso, October 9, 1837; Galavas to Prefect del Paso, October 12, 1837.

19. Juarez Archives, R8, Galavas to Prefect del Paso, October 12, 1837; Varela to Prefect del Paso, October 26, December 11, 1837; List of Serviceable Firearms, Chihuahua City, October 21, 1837; AHSH, Bustamante to Governor of Sonora, August 18, 1837.

20. SA, R14, de la Vega to Governor of Sonora, October 11, 1837.

21. SA, R14, Simón Elías González to Governor of Sonora, May 30, 1837, contains the reference to McKnight's criminal conduct; JA, R28, Zuloaga to Military Commander, Janos, March 7, 1838; Griffen, *Apaches at War and Peace*, 173, 175–76; William B. Griffen, *Utmost Good Faith*, 54–55; Sweeney, *Cochise*, 38–41; Boyer and Gayton, *Apache Mothers and Daughters*, 26.

22. This same party evidently continued west into Sonora and arrived at Santa Cruz, where they told authorities that they were going to the Colorado River to trap beaver. Near the deserted San Pedro ranch they ran into a party of Western Apaches returning from a raid into Sonora and attacked them, killing and wounding several and confiscating their booty. *El Restaurador Federal*, May 1, 1838.

23. *El Noticioso de Chihuahua*, July 17, 1838.

24. William H. Emory, *Report on the United States and Mexico Boundary Survey*, I, 97–98.

25. Herbert E. Ungnade, *Guide to the New Mexico Mountains*, 162; Basehart, "Chiricahua Apache Subsistence," 79.

26. *El Noticioso de Chihuahua*, April 12, July 19, 1838.

27. George W. Kendall, *Across the Great Southwestern Prairies*, I, 429.

28. *El Noticioso de Chihuahua*, April 12, July 19, 1838.

29. AHSH, Folder 214, Samaniego to Governor of Sonora, April 7, 1838; Griffen, *Apaches at War and Peace*, 176.

30. Griffen, *Apaches at War and Peace*, 176; Sweeney, *Cochise*, 40.

31. Cremony, *Life among the Apaches*, 32; Ball, *In the Days of Victorio*, 46. See Sweeney, *Cochise*, 408–409 n. 11, for a discussion of Cremony's tendency to exaggerate.

32. Boyer and Gayton, *Apache Mothers and Daughters*, 26; Frederick A. Wislizenus, *A Tour to Northern Mexico Connected with Col. Doniphan's Expedition in 1846–47*, 58; Bartlett, *Personal Narrative*, I, 228–29; NA, RG75, M234, R547, Steck to Pelham, October 4, 1855.

33. *El Noticioso de Chihuahua*, November 23, 1838.

34. Manuel María Gándara, born in 1801, entered public life in 1829 and two years later briefly held the post of provisional governor of Sonora. He owned two large haciendas near Hermosillo and in 1837, supported by many of Sonora's wealthy ranchers, he was appointed governor by Mexico's President Anastasio Bustamante. After Urrea displaced him in 1838, he began to marshal his forces for the first of many bouts against the Urreas. A pragmatist and supreme opportunist with few scruples, he incensed many of Sonora's citizens because he had

allied himself with its Indian population solely for his personal goals and ambitions. He catered to them, unleashing them whenever he felt threatened. His administrative record was poor, and he favored the church and large ranchers at the expense of the mining and business factions. Sonora floundered under his leadership, although he and his cohorts fared well financially. His coalition began to dissolve in the early 1850s, although he remained a major political factor into the late 1850s. He died at Hermosillo on October 4, 1878. Almada, *Diccionario sonorenses,* 255–61; Rodolfo F. Acuña, *Sonoran Strongman: Ignacio Pesqueira and His Times,* 17–18.

35. José C. Urrea Elías González was truly one of Sonora's remarkable men of his time. Born March 19, 1797, into a prominent military family, probably in Tucson, he began his military career at the age of twelve. Urrea fought in many major battles in Mexico's War for Independence, though initially he had fought to suppress the movement. He retired from the military in 1827, citing illness and family problems, but in 1830 he applied for reinstatement. He participated in Santa Anna's invasion of Texas and returned to Sonora a national hero for his erstwhile and noble service. After the fighting in 1838 he left Sonora for Durango. For most of 1839 and 1840 he continued to fight for the federal cause. He would return to govern Sonora from 1842 to 1845 and took this opportunity to initiate several reforms: improving schools, hospitals, agriculture and the judicial system despite facing continual opposition from Gándara's forces, the Apaches, and the Seris. His forces were defeated near Hermosillo in November 1845, and once again he left Sonora. He fought the Americans during the Mexican War of 1846–48. He contracted cholera and died on August 1, 1849. In the words of his biographer, Patricia Roche Herring, he was a "noble and idealistic" man who "tried to make Sonora a model of federalism. . . . He left behind an illustrious and honorable legacy." Patricia Roche Herring, "Tucsonense Preclaro (Illustrious Tucsonian), General José C. Urrea, Romantic Idealist," *Journal of Arizona History* 34 (Autumn 1993).

36. Voss, *On the Periphery,* 96–100; Acuña, *Sonoran Strongman,* 9–10, 17; Officer, *Hispanic Arizona,* 151–54; Patricia Roche Herring, "José C. Urrea," 307–15.

37. Sweeney, *Cochise,* 41; Officer, *Hispanic Arizona,* 145.

38. AHSH, Folder 96, Elías to Governor, June 19, 1839; Prefect of Bavispe to Governor, August 19, 1839.

39. AHSH, Folder 104, Gándara to Governor, December 3, 1839.

40. AHSH, Folder 110, Governor to Moreno, August 20, 1840.

41. Griffen, *Utmost Good Faith,* 189–90.

42. James Hobbs, *Wild Life in the Far West,* 81. For a discussion of Kirker's motives, see Sweeney, *Cochise,* 409 n. 19.

43. Juarez Archives, R9, de la Vega to Prefect, Paso del Norte District, April 2, 1839; Sweeney, *Cochise,* 42.

44. *El Antenor,* December 31, 1839.

45. JA, R28, Arce to Military Commander, Janos, January 4, 1840.

46. Gregg, *Commerce on the Prairies*, 202–203.

47. JA, R28, Arce to Military Commander, Janos, January 4, 1840; *El Antenor*, January 21, 1840.

48. JA, R28, Simón Elías González to Military Commander of Janos, February 6, 1840.

49. JA, R28, Elías González to Military Commander, Janos, February 19, 1840.

50. *El Antenor*, April 14, May 19, 1840.

51. JA, R28, Diary of Movements, February, May 1840; JA, R30, Varela to Prefect, Paso, July 28, 1840; Juarez Archives, R9, de la Vega to Prefect del Paso, June 23, 1840.

52. *El Antenor*, July 14. 1840.

53. Sweeney, *Cochise*, 42–43.

54. Yrigóllen was an important Chokonen leader from the late 1830s until his death at the hands of Sonoran troops in March 1851 at Janos. He was a moderate Chokonen leader until Kirker's massacre of Chiricahuas (in which he lost kinfolk) at San Buenaventura in July 1846, when he became a leader, with Miguel Narbona, of the militant Chokonens. By 1850 he had grown weary of war and made peace with José María Elías González in Sonora. Late that summer he brought his followers to Janos, where on March 5, 1851, his ranchería was surprised by Sonoran troops under Colonel José María Carrasco. He was killed in his camp. Sweeney, "I Had Lost All," 35–52.

55. Esquinaline was a Chokonen local group leader who enjoyed close ties to Mangas Coloradas and Cochise throughout his life. Born about 1800, he with his local group followed Mangas Coloradas during the 1840s and 1850s, often joining him during his forays into Mexico. Like Mangas, he preferred to maintain friendly relations with Americans while continuing to make war on Mexico. In 1859 one American described him as a "rather good looking specimen of an Apache, about sixty years of age, and speaks Spanish, very imperfectly, however." He died in the early 1860s. *Missouri Republican*, August 29, 1859.

56. Sweeney, *Cochise*, 46–47; Officer, *Hispanic Arizona*, 155–56.

57. Griffen, *Apaches at War and Peace*, 189.

CHAPTER 5

1. Cremony, *Life among the Apaches*, 177.

2. Opler, *Life-Way*, 470.

3. For example, Cremony wrote of Mangas's reputation below the border:

The northern portions of Chihuahua and Sonora, large tracts of Durango, the whole of Arizona, and a very considerable part of New Mexico, were laid waste, ravished, destroyed by this man and his followers. A strip of country twice as large as all of California was rendered almost houseless, unproductive, uninhabitable, by his active and uncompromising hostility. Large and flourishing towns were depopulated and ruined. Vast ranchos, such as that of Babacomori and San Bernardino, once teeming with wealth and immense herds of cattle, horses, and mules, were turned into waste places and restored to their pristine solitudes. The name of Mangas Coloradas was the tocsin of terror and dismay throughout a vast region of country. [Cremony, *Life among the Apaches*, 177–78.]

Although Cremony's propensity to embellish is apparent (for example, I have not come across record of any Chiricahua raids into Durango during the nineteenth century), much of what he observed was based on his experiences while he was stationed in New Mexico and Arizona in the early 1850s and early 1860s. He overstates the deeds carried out by Mangas Coloradas, attributing the deplorable frontier conditions solely to Mangas's war parties, when the other Chiricahua bands, notably the Chokonens, had an equal if not greater hand in these depredations, particularly in Sonora.

4. Bartlett, *Personal Narrative*, I, 319; NA, RG75, M234, R546, Bartlett to Secretary of the Interior, February 19, 1852.

5. Bartlett, *Personal Narrative*, I, 327.

6. Cremony, "Some Savages," 202; Cremony, *Life among the Apaches*, 48; Goodwin, *Social Organization*, 13.

7. H. B. Wharfield, *Cooley: Army Scout, Arizona Pioneer, Wayside Host, Apache Friend*, 7; Allan Radbourne letter to author, September 1, 1983.

8. Griswold, "Fort Sill Apaches," biographies of Cochise, 24; Dos-teh-seh, 32 (although her year of birth must have been about 1820 and not 1838); Sweeney, *Cochise*, 45.

9. Griswold, "Fort Sill Apaches," biographies of Nah-ke-de-sah, 102; Gonah-hleenah, 51; Sethmooda, 123. According to Apache recollections, Gonah-hleenah died at San Carlos in the 1870s. Yet, according to Mexican documents, there was a Clo-nah-gah-yo-gathe who was captured at Casas Grandes, Chihuahua, in the spring of 1882, some six months after the Chiricahuas had left San Carlos in September 1881. He was a member of Bonito's Bedonkohe band in the 1880 census at San Carlos. SA, R21, List Of Chiricahua Apaches held captive in Mexico.

10. Sweeney, *Cochise*, 110.

11. Griswold, "Ft. Sill Apaches," biography of Sethmooda, 123.

12. Sweeney, *Cochise*, 217.

13. Salvador followed in his father's footsteps to become an important fighting man of the Chihennes. Born about 1830, he was a voice for peace in the ill-fated parleys at Pinos Altos in early 1865. The next year he led a war party of 125 warriors that assaulted Pinos Altos. Yet, like his father, he understood that the survival of his people could only be achieved if

they made peace with the Americans. With Loco in 1868 he opened negotiations at Fort Craig and patiently waited for Americans to set aside a reserve for his people near Cañada Alamosa. Finally, in November 1870 he left the temporary reservation with his brother-in-law Cochise and returned to Arizona. In late February 1871 he was killed in a fight with American citizens in the Mogollon Mountains. Sweeney, *Cochise*, 287–88, 301–307, 448 n. 17.

14. Griswold, "Fort Sill Apaches," biography of Carl Mangas, 92; Boyer and Gayton, *Apache Mothers and Daughters*, 60–61.

15. Griswold, "Fort Sill Apaches," biography of Ilth-too-da, 60.

16. Griffen "Chiricahua Apaches," 567; AHSH, Folder 127, Elías to Governor, January 26, May 14, 1842.

17. Griffen, "Chiricahua Apaches," 564; JA, R28, Ugarte to Madrigal, April 26, 1842; JA, R29, Aguirre to Janos Commander, May 15, 1842; *La Luna*, April 19, 1842.

18. Vicente's party may have been referring to an incident at Paso del Norte in November 1834 when Chihuahua's military seized the Chiricahua leader Jasquedegá and fourteen others who had come in to discuss a truce. They were released the following summer in accordance with the peace treaty of March 31, 1835 (see chapter 3). The reliable Josiah Gregg described an incident that occurred during the summer of 1839 when authorities enticed several Apaches into an ambush at Paso del Norte and murdered some twenty warriors "in cold blood." Gregg, *Commerce of the Prairies*, 206–207.

19. JA, R29, Madrigal to Commanding General, District of El Paso, May 26, 1842.

20. *La Luna*, June 28, July 15, 19, 1842.

21. Ponce, also known as José María Ponce, was a literate Chihenne leader, described by one American as speaking "pure Castilian Spanish," a benefit of an education provided by the Mexican government. He was the brother of Poncito, a Chihenne or Nednhi local group leader, and likely the father of Ponce, one of the two Apache scouts who guided General O. O. Howard to Cochise's camp in the Dragoon Mountains in September 1872. Born about 1800, the senior Ponce was one of the more important Chihenne band leaders of the midnineteenth century. His local group territory was the eastern portion of Chihenne territory; hence, he maintained friendly relations with the Mescalero Apaches east of the Rio Grande. Generally a moderate chief, he made peace with Mexicans at Janos in 1842 and 1851, held several talks with Boundary Commissioner John R. Bartlett during the summer of 1851, and signed peace treaties with Americans in 1852 and 1853. He was killed by one of his own people "in a drunken frolic" in late June or early July 1854. Jerry D. Thompson, ed., "With the Third Infantry in New Mexico, 1851–1853: The Lost Diary of Private Sylvester W. Matson," *Journal of Arizona History* 31 (Winter 1990), 372; Sweeney, *Cochise*, 46, 51, 410; National Archives, Record Group 75, Records of the New Mexico Superin-

tendency of Indian Affairs, 1849–1880, Microcopy T21 (hereafter cited as NA, RG75, T21, and roll number), Roll 2, Steck to Meriwether, July 8, 1854.

22. Griffen's excellent analysis carefully examines Apache raids in Chihuahua from September 1842 through February 1845. He concludes that Chihuahua showed a "dramatic drop in hostilities." Griffen, *Utmost Good Faith*, 78.

23. AHSH, Folder 127, Ignacio Elías to Governor, May 14, 1842; Juarez Archives, R11, Varela to Prefect, District of El Paso, June 4, 1842.

24. SA, R14, Aguayo to Urrea, June 27, 1842; JA, R30, Janos Commander to Governor of Chihuahua, August 1, 6, 1842; Juarez Archives, R11, Varela to Prefect, District of El Paso, July 30, 1842.

25. Manuelito, a Chokonen leader, was born in the early 1790s. He was listed on the Janos census rolls as early as 1810 as a member of Asquienalte's group. A moderate Chokonen, he led the band that bore the brunt of Elías González's attack near Janos in August 1844. He met American Captain Philip St. George Cooke in early December 1846 near the San Bernardino ranch in southeastern Arizona. With the emergence of Yrigóllen, Miguel Narbona, and Esquinaline, his influence began to wane in the late 1840s. He died, supposedly of natural causes, during the winter of 1849–50. *Revista Oficial*, September 24, 1844; *Revista Oficial*, Supplement to no. 35, August 28, 1844; Philip St. George Cooke, *Exploring Southwestern Trails, 1846–54*, 122, 129–30.

26. JA, R30, Janos Commander to Governor of Chihuahua, July 16, August 1, 1842; Juarez Archives, R11, Varelo to Prefect, District of El Paso, July 30, 1842.

27. JA, R30, Janos Commander to Governor of Chihuahua, August 6, 1842. Officer, *Hispanic Arizona*, 156–58.

28. JA, R30, Janos Commander to Governor of Chihuahua, September 1, 1842; Conde to Commander, Janos, September 22, 1842; Diary of Movements, August 1842.

29. JA, R30, Janos Commander to Governor of Chihuahua, September 1, 7, 1842.

30. AHSH, Folder 127, Escalante to Governor of Sonora, August 24, 1842.

31. JA, R30, Janos Commander to Governor, September 1, 1842.

32. Griffen, *Apaches at War and Peace*, 195; Sweeney, *Cochise*, 47–48.

33. Griffen, *Apaches at War and Peace*, 205–206.

34. JA, R30, Madrigal to Governor, September 29, 1842.

35. JA, R29, Conde to Military Commander at Janos, October 6, 1842.

36. JA, R30, Madrigal to Governor, November 18 (?), 1842; Officer, *Hispanic Arizona*, 158–59.

37. JA, R30, Madrigal to Governor, November 18 (?), 1842.

38. Officer, *Hispanic Arizona*, 158–60; Griffen, *Utmost Good Faith*, 78–79.

39. Griffen, *Utmost Good Faith*, 78.

40. Soquilla was a leader of a Janeros local group of Nednhis. Born about 1800, he had matured during the presidio system of the early 1800s. He assumed leadership of his group after Johnson's massacre of 1837, becoming a prominent war leader by the early 1840s. His followers apparently settled at Galeana in 1843, where they remained until smallpox broke out. They relocated to Corralitos and Janos in the fall of that year. He had a wife and four children on the Janos ration lists of 1843. In 1844 he rejoined Mangas Coloradas in his war against Sonora. Elías González's Sonoran soldiers attacked his ranchería near Janos in August 1844, killing several people and recovering stock allegedly stolen from Sonora. He was killed in September 1849 when troops from Janos attacked his camp in the Florida Mountains south of Deming, New Mexico. Sweeney, *Cochise*, 416 n. 54.

41. *Revista Oficial*, February 7, 1843; Griffen, *Utmost Good Faith*, 78–79.

42. José Mariano Monterde was born in Mexico City in 1789 and had a long and distinguished career in Mexico's military. He was named governor of Chihuahua on December 8, 1842, a position he held until January of 1845. He returned to Mexico City and in 1846 was named director of the military college. He fought valiantly in the U.S.–Mexican War of 1846 until Americans captured him in September 1847 during the defense of Chapultepec. He died in 1861. Almada, *Diccionario chihuahuenses*, 457.

43. JA, R28, document entitled "Rancherías of Indians at Peace," March 1, 1843; R30, Monterde to Madrigal, March 3, 1843; Monterde to Madrigal, March 19, 1843; *Revista Oficial*, April 18, 1843.

44. *Revista Oficial*, April 18, 1843.

45. Ibid., June 6, 1843.

46. Griffen, *Apaches at War and Peace*, 197.

47. Agua Hueca is located in the Alamo Hueco Mountains in the bootheel of New Mexico in the extreme southwestern part of the state, some three miles north of Chihuahua. The Chiricahuas knew this range as Dzildatlis, or "Blue Mountain." It was a popular base for raiding into Mexico and an important area for gathering mescal and hunting deer. Basehart, "Chiricahua Apache Subsistence," 76; T. M. Pearce, ed., *New Mexico Place Names: A Geographical Dictionary*, 4.

48. *Revista Oficial*, June 6, 1843.

49. Ibid.; JA, R30, Arce to Janos Commander June 9, 1843.

50. *Revista Oficial*, June 6, 27, 1843.

51. AHSH, Folder 134, Ignacio Elías to Governor; JA, R30, Monterde to Madrigal, June 8, 1843; Griffen, *Apaches at War and Peace*, 199; Sweeney, *Cochise*, 48–49.

52. JA, R30, Monterde to Madrigal, June 2, 8, 1843.

53. Griffen, *Apaches at War and Peace*, 207–208.

54. JA, R30, Diary of Movements, July 1843. José Mentisa [Mentira] was considered a loyal Chiricahua scout by Janos authorities. Not so with Sonora, however. Elías González's command captured him near Janos in

August 1844 despite the objections of Captain Mariano Rodríguez Rey, who wrote of the unjust "imprisonment of the Chieftain José Mentisa, who, as we guaranty and can prove with facts when we have a chance, has not left the fort at Janos since he made peace." Despite Rey's strong protest, civilian troops executed Mentisa en route to Bavispe, Sonora. *Revista Oficial*, Supplement to no. 35, August 28, 1844; Griffen, *Apaches at War and Peace*, 213–14.

55. National Archives and Records Center, Record Group 393, Records of the United States Army Continental Commands, 1821–1920, Microcopy 1102, Letters Received, Ninth Military Department (hereafter cited as NA, RG393, M1102, with roll number), Steen to McLaws, September 3, 1850.

CHAPTER 6

1. Griffen, *Utmost Good Faith*, 224–25.

2. Bancroft Library, Louis Alphonse Pinart Microfilm Collection, Document 80, Testimony of Cesario Corella, October 19, 1844; AHSH, Folder 134, Corella to Governor, September 18, 1843.

3. JA, R30, various ration lists, November 27, 1843, through January 15, 1844.

4. Officer, *Hispanic Arizona*, 163–65; Voss, *On the Periphery*, 101–103.

5. Sweeney, *Cochise*, 50–51; Hubert Howe Bancroft, *History of Arizona and New Mexico*, 327–29; Griffen, *Apaches at War and Peace*, 205–206.

6. Sweeney, *Cochise*, 51.

7. Griffen, *Apaches at War and Peace*, 208–209; JA, R31, Madrigal to Commanding General, January 20, 1844; Pinart Collection, Document 77, Subprefect of Moctezuma to Èlías González, November 22, 1844.

8. Pinart Collection, Document 69, Moreno to Elías González, October 29, 1844; Document 73, Narbona to Elías González, October 3, 1844; Salazar to Elías González, November 13, 1844; de Aros to Elías González, November 2, 1844; SA, R14, Lapisco to Governor, October 4, 1844; Barelos to Subprefect of Oposura, October 9, 1844.

9. López de Aros was a veteran officer of Sonora's northern frontier. At various times he commanded the presidios of Altar, Tubac, and Fronteras. His descendants were prominent citizens of southern Arizona after the United States purchased it from Mexico. As with many of Sonora's military men, he would fall victim to the Apaches near Cocospera in late December 1855. Officer, *Hispanic Arizona*, 373 n. 20; *La Voz de Sonora*, January 11, 1856.

10. Pinart Collection, Document 76, Justice of the Peace (?), Fronteras, to Elías González, November 2, 1844; Document 72, de Aros to Elías González, November 2, 1844; SA, R14, Lapisco to Governor, October 4, 1844.

11. Griffen, *Apaches at War and Peace*, 209.

12. Pinart Collection, Document 72, de Aros to Elías González, November 2, 1844; Document 76, Justice of the Peace (?), Fronteras, to Elías González, November 2, 1844; AHSH, Folder 146, Corella to Governor, March 14, 1844.

13. Griffen, *Apaches at War and Peace*, 210–11; Pinart Collection, Document 74, Rodríguez to Moreno, October 18, 1844.

14. Pinart Collection, Document 74, Rodríguez to Moreno, October 18, 1844; Acuña y Ortiz to Moreno, October 18, 1844; Document 69, Valencia to Romero, October 13, 1844.

15. Pinart Collection, Document 73, Granillo to Narbona, November 13, 1844; Salazar to Narbona, November 13, 1844; Seyba to Narbona, November 13, 1844; Document 71, Andrada to Subprefect of Sahuaripa, November 1, 1844; AHSH, Folder 146, Corella to Governor, May 3, 1844; SA, R14, Lapisco to governor, October 4, 1844.

16. Basehart, "Chiricahua Apache Subsistence," 73–74, 80.

17. JA, R31, Rey to Chávez, July 4, 1844.

18. Pinart Collection, Document 68, Campillo to Governor, October 17, 1844; Park, "Apaches in Mexican-American Relations," 135; Sweeney, *Cochise*, 52; Officer, *Hispanic Arizona*, 179.

19. JA, R30, Monterde to Madrigal, August 18, 1843.

20. Ibid.; AHSH, Folder 134, Governor of Sonora to Secretary of War and Navy, September 26, 1843; SA, R14, Bozanegra to Governor of Sonora, December 6, 1843.

21. SA, R14, Bozanegra to Urrea, February 8, 1844.

22. The Pinart Collection, Bancroft Library, has several references to Apaches' boasting of their victories to Sonoran citizens who had gone to Janos or Corralitos on business. For example, in Document 73 is the testimony of Deciderio Escalante, the justice of the peace at Fronteras, who knew several Chiricahuas on a personal basis. When at Janos on business he conversed with the Chokonen warrior Chino, a brother of Posito Moraga, who openly admitted that he and his brother had killed a man near Fronteras. Chepillo and the Chokonen band leader Yrigóllen told Escalante that although he was safe at Janos, if they saw him near his home (Fronteras), they would kill him.

23. Luis García was one of those peripheral frontier characters of northern Sonora who, because of business relationships at Janos and Corralitos, became well acquainted with the Chiricahuas. A commander of Sonora's local militia, or national guard troops, he frequently led campaigns against the Apaches. In February 1851 Sonora's officials sent him to Janos to investigate Apache affairs there, and he wrote an objective report giving his opinion that the Apaches were abiding by their peace treaty, although a month later (March 1851) Sonoran troops under Colonel José María Carrasco invaded Janos and attacked Apaches there. He continued to lead troops against the Apaches until he was killed by a Chiricahua war party under Cochise at Lagartos Canyon about fifteen miles northeast of Bavispe on April 6, 1865. Sweeney, *Cochise*, 101, 230.

24. Pinart Collection, Document 69, Testimony of Gervacio Valencia, October 13, 1844.

25. *Revista Oficial*, Supplement to no. 85, August 28, 1844.

26. Ibid.

27. *Revista Oficial*, September 24, 1844; Pinart Collection, Document 68, Testimony of Francisco Campillo, October 17, 1844.

28. *Revista Oficial*, Supplement to no. 85, August 28, 1844.

29. Ibid.

30. JA, R31, Rey to Chávez, July 4, 1844.

31. Pinart Collection, Document 73, testimony of Juan José Granillo, November 13, 1844.

32. Griffen, *Utmost Good Faith*, 224–25.

33. Officer, *Hispanic Arizona*, 180.

34. See the Pinart Collection, Bancroft Library, for various letters justifying Elías González's actions.

35. José María Zuloaga, born into a prominent family in Chihuahua City in 1804, enjoyed a long military career until his retirement in 1839 at the rank of captain. He owned the mines at Corralitos and eventually became the most important political leader of northwestern Chihuahua in the 1840s and 1850s. His brother Félix served as president of Mexico for a short time in 1853; another relative, Luis, was governor of Chihuahua in 1845. Like most citizens of the Janos, Corralitos, and Galeana area, he had mixed policies toward the Apaches. Ideally, he would have preferred to exterminate every Apache on the frontier, but, finding this impossible to carry out, he maintained a shaky alliance based solely on trade. Yet there were times when this peaceful coexistence would be disrupted; then he was unyielding and had no compunctions about exploiting the Chiricahuas whenever the ends justified the means. Oftentimes his militant policies and his embracing of genocide and scalp hunters repudiated those policies that the military was trying to carry out. Beginning in 1844 Sonoran and American officials made numerous accusations regarding his contraband trade with the Chiricahuas. As late as 1864 American General James Carleton pointed an accusing finger at Zuloaga. Zuloaga died on June 3, 1868. Almada, *Diccionario chihuahuenses*, 576.

36. See Sweeney, *Cochise*, 411 n. 52, for a discussion of the stolen stock that his command found in the Apache villages and in the possession of public officials at Janos and Corralitos.

37. AHSH, Folder 143, Justice of the Peace, Altar to Subprefect of Altar, September 6, 1844.

38. SA, R14, Lapisco to Governor, October 4, 1844; Pinart Collection, Document 79.

39. Griffen, *Apaches at War and Peace*, 213–14.

40. Pinart Collection, Document 82, García to Elías González, January 1, 1845.

41. Herring, "Tucsonense Preclaro," 317–18.

42. SA, R14, Urrea to the Governors of Chihuahua, Durango, and New Mexico, February 3, 1845.

43. State of New Mexico Records Center, Santa Fe, Mexican Archives of New Mexico, Roll 41, Frame 548, Investigations of various persons from Socorro area trading with Apaches.

44. *Revista Oficial*, June 3, 1845.

45. *La Restauracion*, October 28, 1845.

46. Officer, *Hispanic Arizona*, 184–85.

47. SA, R14, Barelos to Subprefect of Oposura [Moctezuma], October 9, 1844; AHSH, Folder 153, Grijalva to Urrea, February 23, 1845; Folder 153, Prefect of Ures to Elías González, June 30, 1845.

48. Officer, *Hispanic Arizona*, 185–86.

49. Goodwin Collection, "Place Names."

50. *Revista Oficial*, July 1, 1845; JA, R31, Ugarte to Padilla, June 20, 1845; Conde to Padilla, July 20, 1845.

51. Griffen, *Utmost Good Faith*, 94.

52. *La Restauracion*, October 28, 1845.

53. Mexican Archives of New Mexico, R41, Frame 548.

54. Griffen, *Utmost Good Faith*, 208–10.

55. AHSH, Folder 155, García to Campoy, October 9, 1845.

56. AHSH, Folder 156, Morales to Governor, September 23, 1845; *El Iris de Paz*, October 9, 1845.

57. *La Restauracion*, November 4, December 9, 30, 1845.

58. Sweeney, *Cochise*, 54–55.

59. Ibid.

60. Kirker's report can be found in *El Provisional*, July 21, 1846. Cásares's report was published a week earlier in *El Provisional*, July 14, 1846. Ruxton's report is in George Frederick Ruxton, *Adventures in Mexico and the Rocky Mountains, 1846–47*, 153–54. Yrigóllen briefly referred to the Kirker massacre during the 1850 negotiations with Elías González, calling it the "double cross at Galeana." AHSH, Folder 221, Elías González to Governor, March 22, 1850; Jason Betzinez's version is in *I Fought with Geronimo*, 3. Betzinez placed the massacre at Kintal, which he incorrectly believed was Ramos. Ramos was never more than a hacienda and at no time could have contained eight hundred to one thousand inhabitants, as Betzinez asserted. Investigation reveals that the Chiricahua name for Casas Grandes was Kin-n-teel ("House Broad"), and the massacre occurred southeast of there at Galeana. Mangas Coloradas's version was published in *Conditions of the Indian Tribes: Report of the Joint Special Commission*, 328.

61. Ibid; Ruxton, *Adventures in Mexico*, 154.

62. *El Provisional*, July 14, 1846.

63. Betzinez, *I Fought with Geronimo*, 1.

CHAPTER 7

1. *El Sonorense*, August 7, 1846.
2. AHSH, Folder 160, Barrios to Governor, August 18, 1846.
3. Ibid.
4. Born in Newark, New Jersey, in 1794, Kearny saw his first action as a Lieutenant in the Thirteenth Infantry in the War of 1812. He was wounded and captured by the English at Queenston Heights, October 13, 1812. He served with distinction in many Indian campaigns during the 1820s and 1830s. In 1836 he was promoted to colonel and six years later became the commander of the Third Military Department, Great Plains region. He served honorably in the pacification of California, which he left in August 1847. He returned to Fort Leavenworth for a short time before embarking to Vera Cruz, Mexico, and then Mexico City. While on duty, he contracted a tropical disease and returned to Saint Louis, where he died on October 31, 1848. *Webster's American Military Biographies*, 212–13.
5. Robert W. Larson, *New Mexico's Quest for Statehood 1846–1912*, 1–2; William A. Keleher, *Turmoil in New Mexico, 1846–1868*, 3–4.
6. Sterling Price, born in Virginia in 1809, attended Hampden-Sydney College in 1826–27, where he studied law. In 1831 he moved to Missouri. Soon after, he became involved in state politics and in 1844 was elected to Congress. He resigned his seat in August 1846 to serve in the Mexican War. He followed Kearny's command to Santa Fe and soon found himself in command when Kearny headed to California and Colonel Doniphan left for an invasion of Chihuahua. After putting down a revolt in New Mexico, he was promoted to brigadier general of volunteers in July 1847. He won an important victory over Mexican troops at Santa Cruz de Rosales on March 16, 1848. Four years later he was elected governor of Missouri. During the Civil War he initially tried to maintain a neutral stance, but this proved impossible because of the border bloodshed in Missouri. He fought gallantly for the South in several major campaigns in Missouri and Arkansas. At the end of the war he moved to Mexico, "where he attempted to establish a colony of Confederate veterans." He returned to Missouri in 1866, and died at Saint Louis on September 27, 1867. *Webster's American Military Biographies*, 333.
7. Fitzpatrick was born in Ireland in 1799. He came to America about 1816 and moved west, becoming one of the "greatest of all frontiersman of his period." During his years in the West he became a trapper, trader, guide, Indian fighter, and Indian agent. He was well acquainted with and respected by the Indian tribes of the Rocky Mountains, including the Flatheads, Blackfeet, and Crows. His nickname, "Broken Hand," was a result of a firearms accident that left his left hand disabled. In 1843 he became Frémont's guide for his second expedition, visiting Oregon and California. In 1847 he was appointed Indian agent for the Upper Platte and Arkansas Rivers and was instrumental in organizing the Fort

Laramie conference of 1851. Two years later he negotiated a treaty with the Southern Plains tribes of Comanches and Kiowas, and when at Washington he died suddenly of pneumonia on February 7, 1854. He left a wife of mixed French-Snake ancestry and two children. Thrapp, *Encyclopedia*, I, 496–97.

8. Larson, *New Mexico's Quest for Statehood*, 2–3.

9. Harvey Lewis Carter, *Dear Old Kit: The Historical Kit Carson*, 111–12.

10. Carter, *Dear Old Kit*, 111–12; Dwight L. Clarke, ed., *The Original Journals of Henry Smith Turner*, 79–80; Ross Calvin, *Lieutenant Emory Reports*, 86–87; Keleher, *Turmoil in New Mexico*, 27–28.

11. Clarke, *Original Journals of Turner*, 84–85.

12. John S. Griffin, *A Doctor Comes to California*, 23–24.

13. Ibid.; Clarke, *Original Journals of Turner*, 85.

14. Clarke, *Original Journals of Turner*, 84–87; Calvin, *Lieutenant Emory Reports*, 99–100.

15. U.S. Congress, House, H. Exec. Doc. 41, 30th Cong., 1st Sess., 579.

16. Calvin, *Lieutenant Emory Reports*, 100.

17. Pauline Weaver was born in Tennessee in 1800 to an American father and a Cherokee mother. He came west as a member of the Hudson's Bay Company and was one of the first Anglo-Americans to explore Arizona. He died in 1867 near Camp Lincoln (later Camp Verde), Arizona. Thrapp, *Encyclopedia*, III, 1525.

Antoine Leroux was one of the Southwest's most famous mountain men. Born in Saint Louis, he came to New Mexico in the early 1820s, eventually settling at Taos. For the next twenty years he trapped and hunted throughout the Southwest. In 1852 he served as guide to Bartlett's boundary survey on its return from San Diego. He died in New Mexico in 1861. Thrapp, *Encyclopedia*, II, 847–48.

18. Bartlett, *Personal Narrative*, I, 300–301.

19. Philip St. George Cooke, *Exploring Southwestern Trails, 1846–1849*, 127–29.

20. Thrapp, *Encyclopedia*, I, 103.

21. Betzinez refers to Colonel José María Carrasco's invasion at Janos in March 1851 which killed some twenty-one Chiricahuas and captured another sixty-two. For the events leading up to the attack, see Sweeney, "I Had Lost All," 35–52.

22. Betzinez, *I Fought with Geronimo*, 1–3.

23. Ibid., 4–8.

24. Opler, *Life-Way*, 352–53.

25. Betzinez, *I Fought with Geronimo*, 4–8.

26. Henry F. Dobyns, ed., *Hepah, California! The Journal of Cave Johnson Couts, 1848–1849*, 41–42.

27. Ralph Bieber, *Southern Overland Trails to California, 1849*, 194–95.

28. Sweeney, *Cochise*, 62.

29. Ibid., 62–63.

30. Robert W. Frazer, *Forts and Supplies: The Role of the Army in the Economy of the Southwest, 1846–1861*, 26.

31. Sweeney, *Cochise*, 62–63; AHSH, Folder 175, Elías González to Governor of Sonora, May 3, 1847.

32. *El Sonorense*, July 30, 1847.

33. Sweeney, *Cochise*, 63–64; James Box, *Captain James Box's Adventures and Explorations in New and Old Mexico*, 56–57.

34. AHSH, Folder 199, Arvizu to Governor of Sonora, March 1, 1848.

35. Officer, *Hispanic Arizona*, 203–207.

36. AHSH, Folder 199, Governor of Sonora to Justice of the Peace, Bacoachi, March 28, 1848.

37. *El Sonorense*, October 25, 1848.

38. Ibid., October 13, 1848.

39. In my biography of Cochise published in 1991, I discussed my reasons why I thought that the Apache leader captured at Fronteras and called Cucchisle was in fact Cochise. There was room for doubt even though the circumstantial evidence seemed to indicate that it was indeed the great Chokonen who had been captured and imprisoned there. A visit to Fronteras in October 1992 further strengthened my hypothesis. When inspecting the hill where the old presidio had been located, I was shown the cave that had served as the fort's prison. I was told that the cave was known as Indio Cochise's cave, undoubtedly referring to the six weeks that he was held in confinement there.

40. Limón blamed his lack of success on the residents of Fronteras, who he believed had warned the Apaches of his campaign. A little more than two years later he would fall victim to an Apache ambush at Cocospera Canyon while he was serving as an escort for the Inez González party. Allan Radbourne, "Ambush at Cocospera Canyon," *English Westerners Tally Sheet* (July 1979), 63–76.

41. Sweeney, *Cochise*, 65–67.

42. Keleher, *Turmoil in New Mexico*, 55.

43. The Treaty of Guadalupe Hidalgo, signed in Mexico City on February 2, 1848, ended the United States–Mexican War of 1846. The United States agreed to pay Mexico fifteen million dollars for the territory ceded by Mexico, to restrain Indians from raiding into Mexico, to repatriate any captives, and to extract compensation from the Indians for any hostile act. With respect to the Apaches, this was an impossible task. The United States would have had to establish a string of forts along the Arizona and New Mexico border, and a penurious Congress was not about to allocate additional funds. Richard N. Ellis, *New Mexico Historical Documents*, 10–20.

44. Annie Heloise Abel, ed. *The Official Correspondence of James C. Calhoun while Serving as Indian Agent at Santa Fe and Superintendent of Indian Affairs in New Mexico*, 54.

45. At Alisos Canyon, sometimes called Alisos Arroyo, occurred one of the more sanguinary encounters in the annals of Chiricahua-Mexican

history. In April 1882 the Chihenne chief Loco led a large band that had bolted from the San Carlos reservation in Arizona, bound for the Sierra Madre in Mexico. With American troops on their heels, on April 29, 1882, they ran into a Mexican ambush set by Colonel Lorenzo García and an army of some two hundred men that succeeded in killing seventy-eight Apaches and capturing thirty-three. The Mexican loss was twenty-two dead and seventeen wounded. Dan L. Thrapp, *General Crook and the Sierra Madre Adventure*, 91–93; Dan L. Thrapp, *Conquest of Apachería*, 248–49; Almada, *Diccionario sonorenses*, 34 (although Almada incorrectly dates the fight one day later on April 30, 1882).

46. SA, R14, Reyes to Governor, September 26, 1848; *El Sonorense*, October 27, 1848.

47. SA, R14, Reyes to Governor, September 26, 1848; *El Sonorense*, October 27, 1848.

48. Sweeney, *Cochise*, 69.

49. Bartlett, *Personal Narrative*, II, 302.

50. SA, R15, Comadurán to Commanding General, December 14, 1848; Comadurán to Elías González, January 26, 1849.

CHAPTER 8

1. JA, R32, Padilla to Governor of Chihuahua, March 22, 29, 1849.

2. JA, R32, Padilla to Governor of Chihuahua, March 29, 1849.

3. SA, R15, Lavadi to Prefect of Ures, January [no date], 1849; *El Sonorense*, January 19, 1849.

4. SA, R15, Tánori to Gándara, January 13, 1849.

5. SA, R15, Gándara to the Minister of War and Navy, January 19, 1849.

6. SA, R15, Davila to Governor, January 25, 1849; Durazo to Prefect of Ures, January 27, 1849; Terán y Tato to Governor, February 10, 1849.

7. SA, R15, list of Mexicans killed, wounded and captured by Apaches in Sonora in 1849.

8. *El Sonorense*, January 19, 1849.

9. Officer, *Hispanic Arizona*, 220–21.

10. SA, R15, Villascuna to Elías González, February 6, 1849; Romero to Prefect of Ures, February 18, 21, 25, 1849; Barragan to Prefect of Ures, February 24, 1849; *El Sonorense*, March 16, 1849.

11. AHSH, Folder 201, Elías González to Governor, March 7, 1849.

12. Officer, *Hispanic Arizona*, 223; *El Sonorense*, June 1, 1849.

13. Merejildo Grijalva was one of early Arizona's most fascinating and adventurous men. An Opata Indian, he was born about 1840 at Bacachi, Sonora, which was near the mining town of Banamichi. He would remain with the Chiricahuas for a decade, becoming well acquainted with Cochise and Mangas Coloradas. In 1859 he escaped from the Chiricahuas and went to New Mexico, where he became interpreter for Apache Agent Michael Steck. During the 1860s and early 1870s he served as scout and

guide for the army, participating in several major campaigns against Cochise. He died at Solomonville, Arizona in 1912. Sweeney, *Merejildo Grijalva*.

14. Ibid., 5–6; Sweeney, *Cochise*, 70.

15. Sweeney, *Merejildo Grijalva*, 7; *The War of the Rebellion: A Compilation of the Official Records of the Union and Confederate Armies*, Series I, vol. 34, 122–23; *El Sonorense*, June 1, 1849.

16. *El Sonorense*, May 4, 1849; SA, R15, Samaniego to Terán y Tato, April 24, 1849; JA, R32, Padilla to Commanding General, March 29, 1849.

17. Limón, a veteran of Sonora's northern frontier, would be killed by Apaches in late September 1850 at Cocospera Canyon while serving as escort for the Inez González party. Radbourne, "Ambush at Cocospera Canyon," 63–76.

18. Sweeney, *Cochise*, 71; *El Sonorense*, June 1, 1849.

19. SA, R15, de Aros to Elías González, May 24, 1849.

20. SA, R15, Reyes to Elías González, April 25, 1849.

21. Sweeney, *Cochise*, 72. For a summary of events leading up to Terán y Tato's attack, the fate of the Apache prisoners, and the fascinating negotiations that would occur in the spring of 1850 between the Chokonen leader Demos and Elías González, see Sweeney, "One of Heaven's Heroes," 209–32.

22. *El Sonorense*, June 1, 1849.

23. JA, R32, Zuloaga to Padilla, February 20, 1849; Padilla to Zuloaga, February 21, 1849.

24. JA, R32, Zuloaga to Padilla, February 21, 1849.

25. JA, R32, Padilla to Governor of Chihuahua, March 22, 1849; Griffen, *Apaches at War and Peace*, 225.

26. One responsibility of a leader is to promote peaceful settlements to problems. Perhaps the two men may have had an altercation, or perhaps relatives of one had committed an offense to the kinfolk of the other, and because they were leaders they felt they had to "lend [their] moral weight towards [a] solution." Opler, *Life-Way*, 460–61.

27. In the spring of 1850 the Chihennes, the Nednhis, and a few Chokonens, essentially the same bands who requested peace in 1849 (plus Delgadito's group), met with Alejo García Conde at Janos. They told him that the "general" Manuelito had died of exposure during the past winter of 1850, but one wonders if the followers of Mangas Coloradas, Miguel Narbona, or Cochise might have killed him when word leaked out of his conversations with Padilla about killing Mangas Coloradas. *El Faro*, July 2, 1850.

28. Bieber, *Southern Overland Trails*, 195–96.

29. JA, R32, Padilla to Commanding General, March 29, 1849.

30. Missouri State Historical Society, Columbia, Thomas E. Breckenridge Memoirs.

31. Bieber, *Southern Overland Trails*, 195–96; SA, R15, Reyes to Elías González, April 25, 1849.

32. *El Paso Herald,* December 23, 1899, courtesy of Jerry Thompson.

33. A. B. Clarke, *Travels in Mexico and California,* ed. Anne M. Perry, 54–55; Harvey Wood, *Personal Recollections of Harvey Wood, Reminiscences of Early Days,* 11; Bieber, *Southern Overland Trails,* 197.

34. University of Texas, Austin, Janos Archives (hereafter cited as Janos Archives, Austin), Trias to Padilla, April 12, 1849; JA, R32, Padilla to Trias, May 26, 1849.

35. Among the early victims killed by scalp hunters was the old Nednhi chief Jasquedegá, who perished with twenty-two others at El Carmen on June 6, 1849. In early July a son of Mano Mocha was killed at Corralitos. *El Faro,* June 23, August 13, 1849.

36. Griffen, *Apaches at War and Peace,* 227–29; Ralph A. Smith, "The Scalp Hunt in Chihuahua—1849," *New Mexico Historical Review* 40 (April 1965), 116–40; Missouri Historical Society, Saint Louis, Solomon Sublette Papers; Griffen, "Chiricahua Apaches," 621.

37. Janos Archives, Austin, Zuloaga to Padilla, June 8, 11, 24, 1849; JA, R32, Zuloaga to Padilla, June 11, 1849.

38. At 8:00 A.M. on June 12, 1849, a force from Bavispe under Captain Reyes Cruz surprised a ranchería near the San Pedro Mountains in Chihuahua and in a five-hour fight killed four Apaches while suffering a loss of three men. SA, R15, Elías González to Governor, June 22, 1849.

39. JA, R32, Padilla to Zuloaga, June 30, 1849.

40. JA, R32, Padilla to Commanding General, June 30, 1849; Zuloaga to Padilla, June 12, 1849; Padilla to Inspector of the Military Colonies, July 1, 1849; Janos Archives, Austin, Zuloaga to Padilla, June 11, 14, 1849.

41. Harris, *Gila Trail,* 65–66, 70.

42. *El Faro,* August 14, 1849; Griffen, *Apaches at War and Peace,* 227–28.

43. Harris, *Gila Trail,* 68; John W. Caughey, *Rushing For Gold,* 27.

44. Jack Gordon, whose real name was Peter Worthington, was born about 1822 to a prominent Virginia family. After killing a man there, he fled west about 1839 and assumed the name of Jack Gordon to conceal his real identity. After serving with Colonel Alexander Doniphan's command during the Mexican War, he allegedly killed a man near El Paso and was imprisoned. Soon after, he escaped and went to the Apaches, married an Apache woman, likely a Chihenne of the Chiricahuas, and joined them in their forays against their enemies, Americans and Mexicans. He became well acquainted with the Chihenne leaders, including Mangas Coloradas. In early 1850 he went to California. He died on December 14, 1864, shot by a business partner in California. Thrapp, *Encyclopedia,* II, 572–73.

45. Harris, *Gila Trail,* 69–70; Caughey, *Rushing for Gold,* 27–28.

46. SA, R15, Elías González to Governor, July 9, 23, 1849. In late summer 1849, James Calhoun met several Mexican traders at Zuñi who told him that they had just come from Apache country. They said that

the Apaches were "friendly and peaceably disposed" toward Americans. U.S. Congress, House, H. Exec. Doc. 17, 31st Cong., 1st sess., 219.

47. *El Sonorense,* August 24, 1849; SA, R15, Elías González, August 13, 1849; Pinart Collection, Document 112.

48. NA, RG393, M1102, R1, Sacket to AAG, Dept. of New Mexico, June 12, 1849.

49. C. C. Cox, "From Texas to California in 1849," *Southwestern Historical Quarterly"* 29 (1925), 135–37; *Arkansas State Gazette,* April 26, 1850.

50. Enoch Steen was born in Kentucky in 1800 and moved west to Missouri. He joined the Mounted Rangers as a lieutenant in 1832 and transferred to the First U.S. Dragoons the following year. He was promoted to captain on December 31, 1840. After seeing much hard duty in the West, Steen fought in the Mexican War and earned a brevet to major in the battle of Buena Vista, February 22–23, 1847. After the war he was assigned to New Mexico, reaching Santa Fe on July 11, 1849, and then continuing on to his station at Doña Ana. The next month he was wounded in a fight with Apaches near Santa Rita del Cobre, which place two years later he would recommend as a site for a military post. He was involved with the peace treaty signed with the Apaches at Fort Webster on April 7, 1853, and by then had met Mangas Coloradas several times.

In the fall of 1856, Steen went to Arizona to establish a new post near Tucson. Instead, he chose a site near the Mexican border, which incensed the Anglo citizens of Tucson. Steen did not wince at their complaints and justified his selection to his superiors as a site that would better control the Apaches. He left Arizona in April 1858, later serving in the Northwest, and was promoted to lieutenant colonel of the Second Cavalry on September 28, 1861. Stein's Peak in the Peloncillo Mountains was named for him.

Steen was an independent and opinionated officer for his time and thus was frequently in the middle of controversy, especially as a military officer whose decisions sometimes conflicted with the views of local citizens. He officially retired on September 23, 1863, but continued to serve in various roles until 1866. He died in 1880. His son Alexander Early Steen was a brigadier general for the Confederacy and was killed at the battle of Kane Hill, Arkansas, on November 27, 1862. Thrapp, *Encyclopedia,* III, 1383–84; Constance Wynn Altshuler, *Cavalry Yellow and Infantry Blue: Army Officers in Arizona between 1851 and 1886,* 316–17.

51. Thrapp, *Encyclopedia,* III, 1363; Thrapp, *Victorio and the Mimbres Apaches,* 23; John Nugent, "Scraps of Early History—III," *The Argonaut* 2, nos. 10–11 (1878).

52. Missouri State Historical Society, Columbia, John Lewis Robards Journal.

53. Geronimo was clearly referring to this incident in his autobiography when he wrote that "four warriors who were captured once at a place

north of Casa Grande, called by the Indians 'Honas' [Janos] were kept in chains for a year and a half, when they were exchanged for Mexicans whom we had captured." Barrett, *Geronimo's Story*, 67.

54. Griffen, *Apaches at War and Peace*, 241–43.

55. JA, R31, Military Record of Félix Padilla; JA, R37, Padilla to Commanding General, September 12, 1849; El Faro, October 6, 1849.

56. Griffen, *Apaches at War and Peace*, 241–42 n. 19.

57. Ibid., 244 n. 31.

58. JA, R32, Padilla to Inspector of the Military Colonies, September 15, 1849; Janos Archives, Austin, Diary of Movements, September, 1849.

59. SA, R15, de Aros to Governor, October 30, 1849.

60. Ibid.

61. Ibid.

62. Hays, born in Tennessee in 1817, had arrived in Texas shortly after the defeat of Santa Anna's forces at San Jacinto. For the next few years he worked as a surveyor, but because of his fighting abilities he eventually became a captain in the Texas Rangers. He earned his reputation as one of the Rangers' best officers during several fights and skirmishes with the Comanches and Mexican forces along the border. He fought in the Mexican War of 1846, after which he was appointed to a boundary commission to settle a boundary dispute between Texas and the United States with regards to New Mexico. He was named first agent for the Gila Apaches on April 11, 1849, but was unable to establish contact with the skittish Chiricahuas. His party was one of the first to travel through Apache Pass instead of following the traditional Cooke's route into northern Sonora. In late 1849 he went to California, resigned his position, and settled in the Oakland–San Francisco area. He died near Piedmont, California, on April 25, 1883. Thrapp, *Encyclopedia*, II, 634; *Alta California*, February 1, 1850.

63. John Nugent, "Scraps of Early History," *The Argonaut* 2, no. 10–11 (1878); Wayne R. Austerman, "Unholy Terror Cornered," *Wild West*, June 1991.

64. Robert Eccleston, *Overland to California on the Southwestern Trail, 1849*, ed. George P. Hammond and Edward H. Howes, 175.

65. Ibid., 175–76; SA, R15, de Aros to Governor, October 30, 1849.

66. Nugent, *Scraps.*

67. Eccleston, *Overland to California*, 175–76.

68. Sweeney, *Cochise*, 75; SA, R15, de Aros to Governor, October 30, 1849.

69. Sweeney, *Cochise*, 76–77, has a full report of what happened, including the version of a participant, a Mr. Thompson.

70. Born in South Carolina in 1819, Glanton was a contemporary of John Coffee Hays and participated in many of the fights against Santa Ana's forces in 1837. He was about five feet, eleven inches tall and somewhat thickset. He was engaged to marry a Mexican girl at San Antonio, but she was captured and killed by Lipan Apaches, after which

he had a life-long hatred of Apaches. He fought with the Texans against the Mexicans in the Mexican War of 1846, was mustered out April 30, 1848, and returned to San Antonio, where in November of that year he killed a man. Fleeing to Chihuahua, he left behind a wife and a daughter. The next year he got into the lucrative scalp hunting business, joining Michael Chevallie in several attacks on the Carrizaleño local group of Nednhis at Agua Nueva and Encinillas in the spring and summer of 1849. He was killed by Yuma Indians on the lower Colorado River in 1850. Ralph A. Smith, "John Joel Glanton: Lord of the Scalp Range," *The Smoke Signal*, Fall, 1962; Thrapp, *Encyclopedia*, II, 564.

71. Janos Archives, Austin, Diary of Movements, 1849; Griffen, *Apaches at War and Peace*, 231–32.

72. NA, RG393, LR, M1102, R1, Captain Charles May to McLaws, December 19, 1849.

73. Thrapp, *Victorio and the Mimbres Apaches*, 22.

CHAPTER 9

1. The Jaramillos were one of Doña Ana's oldest families, having come from Spain and settling in southern New Mexico. They were influential business and government leaders of the region.

2. El Jornada del Muerto, or "The Journey of Death," was a waterless stretch of ninety miles from Rincon to San Marcial in south central New Mexico. Pearce, *New Mexico Place Names*, 77. For a history of this region, see Brodie Crouch, *Jornado del Muerto: A Pageant of the Desert*.

3. AHSH, Folder 221, Martínez to Elías González, April 23, 1850; *Santa Fe Weekly Gazette*, March 19, 1853.

4. NA, RG393, LR, M1102, R2, Steen to McLaws, February 28, March 24, 1850.

5. Box, *Captain James Box's Adventures*, 34–36.

6. AHSH, Folder 221, Martínez to Elías González, February 13, 1850; Martínez to Elías González, February 27, 1850.

7. AHSH, Folder 221, Elías González to Governor, March 22, 1850; Sweeney, "One of Heaven's Heroes," 227–28.

8. AHSH, Folder 221, Ybarra to Elías González, March 17, 1850.

9. *El Sonorense*, May 10, 1850.

10. *El Sonorense*, April 15, 1850.

11. Major Horace Bell, *Reminiscences of a Ranger, or Early Times in Southern California*, 270–71.

12. *El Sonorense*, May 3, 1850.

13. Bell, *Reminiscences of a Ranger*, 271.

14. AHSH, Folder 407, Martínez to Elías González April 11, 1850; Elías González to Martínez, April 24, 1850; Folder 408, Elías González to Governor, April 15, 1850.

15. AHSH, Folder 221, Elías González to Governor, April 15, i850.

16. Ibid., Elías González to Governor, April 30, 1850.

17. Griffen, "Chiricahua Apaches," 654; SA, R16, de Aquillar to Elías González, May 13, 1850.

18. *El Faro*, June 25, 1850; *El Sonorense*, June 7, 1850; AHSH, Folder 221, Elías González to Commissioner of Peace at Janos, July 11, 1850.

19. Manuel Valenzuela, correspondence with author, July 1, September 26, 1992.

20. *El Faro*, June 25, 1850; AHSH, Folder 221, Elías González to Commissioner of Peace at Janos, July 11, 1850; *El Sonorense*, June 7, 1850.

21. AHSH, Folder 221, Elías González to Governor, June 25, 1850.

22. Ibid., Martínez to Elías González, July 2, 1850; Griffen, "Chiricahua Apaches," 655.

23. AHSH, Folder 221, Zozaya to Elías González, July 15, 1850.

24. AHSH, Folder 231, Martínez to Elías González.

25. SA, R16, Martínez to Elías González, July 22, 1850.

26. JA, R33, Padilla to Commanding General, April 30, 1850; Padilla to Justice of the Peace, Galeana, April 8, 1850; Landley to Padilla, February 18, 1850.

27. Lister and Lister, *Chihuahua*, 136; *El Faro*, August 17, 1850.

28. JA, R33, Record of Movements, May 1850; *El Faro*, May 7, July 27, 1850.

29. *El Faro*, July 2, 1850.

30. JA, R33, Record of Movements, May 1850.

31. *El Faro*, August 17, 1850.

32. *El Faro*, July 27, 1850; AHSH, Folder 221, Elías González to Governor, July 15, 1850.

33. AHSH, Folder 221, Ramirez to Elías González, August 30, 1850; Elías González to Governor, August 19, 1850.

34. Ibid., Elías González to Governor, July 15, 1850; Elías González to peace commissioners at Janos, July 15, 1850.

35. NA, RG393, LR, M1102, R2, Steen to McLaws, September 3, 1850.

36. SA, R16, Navamuel to Governor, October 5, 1850; *El Sonorense*, November 15, 1850; AHSH, Folder 221, Terán y Tato to Governor, November 1, 1850.

37. *El Sonorense*, November 15, 1850; AHSH, Folder 221, Terán y Tato to Governor, November 1, 1850; Elías González to Governor, October 28, 1850; SA, R16, Terán y Tato to García, January 28, 1851.

38. SA, R16, Terán y Tato to Governor, February 19, 1851.

39. AHSH, Folder 202, Elías González to Governor, October 20, 1850.

40. Ibid.

41. *El Correo*, May 1, 1851; SA, R16, Military Commander of Bavispe to Terán y Tato, January 4, 1851.

42. Acuña, *Sonoran Strongman*, 7–8, 17–19; Sweeney, *Cochise*, 82.

43. Carrasco, born about 1813, reached the rank of lieutenant in 1833 and fought with honor against the Americans in the U.S.-Mexican War. In 1849 he served at the Colorado River crossing in Arizona. During the short time that he was in command of Sonora's armed forces he

implemented several reforms in an attempt to improve morale and eliminate desertions. He died of cholera in July 1851. Almada, *Diccionario sonorenses*, 128; Officer, *Hispanic Arizona*, 252–55.

44. Sweeney, "I Had Lost All," 52 n. 32.

45. Pesqueira, born December 16, 1820, in Arispe, was educated in Europe. He returned to Sonora in 1839 and joined the local militia, or national guard. By 1845 he had risen to the rank of captain and, as his biographer notes, "was suddenly catapulted from obscurity to statewide prominence" after the Pozo Hediondo fight. In 1857 he became governor of Sonora, a position he held throughout most of the 1860s and into the 1870s. He died on January 4, 1886. Acuña, *Sonoran Strongman*.

46. In October 1992 at the Agua Caliente ranch I was fortunate to interview a man in his eighties who told me that his father had told him that when the older man was a boy, he had found military artifacts on the ridges among the hills south and east of the ranch.

47. Corella, born at Arispe in 1817, began his military career in 1842, fought the Seris in the mid-1840s, and became prefect of Arispe in 1846 and 1847. He suffered four wounds in the Pozo Hediondo battle. He was appointed prefect of Arispe in 1856, joined Pesqueira to fight Gándara's forces in 1856–57, and in the fall of 1857 was named peace commissioner to deal with the Chiricahuas. He continued to enjoy a long and successful military and political career into the 1880s until his death at Arispe on November 4, 1891. Almada, *Diccionario sonorenses*, 167–68; Sweeney, *Cochise*, 107–109.

48. *El Sonorense*, January 31, 1851; *El Correo*, February 11, 1851; Eduardo W. Villa, *Compendia de historia del Estado de Sonora*, 242–44. Villa errs in placing the fight on January 7, 1851. In an issue dated May 30, 1851, *El Sonorense* charged that "Anglo Scoundrels" had armed and led the Apaches, who were well armed with rifles and six-shooters. The Indians killed fifteen and wounded twenty-five of the fifty soldiers from Bacoachi and killed eleven and wounded twenty-two of the fifty nationals from Arispe. AHSH, Folder 224, Villascusa to Governor, April 28, 1851.

49. *El Sonorense*, February 14, 1851.

50. Arvizu was born in the early 1840s. After Mangas Coloradas traded him to the Navajos, he became an important interpreter during the 1860s and 1870s. He died in 1932. Virginia Hoffman, *Navajo Biographies*, I, 155–56. Frank McNitt, *Navajo Wars: Military Campaigns, Slave Raids, and Reprisals*, 406–407.

51. *El Sonorense*, January 31, 1850; Almada, *Diccionario sonorenses*, 61; Hoffman, *Navajo Biographies*, I, 155–56; SA, R16, Terán y Tato to Governor, January 28, 1851.

52. *El Correo*, April 1, 1851; SA, R16, Gonzales to Commander and Chief of Sonora, February 5, 1851; NA, RG393, LR, M1102, R6, Craig to Scott, September 4, 1851.

53. Craig was born in Virginia and became a second lieutenant in the Second Dragoons on October 14, 1837. The next year he transferred to the Third Infantry. He became a captain in 1846 and served with distinction in the Mexican War. He would remain with Bartlett's command until he was killed by deserters near San Diego on June 6, 1852. Fort Craig (1854–85) on the Rio Grande was named for him. Thrapp, *Encyclopedia*, I, 335–36.

54. NA, RG393, LR, M1102, R6, Craig to Scott, September 4, 1851.

55. Fred J. Rippy, "The Indians of the Southwest in the Diplomacy of the United States and Mexico, 1848–1853," *Hispanic-American Historical Review* 2 (August 1919), 388.

56. *El Sonorense*, April 15, 1850, lists five of the nine districts of Sonora, from which 5,654 men had left for California, including over 2,000 from the districts of Arispe and Moctezuma, the Chiricahuas' normal raiding areas.

57. Griffen, "Chiricahua Apaches," 656.

58. SA, R16, Terán y Tato to García, January 28, 1851.

59. *El Sonorense*, February 7, 1851; *El Correo*, February 18, 1851; Sweeney, "I Had Lost All," 44–45.

60. *El Sonorense*, February 28, 1851.

61. Elías González agreed with Carrasco that his men lacked discipline, but he took the new commander to task for suggesting that his troops lacked the courage to fight. The rest of his response was printed in *El Sonorense*, March 21, 1851. Terán y Tato defended his honor and that of the national guard in a letter to the governor dated March 4, 1851. SA, R16, Terán y Tato to Governor, March 4, 1851.

62. *El Correo*, April 1, 1851.

63. Barrett, *Geronimo's Story*, 43–44; Sweeney, "I Had Lost All," 44–49.

64. *El Correo*, March 8, April 1, 1851.

65. See Sweeney, "I Had Lost All," for an analysis and discussion of Carrasco's attack and the ramifications for Geronimo.

66. Barrett, *Geronimo's Story*, 44–45.

CHAPTER 10

1. JA, R33, Carrasco to Prefect of Galeana, March 6, 1851.

2. Ibid., Aguirre to Carrasco, March 7, 1851.

3. AHSH, Folder 234, testimony taken at Janos by Colonel José María Carrasco and Lieutenant Colonel Prudencio Romero, March 6, 1851.

4. *El Correo*, April 5, 15, 22, 1851.

5. Ibid., April 1, 1851.

6. *El Sonorense*, April 11, 1851; *El Correo*, April 15, 1851. A few months later Carrasco told John R. Bartlett that the prisoners "were sent to the interior, and there distributed among the haciendas and ranchos as servants." Bartlett, *Personal Narrative*, I, 268.

7. AHSH, Folder 421, Carrasco to Minister of War and Navy, March 28, 1851.

8. *El Correo*, April 29, 1851. Bartlett also heard that the "central government . . . approved of Carrasco's course." Bartlett, *Personal Narrative*, I, 268.

9. *El Sonorense*, May 2, 1851.

10. Ibid., March 28, 1851.

11. *El Correo*, April 22, 1851.

12. Bartlett, *Personal Narrative*, I, 267–69.

13. *El Correo*, June 28, 1851; AHSH, Folder 230, Carrasco to Governor, June 18, 1851.

14. AHSH, Folder 230, Campos to Governor, July 21, 1851; Sweeney, *Cochise*, 87–88.

15. AHSH, Folder 231, Reyes to Carrasco, June 20, 1851; *El Correo*, June 28, 1851; Bartlett, *Personal Narrative*, I, 295–96, 301–302; Cremony, *Life among the Apaches*, 43.

16. Odie Faulk, introduction in Bartlett, *Personal Narrative*, I; Robert V. Hine, *Bartlett's West: Drawing the Mexican Boundary*, 1–14.

17. Hine, *Bartlett's West*, 1–14. I wish to extend my warmest thanks to Jim "Santiago" Brito of Las Cruces, New Mexico, for providing documentation regarding his grandfather's activities working for Bartlett's Boundary Commission and at Pinos Altos.

18. Cremony, *Life among the Apaches*, 23–26; Bartlett, *Personal Narrative*, I, 154, 178; NA, RG393, LR, M1102, R6, Craig to Scott, September 4, 1851.

19. Bartlett, *Personal Narrative*, I, 298–99.

20. Cremony, *Life among the Apaches*, 33.

21. NA, RG75, M234, R546, Bartlett to Secretary of the Interior, February 19, 1852; Smithsonian Institute, Bureau of American Ethnology, Manuscript 121, "Vocabulary [of] Mimbreno Language from Mancus [Mangus] Colorado [Coloradas] Chief of the Coppermine Apaches.

22. Bartlett, *Personal Narrative*, I, 319–20.

23. Cremony, *Life among the Apaches*, 52; Boyer and Gayton, *Apache Mothers and Daughters*, 43–44; Opler, *Life-Way*, 398–99, has a discussion about gambling as a Chiricahua practice.

24. Bartlett, *Personal Narrative*, I, 303–10, 398–405; Cremony, *Life among the Apaches*, 53–58; Radbourne, "Ambush at Cocospera Canyon," 63–76.

25. Cremony, *Life among the Apaches*, 59–61; Bartlett, *Personal Narrative*, I, 310–12.

26. Bartlett, *Personal Narrative*, I, 312–17; Brown University, Providence, R.I., John Russell Bartlett Papers, Bartlett's personal journal.

27. In his *Personal Narrative*, Bartlett claimed that the wounded man died about a month later. Yet in his personal journal, entry of July 19, a note indicates that the Indian who was shot on July 6 died on July 19.

Bartlett, *Personal Narrative*, I, 333; Bartlett Papers, personal journal, entry of July 19, 1851.

28. Bartlett Papers, personal journal, entry of July 11, July 21, 1851.

29. Ibid., entry of July 23, 1851.

30. Bartlett, *Personal Narrative*, I, 334–39.

31. Bartlett Papers, personal journal, July 31, 1851; Bartlett, *Personal Narrative*, I, 344–45; Cremony, *Life among the Apaches*, 81–82.

32. Bartlett, *Personal Narrative*, I, 329–30; Cremony, *Life among the Apaches*, 49–51.

33. NA, RG393, LR, M1102, R6, Craig to Scott, September 4, 1851.

34. Ibid., R4, Craig to Buell, September 1, 1851.

35. *El Correo*, August 16, 1851.

36. Ibid., August 5, 23; October 4, 1851.

37. Opler, *Life-Way*, 360–62.

38. Sweeney, *Cochise*, 88–89; *Santa Fe Weekly Gazette*, November 20, 1852.

39. NA, RG75, M234, R546, Greiner to Lea, July 31, 1852.

40. Bartlett, *Personal Narrative*, I, 450–51; *El Sonorense*, December 26, 1851.

41. Arizona Historical Society, Hayden Files (hereafter cited as AHS, Hayden Files), José Miguel Castañeda file.

42. Edwin Vose Sumner, born in Boston in 1797, was commissioned a second lieutenant in the Second Infantry in 1819. He worked his way up the ladder and at the outbreak of the Mexican War was major of the Second Dragoons. He accompanied Kearny to New Mexico and later joined Winfield Scott in Mexico. After the war he was promoted to lieutenant colonel of the First Dragoons. He was assigned to command the Ninth Military Department in 1851 and arrived at Santa Fe on July 19 of that year. It was his intolerance of civilian officials that finally forced the War Department to transfer him to another post. He fought well against the Cheyennes in 1857 at Solomon's Fork on the Kansas River, and in 1861 he was named brigadier general. He served early in the Civil War before asking to be relieved from duty. He died at Syracuse on March 21, 1863. One of his sons, Samuel Storrow Sumner, was present at the historic peace treaty made with Cochise on October 12, 1872. Thrapp, *Encyclopedia*, III, 1390–91; Sweeney, *Cochise*, 383–85.

43. Frazer, *Forts and Supplies*, 61.

44. Robert M. Utley, *Frontiersmen in Blue: The United States Army and the Indians, 1848–1865*, 86–87.

45. Richardson, born at Fairfax, Vermont, in 1815, graduated from West Point in 1841. A popular officer with his men, he had earned brevets for meritorious conduct in the Mexican War. He rose to the rank of major general during the Civil War. He was mortally wounded at the battle of Antietam and died on November 3, 1862. Jerry D. Thompson, ed., "With the Third Infantry in New Mexico, 1851–1853: The Lost

Diary of Private Sylvester W. Matson," *Journal of Arizona History* 31 (Winter 1990), 396.

46. Thompson, "Matson Diary," 355–57, 361; NA, RG75, M234, R546, Calhoun to Lea, January 31, 1852; Thrapp, *Victorio and the Mimbres Apaches*, 26–27; Dale E. Floyd, *Chronological List of Actions Etc., with Indians from January 15, 1837, to January, 1891*, 14. Floyd places the casualties at five dead: two on January 24, two on January 25, and one who died from wounds on February 19, 1852.

47. Thompson, "Matson Diary," 361–63.

48. Thompson, "Matson's Diary," 363–65; Floyd, *Chronological List*, 14, places the fight on February 6, 1852, but Matson's diary states January 26, 1852.

49. NA, RG393, LR, M1102, R6, Miles to McFerran January 31, 1852.

50. Ogle, *Federal Control*, 32–33; Abel, *Official Correspondence of James C. Calhoun*, 485–88.

51. James A. Bennett, *Forts and Forays: A Dragoon in New Mexico, 1850–1856*, ed. Clinton E. Brooks and Frank D. Reeve, 33, 36 n. 60; NA, RG393, LR, M1102, R5, Emory to Sumner, February 27, 1852.

52. Bennett, *Forts and Forays*, 34–35; Thompson, "Matson Diary," 366. Bennett's diary is frequently off by a few days to a week because he copied his notes after some years had elapsed and destroyed the originals. He said that they arrived at Fort Webster on February 20, but they actually arrived a week later, on the February 27, according to Matson's diary and "on or about the 28th according to Major Gouverneur Morris." Thompson, "Matson's Diary," 366; NA, RG393, LR, M1102, R5, Morris to AAG, Dept. of New Mexico, March 16, 1852.

53. NA, RG393, LR, M1102, R5, Morris to Howe, March 2, 1852; Morris to McFerran, March 3, 1852.

54. Bennett, *Forts and Forays*, 35–37; Thompson, "Matson Diary," 366–68.

55. NA, RG393, LR, M1102, R5, Morris to McFerran, March 16, 1852.

56. *El Sonorense*, March 19, 1852; *Boletin Oficial*, March 29, 1852.

57. SA, R16, document entitled, "Plans for the Expedition against the Savages in March [1852]."

58. Manuel Gallegos was later an officer in the Arizona Volunteers in 1865–66 and an important military officer in Sonora in the early 1870s.

59. Sweeney, *Cochise*, 89–90.

60. SA, R16, García to Prefect of Arispe, March 31, 1852.

61. SA, R16, Lozada to Blanco, April 12, 1852; *Boletin Oficial*, April 27, 1852; *El Sonorense*, April 16, 1852.

62. NA, RG393, LR, M1102, R5, Morris to AAAG, June 16, 1852.

63. Thompson, "Matson Diary," 372.

CHAPTER 11

1. John Greiner, born in Philadelphia on September 14, 1810, eventually became state librarian of Ohio. In 1849 he was appointed Indian agent in New Mexico. In 1865 he become editor of the *Zanesville (Ohio) Times* and would become known for writing political slogans and lyrics. He died on May 13, 1871. Thrapp, *Victorio and the Mimbres Apaches*, 330 n. 2.

2. Juarez Archives, R17, Alvarez, Justice of the Peace, Bravos, June 12, 1852.

3. NA, RG393, LR, M1102, R5, Morris to AAAG, June 16, 1852; Thompson, "Matson's Diary," 372–74.

4. James S. Calhoun, born in South Carolina in the early 1800s, came to New Mexico in 1849 as Indian agent after a distinguished political career in Georgia. On March 3, 1851, he became governor of New Mexico. Calhoun was a competent and diligent public official who refused to back down from Colonel Sumner's bullying tactics. In failing health, he left Santa Fe for Washington on May 29, 1852 (bringing a coffin with him), but he died along the way near Independence, Missouri, on June 30, 1852. Keleher, *Turmoil in New Mexico*, 130–31; Thrapp, *Victorio and the Mimbres Apaches*, 330–31.

5. Keleher, *Turmoil in New Mexico*, 61–65; Larson, *New Mexico's Quest for Statehood*, 78–79; NA, RG75, M234, R546, Grenier to Lea, April 30, 1852.

6. Annie Heloise Abel, "The Journal of John Greiner," *Old Santa Fe* 3, no. 11 (July 1916), 220–23.

7. Josiah Gregg described Ácoma as standing "upon an isolated mound whose whole area is occupied by the village, being fringed all around by a precipitous *ceja* or cliff. The inhabitants enter the village by means of ladders, and by steps cut into the solid rock upon which it is based." One of the bloodiest engagements between Spaniards and the Pueblo Indians took place here in January 1599 when Spanish soldiers burned the pueblo and killed hundreds while capturing over five hundred. Gregg, *Commerce of the Prairies*, 193; for a history of Ácoma, see Ward Alan Minge, *Ácoma: Pueblo in the Sky.*

8. Martine, a Nednhi, was born about 1858, probably in Mexico. He served as a scout for Lieutenant Charles Gatewood and acted as his personal emissary to Geronimo and Naiche in August 1886. Griswold, "Fort Sill Apaches," 94.

9. Albert H. Schroeder, *A Study of the Apache Indians*, Part 4, 271.

10. Hoffman, *Navajo Biographies*, I, 163–65; McNitt, *The Indian Traders*, 132–24; McNitt, *Navajo Wars*, 407–408; *Santa Fe Weekly Gazette*, November 20, 1852.

11. Abel, "Greiner's Journal," 227–28. Opler, *Life-Way*, 398–400, contains a discussion of Chiricahua gift-giving. His informants emphasized that in the old days, especially within one's local group, gift-giving was

more important than selling. Implied in this practice was the feeling of reciprocity, though not based on equal value, however. Not only were generosity and kindness essential characteristics of a leader, but they also helped to enhance his "reputation and social standing."

12. Bennett, *Forts and Forays*, 39.

13. NA, RG75, M234, R546, Greiner to Lea, July 31, 1852.

14. *Santa Fe Weekly Gazette*, November 20, 1852.

15. Steck Papers, Box 1, Folder 1, "Articles of Treaty between Apaches and Colonel E. V. Sumner"; *Santa Fe Weekly Gazette*, January 26, 1856; Charles J. Kappler, ed., *Indian Affairs: Laws and Treaties*, II, 598–600. This treaty was ratified by the Senate and signed by President Franklin Pierce on March 25, 1853, Thrapp, *Victorio and the Mimbres Apaches*, 27.

16. Mangas is likely referring to the massacre at Bavispe of Tapilá and his local group eight months earlier, in November 1851, which is discussed in chapter 10.

17. NA, RG75, M234, R546, Greiner to Lea, July 31, 1852. Mangas Coloradas told Second Lieutenant Laurence W. O'Bannon that Colonel Sumner had given him "permission to fight Mexicans." RG393, LR, M1102, R5, Miles to AAAG, August 16, 1852.

18. Robert M. Utley, "Captain John Pope's Plan of 1853 for the Frontier Defense of New Mexico," *Arizona and the West* 5 (Summer 1963), 155 n. 12.

19. Boyer and Gayton, *Apache Mothers and Daughters*, 33.

20. Thompson, "Matson's Diary," 374–75.

21. Ibid., 375–76.

22. Ibid., 375; SA, R16, Blanco to Governor of Sonora, June 26, 1852; in the earlier fight, troops from Bavispe battled Apaches and suffered a loss of three dead and twelve wounded, some in hand-to-hand fighting. Reinforcements from Bacerac arrived and followed the Indians toward the Pitaicache Mountains, where they apparently surprised them and killed several warriors. SA, R16, Blanco to Governor of Sonora, June 26, 1852. A party from Huasabas attacked a ranchería in the Teras Mountains on July 9, 1852, and confiscated much material and stock. SA, R16, Durazo to Prefect of Moctezuma, July 11, 1852.

23. Thompson, "Matson's Diary," 377; NA, RG75, M234, R546, Greiner to Lea, August 31, 1852.

24. Thompson, "Matson's Diary," 377.

25. NA, RG393, LR, M1102, R5, Morris to AAAG, May 31, 1852.

26. Frazer, *Forts and Supplies*, 65–66; Robert W. Frazer, ed., *Mansfield on the Condition of the Western Forts, 1853–54*, 62–63.

27. Thompson, "Matson's Diary," 377; Boletin Oficial, September 3, 1852. For information concerning the establishment of Fort Webster, see Lee Myers's two excellent articles: "Fort Webster on the Mimbres River," *New Mexico Historical Review* 41 (January 1966), 47–57, and "Military Establishments in Southwestern New Mexico," *New Mexico Historical Review* 43 (January 1968), 6–8.

28. NA, RG393, LR, M1102, R5, Miles to Sumner, October 12, 1952; Morris to AAAG, September 19, 1852; Miles to AAAG, August 16, September 19, 1852.

29. Born in Maryland in 1804, Miles graduated from West Point in 1824 and was assigned to the Fourth Infantry. He was the quartermaster during the Seminole War from 1839 to 1842 in Florida and received brevets for his actions during the Mexican War. He became lieutenant colonel of the Third Infantry on April 15, 1851. He would participate in the Bonneville campaign of 1857, command an expedition against the Navajos the following year, and receive a promotion to colonel, Second Infantry, in 1859. He was killed at Harpers Ferry, Virginia, on September 16, 1862, by an exploding shell in an accident after surrendering to the Confederates. Thrapp, *Encyclopedia*, II, 984–85; Altshuler, *Cavalry Yellow and Infantry Blue*, 228–29.

30. Edward K. Eckert and Nicholas J. Amato, eds., *Ten Years in the Saddle: The Memoir of William Woods Averell, 1851–1862*, 193.

31. NA, RG393, LR, M1102, R5, Miles to AAAG, August 16, 1852; Thompson, "Matson's Diary," 377–78.

32. NA, RG393, LR, M1102, R6, Ewell to AAAG, January 18, 1853.

33. Steck Papers, Sánchez to Indian Agent, Fort Webster, December 16, 1852; Keleher, *Turmoil in New Mexico*, 132 n. 67.

34. Lane was born in Pennsylvania in 1789, studied law and medicine, and became the first mayor of Saint Louis. He was an unabashed extrovert and an idealistic man who enjoyed public life, either in medicine or through politics. Yet he was also a restless man open to new challenges and opportunities. In 1846, after his only son, Victor, died, Lane endured a period of despondency by spending "as much time as he could wandering about the country." He happened to be in Washington when news of Governor Calhoun's death reached there. President Fillmore offered the post to Lane, who saw it as an opportunity to leave his bad memories in Saint Louis and once again serve the nation. He died in Saint Louis on January 6, 1863. William G. B. Carson, ed., "William Carr Lane Diary," *New Mexico Historical Review* 39 (July 1964), 181–234; Ralph P. Bieber, "Letters of William Carr Lane," *Historical Society of New Mexico* (April 1928), 179–203.

35. Larson, *New Mexico's Quest for Statehood*, 75–77; Keleher, *Turmoil in New Mexico*, 131 n. 66.

36. Annie H. Abel, "Indian Affairs in New Mexico under the Administration of William Carr Lane," *New Mexico Historical Review* 16 (April 1941), 221.

37. Thrapp, *Victorio and the Mimbres Apaches*, 29.

38. Ibid.

39. NA, RG393, LR, M1102, R5, Lane to Wingfield, October 28, 1852.

40. NA, RG75, M234, R547, Wingfield to Lane, December 20, 1852; May 3, 1853.

41. *El Boletín*, November 19, 1852.

42. NA, RG75, M234, R547, Wingfield to Lane, December 20, 1852.

43. Frazer, *Forts and Supplies*, 66.

44. NA, RG75, M234, R547, Wingfield to Lane, May 3, 1853.

45. Missouri Historical Society, Saint Louis, William Carr Lane Papers, Steen to Lane, January 10, 1853.

46. Carson, "William Carr Lane Diary," 190–91.

47. Richard Stoddart Ewell, born at Georgetown in 1817, was appointed to West Point by President Jackson and became a second lieutenant on November 1, 1840. He fought in the Mexican War, became a captain in 1849, and was sent to New Mexico. He was a popular officer who fought the Mescaleros in 1855, participated in the Bonneville campaign of 1857, and campaigned against the Western Apaches in Arizona in 1859 and 1860. In late 1860 he took sick leave and went home, and he joined the Confederacy in 1861. He fought with distinction during the Civil War, ending the conflict as a lieutenant general. He died from influenza at his wife's family farm in Tennessee on January 24, 1872. Thrapp, *Encyclopedia*, I, 475–76.

48. RG393, LR, M1102, R6, Ewell to AAAG, January 18, 1853.

49. Ibid., R7, Steele to Howe, February 1, 1853; Thompson, "Matson's Diary," 382.

50. NA, RG75, M234, R547, Wingfield to Lane, May 3, 1853; RG393, LR, M1102, R7, Steen to Sumner, March 16, 1853.

51. Larson, *New Mexico's Quest for Statehood*, 80–82; Carson, "William Carr Lane Diary," 188–92.

52. NA, RG393, LR, M1102, R7, Miles to Sumner, October 19, 1852.

53. Ibid., Miles to Melendres, February 5, 1853; Miles to Alcalde of Mesilla, February 6, 1853; Miles to AAAG, February 8, 1852; Nona Barrick and Mary Taylor, *The Mesilla Guard, 1851–61*, 12–13; Carson, "William Carr Lane Diary," 217–18.

54. Pablo Melendres, born about 1800, was the leader of thirty-three colonists from El Paso who settled Doña Ana in 1843. A hardy frontiersman, Melendres became the alcalde of Doña Ana in 1846 and probate judge for Doña Ana County in 1855. He died on July 7, 1868, at Doña Ana. Paxton P. Price, *Pioneers of the Mesilla Valley*, 65–68.

55. Carson, "William Carr Lane Diary," 218–23.

56. NA, RG75, M234, R546, Lane to Commissioner of Indian Affairs, May 21, 1853; Thrapp, *Victorio and the Mimbres Apaches*, 30.

57. José Nuevo, a brother of Josécito, was apparently a Chihenne who married into the Janeros group of Nednhis. He was in New Mexico for most of 1854 and 1855 when he was not raiding in Mexico. Agent Michael Steck issued rations to his band on numerous occasions during this period. Chihuahuan troops under Joaquín Terrazas captured him near Agua Nueva in June 1861, and he probably perished in a Chihuahuan prison. Steck Papers, various rations lists, 1854–1855; *La Alianza de la Frontera*, June 20, 1861.

58. Riñón (Rinyon, Rincon, Ruñon) was a prominent Chihenne leader from the early 1850s until the late 1860s. Possibly a son of Cuchillo Negro, he was from the Warm Springs local group. When Cuchillo Negro and Itán passed from the scene, he became chief of one Chihenne local group. He also made important alliances with both Delgadito and Nana, as he had married daughters of both. He fought Americans throughout the mid-1860s before Chihuahuan troops killed him, likely in the late 1860s. William H. Mullane, *Indian Raids As Reported in the Silver City Enterprise, 1882–1886*, 38.

59. NA, RG75, M234, R546, Lane to Commissioner of Indian Affairs, May 21, 1853.

60. According to Enoch Steen, Fletcher had been "a trapper for several years among the Coyotero Apaches and knows most of the principal men, speaks their language some and knows the whole country and has great influence with the Indians." NA, RG393, M1120, R5, Steen to Nichols, August 17, 1856.

61. Carson, "William Carr Lane Diary," 223.

62. Carson, "William Carr Lane Diary," 196; Robert M. Kvasnicka and Herman J. Viola, ed., *The Commissioners of Indian Affairs, 1824–1977*, 51, 57–58.

63. SA, R16, Samaniego to Terán y Tato, February 24, 1853; *El Sonorense*, February 11, 1853.

64. Officer, *Hispanic Arizona*, 270–71.

65. *El Sonorense*, March 18, 1853.

66. SA, R17, Samaniego to Terán y Tato, February 19, 1853; Governor of Sonora to Commanding General, March 4, 1853.

67. *El Sonorense*, April 15, 1853; Chomina, *Compendio de datos históricos de la familia Elías*, 146–47.

68. SA, R16, Prefect of Arispe to Governor, April 12, 1853; Pesqueira to Gándara, April 16, 1853.

69. Ibid., García to Governor, April 14, 1853; *El Sonorense*, April 22, 1853.

70. Mangas told Captain Enoch Steen that he had lost three warriors, but that number may have included only members of his Bedonkohe or Chihenne bands and not any Chokonen casualties. NA, RG75, M234, R546, Steen to Lane, May 20, 1853.

71. Opler, *Life-Way*, 351.

72. Cañon de Las Paces (either Turkey Creek or Cave Creek canyon in the Chiricahua Mountains) received its name from a peace treaty made in June 1695 between Spanish soldiers and Indians, some of whom may have been the ancestors of the Apaches. Thomas H. Naylor and Charles W. Polzer, *The Presidio and Militia on the Northern Frontier of New Spain, 1570–1700*, 594.

73. SA, R16, Pesqueira to Governor, May 10, 1853.

74. NA, RG75, M234, R546, Steen to Lane, May 20, 1853.

75. Ibid., Wingfield to Lane, April 17, 27, May 3, 1853; Steen to Lane, May 2, 1853.

76. Ibid., Steen to Lane, May 2, 16, 1853; JA, R34, Padilla to Zuloaga, April 30, 1853. The Florida Mountains and the nearby Tres Hermanas range were important places in which to gather mescal. Basehart, "Chiricahua Apache Subsistence," 78–79.

77. NA, RG75, M234, R546, Steen to Lane, May 16, 1853.

78. Ibid., Wingfield to Lane, May 18, 1853.

79. Ibid.; Steen to Lane, May 20, 1852.

80. Ibid., Wingfield to Lane, May 28, 1853; NA, RG393, LR, M1102, R7, Steen to Miles, June 1, 1853.

81. NA, RG75, M234, R547, Wingfield to Lane, May 28, 1853; RG393, LR, M1102, R7, Steen to Miles, June 1, 1853.

82. Thompson, "Matson's Diary," 388–89.

83. Abel, "Indian Affairs in New Mexico," 342, 345. Wingfield had written Lane on May 15 that he wanted to leave by December 31, 1853. NA, RG75, M234, R547, Wingfield to Lane, May 15, June 15, 1853.

CHAPTER 12

1. Utley, *Frontiersmen in Blue*, 153.

2. Michael Steck, born in Hughesville, Pennsylvania, in 1818, graduated from Jefferson Medical College at Philadelphia about 1843 and practiced medicine for the next six years. He went to New Mexico in 1849 as an army contract surgeon and three years later was appointed Indian agent for New Mexico by President Fillmore upon the recommendation of Luke Lea, the commissioner of Indian affairs. When Governor David Meriwether arrived in New Mexico he brought with him two Indian agents, one of whom replaced Steck. Steck returned east. But his fine reputation earned him a new appointment by President Franklin Pierce on May 9, 1854, as the agent for the Mimbres and Mescalero Apaches. He was arguably the best agent ever assigned to the Chiricahuas. He combined honesty with diplomacy to gain the trust and respect of the Chihennes and Bedonkohes. He also provided some of the early ethnological data that we have on the Apaches. Besides that with Mangas Coloradas, he developed a good relationship with Cochise before leaving his post in early 1861. In 1863, Abraham Lincoln appointed him superintendent of Indian affairs of New Mexico. As Lane and Greiner had with Sumner, Steck repeatedly clashed with General James Carleton, the military commander of the department. He died in Virginia in 1883. Thrapp, *Encyclopedia*, III, 1361–62.

3. Abel, "Indian Affairs in New Mexico," 350–52.

4. Steck Papers, Steck to Lane, July 16, 1853.

5. Ibid., Lane to Steck, July 11, 1853.

6. Carson, ed., "William Carr Lane," 196; NA, RG75, M234, R547, Wingfield to Lane, June 15, 1853.

7. Lane Papers, Steck to Lane, August 3, 1853.

8. NA, RG75, M234, R547, Wingfield to Lane, July 8, 1853.

9. Steck Papers, Steck to Lane, undated but probably August 3, 1853; Steck to Lane, August 13, 1853.

10. Ibid., Steck to Lane, August 13, 1853.

11. Steck Papers, Abstract of Provisions, quarter ending September 30, 1853.

12. Juarez Archives, R4, Cubero to Political Chief of District of Bravos, August 23, 24, 1853; Barrick and Taylor, *The Mesilla Guard*, 13–14.

13. There were two Apaches known as Ratón or Ratton. One was a member of Delgadito's Chihennes and the other apparently a member of Láceres's Nednhis. This man, along with Costales, was on a mission for Agent Steck when Mexicans killed them in their sleep, crushing their skulls and slitting their throats, in late December 1856 at San Diego Crossing on the Rio Grande about ten miles south of Fort Thorn. Thrapp, *Victorio and the Mimbres Apaches*, 52–53.

14. NA, RG75, M234, R546, Smith to Meriwether, September 10, 1853.

15. Ibid., Smith to Meriwether, September 5, 1853.

16. Ibid. Thrapp, *Victorio and the Mimbres Apaches*, 35–36, has most of Smith's account.

17. *El Nacional*, July 22, August 5, 1853.

18. NA, RG75, M234, R546, Smith to Meriwether, September 8, 1853.

19. Meriwether, *My Life in the Mountains*, 82–104.

20. Garland, born in Virginia in 1792, was commissioned a first lieutenant in the Thirty-fifth Infantry Regiment in 1813. He participated in the War of 1812 and the Black Hawk War of 1832, in which he escorted the Sac and Fox leader Black Hawk to prison at Rock Island, Illinois. He also fought the Seminoles in the late 1830s and early 1840s and helped end that war through deceit, inviting the Seminoles in for a feast and springing a trap. Garland became a captain in 1817, a major in 1836, a lieutenant colonel in 1839, and a colonel ten years later. He had also won brevets to brigadier general for action in four battles. After Sumner's tumultuous regime, Garland brought reason and stability to military affairs in New Mexico. He died in New York on June 5, 1861. Thrapp, *Encyclopedia*, II, 537; Francis B. Heitman, *Historical Register and Dictionary of the U.S. Army*, I, 447.

21. Frazer, *Forts and Supplies*, 88–91; Frazer, *Mansfield on the Condition of the Western Forts*, 25–26, 51–54; Robert W. Frazer, *Forts of the West: Military Forts and Presidios and Posts Commonly Called Forts West of the Mississippi River to 1898*, 106–107; Thrapp, *Victorio and the Mimbres Apaches*, 37.

22. Thrapp, *Victorio and the Mimbres Apaches*, 333 n. 29.

23. SA, R17, Samaniego to Terán y Tato, August 8, 1853.

24. SA, R16, Gándara to Minister of Relations, Mexico City, August 19, 1853.

25. NA, RG393, M1120, R3, Garland to Gadsden, December 25, 1853.

26. Estevan Ochoa was one of the Southwest's noted merchants. Born in Chihuahua in 1831, he learned English while accompanying his brothers' wagon trains to Independence, Missouri. He became well acquainted with the Chihennes in the late 1850s and early 1860s, at times filling in for Agent Michael Steck. In 1864 he formed the respected Tucson mercantile firm Tully, Ochoa & Co. The coming of the railroad in 1880 doomed his operation, which went out of business. He died at Las Cruces on October 27, 1888. Thrapp, *Encyclopedia*, II, 1072.

27. NA, RG393, LR, M1102, R7, Richardson to AAG, December 19, 1853.

28. NA, RG393, LR (Unentered), Department of New Mexico, Meriwether to Smith, October 30, 1853.

29. Thompson, "Matson's Diary," 392.

30. *Missouri Republican*, April 18, 1854; *Santa Fe Gazette*, April 8, 1854; John O. Baxter, *Las Carneradas: Sheep Trade in New Mexico, 1700–1860*, 126–27.

31. *El Nacional*, February 3, 1854; SA, R17, Durán to Terán y Tato, January 3, 1854.

32. Opler, *Life-Way*, 335.

33. *El Nacional*, February 24, 1853; SA, R17, Samaniego to Governor, February 2, 1854; Reyes to Governor, February 3, 1854.

34. SA, R17, Samaniego to Governor, April 11, 1854; Prefect of Ures to Governor, May 16, 1854.

35. SA, R17, Samaniego to Governor, March 14, 1854.

36. *El Nacional*, February 17, 1854; SA, R17, Tánori to Terán y Tato, February 13, 1854.

37. Ibid.; SA R17, Justice of the Peace at Alamos to Governor, February 14, 1854; Vasquez y Ballestero to Terán y Tato, February 19, 1854.

38. Box, *Captain James Box's Adventures*, 34–36, 56–57.

39. Wagoner, *Early Arizona*, 324; L. R. Bailey, ed., *The A. B. Gray Report*, 73–75.

40. Costales was a Mexican born about 1825 at El Carmen, Chihuahua. Delgadito's Chihennes captured him in the early 1830s in Chihuahua. A man of medium stature, he grew up with the Chihennes, becoming an important war leader because of his daring actions and superb fighting ability. Governor David Meriwether described him as follows: "Costales is not an Indian but a Mexican by birth; he was captured by these Indians in his infancy and raised by them, He married a squaw, was identified with the Mimbres Apaches, was a prominent man among them, and was of great assistance to Agent Steck in his management of them." He was killed at San Diego Crossing on the Rio Grande by Mexicans when on a mission for Agent Steck in the early morning of December 31, 1856. His murderers scalped him and took the trophy to Chihuahua for the bounty. Sweeney, *Cochise*, 418 n. 46; Reid, *Reid's Tramp*, 175; NA, RG75, T21, R26, Meriwether to Manypenny, January 12, 1857.

41. Griffen, "Chiricahua Apaches," 670–71; *El Nacional,* June 9, 1854; *El Centinela,* July 13, 1854; SA, R17, Prefect of Moctezuma to Prefect of Ures, May 24, 1854; Sweeney, Cochise, 93.

42. See Dan L. Thrapp, *Al Sieber: Chief of Scouts,* for a biography of this Arizona pioneer.

43. SA, R18, Samaniego to Governor, July 14, 1854; *El Nacional,* August 4, 1854.

44. SA, R18, Samaniego to Governor, July 14, 1854; *El Nacional,* August 4, 1854; Terán y Tato to Governor, July 11, 1854.

45. SA, R18, Terán y Tato to Governor, September 5, 1854.

46. AHS, Hayden Files, Diary of J. G. Bell, entries of September 6 and 7, 1854; *San Diego Herald,* September 16, 1854; Griffen, *Apaches at War and Peace,* 249; Schroeder, *A Study of the Apache Indians,* 4, 136.

47. *El Nacional,* October 6, 1854; Officer, *Hispanic Arizona,* 278–79.

48. Thompson, "Matson's Diary," 392. Fort Thorn, about five miles northwest of present-day Hatch, was established on December 24, 1853, on the west bank of the Rio Grande at Santa Barbara. It was named for First Lieutenant Herman Thorn, Second U.S. Infantry, who drowned on the Colorado River on October 16, 1849. It was an unhealthy location, however, and for that reason was abandoned in March 1859. Frazer, *Forts of the West,* 104–105; Giese, *Forts of New Mexico,* 23.

49. NA, RG75, M234, R547, Graves to Manypenny, January 27, 1854.

50. Keleher, *Turmoil in New Mexico,* 88.

51. NA, RG75, M234, R547, Evans to President of the United States, February 24, 1854; Steck to Manypenny, May 12, 1854; Swallon to President Franklin Pierce, February 2, 1854; Steck Papers, Meriwether to Steck, July 23, 1854.

52. Pinckney Randolph Tully, born in Mississippi in 1824, came to Santa Fe in 1846 and went to California in 1849. He eventually returned to New Mexico, became acting Southern Apache agent in 1861, and formed his mercantile business with Estevan Ochoa in 1864. Together they became the largest operation in southern Arizona. The arrival of the railroad in 1880 brought an end to the freighting enterprises. After he liquidated his business, he became a two-term mayor of Tucson. He died in California on November 10, 1903. Thrapp, *Encyclopedia,* III, 1445.

53. NA, RG75, T21, R2, Steck to Meriwether, July 8, 1854; RG75, M234, R548, Steck to Collins, July 26, 1857.

54. NA, RG75, T21, R2, Steck to Meriwether, August 13, 1854.

55. Steck Papers, Steck to Meriwether, August 22, 1854.

56. Juarez Archives, R18, Cubero to Prefect of the Bravo District, August 18, 1854.

57. Price, *Pioneers of the Mesilla Valley,* 22.

58. Juarez Archives, R18, Cubero to Prefect of the Bravo District, August 19, September 8, 9, 1854.

59. Thrapp, *Victorio and the Mimbres Apaches,* 41–42.

60. Steck Papers, Abstract of Provisions, Box 1, Folder 3, entries dated October 25 and 27, November 11, 1854.

CHAPTER 13

1. Ellis, ed., *New Mexico Historical Documents*, 41–45.

2. Bancroft, *History of the North Mexican States and Texas*, II, 693.

3. See, for example, SA, R18, Moreno to Governor June 17, 1856; AHSH, Folder 283, Gómez to Governor, April 7, 1853; Pesqueira to Governor, November 3, 1855.

4. Loco, born in the early 1820s, was a respected Chihenne leader of the last half of the nineteenth century. It would appear that he was of Cuchillo Negro's Warm Springs local group. He lost an eye as a young man during a fight with a grizzly bear. He was considered to be a kind and friendly man, well respected by whites and Indians. He figured prominently in the tragic affairs of the 1870s and 1880s and died in 1905 at Fort Sill, Oklahoma. Griswold, "Ft. Sill Apaches," 87; Thrapp, *Conquest of Apachería*, 231–250. Thrapp, *Victorio and the Mimbres Apaches*, contains much information relative to Loco's life, and Ball, *Indeh*, 38–42, and In the Days of Victorio, 136–45, contain the Apaches' recollection of Loco.

5. NA, RG75, M234, R547, Meriwether to Manypenny, November 30, 1854; Steck Papers, abstract of provisions, quarter ending December 31, 1854; Steck to Meriwether, March 5, 1855.

6. Opler, *Life-Way*, 355.

7. Steck Papers, Steck to Manypenny, report for February 1855.

8. Steck Papers, Steck to Meriwether, March 5, 1855; JA, R36, Padilla to Governor, May 28, 1855.

9. Keleher, *Turmoil in New Mexico*, 76–77.

10. Steck Papers, Steck to Meriwether, April 13, 1855.

11. Ibid., May 15, 1855.

12. JA, R36, Padilla to Governor, May 28, 1855; Sweeney, *Cochise*, 94.

13. NA, RG75, M234, R547, Meriwether to Manypenny, June 26, 1855; National Archives, Record Group 11, General Records of the United States Government, Records Relating to Indian Treaties, Microcopy 668, Ratified Indian Treaties, 1722–1869, Roll 10, Frames 459–63.

14. Meriwether, *My Life in the Mountains*, 217.

15. NA, RG75, M234, R547, Meriwether to Manypenny, June 26, 1855; NA, RG11, M668, R10, Frames 459–63.

16. Thrapp, *Victorio and the Mimbres Apaches*, 43–44.

17. Officer, *Hispanic Arizona*, 274.

18. AHSH, Folder 283. Gómez to Governor, April 7, 1855; Terán y Tato to Governor, April 30, 1855.

19. AHSH, Folder 283, Terán y Tato to Governor, April 30, 1855.

20. *El Centinela*, May 12, 1855; Steck Papers, Steck to Meriwether, July 30, 1855.

21. JA, R36, Padilla to Commander in Chief, Chihuahua, May 28, 1855.

22. Ibid.

23. *El Centinela*, July 23, 1855; National Archives, Record Group 393, Department of New Mexico, Unregistered Letters Received, Records Relating to Indian Affairs, Department of New Mexico, "Examination of a Mexican Boy Who Joined Major Kendrick Near Zuñi," which is the testimony given by Refugio Corrales about November 26, 1856 (hereafter cited as NA, RG393, "Corrales testimony").

24. Opler, *Life-Way*, 219–20, 242–44.

25. JA, R36, Zuloaga to Padilla, August 17, 1855.

26. Steck Papers, Steck to Meriwether, September 12, 1855.

27. Eligio, a brother-in-law of Coleto Amarillo, assumed leadership of one Janeros local group after the death of Coleto Amarillo in 1852. This band, whose usual haunts were the Sierra Madre north to the Animas Mountains and east to Boca Grande and Lake Guzmán, moved north into Chihenne country to avoid Mexican troops. Eligio provides a link and a clue to tracking the movements of the relatively unknown Nednhi band of Chiricahuas. Americans knew little about this band until Juh and Natiza came to the Chiricahua reservation in southeastern Arizona in November 1872. Eligio was a subordinate to Juh. In the spring of 1874 the Nednhi chief sent Eligio to solicit peace at Janos, but there Sonoran troops captured and subsequently executed him during their return trip to Sonora. Thus, it would seem likely that Juh was a member of Coleto Amarillo's group and came into prominence in the 1860s after the death of Láceres, José Nuevo, and Poncito. During the early 1860s Galindo was another important Nednhi headman of the Janeros local group. SA, R20, Ochoa to Governor of Sonora, August 26, 1874.

28. Steck Papers, Steck to Meriwether, July 30, 1855.

29. Steck Papers, Miles to Steck, February 27, 1855; Steck to Meriwether, April 13, 1853; NA, RG393, M1120, R4, Eaton to AAAG, June 11, 1855; National Archives, Records of the U.S. General Accounting Office, Record Group 217 (hereafter cited as NA, RG217), Michael Steck accounts, no. 6967, Steck to Manypenny, January 18, 1856.

30. NA, RG393, "Corrales Testimony."

31. Thrapp, *Victorio and the Mimbres Apaches*, 47.

32. NA, RG393, M1120, R4, Miles to Nichols, November 28, 1855.

33. Ibid.

34. NA, RG393, M1120, R4, Eaton to Nichols, first letter dated December 23, 1855; Steck to Eaton, December 6, 1855.

35. Ibid., Eaton to Nichols, first letter dated December 23, 1855.

36. Ibid., Eaton to Nichols, second letter dated December 23, 1855.

37. Pearce, *New Mexico Place Names*, 166.

38. NA, RG393, M1120, R5, Steck to Garland, January 9, 1856.

39. Thrapp, *Victorio and the Mimbres Apaches*, 48.

40. NA, RG75, M234, R548, Steck to Davis, February 13, 1856; RG393, M1120, R5, Miles to Richards, January 28, 1856.

41. *La Voz de Sonora*, January 18, February 29, 1856.
42. NA, RG393, M1120, R5, Eaton to Nichols, March 17, 1856.
43. Ibid., Steck to Eaton, March 12, 1856; "Corrales testimony"; RG75, M234, R548, Steck to Davis, April 6, 1856; Thrapp, *Victorio and the Mimbres Apaches*, 49–50.
44. NA, RG393, "Corrales testimony."
45. Schroeder, *A Study of the Apache Indians*, IV, 143.
46. Ibid.; Thrapp, *Victorio and the Mimbres Apaches*, 48–50. Thrapp has produced a thorough analysis of the affair and the subsequent investigation. Steck pushed hard to have Chandler censured for his conduct, but to no avail.
47. NA, RG393, M1120, Steck to Davis, April 6, 1856.
48. NA, RG217, Steck accounts no. 6967, voucher dated April 20, 1856.
49. NA, RG393, "Corrales testimony."
50. NA, RG393, M1120, R5, Steck to Eaton, April 18, 1856; RG75, M234, R548, Steck to Manypenny, June 1, 1856; Steck Papers, Annual Report, August 1856, Steck to Meriwether.
51. *El Eco de la Frontera*, June 13, October 9, 1856; JA, R36, Padilla to Steck, November 3, 1856; Steck Papers, Steck to Meriwether, June 30, 1856.
52. Reid, *Reid's Tramp*, 175.
53. Acuña, *Sonoran Strongman*, 19–25; Voss, *On the Periphery*, 130–44.
54. *La Voz de Sonora*, May 30, 1856; SA, R18, Valencia to Governor, May 26, 1856.
55. SA, R18, Moreno to Governor, June 17, 1856.
56. *La Voz de Sonora*, May 30, 1856; Almada, *Diccionario sonorenses*, 167–68; Voss, *On the Periphery*, 137–39.
57. Steck Papers, Abstract of Provisions, quarter ending September 30, 1856; Charles D. Poston, *Building a State in Apache Land*, 66–67; A. W. Gressinger, *Charles D. Poston: Sunland Seer*, 24; Lockwood, *The Apache Indians*, 92–93.
58. Steck Papers, Annual Report, August 1856, Steck to Meriwether.

CHAPTER 14

1. NA, RG75, M234, R548, Steck to Collins, November 25, 1857.
2. Sweeney, *Cochise*, 100.
3. Aguirre, a brother of Yrigóllen, had attended the Janos treaty of 1850 as the representative of his brother and Mangas Coloradas. By the late 1850s he came to recognize Cochise as the Chokonen band leader. Sonoran troops killed him near Janos on October 31, 1868. E*strella de Occidente*, December 4, 1868.

Yrinco, a Chokonen local group leader of the early 1850s, was born in the early 1800s. A member of Pisago Cabezón's band, he appears on the Janos ration lists from 1842 to 1844. Yrinco, like his brother Manuelito, preferred peace to war. He passed from the scene in the mid-1850s.

Parte, a contemporary of Cochise, was a renowned Chokonen war leader. In June 1859 he led the raid which stole eighty to ninety mules and horses from the Sonora Exploring and Mining Company near Patagonia. He made peace at Fronteras in 1861 and died there in February 1862 of smallpox. Sweeney, *Cochise*, 130–31; *Estrella de Occidente*, March 7, 1862.

4. Sweeney, *Cochise*, 130–31; *El Eco de la Frontera*, August 19, 1856.

5. *El Eco de la Frontera*, September 16, 1856.

6. JA, R36, Padilla to Steck, November 9, 1856; Padilla to Zuloaga, September 2, 1856.

7. JA, R36, Padilla to Zuloaga, September 2, 3, 1856.

8. Griffen, *Apaches at War and Peace*, 251.

9. JA, R36, Padilla to Zuloaga, September 3, 1856.

10. JA, R36, Diary of Movements, September 1856.

11. Steck Papers, Padilla to Steck, September 29, 1856; translation taken from Griffen, *Apaches at War and Peace*, 263.

12. Steck Papers, Abstract of Provisions, quarter ending September 30, 1856.

13. NA, RG75, T21, R2, Steck to Meriwether, September 12, 1856.

14. NA, RG75, T21, R26, Meriwether to Winslow, September 24, 1856, "Indian Goods for His Trip to Fort Thorn"; Meriwether to Manypenny, October 28, 1856; Meriwether, *My Life in the Mountains*, 258–59.

15. Steck Papers, Steck to Padilla, October 18, 1856; JA, R36, Steck to Padilla, October 18, 1856; NA, RG75, M234, R548, Meriwether to Manypenny, April 13, 1857.

16. Steck Papers, Padilla to Steck, November 9, 1856.

17. NA, RG75, T21, R26, Meriwether to Manypenny, October 28, 1856.

18. According to Opler, this reciprocal practice, in which the Mescaleros and Chihennes "offered a haven for each other's members," was a frequent event before the reservation period. Morris Opler, *Apache Odyssey: A Journey between Two Worlds*, 9.

19. NA, RG393, M1120, R5, Eaton to Nichols, May 13, 1856; Eaton to Grier, May 15, 1856.

20. Ibid., R5, Eaton to Nichols, May 31, 1856.

21. Ibid., R5, Van Horne to Nichols, March 14, 1856.

22. NA, RG75, T21, R26, Meriwether to Manypenny, May 24, 1856.

23. NA, RG393, M1120, R5, Sprague to Nichols, December 19, 1856.

24. NA, RG75, T21, R26, Meriwether to Steck, June 29, 1856.

25. Ibid., Meriwether to Manypenny, October 28, 1856.

26. Dodge, born Henry Lafayette Dodge in Missouri in 1810, studied law before volunteering for service in the Black Hawk War of 1832. In 1836 he married at Saint Genevieve, Missouri, before moving to Wisconsin, where he became a lead miner. In 1847 he went west without his wife, volunteered once again in the Mexican War, and remained in New

Mexico. He then became well acquainted with the Navajos and became their agent in 1853, establishing his headquarters at Fort Defiance. Soon after, he married a daughter of a Navajo leader, though he apparently had never divorced his first wife. The Navajos liked, trusted, and respected him. Some of his offspring became important leaders among the Navajos. Thrapp, *Encyclopedia*, IV (Supplement), 144–45.

27. Henry Lane Kendrick, born in New Hampshire about 1811, graduated sixteenth in a class of fifty-six from the U.S. Military Academy in 1835. He fought with distinction in the Mexican War, earning a brevet, and became commander of Fort Defiance in 1852. He remained until 1857, when he returned to the academy as a professor of chemistry, mineralogy, and geology. He retired in 1880 and died in New York City in 1891. Altshuler, *Cavalry Yellow and Infantry Blue*, 189.

28. McNitt, *Navajo Wars*, 286–87.

29. NA, RG393, "Corrales testimony."

30. NA, RG393, M1120, R5, Kendrick to Nichols, November 26, 1856.

31. Schroeder, *Apache Indian Series*, IV, 169–70; Steck Papers, Steck to Meriwether, December 17, 1856.

32. NA, RG393, M1120, R5, Kendrick to Van Horne, November 22, 1856; Kendrick to Nichols, November 26, 1856.

33. NA, RG75, T21, R26, Meriwether to Steck, November 28, 1856; Steck Papers, Meriwether to Steck, November 28, 1856.

34. Steck Papers, Steck to Meriwether, December 7, 1856; NA, RG217, Steck accounts no. 6967.

35. Steck Papers, Steck to Meriwether, December 17, 1856.

36. NA, RG393, M1120, R5, Claiborne to Nichols, December 18, 1856.

37. Steck Papers, Steck to Meriwether, January 3, 1857; NA, RG393, M1120, R6, Randall to Roberts, December 4, 1856.

38. Quite possibly this man may have been Ulzana (1821–1909), a noted Chokonen warrior of the mid-1880s who led a famous raid in November 1885 into Arizona from Mexico. Ulzana was a brother of Chihuahua, a Chokonen local group leader during Cochise's lifetime whose territory was near Safford and Duncan. Sweeney, *Cochise*, 368–69, 459–60; Griswold, "Ft. Sill Apaches," 66. For an in-depth account of Ulzana's legendary raid in late 1885, see Daniel D. Aranda, "Josanie—Apache Warrior," *True West*, May–June, 1976, 38–39, 62–64.

39. Steck Papers, Steck to Meriwether, January 3, 1857.

40. McNitt, *Navajo Wars*, 292–95.

41. NA, RG393, Letters Sent, Ninth Military Dept., Dept. of New Mexico, M1072 (hereafter cited as NA, RG393, M1072, with roll number), R2, Bonneville to Thomas, January 31, 1857.

42. Juarez Archives, R20, Abiores to Chief Politician, District of El Paso, January 13, 1857; NA, RG75, M234, R546, Meriwether to Manypenny, January 27, 1857; Thrapp, *Victorio and the Mimbres Apaches*, 52–53.

43. NA, RG393, M1072, R2, Nichols to Morris, December 29, 1856; Bonneville to Thomas, January 31, 1857; Juarez Archives, R20, U.S. Consul, El Paso to Ruiz, January 13, 1857.

44. NA, RG75, M234, R546, Meriwether to Manypenny, January 27, 1857; Steck Papers, Meriwether to Steck, March 24, 1857.

45. Steck Papers, Steck to Meriwether, March 14, 1857; Meriwether to Steck, March 24, 1857; NA, RG393, M1120, R6, Miles to Nichols, March 6, 1857.

46. Steck Papers, Steck to Bonneville, March 14, 1857.

47. NA, RG75, T21, R26, Meriwether to Steck, March 24, 1857.

48. *Santa Fe Weekly Gazette*, February 14, 1857; NA, RG393, M1120, R6, Miles to Nichols, January 27, 1857.

49. NA, RG393, M1120, R6, Gibbs to Whipple, March 11, 1857.

50. Steck Papers, Steck to Bonneville, March 14, 1857.

51. NA, RG393, M1120, R6, Miles to Nichols, March 14, 1857.

52. Ibid., Miles to Nichols, March 29, 1857.

53. Griffen, *Apaches at War and Peace*, 252–53.

54. JA, R37, Janos ration lists, February 1, April 1, 1857; Merino to Steck, February 4, 1857; Janos Archives, Austin, Padilla to Governor of Chihuahua, January 2, 1857; Steck Papers, Steck to Davis, May 6, 1857.

55. Sweeney, *Cochise*, 103–104.

56. Bonneville, born in Paris in 1796, came to the United States with his mother in 1803. He was educated at West Point and graduated in 1815. He enjoyed a long and rewarding career in the West, but not without his share of controversy. He took leave from the army in 1832 to enter the fur trade of the Rocky Mountains and wrote a noteworthy account of his experiences. He afterwards rejoined the army, participated in the second Seminole War in Florida, and served in the Vera Cruz campaign, in which he earned a brevet for "gallantry and meritorious conduct" and also a court martial for "misbehavior before the enemy." He disputed the charges but was found guilty of three of the ten charges. He was ordered to New Mexico in late 1855, taking command of Fort Fillmore. On August 30, 1856, he assumed command of the Department of New Mexico when Colonel Garland went east on leave. in 1860 he was ordered to Fort Clark, Texas. He continued to serve during the Civil War, but in administrative positions. He died at his farm at Fort Smith in 1878. Thrapp, *Encyclopedia*, I, 136–37; Henry P. Walker, ed., "Colonel Bonneville's Report: The Department of New Mexico in 1859," *Arizona and the West* 22 (Winter 1980), 343–62. For a recent biography of Bonneville, see Edith Haroldsen Lovell, *Benjamin Bonneville: Soldier of the American Frontier.*

57. Lee Myers, "Military Establishments in Southwestern New Mexico," *New Mexico Historical Review* 43 (January 1968), 9–12.

58. NA, RG393, M1120, R6, Ewell to Nichols, June 9, 1857; Frank D. Reeve, "Puritan and Apache: A Diary," *New Mexico Historical Review*

24 (January 1949), 29. From the Gila Depot, Bonneville wrote a letter to a friend in San Francisco giving information about his expedition. He placed the northern column at 430 men (300 troops, 100 Navajo and Pueblo scouts, and 30 Mexicans as guides), the southern column at 330 men (300 soldiers and 30 Mexican as guides), and a third detachment from Fort Buchanan of 120 men and an expected 100 Pima Indians. The Pimas were apparently no-shows. *Alta California*, September 7, 1857.

59. See, for example, Percy Gatlin Hamlin, *The Making of a Soldier: Letters of General R. S. Ewell*, 82–83; Frank D. Reeve, ed., "Puritan and Apache: A Diary," *New Mexico Historical Review* 23 (October 1948), 288; 24 (January 1949), 24–25.

60. NA, RG393, M1120, R6, Loring to Bonneville, June 2, 1857.

61. U.S. Department of War, *Annual Report of the Secretary of War*, 1857; Utley, *Frontiersmen in Blue*, 156–57; Thrapp, *Victorio and the Mimbres Apaches*, 54–55.

62. Steck Papers, Steck to Collins, September 4, 1857.

63. NA, RG393, M1072, R2, Garland to Thomas, August 1, 1857.

64. NA, RG393, M1120, R6, Ewell to Nichols, June 9, 1857.

65. AHSH, Folder 310, Noriega to Commander in Chief, June 27, 1857.

66. Ibid., Zuloaga to Cruz, June 4, 1857.

67. JA, R37, Padilla to Municipal President of Janos, June 10, 1857.

68. Sweeney, *Cochise*, 104–105.

69. JA, R37, Janos monthly census lists, July–November, 1857; SA, R19, Commanding General, Chihuahua, to Governor of Sonora, July 15, 1857.

70. Sweeney, *Cochise*, 105–109; Steck Papers, Steck to Collins, November 21, 1857.

71. Sweeney, *Cochise*, 106–107.

72. Ibid., 108–109.

73. NA, RG75, M234, R548, Mowry to Mix, December 7, 1857.

74. Steck Papers, Steck to Collins, November 21, 1857.

75. NA, RG75, T21, R3, Steck to Bonneville, May 16, 1857; NA, RG75, M234, R548, Collins to Denver, May 30, 1857; Steck Papers, Steck to Collins, June 8, 1857; Abstract of Provisions, quarter ending December 31, 1857.

76. NA, RG393, M1120, R6, E. Leonard to the Commander, Fort Fillmore, November 21, 1857.

77. NA, RG75, M234, R548, Steck to Collins, November 25, 1857.

78. NA, RG393, M1120, R6, Willard to Nichols, November 17, 1857; M1072, R3, Nichols to Willard, November 25, 1857.

79. Steck Papers and NA, RG75, M234, R548, Steck to Collins, November 25, 1857.

80. *Conditions of the Indian Tribes*, 328; Sweeney, *Cochise*, 108–109.

81. Thrapp, *Victorio and the Mimbres Apaches*, 57–58.

82. NA, RG75, M234, R548, and Steck Papers, Steck to Collins, November 25, 1857.

CHAPTER 15

1. Opler, *Life-Way*, 470.

2. Steck Papers, Abstract of Provisions, March quarter, 1858.

3. Frank D. Reeve, "The Federal Indian Policy in New Mexico," *New Mexico Historical Review* 13 (July 1938), 281–82.

4. NA, RG393, M1120, R8, Wood to Nichols, May 19, 1858.

5. Ibid., R7, Miles to Nichols, May 2, 1858; Schroeder, *A Study of the Apache Indians*, IV, 179–80.

6. NA, RG393, M1120, R8, Wood to Nichols, April 17, 1858; RG75, M234, R549, Collins to Mix, May 10, 1858. James Collins was not surprised to find that the thirty-six members of the Mesilla Guard had been set free. He had predicted that in "a trial before a jury of their countrymen they will of course, be acquitted." For other accounts of this atrocity, see Averell, *Ten Years in the Saddle*, 139–42; C. L. Sonnichsen, *The Mescalero Apaches*, 96–97; Barrick and Taylor, *The Mesilla Guard*, 31–33; NA, Territorial Records of New Mexico, Microfilm Copy T17, Roll 1, Annual Message of Governor Rencher, December 7, 1859.

7. NA, RG393, M1120, R8, Wood to Nichols, May 19, 1858; *La Voz de Sonora*, June 18, 1858.

8. Sweeney, *Cochise*, 110.

9. William A Duffen, ed., "Overland via 'Jackass Mail' in 1858: The Diary of Phocion R. Way," *Arizona and the West* 2 (Summer 1960), 154–56.

10. NA, RG393, M1120, R5, Steen to Nichols, August 17, 1856.

11. Henry Alexander Crabb, born about 1823 in Tennessee, was the son of a state supreme court justice. He also studied law and went to California in 1849 after being acquitted on the charge of killing a newspaper editor over political differences. He settled at Stockton and became active in California politics. He became an associate of filibuster William Walker and in 1857 organized an expedition into Sonora with sympathies toward Pesqueira's regime. By the time he arrived, however, Pesqueira had bested Gándara's forces, and the former no longer needed Crabb's support, which was potentially very embarrassing to Pesqueira. With fifty-nine survivors, Crabb surrendered at Caborca, eighty-four miles west of Magdalena, under the impression that his men would be escorted to the border and released. Instead, the Mexicans executed all but one man, effectively discouraging future filibusters. Thrapp, *Encyclopedia*, I, 333–34.

12. NA, RG393, M1120, R5, Petition from the Citizens of Gadsden Purchase, Tucson, Complaining of the Conduct of Major Enoch Steen, September 11, 1857; Benjamin Sacks, "The Origins of Fort Buchanan: Myth and Fact," *Arizona and the West* 7 (Autumn 1965), 217–18; see Frazer, *Forts and Supplies*, 123–36, for a discussion of Steen's selection of the site of the post to become known as Fort Buchanan.

13. Jay J. Wagoner, *Early Arizona: Prehistory to Civil War*, 344–50.

14. Roscoe P. and Margaret B. Conkling, *The Butterfield Overland Mail, 1857–1869*, I, 128–31, 140–42; Leroy R. Hafen, *The Overland Mail, 1849–1869*, 86–89.

15. Hafen, *Overland Mail*, 86–89; Wagoner, *Early Arizona*, 352; *Missouri Republican*, October 31, 1859.

16. For a description of this event, see Sweeney, *Cochise*, 111–14.

17. *Los Angeles Star*, October 2, 1858; *San Diego Herald*, September 18, 1858; *San Antonio Daily Herald*, October 23, 1858.

18. NA, RG75, M234, R549, Mowry to Mix, September 14, 1858.

19. Manuel Sandomingo, *Historia de Sonora*, 373–74.

20. Sweeney, *Cochise*, 114–15.

21. Walter B. Lang, *The First Overland Mail: Butterfield Trail, St. Louis to San Francico, 1858-1861*, Part 1, 119; Part 2, 76.

22. Steck Papers, Steck to Collins, undated but probably August or September 1858.

23. NA, RG75, M234, R549, Collins to Mix, February 10, May 11, 1858; Steck Papers, Mix to Collins, July 2, 1858.

24. NA, RG217, Steck accounts no. 8759.

25. NA, RG75, M234, R549, Collins to Mix, December 5, 1858.

26. Debo, *Geronimo*, 57.

27. Lang, *First Overland Mail*, Part 1, 118; NA, RG75, M234, R549, Mowry to Mix, September 14, 1858.

28. *Missouri Republican*, December 3, 1858.

29. For a discussion of Cochise's perception toward Americans and his desires to remain at peace, see Sweeney, *Cochise*, 118–41.

30. James Henry Tevis, born in 1835 at Wheeling in what is now West Virginia, served with filibuster William Walker in Central America before coming to Arizona in the late 1850s. He became station keeper at Apache Pass in late 1858 and had several adventures with Cochise before quitting and heading to Mesilla in late summer 1859. He rushed to the Pinos Altos gold fields about June 1860 and had several encounters there with Apaches, many of whom he had known at Apache Pass. He joined the Confederacy during the Civil War and went into business at Saint Louis after the war. He returned to Arizona in 1880, ran a hotel at Bowie, Arizona, in the 1890s, and died in 1905. He and his wife are buried in Bowie. His account, *Arizona in the '50's*, is a colorful recollection of events at Apache Pass in 1858–59. It cannot be ignored, but it must be used with caution. Thrapp, *Encyclopedia*, III, 1411–12.

31. Sweeney, *Cochise*, 123–25.

32. Barrett, *Geronimo's Story*, 73–74. Although Geronimo's chronology is confusing, it would appear that he accompanied Mangas Coloradas on this raid. According to an escaped captive, the Apaches had come from the Huachuca Mountains. SA, R50, Angel Elías to Military Commander, Fronteras, December 23, 1858.

33. Sweeney, *Cochise*, 115–17.

34. Ibid., 122–25.

35. *La Voz de Sonora*, February 18, 1859.

36. *Missouri Weekly Democrat*, January 13, March 3, 11, 1859.

37. NA, RG75, T21, R4, Steck to Governor, June 15, 1859.

38. Walker, "Colonel Bonneville's Report," 358–59.

39. NA, RG393, M1120, R9, Gordon to Wilkins, July 28, 1859.

40. Ibid.

41. *Missouri Republican*, April 20, 1859.

42. NA, RG393, M1120, R9, Hatch to Commanding Officer, Fort Craig, April 28, 1859.

43. Ibid., Howland to AAAG, Dept. of New Mexico, August 16, 1859. According to Dale Giese, the troops remained until "the grass failed and the cold weather set in." Giese, *Forts of New Mexico*, 18; Frazer, *Forts and Supplies*, 143.

44. Steck Papers, Steck to Collins, August, 1859.

45. NA, RG75, M234, R549, Steck to Collins, November 25, 1859.

46. Steck Papers, Collins to Steck, February 16 and 20, 1860.

47. Steck Papers, Steck to Fauntleroy, March 1, 1860.

48. Steck Papers, Steck to Collins, March 10, 1860.

49. Steck Papers, Steck to Ochoa, March 17, 1860; NA, RG75, T21, R4, Steck to Commissioner of Indian Affairs, March 20, 1860; *Missouri Republican*, April 3, 1860.

50. NA, RG75, M234, R550, Steck to Greenwood, May 11 and 14, 1860.

51. R. S. Allen, "Pinos Altos, New Mexico," *New Mexico Historical Review* 23 (October 1948), 302–303; Dorothy Watson, *The Pinos Altos Story*, 5–6; Thrapp, *Victorio and the Mimbres Apaches*, 66–67.

52. W. Hubert Curry, *Sun Rising on the West: The Saga of Henry Clay and Elizabeth Smith*, 31–33.

53. Opler, *Life-Way*, 444–45.

54. Kajo may have been a Bedonkohe chief named Coha, whom White Mountain Apaches killed in a fight on Christmas Day, 1875, on the Chiricahua Apache reservation. NA, RG75, M234, R16, Jeffords to Smith, May 2, 1876.

55. Curry, *Sun Rising on the West*, 31–33.

56. Constance Wynn Altshuler, ed., *Latest from Arizona! The Hesperian Letters, 1859–1861*, 96; *Alta California*, July 11, 25, 1860; Missouri Historical Society, Saint Louis, Webb Papers, Kingsbury to Webb, June 24, 1860; Curry, *Sun Rising on the West*, 35–39.

57. *Missouri Republican*, February 18, 1860.

58. NA, RG75, T21, R4, Steck to Commissioner of Indian Affairs, March 20, 1860; *Missouri Republican*, April 3, 1860.

59. Juh, born in the early 1820s, was an important leader of the Janeros local group of Nednhis from the mid-1850s until his death in Mexico in 1883. For a first-rate biography of this chief, see Dan L. Thrapp, *Juh: An Incredible Indian*.

60. *Missouri Republican*, May 6, 1860.

61. NA, RG75, T21, R4, Steck to Commissioner of Indian Affairs, March 10, 1860.

62. L. Boyd Finch, *Confederate Pathway to the Pacific: Major Sherod Hunter and Arizona Territory, C.S.A.*, 39; L. Boyd Finch, "Arizona's Governors without Portfolio: A Wonderfully Diverse Lot," *Journal of Arizona History* 26 (Spring 1995), 78–80.

63. NA, RG393, M1120, R12, Hunter to Owings, May 6, 1860.

64. L. Boyd Finch, *A Southwestern Land Scam: The 1859 Report of the Mowry City Association*, 10–11; Finch, *Confederate Pathway to the Pacific*, 39–40.

65. *Missouri Republican*, June 3, 10, and 12, 1860; Finch, *Southwestern Land Scam*, 10–15.

66. *La Coalicion*, September 4, 1860; *Estrella de Occidente*, June 29, July 6, 1860.

67. Sweeney, *Cochise*, 138–40.

CHAPTER 16

1. Ball, *In the Days of Victorio*, 46–47.

2. Boyer and Gayton, *Apache Mothers and Daughters*, 45–46, 49–50.

3. Steck Papers, Ewell to Steck, August 31, 1860; Sweeney, *Cochise*, 135–38.

4. NA, RG75, M234, R550, Steck to Collins, October 7, 1860 (enclosing petition dated September 2, 1860).

5. Ibid.; NA, RG75, T21, R5, Greenwood to Collins, January 5, 1861.

6. Altshuler, ed., *Latest from Arizona!* 136.

7. Steck Papers, Abstract of Provisions, quarter ending December 31, 1860; *Alta California*, November 21, 1860; NA, RG75, T21, R4, Steck to Collins, November 26, 1860.

8. NA, RG75, T21, R27, Collins to Steck, December 2, 1860.

9. James H. Tevis, *Arizona in the '50's*, 206–16; Steck Papers, Lynde to Steck, December 7, 1860; NA, RG393, M1120, R13, Lynde to AAG, Dept. of N.M., December 18, 1860.

10. Tevis, *Arizona in the '50's*, 214. Apache Tejo may have taken its name from a Chihenne leader of the 1770s named Pachiteju, who probably camped near there. It is interesting that this place name survived almost one hundred years in Chiricahua oral history. Alfred Barnaby Thomas, *Forgotten Frontiers: A Study of the Spanish Indian Policy of Don Juan Bautista de Anza, Governor of New Mexico, 1777–1787*, 15.

11. NA, RG393, M1120, R13, Lynde to AAG, Dept. of N.M., October 9, 1860.

12. NA, RG393, M1120, R13, Lynde to AAG, Dept. of N.M., December 18, 1860.

13. Steck Papers, Lynde to Steck, December 7, 1860.

14. NA, RG75, M234, R550, Steck to Collins, December 14, 1860.

15. NA, RG393, M1120, R13, Lynde to AAG, Dept. of N.M., December 15, 18, 1860.

16. NA, RG75, M234, R550, Tully to Collins, January 3, 1861.

17. Betzinez, *I Fought with Geronimo*, 43.

18. NA, RG393, M1120, R13, Lynde to AAG, Dept. of N.M., January 15, 1861.

19. Ibid., Lynde to AAG, Dept. of N.M., February 17, 1861; LS, M1072, R2, Maury to Lynde, December 30, 1860.

20. See Sweeney, *Cochise*, 142–65, for a day-by-day account of the Bascom affair, known to the Chiricahuas as the "Cut the Tent" incident.

21. NA, RG393, M1120, R13, Bascom to Maury, January [February] 14, 1861.

22. Barrett, *Geronimo's Story*, 116–17.

23. AHSH, Folder 363, Corella to Governor, February 13, 1861.

24. For an analysis of Cochise's activities leading up to the Bascom affair, see Edwin R. Sweeney, "Cochise and the Prelude to the Bascom Affair," *New Mexico Historical Review* 64 (October 1989), 427–46.

25. NA, RG393, M1120, R17, Shaw to AAG, Dept. of N.M., September 20, 1862.

26. Cremony, *Life among the Apaches*, 173.

27. *Missouri Republican*, December 27, 1861.

28. NA, RG75, M234, R550, Tully to Collins, January 3, 1861.

29. Steck Papers, Abstract of Provisions, quarters ending March 31 and June 30, 1861.

30. NA, RG393, M1102, R13, Tully to Collins, May 26, 1861.

31. For example, NA, RG75, M234, R550, Collins to Greenwood, February 24 and March 3, 1861; Steck to Collins, December 14, 1860; Tully to Collins, February 17, 1861.

32. Tevis, *Arizona in the '50's*; Curry, *Sun Rising on the West*.

33. J. P. Dunn, Jr., *Massacres of the Mountains: A History of the Indian Wars of the Far West, 1815–1875*, 326; Will L. Comfort, *Apache*, 231–34; Wellman, *Indian Wars of the West*, 286–88; Woodworth Clum, *Apache Agent: The Story of John P. Clum*, 30–31.

34. Boyer and Gayton, *Apache Mothers and Daughters*, 32; John U. Terrell, *Apache Chronicle*, 196–97.

35. Thompson, "Matson's Diary," 392.

36. For example, Private John Teal, who served under Cremony in the California Volunteers, did not think too highly of his captain's character: "I do not believe anything he says except when he says he wants whiskey" (Henry P. Walker, ed., "Soldier in the California Column: The Diary of John P. Teal," *Arizona and The West* 13 (Spring 1971), 49). Writing of Cremony's death in 1879, the *Arizona Daily Star* wrote that his unreliability was "greater than [that of] Baron Munchausen" who was renowned for telling absurdly exaggerated yarns (Thrapp, *Encyclopedia*, I, 343).

37. Ball, *In the Days of Victorio*, xiv, 47.

38. NA, RG393, M1120, R13, Buckley to Lane, February 16, 1861.
39. Barrett, *Geronimo's Story*, 117–18.
40. Sweeney, *Cochise*, 169.
41. NA, RG75, M234, R550, Collins to Greenwood, February 24, March 3, April 10, 1861; Collins to Dole, June 8, 1861.
42. Sweeney, *Cochise*, 168–69.
43. Ibid., 170–75.
44. Steck Papers, Collins to Tully, April 29, May 4, 1861.
45. *Mesilla Times*, March 16, 1861; AHSH, Folder 364, García to Governor, March 19, 1861.
46. *Mesilla Times*, May 11, June 8, 1861; NA, RG393, M1120, R13, Tully to Collins, May 26, 1861; Lynde to AAG, Dept. of N.M., May 26, 1861.
47. NA, RG75, M234, R550, Tully to Collins, June 2, 1861.
48. Fort Buchanan was abandoned and burned on July 23, 1861; Fort Breckenridge was evacuated and burned on July 10, 1861; Fort McLane was abandoned on July 3, 1861, and its garrison relocated to Fort Fillmore. Frazer, *Forts of the West*, 4, 6, 100.
49. Sweeney, *Cochise*, 178–79; Ball, *In the Days of Victorio*, 45.
50. NA, RG75, M234, R550, Steck to Collins, July 15, 1861.

CHAPTER 17

1. *Missouri Republican*, December 27, 1861.
2. Sweeney, *Cochise*, 180–89.
3. NA, RG393, M1072, R3, Carleton to AAG, August 14, 1865.
4. *Santa Fe Gazette*, September 22, 1866.
5. Neil B. Carmony, ed., *The Civil War in Apacheland: George Hand's Diary, California, Arizona, West Texas, New Mexico, 1861–1864*, 94–95.
6. University of Arizona Library, Special Collections, AZ 300, Thomas Akers Diary.
7. Austerman, *Sharps Rifles and Spanish Mules*, 179–80.
8. Donald H. Couchman, *Cooke's Peak—Pasarón Por Aquí*, 132–33. Couchman believes that the attack took place on July 21, 1861, which makes more sense than my version in *Cochise*, when I assumed the attack had occurred late July 20, 1861. This excellent book, published by the New Mexico Bureau of Land Management, is one of the best sources for the history of southern New Mexico in the nineteenth century. Rex Strickland, who edited W. W. Mills, *Forty Years at El Paso, 1858–1898*, has a reconstruction of the battle, and he also placed the fight on July 21. See Mills, *Forty Years at El Paso*, 195–96.
9. *San Francisco Evening Bulletin*, September 7, 1861; *Arizona Daily Star*, July 27, 1879, containing William S. Oury's account; Mills, *Forty Years at El Paso*, 195–96; Tevis, *Arizona in the '50s'*, 229–30.
10. AHS, Hayden Files, William Fourr file.
11. Mills, *Forty Years at El Paso*, 53–54.

12. *Arizona Daily Star*, July 27, 1879.

13. New Mexico State University Library, Las Cruces, Rio Grande Historical Collection, Keith Humphries file.

14. Mills, *Forty Years at El Paso*, 53.

15. AHSH, Folder 364, Perez to Governor, November 4, 1861.

16. The primary source for the Ake party's retreat to New Mexico is James B. O'Neil, *They Die But Once: The Story of a Tejano*, in which one of Ake's sons relates his version. Although he claimed there "were 47 men in the company all told when we pulled out from there [Tucson] seven women and sixteen children," he likely meant forty-seven in all. This would put the number of men at about twenty-four, which approximates the recollections of Thomas Farrell (nineteen men); Robert Phillips, who recalled there were twenty-five to thirty men and boys; and Mariano Madrid, who said that the Indians outnumbered the whites ten to one. He estimated the Apaches' numbers at two hundred, thus placing the whites at about twenty. In a later statement Ake indicated that only eight men escaped unharmed, which, if one takes into account the accepted casualties of four whites killed and five wounded, plus the seven men who bolted at the beginning of the fight, would mean that there were about twenty-four men in the party. O'Neil, *They Die But Once*, 36–46; National Archives, Records of the United States Court of Claims, Record Group 123, Indian Depredation Division, Indian Depredation File 3112, T. J. Cassner, Administrator (hereafter cited as NA, RG123, Indian Depredation File 3112).

17. O'Neil, *They Die But Once*, 36, 41; Curry, *Sun Rising on the West*, 57.

18. Unless specifically noted, the primary sources of the Chiricahuas' ambush of Ake's party are to be found in NA, RG123, Indian Depredation File 3112, which the descendants of Felix Grundy Ake filed for restitution for the losses he suffered at the hands of the Apaches. This file contains many colorful anecdotes of the fight. O'Neil, *They Die But Once*, 36–46; University of Arizona Library, Special Collections, Palmer manuscript, AZ 197. For published material, see Sweeney, *Cochise*, 183–85, and Virginia Cullin Roberts, *With Their Own Blood: A Saga of Southwestern Pioneers*, 111–21. Roberts's reconstruction of the fight, based primarily on the Indian Depredation File, is well done and provides exciting reading.

19. Berndt Kuhn of Stockholm, Sweden, has done an immense amount of field work in Cooke's Canyon. His best guess is that the fight between the Chiricahuas and Ake's party took place in "the narrow passage in the canyon which is at the eastern entrance. This, I believe, is the only place which corresponds with the description of a 'narrow gap,' or 'the narrowest portion of the canyon' where the party would have had difficulties in turning the wagons around. The road is here paralleled by a rocky ridge on the north and east side covered with natural ramparts which offer excellent protection for an enemy waiting in ambush." Berndt Kuhn to author, May 19, 1996.

20. AHS, Hayden Files, Thomas Farrell file.

21. Ibid.

22. O'Neil, *They Die But Once*, 45.

23. Ibid., 42–46; NA, RG123, Indian Depredation File 3112; AHS, Hayden Files, Thomas Farrell file.

24. Curry, *Sun Rising on the West*, 55–57.

25. George Wythe Baylor, *John Robert Baylor: Confederate Governor of Arizona*, 12.

26. Samuel Woodworth Cozzens, *Young Trail Hunters*, 176–77.

27. Curry, *Sun Rising on the West*, 55.

28. Ibid., 55–57.

29. AHSH, Folder 366, Sánchez to Governor, September 17, 1861.

30. Baylor, *John Robert Baylor*, 32.

31. Baylor, born in Kentucky on July 20, 1822, moved to Texas in 1840 and became an Indian fighter of some note against the Comanches. He won election to the state legislature in 1853 and the following year was admitted to the state bar. In January 1861 he served as a delegate to the Texas Secession Convention at Austin, and in March he was commissioned lieutenant colonel of the Second Texas Mounted Rifles Regiment, whose mission was to occupy the abandoned Federal forts between San Antonio and El Paso. He hated Indians—all of them—and his policies and actions suggested that he believed the frontier axiom that the only good Indian was a dead Indian. After the war he returned to Texas and died on February 8, 1894. Thrapp, *Encyclopedia*, I, 74–75; Baylor, *John Robert Baylor*.

32. Wagoner, *Early Arizona*, 443–45.

33. Born in Kentucky in 1817, Canby graduated from West Point in 1839 and joined the Second Infantry. He fought the Seminoles in Florida from 1839 to 1842. He was promoted to first lieutenant in 1846 and to captain the following year. He saw much action in the Mexican War, participated in the Mormon expedition of 1857–58, and in 1861 became a colonel. On June 11, 1861, shortly after Colonel William Loring resigned to join the Confederacy, Canby was named the commander of the Military Department of New Mexico. He faced serious problems but carried out his responsibilities honorably and efficiently. He was treacherously murdered by Modoc Indians during a peace conference with their leader, Captain Jack, in 1873. Thrapp, *Encyclopedia*, I, 218–19.

34. Keleher, *Turmoil in New Mexico*, 147–50; Robert Lee Kerby, *The Confederate Invasion of New Mexico, 1861–62*, 29–36; Ray C. Colton, *The Civil War in the Western Territories*, 16–20; Baylor, *John Robert Baylor*, 6–11; Curry, *Sun Rising on the West*, 84–87.

35. As quoted in Wagoner, *Early Arizona*, 425.

36. Curry, *Sun Rising on the West*, 52–54. As usual there is much disagreement about the number of Apaches thought to be in the fight. The only contemporary account appeared in the *Mesilla Times* of October 3, 1861, and it placed the Indians at 250 to 300 warriors. One year later,

Baylor reported them at 400, while Carleton wrote in 1867 that some 500 Apaches were involved. *Mesilla Times*, October 3, 1861; as quoted by James Collins to W. P. Dole, October 6, 1861, in U.S. Congress, 37th Cong., 2d sess., S. Executive Doc. no. 1, pt. 1, 672–73. *Estrella de Occidente*, November 22, 1861, picked up the *Mesilla Times* account. Baylor's account can be found in *The War of the Rebellion: A Compilation of the Official Records of the Union and Confederate Armies* (hereafter cited as *OR*), Series I, vol. 15, pt. 1, Baylor to Magruder, December 29, 1862, 916; Carleton's version was printed in the *Santa Fe Gazette*, July 27, 1867. Tom Mastin died on October 7, 1861 of blood poisoning (*Mesilla Times*, October 17, 1861).

37. Opler, *Life-Way*, 344–45.

38. Curry, *Sun Rising on the West*, 48–49; 37th Cong., 2d sess., S. Executive Doc. no. 1, pt. 1, 672–73; information from Berndt Kuhn, "Apache Chronology," September–October 1861.

39. Sweeney, *Cochise*, 180.

40. Juarez Archives, R23, Ruiz to Ochoa, October 3, 1861.

41. Sweeney, *Cochise*, 190.

42. Ibid., 194.

43. *OR*, Series I, vol. 50, pt. 1, Baylor to Helm, March 20, 1862, 942.

44. Kerby, *Confederate Invasion*, 110–20.

45. Aurora Hunt, *Major General James Henry Carleton, 1814–1873*, 220–25.

46. Darlis A. Miller, *The California Column in New Mexico*, xi.

47. Hunt, *Major General James Henry Carleton*, 220–25.

48. *OR*, Series I, vol. 50, pt. 1, 120.

49. Ibid., 120–22.

50. Larry Ludwig to author, April 10, 1996. Mr. Ludwig has a better grasp than anyone else I know regarding the Battle of Apache Pass on July 15–16, 1862. He is currently working on a manuscript that will give a full account of the battle.

51. For a good account of the life of the Chihenne chief Nana, who was probably a member of Cuchillo Negro's local group, see Stephen H. Lekson, *Nana's Raid: Apache Warfare in Southern New Mexico, 1881*. For the Nednhis under Juh, see Ball, *In the Days of Victorio*, 47; Ball, *Indeh*, 19–20, 52.

52. In *Cochise*, I had placed Roberts's command at sixty-nine men plus a few civilian teamsters. Larry Ludwig's careful study concludes that Roberts's command totaled between ninety-three and ninety-six men, broken down as follows: sixty infantry, twenty infantry assigned to the gun crews (Thompson's company), six to eight cavalry, five or six teamsters, Captain Roberts, and Lieutenant Thompson. Ludwig to author, April 10, 1996. *OR*, Series I, vol. 50, pt. 1, 128–31; *Rio Grande Republican*, January 2, 1891.

53. As usual, accounts vary as to the number of Apaches involved in the fighting at Apache Pass. The *Sacramento Union* (August 14, 1862)

and the *Santa Fe Gazette* (October 4, 1862) put the numbers involved at more than 100. Edward Palmer, who knew the Western Apaches, estimated the combined strength at between 200 and 300 warriors. Two participants, John C. Cremony and Albert J. Fountain, placed the Apaches' numbers at 700 and 800, respectively. As with the fights of the previous summer, the allied Chiricahuas probably numbered about 200, plus or minus 50. About a year after the Battle of Apache Pass a captive who had escaped from Cochise said that he had mustered a following of 180 warriors, which must have included recruits from the Nednhis, Bedonkohes, and Chihennes. At that time the four Chiricahua bands numbered about 350 to 400 warriors. *Sacramento Union*, August 14, 1862; *Santa Fe Gazette*, October 4, 1862; University of Arizona, Special Collections, Palmer manuscript, AZ 197; Cremony, *Life among the Apaches*, 161–67; *Rio Grande Republican*, January 2, 1891; Joseph Miller, ed., *Arizona Cavalcade: The Turbulent Times*, 30–35; Arizona State University Library, copy of Hubert Howe Bancroft, *Scraps*, a collection of Arizona Items clipped from California newspapers, 48.

54. *Rio Grande Republican*, January 2, 1891; Miller, *Arizona Cavalcade*, 35.

55. According to Albert Fountain, a sergeant in the California Column, Cochise told him that "you never would have whipped us if you had not shot wagons at us." *Rio Grande Republican*, January 2, 1891; Miller, *Arizona Cavalcade*, 35. Asa Daklugie told Eve Ball that "after they turned cannon loose on us at Apache Pass . . . my people knew that the Apaches were doomed." Eve Ball, "Cibicu, an Apache Interpretation," in Ray Brandes, ed., *Troopers West: Military and Indian Affairs on the American Frontier*, 123.

56. Fountain's account, in the *Rio Grande Republican*, January 2, 1891.

57. Larry Ludwig to author, April 10, 1996.

58. Ibid.; Henry P. Walker, ed., "Soldier in the California Column: The Diary of John W. Teal," *Arizona and the West* 13 (Spring 1971), 40–41; Konrad F. Schreier, Jr., ed., "The California Column in the Civil War: Hazen's Civil War Diary," *Journal of San Diego History* 22 (Spring 1976), 45.

59. *Rio Grande Republican*, January 2, 1891; *OR*, Series I, vol. 50, pt. 1, 131.

60. Bronson, *The Vanguard*, 85.

61. Larry Ludwig to author, April 10, 1996.

62. U.S., Department of the Interior, National Park Service, unpublished report, "Preliminary Findings of the Battle of Apache Pass, Archaeological Survey."

63. *Rio Grande Republican*, January 2, 1891.

64. Ibid.; Ball, *In the Days of Victorio*, 47; Betzinez, *I Fought with Geronimo*, 42; Ernest Marchand, ed., *News from Fort Craig, New Mexico, 1863: Civil War Letters of Andrew Ryan with the First California*

Volunteers, 34; Walker, "Teal's Diary," 40; Schreier, "Hazen's Diary," 45; Carmony, *The Civil War in Apacheland,* 111–12.

65. *Rio Grande Republican,* January 2, 1891.

66. Walker, "Teal's Diary," 41.

67. Ball, *Indeh,* 19–20; Ball, *In the Days of Victorio,* 47; Cremony, *Life among the Apaches,* 160.

68. *OR,* Series I, vol. 50, pt. 1, 128–32; *Rio Grande Republican,* January 2, 1891.

69. *OR,* Series I, vol. 50, pt. 1, 128.

70. Cremony, *Life among the Apaches,* 164.

71. Betzinez, *I Fought with Geronimo,* 42; Ball, *In the Days of Victorio,* 47.

72. Thrapp to author, December 5, 1975; December 16, 1981.

73. Sweeney, *Cochise,* 206–207.

CHAPTER 18

1. *OR,* Series I, vol. 50, pt. 1, 128–29, pt. 2, 40–41; vol. 9, pt. 1, 565.

2. *Santa Fe Gazette,* October 4, 1862; *OR,* Series I, vol. 9, pt. 1, 565. The victims were Thomas Buchanon and William Smith of Pennsylvania, William Allen of Illinois, Conrad Stark of Ohio, David Berry of Iowa, James Burnes of Wisconsin, James Ferguson, and two Mexicans from Mesilla. Cremony, *Life among the Apaches,* 174–75.

3. Sweeney, *Cochise,* 204–205.

4. Ball, *Indeh,* 20; Cremony, *Life among the Apaches,* 176.

5. *La Alianza de la Frontera,* August 14, September 11, 1862.

6. Opler, *Life-Way,* 470.

7. NA, RG393, M1120, R17, Shaw to AAG, Dept. of N.M., September 20, 1863.

8. Constance Wynn Altshuler, *Chains of Command: Arizona and the Army, 1856–1875,* 31.

9. NA, RG393, M1120, R15, Carleton to West, August 6, 1862.

10. *OR,* Series I, vol. 50, pt. 2, 147–48.

11. NA, RG393, M1120, R17, West to Carleton, October 8, 1862.

12. NA, RG393, Carleton to West, October 14, 1862.

13. *OR,* Series I, vol. 50, pt. 2, 200.

14. AHS, Hayden Files, William Fourr file.

15. Barrett, *Geronimo's Story,* 119–20.

16. Ball, *In the Days of Victorio,* 48; Ball, *Indeh,* 19–20.

17. NA, RG94, M619, R195, Carleton to Thomas, February 1, 1863.

18. *OR,* Series I, vol. 15, pt. 1, 580.

19. Joseph Walker (1798–1876) may have had the "longest and most distinguished career of any frontiersman in American history," according to his biographer, Bill Gilbert. Physically, Walker was a giant for his times, standing six feet, four inches tall and weighing more than two hundred pounds. He was also a giant in terms of reputation, one of the

few frontiersmen whose actions and deeds probably equaled or even exceeded his legend. He left Tennessee in 1819, moved to Missouri, and in 1825 guided a government party which surveyed the Santa Fe Trail. Two years later he helped to found the town of Independence, Missouri, and became its sheriff, and five years later he went to the Rockies to trap and began to earn his reputation as a mountain man. In 1833 he led a band of trappers through the mountains to California and the Pacific, the first Americans to make the overland journey. He also guided Frémont in his second expedition before ranching in California in the 1850s. During this time he encountered Indians on many occasions, and he dealt with them honestly and respectfully, only fighting when it was necessary. He was truly a pathfinder who ranked with Daniel Boone and Jim Bridger in terms of accomplishments. Dan Thrapp wrote that "his impact on the west was immense, his life replete with significant deeds, and Walker was a man of integrity, vision, intelligence, fortitude and great worth" (Thrapp, *Encyclopedia*, III, 1500–1501). For a fine biography, see Bill Gilbert, *Westering Man: The Life of Joseph Walker*.

20. NA, RG393, M1120, R20, Shirland to McCleave, January 22, 1863; Conner, *Joseph Reddeford Walker*, 36.

21. Ball, *Indeh*, 20; Ball, *In the Days of Victorio*, 48.

22. James H. McClintock, *Arizona: Prehistoric, Aboriginal, Pioneer, Modern*, 176–77.

23. Conner, *Joseph Reddeford Walker*, 36–37.

24. NA, RG393, M1120, R20, Shirland to McCleave, January 22, 1863.

25. Huntington Library, San Marino, Calif., William Gillet Ritch Collection, manuscript no. 1735.

26. This version of Clark Stocking's account is in Bronson, *The Vanguard*, 99–100.

27. Conner, *Joseph Reddeford Walker*, 37.

28. NA, RG94, M619, R195, West to Cutler, January 28, 1863.

29. Bronson, *The Vanguard*, 100–101.

30. NA, RG94, M619, R195, West to Cutler, January 28, 1863.

31. McClintock, *Arizona*, 176–78.

32. AHS, Hayden Files, Clark B. Stocking file.

33. Conner, *Joseph Reddeford Walker*, 38–39; AHS, Hayden Files, Stocking file.

34. David B. Sturgeon enlisted as an assistant surgeon, volunteers, on September 11, 1862. He resigned April 3, 1864, when he took the skull of Mangas Coloradas to Toledo, Ohio, where he opened a medical practice. He presented the skull to Professor Orson Squire Fowler for examination. Fowler, a noted phrenologist, in 1873 published the results in his book *Human Science or Phrenology*, pages 1195–97. He wrote that Mangas's skull was "the shortest and broadest human skull I have ever seen, excepting one or two from the Isthmus of Darien, and actually wider than it is long!" Fowler goes on to give his opinion about Mangas's intellectual capabilities, concluding that his "head says that as a scout and spy he had

no equal." He also noted that Mangas's under jaw was "monstrous—probably because he used it in eating a great deal of dry hard meat." Heitman, *Historical Register*, I, 974; *Boston Evening Transcript*, February 4, 1873; U.S. Smithsonian Institution, National Museum of Natural History, report "The Skull of Mangas Coloradas," by L. E. St. Hoyme.

35. U.S. Smithsonian Institution, National Museum of Natural History, report "The Skull of Mangas Coloradas."

36. Bronson, *The Vanguard*, 101.

37. NA, RG94, M619, R195, West to Cutler, January 28, 1863.

38. Although in 1865, after the *Santa Fe New Mexican* published a letter from Judge Joseph G. Knapp to Carleton that not only criticized the general's "Black Flag" policy toward the Chihennes but also stated that the troops had killed Mangas in cold blood, Carleton sent a copy of the article to West for his comments. By this time the men had become archenemies, and West was no longer under Carleton's command. In response, West labeled Knapp's accusations "totally false" and referred Carleton to his official report of January 28, 1863. *Santa Fe New Mexican*, April 14, 1865; NA, RG393, M1120, R27, West to Carleton, May 27, 1865.

39. Stocking's account is in McClintock, *Arizona*, 178; Crouch's and Martin's accounts are in the Huntington Library, Ritch Collection, manuscript no. 1735; Townsend's account is manuscript no. 1410.

40. McClintock, *Arizona*, 178.

41. Conner, *Joseph Reddeford Walker*, 41.

42. Miller, *California Column*, 17.

43. AHS, Hayden Files, Fourr file.

44. *Santa Fe New Mexican*, April 14, 1865.

45. *Conditions of the Indian Tribes*, 328.

46. AHS, Charles Connell File.

47. Conner, *Joseph Reddeford Walker*, 41.

48. John Quincy Adams, "Surgeon to the Indian Fighters," *True West*, September 1982.

49. NA, RG393, M1120, R20, McCleave to West, January 22, 1863; Shirland to McCleave, January 22, 1863.

50. NA, RG75, M234, R554, Hackney to Commissioner of Indian Affairs, January 31, 1867; Conner, *Joseph Reddeford Walker*, 41.

51. Carmony, *The Civil War in Apacheland*, 101.

52. Barrett, *Geronimo's Story*, 119.

53. Ball, *In the Days of Victorio*, 48.

54. Ball, *Indeh*, 20.

55. Opler, *Life-Way*, 477–78; also, see Morris E. Opler, "Myths and Tales of the Chiricahua Apache Indians," *Memoirs of the American Folk-Lore Society*, 1942, 82–83.

56. Thrapp, *Victorio and the Mimbres Apaches*, 83.

57. *Santa Fe New Mexican*, April 14, 1865; NA, RG393, M1120, R19, Morrison to AAG, Department of New Mexico, June 24, 1863.

BIBLIOGRAPHY

MANUSCRIPT MATERIALS, UNPUBLISHED DOCUMENTS,
COLLECTIONS

Akers, Thomas. Diary (AZ 300). Special Collections, University of
Arizona Library, Tucson.
Archivo Historico de Sonora (AHSH), Hermosillo, Sonora.
Arizona Historical Society, Tucson. Hayden Files or collections: Diary of
J. G. Bell, Diary of John G. Bourke, Charles T. Connell, José Miguel
Castaneda, Thomas Farrell, William Fourr, Clark B. Stocking.
———. Sonoran State Archives, Rolls 12–19.
Arizona State University Library, Tempe. Copy of Hubert Howe Ban-
croft, Scraps, a collection of Arizona items clipped from California
newspapers.
Bartlett, John Russell. Papers. Brown University, Providence, R.I.
Basehart, Harry W. "Chiricahua Apache Subsistence and Socio-Political
Organization." A report of the Mescalero-Chiricahua Land Claims
Project. Contract Research No. 290-154. University of New Mexico,
Albuquerque, March 1959.
Breckenridge, Thomas E. Memoirs. Missouri State Historical Society,
Columbia.
Correspondence with author: Eve Ball, Jim Brito, William B. Griffen,
Berndt Kuhn, Larry Ludwig, Morris Opler, Allan Radbourne, Dan
Thrapp, Manuel Valenzuela.
Goodwin, Grenville. Collection at Arizona State Museum, Tucson.
Griffen, William B. Unpublished manuscript, "Chiricahua Apaches."
Griswold, Gillett M. "The Fort Sill Apaches: Their Vital Statistics, Tribal
Origins, Antecedents." Unpublished manuscript, Field Artillery
Museum, Fort Sill, Okla., 1970.
Huntington Library, San Marino, Calif. William Gillet Ritch Collection.

Lane, William Carr. Papers. Missouri Historical Society, Saint Louis.
New Mexico State University, Las Cruces. Rio Grande Historical Collection, Dan Aranda file, Keith Humphries file.
Palmer, Edward. Manuscript (AZ 197). Special Collections, University of Arizona Library, Tucson.
Pinart, Louis Alphonse. Microfilm Collection. Bancroft Library, University of California, Berkeley.
Robards, John Lewis. Journal. Missouri Historical Society, Columbia.
State of New Mexico Records Center, Santa Fe, Mexican Archives of New Mexico.
Steck, Michael. Papers. Zimmerman Library, University of New Mexico, Albuquerque.
Sublette, Solomon. Papers. Missouri Historical Society, Saint Louis.
United States, Department of the Interior, National Park Service. "Preliminary Report on the Battle of Apache Pass, Archaeological Survey."
United States, National Archives and Records Center, Washington, D.C. Record Group 94, Records of the Adjutant General's Office (AGO), 1780s–1917, Letters Received, Main Series, Microcopy 619, Rolls 195, 284.
———. Record Group 75, (RG75) Records of the Bureau of Indian Affairs, Microcopy 234, Letters Received, 1824–80, New Mexico Superintendency, 1849–80, rolls 546–64; Microcopy T21, Records of the New Mexico Superintendency of Indian Affairs, 1849–80.
———. Record Group 11, General Records of the United States Government, Records Relating to Indian Treaties, Microcopy 668, Ratified Indian Treaties, 1722–1869.
———. Record Group 123, Records of the United States Court of Claims, Indian Depredation Division, Indian Depredation File 3112, T. J. Cassner, Administrator.
———. Record Group 148, Records of the Office of the Secretary of the Interior; State Department Territorial Papers, New Mexico.
———. Record Group 217, Records of the U.S. General Accounting Office.
———. Record Group 393, Records of the United States Army Continental Commands, 1821–1920, Arizona: District of Arizona, Unregistered Letters Received; Records Relating to Indian Affairs, Department of New Mexico; Department of New Mexico Unentered Letters Received, 1848–1866; Unregistered Letters Received; New Mexico: Microcopy M1072, Letters Sent, Ninth Military Department, the Department of New Mexico and the District of New Mexico, 1849–80; Microcopy 1102, Letters Received, Ninth Military Department; Microcopy 1120, Letters Received, Department of New Mexico.
United States, Smithsonian Institution, National Museum of Natural History. Unpublished report by L. E. St. Hoyme, associate curator of physical anthropology, "The Skull of Mangas Coloradas"; Bureau of

American Ethnology, Manuscript 121, Vocabulary [of] Mimbreno Language from Mancus [Mangus] Colorado [Coloradas] Chief of the Coppermine Apaches.

University of Texas at Austin, Janos Collection.

University of Texas at El Paso. Janos Collection (JA), 37 rolls; Juarez Collection, 12 rolls; Periodico Oficial de Chihuahua, Rolls 1–8.

Webb, James J. Papers, Missouri Historical Society, Saint Louis.

Wilson, Benjamin. "Observations of Early Days in California and New Mexico," Bancroft Library. University of California, Berkeley.

UNITED STATES GOVERNMENT PUBLICATIONS

Abel, Annie Heloise, ed. *The Official Correspondence of James C. Calhoun While Indian Agent at Santa Fe and Superintendent of Indian Affairs in New Mexico.* Washington: Government Printing Office, 1916.

Conditions of the Indian Tribes: Report of the Joint Special Commission. Washington: Government Printing Office, 1867.

Heitman, Francis B. *Historical Register and Dictionary of the United States Army from Its Organization, September 20, 1789, to March 2, 1903.* 2 vols. Urbana: University of Illinois Press, 1965.

Hodge, Frederick Webb. *Handbook of American Indians North of Mexico.* 2 vols. Washington: Government Printing Office, 1907.

Kappler, Charles J. *Indian Affairs, Laws and Treaties.* Washington: Government Printing Office, 1903.

United States, Congress, 37th Cong., 2d sess., S. Executive Doc., No. 1, Pt. 1.

———, Congress, 30th Congress, 1st sess., H. Executive Doc., No. 41.

———, Congress, 31st Congress, 1st sess., H. Executive Doc., No. 17.

———, Department of War. Report of the Secretary of War, 1857.

The War of the Rebellion: A Compilation of the Official Records of the Union and Confederate Armies. Series I, 53 vols. Washington: Government Printing Office, 1880–1901.

AMERICAN NEWSPAPERS

Boston Evening Transcript
El Paso Herald
Los Angeles Star
Mesilla Times
(Las Cruces) *Rio Grande Republican*
Sacramento Daily Union
San Antonio Herald
San Diego Herald
(San Francisco) *Alta California*
San Francisco Evening Bulletin
Santa Fe Weekly Gazette

Santa Fe New Mexican
(Saint Louis) *Missouri Weekly Democrat*
(Saint Louis) *Missouri Republican*
(Tucson) *Arizona Daily Star*

MEXICAN NEWSPAPERS

SONORA (BANCROFT LIBRARY, UNIVERSITY OF CALIFORNIA, BERKELEY)

(Ures) *El Iris de Paz*
El Nacional
El Restaurador
El Sonorense
Estrella de Occidente
La Voz de Sonora

CHIHUAHUA (UNIVERSITY OF TEXAS AT EL PASO MICROFILM COLLECTION, OFICIAL
PERIODICO DE CHIHUAHUA)

El Antenor
El Boletin Oficial
El Centinela
El Correo
El Eco de la Frontera
El Fanal de Chihuahua
El Faro
El Noticioso de Chihuahua
El Provisional
La Alianza de la Frontera
La Luna
La Restauración
Revista Oficial

BOOKS: PRIMARY SOURCES

Altshuler, Constance Wynn, ed. *Latest from Arizona! The Hesperian
    Letters, 1859–1861.* Tucson: Arizona Pioneers' Historical Society, 1969.
Averell, William Woods. *Ten Years in the Saddle: The Memoir of William
    Woods Averell, 1851–1862.* Ed. Edward K. Eckert and Nicholas J.
    Amato. San Rafael, Calif.: Presidio Press, 1978.
Bailey, L. R., ed. *The A. B. Gray Report.* Los Angeles: Westernlore Press,
    1963.
Ball, Eve. *In the Days of Victorio: Recollections of a Warm Springs
    Apache.* Tucson: University of Arizona Press, 1970.
———, with Nora Henn and Lynda Sanchez. *Indeh: An Apache Odyssey.*
    Provo, Utah: Brigham Young University Press, 1980.
Barrett, Stephen M., ed. *Geronimo's Story of His Life.* New York: Garrett
    Press, 1969.

Bartlett, John Russell. *Personal Narrative of Explorations and Incidents in Texas, New Mexico, California, Sonora, and Chihuahua, Connected with the United States and Mexican Boundary Commission during the Years 1850, '51, '52, and '53.* 2 vols. 1854; reprint, Chicago: Rio Grande Press, 1965.

Bell, Major Horace. *Reminiscences of a Ranger, or Early Days in Southern California.* Los Angeles: Yarnell, Caystile, and Mather, 1881.

Bennett, James A. *Forts and Forays: A Dragoon in New Mexico, 1850–1856.* Ed. Clinton E. Brooks and Frank D. Reeve. Albuquerque: University of New Mexico Press, 1948.

Betzinez, Jason, and Wilber Sturtevant Nye. *I Fought with Geronimo.* New York: Bonanza Books, 1959.

Bieber, Ralph, ed. *Southern Trails to California in 1849.* Glendale, Calif.: Arthur H. Clark Co., 1937.

Box, James. *Captain James Box's Adventures and Explorations in New and Old Mexico.* New York: James Miller Publishers, 1869.

Boyer, Ruth McDonald, and Narcissus Duffy Gayton. *Apache Mothers and Daughters: Four Generations of a Family.* Norman: University of Oklahoma Press, 1992.

Bronson, Edgar Beecher. *The Vanguard.* New York: George H. Doran Company, 1914.

Calvin, Ross, ed. *Lieutenant Emory Reports: Notes of a Military Reconnaisance.* Albuquerque: University of New Mexico Press, 1968.

Carmony, Neil, ed. *The Civil War in Apacheland: Sergeant George Hand's Diary, California, Arizona, West Texas, New Mexico, 1861–1864.* Silver City, N.M.: High-Lonesome Books, 1996.

Caughey, John Walton, ed. *Rushing for Gold.* Berkeley: University of California Press, 1949.

Chomina, Armando Elías. *Compendio de Datos Historicos de la Familia Elías.* Hermosillo, Sonora: privately printed, 1986.

Clarke, A. B. *Travels in Mexico and California.* Ed. Anne M. Perry. College Station: Texas A&M University Press, 1988.

Clarke, Dwight L., ed. *The Original Journals of Henry Smith Turner with Stephen Watts Kearney to New Mexico and California, 1846.* Norman: University of Oklahoma Press, 1966.

Conner, Daniel Ellis. *Joseph Reddeford Walker and the Arizona Adventure.* Ed. Donald J. Berthrong and Odessa Davenport. Norman: University of Oklahoma Press, 1956.

Cooke, Philip St. George. *Exploring Southwestern Trails, 1846–1854.* Ed. Ralph Bieber. Philadelphia: Porcupine Press, 1974.

Cortés, José. *Views from the Apache Frontier: Report on the Northern Provinces of New Spain.* Ed. Elizabeth A. H. John. Norman: University of Oklahoma Press, 1989.

Cozzens, Samuel Woodworth. *Young Trail Hunters, or the Wild Riders of the Plains.* Boston: Lee and Shepard, 1877.

Cremony. John C. *Life among the Apaches*. Tucson: Arizona Silhouettes, 1954.

Curry, W. Hubert. *Sun Rising on the West: The Saga of Henry Clay and Elizabeth Smith*. Crosbyton, Texas: Crosby County Pioneer Memorial, 1979.

Dobyns, Henry F., ed. *Hepah, California! The Journal of Cave Johnson Couts, 1848–1849*. Tucson: Arizona Pioneers' Historical Society, 1961.

Eccleston, Robert. *Overland to California on the Southwestern Trail, 1849*. Ed. George P. Hammond and Edward H. Howes. Berkeley: University of California Press, 1950.

Ellis, Richard N., ed. *New Mexico Historic Documents*. Albuquerque: University of New Mexico Press, 1975.

Emory, William H. *Report on the United States and Mexican Boundary Survey*. 3 vols. Austin: Texas State Historical Association, 1987.

Frazer, Robert W., ed. *Mansfield on the Condition of the Western Forts, 1853–54*. Norman: University of Oklahoma Press, 1963.

Gregg, Josiah. *Commerce of the Praries*. Ed. Max L. Moorhead. Norman: University of Oklahoma Press, 1954.

Griffin, John S. *A Doctor Comes to California: The Diary of John S. Griffin, M.D., 1846–1847*. San Francisco: California Historical Society, 1953.

Hamlin, Percy Gatling, ed. *The Making of a Soldier: Letters of General R. S. Ewell*. Richmond, Va.: Whitter & Shepperson, 1935.

Harris, Benjamin Butler. *The Gila Trail: The Texas Argonauts and the California Gold Rush*. Ed. Richard H. Dillon. Norman: University of Oklahoma Press, 1960.

Hobbs, James. *Wild Life in the Far West*. Glorieta, N.M.: Rio Grande Press, 1969.

Indian Raids as Reported in the Silver City Enterprise. Silver City, N.M.: Willam H. Mullane, 1968.

Kendall, George W. *Across the Great Southwestern Prairies*. 2 vols. N.p.: Readex Microprint Corporation, 1966.

Lang, Walter. *The First Overland Mail: Butterfield Trail, St. Louis to San Francisco, 1858–1861*. N.p., 1940.

McCall, George Archibald. *New Mexico in 1850: A Military View*. Ed. and intro. Robert W. Frazer. Norman: University of Oklahoma Press, 1968.

Marchand, Ernest, ed. *News from Fort Craig, New Mexico, 1863: Civil War Letters of Andrew Ryan with the First California Volunteers*. Santa Fe: Stagecoach Press, 1966.

Meriwether, David. *My Life in the Mountains and on the Plains*. Ed. Robert A. Griffen. Norman: University of Oklahoma Press, 1965.

Miller, Joseph, ed. *Arizona Cavalcade: The Turbulent Times*. New York: Hastings House, 1962.

Mills, W. W. *Forty Years at El Paso, 1858–1898*. Ed. Rex Strickland. El Paso: Carl Hertzog, 1962.

Naylor, Thomas H., and Charles W. Polzer. *The Presidio and Militia on the Northern Frontier of New Spain*. Tucson: University of Arizona Press, 1986.

O'Neil, James B. *They Die But Once: The Story of a Tejano*. New York: Knight Publications, 1935.

Pattie, James O. *The Personal Narrative of James O. Pattie of Kentucky*. Ed. Timothy Flint. Chicago: Lakeside Press, 1930.

Poston, Charles. *Building a State in Apache Land*. Tempe, Ariz.: Aztec Press, 1963.

Reid, John C. *Reid's Tramp*. Austin, Texas: The Steck Company, 1935.

Ruxton, George F. *Adventures in Mexico and the Rocky Mountains*. Glorieta, N.M.: Rio Grande Press, 1973.

Tevis, James H. *Arizona in the '50's*. Albuquerque: University of New Mexico Press, 1954.

Wislizenus, Frederick A. *Memoir of a Tour to Northern Mexico Connected with Col. Doniphan's Expedition in 1846 and 1847*. Glorieta, N.M.: Rio Grande Press, 1969.

Wood, Harvey. *Personal Recollections of Harvey Wood: Reminiscences of Early Days*. Pasadena, Calif.: n.p., 1955.

BOOKS: SECONDARY SOURCES

Acuña, Rodolfo F. *Sonoran Strongman: Ignacio Pesqueira and His Times*. Tucson: University of Arizona Press, 1974.

Almada, Francisco R. *Diccionario de historia, geografía, y biografía chihuahuenses*. Chihuahua: Talleres Gráficos del Gobierno del Estado, 1927.

———. *Diccionario de historia, geografía, y biografía sonorenses*. Hermosillo, Sonora: Instituto Sonorense de Cultura, 1990.

Altshuler, Constance Wynn. *Cavalry Yellow and Infantry Blue: Army Officers in Arizona between 1851 and 1886*. Tucson: Arizona Historical Society, 1991.

———. *Chains of Command: Arizona and the Army, 1856–1875*. Tucson: Arizona Historical Society, 1981.

Austerman, Wayne R. *Sharps Rifles and Spanish Mules: The San Antonio–El Paso Mail, 1851–1881*. College Station: Texas A&M University Press, 1985.

Bancroft, Hubert Howe. *History of Arizona and New Mexico*. San Francisco: History Company, 1889.

———. *History of the North Mexican States and Texas*. 2 vols. San Francisco: History Company, 1889.

Barrick, Nona, and Mary Taylor. *The Mesilla Guard, 1851–1861*, El Paso: Texas Western Press, 1976.

Baylor, George Wythe. *John Robert Baylor: Confederate Governor of Arizona*. Ed. Odie Faulk. Tucson: Arizona Pioneers' Historical Society, 1966.

Brandes, Ray, ed. *Troopers West: Military and Indian Affairs on the American Frontier.* San Diego: Frontier Heritage Press, 1970.

Carter, Harvey Lewis. *"Dear Old Kit": The Historical Christopher Carson.* Norman: University of Oklahoma Press, 1968.

Clum, Woodworth. *Apache Agent: The Story of John P. Clum.* Lincoln: University of Nebraska Press, 1978.

Colton, Ray C. *The Civil War in the Western Territories.* Norman: University of Oklahoma Press, 1959.

Comfort, Will Levington. *Apache.* Lincoln: University of Nebraska Press, 1986.

Couchman, Donald Howard. *Cooke's Peak—Pasarán por Aquí: A Focus on United States History in Southwestern New Mexico.* Las Cruces, N.M.: Bureau of Land Management, 1990.

Crouch, Brodie. *Jornada del Muerto: A Pageant of the Desert.* Spokane, Wash.: Arthur H. Clark Company, 1989.

Debo, Angie. *Geronimo: The Man, His Time, His Place.* Norman: University of Oklahoma Press, 1976.

Dunn, J. P. *Massacres of the Mountains: A History of the Indian Wars of the Far West, 1815–1875.* New York: Archer House, n.d.

Egan, Ferol. *The El Dorado Trail: The Story of the Gold Rush Routes across Mexico.* New York: McGraw Hill Book Company, 1970.

Finch, L. Boyd. *A Southwestern Land Scam: The 1859 Report of "The Mowry City Association."* Tucson: Friends of the Library, University of Arizona, 1990.

———. *Confederate Pathway to the Pacific: Major Sherod Hunter and Arizona Territory, C.S.A.* Tucson: The Arizona Historical Society, 1996.

Floyd, Dale E. *Chronological List of Actions etc. with Indians from January 15, 1837, to January 1891.* Fort Collins, Colo.: Old Army Press, 1979.

Forbes, Jack D. *Apache, Navaho and Spaniard,* Norman: University of Oklahoma Press, 1971.

Fowler, Orson S. *Human Sciences or Phrenology.* Philadelphia: National Publishing Company, 1873.

Frazer, Robert W. *Forts of the West: Military Forts and Presidios and Posts Commonly Called Forts West of the Mississippi River to 1898.* Norman: University of Oklahoma Press, 1977.

———. *Forts and Supplies: The Role of the Army in the Economy of the Southwest, 1846–1861.* Albuquerque: University of New Mexico Press, 1983.

Giese, Dale F. *Forts of New Mexico: Echoes of the Bugle.* Silver City: Dale F. Giese, 1991.

Gilbert, Bill. *Westering Man: The Life of Joseph Walker.* Norman: University of Oklahoma Press, 1985.

Goodwin, Grenville. *The Social Organization of the Western Apache.* Tucson: University of Arizona Press, 1969.

Gressinger, A. W. *Charles D. Poston: Sunland Seer.* Globe, Ariz.: Dale Stuart King, 1961.

Griffen, William B. *Apaches at War and Peace: The Janos Presidio, 1750–1858.* Albuquerque: University of New Mexico Press, 1988. Reprint, Norman: University of Oklahoma Press, 1998.

———. *Utmost Good Faith: Patterns of Apache-Mexican Hostilities in Northern Chihuahua Border Warfare, 1821–1848.* Albuquerque: University of New Mexico Press, 1988.

Hafen, Leroy. *The Mountain Men and the Fur Trade of the Far West.* 7 vols. Glendale, Calif.: Arthur H. Clark Co., 1965–1969.

Hine, Robert V. *Bartlett's West: Drawing the Mexican Boundary.* New Haven, Conn.: Yale University Press, 1968.

Hoffman, Virginia. *Navajo Biographies.* 2 vols. Phoenix: Navajo Curriculum Center Press, 1974.

Hunt, Aurora. *Major General James Henry Carleton, 1814–1873: Western Frontier Dragoon.* Glendale: Calif.: Arthur H. Clark Company, 1958.

Jones, Oakah L., Jr. *Nueva Vizcaya: Heartland of the Spanish Frontier.* Albuquerque: University of New Mexico Press, 1988.

Julyan, Robert. *The Place Names of New Mexico.* Albuquerque: University of New Mexico Press, 1996.

Keleher, William A. *Turmoil in New Mexico, 1846–1868.* Intro. Lawrence R. Murphy. Albuquerque: University of New Mexico Press, 1982.

Kerby, Robert Lee. *The Confederate Invasion of New Mexico and Arizona, 1861–1862.* Tucson: Westernlore Press, 1981.

Larson, Robert W. *New Mexico's Quest for Statehood, 1846–1912.* Albuquerque: University of New Mexico Press, 1968.

Lekson, Stephen H. *Nana's Raid: Apache Warfare in Southern New Mexico, 1881.* El Paso: Texas Western Press, 1987.

Lister, Florence C., and Robert H. Lister. *Chihuahua: Storehouse of Storms.* Albuquerque: University of New Mexico Press, 1966.

Lockwood, Frank C. *The Apache Indians.* New York: Macmillan Company, 1938.

Lovell, Edith Haroldsen. *Benjamin Bonneville: A Soldier of the American Frontier.* Bountiful, Utah: Horizon Publishers, 1992.

Lummis, Charles F. *The Land of Poco Tiempo.* Albuquerque: University of New Mexico Press, 1966.

McClintock, James H. *Arizona: Prehistoric, Aboriginal, Pioneer, Modern.* 3 vols. Chicago: S. J. Clarke Publishing Company, 1916.

McGaw, William Cochran. *Savage Scene: The Life and Times of James Kirker, Frontier King.* New York: Hastings House, 1972.

McNitt, Frank. *The Indian Traders.* Norman: University of Oklahoma Press, 1962.

———. *Navajo Wars: Military Campaigns, Slave Raids, and Reprisals.* Albuquerque: University of New Mexico Press, 1972.

Miller, Darlis A. *The California Column in New Mexico.* Albuquerque: University of New Mexico Press, 1982.

Minge, Ward Alan. *Ácoma: Pueblo in the Sky.* Albuquerque: University of New Mexico Press, 1976.

Moorhead, Max L. *The Apache Frontier: Jacobo Ugarte and Spanish-Indian Relations in Northern New Spain, 1769–1791.* Norman: University of Oklahoma Press, 1968.

—————. *The Presidio: Bastion of the Spanish Borderlands.* Norman: University of Oklahoma Press, 1975.

Murray, John A. *The Gila Wilderness Area: A Hiking Guide.* Albuquerque: University of New Mexico Press, 1988.

Officer, James E. *Hispanic Arizona, 1536–1856.* Tucson: University of Arizona Press, 1987.

Ogle, Ralph Hedrick. *Federal Control of the Western Apaches, 1848–1886.* Intro. Oakah L. Jones, Jr. Albuquerque: University of New Mexico Press. 1970.

Oppler, Morris E. *Myths and Tales of the Chiricahua Apache Indians.* Memoirs of the American Folk-Lore Society, 1942. Menasha, Wis.: George Banta Publishing Company, 1942.

—————. *An Apache Life-Way: The Economic, Social, and Religious Institutions of the Chiricahua Indians.* Chicago: University of Chicago Press, 1965.

—————. *Apache Odyssey: A Journey between Two Worlds.* New York: Holt, Rinehart, and Winston, 1969.

—————, ed. *Grenville Goodwin among the Western Apache: Letters from the Field.* Tucson: University of Arizona Press, 1973.

Pearce, T. M., ed. *New Mexico Place Names: A Geographical Dictionary.* Albuquerque: University of New Mexico Press, 1977.

Perry, Richard J. *Western Apache Heritage: People of the Mountain Corridor.* Austin: University of Texas Press, 1991.

Price, Paxton P. *Mesilla Valley Pioneers, 1823–1912.* Las Cruces: Yucca Tree Press, 1995.

Roberts, Virginia Culin. *With Their Own Blood: A Saga of Southwestern Pioneers.* Fort Worth: Texas Christian University Press, 1992.

Sandomingo, Manuel. *Historia de Sonora.* Agua Prieta, Sonora: n.p., 1953.

Schroeder, Albert H. *Apache Indians*, vol. 4, *A Study of the Apache Indians.* New York: Garland Publishing, 1974.

Sweeney, Edwin R. *Cochise: Chiricahua Apache Chief.* Norman: University of Oklahoma Press, 1991.

—————. *Merejildo Grijalva: Apache Captive, Army Scout.* El Paso: Texas Western Press, 1992.

Terrell, John Upton. *Apache Chronicle.* New York: Thomas Y. Crowell Company, 1974.

Thomas, Alfred Barnaby. *Forgotten Frontiers: A Study of the Spanish Indian Policy of Don Juan Bautista de Anza, Governor of New Mexico, 1777–1787.* Norman: University of Oklahoma Press, 1969.

Thrapp, Dan L. *Al Sieber, Chief of Scouts.* Norman: University of Oklahoma Press, 1964.

———. *The Conquest of Apachería.* Norman: University of Oklahoma Press, 1967.

———. *Juh, an Incredible Indian.* El Paso: Texas Western Press, 1973.

———. *General Crook and the Sierra Madre Adventure.* Norman: University of Oklahoma Press, 1972.

———. *Victorio and the Mimbres Apaches.* Norman: University of Oklahoma Press, 1974.

———. *Encyclopedia of Frontier Biography.* 4 vols. Glendale, Calif.: Arthur H. Clark Company, 1988.

Ungnade, Herbert E. *Guide to the New Mexico Mountains.* Albuquerque: University of New Mexico Press, 1977.

Utley, Robert M. *Frontiersman in Blue: The United States Army and the Indian, 1848–1865.* Lincoln: University of Nebraska Press, 1981.

———. *The Lance and the Shield: The Life and Times of Sitting Bull.* New York: Henry Holt and Company, 1993.

Villa, Eduardo W. *Compendio de historia del estado de Sonora.* Mexico City: Patria Nueva, 1937.

Voss, Stuart F. *On the Periphery of Nineteenth Century Mexico: Sonora and Sinaloa, 1810–1877.* Tucson: University of Arizona Press, 1982.

Wagoner, Jay J. *Early History: Prehistory to Civil War.* Tucson: University of Arizona Press, 1977.

Watson, Dorothy. *The Pinos Altos Story.* Silver City, N.M.: Silver City Enterprise, 1960.

Weber, David J. *The Taos Trappers: The Fur Trade in the Far Southwest, 1540–1846.* Norman: University of Oklahoma Press, 1971.

Webster's American Military Biographies. Springfield, Mass.: G. & C. Merriam Company, 1978.

Wellman, Paul I. *The Indian Wars of the West.* Garden City, N.Y.: Doubleday & Company, 1947.

West, Robert C. *Sonora: Its Geographical Personality.* Austin: University of Texas Press, 1993.

Wharfield, H. B. *Cooley: Army Scout, Arizona Pioneer. Wayside Host, Apache Friend.* El Cajon, Calif.: n.p., 1966.

ARTICLES AND ESSAYS

Abel, Annie Heloise, ed. "The Journal of John Greiner," *Old Santa Fe* 3 (July 1916), 189–243.

———. "Indian Affairs in New Mexico under the Administration of William Carr Lane: From the Journal of John Ward," *New Mexico Historical Review* 16 (April–July 1941).

Adams, John Quincy. "Surgeon to the Indian Fighters," *True West,* September 1982, 20–26.

Allen. R. S. "Pinos Altos, New Mexico," *New Mexico Historical Review* 23 (October 1948), 302–32.

Aranda, Daniel D. "Josanie—Apache Warrior," *True West* 23 (May–June 1976), 38–39, 62–64.

Austerman, Wayne. "Unholy Terror Cornered," *Wild West* 4 (June 1991), 35–41.

Bieber, Ralph P., ed. "Letters of William Carr Lane, 1852–1854," *Historical Society of New Mexico* 6 (April 1928), 179–203.

Carson, Wm. G. B. "William Carr Lane, Diary," *New Mexico Historical Review* 39 (July 1964), 181–234.

Cox, C. C. "From Texas to California in 1849," ed. Mabelle Eppard Martin, *Southwestern Historical Quarterly* 29 (1925–1926), 36–50, 128–46, 201–23.

Cremony, John C. "Some Savages," *Overland Monthly* 8 (March 1872), 201–10.

Duffen, William A. "Overland Via 'Jackass Mail' in 1858," *Arizona and the West* 2 (Spring 1960), 35–53; (Summer 1960), 147–64; (Autumn 1960), 279–92); (Winter 1960), 353–70.

Finch, L. Boyd. "Arizona'a Governors without Portfolio: A Wonderfully Diverse Lot," *Journal of Arizona History* 26 (Spring 1985), 77–99.

Griffen, William B. "The Compás: A Chiricahua Apache Family of the Late 18th and Early 19th Centuries," *American Indian Quarterly* 7 (Spring 1983), 21–49.

———. "Apache Indians and the Northern Mexican Peace Establishments," in *Southwestern Culture History: Collected Papers in Honor of Albert Schroeder*, ed. Charles H. Lange, Papers of the Archaeological Society of New Mexico 10 (1985), 183–95.

———. "The Chiricahua Apache Population Resident at the Janos Presidio, 1792–1858," *Journal of the Southwest* 33 (Summer 1991), 151–199.

Herring, Patricia Roche. "Tucsonense Preclaro (Illustrious Tucsonan): General José C. Urrea, Romantic Idealist," *Journal of Arizona History* 34 (Autumn 1993), 307–20.

Hodgson, Bryan. "Buffalo: Back Home on the Range," *National Geographic* 186 (November 1994), 64–89.

Matson, Daniel S., and Albert H. Schroeder, eds. "Cordero's Description of the Apache—1796," *New Mexico Historical Review* 32 (October 1857), 335–56.

Myers, Lee. "Fort Webster on the Mimbres," *New Mexico Historical Review* 41 (January 1966), 47–57.

———. "The Enigma of Mangas Coloradas' Death," *New Mexico Historical Review* 41 (January 1966), 287–304.

———. "Military Establishments in Southwestern New Mexico: Stepping Stones to Settlement," *New Mexico Historical Review* 43 (January 1968), 5–48.

Nugent, John. "Scraps of Early History," *The Argonaut* 2, nos. 10–11 (1878).

Opler, Morris E. "Chiricahua Apache," in *Handbook of North American Indians* 10 (Southwest). Ed. Alfonso Ortiz. Washington: Smithsonian Institution, 1983.

————. "An Interpretation of Ambivalence of Two American Indian Tribes," *Journal of Social Psychology* 7 (1936), 82–116.

————. "A Chiricahua Apache's Account of the Geronimo Campaign of 1886," *New Mexico Historical Review* 13 (October 1938), 360–86.

————. "An Outline of Chiricahua Apache Social Organization," in *Social Anthropology of North American Tribes: Essays in Social Organization, Law, and Religion.* Ed. Fred Eggan. Chicago: University of Chicago Press, 1937.

————. "The Identity of the Apache Mansos," *American Anthropologist* 44 (October–November 1942), 725.

————, and Harry Hoijer. "The Raid and War-Path Language of the Chiricahua Apache," *American Anthropologist* 42 (October–December 1942), 617–35.

Park, Joseph F. "The Apaches in Mexican-American Relations, 1848–1861," *Arizona and the West* 3 (Summer 1961), 129–46.

————. "Spanish Indian Policy in Northern Mexico, 1765–1810," *Arizona and the West* 4 (Winter 1962), 325–44.

Radbourne, Allan. "Ambush at Cocospera Canyon," *English Westerners Tally Sheet* 25 (July 1970), 63–76.

Reeve, Frank D., ed. "Puritan and Apache: A Diary," *New Mexico Historical Review* 23 (October 1948), 269–301; 24 (January 1949), 12–53.

————. "The Federal Indian Policy in New Mexico, 1858–1880," *New Mexico Historical Review* 13 (July 1938), 261–313.

Rippy, J Fred. "The Indians of the Southwest in the Diplomacy of the United States and Mexico, 1848–1853," *Hispanic-American Historical Review* (August 1919), 363–96.

Sacks, Benjamin H. "The Origins of Fort Buchanan," *Arizona and the West* 7 (Autumn 1965), 207–26.

Schreier, Konrad F., Jr. "The California Column in the Civil War: Hazen's Civil War Diary," *Journal of San Diego History* 22 (Spring 1976), 31–47.

Smith, Ralph A. "The Scalp Hunt in Chihuahua—1849," *New Mexico Historical Review* 40 (April 1965), 116–40.

————. "John Joel Glanton: Lord of the Scalp Range," *The Smoke Signal* 6 (Fall 1962), 9–16.

Stevens, Robert C. "The Apache Menace in Sonora, 1831–1849," *Arizona and the West* 6 (Autumn 1964), 211–22.

Strickland, Rex W. "The Birth and Death of a Legend: The Johnson Massacre of 1837," *Arizona and the West* 18 (Autumn 1976), 257–86.

Sweeney, Edwin R. "I Had Lost All: Geronimo and the Carrasco Massacre of 1851," *Journal of Arizona History* 27 (Spring 1986), 35–52.

————. "Cochise and the Prelude to the Bascom Affair," *New Mexico Historical Review* 64 (October 1989), 427–46.

————. "One of Heaven's Heroes: A Mexican General Pays Tribute to the Honor and Courage of a Chiricahua Apache," *Journal of Arizona History* 36 (Autumn 1995), 209–32.

Thompson, Jerry D. "With the Regulars in New Mexico, 1851–1853: The Lost Diary of Sylvester W. Matson," *Journal of Arizona History* 31 (Winter 1990), 349–404.

Utley, Robert M. "Captain John Pope's Plan of 1853 for the Frontier Defense of New Mexico," *Arizona and the West* (Autumn 1963), 149–63.

Walker, Henry P., ed. "Soldier in the California Column: The Diary of John W. Teal," *Arizona and the West* 13 (Spring 1971), 33–82.

————. "Colonel Bonneville's Report: The Department of New Mexico in 1859," *Arizona and the West* 22 (Autumn 1980), 343–62.

INDEX